D0092348

OPENING MEXICO

THE MAKING OF A DEMOCRACY

JULIA PRESTON AND **SAMUEL DILLON**

Pulitzer Prize–winning reporters for **THE NEW YORK TIMES**

"By combining a nimble narrative with a reporter's eye for detail,
[Preston and Dillon] produce a gripping and insightful history of Mexico's
democratic transition." —Daniel Kurtz Phelan, *The Washington Post*

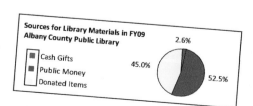

Sources for Library Materials in FY09
Albany County Public Library

- Cash Gifts
- Public Money
- Donated Items

2.6%
45.0%
52.5%

OPENING MEXICO

"Preston and Dillon deserve an immense amount of credit for their achievement here, the payoff of their tireless reporting. At their best, the authors, using exhaustive research, personal testimony, and interviews at every stratum of Mexican society, provide blow-by-blow accounts of seminal moments in modern Mexican history."
— Scott W. Helman, *The Boston Globe*

"Julia Preston and Samuel Dillon . . . have written an extraordinary book on the collapse of one-party rule in Mexico that also serves as an excellent introduction for Americans who want to understand Mexico better. This detailed insiders' account of the slow collapse of what was once called the perfect dictatorship and the messy emergence of a still-imperfect democracy gives readers the most intimate and accessible portrait they are likely to have of Mexico in a time of upheaval . . . The story of how the perfect dictatorship came unglued is one of the most fascinating stories of our time, and the authors tell their story well. The voices of intellectuals, Indians, political dissidents, businessmen and ordinary Mexican citizens fill this densely researched and clearly written book . . . Ms. Preston and Mr. Dillon are magnificent guides to this rebirth of Mexican freedom and paint a compelling picture of the cascading and accelerating change." — Walter Russell Mead, *The New York Times*

"A highly readable and revealing account of the country's dramatic recent history." — Geri Smith, *Business Week*

"Informative, entertaining and sometimes groundbreaking."
— David Gaddis Smith, *The San Diego Union-Tribune*

"A page-turner, a stunning behind-the-scenes look at Mexico and its protagonists as it lurches toward democracy."
— Robert Rivard, *San Antonio Express-News*

"A fascinating case study of the multiple ways public pressure can undermine an antidemocratic regime." — Daniel Wilkinson, *The Nation*

"*Opening Mexico* tells the fascinating inside story of how Mexico became a multi-party democracy after seven decades of single-party rule. Julia Preston and Samuel Dillon, two of America's finest investigative journalists, recount the events that transformed Mexican politics and strengthened democratic momentum at a crucial moment in the history of Latin America. *Opening Mexico* is indispensable reading for those seeking an understanding of contemporary Mexico and would be a valuable addition to the library of any student of how political power is used, abused, or changed." — Madeleine Albright, former U.S. Secretary of State

"Preston and Dillon have produced one of the most important books on Mexico since the publication of Alan Riding's *Distant Neighbors* nearly twenty years ago. It is a clear reminder to U.S. policy makers of why America needs to remain engaged with the destiny of its southern neighbor, and a superb introduction to Mexico for all those who simply want to get to know, and understand, a fascinating country."
— Jorge Castañeda, former Foreign Minister of Mexico

"Americans who think of Mexico as principally an illegal immigration problem will have their eyes opened—and their minds changed—by this story of the heroic struggle Mexicans waged for more than three decades to finally bring democracy to their beautiful but wounded land. *Opening Mexico* recounts the repression, violence, corruption, and inertia inherent in nearly a century of one-party rule. These roadblocks on the path to free elections were gradually overcome by students, intellectuals, journalists, opposition politicians, and even a few working quietly from within the ruling clique. Their crusade culminated with the election of opposition leader Vicente Fox in July 2000, opening a promising new century for Mexico." — Shirley Christian, winner of the Pulitzer Prize for International Reporting, 1981

"*Opening Mexico* takes us on a wonderfully humane and insightful journey, chock-full of vividly portrayed villains and heroes, that brings to life Mexico's own troubled, triumphant journey toward a functioning democracy. Preston and Dillon introduce us to the worst and best of humanity, locked in a historic struggle of entrenched privilege versus individual liberty. This book is a great read for all Americans who are curious about our awakening southern neighbor."
— Richard Feinberg, Director, APEC Study Center, University of California, San Diego

JULIA PRESTON and SAMUEL DILLON
OPENING MEXICO

Julia Preston and Samuel Dillon were Mexico correspondents for *The New York Times* from 1995 to 2000. They were part of the *Times* team that won the 1998 Pulitzer Prize for international reporting.

OPENING MEXICO

OPENING MEXICO
The Making of a Democracy

JULIA PRESTON and SAMUEL DILLON

FARRAR, STRAUS AND GIROUX / New York

Farrar, Straus and Giroux
19 Union Square West, New York 10003

Grateful acknowledgment is made for permission to reprint an excerpt from "Interruptions from the West (3)" by Octavio Paz, translated by Eliot Weinberger, from Collected Poems, 1957–1987, copyright © 1986 by Octavio Paz and Eliot Weinberger.
Reprinted by permission of New Directions Publishing Corp.

Photo credits appear on pages 591–592.

The Library of Congress has cataloged the hardcover edition as follows:
Preston, Julia, date.
Opening Mexico : the making of a democracy / Julia Preston and
Samuel Dillon.— 1st ed.
    p. cm.
Includes bibliographical references and index.
ISBN 0-374-22668-7 (alk. paper)
    1. Mexico—Politics and government—1988–   2. Mexico—Politics and
government—1946–1970.   3. Mexico—Politics and government—1970–1988.
4. Democracy—Mexico.   5. Politicians—Mexico—Biography.   I. Dillon,
Sam.   II. Title.

F1236.P72 2004
972.08'3—dc21

                                                            2003059918

Paperback ISBN-13: 978-0-374-52964-2
Paperback ISBN-10: 0-374-52964-7

Designed by Jonathan D. Lippincott

www.fsgbooks.com

2   3   4   5   6   7   8   9   10

For Emma

Contents

Preface:
Making Mexican Democracy

I t took three decades of pressure, protest, finagling, and occasionally violence for Mexicans to pry open the authoritarian system that had held their country in thrall since
the 1920s. We witnessed the culminating years of this campaign as correspondents for *The New York Times* based in Mexico.

We both had worked for two decades as reporters in Latin America.
We knew that Mexico, although it shared the Spanish language and an
Iberian colonial past with the rest of the region, was a country apart. The
revolution of 1910 had set it on a different course in the twentieth century from its Latin neighbors. After that upheaval Mexico had never
been tempted to adopt a Communist regime like the one Fidel Castro
brought to power in Cuba in 1959. Nor had it succumbed to right-wing
military dictators, such as those who seized control at mid-century in
Central and South America. Mexico had also guarded its independence
from Washington's polarizing policies during the Cold War more zealously than most Latin nations.

Yet Mexico had lived under its own form of closed single-party government. By the time we settled in Mexico City in September 1995, the
oppressive hold of the Institutional Revolutionary Party on every aspect
of Mexican life had made it the world's longest-ruling political organization.

But as it turned out, we had arrived in the midst of a prolonged,
slow-motion, largely peaceful democratic revolution. Mexicans were
remaking their society, institution by institution.

We saw them undertake extraordinary reforms. They transferred control of the elections machinery away from the ruling party, which had

abused it to perpetrate countless frauds, and put it in the hands of an independent agency that devised one of the most modern balloting systems in the world. They created an array of new political parties to challenge the monopoly of the Institutional Revolutionary Party, known as the PRI.

They worked to create a legislature with real clout, replacing a theatrical Congress whose role for seven decades had been to provide ceremonious applause for the President's latest impulse. They were imposing limits on the power of the presidency, which had been so absolute and unrestrained by any legislative, judicial, or popular oversight as to make the Mexican chief executive a kind of Mesoamerican monarch.

We met people from all levels of life who were participating in this grand endeavor. Citizen activists were battling vote fraud. Human rights observers were curbing the abuses of the security forces. Grassroots communities were blocking the devastation of forests and beaches by corporations. Journalists were investigating malfeasance. Neighborhood groups were mobilizing to demand prosecution of criminal gangs and corrupt police. Even the PRI President, Ernesto Zedillo, had opted for a liberalizing role.

In July 2000, nearly five years into our tenure as correspondents for the *Times*, Mexicans took the decisive step toward completing their democratic transition. In the cleanest and most open vote in Mexican history, the nation elected an opposition candidate, Vicente Fox of the National Action Party, to be President, toppling the PRI regime after seventy-one years. Zedillo and his cohorts accepted the result and stepped aside. Mexico's second revolution was accomplished so efficiently and peacefully that not many Mexicans, and even fewer outsiders, really grasped the historic dimension of the event.

The making of Mexico's democracy was distinctive in many ways. There was no Nelson Mandela, no single leader to personify and guide the struggle. Nor was there a single democratic movement, but rather a multitude of initiatives from individuals and groups across the society and the country, which gradually converged as more and more Mexicans became convinced of the need to end the PRI's despotic rule.

Mexico was spared a change of economic system, since it had remained capitalist even after the 1910 revolution. Yet the clash between social classes was not the primary impetus of change. To be sure, along the way rebellions by workers, rural farming people, and Indians—notably the indigenous uprising in the southern state of Chiapas in 1994—served to weaken the authoritarian system. But these protests were part of a broad mix of reform efforts, in which the elite also at times participated. For decades the PRI system served the interests of business, making crony capitalists wealthy. They resisted change. But eventually the corporate class also supported an orderly transition, accepting that an open system could better serve its interests in a globalized economy.

Mexico's passage to democracy did not come about as a victory of the ideas of either the Left or the Right, either liberals or conservatives. At critical moments the Mexican Left, with its bold rejection of the status quo, its nationalism, and its defense of the dispossessed, took the lead in the struggle for greater freedom. But Mexican conservatives, committed to individual rights and a free-market economy and often inspired by Catholic faith, were also tenacious in their pursuit of reform. Over the years the competition among ideologies and factions was channeled into a system of political parties. These parties, when their resolve was tested, shunned violence, agreeing to take their disputes to the halls of local and federal legislatures. Religious fanaticism, which has torn apart many countries in times of transition, never arose to embitter the search for democracy in Mexico.

Mexico's was a negotiated pluralistic transition, with pressure coming from below, from myriad individuals and groups at the grass roots of society, and from above, as the PRI and its successive Presidents responded to dissidence by mandating change. The stalwarts of the system who gave up bits of their control, however, were most often motivated by self-interest, seeking not to reduce their domination but to perpetuate it.

Americans have a large stake in the outcome of Mexico's efforts to create an open society. No country affects the United States' well-being and national security more directly. The border we share is two thousand miles long. Mexico is our second-largest trading partner, after Canada—and ahead of Japan and China. It is a base for thousands of U.S. businesses, which are transforming the country's northern states into an important manufacturing region. It is the place of origin of some 10 million Mexican workers, the United States' largest single immigrant group. It is a destination for American travelers of all kinds. It is a luxuriant but deteriorating biosphere that is vital for the survival of thousands of North American migratory birds, butterflies, and other species.

Both of us have been watching Mexico for many years. Julia Preston first traveled to the country as a wayfaring college student in 1972, when the PRI system was passing from an epoch of growth and stability into cyclical crisis and decline. Sam Dillon began going to Mexico in the early 1980s, when he was a journalist based in El Salvador filing stories to editors at the Associated Press who were based in Mexico City. Julia was living in downtown Mexico City when an earthquake struck in 1985; her apartment rocked, and its windows shattered, raining glass on the street. We both covered the aftermath of that quake, as well as tumultuous gubernatorial elections later in the 1980s in several northern states, where the PRI stoked citizen anger by falsifying the results.

Our account is a journalists' draft of the history of Mexico's opening—its *apertura*, as it is called in Spanish. We have chosen to tell the events through the lives of a number of Mexicans whose activism we witnessed in the course of our reporting. In some places, where we were eyewitnesses to telling events, we recount them in the first person. The individuals we portray in detail were not necessarily the most important figures in the democracy movement; rather, their experiences were representative of the participation of countless other Mexicans in a collective national effort. We made some purposeful omissions. We haven't attempted a systematic study of the country's hermetic armed forces, which remained at the margins of the transition. Nor did we focus our attention on the role of the United States, which has sought stability in its southern neighbor even when that meant overlooking authoritarian abuses. We contend that Mexico's opening to democracy is one of the few major developments in the country's modern history that was *not* shaped by invasion or intervention by the United States.

In the last three decades of the twentieth century, new generations of Mexicans wanted to open their country to democracy. This is the story of how they did it.

OPENING MEXICO

The Day of the Change

No one in the Garza family got any decent sleep the night before Mexico's presidential election on July 2, 2000.

In Mexico City, Conchalupe Garza managed to doze off now and then, but her racing mind kept waking her up in the predawn darkness with anxious questions. "Why can't this country change?" she asked herself. "Why shouldn't it change? Why can't the change happen now, today? If it doesn't happen today, how will we ever work up the energy to try for it yet again?"

She had volunteered to be a poll watcher, and she lay in bed making plans for the task. She would wear sneakers and take extra clothes, she decided, because she would probably be up throughout the night dashing from one voting station to another, trying to prevent the party in power—the party that had been in power for all four decades of her life, and much longer—from fiddling with the ballot count and making off once again with the election.

In Monterrey, the business capital that sits amid gray deserts in northern Mexico, Conchalupe's seventy-three-year-old mother and her sister Beatriz slept equally fitfully. A fervent Catholic, Beatriz rose at dawn and set up a candle "the size of a house," as she described it, on an improvised altar in the living room, beginning hours of prayer for the balloting to bring the peaceful and orderly—but definitive—downfall of the ruling regime.

Conchalupe and her family were members of an opposition group that had worked for generations to defeat the governing party known as the PRI—from the initials of its name in Spanish, Partido Revolu-

cionario Institucional—and the monolithic authoritarian regime it controlled. They were motivated in part by religion: the PRI was the modern
standard-bearer for a tradition, dating back more than a century, of
antagonism between the secular Mexican state and the Roman Catholic
Church. But the Garza family's cause went well beyond their faith. In
the 1930s Conchalupe's grandfather had helped to form the Partido
Acción Nacional, the National Action Party, known as the PAN, an
acronym that means "bread" in Spanish. Its goal was to give Catholics a
moderate voice to challenge the ruling system, and to unite them with
free-market entrepreneurs who resented the PRI government's domination of the economy. In 1946 Antonio L. Rodríguez, her grandfather,
had held one of the first four seats won by the opposition in the federal
Congress, where every seat had been controlled by the ruling party since
its founding in 1929. He had run at a time when the PRI's hegemony
was so seamless and overarching that many Mexicans thought only madmen and masochists would stand against it in an election.

Now, half a century later, the fight that Conchalupe and her relatives
were still waging was more than ever about freedom. A kinetic and garrulous middle-class woman with a head of busy curls, Conchalupe had
devoted her adult life to sharpening the competition with the PRI for a
share of government, in a crusade that was more for pluralism than for
the conservative agenda of the PAN. Over the years, whenever there was
an election, Conchalupe's staid family home in Monterrey would turn
into a bustling forward base of operations for hundreds of volunteer PAN
poll watchers.

"We learned how to make five thousand sandwiches in one day," she
said proudly, giving a precise measure of her effort.

The PRI's monopoly extended down to the elections officials who
presided over the voting stations in city precincts and farming villages
throughout the country. Conchalupe knew from experience that one of
the PRI's favorite tactics was to make all the lights in a polling place go
out just when it was time to open the ballot boxes and count the paper
ballots. While Conchalupe's poll watchers were flailing in darkness, a
PRI official would swiftly remove fistfuls of cast ballots from the boxes
and replace them with ballots all marked for the PRI. She learned to
equip her volunteers with flashlights.

Once, during a race for the mayor of Monterrey, PRI toughs smashed the windows of a campaign car in which she was riding. A few years later, when Conchalupe herself ran for a seat in the congress of Nuevo León, the industrial powerhouse state of which Monterrey is the capital, she stumbled into a band of PRI ward heelers when she was stumping in an open-air market. The place was a rich vein of cash for the PRI, which extorted payoffs from merchants in return for the best stalls and the brawniest protection, and the ruling party was not about to give it up to the opposition. The woman who served as the PRI boss in the market came up behind Conchalupe and yanked on her ponytail hard enough to make her cry. "Bourgeois bitch!" the PRI woman shouted. "Daughter of your whore mother! Get out of here!" Her muscle men shoved Conchalupe into the street as mute shoppers looked on.

At the height of its powers, *el sistema*, as Mexicans called it, was remarkably effective at seducing, dividing, discrediting, intimidating, or simply annihilating any serious opposition. In 1976 the PRI candidate, José López Portillo, ran for President unopposed and won 91.9 percent of the votes cast. So close was the union between state and party that the PRI appropriated the red, white, and green of the Mexican flag for its logo, splashing the colors across adobe walls in every village in Mexico while barring other parties from using them. Mexicans called the PRI the *partido oficial*, the official party, suggesting that other parties lacked fundamental legitimacy.

Seven decades of rule by the PRI system had given Mexico the undeniable benefit of stability. Other major nations in Latin America had descended at some point into civil war or military dictatorship. The PRI regime, born in the aftermath of the chaotic Mexican Revolution that began in 1910, had provided continuity, steering Mexico through major leaps in economic development and fostering a sizable middle class and a sophisticated business elite.

The cost, however, was high. Firmly controlled at the top, Mexican society was permeated with violence at the bottom. In rural states like Guerrero and Oaxaca, the regime suppressed guerrilla rebellions time and again. Across the country, local rule was arbitrary, with few means of popular representation or justice, so that minor village disputes too often could not be resolved peacefully and spiraled into bloody shoot-outs.

Despite its revolutionary name, the PRI system was often harshly indifferent to the poor. Driven increasingly by corruption and patronage, the PRI became a huge, upward-drawing funnel for the public's money. And since the 1980s PRI governments had subjected the Mexican people to a cycle of humiliating economic crises, in which booms fueled by ambitious Presidents would collapse at the end of their six-year terms, leaving the departing leader rich and the taxpayers in ruins.

As a result, over the years the PAN and other opposition groups had made significant gains. In 1997 a veteran PAN politician, Fernando Canales, won the governor's office in Nuevo León. By 2000 the opposition had taken control of eleven of thirty-two statehouses and had gained a majority in the lower house of the Congress. But Conchalupe and her party had never come close to winning *la grande*, the big one, the presidential election—or to being allowed to think that the PRI would ever permit them to claim the victory if they did.

On the morning of July 2, however, Conchalupe had a feeling, alternately gnawing and exhilarating, that this election could be different. Vicente Fox Quesada, a vegetable farmer, boot manufacturer, and former Coca-Cola executive who was then the popular PAN governor of Guanajuato state in central Mexico, had torn up the traditional political calendar by launching a presidential bid in 1997, three years before the vote and only halfway through the term of the sitting PRI President, Ernesto Zedillo. Fox, a towering figure (over six feet six in the cowboy boots that were his staple footgear) with indefatigable personal drive, had taken the PAN by storm, forcing the careful conservative party to make him its presidential candidate by virtue of the sheer momentum of his unlikely campaign.

Fox's vision of lean, clean government was in tune with new political aspirations among the voters, especially a generation of young urban middle-class Mexicans who shopped at Wal-Mart, drove their own cars (although they sweated to pay down the auto loans), and were on-line. These young people liked his proposals to dismantle the PRI kleptocracy and reorient the economy to create better jobs for working people and less wealth for the wealthy. They liked the apparently honest record of his tenure in Guanajuato. Voters also liked the way he dropped the salty vernacular of the streets into his speeches, in contrast to the PRI's pre-fabricated rhetoric, and they liked his macho bravado, which reminded them of a traditional Mexican strongman, or caudillo.

But mainly the voters seemed attracted to the one thing that Fox could absolutely guarantee them he would bring if elected: *el cambio*, a change from the PRI, which by that time had been in power for seventy-one years, making it by far the longest-ruling regime in the world. *"¡Hoy! ¡Hoy! ¡Hoy!"* his followers chanted at his campaign rallies, to say that "Today! Today! Today!" was when they wanted Fox to oust the PRI.

Like the Garza family and many others among his supporters, Fox had known what it was like to be on the outside. When a young man, he never intended to go into politics. He worked for Coca-Cola de México for fifteen years, starting out supervising delivery routes and ending up as chief executive. In 1979 he left Mexico City and moved his family back to Guanajuato to help his brothers manage the big family vegetable farm at a time when the PRI's economic management had put the Mexican peso on a dizzying downward ride. In 1988, fed up with the struggle to turn a profit under the thrall of an inept state, Fox ran for a seat in the Federal Chamber of Deputies.

As soon as he announced his candidacy, government health inspec-tors came around and shut down the family vegetable-packing plant, on the grounds that the employees lacked photographs on their identifica-tion cards. Then the federal social security agency audited Fox's books. Then farmworkers invaded his ranch, encouraged by the PRI to launch an ad hoc local land reform, starting, curiously enough, right there on Fox's farm.

Fox gutted out the harassment and won his congressional race, jump-starting the political career that was culminating on July 2.

This time the PRI candidate Fox had to beat was Francisco Labastida Ochoa, a handsome white-haired politician with a rakishly tilted smile who had accomplished the near impossible: he had made a thirty-seven-year career in PRI government without being seriously tainted by charges of corruption. (Zedillo could not run again because Mexican Presidents are limited by the Constitution to one six-year term.) Unlike most PRI overlords, Labastida was an unpretentious man who disliked chauffeurs, bodyguards, and other trappings of PRI power. He insisted, to the despair of his security contingent, on doing his own driving on the campaign trail. He had a warm way with voters and did well in the suffo-cating crushes that inevitably formed around him at rallies, when hard-core PRI supporters, who regarded their presidential candidate as a dauphin, would push forward to touch his arm. Labastida seemed gen-uinely to want to be a PRI President who would do more than his prede-cessors for Mexico's downtrodden.

His problem was that he didn't stand out enough from the old-time PRI. He favored the finely groomed look and leather windbreakers typi-cal of PRI politicians of his generation (leading the many northern Mex-ico cowboy homophobes in the Fox camp to call him La Vestida, slang for transvestite). In three decades in government he had never rocked the PRI boat even slightly, and his campaign promised changes so in-nocuous as to be almost imperceptible.

There was a third important candidate, Cuauhtémoc Cárdenas of the leftist Party of the Democratic Revolution (Partido de la Revolución Democrática), or PRD, who was making his third presidential bid. Cár-denas, whose natural facial expression was a forbidding glower, was a kind of anti-candidate who persisted, against the advice of exasperated campaign managers, on ignoring the demands of the news media, espe-cially television, and making dourness his distinctive campaign style.

This approach actually served him well the first time he ran, in 1988. As the son of the late President Lázaro Cárdenas, who is beloved by Mexicans for giving land to the peasants and nationalizing the oil indus-try, Cuauhtémoc had a reserve of moral authority in 1987, when he broke with the PRI, which his father had helped found. In his first cam-paign he emerged as a plain dealer, the antithesis of the slick politicos of the PRI. He inspired a popular upswell with his criticism of the PRI's economic policies and his calls for more democracy in the party and the country. Many Mexicans, including Cuauhtémoc himself, believed that Carlos Salinas de Gortari, the PRI candidate, had prevailed against Cár-denas in the 1988 election only by fraud.

But in 1994, and again in 2000, the voters were much less moved by Cárdenas's gravitas and his dated leftist ideas. During the 2000 campaign the polls showed that he never attracted the support of more than about 17 percent of the voters.

However, on the eve of July 2 the polls were not giving much comfort to Fox's followers either. Although the surveys—by Mexican firms as well as respected international pollsters like Harris, Stanley Greenberg, and Zogby—indicated that Labastida had steadily declined throughout the campaign, most polls showed that he remained slightly ahead of Fox as the race ended, although the contest was close enough to be a technical tie. With Election Day looming, Mexican voters seemed to hesitate to embrace change.

"I prefer the devil I do know to the one I don't," said Cristina Luna Flores, a forty-two-year-old working-class housewife who attended Labastida's lavish final rally in the central plaza, or Zócalo, of Mexico City, voicing the peculiar resignation that substituted for enthusiasm in long-time PRI voters.

The Fox campaign had several internal polls that showed its candidate pulling ahead of Labastida. But only Fox himself, with his unsinkable self-assurance, believed them entirely.

There were other reasons for Conchalupe Garza and her cohorts to be nervous. As the poll margins tightened, the PRI had launched a full-

Vicente Fox, the PAN candidate, capped a surprisingly strong campaign with a rally in the Zócalo in Mexico City on June 24, 2000, that drew a huge, hopeful crowd

court vote-buying drive in rural states. The PRI governor of the state of Yucatán, Victor Cervera Pacheco, established a new standard for the price of a vote. Instead of doling out box lunches and promises of government assistance, the common tender of the past, Governor Cervera gave away washing machines. He paid for them unabashedly from the public treasury and handed them out by the thousands in dozens of towns. For effect, in the Yucatecan town of Umán, PRI workers formed a battlement of 1,003 white washing machines (the round kind with the two-roller manual dryers on the top) around the central square and donated them with pomp and fanfare to local housewives, to stop any softening in their loyalty.

Deployments of PRI elections operatives across the country convinced both Fox and Cárdenas that the ruling party was preparing to fix or undermine the vote on Election Day if necessary. Even though the two opposition candidates were insulting each other with brio from the hustings, they formed a common front a few weeks before Election Day to combat chicanery by the PRI.

In the final days before July 2, Labastida remained confident. The elections laws prohibited public campaigning after Wednesday, June 28. On Friday afternoon Labastida gave an interview to *The New York Times* at a campaign retreat in a stylish neighborhood on the edge of Chapultepec Park in Mexico City. The interview was granted with the understanding that if he won, his comments would be published as part of a victor's profile on the day after the election.

If Labastida had some inkling that day that he might not be the victor, he did not betray it. In the morning he had written a first draft of his victory speech, promising to lead a government of unity and reconciliation. His offices already had an executive air. There was no longer any sign of campaign frenzy: no overflowing ashtrays, no posters hanging crooked on smudged walls. The sound system was humming classical music, suitable for a statesman.

Looking fit and dapper, Labastida launched into his plans for his new administration. His main theme, surprisingly, was frustration with his own party. He announced that he did not intend to govern with the PRI alone, but would seek to cement an alliance with one or more of the opposition parties to create a "co-government," as he called it. He intimated that he did not intend to draw his cabinet exclusively from the

PRI and said that immediately after the election he would start to push the party to "rethink itself, redesign itself, and finish transforming itself" to be more democratic in its internal affairs and more in touch with everyday people. The only hint that he had sensed something amiss in the campaign was his prediction that he would have to work hard to "reconquer" young and middle-class Mexicans.

At the end of the interview Labastida rattled off his plans for election night. If the pollsters' quick counts showed that his margin was wide—say, four or five points—he would declare his victory right after the Federal Electoral Institute gave the first official results at 11 p.m. If the race was close, however, he saw no need to rush things. He would hold off his declaration until elections officials had completed their first full count in the dawn hours of Monday.

So, while Conchalupe Garza was fretting in the hours before the vote, Francisco Labastida and his wife, María Teresa, hosted a placid photo opportunity in a parlor at their home, inviting photographers to snap pictures of them as they decided which hero of Mexican independence Labastida would compare himself to in speeches that day, calmly awaiting their coronation.

Vicente Fox, meanwhile, did not get off to such a genteel start. He spent the night at his family ranch in the town of San Cristóbal in Guanajuato, a state famous for exporting leather shoes and immigrant farmworkers to the United States. After working up a sweat on his treadmill, Fox stepped into the shower at 6:30 on a chill country morning and discovered there was no hot water: the pump had burned out. He would not be able to clean up until he reached PAN headquarters in Mexico City hours later.

He wasn't fazed. By a coincidence of the calendar, July 2, the date Mexico decided to hold the presidential election in which Fox would run, was his birthday; he was turning fifty-eight. As soon as he was dressed, his four children, ranging from Rodrigo, age twelve, to Ana Cristina, who was twenty, gathered around him to sing "Las Mañanitas," Mexico's lilting birthday song. Soon a band of mariachi musicians in their silver-buttoned bolero jackets showed up at the front gate to the ranch, and townspeople joined in the birthday chorus.

For breakfast Fox ate tacos stuffed with nopal cactus leaves. He pulled on a pair of azure cowboy boots, specially made in the PAN's party colors. Before leaving the house, he bowed his head to receive a blessing from his eighty-three-year-old mother, Mercedes Quesada, a devout Catholic. Visitors to the ranch noted Doña Mercedes's firm command over the Fox household; at family dinners she sat at the head of the table, not her son Vicente, even when he was a presidential candidate.

As Fox left his ranch that morning, he thought of the election as a final exam. It would be hard, he anticipated, but he felt he had done his homework.

At 8 a.m. the polls opened peacefully and on time in almost all of the 113,000 polling places around the country.

In Mexico City the nine-member citizens council that governed the Federal Electoral Institute was called into session at the same hour by its president, José Woldenberg. The council's order of business for the day was nothing more or less than to hold the elections, in which Mexico was renewing its entire national leadership. The PRI regime centered on an omnipotent President, bolstered by a single national party, which directly controlled the country's main labor, farmworkers, and business federations. Only in the late 1990s had the President's power begun to be checked by the elected representatives in the bicameral Congress. On July 2, Mexicans would choose their President and fill all the seats in both houses of Congress, as well as pick three state governors.

A representative from the PRI (the council included nonvoting representatives from every political party) spoke with assurance of the "pristine" election he was expecting. For their part, the delegates from several opposition parties accused the PRI and the institute of a slew of irregularities. They were especially distressed by the discovery, on the eve of the vote, of a PRI warehouse in the city of Durango packed with fifteen thousand bags of rice, which they took to be currency that the ruling party intended to use for last-minute vote shopping.

Woldenberg listened to the complaints, but they didn't disturb him. He was confident that the council he chaired, and the institute it governed, had organized the vote well. The institute had spent $1.2 billion preparing the election, vastly more than ever before. The agency, once controlled by the government, was now fully supervised by independent citizens like him. In a huge effort it had recruited and trained neutral officials to oversee every polling station in the country and mobilized the opposition parties to place their own poll watchers in the vast majority of them.

As the voting progressed, at around 10:30 in the morning Conchalupe Garza received an urgent call on her mobile phone from a friend reporting trouble. He was at a special polling place in Mexico City set up for registered voters who were not in their hometowns on Election Day. To protect against fraud, these special stations were assigned only a limited number of ballots, 750 each. Conchalupe's friend said that his polling place had filled up with dozens of uniformed policemen who had shoved their way to the front of the line, barking that they were in a rush to return to their duty posts. Other voters were pushed to the back, where they might not get to vote before the ballots ran out. They were jeering and whistling at the police, convinced that the guardians of the public order were there to carry out a PRI plot.

The voting on July 2, 2000, was generally peaceful and orderly. "The vote is free and secret," polling station signs proclaimed

But Conchalupe had a different hunch. She counseled her friend to stay cool and leave the policemen alone, recalling an encounter she had had with police in the Mexico City airport. A manic campaigner, she would buy a newspaper whenever she passed through the airport, just so she could talk Fox up to the newsstand cashier. She would go down the concourse flashing the two-fingered Y (for ¡ya!, meaning "enough!") that Fox had made his campaign logo, and harangue the coffee-shop wait-resses and the cleaning woman mopping the ladies' room. One day five airport policemen came toward her, as if to throw her out.

Instead, checking this way and that for their superiors, the officers had lowered their voices to ask if she had any Fox bumper stickers.

"I may weep tonight that I told you this," she said to her friend on the phone. "But I bet those cops who cut in line are with Fox. I bet they'll vote for change."

In general, the voting was almost too orderly. There was no sense of any upheaval under way. Shortly after noon Labastida, in his candidate's office at the spacious modern complex housing PRI headquarters on Avenida de los Insurgentes, received the results of his own party's first exit polls, based on interviews with Mexicans as they left the voting booths. The surveys showed that he was ahead, although by only one point. An hour later Labastida got a call from Los Pinos, the President's office and residence—the Mexican White House—across the city center in a pine-shaded corner of Chapultepec Park. The caller was Liébano Sáenz, President Zedillo's chief of staff, and Labastida gave him the good news. It was a routine: the PRI candidate reassuring the PRI President that the party was going to retain power once again.

But out in the polling places something unfamiliar was happening. A number of news reporters headed out to Ecatepec, a suburb on the northern edge of the rolling sea of settlement that is the Mexico City me-tropolis. With more than one million voters, Ecatepec is one of the biggest municipalities in all of Mexico. On street after pitted street, Mex-ico's new proletariat, mainly first-generation refugees from failed farms and hungry-dog rural villages, lived in cinder-block houses, crammed in among tortilla stores and tire-repair shops, often lacking water and elec-tricity. Having built their neighborhoods by milking PRI patronage net-works for plots of land, construction materials, and other necessities, these workers had always voted solidly for the ruling party. Even as other Mexico City barrios had turned in recent years to Cuauhtémoc Cárdenas's PRD, Ecatepec remained unfriendly to the opposition.

Now the reporters couldn't seem to find any PRI voters there. People coming out of Ecatepec polling stations either begged to remain silent or announced point-blank that they had gone for *el cambio*. Many didn't mention Fox at all, but spoke only of *el cambio*, as if change itself were their candidate in the race. Even those Ecatepec residents who admitted to voting for the PRI seemed uninspired. When José Luis Caballero, a thirty-nine-year-old city employee, emerged from a polling station with his wife, Gabriela, he confessed his PRI vote to a reporter. His wife turned on him, vexed. "This country needs a change!" she said.

Caballero thought about it for a minute—and immediately repented his vote. Since he was a government employee, he said, he had done it out of habit. "This country needs *many* changes," he agreed.

So it was that by one o'clock in the afternoon, when enough votes had been cast to determine the outcome of the election, a revolution had taken place, very quietly and calmly, in Mexico.

One of the first Mexicans to learn of it was Vicente Fox himself. In the late morning he had flown to Mexico City and gone to the new headquarters of the PAN, in a residential neighborhood on the southern side of the city center. As befit a party that had grown used to the idea that it would never take power, its building wasn't finished. The windows weren't installed, the plumbing wasn't working in whole sections of the square modern structure, and the grounds were a dirt lot surrounded by a hurricane fence.

Fox found an inner room where the lights worked. Sometime after noon the PAN's pollsters arrived. They were grinning. Their exit polls showed that Fox had a clean five-point lead, and the margin seemed to be widening.

A little while later Martha Sahagún came into the room and handed Fox one of her "information notes." Martha was Fox's spokeswoman and had been his most constant companion during the campaign. Her mobile phone had been the real-time link between Fox and the press, and through the press to the Mexican people. The word in the campaign was that the candidate and his spokeswoman were romantically involved.

Martha's note said that Los Pinos, the President's office, had informed her that their own exit-poll results confirmed Fox's lead. Sáenz, the chief of staff, had been cagey over the phone about the exact numbers, apparently fearing that Martha would leak them immediately to the press. But the key, she wrote, was not in Sáenz's numbers but in his words. He told Martha that Zedillo's analysts had concluded that the trend of the voting was "irreversible."

That was his word. *"Irreversible."*

After she saw that Fox had read the note, Martha Sahagún, suspected by all who dealt with her on the campaign trail to be made of titanium, began to cry.

Fox himself was relieved but not overwhelmed, as if there had never been any doubt about the outcome. He began reminiscing with Martha and his staff about the day a year earlier when he had publicly accepted the PAN's presidential nomination, at the official kickoff of what had seemed an utterly quixotic campaign. The rally, hastily convened on a cramped street in the shadow of the Mexico City bullring, had drawn only a few thousand people and been so badly organized that the press had made fun of it.

Just then someone burst in to say that there were hundreds of PAN supporters in the street outside the headquarters who wanted to wish their candidate happy birthday. Fox, contemplating the still-secret vote results, saw an opportunity to exercise his knack for political theater. Stepping out onto a balcony, he greeted the crowd, making no mention of the poll figures. But instead of flashing his two-fingered Y, he held up all five fingers on his right hand, representing his five-point lead at that hour. Many people in the crowd noticed the change of signal, but they would not realize until hours later what it meant.

At 3 p.m. sharp, Woldenberg, the elections council president, went on national television with his first report on the balloting, saying there had been only minor mishaps so far. At Los Pinos, Zedillo's advisers, studying new exit polls, concluded that Fox's lead was widening. Sáenz passed the information along to the President, who was at his residence within the compound, a stone building in a 1950s monumental style that looked more like a central bank than a home. There, Zedillo was following the events intently but not anxiously. Throughout the campaign he had kept a certain distance from Labastida, in a rebuff that had confused and finally offended his party.

The President's detachment stemmed in part from his personal distaste for political glitz and campaigning. A Yale-trained economist, Zedillo enjoyed balancing the budget more than he liked the flesh pressing and deal making of PRI politics. In addition, he did not want to repeat the performance of his predecessor, Carlos Salinas de Gortari. Focused on preserving the glory of his own presidency, Salinas had meddled in Zedillo's campaign and had made some end-of-term economic decisions that Zedillo blamed for turning the first year of his tenure into a nightmare of devaluation and recession.

Six years earlier Zedillo had become the PRI's presidential candidate by a terrible accident. On March 23, 1994, the original candidate, Luis Donaldo Colosio, was assassinated, shot in the head by a gunman who lunged from the crowd at a rally in Tijuana. Rumors swirled that he had been murdered by rivals in the PRI, possibly encouraged by President Salinas himself. Salinas, who had chosen Colosio, cast about for a new candidate and soon discovered that Zedillo was the only member of his cabinet who was both capable and eligible under Mexico's complex laws. So Salinas made Zedillo the candidate.

Although Zedillo had won a credible victory, he remained uneasy about the advantages that the PRI system had afforded his campaign, especially through its control of the media. The events of 1994 convinced him that the regime's methods for the orderly transfer of power were failing. He began to think that the moment had come for Mexico to take a long step toward the genuine democracy that the country had been seeking since its first proclamation of independence in 1810.

Many critics had derided Zedillo as politically maladroit, but they underestimated him. He had moved slowly and deliberately over the course of his term to reach, at the end, a practically unassailable position.

A sweeping set of electoral reforms he had driven through the Congress in 1996 had consolidated the independent elections agency and provided generous public financing for all the parties' campaigns, creating conditions for the opposition to compete on a more level field with the PRI. He had further jolted his party in the year before the election by declining to exercise the ultimate power of PRI Presidents: the *dedazo*, or finger tap, the ritual by which the PRI incumbent (and not the Mexican electorate) chose his successor. Instead, Zedillo made the PRI select its presidential candidate in its first-ever primary election. In a race more hard-fought than anyone expected, Labastida beat out three other candidates in his party. Even though Zedillo never revealed his preference, the party faithful had flocked to Labastida because they believed he was the President's choice.

During the presidential campaign Zedillo had done little to defend Labastida against Fox and Cárdenas. But whenever anyone questioned the fairness of the elections apparatus that he had helped to set up, Zedillo got fighting mad. He had even had a sharp exchange with former President Jimmy Carter, who brought a small observer delegation to Mexico for the elections, when Carter had published a pre-vote report pointing out some problems. Zedillo was convinced that if the elections system worked properly and the results were broadly accepted as clean and fair, he would have made a significant contribution to Mexico's political development.

It was not lost on him, as well, that if the election went smoothly, his reformist legacy would be secured regardless of the outcome: if the PRI won, Zedillo would be remembered as the President who gave Mexico its most open elections and reelected his party. If the PRI lost, he would be the father of Mexican democracy.

So, as the afternoon wore on, the conversations between Zedillo and his aides remained brief and businesslike. Only at one point did Liébano Sáenz, a PRI veteran, pause from his phone calling, sit back in his chair, and take a long breath. "We lost!" he said, stunned, in the one moment of recognition he allowed himself.

Around four o'clock Sáenz took a walk down the cobbled pathway and through the trees between his offices and the President's residence, carrying a memo prepared for Zedillo by his official pollster. It was nothing more than a statistical readout, but it showed clearly that Fox was going to win decisively. Sáenz decided that he should hand it to the President personally.

With that began the second tectonic shift in Mexican politics that night, the fissure that opened between the PRI President and the ruling party, as the system swayed and finally came down.

For Zedillo, to be sure, his party's defeat was strange, untraveled territory. But he had long realized that a real opening of the political system might result in the PRI's downfall, so he had had plenty of time to prepare. No one who accompanied or spoke with Zedillo on July 2 ever saw him hesitate to recognize Fox's victory.

But Zedillo and his men were seriously worried about how the PRI would react. The damage-control scenarios that the President's staff had considered before the election were all tied to a narrow victory by either Fox or Labastida. They hadn't imagined the possibility of a Fox victory so broad that the PRI would be humiliated. Studying the poll results at mid-afternoon, they concluded that it was crucial for Mexico's national security for Labastida to concede as early and gracefully as possible. They saw that an early resolution would benefit Zedillo as well. If the vote count went smoothly, and if Labastida conceded and Fox was a gracious winner, then Zedillo would be able, at the end, to make the speech that would welcome Mexico at last to the realm of modern democracy. It could be the speech that would define his presidency.

So, at 4 p.m., Liébano Sáenz, an affable PRI insider with the touch for negotiation that Zedillo lacked, launched a campaign of telephone diplomacy between Fox and the PRI aimed at achieving the finale that Los Pinos desired. Sáenz's first call was to Labastida, and it did not go well.

"You should be getting ready to make your announcement," Sáenz said. "If you come out now, you will gain the respect of the Mexican people and save the PRI a lot of trouble. Our polls are showing results that are irreversible."

"I have different information," Labastida responded curtly. "I'm going to wait. I am going to respect the orthodoxy of my party."

"Francisco, orthodoxy is for the winner," Sáenz said. "*We lost.*" Already he was using the phrase with more familiarity.

As the afternoon hours passed, phone calls from Los Pinos to PRI headquarters grew more frequent as Zedillo and his advisers observed deepening disarray in the party. The PRI's decision makers were not even in the same room together. Labastida and three or four of his most

trusted aides were sequestered in an office on the third floor of the headquarters complex. Other party chieftains were on the second floor, hun-
kered down around the long committee table in the campaign war room
next to the office of the party president. Labastida did not come down
from his lair to meet with them until after 6 p.m. He didn't even sit
down, but started right in by telling them that the trend was "unfavorable."

The PRI leaders went silent with stupefaction, then murmured in disbelief. "It can't be." "It isn't possible."

Labastida broached the idea that he should prepare a concession
statement. That roused the party leaders, who insisted angrily that he
wait for more results. Although they had never tired of citing poll results
during the campaign when Labastida was ahead, now they scorned the
pollsters, arguing that the PRI's most loyal following had always been the
"green vote" from rural areas, the last ballots to be tallied. At the end of
the day, they told their candidate fiercely, the green vote would pull it
out for the PRI. They expected the candidate to issue a call to arms, not
an admission of defeat.

Labastida, shying away from confrontation with the party machine,
withdrew to his office. Quietly, he summoned a speechwriter and began
to compose his concession.

At about 6:15 p.m. Labastida talked by telephone with Zedillo. "I'm
going to let the whole process run its course, and then decide how to proceed," Labastida said. In a second call with the President, just before
eight o'clock, Labastida acknowledged that he was going to lose but still
gave no timetable for action. Zedillo's tone was cool. Yet he signed off
saying, "*Te mando un abrazo,* I send you an embrace," in the way that
Mexicans have of injecting expressions of affection into the most
strained and impersonal situations.

But the lack of resolve that Labastida had conveyed to Zedillo added
to growing alarm at Los Pinos, where officials had been watching other
signals emanating from PRI headquarters. Labastida abruptly canceled a
press conference with the crowd of reporters who were waiting at PRI
headquarters and refused all phone calls from the press. He called Sáenz
to say that the PRI party president, Dulce María Sauri, would make a
brief statement just after 8 p.m. to acknowledge the party's defeat. The

hour came and went, and Sauri never spoke.

The last polling places in the country closed when it was eight o'clock in Mexico City. (The official closing time was 6 p.m., but there is a two-hour time difference between the capital and Baja California.) Immediately both major national television networks, Televisa and TV Azteca, announced results of independent polls they had commissioned. Vicente Fox had won the election by as much as eight points, both networks reported. In a flash the news was out. Some celebrations erupted.

But many Mexicans held back, waiting to see if the PRI would allow Fox to claim his victory.

Over at PAN headquarters everyone except Fox was struggling to assimilate the events. Fox's supporters were elated, but out of long experience they also remained on guard, bracing for news that the PRI was moving to challenge the election outcome. Conchalupe Garza thought of calling her mother in Monterrey to share the news. But she decided to wait. She thought it would literally break her mother's heart if Fox won and the PRI stole the triumph once again.

At 7:45 President Zedillo put through a call to Fox. He acknowledged Fox's lead but urged him not to act until after 11 p.m., when José Woldenberg would announce the official results from the Federal Electoral Institute. Right after Woldenberg had spoken, Zedillo also told Fox, he intended to address the nation.

Shortly after 8:30 Zedillo called again. Fox stepped into an empty room to find some quiet. The conversation lasted almost ten minutes, with both men addressing each other with the familiar *tú*. Zedillo said he had seen the first official returns from the Federal Electoral Institute. They gave Fox an incontrovertible eight-point margin.

"I congratulate you, Vicente," the President said, straightforward. Fox thanked him cordially, but for the rest of the conversation he struggled to contain his emotions. He barely managed to make a promise to the President that he would not declare victory until after Woldenberg had spoken.

Throughout the afternoon Fox had been all business. But when he emerged into the hallway jammed with his followers, the look on his face produced a hush. "We won," he said simply, and his eyes filled with tears.

He went straight to give a press conference in the headquarters auditorium, which was packed with reporters and sweltering hot. Keeping his pledge to Zedillo, Fox said only that the balloting had been "spotless" and that he was beginning "to feel a sense of great responsibility." He took no questions, but his obvious high spirits left the press satisfied anyway.

However, Fox's sublime moment of glory was to be brief. His two daughters, Ana Cristina and Paulina, had insisted on bringing their mother with them from Guanajuato to the PAN headquarters that day. Fox's marital history was unusual: having been divorced in 1992 from his wife, Lilián de la Concha, after she left him for an affair with another man, Fox had taken custody of all four of the couple's children, all of them adopted. He had been a conscientious single father, but his daughters had never given up hope of brokering a rapprochement between their parents. Although Lilián had not participated in the campaign, the girls, with a bit of encouragement from their mother, decided that the night of Fox's victory was the perfect time to try for reconciliation.

Lilián's ardent congratulatory kiss for Fox was too much for Martha Sahagún, the loyal spokeswoman. A catfight erupted, with the two women yelling. Purses were swung. A few minutes later, when one of Fox's closest advisers approached him to exult and discuss tactical details, Fox barked at him and sent him away. For the rest of the evening Lilián sat as near as she could to the President-elect, smiling winsomely, while Martha Sahagún paced like a lioness.

Labastida, meanwhile, was sealed in the somber quiet of his office, trying to come to grips with his situation. He was the PRI's only losing presidential candidate. The PRI had known defeat in state elections, but the party had never during the lifetime of any of its leaders lost a presidential election.

"Not only the party but also me—I was a man who had never known defeat in his whole life," Labastida said later, recalling the moment. "I never broke down," he insisted. "I've had a lot of tempering. I never broke down."

But he could not move to concede. Ignoring the pressure from Los

Pinos, he decided he would speak after Woldenberg. He would leave it to the newly independent elections authorities to tell the Mexican people who had won—and who had lost.

At about 9 p.m. the men at Los Pinos convened an emergency meeting. Fresh reports from PRI headquarters indicated that the mood in the party was turning sour. They felt that events were running off track.

"In the context of Mexican politics, the uncertainty at that hour was a matter of the highest national security," recalled Federico Berrueto, one of Sáenz's deputies. "We believed that if a war of words broke out, if Fox or the PAN felt that their victory was threatened, things could spin out of control in a matter of minutes. We could have a state of political decomposition that was . . ."—he paused to find the precise word—"unmanageable."

Zedillo's advisers did not know what plans the PRI might have made to respond if Labastida fell behind in the count. They feared that the PRI could signal operatives across the country to disrupt the polling stations or start a campaign of resistance to the results. PAN supporters might rise up to defend their success, and there could be riots, even shooting.

Sáenz called Labastida again. "Listen, Cárdenas is about to concede," he said.

"I know that," Labastida replied, irritated. "I heard the same thing."

"He is going to beat you to it," Sáenz said.

"I don't know if he will beat me to it or not," Labastida said, offended. "This part of it is *not* a race." Labastida said he wanted to consult with PRI governors around the nation to see what they thought he should do. The idea that Mexico's stability was hanging on a straw poll of PRI governors, the field commanders of the regime, alarmed Sáenz even more. He rejected the plan.

"I'm going to come out after the elections authorities speak," Labastida insisted.

"*The President* is going to come out after the elections authorities speak," Sáenz fired back.

"We have to respect the country's institutions," Labastida said bluntly, terminating the conversation.

About five thousand PRI stalwarts were milling around in the broad open courtyard in the middle of the PRI headquarters complex. The plaza had been the scene over the years of dozens of triumphant rallies, self-satisfied displays of esprit de corps, where everyone knew each other and everyone had a red, white, and green banner to wave and a timely PRI slogan to shout. Now the PRI faithful were gathered once again, banners and slogans at the ready. Several giant television screens were set up around the plaza, and every time a news show announced another poll with Fox winning, the crowd hooted and jeered.

"We won't quit! They can't do that to us!" they shouted. They were waiting for instructions, getting ready to change from cheerleaders to militants—even street fighters if necessary.

At 10:20 Cuauhtémoc Cárdenas conceded. Early results indicated that he had won only 17 percent of the vote. In a nationally televised press conference at his headquarters, Cárdenas gave Fox a sour welcome, declining to congratulate him and making no mention of the significance for Mexican democracy of the fall of the PRI. Instead, he pledged the PRD to be "the firmest opposition" to an odd series of abstract evils he said that Fox represented: "anti-nationalism, obscurantism, opportunism, and improvisation."

"We are in a long struggle. What are a few days more?" he asked, referring to the six years of Fox's term. He closed with a phrase evoking Fidel Castro, which all the events seemed to belie.

"We are moving in the direction of history," he said. Asked afterward by reporters why he had not congratulated Fox, Cárdenas said, "Because what is happening is a disaster for this country."

With his first brave, iconoclastic run for President in 1988, Cárdenas had done more than any other Mexican to force the PRI system to open to political diversity. As a result of that race, he was an undisputed champion of the democratic movement. But at the end of his third try at the presidency, Cárdenas seemed to diminish himself, showing that he would only be satisfied to see Mexicans gain greater political freedom if it would bring him and his ideas to power.

As soon as Cárdenas finished, Sáenz called Labastida one last time.

"Listen, Cuauhtémoc has already come out," Sáenz said, implying that it was now Labastida's turn.

"I saw him," Labastida said frostily. "I'm not changing my decision." Both men hung up, furious.

At 10:30 Sáenz reported to Zedillo that Labastida was still delaying and there could be unrest at the PRI. The President was in his office working on the text of his address, and when he heard his aide's assessment, he started over on a second draft, striking out all references to a concession by Labastida.

Sáenz gave orders to clear national airtime for the President's broadcast shortly after 11 p.m. Leaving nothing to chance, Zedillo and his advisers decided that he would pretape the address rather than deliver it live. The cameras started to roll, but Zedillo's aides halted them. The President looked too ruddy, they thought, and not sufficiently anguished about his party's defeat. The camera crew patted some Pan-Cake onto Zedillo's face, giving him just a touch of pallor.

Once the taping was done, there was no changing plans. Zedillo would be on the air at 11:06 p.m.

Promptly at eleven, Woldenberg went on national television to announce that the Federal Electoral Institute had counted enough votes to show that Fox was the winner.

As soon as he finished, the Mexican television networks switched to the main auditorium at PRI headquarters. The cameras showed Labastida in a death march, making his way across the stage through a gantlet of embraces from his followers, many of them sobbing. Labastida reached the podium and waited for the shouts to die down. He put his speech in front of him and started to speak.

"The results of today's votes are not favorable to me or my party—"

Just then, Ernesto Zedillo cut him off. Suddenly the President's address from Los Pinos broke into the broadcast, displacing Labastida. The PRI candidate continued to speak, but the only Mexicans to see him were those watching in the auditorium.

Zedillo, looking sober but composed, was standing at a podium in his office, the centerpiece of a carefully structured tableau. Behind him to his right was a Mexican flag, and just over his shoulder was an oil portrait of Benito Juárez, the great nineteenth-century Mexican President, a liberal whom Zedillo admired.

At first he said nothing of Fox.

"Today we have shown for all to see that ours is a nation of free men and women who believe only in the means of democracy and law to achieve progress and resolve our problems," the President said.

Then it came.

"Just a few moments ago, the Federal Electoral Institute informed all Mexicans that it has data which, although still preliminary, are sufficient and reliable enough to show that Vicente Fox Quesada will be the next President of the Republic."

At Fox headquarters pandemonium at last erupted, both inside the building and outside, where thousands of his supporters had blocked the streets. There was no longer any doubt. Fox had won. The President had spoken. The PRI would leave, and Fox would govern. Democracy would be given a chance.

"¡Hoy! ¡Hoy! ¡Hoy!" Fox's fans shouted. "Today! Today! Today!"

Zedillo pledged to work with Fox to achieve a "transparent, clean, and efficient" turnover of government at the end of his term on December 1, and to make sure that the country was in good order when that time came. He referred to himself as *un servidor*, your servant, using a

President Ernesto Zedillo appeared on a nationwide television broadcast just after 11 p.m. on July 2, 2000, to announce that Vicente Fox had unseated the PRI

gracious Mexican expression of humility. Praising Labastida, he said the PRI candidate had "fought gallantly," and stated his "unvarying affection" for him. He thanked the PRI, which he said had "contributed to social peace, political stability, international prestige, and economic development for Mexico."

As soon as Zedillo finished speaking, the television networks cut back to PRI headquarters, where Labastida was just coming to the end of his own statement.

"The citizens have taken a decision that we should all respect," he had told the morose gathering. "Our party is still alive," he had reported to the followers, who only hours before had no reason to think it faced any risk of death. He predicted that the PRI would one day "recover its vitality," but in the meantime he summoned party members to "profound reflection."

Most Mexicans had not seen Labastida say these words. What the television cameras suddenly showed was a panoramic display of the PRI laid low, a sight most Mexicans never dreamed they would see. The shouts of "¡Duro! ¡Duro! Give it to them! Give it to them!," the PRI rallying cry, sounded weak and hollow. The faithful tried to sing the Mexican national anthem, but it came out as a dirge. Labastida turned to exit with his head held high, but he could not. When his wife touched his elbow, he faltered, stricken with grief.

At the sight of Labastida stumbling, the men at Los Pinos, and many other Mexicans who were watching, realized that the PRI insurrection they feared had not coalesced. Later, Zedillo government officials would learn of plans for local PRI groups to challenge the vote by creating havoc with militant protests. But so confident were the party's leaders that night that by the time they came to grips with the results of the vote, it was too late to react.

At 11:30 p.m. José Woldenberg gaveled the meeting of the elections council to a close. The council members had expected to be up all night struggling over a close vote tally, but now there was nothing for them to do. They shook hands with each other, dispensing with exultation. They had done their assigned task, and it had worked.

At PAN headquarters Fox fielded congratulatory calls and gave press interviews. At midnight he stepped out onto the balcony to greet his followers in the street, who numbered many thousands and had stopped traffic for blocks in all directions. Behind him an enormous video screen projected his image. It was Fox at his best: folksy and warm, but larger than life nevertheless. A master of ceremonies introduced him as "the President of the Republic."

"Wow, that sounds really good!" he said. He threw back his head and took a sloppy swig on a bottle of champagne. "Tequila is better!" he shouted, and the crowd rejoiced. He pledged with a belly laugh to start acting presidential.

"I promise I'm going to stop swearing," he said, and the crowd came back, shouting, "No! No!"

"Everyone is asking me how I feel," Fox said. "¡Me siento a toda máquina, la verdad! I feel I'm going full speed ahead, that's the truth!"

"¡Arriba! ¡Abajo! ¡El PRI se va al carajo! The PRI is going to hell!" echoed the crowd's jubilant slogan.

Fox had praise for Zedillo. "You all know that I don't go around flattering people. But President Zedillo acted tonight without hesitating even once." He said that he hoped to "complete the transition without rancor or resentment."

Conchalupe Garza finally felt free to call home. On hearing all the news, her mother, despite her septuagenarian years, rushed to her bedroom and jumped up and down on the bed.

At about 1 a.m. Fox addressed a crowd that had gathered on the steps at the base of the Angel de la Independencia, the monument of a winged angel perched atop a tall pillar that is to Mexico City what the Eiffel Tower is to Paris. He found a mellow gathering, with no pushing or shoving, no uncontrolled crush. There were lots of young people in loafers with cellular phones, a core Fox constituency. Despite the late hour, many parents had roused their children out of bed and brought them in their pajamas to the angel so they could witness the moment. One man danced a mambo with his mastiff.

Some PAN supporters went down the Paseo de la Reforma tearing down PRI posters as the police stood by, smiling. Another group came shouldering a wooden coffin with a papier-mâché cadaver of the PRI laid out inside.

By three in the morning the crowd had gone home.

The next morning, citizens across the country went about their lives as usual. They steered plows across farm fields and labored in gritty factories and sleek business offices, just as on any other day. They were satisfied with Zedillo and had soaring expectations for Fox. But all in all, it looked as though not much had changed.

Mexicans who had worked for decades to make democracy knew differently.

2

From Disorder to Despotism

The tranquil outcome of the election of July 2, 2000, was remarkable in light of the longevity of the regime that the voters unseated. Up to that point the PRI system had given Mexico twelve consecutive Presidents. But the day's events went far beyond the fall of the PRI in their significance. They marked the first time in its history that Mexico had achieved a peaceful transfer of state power from the rulers to the opposition by means of free elections with full suffrage. Until then, political change had brought conflict and often violence.

The July 2 vote was not only a break with the past, but also held meaning for the future. At long last the working parts of Mexico's democracy were in place. The President, Vicente Fox, was directly responsible, for the first time, to the voters. To limit his power, there was a feisty legislature with an opposition majority in the lower house; the courts were also moving slowly but steadily toward independence. There was pluralism in state government, where the elected governors came from the PRI, the PAN, and the PRD. The independent elections organization was established. An irreverent press was ready to scrutinize the performance of public officials, and civic groups were there to press their agendas on the government.

By consolidating the means to resolve their differences through politics, Mexicans had overcome a heavy legacy of their history. To a sobering degree, Mexico's national pantheon is filled with heroes whose struggles to advance the people's cause brought them exile, at best, or terrible death. The stories that Mexican schoolchildren learn about their forefathers all too frequently end in "rivers of blood," to take a phrase from Miguel Hidalgo, the Catholic parish priest who was the father of Mexican independence.

Hidalgo himself was an example. On the morning of September 16, 1810, he ignited a rebellion against the Spanish Crown by the poorest Indians and peasants, proclaiming, "Death to the Spaniards!" from the

In the town of Dolores in 1810, Miguel Hidalgo, a Catholic priest, raised the cry of rebellion that started Mexico's wars for independence from Spain

steps of his church in the town of Dolores. Within weeks he was leading an army of the aggrieved—small farmers fighting to defend their land and autonomy from the depredations of colonial barons—which came close to capturing Mexico City. But Hidalgo, a theologian and not a General, fell before long into the hands of royalist troops, and on July 30, 1811, he was executed by a firing squad. His severed head remained on display in a cage in the city of Guanajuato until 1821, when Mexico finally won the independence that Hidalgo had sought.

In a Constitution written in 1857, after the decades following independence brought more civil tumult and a war with the United States, Mexicans codified their desire to live in peace in a liberal, federalist, and representative democracy. But their country, lacking steady institutions rooted in popular will, remained trapped in a cycle of excesses, in which periods of near anarchy were succeeded by the rule of despots who imposed order but suppressed popular representation. The PRI regime, created to control the disarray of the Mexican Revolution of 1910, was the latest in a series of autocratic governments that maintained stability at the price of postponing democracy.

In July 2000, 143 years after Mexico's first democratic constitution, its goals were finally met.

The heritage of disorder and despotism weighed heavily on Mexico because of the singular place that history occupies in the country's modern life. History does not merely influence Mexico's present; it is *part* of the present. Carlos Fuentes, the novelist, wrote about the simultaneity of past and present in a 1971 book of essays called *Tiempo mexicano* (Mexican Time). "Among us," he wrote, "there is no single time: all of our times are alive, all of our pasts are present." Fuentes believed that Mexico's present was infused with its past because each historical period had been left unfinished, with core objectives frustrated. He wrote: "The coexistence of all the layers of history in Mexico is only an external sign of an unconscious decision of this land and this people: all of our times should be maintained. Why? Because no Mexican time has yet fulfilled its promise."

Octavio Paz, the poet and thinker who was awarded the Nobel Prize in literature in 1990, said that his poetry was an exploration of Mexico's simultaneous times. "In Mexico the Spaniards encountered history as well as geography," Paz said in the lecture he gave upon accepting the Nobel Prize in Stockholm. "And that history still lives: it is a present rather than a past. The temples and gods of pre-Columbian Mexico may be a pile of ruins, but the spirit that breathed life into that world has not disappeared; it speaks to us in the hermetic language of myth and legend, in forms of social coexistence, in popular art, in customs. Being a Mexican writer means listening to the voice of that present—that presence."

The immediacy of the past is everywhere evident. Among the Mayan ruins at Uxmal on the Yucatán Peninsula are bas-relief stone carvings that show the oval-shaped, stick-walled, thatched-roof houses where ordinary people dwelled at the time when the site flourished, in the eighth century. Alongside the road that leads to the ruin today stand contemporary Mayan dwellings, constructed in the same oval shape, using the same sticks and thatch.

In the Mexico City Zócalo, its vast central square, all of Mexico's eras coincide elegantly, and the country's splendid sense of style is on full display. On the edges of the plaza stand the ruins of the Templo Mayor, the Aztecs' greatest pyramid; and the Roman Catholic cathedral with its Sagrario chapel, whose Baroque facades express the effervescent spirit that percolated under the strictures of seventeenth-century Spanish colonial rule; and the long and stately National Palace, built in the eighteenth century, when the people of New Spain were gaining a separate identity and aspiring to become a separate republic. Most any day the Zócalo reverberates with drumbeats as bands of dancers costumed in loincloths and high peacock-feather headdresses bow and step to rhythms from preconquest times. Vendors lay out their wares on straw mats, forming a small market, a *tianguis*, much like the one that the conquistador Hernán Cortés found on the same site in 1519, when he first reached what was then Tenochtitlán, the Aztec capital. In the modern Zócalo the goods on sale span the ages: you can buy herbal amulets from an Indian healer to cure impotence and lumbago; or an image of the Virgin of Guadalupe, Mexico's dark-skinned patroness, encased in the pendant or key chain of your choice; or a rabbit-ear antenna, a hand-sewn leather cell-phone sheath, or a pirated version of the latest Madonna CD.

In the museum adjacent to the Templo Mayor a diorama depicts the hustle and bustle in the great plaza on the eve of the conquest, under the shadow of surrounding pyramids. In the midst of the exhibit a mannequin of a young woman grinds maize on a rounded gray stone raised on four stubby legs. Across an alleyway from the museum and up the sagging stairs of a colonial town house is a smart nouveau-Mexican restaurant. In one corner stands a woman in an apron who closes the circle of time: she is grinding maize to make tortillas for tacos on a rounded, four-legged stone identical to the one used in the Aztec market.

Mexico chose the Zócalo as the venue for its festivities on the night of December 31, 1999, to welcome the new millennium. There were, of course, several hundred silver-buttoned mariachis blowing trumpets and strumming guitars. But the highlight of the extravaganza was a troupe of Mexican acrobats in silver spandex bodysuits, who performed a daring ballet on the facade of one of the square's venerable colonial buildings by maneuvering up and down ropes hung from the roof. It was a mesmerizing twenty-first-century rendering of the *voladores*, the pre-Hispanic fliers who achieved psychic lightness by sailing around a giant maypole hanging from their heels. The performance that night of the millennial *voladores* was not about the past shaping the present; it was the past being present in the present.

Julia writes:

Aside from our reporting as correspondents in Mexico for *The New York Times*, we also participated in the routines of Mexican society as parents of our young daughter, Emma. She led us into many corners of everyday life in Mexico City, where we encountered the proximity of history time and again.

Once, when Emma was six, I took her to a children's book fair at the National Arts Center in what used to be the Churubusco movie studios in Coyoacán, a pleasant borough in the southern part of Mexico City. Under a white tent we found a storyteller who seemed to have an audience of Mexican youngsters and their parents spellbound.

Emma and I took seats toward the front of the audience. The story that our raconteur began to tell was not a fairy tale, as it turned out, but an Aztec myth, and quite an important one: it told of the birth of Huitzilopochtli, the fearsome god of the sun who inspired the Aztecs to go to war and take captives for sacrifice, so they could offer the human blood to fuel and sustain the solar cycle.

"Huitzilopochtli was the son of Coatlicue, the Earth Mother," the storyteller began, with an arpeggio of pre-Hispanic syllables that flowed off his tongue as if he were speaking of his own family. We learned that Coatlicue, although she was a rather fertile female, was not at all the warm bosom that we expected from someone bearing the Earth Mother title. Her name meant "Woman of the Serpent Skirt," and she lived up to it faithfully by draping her abdomen with writhing snakes.

While Coatlicue was still a young woman, the storyteller recounted, she had given birth to 401 children, including four hundred sons who were stars and one daughter named Coyolxauhqui, who was the moon. Then one day, while Coatlicue was sweeping out her temple on the top of a high hill, a ball of feathers came wafting down from the sky and impregnated her, "gave her another baby" was how the storyteller explained it to the children.

When Coyolxauhqui learned that her mother was pregnant again, she became furious. The moon daughter felt that 401 children were already too many for one mother—a sentiment with which I initially agreed. But then, the storyteller said, "Coyolxauhqui, the moon, summoned her four hundred brothers, the stars, all together. She persuaded them that their mother had betrayed and dishonored them by seeking to have yet another baby. Coatlicue's sons, whipped up into a fury by their sister, decided they would conspire and kill their mother."

The matricide theme was making me just a bit nervous. I moved closer to Emma, who seemed enthralled.

By this time the storyteller had really started to roll with his tale. "Coatlicue's children crept up to her temple when she was sleeping. She awoke just seconds before her sons cut off her head with a sharp knife. Blood gushed from her neck and turned into serpents that slithered all over the floor." The storyteller waved his arms sinuously to show the serpents slithering.

At this image, Emma and I took hold of each other's hands. Around us Mexican children and their parents were laughing and shivering at the thought of all those loose snakes.

"Coatlicue surprised her jealous children," the storyteller continued. "Even without her head, she was able to give birth to her son Huitzilopochtli. And he was born already decked in all of his armor and wielding the powerful fire serpent, the most dangerous weapon of all."

It was a difficult labor by any standards. To avenge his mother, Huitzilopochtli immediately attacked his star brothers and flung them back up into the sky, where they belonged. Then he confronted his killer sister, and with her he was merciless.

"With his fire-serpent sword he cut off her head and flung the rest of her body down the side of the tall mountain. Coyolxauhqui's body broke into many pieces as it rolled down the slope.

"Since then Huitzilopochtli, the sun, has always been the brightest sovereign of the sky," the storyteller concluded. "His star brothers and moon sister only come out at night, and they are pale, distant, and cold in comparison to him."

At the end of the tale Emma and I, slightly shaken, decided to move on, while the Mexican families stayed to enjoy another yarn.

It seemed to me that as a unifying national legend, this saga was a far cry from George Washington's cutting down the cherry tree. A Mexican version of the universal myth about the face-off between the sun and the moon, it told of jealous violence countered by vengeance; of mob insurrection quelled by the ascent of a single awesome ruler, more feared than loved. Since the tale had come down from the time of the Aztecs, the last Indian rulers before the conquest in the early sixteenth century, I could only assume that these ideas were well embedded in the political backdrop against which Mexicans' search for greater freedom in the last decades of the twentieth century was taking place.

Julia:

Another episode I witnessed because of Emma gave me reason to reflect again on how little prepared Mexicans were by history and experience for the democratic challenge they had undertaken. It was a play

that Emma's class put on, when she was in second grade, at her small
private bilingual school in the capital city.

The short play, in Spanish, had been selected by her Mexican
teacher and was called *The Mouse Assembly*. The main characters, performed by Emma and her mainly Mexican classmates, are members of a
community of mice who have become fed up with the tyranny of a foul-
tempered local tomcat. Determined to free themselves from the oppres-
sion, the mice come together in an assembly to debate alternative ways
to subvert, if not defeat, the dangerous feline.

From the outset the assembly is chaotic, with all the mice speaking at
once and no one with sufficient moral or political authority to impose order. One mouse proposes that they attempt to tie up the cat, but the rest
immediately reject that idea.

"We are too small!" they protest.

After much chattering, another mouse suggests that they tie a bell on
the cat's tail, so at least they will know where he is. The others at first approve. But the consensus collapses when Mouse Pérez, who is emerging
as something of a leader, asks who will take on the task of placing the
bell on the tail.

"I can't. I'm half deaf!" pleads one mouse.

"I'm completely deaf. And blind!" says another.

Suddenly, just when Mouse Pérez begins to get the assembly calmed
down again, out leaps the cat. He catches one mouse and begins to gnaw
on him. The others scatter, shrieking piteously.

"Every mouse for himself!" are Mouse Pérez's parting words.

And that is the end of the play.

While the other parents clapped, I sat there dumbfounded. As an
American, I had been taught in childhood a national history in which
every morality tale about democracy always, sooner or later, got a happy
and uplifting ending. I raged privately at the Mexican teacher who had
subjected our daughter to such a disheartening lesson about the efficacy
of democratic discourse.

—   —   —

But to look back at history was to see that the teacher could not have
been expected to do otherwise. Rule by the people for the people had

been notably absent in Mexico. Instead, from the age of the Aztec emperors to the Spanish conquest of 1521, through three centuries of colonial rule, to the nineteenth-century era of civil strife and foreign intervention, through the thirty-year dictatorship of Porfirio Díaz and its overthrow in the Mexican Revolution of 1910, the country's political life has been dominated by gyrations between anarchy and authoritarianism, between the rise of local diversity and the imposition of central power, between revolutionaries and dictators. Mexicans had too often advanced their aspirations, whether for economic enfranchisement or political rights, only when they resorted to armed resistance and rebellion. Their progress was curbed time and again by mighty leaders who arose amid disarray to reinstate oppressive order.

Authoritarian traits appeared in Mexican politics as far back as the Aztecs, if not earlier. Moctezuma II, the Emperor who sat on the Aztec throne when Cortés and his forces landed in Mexico in 1519, was a conqueror himself, reigning over 370 tribes and towns across central Mexico that Aztec warriors had subjugated. The Aztecs suppressed the religions and destroyed the codices of the Mesoamerican peoples they took over, imposing the cult of their sun god, Huitzilopochtli, and carrying out purges of earlier beliefs that would become a regular feature of the political cycle in later centuries. Ceremonial ritual and splendor were fundamental to the Aztecs' exercise of theocratic power, as their priest-lords sought to feed and placate the sun and other demanding gods to keep the universe from expiring.

Ruling by divine right, Moctezuma was an eccentric leader, both contemplative and cruel. A key factor in Cortés's defeat of the Aztecs in 1521 was Moctezuma's morose belief that Cortés was the sun god's exiled rival, Quetzalcoatl, making an apocalyptic return; the Emperor offered weak resistance to Cortés's advance. Even though the conquistador had only a few hundred Spanish troops, he was aided by Indian peoples eager to throw off Aztec domination.

Born in the trauma of the conquest, the colony of New Spain that Cortés founded would last three hundred years. He had laid waste to Indian cities in his war to vanquish the Aztecs, but after his triumph Cortés moved to implement a new vision of empire, discouraging wanton pillage by his forces and working to establish an orderly dominion for

Spain. Cortés, however, was soon forced to the sidelines by a jealous Crown, and the conquest was completed by smallpox and other diseases the Spaniards had brought. According to one study, by 1650 the Indian population had decreased to 13.6 percent of what it was on the eve of Cortés's arrival.

Under the colony the Indians were reduced to laborers for Spain's agriculture and mining enterprises, at first by slavery and later through forced labor and debt peonage. During the first decades the Crown turned over whole villages, and the villagers in them, to Spanish colonists, in what were called *encomiendas*. Later the monarchy endowed the criollos (those of Spanish blood born in the New World) and their descendants with rights to land to form huge agricultural estates, the haciendas.

Catholic missionaries came close behind the conquistadores. The priests carried out new purges to eliminate native religions; the Franciscan friars who arrived shortly after Cortés burned many thousands of Aztec books and records. Some churchmen—most notably, the Dominican bishop of Chiapas, Bartolomé de Las Casas—argued for more humane treatment of the Indians. In the long run the missionaries were successful; Mexicans became a profoundly devout Catholic people. By the seventeenth century the Church had become almost as wealthy and powerful as the Viceroyalty, the master of its own great estates, and one of the colony's chief bankers.

As colonial society became more diverse, it organized along corporatist lines. The growing class of mixed-blood mestizos formed craft guilds, land associations, church societies, and even local militias. But these groups had little power except that which they derived from their ties to colonial masters; they were allowed to petition but not to participate. When the German scientist Alexander von Humboldt traveled through Mexico in 1803, in the last years of the colony, he called it "the country of inequality." Spanish rule had opened an abyss between rich and poor that would long endure.

The encroachment of the haciendas on struggling peasant farms and Indian villages spurred the rebellion that started the war for independence, with Hidalgo's battle cry, or *grito*, in 1810. For Hidalgo the quest for a separate republic was also a fight for equality for the downtrodden.

He declared the abolition of slavery in Mexico in 1810, probably the earliest such proclamation in the Americas.

Another rebel Catholic priest, José María Morelos y Pavón, pressed on with the fight for independence after Hidalgo was put to death, and he, too, was a progressive thinker. (Like the iconic portrait of Hidalgo in his priestly collar and black waistcoat with his fist raised in the air, Morelos's image is striking because of the bandanna he wrapped around his head.) In 1812, in the midst of fierce clashes with royalist troops, Morelos convened his lieutenants at the town of Chilpancingo, in what is now Guerrero state, to form a representative Congress for the new nation, even though it was not yet born. In his address to the assembly Morelos described his vision of a free republic "governed by the will of the people." He proposed to make all Mexicans equal and to break up the rural haciendas, distributing land to the peasants and passing laws that would "increase the daily wages of the poor." Morelos was another leader who died by violence, when he was captured by the forces of the Viceroy and executed by a firing squad in 1815.

From the anticolonial turmoil emerged a hard but flamboyant criollo General, Agustín de Iturbide, who united the disparate forces seeking to oust the rule of Spain and led them to independence in 1821. But only a year later, Iturbide waylaid the new nation by crowning himself—in the tradition of Moctezuma and Cortés—the "Constitutional Emperor of Mexico." Iturbide, too, was eccentric: though he was fierce on the battlefield, his resolve to rule faded when he faced staunch opposition from Mexican republicans. After ten months in power Iturbide lost his empire, and he also died before a firing squad. A nineteenth-century Mexican historian, Lucas Alamán, said that Iturbide's reign was more like "a theatrical performance or a dream" than a government.

Iturbide, however, initiated a style of rule that would prevail, in the absence of institutions of popular self-government, for the better part of two centuries. Mexico's strongmen, or caudillos, governed by the force of arms and personality and were rarely guided by consistent ideology or commitment to the citizens' causes. The caudillos' purpose was to hold power in a country in chaos, making principle a matter of secondary concern.

The man who most spectacularly exemplified the anti-ideological streak of the caudillo was Antonio López de Santa Anna, who took eleven turns as President between 1833 and 1855. In one term he assailed the wealth and privileges of the Catholic Church, embracing a core liberal cause. In the next he swung to a defense of the Church's rights, a creed of the conservatives. Santa Anna styled himself as an impassioned nationalist, yet his military campaigns to defend the nation's sovereignty achieved the opposite. Routed by the forces of Sam Houston, he signed away Texas in 1836, and then lost the rest of Mexico's northern territories, including California, in the war with the United States over the next years.

Under the caudillos' patriarchal authority there was little ground for rule of law to develop. A caudillo, or his equivalent at the village level, the cacique, could not be on the wrong side of the law, since he was the law. Impunity for the powerful became a social norm. While the institutions of justice were weak, government bureaucracy expanded, generally responsive to the interests of the elite and indifferent to the needs of the poor.

At the grass roots the striving for self-government was constant. In many rural villages and Indian enclaves the local leaders were elected and had great influence in community affairs. Peasants were at times able to secure their lands and livelihood by backing a regional caudillo against his rivals, exacting property titles and village autonomy in return. In some cases local groups resisted the domination of central authority for decades, like the Yaqui Indians in the north and the Maya in the Yucatán.

But the social hierarchy remained rigid, and the struggles for position of emerging classes of mestizo farmers and entrepreneurs very often generated conflict.

Julia:

I ran into history again on a reporting trip I took through the countryside of the state of Oaxaca in the weeks before federal elections in July 1997.

Mexico was electing a new Congress as well as many new governors and township mayors across the country, and I was trying to gauge

Benito Juárez, who served twice
as Mexico's President in the
1860s, enacted liberal reforms
that curbed the power of
the Catholic Church and
established the principles of
individual rights and rule of law

whether the rural vote, the famous *voto verde*, would once again favor
the PRI. Driving down a cactus-lined road, I spotted an elderly Indian
farmer in grimy muslin pants guiding an ox and a wooden plow through
a dry field, preparing to plant corn. The earth was unyielding, and yellow
foam oozed from the ox's mouth as the plow repeatedly jammed in the
soil or jumped out of the furrow.

When he came to the end of a row, the farmer stopped to clear the
sweat from his brow and reluctantly take my questions about the elections. He answered in grumbles, saying he was fed up with politics and
didn't pay attention to it anymore. No matter who was in power, he said,
conditions for country people like him just kept going from bad to worse.

"Recently," he said, "we've had nothing but lousy Presidents. We
haven't had a good President for a number of years now."

To see whether he had ever been more politically engaged, I asked
him if there had been any "recent" President he *had* liked. He reflected
for a moment, nodding in thought. Then he said: "The one I liked was
Benito Juárez. *Ese fue el mero chingón.* He was one real motherfucker."

His estimate of the period of misrule was longer than I expected: Juárez had been President in the 1860s. But the farmer's affection for Juárez was interesting: he was one Mexican leader who was both caudillo and statesman, a General who had recaptured Mexico from invading foreign troops as well as a man of laws whose reforms laid the basis for the modern Mexican state. The farmer remembered Juárez as a President who understood a workingman's interests. It also helped that Juárez, like himself, was a Zapotec Indian from Oaxaca.

— — —

Born in 1806 in a mountain village in Oaxaca, Juárez was orphaned when a small boy. Franciscan monks paid for his education and sent him to law school. His determination to pursue politics was strengthened by his failures as a lawyer to achieve justice for poor villagers in disputes with landowners and the clergy.

Juárez's first presidency was interrupted in 1862 by the invasion of French troops supported by his rivals, the Mexican conservatives, who brought the Austrian Archduke Maximilian to Mexico as Emperor. In 1867 Juárez led the liberal armies back to Mexico City. He resumed the presidency, while Maximilian became the latest of the country's fallen rulers to face a firing squad.

Juárez enacted sweeping liberal reforms that canceled the rights and privileges of the Catholic Church, expropriating church properties and shutting down monasteries and schools, laying the basis for the most rigorous separation of church and state in any country in Latin America. He encouraged trade and opposed entrenched economic interests that constrained growth. He engraved the idea of individual rights in Mexico's political canon and argued that law was the foundation of progress. "Respect for the rights of others is peace" was the phrase from Juárez that every Mexican schoolchild learns to recite.

His death was as exceptional for a Mexican leader as his life: he died of natural causes—a heart attack—in 1872. His concept of a state founded on the exercise of law rather than power would fall back into disuse for more than a century. But after the country had been dismembered and demoralized by foreign intervention, Juárez's leadership gave Mexico a new sense of being a nation.

Internecine dissension soon surged again, and Mexico fell under the control of its greatest caudillo of all in the three-decade dictatorship of Porfirio Díaz. With his dictum *"poca política, mucha administración*, little politics, much administration," Díaz was a master of the Mexican art of pragmatic politics. He regarded political debate as so much "scandal" that distracted from his modernizing program to maintain order, expand the economy, and unify the nation with national roads and railways.

Díaz systematically centralized the government and subdued fractious regional caudillos by allowing them economic privileges that made them rich even while their political influence declined. He eliminated much of the democracy that had grown up at the village level by replacing elected leaders with his own appointed ones. Governing through autocratic decision making and calculated displays of pomp, he did not hesitate to use violence when necessary.

"Sometimes we were relentless to the point of cruelty," he told the American journalist James Creelman in an interview as he described the summary shootings and hangings of those caught stealing from the crews who were stringing telegraph wires. "But it was all necessary then to the life and progress of the nation . . . The blood that was spilled was bad blood; what was saved was good blood."

Early in his career Díaz had coined the slogan "*Sufragio efectivo, no reelección*, Effective suffrage, no reelection" as the rallying cry for an unsuccessful uprising against Juárez when he stood for reelection in 1871. After Díaz seized power five years later, he held a vote to ratify his position, and then had himself reelected seven times before the end of his rule, initiating the routine of fake elections in Mexico.

During his reign Don Porfirio integrated Mexico as a nation and brought economic progress and growth but suppressed popular efforts for a greater voice in government. At the end the excesses of his industrial policies, which imposed severe hardships on workers and farm laborers, stirred mass unrest once again.

A political manifesto published in 1908 galvanized the rebellion against the Díaz dictatorship. It was written by Francisco I. Madero, the revolutionary who most clearly articulated for the Mexican people the ideal of democracy based on free elections and individual liberties.

Madero came from provincial aristocracy, a prosperous mining and cattle family in the northern state Coahuila. He studied abroad, then returned to Mexico to lead an emerging professional class that was chafing against Díaz's rule. Madero warned that Díaz's long dictatorship was making children of the Mexican people by eroding their capacity to govern themselves. In his 1908 broadside, *The Presidential Succession of 1910,* Madero said that Díaz's tyranny had infected Mexicans with "corruption of the spirit, disinterest in public life, disdain for the law and a tendency toward dissimulation, cynicism and fear."

What distinguished Madero from other anti-Díaz dissidents was the clarity of his proposals. At the beginning of his campaign he demanded free elections, avoiding a call to arms. He defended the rights of a new urban middle class to organize political parties and enjoy representative government, and he founded a party of his own to reclaim the slogan that Díaz had coined and betrayed: *Sufragio efectivo, no reelección.* Only after he was harassed and jailed by Díaz did Madero issue a summons to revolt, on November 20, 1910.

Madero's rebellion swept across Mexico in armed uprisings that united rough-handed peasants with country gentry and city intellectuals. On May 26, 1911, Díaz resigned and left Mexico. In yet another of the country's cyclical purges, the revolutionaries disowned the success of his regime and denied him a place of rest in his own country; his bones lie in a grave in Paris.

On October 1, 1911, Madero became President by the means he had championed, in the most open election to that time. Yet he proved to be a mild, almost naïve leader, whose moderate temperament was ill suited to the hard-edged times. Madero insisted on trying to govern democratically in a nation with little experience of representative government and still dangerously divided among ambitious Generals, ruthless caudillos, militant workers, and insurrectionary peasants.

In one case President Madero fell out with Emiliano Zapata, the mustachioed leader of an army of cowboy farmers from the southern state of Morelos who rose up, in bullet belts and sombreros, to defend their rights to land. Insisting that Mexico was ready for peace, Madero demanded that Zapata and his men give up their guns before his government had resolved their land disputes. Madero ended up on the wrong side of the movement whose slogan, *¡Tierra y libertad!* (Land and liberty!), had drawn peasants across Mexico to the revolutionary cause.

During fifteen months in office Madero put down one conspiracy against him after another. Yet he declined to shoot his enemies, until finally one of them, a General named Victoriano Huerta, who was supported by the U.S. ambassador, had Madero shot.

The fighting that Madero had unleashed raged for another eight years. The Mexican Revolution was not a clear class conflict of laborer against bourgeois, although there were attacks by insurgents in many states on the haciendas of Mexican oligarchs and estates and mines owned by wealthy Americans. Unlike other great revolutions of the twentieth century, Mexico's was never driven by an anticapitalist ideology or program like Communism or Maoism. After Madero's assassination the revolution broke down into a series of regional rebellions and counter-rebellions, a free-for-all of revolutionaries clashing among themselves in the struggle to reestablish central power.

General Huerta was soon spurned by other revolutionaries as a usurper who had commandeered the revolution for his own ambitions. He and the forces loyal to him within the federal army were defeated in 1914. Over the next years two forces clashed within the revolution. On one side were the villagers arrayed around Zapata, the leader of serfs and sugar workers from the south whose fight was for land and freedom. Zapata formed an alliance with Pancho Villa, a rowdy but shrewd muletrain driver operating in the northern states of Chihuahua and Durango. Villa rallied settlers, cowhands, miners, and sharecroppers across northern Mexico behind his own vision of grassroots justice, calling for fair wages for workers, restitution of land rights, and agrarian reform. Part bandit and part generalissimo, Villa proved to be a formidable field marshal of his people's army. But neither he nor Zapata ever put forth a cogent plan for central state power. They were leaders of el México bronco—as the insubordinate masses were called by those who feared them—seeking justice for the Mexican village.

They were opposed by the Constitutionalists, army Generals whose goal was to restore constitutional order in a reformed Mexican state. Hailing from the northern ranching states of Coahuila and Sonora, these officers represented provincial landed and bureaucratic elites. Among their leaders were Venustiano Carranza, a patrician landowner with a white beard who was governor of Coahuila; Plutarco Elías Calles, a steely military man from Sonora; and Álvaro Obregón, a former small rancher who came from an emerging, and therefore cautious, Sonoran middle class. Trained and tempered in the armed forces, these were men of strategy and institution, and they had a vision for the reform of central power that was nationalist and capitalist. Among the insurgents, they were the new forces of order.

Carranza led the triumphant Constitutional forces to take Mexico City from Huerta in August 1914, and he became President. His movement's popularity surged because he and his Generals resisted the U.S. occupation, in April of that year, of Veracruz. The Constitutionalists remained true to the revolution by espousing nationalist control of the country's resources and moderate agrarian reform and labor rights. But they were also true to their origins, defending private property and opposing the land expropriations that Zapata demanded. They regarded Villa as nothing better than an unwashed outlaw.

Although Zapata and Villa were backed by swells of support from the poorest rebels, they were ultimately defeated by Carranza's Constitutionalist federal troops. Carranza was helped by the Constitution written in 1917 at a convention he called together. The new Magna Carta incorporated and enlarged the political rights and democratic ideals of the 1857 Constitution. It retained the liberal distrust of the Catholic Church, mandating a broad separation of church and state. But, responding to the radical agitation of the Zapatistas, Villistas, and anarchist labor movements, the 1917 Constitution also codified social and labor rights, including the right to strike and the right (and obligation) to free secular public education. The Mexican nation became the owner of its subsoil and natural resources. Agrarian clauses established the legal foundations for land reform in the public interest. At the same time, at the insistence of Carranza and his Generals, the revolutionary Constitution provided for a strong central executive.

The 1917 Constitution, one of the most advanced charters in the world at the time, was the great success of the revolution, the achievement for which so many Mexicans had died. It was also a synthesis of the conflicting tendencies of the Mexican political cycle: it recognized the social claims of the insurgent masses but also laid the groundwork for the restoration of rigorous central authority.

The Constitution, however, did not stop the bloodshed. On April 10, 1919, an assassin sent by Carranza set a trap for Zapata and killed him. Villa yielded in 1920. When the smoke began to clear from the battlefields that year, the clear winners were the Constitutionalist caudillos. Now, however, Mexico was dominated not by one strongman like Porfirio Díaz, but by dozens of revolutionary Generals.

In May 1920 Carranza himself was shot to death, apparently by a gunman loyal to Álvaro Obregón. The latter was elected President that year, emerging from the revolution as the strongest among strongmen. Obregón served four years as President. But on July 17, 1928, as he was preparing to return for a second presidential term, Obregón himself was assassinated by a Catholic fanatic.

After the years of bloodletting, Obregón's murder finally seemed to be one death too many. It moved other Generals to see that their interests might now be served by setting aside rivalries and joining forces behind a strong centralized state.

There was considerable support in Mexican society for a government that would stabilize the country—even if it meant postponing the egalitarian ideals for which many had fought. The revolution had disrupted life across Mexico. The death toll from *la bola*, as the flux of the revolution was called, was immense: census figures show a real decrease in the population, from 15.2 million to 14.3 million, between 1910 and 1921. Mexicans acquired a collective memory of the mayhem, which left them with an enduring longing for predictable political control and a fear of rapid change that could unleash disorder again.

Plutarco Elías Calles, a revolutionary General with a close-clipped square mustache, was President when Obregón was slain and had been preparing to make Obregón his successor. After the assassination Calles decided Mexico needed an official party to steady and bolster the government. He previewed his intentions in his annual State of the Union address on September 1, 1928, in a speech filled with rhetoric that contradicted reality. "This [present] circumstance, that perhaps for the first time in history Mexico faces a situation in which the dominant note is the absence of caudillos, should allow us, *will* allow us, to steer our country's politics on the course of a true institutional life," Calles said. "We will strive to pass, for once and for all, from the historic condition of a 'country of men' to that of a 'nation of institutions and laws.' "

There was apparently no doubt that Calles was still a caudillo, and he would prove it by installing three successive puppet Presidents, earning himself a new strongman's title: *el jefe máximo de la revolución*, the Maximal Chief of the Revolution. Calles carried out a three-year scorched-earth campaign to subdue an uprising by Mexican Catholics, *los cristeros*, who rejected the anticlerical terms of the 1917 Constitution. A photograph from the time shows a row of light poles stretching across an arid plateau in central Mexico, with a hanged Catholic rebel swinging from each one. By 1929 the *cristeros'* rebellion had subsided after at least 100,000 of them were killed, leaving deep resentment between the Mexican state, on the one hand, and the Catholic hierarchy and its flock, on the other.

On March 4, 1929, Calles and a conclave of revolutionary warlords in the city of Querétaro founded the Partido Nacional Revolucionario, the National Revolutionary Party. Although the new party was robed in the populist tenets of the revolution, the Generals who created it were not primarily concerned with ideals. Their objective was to bind together their disputatious provincial fiefdoms into one powerful national whole.

Within the authoritarian cycle, other continuities had emerged in the tumult of Mexican politics. After the nation fought several wars with foreign invaders in its first century and lost half its territory by amputation to the United States, Mexicans had become nationalists, favoring forceful leaders to defend them from outside aggression. Mexico's rulers had an enduring sense of ceremonial grandeur, inherited from their pre-Hispanic and colonial forebears, which they used as a tool of government to enhance their appearance of strength in the people's eyes. But as a corollary, a gap persisted between the high progressive rhetoric of the regimes in Mexico City and the reality of their arbitrary rule for ordinary citizens.

The state dominated the economy and subjected it to the vagaries of politics, so that a country graced with abundant natural resources—petroleum, silver, vast forests—often struggled with bankruptcy. Corruption was a common lubricant for the slow-moving government bureaucracy that controlled much economic activity.

All these continuities would converge in the political system that was born at the caudillo summit of 1929.

After Calles, in the first years of the regime a revolutionary caudillo became President who both embraced the goals of the 1917 Constitution and sought to realize them. After taking office in 1934, Lázaro Cárdenas (a man with a distinctively long face and large ears) carried out the agrarian reform promised in the Constitution, distributing land during his six-year tenure to about one-third of the population. In 1938 he nationalized the foreign oil companies, finally giving Mexicans confidence in their sovereignty.

In March 1938, just twelve days after this bold stroke, Cárdenas refounded and renamed what had already become a wide-reaching government party, calling it the Partido de la Revolución Mexicana, the Party of the Mexican Revolution. Under Cárdenas, the official party became both more popular and more authoritarian. Under its umbrella he drew the huge national federations that served to organize different sectors of society, with rural farmers in one, factory workers in another, and public-school teachers and government bureaucrats in a third. Cárdenas encouraged activism from the workers and farmers at the base of this pyramid but also tightened the mechanisms of his control from the top. It was Cárdenas who pioneered the *dedazo*, choosing his own successor (Manuel Ávila Camacho) and then having him anointed by the party.

In 1946 the party was restructured once again and became the Partido Revolucionario Institucional, the Institutional Revolutionary Party, an oxymoron that recaptured the contradictions and latent fascism of Calles's original project. Mexicans were soon referring to the PRI and its governments as *el sistema*, not a system but *the* system. Its rules of conduct became part of the civic decorum, as routine as Sunday Mass for Catholics.

A quasi-single-party system, the PRI centralized power in the President, who ruled through his control over the state governors and the party, which was hegemonic. Small parties survived on the fringes, but for decades they posed no effective opposition.

The President's powers were almost those of a monarch. The legislature convened only to rubber-stamp his decisions and maintain democratic appearances; in popular parlance the lawmakers were called *levantadedos* for the fingers they raised to approve the President's edicts. PRI candidates for congressional posts were selected by the President, making all the party's legislators beholden to him. Being a senator was a form of early retirement, a reward from the President for years of service. The lower house, the Cámara de Diputados, or Chamber of Deputies, was a respectable holding position for rising PRI politicians awaiting attractive openings in the government secretariats. The Supreme Court, whose magistrates were appointed by the President, attended to minor judicial matters, careful never to cross *el Señor Presidente*.

The only significant restraint on the President's power was the rule in the revolutionary Constitution that barred reelection, limiting the chief executive to one six-year term, a *sexenio*. Thus the PRI system invested power in the office, not the politician, and the *dedazo* allowed it to perpetuate itself while carrying out a regular rotation of its leaders. The *dedazo* rituals were performed every six years in the inner sanctum of Los Pinos, out of public view. Only a handful of PRI initiates were considered by the President as contenders to succeed him, and, obeying unwritten rules, they declined to comment about it afterward. Until very recently Mexicans knew only through gossip and speculation how one incumbent President had decided who would be the next one.

One of the PRI President's main activities was to hold court. Since his was the only authority above appeal, Mexicans all wanted to take their problems, no matter how local, to the President. A vast range of issues landed at the door of Los Pinos, from village land feuds to arcane intellectual arguments. The President spent a lot of time on *giras*, tours around the country that had the air of visits from a king. In a tradition started by Lázaro Cárdenas, it was not unusual for the President to preside over ribbon-cutting ceremonies at ten-bed health clinics, primary schools, municipal sports fields, and other apparently unexceptional public works. It was the President's way of maintaining some contact with his constituents, while for them unmediated contact with the President, even for a few minutes, could radically improve the life of a village or barrio. A villager lucky enough to have his picture taken with the President could use the snapshot for a lifetime to negotiate from a position of strength with bureaucrats, the police, or the courts.

The party was guided by the central principle of loyalty to the President and followed *la línea*, the party line, which he handed down. The PRI was largely unencumbered by doctrinal commitments, making it exceptionally adaptable. (The same party that revered Lázaro Cárdenas, the nationalist who expropriated American oil companies, later glorified Carlos Salinas, who made a partnership with the United States in the North American Free Trade Agreement.)

Internally the party was an expansive forum where disputes among competing regional and class factions—of the sort that had torn the nation apart in earlier periods—were vented and managed. Groups would organize around some ascendant figure within the party, a suit-and-tie caudillo in training. Moving among the party, the legislature, and the government, these leaders and their groups were able to showcase their party discipline and infighting talents. The rising PRI politician acquired essential skills, learning to rouse crowds with revolutionary eloquence, distribute government patronage effectively, and strike the correct attitude of respect with the President.

In the 1930s, when they still led the system, the revolutionary Generals made a strategic decision to remove the armed forces from PRI politics. The neutrality of the Mexican military endured and became a key factor in the regime's stability.

Meanwhile, the PRI system derived much of its strength from its command over the three social sectors, especially organized labor. Calles did not apply the rule of no reelection to labor, to ensure that it would be controlled by loyal leaders from one presidency to the next. His strategy worked well. Fidel Velázquez, the head of the Confederación de Trabajadores Mexicanos, the Mexican Workers Confederation, or CTM, dominated the labor movement for almost six decades, from 1941 until his death in 1997 at the age of ninety-seven. PRI labor groups, with millions of workers and millions of voters at election time, provided a base of support for the system. In its first decades the official labor movement helped workers to obtain new jobs, higher wages, and the advanced job benefits and security offered by the postrevolutionary labor code. Later, in the years of economic crisis, Velázquez used his authoritarian clout to keep labor in check through a three-decade slide in the real value of workers' wages. "We came to power by the force of arms," Velázquez was quoted as saying of the PRI regime, "and nobody is going to get us out of here at the point of a speech."

From its earliest years the system was also a well-tuned electoral machine, although one not designed to compete against other parties in fair voting. Rather, its job was to preserve the regime's image as a revolutionary democracy by putting on, every six years, a convincing stage play of a presidential election, and to win that and every gubernatorial and municipal vote, by persuasion if possible, by coercion if necessary.

From the *sexenio* of Lázaro Cárdenas through the 1960s, the PRI system made extraordinary gains, delivering stability and economic growth for most Mexicans. Its social-welfare programs provided decent health care, housing, recreation, and even funeral services for working people. In a brilliant foreign policy, Mexico defended anti-imperialist and democratic causes overseas, gaining stature as an enlightened nation in the developing world and maintaining its independence from the American colossus to the north. Leftist exiles from the Spanish civil war, and later from South American military regimes, were welcomed—as long as they did not criticize Mexico or participate in its politics.

In the postwar period the Generals' reign came to an end. In 1946 the PRI chose a career politician as President, Miguel Alemán Valdés. Reorienting Cárdenas's model of state-led industrialization, Alemán aggressively courted foreign investment and made alliances with Mexican capitalists while working to weaken and co-opt the labor movement. With his many personal business deals that benefited from government support—like his investments in Acapulco, which soared in value after his government developed the resort there—Alemán brought corruption into the heart of the system and established the custom that the PRI President should get rich while in office.

Nonetheless, Alemán's term was the beginning of two decades of sustained economic growth (consistently above 5 percent annually) that were called the Mexican Miracle. The peso remained steady at 12.5 to the dollar from 1954 into the 1970s. PRI governments built roads, dams, airports, telecommunications networks, a national electric grid, and a nuclear power plant. Pemex, the nationalized oil industry, thrived. The National Autonomous University of Mexico, commonly called the National University or the UNAM, moved to a vast modernist campus in southern Mexico City, grew exponentially, and attracted intellectuals from all over Latin America. Mexico became an international tourist destination after the government built up beaches in remote places like Ixtapa and Cancún.

In 1958 the PRI gave Mexico a President, Adolfo López Mateos, who momentarily moderated the corruption and enchanted Mexicans with his populist joie de vivre. By the 1960s Mexico had changed a great deal. The population had nearly tripled since the revolution, while the infant-mortality rate dropped by about 50 percent. The country was losing the agrarian identity that had defined it during the revolution, since more than half of Mexicans lived in urban areas; Mexico City alone concentrated 18 percent of the population in 1960. The postwar economic boom gave birth to an urban middle class of office workers and government functionaries.

The system continued to rest on unifying factors in Mexican society. There was no longer a threat of religious rift. More than 90 percent of Mexicans professed to be Catholic, and they had become reconciled to an uneasy coexistence with the anticlerical PRI. National ethnic strife was also unlikely. The Indian peoples, although they made up about 18 percent of the population and were mistreated and marginalized, were divided among dozens of tribes and language groups.

Yet polarizing forces were at work.

The perennial distance between rich and poor was widening. Conditions for many blue-collar laborers remained harsh, and those who did not accept the control of the PRI's *charro* unions faced ostracism or repression. In 1952 protesting miners from the north marched on Mexico City, and for two years after 1956 strikes by teachers and telephone, electric, and railroad workers swept the country.

Rural farmers were given land during the Cárdenas era, but subsequent PRI administrations favored aggressive industrialization, holding down food prices and undermining the economics of small farms. The flow of labor migrants to the United States became a flood. Rubén Jaramillo, a farmer who had fought with Zapata in the revolution, rose up in arms again in Morelos to defend the agrarian reform from local caciques and was murdered by army troops in 1962.

The system, at its apex, was an electoral democracy with no fair elections; a federation in which all power was centralized in the presidency; and a revolutionary state where the workers were dominated and demobilized. Yet Mexicans were accustomed to a gap between government rhetoric and performance. The PRI regime had given them three decades with progress and no upheaval, and it continued to govern with the consent of most Mexicans.

Julia:

Although we quickly learned of Mexicans' discontent with the PRI, we also saw that they took a certain pride in the sophistication of their unique system. To understand a regime that at first seemed inscrutable, we had to learn its protocols and lexicon. For example:

acarreo: the PRI practice of hauling people to its rallies and elections with promises of bag lunches or better

alquimistas: PRI alchemists, or experts in rigging elections

cargada: the piling on of PRI followers behind a candidate nominated by the President

carro completo: a full house, in which the PRI wins every election in a state or district

charro: a PRI labor leader, from a Mexican term for "cowboy"

destape: the unveiling of the PRI presidential candidate chosen by *dedazo;* before the unveiling, the candidate was *el tapado,* the one behind the cover, and Mexicans tried to guess who would be *el bueno,* the right one

dinosaurio: dinosaur, a term coined in the 1980s to describe members of the PRI old guard, who opposed the trade opening with the United States and the rise of the technocrats

grilla: politicking PRI-style, more talk than results

hueso: a bone, or patronage job

mayoriteo: when the PRI used its majority in the Congress to crush an opposition initiative

Among the system's basic codes of conduct, corruption seemed to be one of the most fundamental, with impunity starting at the highest level. We learned that it was an inviolable unwritten rule that former Presidents and their families would not be criticized, let alone prosecuted. Once a President was out of office, he was home free.

"A politician who is poor is a poor politician" was the oft-cited maxim of Carlos Hank González, a former Mexico City mayor and renowned PRI dinosaur who applied this principle vigorously in his own career. Hank started out as a rural schoolteacher but became vastly wealthy as mayor by contracting city construction projects to his own companies. Mexicans continued to refer to him, but now with irony, as El Profesor, as if to point up the discrepancy between his modest origins and his later prosperity.

Using money to circumvent the rules was a cultural norm. Paying a *mordida*, a bribe, to a policeman or functionary was far easier than going through the legal procedures—if there were any—to pay a traffic ticket, get a driver's license or a construction permit, or register a property title or a newborn baby. Mexicans were constantly induced to bend the law to perform the essential tasks of life, becoming involuntarily complicit in the grander corruption of their politicians.

One incident I heard about in my reporting for the *Times* showed how the endemic corruption did the most damage to the poorest Mexicans. In October 1999 President Ernesto Zedillo inaugurated a twelve-bed hospital in the town Santa Catarina Juquila, on a mountaintop in Oaxaca. The people of Juquila had waited twenty years for their hospital, praying for it to a celebrated virgin around whose shrine the town had grown. It took thirteen years of treks to meetings with PRI bureaucrats in Oaxaca City to get the project launched. The construction took another seven years and cost more than $2 million, enough time and money to build three hospitals that size.

Three days after Zedillo cut the ribbon, when the first patients were lining up for care, an earthquake struck the town. The hospital's flimsy walls cracked open, injuring ten patients. The building had to be condemned. Federal inspectors determined that about $1.3 million had been siphoned out of the hospital budget through contract overpayments and kickbacks to local politicians.

The decades of PRI rule had engendered a broader culture of lawlessness. This was evident in the frightening plague of kidnappings and drug crimes that was under way. But we also experienced it as we sought to get around Mexico City, negotiating the Darwinian driving patterns in the streets there.

We discovered that for many Mexican drivers, a red light was not a command to stop but the opening play in a contest of wits. A driver approaching a red light would attempt to measure his (or her) forces against those of cars on the cross street whose light was green, to see if his greater speed and dexterity might allow him to shoot through the intersection despite the tedious traffic signal. If, for instance, I put on my blinker before making a turn, I was weakening my defense, giving the driver behind me a chance to speed up to block my move. Since speed-limit and other traffic signs carried no weight, there was a proliferation of speed bumps, physical obstacles across the roadway that would gut the bottom of any car that went over too fast.

Mexicans' basic assumptions about politics had also been shaped by the long tenure of the PRI system. For one thing, they were masters of the conspiracy theory. Although the assassination of the PRI presidential candidate, Luis Donaldo Colosio, was far from solved and the evidence was confusing, most Mexicans were certain that he could only have been the victim of a plot laid by the PRI. While the press had become quite combative, there was still a dearth of hard information from Los Pinos about the President's activities, leaving Mexicans with their belief that Ernesto Zedillo, like PRI Presidents before him, was all-seeing and omnipresent and continuously scheming to undo his rivals. When a shadowy guerrilla group carried out coordinated attacks across the country on the eve of Zedillo's State of the Union address in 1996, creating a major problem for the President, there was a swift storm of speculation that Zedillo had ordered his own intelligence services to create the group, supposedly to discredit the mainstream leftist opposition.

The PRI system also fed the fatalism that had been part of Mexico's outlook since Moctezuma lost his empire to the Spaniards because of his premonitions of doom. The PRI was a patronage pyramid that doled out favors in return for allegiance, and it discouraged community people from organizing to help themselves. Communities that showed signs of independence ran the risk of being eliminated by PRI authorities from the running for new roads, water systems, electric projects, or schools. I heard people say time and again that the only way they could progress was if the government helped them, and they seriously doubted that the government ever would.

I went once to a proletarian settlement of 2 million people on the edge of Mexico City called Ciudad Nezahualcóyotl, named for the Aztec monarch and poet who once ruled over a kingdom in the same location. Today Neza, as it is now known, is bordered on one flank by a desiccated lake bed that was allowed many years ago, by municipal omission, to become an unregulated open-air dump. Fetid refuse had accumulated in enormous mounds alongside an open sewer canal filled with viscous black water. Toxic dust from the dump rained down on Neza residents, sickening them.

The people of Neza said they were well aware of the grave threat to their health, but everyone I spoke with intoned a unified refrain. "Of course it bothers us," said Alejandra Pérez, an eighteen-year-old resident, as she led her wheezing baby sister down a gritty street. "But what's the point of saying something about it? No one in power would pay any attention to us if we did."

—   —   —

From the earliest years of the system, iconoclastic individuals tried from time to time to advance the democratic agenda. Their efforts met with repression, and the PRI powers saw to it that their stories were written out of official history.

José Vasconcelos served as Secretary of Education during the 1920s. An ally of Madero's during the revolution, he dared to run for President in 1929, challenging the candidate of Calles, the Maximal Chief. Vasconcelos was an eloquent advocate of free secular public education, and as Secretary he had laid down the philosophical foundations of the public school system in Mexico. But the regime closed ranks against his maverick presidential bid and began to develop its skills in electoral fraud. The rigged results gave Vasconcelos only 105,655 votes out of 1.9 million cast, and he was forced to flee into exile.

However, as soon as Vasconcelos's dissent was neutralized, PRI leaders began to lionize him in official hagiographies as the Father of Mexican Education. Vasconcelos died in 1959, his clash with the regime all but forgotten, immortalized as the PRI's official educator.

A decade later, in 1940, a revolutionary General, Juan Andrew Almazán, attempted another independent presidential run. Backed by the business class of northern Mexico and the PAN, then a newly formed opposition party, Almazán blasted the government and its party as "totalitarian." The system mobilized its machine against him and overwhelmed him at the polls.

Another dissident campaign was led by Miguel Henríquez Guzmán, a PRI politician who ran against the party's official candidate in the presidential race of 1952. Henríquez disagreed with his party's slide into corruption and defended the right of unions to organize independently of the system. The PRI tolerated his campaign but not the protests of his followers, who decried the vote as fraudulent. The security forces opened fire on a demonstration at one of the major promenades in downtown Mexico City. Exactly how many were killed has never been known, but the wounded were in the dozens.

Although the PRI never ruled out violence against adversaries, in general the party was known for the subtlety with which its leaders calibrated coercion, rarely employing more than necessary. However, thirty years after the regime was founded, a shift occurred in its approach. A hard new man, Gustavo Díaz Ordaz, took control of Mexico's security apparatus. He held it for twelve years, first as Government Secretary, the Mexican equivalent of Interior Minister, and, after 1964, as President.

A short man with horn-rimmed glasses and a brooding temperament, Díaz Ordaz was less skilled than his predecessors at gauging the real dangers posed by dissidents. He tended to see subversive threats on all sides and often preferred force over negotiation to meet them.

In 1959 two Communist leaders of the union representing workers at the state-owned railroads, Demetrio Vallejo and Valentín Campa, sought to obtain better wages and benefits and to oust the PRI's *charro* bosses. To stop a threatened strike, Díaz Ordaz summarily fired thirteen thousand workers. As Campa and Vallejo pressed their campaign, Díaz Ordaz ordered a massive roundup on March 28, 1959, arresting both men and some ten thousand workers, sending them all to military prison camps. Both Campa and Vallejo spent the next decade in jail.

It happened, however, that Díaz Ordaz began to put his repressive stamp on the PRI system just as the changes in the country were generating new kinds of dissidence. The middle class was increasingly cosmopolitan, and its youths were attuned to the cultural rebellion that swept the West after the straitlaced 1950s. A thriving Mexican hippie movement adopted the white muslin clothing of the poorest Indians. The country had its own *rocanroleros*, as rock musicians were called. Mexican teenagers did not have to import marijuana and mushrooms to heighten their reveries, since these were in abundant supply in the mountains and deserts of northern Mexico.

Díaz Ordaz was ill suited by both disposition and political training to comprehend the ferment. Not long into his presidency, he summoned the strong-arm methods he had used against workers and turned them on urban dissenters. He deployed riot police to oust striking physicians and nurses from government hospitals. Then he sent paratroopers to put down protests by middle-class university students in the states of Michoacán, Sonora, and Tabasco. While the demonstrators' demands varied, complaints against police and military brutality were a common denominator.

With its customary resilience, the PRI system emerged from the early confrontations of Díaz Ordaz's *sexenio* with its hegemony and prestige intact. In fact, in 1968 Mexico was getting ready to become the center of world attention as the first developing country ever chosen to host the Olympic Games.

3

Tlatelolco, 1968

Luis González de Alba was a twenty-four-year-old psychology major at the National Autonomous University of Mexico when he first glimpsed the beginnings of the student revolt in July 1968. A slender student with a black Zapata-style mustache, the son of a Guadalajara pharmacist, González de Alba was in a lounge at the university campus in the southern suburbs of the capital the evening of July 26 when word arrived that street battles were raging all over downtown Mexico City. He decided to drive into the city in a friend's Volkswagen Beetle to see for himself.

Arriving at the edge of the colonial center at 11 p.m., González de Alba found streets littered with rocks and broken glass, several buses in flames, and squadrons of helmeted riot police menacing from every corner. He parked near the Zócalo and walked the cobbled streets to San Ildefonso, an eighteenth-century colonial palace housing two high schools administered by the UNAM. As he entered San Ildefonso, riot police charged down the street, and a panicked group of teenagers pulled the heavy wooden doors shut and barred them. Inside, the building resembled a medieval castle under siege. Students were wandering through the corridors, dazed. Moving in the darkness past murals by the revolutionary painter José Clemente Orozco, teenagers were hauling stones and bricks to the roof to hurl down on police. Others were assembling Molotov cocktails.

An antiauthoritarian mutiny was under way. It had begun four days earlier, when teenagers from two rival high schools had gotten into a brawl during a touch-football game in a downtown park. Riot police had waded in, swinging their clubs. When the students retreated into a nearby vocational school, the police had charged through the school-house doors after them, beating teachers and students alike. That led to days of skirmishes between hundreds of stone-throwing adolescents and the police.

Those protests provoked more repression, which provoked more protests. Now students had declared strikes at San Ildefonso and several other downtown high schools. Street fighting had paralyzed the city center. Police were beating practically every pedestrian they could corner. Students built barricades. Along some streets, neighborhood women lobbed flowerpots down on the heads of police from their balconies. The air was foul with tear gas and the smoke of burning vehicles.

The spectacle of longhaired students taunting authorities in the streets outside the National Palace infuriated President Gustavo Díaz Ordaz. As a personality, he was obsessive about order and discipline. In sharp contrast to his playboy predecessor, Adolfo López Mateos, Díaz Ordaz was an ascetic, never seen to enjoy a stiff drink or a rich meal. With a prominent deck of buckteeth, he was genuinely unattractive and had few close friends. The world kept its distance from him, and he in turn regarded the world with suspicion. He believed that the fundamental job of the Mexican President was to preserve order, and he could not tolerate the rowdy protesters who were thumbing their noses at him and his office.

So, characteristically, Díaz Ordaz responded to the strike at San Ildefonso with overwhelming force, sending army troops to take up positions in front of the high school's three-hundred-year-old wooden door, ornately carved by indigenous craftsmen. The soldiers blew the door apart with the blast of a bazooka and rushed in to beat and detain the terrified teenagers inside. Troops invaded several other high schools, clubbing and arresting students. By the end of the day four hundred people had been hospitalized and one thousand arrested.

The country had seen Díaz Ordaz suppress dissent before. But the army attack on a high school stunned many Mexicans. The rector of the university, Javier Barros Sierra, a distinguished and politically moderate engineer, ordered the flag on the campus commons lowered to half-mast. The following day he walked at the head of a march of more than fifty thousand students and professors through the city's southern neighborhoods.

The rector's dignified protest earned him Díaz Ordaz's contempt and later that summer cost him his job. But it inspired thousands of previously apathetic students into fervid political action. Overnight, the UNAM, the largest university in Latin America, with more than 100,000 students, became virtually united in opposition to the Díaz Ordaz government and its violent tactics.

Thirteen miles across Mexico City at a campus on the far northern edge of the metropolis, the country's other large federal center of higher learning, the National Polytechnic Institute, the Politécnico, was also in rebellion. Raúl Álvarez Garín, then a twenty-seven-year-old physics student, was attending a mathematics seminar outside Mexico City during the first student-police clashes. But when word reached him of the bazooka attack on the San Ildefonso school, he rushed back to the Politécnico and, offering direction to an inchoate, virtually leaderless movement, began to help draw up a list of student demands.

Álvarez Garín, a stocky, mustachioed fellow, came from a radical family. His grandfather had been an aide to the revolutionary General Álvaro Obregón, his parents were Communists, and his wife was the daughter of Valentín Campa, a leader of the railway strike that Díaz Ordaz had crushed when he was Government Secretary in 1959. Álvarez Garín showed himself to be a natural strategist, and he helped to outline a concise list of straightforward demands: the government should free jailed students as well as railway union leaders imprisoned since 1959, pay compensation to the families of injured protesters, disband the riot police, and repeal vague laws used to jail dissenters.

Álvarez Garín was not a great speaker; sometimes he stuttered. But when he first outlined the demands in a speech before students and faculty on the Politécnico campus, he electrified the crowd. Thousands of voices drowned him out with roars of approval and defiant chants.

"It was one of those emotions that you experience only a few times in life," Álvarez Garín said of that moment. "They interrupted me ten or fifteen times in the few minutes that I spoke."

The demands Álvarez Garín helped to conceive were quickly taken up by the movement as a whole. The simplicity and elemental justice of the students' petitions gave them tremendous moral authority. Over the next weeks, as the students resisted escalating attacks from the government, their street demonstrations and raucous public presence became a symbol to many of criticism of the PRI system that the wider public had felt but left unspoken. Suddenly the regime that had presented itself as the Mexican people's revolutionary benefactor looked like an emperor parading with no clothes.

In the days following Álvarez Garín's stirring speech, students declared strikes at the Politécnico, the UNAM, and virtually every other college, preparatory, and private school in and around Mexico City. University campuses in many of the thirty-one Mexican states were also shut down. Almost overnight, students at dozens of schools sent representatives to a two-hundred-member National Strike Council.

The council's first major test came when it called for a march and rally on August 13, setting its destination at the Zócalo in Mexico City. Student leaders had no way of knowing how the public would react to their impertinent invitation. But the depth of public disaffection with decades of PRI government became clear along the route, when thousands of onlookers cheered the marchers from balconies and sidewalks. Eventually 200,000 Mexicans marched into the central square. Many were parents of protesting students. Others were teachers, nurses, and independent workers of all stripes.

The unexpected size of the crowd proved that the students were voicing frustrations felt by Mexicans of all ages in a modernizing Mexico. Like Álvarez Garín and González de Alba, many of the student leaders considered themselves revolutionaries, à la Fidel Castro and Che Guevara. But they attracted wide public support because the demands they pressed publicly were not to overthrow the government but to make it more democratic.

During August the campuses became centers of feverish political activity. By day at the Politécnico, Álvarez Garín was working to arrange a disciplined strike; he helped organize student brigades, a communal kitchen, and the purchase of a sound system for rallies. By night he was sleeping in one of his professors' cubicles.

At the UNAM, González de Alba, who had been chosen to represent the philosophy department on the National Strike Council, began living on the eighth floor of the Humanities Tower in a carpeted hallway where he could close the doors at night to shut out the incessant whine of the mimeograph machine printing the students' latest handbill.

For González de Alba the student movement was not all protest and persecution. It was also an exhilarating cultural revolution, in which he and a whole generation of students broke gloriously out of the stifling, static confines of mid-century Mexican society. "It was a party," González de Alba said, "an explosion after fifty years of good behavior."

"We slept in the dean's leather chairs; we breakfasted without paying in cafeterias that we'd taken over," González de Alba recounted. "We went to the rally feeling like a bullfighter before the pens were to be opened to let in the bull-as-riot-policeman; we boarded the buses to give speeches to people, to sing, to present skits; we fled from the bull, delighted, when a patrol car would stop the bus; at night we'd light campfires and sing songs of the Spanish civil war; we'd form couples, and we'd look for the vacant cubicle to be alone with our lover; we'd swim at the pool without a credential. We did everything without any ticket or any permission."

On August 27, another march to the Zócalo drew an overwhelming crowd: 400,000 Mexicans, who tramped into the square for four straight hours. Students climbed into the tower of the sixteenth-century cathedral and set its ancient bells ringing. Some demonstrators gathered under the National Palace's central balcony, where Mexican Presidents by tradition officiate over Independence Day ceremonies, to hurl personal insults at Díaz Ordaz.

"*¡Sal al balcón, chango hocicón!*" they shouted. "Come on out, monkey big-snout!"

Díaz Ordaz was not amused. By late evening most of the protesters had gone home, but a few thousand stayed behind, building bonfires and vowing to maintain an encampment to pressure the President to respond to their demands. At midnight three battalions of federal troops marched out of the National Palace and converged on the Zócalo, joined by twelve armored personnel carriers from other garrisons. Shouting through loudspeakers, they ordered the youths out of the Zócalo. Most fled; those who dawdled were chased down and beaten.

In his annual State of the Union message the following Sunday, September 1, Díaz Ordaz issued an unmistakable threat: "We can't allow our legal order to continue to be ruptured so inexcusably," he said. "We wouldn't like to find ourselves in a situation where we would have to take measures we don't want. But we'll take them if we have to. We'll go as far as we have to go."

If at first the protests had angered Díaz Ordaz simply because of the challenge they posed to his authoritarian views, as the summer closed he saw in them a larger threat. The government regarded Mexico's designation to host the Olympic Games as an extraordinary opportunity to portray the country as a success story in economic development with social justice. The Games were scheduled to begin October 12. Díaz Ordaz was determined to quiet the student protests well before that date, so in the days after his annual address the authorities cracked down hard.

The government-controlled papers attacked the student movement with mounting vehemence, and scores of activists were arrested. One of the university leaders whom Díaz Ordaz's secret police, the Dirección Federal de Seguridad, or Federal Security Directorate, pursued most relentlessly was Heberto Castillo Martínez, a professor of mechanical engineering.

Castillo was well known in Mexico not only for his distinguished engineering career but also because of his close association with General Lázaro Cárdenas, the immensely popular President who, after nationalizing Mexico's petroleum industry in 1938, had for decades thereafter been a senior statesman in the country's leftist causes. Cuauhtémoc Cárdenas, the General's son, had been a student of Castillo's in the 1950s, and through Cuauhtémoc, Castillo had met General Cárdenas, with whom he formed a warm political association and friendship. From 1959 through 1964 Castillo had been the General's personal secretary.

Castillo had embraced the 1968 student strike enthusiastically, and in the tumultuous assemblies of the students' National Strike Council he often stood to outline his own and other leftist professors' views.

Castillo's involvement in the protests especially infuriated Díaz Ordaz. The President used the memoirs he wrote in his private moments to vent his envy of the professor, raging about all the adulation Castillo was receiving.

On one occasion Castillo helped to organize a meeting at General Cárdenas's Mexico City home between the General and a dozen student leaders, including González de Alba. General Cárdenas, who was following the movement's development with great interest, spoke to the students with respect but also with considerable concern. He had been a General during the revolution, a leader of the Mexican left, and a respected member of the PRI elite, and he saw that the movement was rattling the postrevolutionary society he had helped build.

After the meeting Cárdenas encouraged Castillo to continue to support the protesters. He also pooh-poohed Castillo's worries that Díaz Ordaz might deploy the army against the UNAM.

That proved to be a miscalculation. On September 18, tanks rumbled onto the UNAM campus, and troops arrested five hundred students. Castillo barely escaped capture.

He was in the science department that night, writing the script for a documentary film about the movement, when a panicked student rushed in with the news. Castillo raced out of the building toward the edge of campus, where, at an overpass, a soldier on the turret of a tank shined a spotlight on him.

"Halt!" the soldier called.

"If I stop, they'll kill me—and if I don't, maybe not," Castillo told himself. He sprinted a few paces, dived into a gully, and crawled through rocks and shrubs to escape. He spent several harrowing days hiding in the cactus-covered hills around the campus, finally approaching a taxi that drove him to the home of sympathizers who gave him lodging.

The army takeover of the UNAM met with no resistance. But when authorities sought to seize the Politécnico days later, students defended the campus fiercely, hurling Molotov cocktails and setting police vehicles on fire. When army troops arrived in reinforcement, residents of nearby buildings hurled garbage, bottles, and pots of boiling water down on the tanks. The clashes lasted three days.

In the last days of September, Mexico City was in a de facto state of siege. There were scores of illegal arrests, detainees were held without access to lawyers, and state security agents routinely searched homes and cars with no warrant. Yet most of the strike leaders were still free. And González de Alba, Álvarez Garín, and others on the National Strike Council scheduled another protest rally for October 2 in the central commons of a downtown housing project known as Tlatelolco.

They picked the site because the thirteen-story Chihuahua apartment building overlooking the square had a broad third-floor balcony that would serve well as a speaker's platform. But the commons, the Plaza de las Tres Culturas, was a space with extraordinary historical significance: it was the site where, in the 1521 battle of Tlatelolco, the conquistador Hernán Cortés conquered Cuauhtémoc, the last of the Aztec Emperors. When, in the early 1960s, the government inaugurated the vast modern Tlatelolco project around the ruins of an Aztec ceremonial temple, a plaque was erected to commemorate that fateful battle between Aztec and Spaniard. "It was neither a triumph nor a defeat," the plaque says. "It was the painful birth of the mestizo nation that is Mexico today."

The student rally on October 2, 1968, at the Tlatelolco plaza proved to be another painful birth: that of a new Mexican generation.

The rally was to start at 5 p.m. When González de Alba arrived half an hour late, a light drizzle was falling and leaders of the strike council were already making speeches.

"The movement will continue!" a student was telling the crowd. González de Alba climbed the stairs of the Chihuahua building to the third-floor balcony, which student leaders had equipped with a sound system. Perhaps twenty other leaders of the strike council were already on the balcony, along with many Mexican journalists. With the Olympic Games approaching, some one hundred foreign reporters were also present at the rally, and many were crowded onto the balcony as well.

From the Chihuahua building González de Alba had a great view of the rally. To the left of the plaza was a sixteenth-century stone chapel; towering behind it was the white twenty-story building housing the Foreign Relations Secretariat, completing the plaza's three cultures: Aztec, Spanish colonial, and modern. To the right were more blocky apartment buildings. Perhaps eight thousand demonstrators were packed into the plaza, some holding protest banners, others huddling under umbrellas. Mingling with the students were residents of the housing project, including many children.

At the same time, hundreds of plainclothes state security agents were also visible, betrayed by their military haircuts and, on this occasion, another curious detail: many were wearing one white glove. Uniformed troops in light tanks and jeeps had taken up positions in parking lots and streets on all sides of the housing project. Analysts calculated later that more than ten thousand soldiers and police were at Tlatelolco.

The military presence was so ominous that shortly after González de Alba's arrival, a student approached him to urge that the rally be canceled immediately. González de Alba brushed the suggestion aside. After all, the student movement had seen plenty of troops and police at previous demonstrations that summer.

Two military helicopters had been circling the zone. At 6:10 p.m. they moved down to hover menacingly above the plaza, well below the roofs of the surrounding buildings. At that moment two military flares crackled in the air, panicking the demonstrators.

"Don't run, *compañeros!*" a student shouted over the sound system. "Keep calm! It's a provocation!" The multitude began to run anyway. Soldiers with bayonets, however, were advancing in formation toward the plaza from several sides, blocking the few escape routes between the surrounding buildings. The crowds were turned back, forming a vast whirlpool of terrified humanity.

Shots rang out amid the shouts and cries, first the sharp pinging of light weaponry, then the rhythmic rattle of machine-gun fire. Gunmen posted on the rooftops were firing on the crowd; so were some soldiers on the ground.

Dozens of the white-gloved state security agents charged up the stairs onto the balcony of the Chihuahua building, brandishing pistols and automatic rifles. "Don't turn around or we'll blow your heads off," they. shouted, throwing students and journalists alike against the wall and ripping out the wires of the sound system.

His head pressed against the wall, González de Alba nonetheless was able to see some of what was happening on the balcony out of the corner of his eye. After detaining him and the other student leaders, the state security agents moved to the edge of the balcony, raised their weapons, and began shooting down on the crowd. To the agents' apparent surprise, however, their shots were immediately returned by soldiers firing automatic rifles and machine guns.

The balcony was engulfed in chaos. Many of the white-gloved agents dived to the cement floor, ordering the detained students down as well to avoid the bullets slamming into the balcony. Even so, some students were hit. Machine-gun fire punctured the building's water pipes, and water rained down on the students' heads. The stairwells became waterfalls.

"Olympia Battalion!" some of the state security agents shouted. "Don't shoot!"

Álvarez Garín had joined the rally at a spot at the southern edge of the plaza, near the chapel. When the shots began to rain down on the crowd from the rooftops and from several flanks, he and hundreds of other demonstrators sprinted along the stone wall, seeking to escape the plaza along the church's eastern edge. But when the protesters rounded the corner of the chapel, they faced a line of bayonet-carrying troops twenty-five yards away, shouting for them to halt. Many protesters were hit there by gunfire. Álvarez Garín saw the dead fall into a heap, one on top of the other, at the corner of the church.

During the first minutes of riotous gunfire from hundreds of weapons, students dropped to the ground and found it wet with blood. "When the gunfire was most intense, you couldn't even lift your head," one student said. "We covered ourselves with the bodies of the dead."

Amid this firestorm a little girl appeared, clutching a bag of bread and wandering, dazed, through the bodies. Frantic students screamed at her to get down, but she appeared not to hear.

The machine-gun fire was so intense that four upper floors of the Chihuahua building caught fire, forcing many families to flee the building. The gunfire continued intermittently for ninety minutes, until 7:45 p.m.

Students detained on the balcony saw state security agents dragging bodies by the legs down the stairwell of the Chihuahua building. Many residents were killed or wounded in their homes as machine-gun fire tore through the Chihuahua and at least seven nearby apartment buildings. A young woman seeking to drive away was killed by gunfire in her car. The horn shrieked as she slumped on the steering wheel. Many of the victims were later found to have been killed by bayonets; a photographer for the newspaper *Excélsior* was bayoneted in the hand.

At 11 p.m., when the first of the 2,360 persons detained at the rally were being kicked and beaten aboard army trucks and buses, the government forces fired on the plaza again, this time for about an hour.

At one point after his detention but before he was trucked away to a military camp, Álvarez Garín watched army troops strafing the front wall of the Chihuahua building with tracer bullets from a machine gun. Their objective, if they had one, was not clear. When the last detainees were bused from the plaza, soldiers were setting up camp along the streets surrounding the housing project. Some were eating. Some shouted insults at the student prisoners.

Until ten o'clock the night of the massacre, Mexican radio and TV stations reported that the army had dispersed a student rally with gunfire and that there were many dead. But the newscasts thereafter and the newspapers the following day reported a revised government version of the events: that "terrorist" snipers located in buildings overlooking the plaza had fired on the army, forcing the army to shoot back in self-defense; the government implied that the terrorists were students but

October 2, 1968: Detainees at the Chihuahua building

produced no evidence. The official body count: twenty dead and seventy-six wounded. Among the wounded was General José Hernández Toledo, the commander of the paratroop battalion that participated in the Tlatelolco operation.

President Díaz Ordaz followed the media coverage in minute detail. Televisa, the television monopoly, had broadcast no taped footage of the attack on the students, and Jacobo Zabludovsky, the network's anchorman, had faithfully conveyed the government's version of events. But Díaz Ordaz noticed that Zabludovsky was wearing a solid black tie. Zabludovsky always wore a plain black tie on the air, but Díaz Ordaz didn't know that. Imagining enemies on all sides, the President viewed the newscaster's tie as a surreptitious sign that Zabludovsky disapproved of the killing. Díaz Ordaz called Zabludovsky and chewed him out ferociously.

Heberto Castillo was not at the plaza, because he was already in hiding on the night of October 2, sheltered at the home of a sympathetic university professor. He sat in anguish listening to the sketchy radio reports of the violence. Telephoning friends, he learned that the government had unleashed all its fury on the movement.

General Cárdenas, who had helped build the modern Mexican army and had been increasingly distraught throughout the summer of 1968 as he watched it deployed with mounting ferocity against the student protesters, was at his Polanco home the night of the Tlatelolco operation. His wife stayed up with him until three o'clock in the morning as the General paced fitfully, unable even to lie down. At that point a friend of the General's who had been at the plaza burst in, pouring out his account. He told General Cárdenas how "in the staircases they had chased the boys down and left them there dead." The man broke down in tears.

"And I believe that the General shed some tears, too," Cárdenas's wife said.

On the evening of October 2, Elena Poniatowska, a thirty-five-year-old reporter for the newspaper *Novedades*, heard sobbing at the door of her home in Coyoacán, in the south of Mexico City. On the step she found two of her friends, both anthropologists, weeping and mumbling about events they had seen at the Tlatelolco rally. The two were crying so hysterically that it took a while for Poniatowska to form a clear picture of what had happened: soldiers bayoneting students; tanks firing at apartment buildings; rivers of blood.

One of the women, Margarita Nolasco, told Poniatowska that she had watched as crowds stampeded toward her to escape gunfire from soldiers on the far side of the plaza, only to turn and race away, falling over each other, when they heard bullets raining down on them from snipers above. Women and children had been cut down by gunfire before her eyes.

Nolasco's companion lived in a flat on the fourth floor of the Chihuahua building. Amid the gunfire and screaming, she and Nolasco had somehow managed to climb the stairwell back to her apartment. There, from a window, Nolasco had watched soldiers dragging bodies through the rain and laying them out in pools of blood on a sidewalk below. She had counted sixty-eight dead, she told Poniatowska.

What made Nolasco most distraught was that her teenage son had gone missing at the plaza. After telling their story, the two women headed back out into the rain to search for him.

"They were so beside themselves, I thought they were crazy," Poniatowska said.

Poniatowska was not a typical newspaper reporter. She had been born in Paris to French aristocrats with noble roots tracing back to a Polish king. Her father was a senior executive in the Belgian branch of International Telephone and Telegraph. Her maternal grandparents were wealthy sugar planters who fled from Mexico to Paris after the 1910 revolution, when Emiliano Zapata's rebels attacked their vast plantation in the state of Morelos. Poniatowska had first come to Mexico in 1942, at age nine, when her mother fled wartime Europe with Elena and her brother. Attending elementary schools in Mexico City, she never lost her French accent. She was sent to high school at the Sacred Heart Convent in Philadelphia. Her father came to Mexico and brought Elena back from North America before she got her high-school diploma, urging her to take advantage of her fluency in French, English, and Spanish by becoming an executive secretary.

Poniatowska, however, had her own ideas. She wanted to be a journalist. She took the only newspaper job open to aspiring young female reporters in Mexico of the 1950s, writing about society luncheons and debutantes for the social column of the newspaper *Excélsior*.

After one year she left the paper to write as a freelancer for *Novedades*, a yellow broadsheet that nevertheless allowed her to write about politics. As a reporter, she had a knack for insinuating herself into the right place at the right time. On first impression, she seemed like a harmless, light-headed housewife, an appearance that helped her gain access to all sorts of difficult situations. She also branched out, publishing short stories and essays. By 1968 Poniatowska had become a seasoned journalist who had interviewed many of the era's prominent figures, including Lázaro Cárdenas and Fidel Castro.

Although her friends' account of the events at the Tlatelolco plaza sounded exaggerated, Poniatowska wanted to see for herself. She rose at five the next morning and took a taxi north toward Tlatelolco.

Along the way she bought a copy of *Novedades*, which, like most Mexican newspapers of the period, adhered strictly to daily editorial "suggestions" from the Government Secretariat and other PRI authorities. FIREFIGHT BETWEEN SNIPERS AND THE ARMY IN TLATELOLCO! the headline said.

Poniatowska reached the plaza at dawn. Dozens of tanks and jeeps jammed the surrounding streets, and soldiers milled around, but nobody prevented her from walking into the housing project. Hundreds of windows were smashed. Building facades were pockmarked from thousands of bullet holes. Women from the project were lined up with buckets at a single outside water faucet; high-caliber shells had destroyed the plumbing in the apartment buildings. An anguished soldier was talking into a pay phone. "I don't know how many days I'm going to be here," he said. "Let me talk to my son. I want to hear his voice."

The bodies Nolasco had seen soldiers lay out on the cement had been trucked away. But dozens of shoes—women's pumps, boys' tennis shoes—were piled in the trampled mud of the pre-Hispanic ruins, where crowds had sought refuge from the shooting.

Poniatowska was familiar with repression: in 1959 she had covered the strike in which Díaz Ordaz, then Government Secretary, had ordered the arrest of ten thousand railroad workers. Still, Poniatowska never imagined that the authorities would send soldiers to fire on a peaceful crowd in the heart of Mexico City.

Poniatowska had a four-month-old baby, whom she was breast-feeding, and she had been working only part-time. But now, sensing the significance of the events, she shifted into overdrive.

In *Excélsior* she read that Oriana Fallaci, a prominent Italian jour-nalist in the country to cover the Olympic Games, had attended the Tlatelolco rally and had been wounded. Poniatowska went to interview her in her hospital bed and found Fallaci seething with fury.

"What savagery!" Fallaci told Poniatowska. "Police dragging students away by the hair. I saw many people get hit, until I was hit, too. I lay in a pool of my own blood for forty-five minutes." Instead of helping, she said, the white-gloved state security agents stole her watch from her wrist, then moved on. Poniatowska wrote up the interview and took it to *Novedades*.

Her editor rejected the article immediately. "There's an order," he said. "We're going to concentrate on the Olympic Games. We're not printing anything more about Tlatelolco."

The International Olympic Committee learned of the Tlatelolco vio-lence, both from the international press and from a senior committee of-ficial who was in Mexico on October 2 and drove to the plaza, where he saw soldiers piling bodies onto trucks. The committee considered how to respond during a four-hour emergency session on October 3. Members of the Italian delegation were indignant, partly because Fallaci's experi-ences had received much coverage, and Italian and Australian members sent a protest, albeit tepid, to the Mexican government. But the commit-tee nonetheless resolved that the Games should proceed as scheduled on October 12. And they did.

Díaz Ordaz formally inaugurated the Nineteenth Olympiad before a crowd of 100,000 at a newly constructed stadium near the UNAM cam-pus. *The New York Times* described "a setting of pageantry, brotherhood and peace." A British television documentary took a similar tone:

It was an impressive ceremony, but one of apprehension, for the threat of a civil disturbance was present. As the flag was raised

above the heads of the crowd, hopes for a peaceful ceremony began to run high. The excitement of the occasion was electric . . .
Forgotten were the underlying threats, forgotten the huge force of
plainclothes police mingling with the crowd. As thousands of
doves soared away from their captivity, the Olympic flame burned
brightly . . . All was well in Mexico, the city of 1968.

Sports fans would remember those Games for the debate they provoked
about the effects of Mexico City's 7,350-foot altitude. Perhaps the biggest
story for Americans was the Black Power protest by Tommie Smith and
John Carlos, winners of the gold and bronze medals in the two-hundred-
meter race, who stood barefoot during the playing of the "Star-Spangled
Banner," each raising one black-gloved fist. The International Olympic
Committee expelled them for their protest.

Elena Poniatowska paid no attention to the Olympics; she was too busy
interviewing people who had witnessed the massacre. Margarita Nolasco
had found her son unhurt, and now, considerably more composed,
she sat down in Poniatowska's living room to recount her experiences
in more detail. Word got around, and the mothers and sisters of the
Tlatelolco dead began to show up at Poniatowska's door. Poniatowska
conducted scores of interviews, but no paper wanted her stories. Months
later, she shared her work with a friend, Neus Espresate, the daughter of
a book publisher, who encouraged her to shape the interviews into an
oral history.

She needed to talk with the student leaders. Scores had been arrested
at Tlatelolco (along with some two thousand protesters) and held for ten
days at Mexico City's Military Camp No. 1. Many leaders had been
beaten or threatened with summary execution during their interroga-
tions, although few if any had been tortured savagely as in other Latin
American countries. By the time the Olympics ended on October 27,
most detainees had been released. But Álvarez Garín, González de Alba,
and more than one hundred other student leaders labeled "dangerous"
were trucked to the Lecumberri penitentiary, constructed by Porfirio
Díaz in the nineteenth century on land a mile or so east of the Zócalo.

They were being held pending trial on murder, sedition, and other fabricated charges.

Poniatowska gained entrance to Lecumberri by posing as a prisoner's wife. She befriended Álvarez Garín, who liked her book project. He allowed her to use his cell for interviews and persuaded other political prisoners to talk with her. Poniatowska also met Heberto Castillo, whom Díaz Ordaz's secret police had finally tracked down and arrested. Poniatowska found him at peace and taking pleasure in small luxuries: the smell of flowers in the prison garden, the soft light of sunset through a window in his cell.

She found González de Alba at a typewriter in his cell, putting the finishing touches on a manuscript of his own. It was *Los días y los años* (The days and the years), a first-person account of his experiences in the student movement. Poniatowska, now pregnant with her third child, smuggled González de Alba's manuscript out of Lecumberri under her large skirt and arranged for its publication in early 1971, shortly after Díaz Ordaz had left office. It became an immediate best-seller.

But Poniatowska's book *La noche de Tlatelolco* (The night of Tlatelolco; published in English as *Massacre in Mexico*), which came out months later, was an even more sweeping success, going through several editions in its first year. Mexicans were in anguish over the events at Tlatelolco, and they craved hard information. The newspapers had been too muzzled to investigate. Poniatowska's book was a breakthrough, the first time a journalist had pierced the official shield of secrecy in such a compelling way.

She published verbatim the judicial statement of an army captain wounded at Tlatelolco who said the government had deployed scores of plainclothes soldiers wearing white gloves that identified them as members of a secret army unit, the Olympia Battalion, to arrest student leaders when military flares gave the signal. Her book included many eyewitness accounts describing soldiers and police firing point-blank at demonstrators. She cited an investigation by the British newspaper *The Guardian* indicating that as many as 325 people had been killed.

The evidence she amassed left no doubt that authorities had planned in advance to crush the student movement once and for all at Tlatelolco, whatever the cost. It demolished the official story that the security forces had merely responded to an attack mounted by the demonstrators.

Yet the authorities fiercely guarded their secrets, forcing the country to puzzle out events for decades thereafter. Who had coordinated the complex attack, and on whose orders? Who were the snipers who had fired on both protesters and government troops alike, and to whom did they answer? How many Mexicans had finally perished in the fury and impotence of that nightmarish plaza?

Only one Mexican official stood up to protest the Tlatelolco atrocities: Octavio Paz, the poet and essayist who was serving in 1968 as Mexican ambassador to India.

Born in 1914 in Mexico City, Paz studied law but became a poet instead. In 1944 he entered the Mexican foreign service, which had a tradition of nurturing talented writers within its embassies. Six years later Paz received worldwide acclaim for *El laberinto de la soledad* (*The Labyrinth of Solitude*), a portrait of the Mexican character that was neither history nor anthropology nor sociology but the vision of a poet borrowing freely from those and other disciplines.

Paz was fifty-four years old and had been posted in New Delhi for six years when student demonstrations began in the spring of 1968, first in Paris and then across the developed world. From the beginning Paz sympathized with this revolt of the young; the new generation's irreverence for the status quo reminded him of the surrealist movements he had admired in his youth.

"We were experiencing a kind of earthquake—not in the earth, but in the human conscience . . . in the psychic subsoil of Western civilization," he wrote later.

Vacationing with his French-born wife that summer in a hotel on the slopes of the Himalaya, Paz followed the course of the upheavals through shortwave newscasts of the BBC. Upon his return to the Indian capital, he learned of the first student-police clashes in Mexico City. Then, in late August, a cable arrived in New Delhi from Antonio Carrillo Flores, Díaz Ordaz's Secretary of Foreign Relations, requesting reports from all Mexican ambassadors serving in countries that had seen student turmoil, including India.

Paz poured himself into the assignment. On September 6, he dispatched a lengthy report to Carrillo Flores, in which he not only discussed the Indian government's handling of youth unrest, but added an analysis of the student upheavals worldwide, with insights about events in Scotland, France, West Germany, Italy, Poland, Czechoslovakia, Hungary, Yugoslavia, the United States, and even Japan.

With regard to Mexico, Paz urged his government to respond positively to the protesters' demands for democracy and warned against using force. In closing, he apologized for presenting "reflections that nobody has asked me for . . . But if I have exceeded my duties as an official," he added, "I have complied with my duties as a citizen."

In Mexico City, Carrillo Flores read parts of Paz's lengthy essay aloud to Díaz Ordaz and wrote back to Paz in mid-September to convey the President's response. "Poets sometimes have the most accurate intuitions," he had said. But if Díaz Ordaz respected Paz's insights, the President did not allow them to influence his plans. Two days later troops invaded the university on his orders, beginning the crackdown that culminated with the October 2 massacre.

Paz heard the first accounts of the Tlatelolco killings in a BBC newscast on October 3 and read about them in Indian newspapers the next day, whereupon he resigned his post without delay. "I will not describe to you my state of mind," Paz wrote in his resignation letter. "I imagine that it is the same as a majority of Mexicans: sadness and fury.

"In the face of these most recent events, I have had to ask myself if I could continue to serve the government with loyalty and without intellectual reservations," he wrote. "I am not in agreement in the slightest with the methods used to resolve (in reality, to repress) the demands and problems that our youth have expressed."

Paz's next move was to sit down at a desk and scribble twenty-four lines of verse. The promoters of the Nineteenth Olympiad had organized cultural events to coincide with the Games, including art exhibitions, concerts, and a meeting of poets from around the world, and Paz had been invited to submit "a poem that would exalt the Olympic spirit" for recitation during the Games.

Paz had politely declined. Prompted by the Tlatelolco violence, however, he changed his mind, and on October 7 he sent "a little poem to commemorate these Olympic Games":

Lucidity
            (perhaps it's worth
writing across the purity
of this page)
            is not lucid:
it is fury
            (yellow and black
mass of bile in Spanish)
spreading over the page.
Why?
            Guilt is anger
turned against itself:
                        if
an entire nation is ashamed
it is a lion poised
to leap.
            (The municipal
employees wash the blood
from the Plaza of the Sacrificed.)
Look now,
            stained
before anything worth it
was said:
            lucidity.

Paz asked that the poem be distributed to the poets attending the Mexico City event. It is not known whether it was. But officials in the Díaz Ordaz government did read Paz's poem in any case and, not surprisingly, they began to vilify him.

Officials passed out a bulletin saying that Paz had not resigned but been fired for making intemperate remarks. Díaz Ordaz himself, in a letter to Zakir Husain, the President of India, claimed that he had called Paz home. "I have decided to end Señor Paz's mission," Díaz Ordaz wrote.

Paz prepared to travel to France, where he had many friendships dating from an earlier posting in Mexico's Paris embassy. Indira Gandhi, India's Prime Minister, invited him and his wife to a dinner with her son Rajiv and other Indian leaders, and a group of writers and artists also organized a goodbye party to pay him homage.

Sometime in November, Paz and his wife finally boarded a train from Delhi to the port of Bombay. At stations along the route, Indian students gathered by the railroad tracks to cheer him and show solidarity with the Mexican students. Some gave him flowers. From Bombay, Paz set sail for Europe, following the long route around the Horn of Africa (the Suez Canal was closed because of war in the Middle East). He landed in Barcelona, where a crowd of writers who wished to express their solidarity with Paz, including Carlos Fuentes and Gabriel García Márquez, the Mexican and Colombian novelists, greeted him on the dock. He arrived in Paris in January 1969.

Just before leaving New Delhi, Paz gave a candid interview to Jean Wetz, a correspondent for the Paris newspaper *Le Monde*. "The massacre of the students was a ritual sacrifice," Paz said, "an act of terrorism, pure and simple, carried out by the state." The time has come, Paz said, "to carry out reforms that can lead to the disappearance of the PRI and the personal power conferred on each President." Citing Paz, *Le Monde* headlined the article MEXICO: THE GOVERNMENT PARTY IS AN OBSTACLE TO THE COUNTRY'S DEVELOPMENT.

In Paris the ambassador Silvio Zavala, a distinguished historian with a sycophantic streak, had worked throughout 1968 to prove his loyalty to Díaz Ordaz and the PRI, cabling reports to Mexico City on the student protests in France and the French press's interpretation of the violence in Mexico. When he read Paz's statements to *Le Monde*, Zavala was beside himself. Searching for ways to repair the damage to Mexico's image in France, Zavala arranged for a speech by Alfonso Martínez Domínguez, the president of the PRI, to be translated into French and thousands of copies distributed in villages across France. It was an inscrutable harangue on an arcane topic, filled with Mexican revolutionary jargon, which can only have puzzled its French readers.

When an embassy economist spoke too freely at a dinner with colleagues, asking if the government "was still murdering students," the embassy relayed his statements to Mexico City, and he was fired.

While in Paris, Paz gave an interview to the literary supplement of the newspaper *Le Figaro*. The PRI, Paz said, had become "a privileged bureaucracy, an apparatus that is increasingly sclerotic."

Zavala cabled to Mexico City, floating the possibility of taking legal action in the French courts to muzzle Paz. That spring, Paz and his wife left Paris for the United States, where he took jobs at the University of Pittsburgh and later at the University of Texas at Austin. All the while he was ruminating on the massacre. In October 1969, he gave a lecture in Austin that became the basis for a short book, *Posdata*, published in Mexico City three months later.

The protests in Mexico, Paz argued, had been most similar not to those in the United States, France, or Germany but to those by students in the Communist bloc. In Mexico, as in the Soviet Union, an authoritarian party had presided over decades of extraordinary economic progress. "But the experiences of Russia and Mexico are conclusive: without democracy, economic development makes no sense," he said. "On October 2, 1968, the student movement in Mexico came to an end. So did an entire period of Mexican history."

"These days will later be remembered like a scar," Luis González de Alba wrote in *Los días y los años*. He was right. The student protests and the massacre that crushed them marked an entire generation of Mexicans, changing forever the way they viewed themselves and their society.

Before 1968, most Mexicans had been proud of their system of government and its achievements. In 1959 a poll carried out by American academics found that although many Mexicans expressed cynicism about politics and corruption, most viewed their Presidents as benign.

But in 1968 the PRI system lost legitimacy in the eyes of many Mexicans, especially the middle class. The mass democratic movement that emerged was the first of its kind in Mexico: hundreds of thousands of citizens participated in antigovernment demonstrations that (unlike the uprisings in the Mexican Revolution) were essentially peaceful. The Tlatelolco killings dramatized to Mexicans as never before the closed and repressive nature of their government and the PRI clique that controlled it.

"Democracy in Mexico is just a concept, another formalism," the National Strike Council said in its final communiqué in December 1968, when most of its leaders were dead or in jail. "Politics is carried out behind the backs of the popular majorities and of their aspirations, interests, and demands."

Throughout that summer virtually every Mexican institution had proven servile to presidential despotism. Mexicans saw their Congress leap up with applause when Díaz Ordaz threatened to use military force against the students. They watched the media parrot government propaganda. They saw a Catholic Church so supine that some priests even refused to celebrate Mass in remembrance of Tlatelolco victims.

Mexicans saw the full scope of the regime's internal security apparatus—the President's secret police, the Government Secretariat's red squad, the Mexico City riot police, and even the once-admired army, born of the revolution—deployed against the country's own citizens. And after the Tlatelolco massacre, they saw the federal judiciary mount a kangaroo court, with judges convicting student leaders of homicide, sedition, and other felonies on the basis of blatantly phony evidence. Hundreds of students detained on October 2 were formally charged with murder and imprisoned for several years, and in every case the victims were the same two soldiers who died at Tlatelolco.

For all the turbulence, no Mexican institution had enough power in 1968 to challenge the PRI system. But millions of young Mexicans had been touched in one way or another by the protests.

One was Ernesto Zedillo, then sixteen years old. After riot police beat classmates and teachers inside his Vocational School No. 5, which was administered by the Politécnico, he joined the protests, boarding buses and strolling through restaurants with a tin can to collect donations for the strike council. During one street skirmish a photographer captured images of Zedillo, shaggy-haired, cringing against a wall as helmeted troops threatened him with bayonets.

Vicente Fox also caught a brief glimpse of the protests but was slow to grasp their importance. In 1968 he was twenty-six years old, a gangling fellow with bushy sideburns, working as a rural route supervisor for Coca-Cola de México. The son of a rancher, he had not yet betrayed the slightest interest in politics. Ever since he had abandoned his business studies at Mexico City's Jesuit-run Iberoamerican University to work for

Coca-Cola four years earlier, he had been transferred from town to town across Mexico. In 1968 he was living with two roommates in the Gulf Coast port of Tampico. Visiting an aunt in Mexico City, Fox "ran into one of those demonstrations," he recalled in a 1999 autobiography.

"I was totally out of that world, so all I could do was observe and make judgments that were inconclusive," he said. "Now that time has passed, I'm convinced the government was responsible for that massacre, and not just when it used violence to quiet the students. The lack of democracy and its dictatorial attitudes were what fed the movement."

Another young Mexican, Sergio Aguayo, saw his worldview change profoundly that summer. Growing up in a tough, working-class neighborhood on the outskirts of Guadalajara, where his mother bred sows and fighting cocks, Aguayo was a leader in a local gang known as Los Vikingos, the Vikings, often mixing it up with the members of a PRI-sponsored youth group. In 1968 Aguayo turned twenty-one, and during a visit to Mexico City he participated in the July 31 protest march through residential streets near the UNAM, led by the rector, Javier Barros. The demonstration, and the way Mexicans along the marchers' route shouted their support and threw confetti down from apartment balconies, thrilled Aguayo, helping him to clarify his inchoate antiauthoritarian resentments. Returning to Guadalajara, he attempted to organize similar protests there—and was so convincingly threatened by a paramilitary group that he fled into exile, to Milwaukee, where he spent a year washing dishes in a Chinese restaurant.

When Aguayo returned to Guadalajara in 1969, he was stunned to find childhood friends joining underground guerrilla groups. One day a close friend brought him a rifle and pressed him to take it. He refused, not because he was afraid, he later recalled, or because his antiauthoritarian bitterness was cooling, but because he was already beginning to understand that to help change Mexico he needed more than a rifle.

"This is crazy," Aguayo told his friend. "We'll all just get killed. It won't get us anywhere. It's suicide."

Instead of taking up arms, he turned to his books, studying obsessively for a year and scoring highly on an entrance exam that earned him admission to the Colegio de México, an elite state-financed university. His academic training would mold him into one of the PRI's most tenacious antagonists.

In the bitter months after Tlatelolco, however, many other young Mexicans formed rebel armies or joined the tiny armed groups already in operation. In June 1971, six months after Luis Echeverría Álvarez succeeded Díaz Ordaz as President, paramilitary soldiers carried out another massacre, attacking scores of young protesters as they marched from the Politécnico through Mexico City's northern San Cosme neighborhood and leaving twenty-nine dead. That bloodletting convinced hundreds of youths that peaceful protest would never bring political change.

One student who despaired of nonviolence was Jesús Piedra Ibarra, a young man with a serious but slightly boyish look. His disaffection had started in high school, when he and some friends had joined a demonstration in his hometown of Monterrey to mark the first anniversary of the 1968 massacre. When the youths shouted slogans at the police, the police clubbed them. Jesús was in medical school in Monterrey when news of the student killings of June 1971 filled him with rage. His mother, a voluble housewife named Rosario Ibarra de Piedra, began to notice his absences from home. Then, one evening in late 1973, she sent him out to buy some cheese. At midnight the police came to the door. Jesús had been in a shoot-out with their agents, they said, but had escaped alive. Rosario Ibarra never saw her son again.

She learned that he had been working with an urban guerrilla group, the Liga Comunista 23 de Septiembre. (Its name commemorated a September 23, 1965, attack by a column of leftists on a mountain garrison in Chihuahua state; the army had wiped out the rebel attackers.) Over the next sixteen months Jesús called home a few times to let his mother know he was alive. Then Rosario read a newspaper story saying that Jesús, by then twenty-one, had been arrested on April 18, 1975. His phone calls stopped. He became one of the *desaparecidos*, the disappeared, people who went missing after being detained by the authorities.

Mexican rebel groups like the Liga never achieved the combat capacity of their counterparts in Central and South America. In part that was because the Cuban leader Fidel Castro, grateful for the support Mexico shrewdly gave him against the United States, never lent Mexico's rebels the backing he offered armed leftist groups elsewhere. But it was also because the successive PRI regimes were cunning and ruthless in exterminating the rebels. During the 1970s hundreds of Mexican rebels were killed by the security forces and hundreds of others disappeared after detention. At least 143 rebels were executed on army bases and their bodies dumped into the sea from government helicopters.

Perhaps it was because of Rosario Ibarra's father, who had regaled her with stories of his participation in the Mexican Revolution, or her husband, who defied custom by encouraging her independent spirit, but unlike most frightened relatives of young Mexicans who vanished in the government's 1970s antiguerrilla campaigns, Ibarra never gave up her search for Jesús. Days turned to years, but she staged protests and hunger strikes, even ran twice for President, to keep hammering at the government to give back her son.

Because the PRI's foreign policy skillfully projected an image of Mexico's government as progressive and tolerant, the Mexican counterinsurgency never drew much international attention. During those years Rosario Ibarra was met with disbelief when she tried to tell people outside Mexico how her son and many others had disappeared.

Other veterans of the 1968 movement found different battlegrounds against authoritarianism. As Echeverría, early in his presidency, sought a tactical rapprochement with some of the regime's critics, Mexican journalism started to publish more independent thought. Some of Mexico's sharpest writers began to appear in *Excélsior*; even Octavio Paz, returned from exile in 1971, found his intellectual home there, as the founder of *Plural*, a cultural supplement.

Yet in his last months in office, Echeverría tightened his grip again. He engineered the ouster of *Excélsior*'s independent-minded editor, Julio Scherer García, degrading the newspaper into a pro-government rag. But Scherer soon founded the weekly newsmagazine *Proceso*, which began almost overnight to publish outspoken journalism of a quality that Mexico had not seen since the advent of PRI rule.

Paz left *Excélsior* in solidarity with Scherer and started his own monthly magazine, *Vuelta* (Turn), which promoted democratic change from an anti-Communist viewpoint. Soon several writers and scholars formed a rival monthly, *Nexos*, which became a forum for reasoned criticism from the Left.

Still another group of *Excélsior* refugees founded *Unomásuno*, an irreverent leftist daily newspaper. Among them was Luis González de Alba, and he struck another blow for pluralism. Reporting in his weekly column on the police's brutal tactics during a 1977 raid on a Mexico City gay bar, González de Alba came out of the closet as a homosexual. It was an unprecedented action in a country where gays had been beaten and even lynched.

Arturo Alcalde Justiniani sought to build democracy in the labor movement. Born into a somewhat threadbare, devoutly Catholic Chihuahua household, he was studying industrial relations at the Iberoamerican University during the 1968 student protests and working part-time in a bank to pay tuition. Whenever he showed up for strike meetings at the UNAM in a suit and tie, he was jeered at by other students.

The following year, at age twenty-one, he took a job as a personnel manager for a national corporation operating thirty factories. He began to travel the country negotiating contracts, an experience that impressed upon him the contrasts between Mexico's pro-worker labor laws and its harsh workplace practices. When it was time to open a new factory, Alcalde's corporate colleagues would identify the local labor leader considered most subservient to management and offer to sign a sweetheart contract with him. Some companies even installed one of their own executives as their "union leader."

Some companies would sign a collective-bargaining agreement with a labor leader of their choosing before hiring a single worker. The contract was then filed with the local PRI-controlled labor board, where, by law, it became a secret document. When they were eventually hired, the workers covered by it had no legal right to read it or to know the name or address of their union. Union dues, deducted from workers' paychecks, were considered the union leader's rightful reward.

Alcalde helped to negotiate about thirty contracts a year. These were private talks between executives and the labor leader chosen by them; workers were completely excluded. The company's goal was to keep labor costs minimal, the leader's to obtain a lucrative bribe. "Heading a union was like running a little business, like owning a toy store," Alcalde recalled.

He worked as an industrial-relations manager for three companies in five years, his Catholic ideals in constant revolt against his corporate duties. Finally, he showed up unannounced at his boss's home at one o'clock one morning, apologized profusely, and quit. His boss thought he had gone mad.

In a way he had. He took a job with the Frente Auténtico del Trabajo, the Authentic Labor Front, known by its acronym, FAT, which rhymes with the English word "dot." It was a tiny, beleaguered federation of independent unions. Its leader, Alfredo Domínguez, welcomed Alcalde because of his experience as a negotiator but could offer no salary. Alcalde borrowed rent money from siblings, working for the FAT as he studied for a law degree, then returned to the world of industrial relations as a labor lawyer.

Over the years that followed, Alcalde passed thousands of hours before the grimy labor tribunals, seeking to wrest from authorities the all-important *registros* that allow unions to operate in Mexico. To leaders of unions affiliated with the PRI, these were handed out with no more paperwork than a vendor's license. Independent workers seeking to form a union had to battle for recognition.

Only once did Alcalde obtain a *registro* as a result of official largesse. After a devastating flood inundated dozens of sewing factories in central Mexico, the FAT led a cleanup effort, which inspired the admiration of Echeverría. He invited Domínguez, Alcalde, and two other FAT leaders to dinner at Los Pinos.

Alcalde suspected that Echeverría would offer gifts in an attempt to co-opt, and he was not mistaken. The President said he would build their federation a new headquarters. Domínguez demurred, but rejection only whet Echeverría's appetite for political seduction. He conversed with his guests until past midnight, proposing other lavish subsidies, each politely rejected. Eventually he insisted they wait while he bathed. Returning in his bathrobe, Echeverría offered Alcalde a government fellowship to travel to Peking to study the Chinese labor system. "No, but I'd like to ask a different favor," Alcalde responded.

Porfirio Muñoz Ledo, Echeverría's Labor Secretary, had repeatedly refused the FAT's request for a national *registro* that would allow the federation to represent workers in the steel industry, Alcalde said. Would the President help? Echeverría reached for the phone, roused Muñoz Ledo out of bed, and the FAT got its steel industry *registro*.

Several prominent participants in the 1968 protests, including Heberto Castillo (who was released from prison in 1971), formed leftist political parties. They failed to gain much support, however, mostly because they were perpetually involved in sectarian bickering.

By 1976 the weakness of the opposition parties had become an embarrassment to the PRI. National Action, the largest opposition party, decided that year not even to field a presidential candidate, and the Communist Party, the second largest, had long been outlawed. The PRI's candidate, José López Portillo, was the only one on the ballot, so it wasn't surprising when he won 91.9 percent of the votes cast.

López Portillo and his advisers sensed that they could face trouble if they did not cede at least a little power, if only to ease the discontent in Mexican society. In 1977 López Portillo freed some political prisoners and allowed his Government Secretary, Jesús Reyes Heroles, a respected and seasoned PRI statesman, to craft an electoral reform.

"Intolerance is the sure path to return to a wild and violent Mexico," Reyes Heroles said, announcing a series of public hearings on the reforms. For the first time, a public political debate included groups like the Communist Party that had never previously been allowed to register as parties.

In December 1977 Reyes Heroles's reforms were enacted in constitutional amendments and political reform laws. Citizens' rights to organize parties were codified in the Constitution. Restrictive preconditions for party registration were abolished; if a party won 1.5 percent of the votes in a presidential election, it could register. Perhaps most significant, the reform authorized proportional representation in the legislature. Even a tiny party could gain a few seats, at least a toehold in the congressional game.

López Portillo spoke of the reforms grandly. "We want to make it understood that dissidence is not synonymous with violence, and opposition should not be associated with crime," he said—even though only the PRI had ever suggested as much.

In the short term, the reforms provided only a narrow opening to the opposition and suited the PRI's interests. Their effect was to boost a number of disputatious micro parties on the Left at the expense of the PAN, a much more serious opposition to the PRI at that time. Still, the reforms built a foundation for legitimate political action by opposition parties that proved crucial in drawing dissidents away from violent rebellion.

Two years later, in 1979, National Action elected 43 deputies, and five leftist parties won another 61 seats, giving the opposition a total of 104 seats in the 400-seat Chamber of Deputies. The opposition deputies were able to make fiery speeches but never to block PRI legislation or pass their own, so the PRI monopoly was unaffected. But opposition politicians, whether leftist or conservative, never forgot the contact with everyday Mexicans they experienced in their quixotic campaigns, or the thrill of the few victories they were allowed to keep. The 1977 reforms started a pattern. After that, the opposition pressed relentlessly for more legal space, and each PRI President was forced to enact new reforms, conceding bit by bit the advantages the PRI enjoyed in Mexican law.

In the years after 1968 the PRI tried hard to pull its critics back under its wing. But many of the students of 1968 remained determinedly outside the system. Aguayo, after earning his B.A. at the Colegio de México, had gone on to study at Johns Hopkins University in Baltimore and at its institute in Bologna, Italy. When he returned to Mexico with a master's degree in international relations in 1977, Aguayo was a sought-after young technocrat: he received job offers from the Treasury and Education Secretariats and from Carlos Salinas de Gortari, a young economist with a Harvard doctorate who was advancing rapidly through the bureaucracy. Sensing his reservations about working for the government, Aguayo's prospective employers argued that if he wanted to change the system, he could best do it from within. But Aguayo rejected all the offers.

"I saw how they degraded everybody who worked for the government," he said. "Nothing had changed since 1968: to be in the system, you had to humiliate yourself, to surrender your integrity, and I couldn't do it."

4

Earthquake, 1985

In the first half of the 1980s, when the authoritarian system seemed fully recovered from 1968, it was jarred again, this time by two seismic events, one financial and the other geological.

President José López Portillo created a government of splendor and prosperity that turned out, as many presidencies had before, to be based on illusion. Early in his term, after new exploration in the Gulf of Mexico increased the country's oil reserves tenfold to more than 70 billion barrels, López Portillo announced that his job would be to "administer abundance." Jorge Díaz Serrano, the head of Petróleos Mexicanos, or Pemex, the national oil company, was even more optimistic: oil would give Mexicans a chance at "the creation of a new country," a nation with full employment and a television in every home. López Portillo opened a gusher of government spending, much of it on industrial infrastructure and no small part on corruption.

But in 1981, the fifth year of his presidency, oil prices crashed. Stubbornly, López Portillo refused to cut the budget, and his abundance quickly turned to chaos. The economy sank, inflation soared, the foreign debt swelled to $76 billion, and López Portillo searched for an enemy to blame. In his final *informe*, his report to the nation on September 1, 1982, López Portillo pointed to "a group of Mexicans" who were "headed, advised, and supported by the private banks." He claimed that they had "taken more money out of the country than all the empires that have exploited us since the beginning of our history."

"It is now or never," he thundered at the congressional hall. "They have plundered. But Mexico is not done for yet. They will never plunder again."

Then, with one sweeping presidential decree, he nationalized the banks. He also ordered that dollar bank accounts be converted to pesos at rates far below the market.

As a display of the unfettered might of the PRI President, López Portillo's bank nationalization was never matched. He was a lame duck when he did it, with barely three months left to serve. He hardly consulted with his cabinet or his party. His anointed successor, Miguel de la Madrid, strongly opposed it. Lacking financial logic, it was an act of pure presidential spleen.

The economy, already sputtering, ground to a virtual halt. The forced conversion of dollar accounts to pesos amounted to an expropriation of the nest eggs of all the Mexicans who had struggled to arrive in the middle class during the boom years of the *sexenio*. Although the nationalization was designed to punish moneyed Mexicans who had sent some $22 billion in capital out of the country in the final two years of López Portillo's term, in practice those hardest hit were working people who lost their jobs and savings.

The populace turned on López Portillo with a fury. In Mexico City and in the south, where there were few political alternatives to the PRI, popular discontent seethed with no outlets. Across northern Mexico, ranchers, farmers, and entrepreneurs saw their dollar savings gutted and their businesses crippled by the lack of liquidity and credit after the nationalization. They fled the government party, which they believed was heading toward socialism, and flocked to the PAN.

As a result of López Portillo's mismanagement, President Miguel de la Madrid had little choice in the first years of his term but to impose a severe and intensely unpopular adjustment program of federal-spending cutbacks, price increases, and peso devaluations.

Then, in 1985, just when Mexico seemed to regain its footing, the floor moved once again. Only this time the movement was not metaphoric.

Cuauhtémoc Abarca was out early. The Mexico City marathon was coming up, and he had agreed to meet two friends for a morning training jog. A chunky man, Abarca was in decent shape but would still have to work hard to finish the race. He was stretching his hamstrings in the shadow of a tall apartment building when he felt the earth begin to rock. As a resident of the capital city for twenty years, Abarca had been through countless earthquakes. But this one didn't just slide sideways like the others. This one bucked up and down, and it didn't end. Thirty seconds went by, then a minute. Abarca heard glass breaking, and he wondered distractedly if his neighbors had decided to throw their dinner plates out the window.

Then his eye went to the swaying of the apartment tower right above him. Suddenly, as he watched, the building crumpled in the middle. Four floors halfway up compressed into one. With another buck from the earth, the building split in two. The top half came down and landed with an ear-lacerating crash on the avenue. The bottom half toppled the opposite way, burying a garden just a few hundred feet from where Abarca was standing.

"For a moment there was only dust, and total silence," Abarca remembered later. "There wasn't a sound. The voices were silent. The cars were silent. The birds were silent. Then the building heaved a loud groan.

"Even so, I still couldn't comprehend what had happened," he said. "I went over to touch a fallen wall. That was when I heard the screams. They were coming from somewhere deep inside that mountain of concrete. They were my neighbors. They were screaming."

The earthquake that struck Mexico City at 7:19 a.m. on September 19, 1985, with a force of 8.1 on the Richter scale, brought Mexican history back to Tlatelolco once again. After the massacre of 1968 many residents had moved out of the buildings ringing the Plaza de las Tres Culturas. For years the Chihuahua building, where army troops had taken up shooting positions, sat nearly empty; Mexicans had an aversion to buying or even renting apartments there. By the late 1970s the apartments, with rock-bottom rents, had gradually begun to fill again. In 1985 one Tlatelolco building that was fully occupied, with twelve hundred residents, was the Nuevo León, just down a walkway from the plaza.

Abarca came from a humble family of schoolteachers in the mountain state Guerrero. While studying medicine at the UNAM, he had dabbled in radical leftist politics. Soon after settling in Tlatelolco, he had become president of the cooperative association in a twin building adjacent to the Nuevo León—which somehow escaped major damage in the temblor. Now he stood in shock a long while, his hands placed on the fallen building as though he were palpating for vital signs. The quake had turned the apartment tower inside out, disgorging shoes, bed pillows, hair dryers, dining room chairs, children's playthings. Some residents had hurled themselves out their windows as the building began to founder, and bodies were strewn like broken toys around the building.

Many of the 102 buildings in the Tlatelolco complex had been damaged, but only the Nuevo León had collapsed and killed people. Abarca instinctively began organizing a rescue effort, enlisting anyone, neighbor or stranger, who appeared at the site. He dispatched one group of volunteers to get ambulances and medicines, another for food and water, a third for shovels and spades to start digging out survivors. A fourth group went for pencils and notebooks to make a census of the dead and injured.

For most of that day the people of Tlatelolco did not know the extent of the damage in the rest of Mexico City. They didn't know that more than 370 buildings had collapsed, including the main pavilions of two public hospitals, scores of government offices, the main studios of Televisa, several tourist hotels, and the central telephone switching station, which controlled local and long-distance telephone communications for the whole city. They only knew that their phones were dead, their electricity was off, and their water wasn't running. As they began to scrape and pry at the ruins of the Nuevo León, they found both mangled bodies and mutilated survivors, many dozens of them. But neither hearses arrived for the dead nor ambulances for the wounded.

Stunned and grieving, Abarca and his neighbors immediately thought to seek help from the authorities. They assumed the government would take charge of coping with the emergency. Under the PRI system, citizens were discouraged from organizing to solve problems on their own; officials made it clear in countless ways that they had a monopoly on power to make things happen. So Abarca sent off a group of his neighbors to summon the director of the Fondo Nacional de Habitaciones Populares, or FONHAPO, the agency that managed the Tlatelolco housing development.

They were back an hour later. The FONHAPO director, they reported, was too busy to see them. He had sent word that he would try to fit them into his schedule later in the week.

Abarca and his neighbors stood amid the foul dust rising from the Nuevo León and considered this response. They were astonished, then indignant. On the spot, Abarca called a protest demonstration for the following day. The Tlatelolco residents would march to the FONHAPO offices and force the director to see them.

On September 20, hundreds of residents gathered, and by that time they had become very angry. Some ambulances had finally come to the complex, but the excavation of the Nuevo León was still being carried out by residents with a few old shovels. Army troops and jeeps had arrived to cordon off the wreckage, but they did not join in the rescue work. They gave residents the feeling that Tlatelolco was occupied once again, seventeen years after 1968, by military guards.

Among the marchers to the housing agency were a few people who had managed to crawl out of the wreckage of the Nuevo León. They had come back from the dead, and they looked it, still dressed in bloody tatters and caked with stucco. Elbowing their way into the agency's offices, the residents found an ashen-faced, stammering bureaucrat, Enrique Ortiz Flores, who admitted he was administratively paralyzed. "This goes way beyond me," he said contritely. "I have to await instructions."

His immobility infuriated the residents. They reminded Ortiz Flores of his agency's response after an earthquake several years earlier had tilted the Nuevo León and damaged its foundations. After a thousand arguments the agency had finally made some repairs. But pipes still leaked, and floors were still cracked. The residents had hung a banner down the side of the building denouncing the faulty job. When they went back to FONHAPO to complain, an agency engineer had dismissed their concerns, calling the Nuevo León "one of the three safest buildings in Mexico City."

The banner warning of the dangers of the Nuevo León building had been one of the first items recovered from its rubble.

In the midst of the yelling with Ortiz Flores, one resident called for quiet. Through a door behind the director he had spotted the engineer who had made the lofty claim about the solidity of the Nuevo León.

"Mr. Director, we don't have anything against you personally," the man said to Ortiz Flores in a low, controlled voice. "We understand that the earthquake is not your fault.

"But, Mr. Director, if I ever again lay eyes on that son-of-a-bitch motherfucker who told us that the Nuevo León was safe," the man said coolly, "I will murder him with my own hands."

Just when the meeting seemed headed for violence, at 7:38 p.m. another earthquake struck. It was 6.5 on the Richter scale, somewhat less forceful than the first—but far more terrifying. The people of Tlatelolco ran screaming from the FONHAPO offices, and Abarca had to step in to block several from flinging themselves out the windows. Elsewhere, people who had survived the first quake died of heart attacks with the second. Hundreds of people who were trapped alive in the rubble died when the ruins shifted again.

For almost thirty-six hours after the first quake, President Miguel de la Madrid seemed absent. There were news reports that he toured the damage zones in the hours after the quake, first by helicopter and then by bus. Some people in Tlatelolco saw him just before noon on the nineteenth, when he passed through the housing complex followed by a platoon of bodyguards. They greeted him respectfully but begged him for machinery to lift the debris. They noted that he was wearing an elegant leather bomber jacket and didn't come close enough to the rubble to get it dusty.

De la Madrid was a President of a new type. The PRI's earliest Presidents, from Plutarco Elías Calles in the 1920s through Manuel Ávila Camacho in the 1940s, were Generals from the revolution. Then, over the next three decades, all the men who ascended to the presidency came from the Labor or the Government Secretariat, where they were forced to mix it up in earthy power struggles. López Portillo, in contrast, was a lawyer and bureaucrat who had gained his more limited political experience from negotiating budgets in the Treasury Secretariat. He picked de la Madrid to succeed him in 1982, when Mexico's economy was in such a shambles that even López Portillo could see the need for a cool administrator with good connections to foreign banks.

That was de la Madrid. The son of an attorney, he had been a reserved and colorless law student at the UNAM. But during the 1960s he had enhanced his résumé considerably by taking a master's degree in public administration from Harvard University. Back in Mexico he spent a decade and a half crunching numbers in the Treasury and Budget Secretariats, well removed from any political hurly-burly, until López Portillo made him President. During his first three years in office he had remained aloof as he devoted himself resolutely and without emotion to the task of imposing order on the chaotic economy he inherited.

On September 19, after visiting Tlatelolco, he had gone to the Multifamiliar Juárez, another badly battered public housing development. Irate people there had shouted their demands at him, and he turned and left.

De la Madrid made no general address to the Mexican people that day. He did make a brief statement in the afternoon to the press. "We are ready to return to normal life," he said, exuding presidential composure. "We are prepared to deal with this situation, and we don't need outside aid."

De la Madrid remained out of sight for most of September 20. Finally, two hours after the second quake, the President went on national television, looking more sober than the day before. "The truth is that in the face of an earthquake of this magnitude, we don't have enough resources to confront the disaster quickly and efficiently," the President acknowledged. He gave a nod of recognition to spontaneous citizen rescue efforts that were starting up across the city, but he advised people to continue to rely on the government. "Be patient with us, as you have been up to now," he said.

After the second quake, relations between the Tlatelolco residents and the authorities deteriorated rapidly. Instead of rolling up their sleeves to dig, many army troops spent their time blocking citizen volunteers from approaching the Nuevo León rubble pile. The soldiers were assigned to prevent looting, but often they became looters. One afternoon Abarca was standing on the roof of his own building, next to the Nuevo León,

When the PRI government appeared paralyzed after the 1985 earthquake, citizens formed their own rescue brigades to search for survivors in the rubble

with a camera crew from the UNAM. With film rolling, they watched a jeep full of soldiers pull up to one side of his building where several apartments had been left unoccupied. After looking this way and that, the soldiers kicked through the door of one apartment. They soon came out with two bags of booty and sped away.

One relative who came from afar to dig for survivors in the Nuevo León was Plácido Domingo, the Spanish-born tenor who was raised in Mexico. Some of his cousins lived in the building. As soon as he arrived, he perceived the government's failure to act. He tied a bandanna over his mouth to save his throat from the dust, strapped on a helmet, and went to work lifting drywall and chunks of concrete with his hands. Later he led an effort to raise international aid and used his moral authority to denounce and shame government officials who stole some of it. The opera star's presence in the rescue effort was inspiring to Mexicans, an example of what the high and mighty could accomplish if they went shoulder to shoulder with the people.

By September 22, three days after the quake, thousands of Tlatelolco residents had realized that they would not be able to return to their homes and had become *damnificados*, damaged people, the term for earthquake refugees. They held an assembly in the Plaza de las Tres Culturas. By informal consensus Abarca became their leader.

"In a way we had never done before, we had to make our own decisions," Abarca said. "The earthquake hit, and then we found out that the FONHAPO director couldn't see us, the borough president was not in his office, the mayor wasn't taking visitors. All of a sudden we were living in a city without a government."

The assembly settled on a list of demands. They called on the government to rescue all the survivors and as many bodies as possible from fallen buildings; to prosecute officials they held responsible for the structural weakness of the Nuevo León; and to expropriate and rebuild as many damaged homes as possible, instead of attempting to relocate tens of thousands of people elsewhere.

Within a week 472 bodies were recovered from the Nuevo León—"only 472 dead," as the Tlatelolco authorities stated, with a revealing lack of tact, in a wall mural they painted in the complex several weeks after the quake. Fewer than half of the bodies could be identified. Dozens of residents were never accounted for, but the authorities refused to include the disappeared in the death toll.

One week after the quake thousands of victims from Tlatelolco and other neighborhoods marched to Los Pinos. Police on horseback blocked most of them from reaching the entrance. But a small commission managed to skirt the security cordon and talk their way inside, where they presented their demands to several cabinet officials, making themselves heard at a level they would never have dreamed of reaching before the quake.

Within days a nascent citizens movement, spreading across the city, took up the Tlatelolco demands. The network of community groups that sprang up to defend the earthquake victims' interests was the most vigorous grassroots activism Mexico had seen since 1968. Its logic was very different from the system's. Under the PRI, unions and social organizations were organized from the top down. Their job, fundamentally, was to follow the bidding of the President and jockey for jobs, gifts, and other perks from the PRI's uniquely varied reserve of patronage. The pressure groups that formed in the weeks after the earthquake had no organic link to the government or the party, and they were born with a deep suspicion of the system's motives.

"The earthquake threw down walls, and it also threw down barriers between communities," Abarca said. "Instead of lines of communication from the top down, suddenly we had lines of communication that were horizontal, between different organizations and barrios, or, better yet, from the bottom up."

On October 24, the citywide movement inaugurated itself as the Co-ordinadora Unica de Damnificados, the Unified Coordinating Committee of Earthquake Refugees. To flex its muscles, the committee called a march to Los Pinos on October 26, and forty thousand people showed up. The PRI authorities, forced to negotiate, took precisely the position the residents had anticipated. They announced that their inspection had revealed that twenty-three buildings would have to be evacuated and leveled, and they promised to move the residents to "equivalent housing" in the State of México, as much as seventy miles away. The authorities planned to construct new office towers on the razed site, meaning many contracts for builders associated with the PRI.

When the people protested the plan, PRI officials went on the attack, as though they were embroiled in an elections campaign and not a human tragedy. Guillermo Carrillo Arena, who as head of the federal environmental agency was a key player in the earthquake recovery, denounced the earthquake movement, saying it was full of "bad Mexicans" and "seditious leaders moved by murky interests." Carrillo Arena, an architect, had been the top official to approve the plans for several of the recently constructed government hospital buildings that fell down, killing hundreds of people. At one press conference reporters asked him whether he felt responsible for their collapse.

"The only thing I can say about that question is that whoever is asking it is a prostitute and an imbecile," he replied. "Write that down, please."

As time wore on, the Tlatelolco residents' distrust of the government became so acute they adopted irrational tactics that put them in new danger. Desperate for some form of protest that would force the government to abandon its plans to relocate them, they moved, en masse, in the first week of January 1986, back into their unrepaired apartments, with the plaster dangling from the ceilings and the walls still scarred with fissures.

The kamikaze protest was risky, but it worked. Within days President de la Madrid fired Carrillo Arena. A new team of officials opened negotiations that included all the community groups on a plan for the "Democratic Reconstruction" of Tlatelolco and many other damaged neighborhoods. The plan put much more emphasis on restoring structures that could be fixed, so that the homeless would not have to suffer the additional trauma of starting life again in a distant location.

"People woke up," Abarca said. "They began to see the government not as something superior to them but as an equal with whom you could talk, negotiate, and even win a round or two. No one could remember ever seeing a government project defeated as categorically as we defeated the plan to move us out of Tlatelolco."

At year's end there were 180,000 homeless refugees living in tin lean-to shelters in streets and parks across Mexico City. The frenetic activity of the new movement had buoyed them throughout the fall, but depression took hold as Christmas approached. Leaders of the earthquake campaign, fearful of losing their momentum, summoned Mexican artists and actors to stage traditional Christmas plays, called *pastorelas*, in the shelters. According to custom, the plays end when Mary and Joseph arrive in Bethlehem and stand outside the door of the inn, asking, in song, for shelter. Voices from inside respond with insults to drive them away. In December 1985 the plea for shelter had an immediate personal meaning for thousands of people who were still homeless. To cheer up, they used the Christmas carol to lampoon the authorities.

"In the name of the Lo-o-o-ord, we ask you for she-e-el-ter" went the chorus.

The response came back: "I am just the ma-a-a-yor. Why should I do you a fa-a-a-vor?"

Years later, when he thought about the earthquake Christmas, Cuauhtémoc Abarca would burst into that song.

Parallel to the victims' mobilization, a more militant movement came out of the National University, led by students like Imanol Ordorika.

Ordorika came from a family of politically active university professors. His parents had been brought to Mexico when young children, refugees from the Spanish civil war. Both his paternal grandfather and his father had taught at the UNAM. When a boy, Ordorika had seen some of the street protests of 1968 and had never forgotten them. In 1985 he was twenty-six, an undergraduate in physics.

On the morning of September 19, as soon as the shaking stopped, Ordorika had headed, by instinct, for the giant UNAM campus at the southern end of the capital. With more than 200,000 students, the UNAM was a sociopolitical universe unto itself. For Ordorika and his crowd in the School of Sciences, it was primarily a laboratory for leftist politics, a testing ground for the ideas of an array of squabbling revolutionary sects. Some of these groups were so immersed in radical Marxist philosophy that they were on the brink of going over the line into *la lucha armada*, the clandestine armed underground. But Ordorika was in a faction that had sought to extend its ties to the masses outside the university by doing social work. So it came naturally to him to assemble with his friends at the UNAM campus on the morning of the quake and head out to the streets to see what they could do to help. They ran immediately into a confrontation with the government.

Their first clashes were with army troops. Within forty-eight hours after the quake, the army command ordered the ruins off-limits to volunteers, on the grounds that they were unstable and filled with bodies that could spread infection. But brigades of UNAM students were already working at public housing developments and hospitals, side by side with anguished survivors who wanted to be sure that they had done everything possible to rescue their living loved ones and recover the remains of their dead.

One day the army moved in to close off a street in a residential neighborhood where Ordorika's brigade was working in flattened homes. When the students refused to leave, the soldiers shoved them with their rifles; the students fought back with fists and stones. The soldiers blasted tear gas, but the students held their ground. The news traveled by word of mouth, and the city celebrated the students' resistance.

The students also challenged the bulldozers. The authorities, focusing on the dead as potential sources of disease, were eager to send in heavy equipment to compact the rubble and carry it away. At the Juárez hospital, a government facility where a twelve-story pavilion had crumbled, UNAM students lay down on the ruins to block the bulldozers from going to work. As the students held off the machines, expert rescuers from France tunneled through the hospital wreckage. After nightfall on September 23, four and a half days after the first quake, one rescuer came upon a survivor trapped under two corpses in the chill darkness of the debris. Led back through the maze, the youth appeared, deathly pale, like a specter at the mouth of the tunnel, then mobilized his energy for one last lunge to freedom. It turned out he was a twenty-three-year-old medical student named Juan Hernández Cruz.

Despite this example, the authorities insisted on bulldozing the ruins. On September 24, the machines worked for a few hours, but the students managed to stop them again. During the break, rescuers finally tunneled through to the maternity ward. In a half-flattened room full of cribs they found a baby whose flesh was still warm. According to a tiny wrist bracelet, the still-unnamed son of Inés Cruz Soriano had been born on September 18. After nearly six days in the rubble, he was still alive. In all, eight babies were pulled alive from the maternity ward, forty-eight hours after government officials had ordered the pavilion leveled.

With these victories, the first weeks after the earthquake were a heady time for Ordorika and the UNAM brigades. "The city was ours," Ordorika recalled. "We were in control. We directed traffic in the streets. We commandeered public buses when we needed them. We organized the food lines in damaged neighborhoods. We fought with the powers that be."

University brigades helped repair telephone lines and the electric grid, published a crisis newspaper, and kept an alternative census of the death and damage toll. The radical students in Ordorika's School of Sciences brigade were among the volunteers who took the greatest risks by becoming "moles" who tunneled into the ruins. "We would crawl in between two slabs of concrete held apart by a board or a table leg with our feet tied to a rope that supposedly they could use to pull us out quickly—supposedly," Ordorika said, rolling his eyes at the thought of the danger he had plunged into. "After a few days there was a smell of decomposition in the rubble that still comes back to me sometimes."

Despite his wild curly hair and unkempt look, Ordorika was embraced by the people at the sites where he worked. While the food

shortages in the city were critical, Ordorika feasted on dishes that neighborhood señoras prepared for him and other volunteers.

"There was a general sensation that even in the face of an event as
implacable and inevitable as an earthquake, we could act," he explained.
"We had a sense of the possibility of action and a conviction that we had
to act collectively."

Because of his rescue work, Ordorika gained a new understanding of
the lengths to which the PRI system would go in order to neutralize its
critics and draw them into its fold, one way or another. He and many students in the UNAM brigades stayed with the relief effort for more than
a month after the quake. Through it all, they thrashed the President
incessantly. But one day in November a messenger brought Ordorika
a large envelope of embossed parchment. Inside was a letter from
President de la Madrid informing Ordorika that he had been named a
"Hero of Solidarity" for his rescue work and inviting him to receive a
medal and a diploma at a ceremony in the Campo Marte, the military
parade grounds along a leafy boulevard near Los Pinos. Ordorika's chief
political enemy was offering to decorate him as a national hero in a bastion of the army with which he had been locked for weeks in running
battle.

Some sixty students from the UNAM brigades, as well as hundreds of
other citizens who joined the rescue effort, had been selected as national
heroes. Ordorika and the other students decided they would go to the
Campo Marte. At the moment they were called to receive their medals,
they began shouting slogans at de la Madrid:

¡Terremoto al presidente
Pa'que vea como se siente!

Earthquake to the President
Let him know how it feels to live in a tent!

The chant spread through the crowd of heroes. The commanders of the
Presidential General Staff, an elite corps in charge of the President's security, rushed to detain the instigators. After a scuffle the UNAM students managed to slip away without arrest.

Two weeks later, de la Madrid's office sent Ordorika his hero's medal in the mail.

In September 1985 Elena Poniatowska was still reporting for *Novedades* newspaper, mainly because nothing had happened to force her to change. The earthquake devastation immediately drew her into the streets. She started to pound out stories about the search for survivors and the new cooperation among everyday people, as well as their disappointment with the government's response to the disaster. About a week after the quake she had an experience of déjà vu. Her editor at *Novedades*, the same man who had suppressed her stories in 1968, instructed her to stop writing about the damage and the disarray. Word had come down from President de la Madrid, he said, that it was time for Mexico City to "return to normal." The editor told Poniatowska that her stories about the survivors' struggles were demoralizing the public.

"Out in the streets I could see that everyone was looking for bodies, and the heavy machinery was going into the ruins and coming out with legs and arms mixed in the rubble," Poniatowska recalled. "I went out at night and I saw that street gangs and punks and student radicals, people whom the society at large had rejected, were out there helping, forming bucket brigades to remove debris."

She had not pressed the issue in 1968, but now she was an older and more accomplished journalist. She decided to take her earthquake stories across Calle Balderas to the offices of an upstart newspaper called *La Jornada*. It had been founded exactly one year before the earthquake, on September 19, 1984, by a group of leftist intellectuals who split off from *Unomásuno*, the alternative paper that had started out bravely in November 1977 but then slipped back into the grip of the government. *La Jornada* (it means "workday" in Spanish) was modeled on sophisticated leftist daily tabloids in Spain and France. In comparison to *Novedades*, it was a crude operation, with no press of its own and edited on a dozen secondhand computers. Poniatowska just left off her latest earthquake story at the front door and went back to *Novedades*. An hour later she got a call asking her for another story the following day. She wrote reports for *La Jornada* every day for four months.

While other Mexico City papers were combing the city for signs of normalcy, *La Jornada* was devoting full pages every day to stories about social trauma, official ineptitude, and the burgeoning popular movement. When the Tlatelolco residents moved back into their teetering buildings, *La Jornada* held its presses to get the late-breaking story on the front page. For Cuauhtémoc Abarca it was surprising and satisfying to see something of his reality reflected for the first time in the press. "The people of Mexico City never existed for the press except in the murder and mayhem pages," he said. "Suddenly here was a newspaper treating us like citizens whose views were worth recording."

Here and there Poniatowska ran into friends from 1968. Raúl Álvarez Garín, the former student leader, set up an information center where people could file complaints and petitions for assistance. Heberto Castillo summoned his engineering expertise to explain how the seismic shock waves of the September 19 earthquake had made it especially damaging to buildings of a certain height standing on the soft subsoil of downtown Mexico City.

Of all the stories Poniatowska wrote, the one she found most compelling was on the plight of the sewing-machine operators who worked in a warren of sweatshops on Calzada San Antonio Abad. The women's long workday started at 7 a.m., so some eight thousand of them were already sewing when the quake struck. Whole blocks of warehouses filled with whirring machines had broken apart like dollhouses. The shop owners, instead of trying to find out how many of their workers were killed or ensure that survivors were rescued, hired heavy equipment to extract their machines and inventory. Many sweatshops had no licenses to operate, so, to avoid indemnifying victims' families, the owners argued that women who were killed were never on their payroll.

The army searched the rubble for two days, then gave up. On September 23, one woman clawed her way out of the ruins, saying that she had heard other voices under the wreckage.

The earthquake accomplished for the seamstresses what demeaning work conditions could not: it convinced them to organize a union. They saw Poniatowska so often as she came to report on their travails that they decided to name her their treasurer.

"I'm awful with accounts," Poniatowska said. "But they made me treasurer for a sad reason. They were sure that I at least was not going to steal their money."

Homero Aridjis, a poet and novelist, never expected to lead an antigovernment organization. As an intellectual, he didn't admire the PRI system, yet he had served it in the 1970s, as Mexican ambassador to Switzerland and then to the Netherlands. Then, in late February 1985, an ocher cloud of air pollution had settled over Mexico City. Because the government did not measure atmospheric pollution at that time, Aridjis couldn't be sure in scientific terms how bad the air was. But he knew he couldn't draw a deep breath. He and his city were suffocating.

He made some telephone calls to friends and soon had a petition to the government for relief from the smog signed by one hundred people, including the cultural cream of Mexico City: painters of the stature of Rufino Tamayo, Francisco Toledo, Alberto Gironella, and José Luis Cuevas; and writers like Juan Rulfo and Gabriel García Márquez, a Colombian who had made a second home in the Mexican capital.

"We who live beneath this viscous mushroom that covers us day and night have a right to life," the petition said. "What astounds us most is the lack of action on the part of the authorities."

The petition was published as a paid advertisement in several Mexico City newspapers on March 1, 1985. Aridjis received a torrent of calls and letters of support. Over the following months the Group of 100, as it came to be called, published other petitions, decrying air pollution, deforestation, and dolphin killing. The new environmental group had its headquarters in the study of Aridjis's home in the Lomas de Chapultepec neighborhood of Mexico City. Aridjis became its director and his American wife, Betty Ferber, the chief operating officer.

The government responded by doing nothing. Officials either dismissed Aridjis's group as silly or accused it of being a front for foreign interests.

"When it was founded, the Group of 100 was an anomaly in Mexico," Aridjis said. "It was a group where people participated voluntarily. The government couldn't figure that out. They couldn't understand the idea of volunteer work or disinterested civic action. It was never enough for us just to have a cause. They always thought there was some hidden agenda. They thought that we must be paid by the CIA or that we wanted money for ourselves."

Aridjis remembered a meeting with Pedro Ojeda Paullada, the Secretary of Fisheries under President de la Madrid.

"What do you want?" Ojeda Paullada had asked, wasting no time.

"I want you to make the fishing fleet stop killing dolphins," Aridjis replied.

Ojeda Paullada laughed. "Okay, let's talk seriously," he said. "What do you *really* want?"

"I *really* want you to stop killing dolphins," Aridjis persisted.

Ojeda Paullada seemed to Aridjis to get impatient. "Come on, now," he said. "Just tell me what you want me to do *for you.*" The Fisheries Secretary couldn't believe that Aridjis was taking up his time to plead for a bunch of sea creatures.

When the earthquake struck, Aridjis and his wife began to note the pattern of the buildings that had fallen down. About half of the nearly four hundred buildings destroyed had been built by the government: office towers, housing developments, hospitals, and schools. Aridjis summoned some independent architects, and soon the Group of 100 published another paid newspaper statement.

"Corruption is a bad builder!" they wrote. Mexico's building codes were adequate, they contended, but lax enforcement and outright corruption had allowed government contractors to circumvent the codes in countless ways. Their charge echoed widely with the public.

After that the government never again failed to take the Group of 100 seriously. Nongovernmental interest groups like the Group of 100 became common. Aridjis's idea, that defending the environment was a way to defend the quality of human life, no longer seemed so elitist to average Mexicans. After 1985 Aridjis was harassed, ridiculed, consigned to literary exile, and accused of being an agent of foreign imperialism, but he was never ignored.

The Aztecs called their universe the fifth sun. Before their time, the Aztecs believed, the world had been created and destroyed four times by different forces of nature. The myth predicted that the fifth sun would be destroyed by an earthquake. On September 19, it seemed at first that the Aztec prophecy was being fulfilled. Probably twenty thousand people perished in all, although the figures (like the death toll from the 1968 massacre) were suppressed by the government and have never been fully revealed. There are still sad vacant buildings and empty lots along the Paseo de la Reforma, scars on the city's heart. The Mexicans who lived the worst of the earthquake lost their sense of security and would never recover it.

Yet the earthquake was also invigorating. In its wake, because of the government's failure to respond, there emerged a new form of popular political action, called *autogestión*, do-it-yourself politics. The notion that a community could band together to lobby the government in defense of its interests was not original, but it was new in PRI-controlled Mexico. The earthquake forced the capital city to shake off its dependence on the PRI system.

If the 1968 Tlatelolco massacre had revealed the repressive core of the system, the earthquake exposed its depths. On September 20, rescuers came upon the bodies of six men (two Mexicans and four Colombians) in the rubble-filled basement of the Procuraduría General de la República, Mexico's equivalent of the Justice Department, headed by the federal Attorney General. The men had been arrested by federal police four days before the quake. Medical examiners announced, indiscreetly, that all of them showed signs of torture. Two had died of it.

On September 22, after another body with torture wounds turned up in the trunk of a car parked in the basement, the Attorney General, Victoria Adato, made a telling remark: "It's absurd to suggest we tortured them," she said. "They had already confessed."

The new force that emerged from the earthquake was civil society. The citizens groups that formed were independent of the PRI, but they had no direct ties to opposition parties either. They mobilized Mexicans across class lines. The poorest of the poor, who had lived in decaying tenements in the old city center, joined with groups from solidly middle-class neighborhoods. And after the quake shattered their homes and lives, many Mexicans were willing to try tactics they had never considered before. Workaday citizens regularly clogged the streets with insolent

sit-ins and marches. When President de la Madrid inaugurated the
World Cup soccer games in Mexico City in 1986, the crowd jeered and
whistled at him.

The symbol of this irreverent new politics was Superbarrio, a masked
figure in a spangled red costume and cape, a hybrid between Superman
and a show wrestler. The figure, whose name might be translated as "Su-
perhood," showed up at opposition demonstrations as well as government events, entertaining the people and taunting government officials
with sassy clowning and doggerel. Superbarrio was modern Mexico's first
homegrown masked man.

The earthquake also generated a new class of PRI politicians. Mexico
City mayor Ramón Aguirre Velázquez, a PRI functionary since 1956,
was confounded by the cheeky new opposition. He was slow to respond
to citizens' demands and seemed to think his main task was to reestablish
the government's tattered authority and channel relief resources through
the PRI.

In contrast, Carlos Salinas de Gortari, the young Secretary of Planning and Budget, quickly grasped the opportunity the new forces offered.
Groomed since boyhood by his father, a former cabinet secretary, to be
President, Salinas had completed a doctorate in political economy at
Harvard in 1978 and shot up to the cabinet in just a few years in government. Under de la Madrid, he showed that he was an implacable budget
cutter and calculating bureaucratic infighter. But unlike many PRI veterans who felt that power was theirs by entitlement, Salinas saw the need
to build his own political base. During the earthquake he proved to be a
dynamic administrator who was more willing than most officials to listen
to citizens groups, which he saw as part of his future constituency.

One of Salinas's most effective aides was another ambitious young
politician, Manuel Camacho Solís. He was detailed one day to accompany President de la Madrid at the inauguration of some of the first
houses the government had built for earthquake victims. While de la
Madrid was cutting the ribbon, some community leaders approached
Camacho to complain that the new houses had been built not by the
government but by the Red Cross, with international relief donations.
City officials had taken down the Red Cross emblem just before the
President arrived. Days later Camacho was sent to attend a meeting be-

tween city and federal officials and earthquake movement leaders, in a stifling room with no chairs. "The point of this meeting," one official whispered to Camacho at the start, "is to break them."

After Carrillo Arena was fired from the federal environmental agency, Salinas saw to it that Camacho was named to take over, even though he knew nothing about the environment. Camacho immediately opened his doors to earthquake groups and listened intently to their petitions, then crafted a "Democratic Reconstruction" plan that included many of their demands. He reached across political lines to name Heberto Castillo to head a commission of architects and engineers in charge of assessing the damage to buildings in Tlatelolco. He built almost fifty thousand dwellings for the homeless in one year. Together, Salinas and Camacho stopped the earthquake from permanently undermining de la Madrid's presidency.

The earthquake also spawned a new generation of community leaders. Some, like Cuauhtémoc Abarca, stayed in their neighborhoods. Abarca never left Tlatelolco. He continued to work with tenants groups, made an unsuccessful run for local elected office, and eventually founded an organization for street children. Others who emerged as leaders of groups like the Popular Union of New Tenochtitlán and the Barrio Assemblies (René Bejarano, Dolores Padierna, Javier Hidalgo, and Marco Rascón, to name a few) went on to careers as elected opposition officials.

The movement of nongovernmental organizations also received a tremendous boost. Since the 1970s, women's groups and human rights organizations, for example, had been working away on their issues, to little effect. After 1985 they acquired new collective momentum. As for Imanol Ordorika and his friends, they never looked back to the shrill, abstract radicalism they had practiced at the UNAM. After the quake they still espoused a leftist agenda, but they were committed to achieving it through the movement for democracy.

5

Chihuahua, 1986

During the summer of 1986 the gravitational center of Mexican politics shifted from its traditional pole in Mexico City up to the north, to the desert state of Chihuahua.

Over the fifty-seven years since the PRI was founded, the party had never lost a state governor's seat to an opposition party. The governors were the President's operators in the states, providing a vital link between the all-powerful central authority and the sometimes fractious provinces. The President in effect selected the governors, since he had the final say in deciding the PRI's gubernatorial candidates. Governorships were among the richest treasures in the President's storehouse of patronage, mainly because of the moneymaking opportunities they offered, and the chief executive used them to reward his most loyal and effective allies. The PRI had never so much as considered giving one of them up.

But in 1986 the PAN, Mexico's largest opposition party, suddenly emerged as a serious contender for the statehouse in Chihuahua, the sprawling state of spruce-covered mountains and boundless prairies that borders Texas and New Mexico.

PAN, the National Action Party, had been around since 1939. Its founder, Manuel Gómez Morín, was a philosopher-politician who as an Undersecretary of Finance under President Álvaro Obregón during the 1920s had created Mexico's central bank, modeled on the U.S. Federal Reserve. He founded the party in opposition to President Lázaro Cárdenas's efforts to compel peasants, unionized laborers, and nearly everyone else to participate in the official party. The PAN had always been a low-budget operation run by a clannish group of Catholic lawyers and their wives. Its leaders had plenty of democratic convictions and pluck, but to many Mexicans the PAN seemed like a debating society.

The party had occasionally, over its long history of opposition to PRI rule, fielded local candidates in town mayoral elections who proved sufficiently popular to attract a majority of votes. But when that happened, PRI authorities as often as not stole the elections. Sometimes such frauds had stirred the citizens to react with rage, even to riot, but the protests had always died out within a few days.

Only in a handful of instances had the government certified PAN victories, and never for any office as important as state governor. But by 1986 the situation had begun to change dramatically due to the financial crisis. Especially in the northern border states, Mexicans had begun to

Antifraud protesters
block a Chihuahua
highway, 1986

demonstrate a tenacious defiance of the PRI, and the PAN had become the main beneficiary of citizens' emboldened attitudes.

Gubernatorial elections were scheduled for July 1986 in Chihuahua, and at least one poll had suggested that if the vote was fair, the PAN would beat the PRI by a three-to-one margin. Mexico's hitherto beaten-down and belittled opposition would for the first time win control of a state governor's office—if President Miguel de la Madrid would permit it.

The PAN in Chihuahua was led by Luis H. Álvarez, a textile manufacturer who had studied engineering at the University of Texas. By 1986 Álvarez had been jousting with the PRI for thirty-two years.

In 1956, when he was thirty-seven years old, Álvarez had attended the PAN's Chihuahua state convention, where he was thrilled to meet Gómez Morín and to see that the PAN's legendary founder paid keen attention to his views. But Álvarez was astonished when, later that afternoon, Gómez Morín asked him out of the blue if he would run for governor.

"I'm not even a party member!" Álvarez said—then accepted the offer. Only later did he realize that no party member was willing to run against the PRI.

Not surprisingly, his PRI opponent overwhelmed him in the 1956 governor's race. Official results from remote communities in Chihuahua's Sierra Madre showed that fifty thousand Indian villagers had supposedly voted for the PRI—and not one person for the PAN. Still, Álvarez's spirited campaign earned him admiration. Two years later, in 1958, with many Mexican voters disgruntled over a decline in worker salaries, Gómez Morín and the PAN's other national leaders nominated Álvarez to run for President.

The party's eagerness to thrust its highest responsibilities on him, almost overnight, left Álvarez breathless. But he again accepted the challenge. After all, besides the outlawed Communist Party, National Action was the PRI's only real opposition.

"What good was it to be a critic if I wasn't willing to act?" Álvarez asked himself.

The Mexican President had chosen Adolfo López Mateos, the Labor

Secretary, to be the PRI candidate. López Mateos was a handsome man and a gifted orator, and his campaign would want for absolutely nothing. The army dispatched officers all over Mexico to reserve hotel rooms, map out parade routes, oversee the construction of speaker platforms, and handle other logistics for the PRI candidate and his vast train of fixers, speechwriters, and valets. The Banco de México, the ostensibly non-political central bank, put its airplanes at his service. Television and radio stations, without exception, broadcast only flattering news about López Mateos. They mostly ignored Álvarez.

For its part, the PAN had few resources to offer Álvarez. The party's full-time staff in 1958 consisted of the party president and a secretary, who answered the phone in the party's rented Mexico City offices. The PAN did not have enough money to pay for a single campaign advertisement for Álvarez in the newspapers.

The PAN had always been broke. Gómez Morín was a free-marketeer and personally knew many of Mexico's wealthiest businessmen, but they were afraid to associate themselves publicly with his party and lose the government contracts that were key to business success. That left the PAN a threadbare organization of overworked volunteers who paid the rent at party headquarters by selling raffle tickets to middle-class friends. They could barely scrape together the pesos necessary to publish the party's weekly paper.

If Álvarez wanted to campaign, he would have to foot most of the bills himself. But he was a man of some means—he owned a jeans factory in Ciudad Juárez on the U.S.-Mexico border—and he put together plans for a national tour. He would travel with his wife, Blanca, and no more than two or three volunteer aides. He would rarely fly, partly because Mexicana airlines offered only a few air routes in those days. Mostly he would barnstorm Mexico by car, making roadside and town park speeches from the bed of a pickup truck. To get to one riverside village in the gulf state of Veracruz, Álvarez and his wife had to clamber aboard a canoe.

But Álvarez's biggest obstacles came not from Mexico's physical landscape but from its political geography. The country was a patchwork of fiefdoms, each controlled by a PRI cacique. Some were more civilized than others, but as a species these were ornery and often violent men who believed their advancement depended on stamping out all political dissidence.

As a result, the campaign was an endless string of aggravations. As often as not, when Álvarez's campaign car would pull into a town for a rally past sundown, local authorities would simply shut off the municipal electricity, leaving Álvarez to speak by the glimmer of a kerosene lamp. In other settlements, hotel owners refused him lodging, fearing reprisals. Often he spent the night in the homes of local supporters.

In Acapulco, Álvarez found several thousand PAN sympathizers awaiting him in a bayside park. But when he mounted a platform to speak, the town's brass band, controlled by the PRI, marched up next to his podium and began blowing their tubas and bashing their drums. They played for hours, drowning out Álvarez's speech.

The reception was uglier in Tonila, overlooking a volcano in Jalisco state. There, after Álvarez finished addressing the locals, the town cacique approached, brandishing a .45 revolver and accompanied by deputies carrying Mauser rifles. The cacique, Emilio Alonso Díaz, barked a string of insults. Álvarez identified himself as the presidential candidate of the National Action Party and asked Alonso to cool off.

"Come any closer and you're going to get burned!" Alonso shouted as his men grabbed two of Álvarez's aides. The gunmen shoved the two aides down a street to a cage of wood and iron that served as the local lockup. Along the way a young PAN activist and his mother who had accompanied Álvarez to the rally began to protest the rough treatment of their friends—and Alonso's men detained them too.

In all, five of Álvarez's people were jailed. Alonso and his *pistoleros* then returned to the Tonila square to disperse the crowd. "We're the government here," Alonso bellowed. "Nobody comes in here from outside to offend our authorities."

In Jalpa, Zacatecas, Álvarez was delivering a speech in the town plaza when he saw several local police, pistols in hand, detaining one of his campaign aides. Álvarez left the microphone, elbowed his way through the crowd, and confronted the police. "Why are you arresting *him?*" Álvarez asked them. "I'm the candidate."

"Are you running for President of Mexico against the PRI?" one of the policemen inquired.

"Yes, I am," Álvarez confirmed.

"Right. You're under arrest," the officer said, and led him off to jail. Álvarez was released hours later, after PAN leaders in Mexico City telephoned the Government Secretary's office to complain.

In many towns Álvarez gave more or less the same speech, outlining the PAN platform: he pledged to defend private factories, farms, and ranches from confiscation; to promote profit sharing and union democracy for workers; and to provide better schools and clinics for the poor and unemployed. But because his tiny campaign had suffered so many abuses, Álvarez boiled down many of his speeches to humble appeals for democracy.

"The authorities scorn our civic efforts," he told a crowd in Guadalajara a few days after his brief incarceration. "They sneer at the insignificance of the independent candidate. And that's true, I'm no superman. I'm just a candidate who loves freedom and is doing everything he can to end injustice."

In the days before the July 1958 vote, the PRI attacks grew more violent. A leader of the PAN's youth movement in Chihuahua, Jesús Márquez Monreal, was shot dead as he pasted up a campaign poster along a main thoroughfare of the state capital. Álvarez flew to Chihuahua to preside over a gathering that drew thousands into the streets to mourn the youth. The authorities never charged anyone with the killing. In Mexico City party workers hung a protest sign on the facade of the PAN headquarters: MURDERERS, THE PEOPLE WILL NOT SURRENDER! LONG LIVE CHIHUAHUA, YOU MISERABLE BASTARDS!

After the 1958 balloting, the authorities announced the official results: 705,000 votes for Álvarez, 6.8 million for López Mateos. PAN officials denounced the results as fraudulent. Álvarez had drawn large crowds at many of his rallies, and even academics sympathetic to the PRI concluded that the results looked phony.

Álvarez's experience in 1958 was typical. During the forty years after 1943, when the party first ran candidates, there were about thirty-two thousand municipal elections in Mexico's twenty-four hundred cities and towns. Authorities recognized PAN victories in just eighty-eight cases.

During the congressional elections held every three years during the 1940s and 1950s, the PAN never won more than 6 of the 150 or so seats at stake in the Chamber of Deputies. Eventually the lack of a more credible opposition became awkward for the PRI, and in 1963 the government slightly altered the electoral laws in a way that allowed the PAN to elect at least twenty deputies in most elections during the 1960s and 1970s.

Still, the PRI excluded PAN deputies from the Chamber's committees, although there was not much congressional work anyway, since most legislation was written by the President's aides in Los Pinos. National Action felt so bitter that for more than three decades, PAN deputies refused to talk to their PRI counterparts in the Chamber and averted their eyes when meeting members of the official party in hallways.

Following his 1958 presidential defeat, Luis H. Álvarez returned to Chihuahua and to his business. Over the next twenty-five years he worked endlessly for his party, attending meetings, seeking recruits, searching for new strategies. Yet the party grew only marginally. It remained difficult for the average Mexican to see the PAN as a serious alternative.

That's why Álvarez and other PAN leaders were as surprised as everybody else when suddenly, in the early 1980s, the political winds began to shift their way.

The economic crisis José López Portillo wrought in the final months of his presidency was Mexico's worst since the worldwide depression of the 1930s. The President promised to defend the peso "like a dog," but the currency, which had been worth about 4 American cents for several years, fell in February 1982 by nearly half to about 2.2 cents. Following the election that summer of López Portillo's successor, Miguel de la Madrid, the peso plunged further, and Mexico suspended payments on its foreign debt. After nationalizing the banks, López Portillo imposed exchange controls in an attempt to stabilize the currency, but the move merely stimulated a black market. In December 1982, when López Portillo left office, the peso was trading at 0.7 cents.

Mexico was bankrupt, and so were many Mexican families. López Portillo, meanwhile, had plundered the public coffers in a way extreme even by Mexicans' tolerant standards. Before relinquishing control over the national treasury, he built himself a retirement compound, including five mansions, tennis courts, swimming pools, stables, and a gym, all perched on a hill in a western Mexico City suburb above a road traveled by commuters. Enraged, Mexicans dubbed it Dog's Hill.

The anti-PRI fervor was running especially high in Chihuahua. By the early 1980s the state's 2.3 million residents viewed their federal government with about as much affection as the people of Wyoming have for the Beltway bureaucracy.

The peso devaluation aggravated these regional resentments, punishing border states more severely than regions farther south. Daily life in places like Ciudad Juárez, which faces El Paso, Texas, depended on considerable routine commerce involving dollars. The crisis sent prices for all basic goods, everything from milk and chicken to toothpaste and toilet paper, spiraling upward. Many border businessmen had borrowed dollars during the López Portillo boom, and with the devaluation their peso revenues were falling far short of their dollar-denominated interest payments.

A political backlash was brewing, and Luis H. Álvarez smelled it. Twenty-five years after his failed presidential campaign, he announced his candidacy for mayor of the city of Chihuahua, the state capital, in elections scheduled for July 1983.

This time Álvarez's candidacy prospered. One powerful factor was the Catholic Church, which after years of watching PRI fraud and corruption in silence had been emboldened by the peso crisis to speak out and began urging parishioners to vote for change. The Chihuahua Archbishop, Adalberto Almeida Merino, distributed thousands of copies of a pamphlet titled *Vote with Responsibility*, urging Catholics to vote for "the party seeking profound changes in the society."

At the same time, local businessmen who had for years declined to contribute to National Action candidates were suddenly making generous donations. Money allowed Álvarez and other PAN candidates in Chihuahua to build a campaign organization that could spread their message, mobilize supporters on Election Day, and, to a degree, defend against fraud.

In the July 1983 vote Álvarez won by a landslide, with most precincts in the capital voting for him by a two-to-one margin. His victory was all the more dramatic because PAN candidates swept over the PRI in six of Chihuahua's seven largest cities; a small leftist party won the seventh. It was the most jolting election defeat the official party had ever suffered.

Álvarez's PRI opponent, Luis Fuentes Molinar, acknowledged his defeat in a press conference the day after the balloting. That stirred public admiration; many citizens put ads in local papers thanking Fuentes for his unusual honesty. But within the PRI Fuentes's quick concession aroused only backbiting. Why had Fuentes not waited a bit to see how the party could arrange things?

In Juárez the mayor-elect was Francisco Barrio Terrazas, thirty-two years old, who had joined the PAN only months before the election. An accountant with broad shoulders and a shock of bushy brown hair, Barrio had come of age during the 1970s, when Juárez was exploding with construction of American-owned assembly factories known as maquiladoras (derived from the verb *maquilar*, to contract out piecework, especially in the garment industry), which transformed a once-somnolent border town into one of Mexico's most important industrial centers. He had seen the inside of the PRI system when he worked as an accountant in the Juárez office of the federal low-income housing program, where he watched a senior PRI official demand huge bribes before approving contracts with suppliers of building materials. During the years just before his entry into politics, he had been the president of Juárez's most important business association, as well as the CEO of a supermarket chain and several other businesses owned by Jaime Bermudez, a wealthy PRI supporter. Barrio had joined the PAN out of outrage over the bank nationalization.

When he threw his hat in the ring for mayor of Juárez, Barrio enlisted several dozen of his middle-class friends to coordinate his campaign. A real-estate agent drove across the bridge into El Paso, went to the public library, and checked out a book on U.S.-style campaign tactics. It described how to recruit volunteers, plan a campaign rally, set up precinct poll-watching committees, and other political basics. "That book became our bible," Barrio recalled later.

Barrio was part of a generation of energetic businessmen, most of them thirty-somethings, whose sudden opposition activism in the months after the 1982 peso crisis marked a watershed. They were not Mexico's multimillionaires—the super-rich had too many links to the PRI to risk change—but rather the owners or executives of midsize enterprises powerful enough to build effective political organizations, but not so powerful that they had government contracts to lose.

Their rebellious voices began to be heard all across northern Mexico. In Baja California, Ernesto Ruffo Appel, the thirty-one-year-old CEO of an Ensenada-based company with a small tuna-fishing fleet, joined the PAN in 1983, launching a political career that would years later lead him to become state governor. In Durango, Rodolfo Elizondo Torres, a lumberman and owner of a regional airline, was elected as mayor of the state capital (and later federal deputy and senator). In Sinaloa, Manuel Clouthier del Rincón, then forty-nine, was a vegetable rancher who had been the national president of the Consejo Coordinador Empresarial, the Business Coordinating Committee, Mexico's most influential business lobby. He helped his uncle campaign as the PAN candidate for mayor of the state capital in 1983 and later became a candidate himself, for governor and then for President. And in Guanajuato, Vicente Fox, struggling to make payments on his family's broccoli-packing plant, turned to politics.

The PAN victories across Chihuahua in 1983 had blindsided the PRI, but the party's leaders would not be surprised twice. President de la Madrid, the economist, was engrossed in the financial crisis, but he had a vigorous lieutenant who would take charge of the government's response to the opposition insurgency: Manuel Bartlett Díaz, his Government Secretary.

Bartlett was the son of Manuel Bartlett Bautista, a Supreme Court justice whose ruling against the international oil companies in 1938 ignited a nationalist movement, leading to Mexico's expropriation of the petroleum industry. During the early 1950s Bartlett's father was serving as the PRI governor of the state of Tabasco when Manuel began studying law at the UNAM. De la Madrid had begun his law studies there two years earlier.

Those who knew the two law students during that period would never have guessed that de la Madrid, a colorless, plodding fellow, would go further in politics. Bartlett was a much-admired campus leader, immersed in politics even as he built a brilliant academic record. After law school Bartlett polished his elegant French while studying at the University of Paris and his British English while writing his doctoral thesis at the University of Victoria. During his early career in government he proved himself a talented analyst and an audacious strategist. He was a true believer, unlike many party colleagues who cared little about ideology. He viewed the PRI as the heir to a line of nationalist patriots reaching back beyond the 1910 revolution to Juárez, Hidalgo, and Morelos. Once he assumed the powers of the Government Secretariat, pride of party translated into unabashed authoritarianism.

Bartlett believed that stopping the rise of the PAN in Chihuahua was a matter of the gravest national security for the de la Madrid government. He attributed the PAN victories there to a treasonous alliance among wealthy businessmen, the Catholic hierarchy, and rightists north of the border who would be eager to annex Chihuahua to Texas if given a chance. Chihuahua is a border state, Bartlett stressed. We can't surrender it to the conservatives, with their history of traitorous ties to the United States. Mexican intellectuals said later that Bartlett told them that electoral fraud in Chihuahua, if committed, could be justified as "patriotic fraud."

Sure enough, over the months after the 1983 PAN victories in Chihuahua, opposition candidates reported foul play in elections in Baja California, Sinaloa, Oaxaca, Puebla, Yucatán, Coahuila, Sonora, and San Luis Potosí. After a fraudulent election in Chemax, Yucatán, a mob of one hundred local men seized a PRI official who had attempted to steal a ballot box and, one by one, urinated in his face. Some fifteen hundred PAN members later blocked a nearby highway. After 1985 balloting in the border town of Agua Prieta, Sonora, the city hall was burned, and scores of PAN members, pursued by PRI gunmen, fled into Arizona.

Hooliganism, however, was by no means the PRI's basic electoral tactic. The party won most elections by transporting members of its peasant federations and labor unions to the polls, often standing them shoulder to shoulder in the beds of government-owned garbage or dump trucks. In many rural areas voters were made to mark their choices on a table in full view of the local PRI authorities. In elections in which the party knew it faced serious competition, its precinct captains made sure that thousands of the party faithful voted several times.

José Newman Valenzuela saw how the system worked during his 1980s tenure as the director of the National Voter Registry, the arm of the Government Secretariat responsible for maintaining the voter rolls and issuing election credentials. Newman came from a family with longtime PRI ties, but he attended Catholic lower schools, where most of his class-mates and teachers were *panistas*, and the UNAM, where his friends were leftists. There the experience of Díaz Ordaz's repression raised questions for him about the party's authoritarian rule.

"Nineteen sixty-eight marked us," he said later. "How could we adjust our thinking about a party in whose culture we'd grown up but whose leaders suddenly turned their aggression on us?"

During the 1970s Newman pursued academics, studying mathematics and philosophy, obtaining a degree in psychology and, when he was twenty-six years old, a doctorate in science from the University of London. All the while, Newman worked for Jesús Reyes Heroles and Enrique Olivares Santana, López Portillo's two Government Secretaries. He helped Reyes Heroles to carry out the political reforms enacted in 1977, and in 1980 Olivares Santana appointed him to head the voter registry.

This was an agency that enjoyed little prestige but had an extraordinary network of grassroots employees, with full-time representatives working in dusty little offices in every one of Mexico's thirty-one state capitals and three hundred legislative districts, as well as each of its twenty-four hundred towns. With all these local officials phoning in a steady stream of political chitchat to the Government Secretariat, the registry functioned a bit like the nervous system of Mexico's body politic. As a result, although Newman was no novice when he took over his post, he soon had to acknowledge his previous ignorance about some practical details of the voting system.

The Reyes Heroles election reforms had mandated the creation of a new national voter list and the replacement of the country's voter identi-fication cards, previously just slips of paper, with new plastic-covered credentials. These became Newman's first major tasks. To his surprise, his efforts irritated some PRI governors. After several called the Government Secretariat to complain, Newman asked a party veteran to explain.

"Before, it was easy," the politician told Newman. "A few weeks in advance of an election, I'd go to the voter registry official in my town. 'Listen, brother,' I'd say, 'These elections are looking tough. Can you give me a hand? Give me some extra voting credentials.' "

It had been standard practice, Newman learned, for the registry's local offices to issue thousands of blank voting cards to PRI officials in the weeks before an election. The party bosses could fill the cards out with any names they wished, load up buses or trucks with, say, PRI schoolteachers, and travel from precinct to precinct on Election Day, at each polling place giving the teachers a phony new card. The teachers might vote as many as five or six times each.

Now the Reyes Heroles reforms had changed the system a bit. The new plastic credentials were produced by a computer, and the only names the computer would print on them were those registered on the new voter list. It was no longer possible for registry officials to simply hand out stacks of blank voter IDs.

Still, the new laws had plenty of loopholes, and Newman figured out quickly how PRI officials would take advantage of them. Virtually all of the registry's twenty-seven hundred local officials were PRI members. To obtain phony new credentials, all a local party boss needed to do was to persuade the local registry representative to waive the requirement that citizens appear personally to register, accepting instead a list of names and addresses provided by the party. The computer, fed names, would spit out credentials, whether or not they were backed by living voters.

Newman had worked hard directing the national door-to-door canvassing effort that had compiled 27.8 million names on the new national voters list. He had overseen the list's computerization, storing the data on three hundred bulky magnetic tapes, one for each electoral district, used by Mexico's 1970s-era mainframe computers. Realizing that PRI officials would now begin to muddy this computerized registry with thousands of phony names, Newman came up with a plan that would allow him to accurately determine the number of real voters and thus protect the sanctity of his hard-won list.

Each phony name entered into the list at the PRI's behest would be marked, he decided. To prevent opposition parties from detecting the marks, Newman devised a computer program that assigned a different code for the false names in each of the country's electoral precincts (which numbered thirty-seven thousand at the time), with a key to decipher it all.

Although Newman ordered his local officials to use the system, some of them, apparently considering the exercise a waste of time, continued to enter thousands of false names with no coding, making trouble for Newman. One day an alert PAN official came to Newman with questions about the voters list for the state of Sonora, across from Arizona. The PAN official had noticed that thousands of the voters on the Sonoran list had Mayan Indian names like Juan Choc or Maria Chuc. This cannot be, the PAN official told Newman; Sonora has no Mayan population. Newman, embarrassed, reassured the angry *panista* that the computer must have made an error and that he would correct it.

Checking, Newman discovered that an entire swath of the Sonoran voters list was identical with the list for the gulf state of Campeche. The Reyes Heroles election reforms had modernized the system, if only a bit. But the PRI's electoral machine was adapting shrewdly to changing circumstances.

As Chihuahua prepared to elect a new governor to a normal six-year term in balloting scheduled for July 6, 1986, the PAN felt confident of victory. Álvarez and Barrio had governed the state's two largest cities with honesty and imagination, and their popularity as mayors had increased steadily. A PAN convention nominated Barrio as its gubernatorial candidate, and Álvarez endorsed the decision. The PRI seemed to pick a candidate who would appeal to PAN voters: Fernando Baeza Meléndez, a forty-four-year-old lawyer, educated by Jesuits, who had even belonged to the PAN early in his career.

But events suggested that the PRI was preparing more dirty tricks. Óscar Ornelas, the governor of Chihuahua who had certified the PAN's 1983 victories, resigned under pressure from the PRI. He was replaced by Saúl González Herrera, who immediately rammed through the

PRI-controlled Chihuahua legislature twenty-five changes to the state's electoral laws, making it tougher for opposition parties to recruit poll watchers and easier to falsify balloting documents. Álvarez, Barrio, and their followers organized protests, which gained in fervor as the day of the vote approached.

The election was becoming a thrilling news story, yet there was little coverage of it on Televisa or on the other broadcast stations and newspapers under PRI control. But there were now independent voices in the media, and one of the most influential that summer was the weekly magazine *Proceso*. Julio Scherer, the magazine's founder and editor, assigned one of his most experienced reporters, Francisco Ortiz Pinchetti, to travel to Chihuahua to report the story.

Ortiz Pinchetti, a dark-eyed man with thick hair that he swept to one side, had been reporting at the Tlatelolco plaza on October 2, 1968, when the gunfire began and minutes into the mayhem had been hit by a ricocheting bullet. Doctors had removed fourteen bullet fragments from his leg. In May 1986, when he stepped off a plane at the Chihuahua airport, the blazing desert sun had raised temperatures to one hundred degrees, and as he rode into the city center, he saw army troops patrolling the streets. The state seemed to be girding for battle.

A café in the downtown Hotel San Francisco became a gathering place for reporters and politicians eager to trade information. Over breakfast there a few mornings later, Ortiz Pinchetti met Alberto Aziz Nassif, a professor and Chihuahua native who had written his doctoral thesis on Mexico's electoral system and had also traveled from Mexico City to observe the voting. Ortiz Pinchetti and Aziz began to collaborate, often conducting interviews and attending political rallies together. Both of them knew they were into something new.

One leader who was acutely sensitive to the fresh winds blowing across Chihuahua was Antonio Becerra Gaytán, a fifty-three-year-old Marxist who wore cowboy hats and was the local leader of Mexico's main socialist party, the Partido Socialista Unificado de México, known by its Spanish acronym, PSUM. In an interview with Aziz, Becerra described the grumbling among his party's leaders in Mexico City about his decision to support the Chihuahua PAN in the fight against fraud. "They're having trouble understanding," Becerra said. "They're going with the analysis we've always made: the PAN is a party of right-wingers and fascists. But you just can't explain what's happening here in those terms anymore. A few years ago the PAN couldn't mobilize young people or women or peasants—not even the senior citizens. And now it's a center of political attention that you can't help but envy!

"I stand on the street corner and watch these people, and I can only say, What enthusiasm! What combativeness! What euphoria! What confidence! They've got people who've never shown any interest in politics shouting for democracy!"

The PRI, in contrast, was in trouble. Ortiz Pinchetti attended a rally at which the main speaker was Adolfo Lugo Verduzco, the PRI's national party leader. Busing entire villages of peasants to the meeting with promises of free sandwiches and beer, PRI organizers had succeeded in filling a gymnasium's six thousand seats—but only briefly. By the time Lugo Verduzco stood to speak, thousands of people had already eaten their sandwiches and drifted away.

"What has put the PRI up against the wall in Chihuahua is its own discredit in the eyes of a citizenry demanding the one thing the official party cannot give: respect for democracy," Ortiz Pinchetti said in the first dispatch he sent to *Proceso* that summer.

Chihuahua's Archbishop Almeida had issued a new pastoral letter, "Christian Coherence in Politics," condemning electoral fraud as a sin. Ortiz Pinchetti took a taxi from his downtown hotel over to the Archbishop's residence to interview him. The seventy-year-old prelate told him that just a few days earlier, Manuel Gurría Ordoñez, the PRI's top representative in Chihuahua, had also paid him a personal visit. "He invited me to join the PRI," Almeida told the *Proceso* reporter. "You've got to be with the PRI. Help us!" Gurría had said.

"Look, *licenciado*, that's not our place," the Archbishop replied, careful to use a title of respect for lawyers and other professionals. "We don't get involved in party politics."

"Well, start getting involved!" Gurría had told the Archbishop.

The PRI wanted Catholic votes so badly that Baeza had begun including religious moments in his own rallies, another break with the party's anticlerical traditions. In one speech he scoffed at opposition claims that the official party was preparing to steal the election, then closed with a prayer. "Lord, forgive them, for they know not what they do," Baeza said.

The PRI appeared ready to use any tactic to retain control. In many previous elections, authorities had prevented voters in strongly opposition districts from casting ballots simply by leaving them off the lists of registered voters. So PAN leaders repeatedly demanded the lists, without satisfaction. Finally, after two hundred PAN women conducted a sit-in in the Chihuahua offices of the National Voter Registry, the authorities turned over the registered-voter rolls. PAN leaders identified gross errors, including the omission of thousands of names. But with just days left before the balloting, there was no way to correct the errors.

Meanwhile, Becerra's socialist party had supported National Action's demands to see the voter list, by lodging its own complaints. PRI authorities responded by disqualifying all of the four hundred PSUM activists registered to work as poll watchers in Juárez and the state capital. That left the PAN as the only opposition presence at most polling places on Election Day.

The signs of impending fraud were so blatant that a week before the vote, Luis H. Álvarez left the mayor's office, climbed the steps of a kiosk in Chihuahua's downtown Lerdo Park lugging a sleeping bag, and began a hunger strike.

July 6 was a Sunday. Ortiz Pinchetti and Aziz met early at the Hotel San Francisco, guzzled some coffee, and headed out to watch the balloting.

They took a cab to a proletarian neighborhood with dirt streets on the outskirts of the capital. There, at polling place 95-B, a piece of political theater unfolded. The PAN's poll watcher, Lourdes Cerecero, twenty-one years old, had arrived minutes before voting was scheduled to begin at 8 a.m. To her surprise, the other poll watchers and authorities—all from the PRI—told her that voting had begun half an hour earlier, before the legal voting hour. They shrugged off her protests and refused to let her examine the corrugated-cardboard ballot boxes, even though a document on the polling table indicated, falsely, that she had helped inspect them before the balloting began.

At 8:15 a.m. a bricklayer who was one of the first voters made a ruckus. He had marked his ballot, but then had trouble inserting it into the slot atop a ballot box. He soon discovered why: all the boxes were already filled with ballots. Indignant, he shouted out his discovery, and an infuriated crowd gathered around the polling place, chanting, "Magic! Magic!"—a reference to alchemy, Mexican slang for the PRI's mysterious powers to transform the lead of electoral loss into the gold of triumph.

Soldiers arrived, and the voting came to a halt. Only forty-five voters had cast ballots.

The president of the polling station, Emma Ramírez, a fifty-year-old neighborhood housewife recruited by the PRI, acknowledged to Ortiz Pinchetti that the ballot boxes had come sealed with tape. No one had inspected them to ensure that they were empty before voting began, she said.

Ramírez's neighbors began to shout at her to cancel the balloting. "Don't preside over this fraud," they said. "You'll regret it your whole life."

Ramírez was torn. PRI poll watchers surrounded her, insisting that she ignore her neighbors. Finally the crowd prevailed, and she ordered the voting canceled and the ballot boxes annulled. Just then, however, a delegate from the PRI-controlled election agency arrived and took command.

"Nothing will be canceled!" he proclaimed. "If the señorita representing National Action wants to lodge a protest, let her do it in writing, and we'll attach it to our electoral report. Now let's get on with the voting."

"Why should we vote if our ballot is going to be wasted?" someone shouted. And the embittered crowd, surrounding the polling place, prevented anyone else from voting that day.

After the polls closed, Ortiz Pinchetti retrieved the official results from the precinct. They showed that the PRI received 660 votes, the PAN 29. And soon it became clear that precinct 95-B was representative of hundreds of precincts all across Chihuahua. The polling results from many working-class neighborhoods were equally lopsided. Ortiz Pinchetti phoned fellow journalists in Juárez and other cities. All told of voting abuses. At scores of the state's eighteen hundred polling places, authorities had simply ejected the PAN representatives, often violently.

At one precinct a PAN poll watcher who had been shoved bodily from the balloting area returned with a lawyer to draft a notarized document reporting his expulsion. But PRI hooligans abducted the lawyer.

At 7 p.m. Aziz and Ortiz Pinchetti attended a news conference at which Gurría, the PRI leader, announced triumphantly that his party had won almost every office at stake that day. Reporters, including many foreign correspondents, shouted questions. "Would you dare to characterize these elections as clean?" one journalist asked.

Gurría paused. "I'd call them legitimate," he responded.

At first the PAN seemed paralyzed with disbelief. Barrio, looking pale, mumbled to journalists about reports of "serious irregularities" but acted confused and defeated. Ortiz Pinchetti stopped by the kiosk in Lerdo Park. Mayor Álvarez, one week into his hunger strike, was the very picture of desolation.

The day after the elections, rank-and-file voters demanded action. Hundreds gathered outside the PAN's local headquarters, where party leaders were meeting. The crowd hollered and carried on in the streets until finally Barrio emerged. Their fury seemed to bring him alive.

"An outrage has been committed against the Chihuahuan people," he shouted, and he announced a sudden decision: the PAN would demand that the vote be annulled. Over the next hours the Catholic bishops and the main business groups endorsed Barrio's call for annulment, and the PSUM and an alliance of thousands of peasants led by the Reverend Camilo Daniel Pérez, a radical parish priest, announced antifraud actions.

A couple of days later, thirty-five thousand angry Chihuahuans massed in front of the cathedral. Businessmen and peasants, socialists and *panistas*, priests and housewives, all were chanting, "Democracy! Democracy!"

Barrio stepped to the microphone. Standing before the multitude, his hair blowing a bit in the summer breeze, Barrio absolutely set the crowd on fire, Ortiz Pinchetti recalled.

"Listen to me, Miguel de la Madrid," Barrio bellowed. "We Chihuahuans have decided that we've had enough!"

The crowd began to chant "Barrio! Barrio!," drowning him out for a time.

"We aren't going to put up with fraud anymore!" Barrio went on. "The authorities are going to learn what it means to mess with Chihuahua!"

The state immediately erupted in protests. At designated hours, hundreds of angry voters stopped their cars and honked their horns at downtown intersections in the state capital, in Juárez, and in other cities, paralyzing traffic in a cacophony of civic anger. The army had deployed several battalions from surrounding states to Chihuahua, equipping them with shields and tear gas for antiriot duty. But the troops were powerless to unsnarl the traffic.

Soon the blockages spread to the state's biggest highways. Three thousand PAN backers drove out to the four-lane divided thoroughfare connecting the state capital with Mexico City, turned their cars sideways across the pavement and the median strip, and shut off their ignitions. At the same hour protesters were blocking the main highways leading out of Juárez and other cities.

A Federal Highway Patrol commander landed his helicopter near the vast snarl-up outside the state capital. His mission: to get traffic moving. He was immediately surrounded by demonstrators. Looking confused, the commander smiled, urged the demonstrators to give Barrio his cordial greetings, raised two fingers in the V for victory sign, climbed back into his helicopter, and flew away.

Over the following weeks the street and highway blockages became a daily ritual. In Juárez, twenty thousand PAN backers flooded onto the Córdoba International Bridge over the Rio Grande, interrupting traffic with El Paso, Texas, for six days. Thereafter demonstrators blocked that and a second bridge several times. Entrepreneurs shuttered one thousand factories and other businesses to protest the fraud and urged citizens to stop paying taxes. Becerra, the socialist leader, and Pérez, the leftist priest, led a sixty-mile march to Chihuahua by peasants from villages northwest of the state capital.

And Mayor Álvarez's hunger strike became a powerful symbol of the democratic struggle, although he did not like to admit it. "I'm not a symbol of anything," he insisted in an interview with Ortiz Pinchetti. "I'm

Luis H. Álvarez on hunger strike, Chihuahua, 1986

just a man who believes in democracy. Circumstances have thrust me into prominence, but my efforts and my sacrifice are no greater than those of many Chihuahuans." Still, seated in the Lerdo Park kiosk in a white shirt and windbreaker, appearing paler and thinner by the week, Álvarez was a focus for embittered Chihuahuans looking for leadership. Day after day he was surrounded by citizens eager to shake his hand and thank him for the stand he was taking.

Perhaps the most extraordinary protest was announced by Archbishop Almeida. Immediately after the Chihuahua vote, the white-haired, bespectacled church leader told reporters that a candidate like Baeza, who had been devoutly professing his Catholicism at rallies, simply could not in good faith take office knowing that he had won through fraud. The following Sunday, Almeida stood before the faithful in the cathedral.

"Last Sunday someone was seized by assailants," he said, reading aloud from a statement that priests also recited to parishioners in every Catholic church in Chihuahua. "Someone suffered abuse, mistreatment, scorn, and insult. Someone was threatened and lied to. That someone is the Chihuahuan people." Almeida announced that the Archdiocese would not celebrate any Masses the following weekend in protest.

"For all the hypocrisy and deceit, for the fraud, for the violation of so many human rights, forgive us, Lord," he said.

But the Chihuahuan church underestimated the power of a strange and unholy complicity between the PRI government, anticlerical from inception, and the Catholic hierarchy in Rome. The Catholic activism in Chihuahua incensed Secretary Bartlett. He phoned Monsignor Girolamo Prigione, the Vatican's apostolic delegate to Mexico, who had cultivated warm ties to the PRI government, even though Mexico did not even have diplomatic relations with Rome. Bartlett asked Prigione to intervene. Prigione called Archbishop Almeida and informed him that the Vatican had ordered the protest canceled.

Bartlett's unflinching tactics with the Catholic Church were characteristic of his attitude to the clamor in Chihuahua generally: he was unmoved. Under his orchestration, the PRI electoral machinery ground forward like a steamroller, flattening all objections.

The PAN had filed 920 formal complaints, documenting practices like the start of balloting at precinct 95-B before the scheduled hour, the failure to allow the inspection of ballot boxes before voting, and the expulsion of opposition poll watchers from balloting places. The PRI-controlled state commission in charge of certifying the vote summarily dismissed 888 of the 920 complaints.

"Notoriously honest," the commission said of the balloting in its final report.

But as the authorities were putting their good-housekeeping seal on the elections, an unusual flirtation was under way between Chihuahua's PAN insurgents and the Mexican Left, many of whose leaders had seemed to swallow Bartlett's claims that the revolt had been sparked not by electoral chicanery but by reactionary Catholic bishops and U.S. Republicans.

Heberto Castillo, who by the mid-1980s had become the leader of the tiny, socialist Partido Mexicano de los Trabajadores (the Mexican Workers Party, or PMT), had been watching Chihuahua with mounting interest. Six weeks after the elections Castillo flew to Juárez—with Ortiz Pinchetti at his side recording the events—and walked out onto the Córdoba Bridge, connecting Juárez to El Paso, on whose arching span hundreds of PAN protesters were blocking traffic.

Castillo, who was fifty-seven years old and one of Mexico's most prominent socialists, embraced Barrio and several of his aides, most of whom had recently given up business careers to join the PAN, the party known as the country's most conservative. The cordial encounter, and the pluralism of the interchanges that ensued, had few precedents at that time in a country where ideological sniping was a favorite political sport.

"The problem in Mexico is not one of lefts and rights but of a struggle for democracy," Castillo told Barrio and the other protesters. "In that, I agree with the PAN, and I'm not afraid to be identified with it. The democratic struggle is for all Mexicans."

"That's the bible," seconded Fernando Benítez, a prominent writer who also witnessed the encounter. Barrio thanked Castillo for the solidarity.

"We don't have your knowledge or your intellectual capacity," Barrio said. "But what we do have, just like you all, is the decision to carry forward the battle for democracy, whatever the cost."

Castillo then flew south to Chihuahua with Ortiz Pinchetti and took a taxi straight to the Lerdo Park kiosk. Álvarez, emaciated in the thirty-eighth day of his hunger strike, struggled to his feet and welcomed the white-haired leftist with an embrace. Castillo spoke to Álvarez in the same philosophical terms he had used in Juárez but now added a tactical proposal: he urged the Chihuahua mayor to abandon his fast and regain his strength.

"Let's launch a national campaign for democracy," Castillo told Álvarez. "In Mexico democracy is the only road for the forces of the Left and the Right. Let's fight together to achieve it."

The dialogue that Castillo opened with Álvarez and others in the PAN was one of the first important links across the country's left-right divide. Many more would follow over the next decade and a half as opposition forces sought to unite against the PRI's authoritarian monopoly.

After Castillo's visit Álvarez agonized with indecision for three days. He had found Castillo's proposal inspiring, but abandoning a hunger strike with demands left unsatisfied seemed by definition humiliating. And there was no camouflaging the facts: the authorities had thumbed their nose at him and at Chihuahua's citizens' revolt.

On the forty-first day of his fast, thirty thousand people gathered in

Lerdo Park around Álvarez's kiosk. Barrio addressed the multitude first, announcing that a new period of civil resistance was beginning and that "it could last months or years."

Then Álvarez rose. "I know that my small efforts, limited by my own human weaknesses, have achieved little," he said, his voice quavering. "But now I put my confidence in God on high. I'm going to accept new challenges, and I'm giving up this fast."

Years later Ortiz Pinchetti recalled that moment as the most extraordinary of the Chihuahua summer. Barrio and hundreds of other demonstrators wept openly as Álvarez staggered out of the kiosk and through the cheering throng and made his way to a nearby hospital.

Aziz and Ortiz Pinchetti, whose weekly dispatches for *Proceso* had been studied by readers all over Mexico during the blackout imposed by the PRI-controlled media, packed their bags and flew back to Mexico City. The events in Chihuahua had become far more important than the election of a governor, Ortiz Pinchetti wrote in his final article that summer, because thousands of previously apathetic Mexicans had for the first time sought to defend their dignity as citizens. "The desire for democracy," he wrote, "converted this northern state into the scene of a decisive national contest, and it may be a long time before its final outcome is known. The opposition is organizing for more resistance."

Although thousands of Chihuahuans had watched the authorities steal the July 3 elections, they had no legal proof of the fraud. Not, at least, according to the rules set by the PRI authorities. President de la Madrid and Secretary Bartlett were smug in asserting the PRI's victory, offering patronizing civics lectures to journalists and opposition representatives. "The PAN got a lot of votes, but they didn't get a majority, not according to the official data available," de la Madrid told Ed Cody, a *Washington Post* correspondent who interviewed him at the time. "And elections have to be won with votes, not with demonstrations or hunger strikes."

Late that summer, de la Madrid and Bartlett listened impassively to a delegation of eleven PAN leaders who brought their complaints to Los Pinos. Then the President warned the oppositionists not to violate the law in their protests, told Bartlett to carry on without him, and walked out. Bartlett reverted to the official line: if the PAN had any evidence of fraud, he'd love to see it. Please, he said, bring it to my offices at the Secretariat.

"Thieves who steal ballots don't leave a receipt," one of the PAN leaders grumbled to Bartlett.

In public the authorities continued to dismiss the Chihuahua protests as the work of a sinister alliance of businessmen, the Catholic Church, and American rightists. But there were a few breaches in the official truth.

Enrique Krauze, a historian and partner with Octavio Paz at the magazine *Vuelta*, had visited Chihuahua two months before the election. He had published an essay profiling an insurgent PAN, a sclerotic PRI, and a state in intermittent revolt against the domination of Mexico City ever since the Spanish conquest. Krauze urged the de la Madrid administration to respect the voters' will. "Chihuahua today is living the revolution of democracy," he concluded.

When he saw the news out of Chihuahua after the vote, Krauze was infuriated, and he decided to speak out. He wrote a public letter to the government urging the annulment of the elections, and he began phoning respected intellectuals, asking them to co-sign it. Paz of course signed, along with Gabriel Zaid, another writer in the *Vuelta* circle. Krauze also got signatures from José Luis Cuevas, the painter, and from Lorenzo Meyer, a well-known history professor.

But Krauze decided that fighting the fraud in Chihuahua was a cause that could attract intellectuals beyond the traditional circle around Paz and his magazine. So he made a bold move. He reached out to Héctor Aguilar Camín, the editor of *Nexos*, the center-left journal that was *Vuelta*'s ideological arch rival. Krauze and Aguilar Camín had been friends and fellow students at college, but their friendship had been strained by the prolonged duel of ideas that they had joined.

Aguilar Camín agreed with the principle of the petition right away. There was a bit of a tug-of-war over the telephone about exactly what the statement should say; Aguilar Camín argued to Krauze that it was better not to state categorically that there had been fraud in Chihuahua, but only that it appeared so. Eventually the two settled on common language, and Aguilar Camín and other leftist writers on *Nexos*'s board, including Carlos Monsiváis and Elena Poniatowska, also signed the statement:

The official results of the recent balloting in Chihuahua showed victories for the PRI in 98 percent of the posts up for election. From a distance, we who have no ties to any of the parties think these figures demonstrate a dangerous obsession for unanimity. A broad and diverse sector of Chihuahua society, being closer and having more information with which to make a reasoned judgment, believes that its vote was not respected. To express its discontent, this sector has carried out peaceful acts of civic bravery, showing the lack of unanimity and raising doubts about the democratic nature and honesty of the elections. The authorities should not ignore the importance of these demonstrations. Today more than ever, voters need to believe their ballots count, that they count more than abstention or violence. That means the losers must be convinced. Citizens as well as the national and international press have documented sufficient irregularities to sow reasonable doubts about the legality of the entire process. To clear away these doubts, which touch the very fiber of the credibility of politics in Mexico, we think the authorities, acting in good faith, should reestablish public harmony and annul the Chihuahua elections.

The statement appeared as a full-page advertisement in several opposition dailies and in *Proceso* during the last week of July, an embarrassment to the de la Madrid government. The twenty-one co-signers included many of the country's most respected writers and artists, several of them well-known leftists. Given their prestige, the government could hardly argue that their call for new elections was just more of the right-wing conspiracy.

Ten days after the statement appeared, an aide to Bartlett invited several of the intellectuals to dinner at a restaurant in Mexico City's bohemian Zona Rosa section. Krauze, Aguilar Camín, Cuevas, Poniatowska, Monsiváis, and a couple of others showed up at the appointed time. Two hours later they were still waiting for Bartlett. Finally the Secretary swept in, accompanied by two of his top deputies.

A long, civilized dinner debate followed. Bartlett warned about the dangerous right-wing alliance in Chihuahua. Krauze and others respectfully dismissed those alarmist claims; they also criticized the longtime practice of allowing the PRI election machine to dip freely from government resources at election time. But the conversation returned again and again to the same point: Bartlett demanded that the intellectuals show him hard evidence that the Chihuahua elections were fraudulent.

"There was no fraud," Bartlett said. "What do you mean, 'reasonable doubts about the legality of the entire process?' That's absurd! Where's your evidence?"

Bartlett's assertiveness put his dinner guests against the wall. "We didn't really know any more about the election than what we'd read in the press," Aguilar Camín recalled.

In contrast, Bartlett spoke with authority, claiming to have studied the complete official election file, precinct by precinct, document by document. "You say in your manifesto that you're judging from a distance," Bartlett went on with just a hint of disdain. "Well, I'm not! I know what I'm talking about! The balloting was perfectly legal."

Then, perhaps growing cocky, he went further. "If you want, I'll make the election documents available to you," he said. "Analyze them. Draw your own conclusions."

Those at the table absorbed Bartlett's offer. The government revealed only what it pleased, which usually was not much. There was no Freedom of Information Act in Mexico, and academics and journalists had to fight to get everything from central-bank figures on the money supply to Health Secretariat statistics on infant mortality. Information became public only when a PRI official decided on a whim to release it—as Bartlett had just done.

"We'd like to look at the documents," Aguilar Camín said.

He knew that Bartlett was no fool; the Secretary had based his offer on the assumption that anyone not directly involved in the organization of the Chihuahua voting would find it virtually impossible to make sense of the official papers.

But Aguilar Camín knew somebody who might put them to very good use.

———

Juan Molinar Horcasitas was an elections whiz. A thirty-one-year-old political science professor with a master's degree from the elite Colegio de México, Molinar had spent half his life studying the mysteries of Mexican politics. Growing up in the early 1970s in the middle-class Polanco neighborhood of Mexico City, the son of a real-estate agent, he had preferred reading Cervantes and Shakespeare to watching television.

During the presidential elections in 1976, when the only name on the ballot was that of José López Portillo, Molinar had worked as a poll watcher. He was appalled.

"Elections with one candidate?" he remembered thinking. "It was like a dramatization of the entire political system. Mexico seemed like the Soviet Union."

The experience deepened his political curiosities, and as a college student he turned into a political junkie. He helped write a political newsletter and attended the evening meetings of the Federal Electoral Commission, the PRI-controlled agency that organized Mexico's elections, in a conference room next to the Government Secretary's office on Avenida Bucareli in downtown Mexico City.

Inevitably, all decisions were taken in votes in which representatives of the PRI and several puppet leftist parties would outvote the opposition. Before the political reform engineered by Reyes Heroles in 1977, the votes were four to one; the PAN was the only opposition. After the reform the PRI still controlled enough votes on the commission to defeat the opposition, invariably, eight to five.

Molinar watched the voting—eight to five, eight to five—and found the process repugnant. Sometimes the *priístas* would explain to him their rationale for their political hammerlock. Mexico was a revolutionary regime, they said, which gave the PRI not only the right but the duty to lead the nation. Granted, some Mexicans dissented from their policies, they would acknowledge to Molinar, but that simply posed a choice: the PRI could treat them harshly, the way dissidents were repressed in Cuba or the Soviet Union, or allow them to have their little parties and participate in the elections. But the PRI, the officials said, had a historical obligation to retain power.

Molinar was developing an association with the PAN. But he maintained a personal rapport with the PRI officials at the commission, and sometimes they would even explain their electoral *ingeniería*, the behind-the-scenes engineering by which they "won" elections. They boasted of issuing duplicate voting credentials to thousands of party district bosses and of their prowess at organizing *los carruseles*, the merry-go-rounds of PRI teachers or bureaucrats carried in party buses to vote at a dozen or more polling places on a single voting day.

As a political scientist, Molinar grappled with the question faced by all those studying Mexican elections: how to analyze the results, knowing that the process was fraudulent? The official figures were cooked; the opposition's were usually incomplete and full of errors. The only approach, Molinar concluded, was to bring sophisticated analytic tools to bear on the official data in hopes of glimpsing bits of truth through the lies.

In an article he wrote for *Nexos* magazine in 1985, Molinar demonstrated his technique, reporting a trend few others had noted: the official presidential election results showed the PRI's voter support dropping from near 100 percent during the 1920s and 1930s to less than 70 percent in 1982. "The official statistics cannot totally hide the electoral reality," Molinar wrote. "The element of truth in them is discernible. The alchemy reveals itself even as it tries to hide."

The morning after the Zona Rosa dinner, Aguilar Camín phoned Molinar and described Secretary Bartlett's offer.

"You think you could find evidence of fraud?" Aguilar Camín asked.

"They have to leave tracks," Molinar answered. "It's just a question of study."

"What will you need?" Aguilar Camín asked.

Molinar said he wanted the voter lists and electoral results, precinct by precinct, for all the elections in Chihuahua from 1982 through 1986. Aguilar Camín phoned the request to one of Bartlett's deputies.

A week later Aguilar Camín summoned Molinar to the *Nexos* offices. There Molinar found a stack of cardboard boxes that reached nearly to the ceiling. There were thousands of pages of electoral data, so much that digesting it all seemed impossible. But Molinar gamely began reading and classifying documents.

Studying other elections, he concluded that the PRI inflated the number of registered voters in regions the party controlled completely, thus providing a margin for ballot-box stuffing, while eliminating registered voters in opposition areas, enabling PRI authorities to turn them away from the polls on Election Day.

But how to test the hypothesis? Molinar pored over the documents for weeks, and then hit on a solution. He began to compare the official voter lists for Chihuahua with the national census, which was carried out by a separate government agency. The process took him several months, but in January 1987 his demographic comparisons had produced fascinating results.

In fifty-three of Chihuahua's sixty-seven towns the number of citizens registered to vote was greater than the total number of adults in the population. One town with 1,128 adults had 2,627 people registered to vote; another with 987 adults had 2,112 registered voters. The rolls had swelled right after the PAN's upset victory in the 1983 municipal elections, rising by more than a third from 1983 to 1986, eight times the rate of growth of the population. Virtually all of the growth had occurred in PRI strongholds.

The 1986 balloting results were also at odds with the census figures. The number of votes cast was far larger than the total adult population in many Chihuahua towns in remote corners of the Sierra Madre, where none of the candidates for governor had campaigned and the PAN had no poll watchers. In those mountain towns more than 80 percent of the votes cast had been for the official party.

Molinar presented his findings to Aguilar Camín, who took a prudent step, characteristic of those authoritarian times: he contacted Bartlett. "Mr. Secretary, we're going to publish an article with some strong criticisms," Aguilar Camín said. "I'd like you to see it before it goes to print." Bartlett told Aguilar Camín to send the article to José Newman, the Government Secretariat's elections expert at the National Voter Registry, and then phoned Newman himself.

"I want you to read this article and destroy it," Bartlett told Newman.

"How do you mean, destroy it?" Newman asked.

"Well, convince this guy that his arguments are off base," Bartlett said. "Tell him that he's an idiot, that he's badly mistaken."

When Newman read Molinar's work, however, he saw that he had a tough job. No study had ever laid bare such authoritative evidence of PRI chicanery.

Newman phoned Molinar. The two had met years earlier at the meetings of the Federal Electoral Commission (as the national agency was then called), and although they were political adversaries, they had a cordial relationship. Newman proposed that they review the article together line by line. Molinar agreed, and during the process Newman pointed out a few errors, the correction of which actually strengthened Molinar's arguments.

Preserving the formalities, Aguilar Camín introduced Molinar's *Nexos* article with an essay thanking Bartlett for so generously sharing the official electoral documents.

When the article, "Return to Chihuahua," was published in March 1987, it caused a stir. Virtually everyone in the Mexican elite studied it, and thousands of international leaders read an account of Molinar's findings in the British magazine *The Economist*. Bartlett was not pleased. Nineteen eighty-seven was the year de la Madrid would use his *dedazo* to pick a successor. His likely choice was Carlos Salinas, the young Planning and Budget Secretary and a fellow Harvard alumnus, but Bartlett was also a contender. Now Molinar's article had hurt his chances.

Bartlett (and many other PRI politicians) suspected that Molinar was working for Salinas and the whole *Nexos* study had been designed to destroy Bartlett's presidential aspirations. He ordered his operatives to investigate Molinar, and they soon realized he had no ties to Salinas. But in the byzantine context of the Mexican succession, evidently no one in the PRI read Molinar's study as a wake-up call about the need for genuine reform.

The turmoil of the 1986 election in Chihuahua was felt long after, and far beyond the state. But it proved to be only a prelude to the events of the presidential vote of 1988.

6
1988

Hours after the polls closed in the presidential election of July 6, 1988, Government Secretary Manuel Bartlett announced that technical problems with a vote-tabulating computer had made the results unavailable. But that was just a cover story. The real problem was that the first results had shown the PRI candidate, Carlos Salinas de Gortari, to be losing. It was such an astonishing development that President de la Madrid secretly ordered Bartlett to withhold public announcement of the balloting figures. Mexicans waited a full week to hear the official results. By then almost no one believed them.

Mexicans remember the 1988 elections as those in which *"se cayó el sistema"*—the system crashed. The phrase has the same sinister overtones in Mexico that "Watergate" does in the United States. Although the words refer primarily to a government computer system, they are also an apt description of the weeks that followed the voting. Before authoritarian control was reestablished, Mexico faced its most profound crisis since the 1910 revolution.

The myth of the malfunctioning government computer became a national legend, but it conveyed an inaccurate account of the events. The 1988 fraud was not a quiet cybernetic exercise. It was a clumsy operation that left messy tracks all across the country: votes were burned, ballot boxes dumped into rivers, tally sheets counterfeited.

Millions of citizens sought to defend their vote in the streets, participating in the largest protest demonstrations in the country's history. But the government and its official party still controlled virtually every gear in the voting machinery. As a result, PRI party discipline, chutzpah, and meanness allowed the authorities to bulldoze over the protesters.

But the cynicism displayed by the ruling system marked the principal contenders indelibly. Carlos Salinas was declared the winner, but in the minds of many Mexicans his personal integrity and political legitimacy were permanently diminished. Cuauhtémoc Cárdenas Solórzano, from whom the authorities stole millions of votes, galvanized a vast movement. In the eyes of many on the Left, he became a democratic messiah.

Cárdenas was a revolutionary prince, the son of Lázaro Cárdenas, the one PRI President Mexicans regarded with almost the same veneration as Benito Juárez or Emiliano Zapata.

Born in 1934, the year Lázaro Cárdenas took office as President, Cuauhtémoc spent his boyhood pushing toy trucks past his father's feet in the presidential palace and bicycling through the wooded gardens at Los Pinos. He was a toddler when his father was barnstorming the country handing out farmlands to peasant communities and four years old when his father expropriated Standard Oil and other foreign oil companies.

He earned a degree in civil engineering at the UNAM and later did graduate studies in France, Germany, and Italy. In 1959 he met Fidel Castro in Cuba with his father and two years later participated in Mexican protests over the Bay of Pigs invasion, again acting only in his father's shadow. He passed most of the 1960s working as the government engineer overseeing construction of a dam in his father's home state, Michoacán, west of Mexico City. During the student movement of 1968, Cárdenas, then thirty-four years old, did not participate in the protests. Soon after they ended, he began to move quietly into politics, constructing a traditional career within the PRI.

He contributed a technical study about development possibilities in Michoacán to Luis Echeverría's 1970 presidential campaign. After his father's death that year, he sought PRI nomination to the Senate, and Echeverría's selection of a rival angered him.

Still, in 1975 he was among the politicians who rushed to congratulate López Portillo for his selection as the PRI presidential candidate and was delighted when López Portillo installed him in the Senate, by *dedazo*, and later, in 1980, sent him to Michoacán as governor, also by *dedazo.* He ruled there generally in the style of other PRI governors. He lived much of the time in Mexico City, flying back and forth to Michoacán in a government-supplied plane.

After federal police in collusion with drug traffickers committed a mass killing of Michoacán villagers in 1985, federal officials sought to cover up the incident, but Cárdenas protested the atrocity in a letter to de la Madrid's Attorney General. Then, at an academic forum, Cárdenas argued that from the day his father left office, successive PRI administrations had abandoned the revolution's commitment to social justice. During his last months as governor and in early 1987, after he had left office and saw no avenue within the PRI to pursue his ambitions, Cárdenas spoke out with mounting vigor. He joined Porfirio Muñoz Ledo, Echeverría's Labor Secretary and later president of the PRI, and other left-leaning leaders to form a dissident group within the party they called the Democratic Current.

The group voiced little criticism of the frauds the PRI perpetrated against other parties, but sought to make the party's nomination procedures more democratic. Its main target was de la Madrid's economic policy, which had pauperized millions of Mexicans. "We are responding to the cries for help from a desperate society that is being bled by the foreign debt and persecuted by inflation, unemployment, and constantly falling salaries," said the Democratic Current's first manifesto, published in late 1986.

Cárdenas and his dissident group were not the only members of the official party upset with de la Madrid's handling of the economy. Yet only Cárdenas and his followers spoke out. At a March 1987 PRI convention in Mexico City, Cárdenas warned in a speech that Mexicans were angry about government policies favoring the rich. The only way the PRI could win back voters, he said, was by allowing its grassroots members to nominate a "democratic and nationalist" presidential candidate.

This was heresy. Jorge de la Vega, the president's handpicked party leader, said at a party convention that those who did not understand the PRI's traditions should leave the PRI, and de la Madrid continued the attack shortly thereafter: "As far as I'm concerned, let them go," he said of Cárdenas and Muñoz Ledo. "Let them form another party."

Cárdenas's public demands for the democratization of the party's nominating process had been ridiculed and rejected but not ignored. In August, Jorge de la Vega broke modestly with tradition by inviting Bartlett, Salinas, and four other top contenders for the PRI candidacy to give breakfast speeches to the PRI's executive committee, discussing national problems. The show came to be known as the *pasarela*, the term used for a parade of beauty contestants. But all the speechmaking changed the process little.

Five weeks later, on October 4, 1987, de la Madrid carried out another classic exercise of the *dedazo*. With the PRI leadership gathered at Los Pinos, de la Vega asked the President to offer his guidance, and de la Madrid said Salinas was the ideal candidate. De la Vega immediately told reporters that he and the party, after careful thought, had settled on Salinas.

Salinas was a brilliant budgetary strategist and a cunning political tactician but a weak candidate. An owlish-looking economist with a squeaky voice, he had little human appeal to voters. And as the man most closely identified with de la Madrid's economic policies, he had earned a nickname: Salinas de Cortari, a pun on the Spanish verb meaning "to cut," as in the budget. But de la Madrid's views were all that mattered. Pundits joked that Mexican politics remained a genuine "one man, one vote" system.

Cárdenas was left with little choice but to kiss the hand of Salinas, whom he detested, or to mount his own candidacy. A week after Salinas's *destape*, Cárdenas announced that he had accepted the nomination of a small party, the Partido Auténtico de la Revolución Mexicana, composed largely of retired army officers who had always allowed themselves to be controlled by the PRI. (Nominating Cárdenas was a rare act of defiance.) The PRI expelled Cárdenas immediately. Porfirio Muñoz Ledo also broke with the PRI. De la Madrid considered them has-beens, but Cárdenas began immediately to attract a following.

Cárdenas had first caught the attention of Imanol Ordorika, the National University student leader, in late 1986, about the time when Cárdenas was finishing his term as governor of Michoacán. Ordorika was leafing through a *Proceso* magazine when his eye fell on an editorial essay written by Cárdenas. It was a frontal attack on de la Madrid, accusing him of betraying the principles of the Mexican Revolution with his harsh economic-adjustment policies.

"Look at this goddamned *priísta!*" Ordorika thought. "He came up with a nice critique!"

By then Imanol and his friends from the UNAM had become celebrities. Reinvigorated by the earthquake rescue, they had gone back to the UNAM to organize among the students. A few months later the president of the university had announced a tuition increase, imposing a real fee after the university had been essentially free. Ordorika, his friend Carlos Imaz, and other veterans of the earthquake brigades all leaped into action, unleashing a protest movement that gathered support both within the university and out in the working-class neighborhoods where the students had helped dig people out of the quake rubble.

During 1987 the students watched with casual interest the feud between Cárdenas and de la Madrid. In the fall, just before Cárdenas announced his candidacy, the students were invited to meet him at a professor's home. Cárdenas told them he was planning to leave the PRI and challenge Salinas as an opposition candidate. He said he supported their defense of free college education and shared their criticism of Mexico's burgeoning foreign debt. At first they were skeptical.

"We just want it to be clear that you're still in the PRI, and so we basically don't trust you," Carlos Imaz said.

Muñoz Ledo, a politician with bombastic reflexes, started to lecture the students. Cárdenas stopped him.

"I didn't expect anything different of you," Cárdenas told the students. To test him, they demanded that he take a position in support of Rosario Ibarra de Piedra's nationwide movement in search of the disappeared. Cárdenas asked them to draft a statement, and then, instead of watering it down, he made their text stronger.

That gesture won Cárdenas the lasting allegiance of Ordorika, Imaz, and the other student leaders. And over the next weeks he confronted the suspicions and won the loyalties of hundreds of other Mexican leftists. In late December six parties formed an alliance to support his candidacy: the Frente Democrático Nacional.

The PAN nominated Manuel Clouthier del Rincón, a millionaire who had been the president of Mexico's main business association. A burly man with a beard, Clouthier had graduated from a California high school, and at the Monterrey Technological Institute he had played American football as a 250-pound tackle. With his wife and ten children, Clouthier ran a prosperous tomato and chile ranch in the western state of Sinaloa. In his first run for office, the 1986 race for Sinaloa governor, Clouthier faced off against Francisco Labastida, then a mid-level man of the PRI machine. After the balloting, Labastida declared himself the victor, but Clouthier's supporters marshaled evidence of ballot stuffing and took to the streets in protest.

Labastida responded by calling Clouthier a "neo-fascist." After he took office, peasants controlled by the PRI invaded Clouthier's ranch lands; it took Clouthier two years to evict the squatters. The experience embittered him, and his presidential campaign became not so much a quest for office as an anti-PRI crusade. He proved to be a tireless campaigner.

Early in the presidential campaign the PRI assumed that the PAN could be as dangerous an adversary as it had been in Chihuahua in 1986. Secretary Bartlett authored electoral legislation that rendered it practically impossible for any party but the PRI to win control of the Congress. The new laws gave the PRI control of an electoral tribunal and an absolute majority on the Federal Electoral Commission, the agency that organized the voting. They empowered Bartlett to name every important election official in the country and made it virtually impossible to prove fraud.

Salinas's nomination was a painful setback to Bartlett. For months he had been maneuvering behind the scenes to improve his own presidential possibilities. He had ordered one of his closest aides, Óscar De Lasse, to organize a network for collecting political intelligence during the presidential campaign and for compiling preliminary results after the balloting.

Bartlett had several more experienced lieutenants in electoral matters, including Deputy Government Secretary Fernando Elías Calles and José Newman, the director of the National Voter Registry. De Lasse, a former rock musician with shoulder-length hair and a resemblance to the rock star Jim Morrison, had worked on PRI campaigns but had never organized a federal election. He often showed up for work wearing a white suit and matching white shoes. He spoke in hip jargon. "What's happenin', Tiger?" De Lasse would greet José Newman when they'd meet at the Government Secretariat.

With Bartlett's backing, De Lasse began to put different parts of the Government Secretariat compound to his own use. Originally housed in a two-story nineteenth-century palace at 99 Avenida Bucareli, the Secretariat had been expanded over the years until it occupied a complex of four connected buildings sprawling over an entire city block and centered on a flagstone central plaza the size of a football field. Bartlett let De Lasse take control of the Secretariat's largest mainframe, a huge Unisys the size of a boxcar, located in a vast basement, and hire hundreds of data-entry workers to feed the whirring monster with political data. De Lasse ordered Newman's three thousand voter registry delegates to start phoning in biographical details on the hundreds of congressional candidates, as well as all the passing rumors about feuding among the opposition parties.

De Lasse called his creation the Sistema Nacional de Información Político-Electoral, known as the SNIPE. (In Spanish the acronym carried none of the unsavory meaning it holds in English.) It aroused considerable puzzlement within the Secretariat. For what purpose was De Lasse collecting all this arcane information? It was not being given to the Salinas campaign, and the SNIPE was separate from the federal intelligence agency. Newman concluded that Bartlett had planned the SNIPE as a resource for his own presidential campaign. After Salinas got the nomination, the Secretary saw no reason to jettison the project, especially since De Lasse promised to provide accurate numerical voting results in the first hours after the polls closed.

That was a new idea in Mexico in 1988. Never in any previous presidential election had the government, television networks, or anyone else sought to provide early results. There had never been any interest, because the outcome of previous elections had never been in doubt. On election night every six years, PRI leaders had always declared their candidate the winner, without providing numbers to back up the claim until days or weeks later.

The official vote-counting procedures were cumbersome and slow. After the polls closed, ballots were counted by hand in each of the country's polling places (there would be fifty-four thousand in 1988), many of them in remote hamlets. The results were then recorded on a tally sheet known as an *acta*, and the ballots and tally sheets were trucked to the nearest of the country's three hundred election district offices, most of which were located in sizable towns or cities. The law allowed rural officials thirty-six hours to deliver their voting packages to their district headquarters. There, four days after the balloting, officials would meet to add up the results from the 180 or so polling places in their district and finally send the results on to Mexico City.

Now, for the first time, the SNIPE was going to shortcut the process by having the voter registry delegates visit as many polling places in their districts as possible on election night to collect voting numbers and call them in to the phone banks that De Lasse had established adjacent to the computer center in the basement at Bucareli.

Salinas campaigned before lackluster crowds in early 1988. He crisscrossed the country, promising to revive the economy, end corruption, and correct every government abuse. But his promises sounded hollow: voters were having to labor forty-eight hours in 1988 to earn what they had received for twenty hours' work in 1976, two PRI presidential terms earlier.

Salinas had elevated his clique of young technocrats to the top campaign posts, excluding the party's more experienced election organizers, those with personal contacts in working-class districts and peasant cooperatives. As a result, the PRI's legendary campaign efficiency had gone slack. Clouthier, who was a rousing stump speaker, was drawing more excited crowds than Salinas.

But Cuauhtémoc Cárdenas was dominating the campaign, even though he had little money and headed a fragile leftist coalition. In any Mexican village all he had to do was step out of his campaign bus and stroll toward the central plaza, and he would be quickly surrounded by throngs of voters shouting reverence and jubilation. In a town in Aguascalientes, in central Mexico, for instance, beaming parents pressed their small children to him.

"Long live the son of the patriot General!" shouted a peasant in sandals. Old men and women wept.

Cárdenas was no great speaker. With the plodding methodology of an engineer, he insisted on reading his speeches, and he rarely smiled. The attraction, however, was not the oratory but the man.

"No matter where we go, no matter how small or remote the place, we find that Lázaro Cárdenas was there, too, fifty years ago," one of Cárdenas's advisers told a reporter. "The historical memory of the lands he distributed and the roads and schools he built is still strong, and it has attached itself not to the PRI but to the figure of Cuauhtémoc Cárdenas."

At the UNAM, where no PRI candidate had been able to appear since 1968 without provoking jeers or rock throwing, Imanol Ordorika and his friends organized a rally that filled the entire campus commons with an ocean of Cárdenas's admirers.

Yet not all the leftist parties were supporting his candidacy. Rosario Ibarra was running for President as the candidate of a tiny Trotskyist party. (Her platform had basically one plank: deliver *los desaparecidos*.) Heberto Castillo was the candidate of his own Partido Mexicano Socialista. His association with Lázaro Cárdenas and his leadership during the 1968 movement had made him an opposition symbol, and he competed fiercely for leftist votes.

But an independent opinion poll—a new phenomenon in Mexico in 1988—changed his mind. In late May, *La Jornada* published a survey of Mexico City voters, carried out by a pollster named Miguel Basañez. It showed Salinas favored by 45 percent of voters, Cárdenas by 26 percent, and Clouthier by 10 percent. Only 2 percent of voters supported Castillo. He looked over the numbers, heaved a sigh, and resigned his candidacy in favor of Cárdenas.

In June, Basañez carried out a nationwide survey. It showed Salinas slipping and Cárdenas gaining momentum. Salinas was favored by 44 percent of voters, Cárdenas by 29 percent, and Clouthier by 17 percent. In Mexico City it showed Cárdenas winning: Salinas was favored by 35 percent, Cárdenas by 38 percent, and Clouthier by 12 percent.

The poll stunned Salinas: no PRI candidate had ever received less than 76 percent of the vote.

The campaign transformed Cuauhtémoc Cárdenas. As a dissident within the PRI, he had sought less authoritarian practices, so that he could seek the party nomination. His democratic commitments deepened, however, when he confronted authoritarian tactics as an opposition candidate.

Salinas's older brother Raúl, then a government bureaucrat detailed to Carlos's campaign, reached into the federal police to hire a commander, Guillermo González Calderoni, to bug the phones of several of Cárdenas's top aides.

Days before the balloting, two of Cárdenas's campaign aides were shot dead in Mexico City. One of them had created a nationwide network of polling-place informants; his murder destroyed Cárdenas's capability to compile independent balloting results. No one was ever charged.

Throughout the campaign Televisa, with Jacobo Zabludovsky as anchorman, aired Salinas's every move in flattering detail. Cárdenas and Clouthier were ignored, insulted, or slandered. The coverage was so biased that Mexicans coined a joke: The Pope visited Mexico and went boating with Cárdenas. A breeze blew the Pope's hat into the water. Cárdenas walked across the waves, retrieved the hat, and delivered it back to the Pope. That night Televisa broadcast footage of the incident, with a terse commentary: Cárdenas doesn't know how to swim. The humor reflected voters' admiration for Cárdenas despite—or because of—the system's sabotage.

Jorge G. Castañeda, the son of a former Foreign Minister who was a prominent political scientist, accompanied Cárdenas late in the campaign. "The impression caused by arriving in Acapulco at 10:30 at night,

three hours late and in terrible heat, and seeing a multitude of fifty thousand souls, waiting for Cárdenas—patient, convinced, combative—goes
beyond my descriptive capacity," Castañeda wrote in *Proceso* just before
Election Day. "Mexico is on the eve of change."

Óscar De Lasse's immense elections computer system was supposed to
be a secret. The election law did not obligate the government to provide
early vote returns, and Bartlett originally had no intention of sharing the
SNIPE's data with the opposition parties. But in the weeks before the
balloting, word got out. For one thing, hundreds of De Lasse's temporary
employees had been pouring out of the Bucareli offices every day at
lunchtime, wearing plastic SNIPE credentials. Asking around, opposition leaders soon learned that Bartlett was assembling a computer system
that would provide early returns.

The news aroused considerable excitement, provoking a tug-of-war at
the Federal Electoral Commission. Bartlett's new elections law had expanded the commission to thirty-one members, although the PRI retained well over half the votes. Bartlett presided over its sessions in
the ornate Hall of the Revolution at Bucareli, at the head of a huge
horseshoe-shaped table. Jorge Alcocer, a congressional deputy, thirty-
three years old, represented one of the parties in Cárdenas's alliance.

At a meeting in mid-June, Alcocer asked Bartlett to explain how the
SNIPE would work and to share its information with the opposition parties. At first Bartlett denied the system existed. But Alcocer repeated his
requests, putting Bartlett on the spot.

On Friday, July 1, at the last commission meeting before the vote,
Bartlett suddenly agreed. Even though the law did not require it, he said
grandiloquently, he would make an extra effort, based on his commitment to pluralism, to provide the parties with preliminary results.

Bartlett's announcement sent José Newman into a panic. Throughout the spring Newman had listened with deepening skepticism to De
Lasse's boasts about the marvels of the SNIPE. Now he feared that
Bartlett's promise to provide results the night of the vote could turn into
a fiasco.

After the commission meeting, Bartlett, De Lasse, and Newman met in the Secretary's office. "Manuel, have you given any thought to how you're going to organize this?" Newman asked.

"Tell him about the terminals, Óscar," Bartlett said confidently.

Óscar De Lasse was bubbling with enthusiasm over what he considered a foolproof cybernetic ruse. To allow the opposition parties to follow the election returns, he said, he would set up computer terminals and keyboards at the voter registry—Newman's agency, located on Avenida de los Insurgentes about five miles south of the Government Secretariat. The opposition parties would be told that the computer running the terminals was on the eighth floor at the registry. In fact the terminals would be connected by phone lines to the SNIPE computer in the basement at the Secretariat. De Lasse would assign technicians to work alongside the opposition representatives at the registry to download precinct-by-precinct results.

Newman's fears only grew. He knew that the first precincts to report results would be in Mexico City, precisely where the PRI's support had declined most precipitously during the 1980s. What if the Mexico City voting went disastrously for the PRI?

De Lasse said he had designed a computer program that would systematically divide the precinct-by-precinct results into two groups. The results of precincts favorable to the PRI, where the official party had received more votes than all the opposition parties combined, would go to a computer file that the opposition parties would be able to view from their terminals at the voter registry. Results from precincts where the PRI was losing, on the other hand, would be sent to a computer file locked safely away by a series of passwords. Those unfavorable figures would only be released when results from PRI strongholds in rural areas had been reported in sufficient numbers to show an overwhelming PRI triumph, De Lasse said.

Bartlett's sudden, inexplicably generous offer to share the preliminary results was a sham; he intended to make public only those vote returns that had been filtered to portray a PRI lead.

De Lasse estimated that he would have returns from more than half the country's precincts by midnight on voting day, well before the 1:45 a.m. deadline for the eight-column headlines of the Mexico City papers.

Newman groaned. "You don't have a clue, Óscar," he said. "You won't get results anywhere near that quickly."

By early afternoon on July 6, it was already clear that this Election Day would be like no other before it. At the Government Secretariat, Newman visited Bartlett in his office, where the Secretary had been calling PRI governors in their state capitals. "It's very close, this election," Bartlett said, uncharacteristically worried.

Not long after, President de la Madrid took a call from his Government Secretary in his office at Los Pinos. Bartlett was blunt. The voting was going poorly for the PRI.

"Well, how bad is it?" the President asked. "Are we going to lose?"

"No, it's not *that* bad," Bartlett answered.

At 6:22 p.m. Bartlett rode his personal elevator down from his second-floor office to the Hall of the Revolution, took his place at the head of the U-shaped table, and called the Federal Electoral Commission to order. Immediately one of the opposition representatives denounced PRI manipulation of the election coverage in several newspapers, printed before a single vote was cast, which were trumpeting Salinas's "clear and decisive victory."

"Interesting essays in futurology," Bartlett said, forcing a smile. But the opposition representatives were in no mood for congeniality. They lodged reports of fraudulent practices all over the country. There were roving brigades of *priístas* casting ballots in multiple precincts; opposition poll watchers expelled from polling places; ballot boxes filled with votes marked for the PRI before the polls had even opened; polling places in opposition neighborhoods that never opened or were closed when hundreds of voters were waiting in line to cast ballots; PRI hooligans stealing ballot boxes.

Bartlett would often sit stone-faced during the meetings, resting his elbows on the table and holding a wooden pencil horizontal in front of him, squeezing it in his fingers while pressing in the center with his thumbs, bending it almost to the breaking point. When he was agitated, he would lose control. That night, as fraud complaints multiplied, Bartlett began to break pencils.

At the voter registry, José Antonio Gómez Urquiza, a thirty-eight-year-old PAN representative, and half a dozen party colleagues were working with a young, apparently apolitical technician whom De Lasse had assigned to operate the PAN's terminal. More than an hour after the polls had closed at 6 p.m., the opposition party representatives had not been able to extract any results from their terminals.

During the afternoon Gómez Urquiza had been peering over the technician's shoulder and had jotted down the half-dozen passwords the technician had used to gain access to different files within De Lasse's system. Now he asked the technician to enter some of the passwords. After several tries the terminal blinked, and a menu appeared on the screen, outlining the path to obtain results from each of the three hundred election districts.

Unbeknownst to Gómez Urquiza, he had penetrated the secret file where the SNIPE was storing voting results unfavorable to the PRI, which meant virtually every precinct in Mexico that had finished counting ballots at that early hour—just as Newman had predicted. Gómez Urquiza asked the technician to retrieve results from his own district in the Coyoacán section of the Federal District. Sure enough, results from two Coyoacán precincts appeared on the screen. Salinas was trailing Cárdenas and Clouthier in both. Telephoning friends who were poll watchers in the districts, Gómez Urquiza confirmed the accuracy of the results.

Delighted, he asked the technician to check results for Monterrey. In the dozen precincts reporting there, Salinas was also faring poorly. They checked results from Aguascalientes, in the center of the country, and from Puebla, to the east. In each district they checked, at least a few precincts had reported results, and everywhere Salinas was losing!

Thrilled with their success, the PAN representatives began to print out the results and to phone colleagues to confirm the accuracy of the figures. The sound of the printer churning and the excited voices in the PAN office drew representatives of other parties, whose terminals were still blank and useless. They began to gather in the PAN's little cubicle.

Suddenly another one of De Lasse's officials, heavyset and middle-aged, appeared in the doorway. He watched for a few moments, an expression of horror dawning across his face. Then he ordered the young technician to close down the PAN's terminal. "You've strayed into the wrong file," he said. "You're damaging the system!"

"That's absurd!" Gómez Urquiza interrupted. He insisted that the young technician continue with his work. The older official disappeared for a minute or two, then returned, this time more aggressive. "I'm ordering you to shut off that terminal!" he told the young technician.

"Don't do it!" Gómez Urquiza interrupted again. "We have credentials to access these results, and we need your help." The technician, caught in the middle, sat impassively at the PAN's terminal.

Suddenly the older official made a lunge for the computer's cables, trying to yank them from the wall. But Gómez Urquiza and his colleagues threw themselves in front of the computer, shoving the official away. Shouts were exchanged. The official slunk away to phone De Lasse, and minutes later Gómez Urquiza's screen went blank. Infuriated, he and the other opposition party representatives began to protest angrily to every official they could find. They tried to climb the stairs to the eighth floor, where they had been told that the computer processing the data was located. But soldiers blocked their way.

At the Federal Electoral Commission, Newman received a panicked call from an assistant, reporting that a commotion had broken out at the voter registry. Newman passed a note to Bartlett and walked out of the session to find De Lasse.

He found De Lasse, serene, in his office, smoking a cigar. "What is going on, Óscar?" Newman asked.

"What're you talking about, Tiger?" De Lasse responded.

"The line went dead to the computers at the voter registry, and it caused an uproar."

"Don't worry," De Lasse said.

Back at the U-shaped table, Diego Fernández de Cevallos, the PAN representative and an attorney famous for his patrician oratory, had the microphone. "Se nos informa que se calló la computadora, afortunadamente no del verbo caer, sino del verbo callar," Fernández de Cevallos said.

"We've been told that the computer has gone silent." He made a word-play on two verbs in Spanish that sound the same in the past tense: *caer*, which means "to crash" when referring to a computer system; and *callar*, which means "to go silent." "Fortunately," he added, "the computer did not crash, it's simply gone silent. And we hope that every best effort will be made to get it working again."

(When recalling the events later, Mexicans always said, *"Se cayó el sistema,"* resurrecting the idea of a computer crash. By the time the phrase made its way into the national folklore, its paternity had also become confused, and it was attributed to Bartlett and not Fernández de Cevallos.)

Bartlett was flustered. "There's no problem. The information is going to flow," he said, but ordered a half-hour recess, beginning at 7:50 p.m. It lasted until 2 a.m.

Bartlett stalked into his office, where De Lasse and Newman were waiting together with Deputy Secretary Calles. "Explain what's happened," Bartlett ordered De Lasse.

"Boss, don't get upset, but things are going badly," De Lasse responded.

"How badly?" Bartlett snapped.

"It's ugly," De Lasse said. The PRI was losing in Mexico City and in the nearby states of México and Michoacán. It was an electoral catastrophe without precedent in the PRI's history.

"And there was a problem with the terminals at the voter registry," De Lasse added. "So I shut them off."

"What do you mean you shut them off, you imbecile?" Bartlett shouted. He had known since mid-afternoon that the PRI was faring poorly in the vote count. But now De Lasse's decision to shut off the terminals had fueled the opposition parties' suspicions of fraud and their determination to see early results.

"I'm going to talk to the President," Bartlett said, stepping into a tiny side room, where he could speak privately to de la Madrid on a direct line. He told the President about the PRI's disastrous showing in Mexico City and nearby states. "I can't release these results," he said. "They're too one-sided." Results from other states would probably reverse the early trends, Bartlett argued. But if he allowed Cárdenas to pile up an early lead now, no one would believe the later returns giving Salinas the victory. He asked permission to suspend the release of more electoral results until they turned favorable for the PRI. The President approved the request.

At about the same time Cárdenas, Clouthier, Luis H. Álvarez, Rosario Ibarra, Heberto Castillo, Porfirio Muñoz Ledo, and other leaders of the main opposition campaigns were meeting at the Fiesta Americana hotel, on the Paseo de la Reforma, just a few blocks from the Government Secretariat. They had pooled their parties' fraud reports and written a joint opposition manifesto, which they intended to present to Secretary Bartlett.

As Bartlett finished his call to the President, Cárdenas, Clouthier, and Ibarra were approaching Bartlett's offices on foot, followed by several hundred supporters. At the Secretariat's main entrance they found the wrought-iron gates chained shut, but they rattled the gates until a security guard with a walkie-talkie got orders to let them in. The multitude poured in through a courtyard and up a grand, white-marble staircase to Bartlett's office.

"Long live President Cárdenas!" somebody in the crowd shouted.

Bartlett met the candidates and ushered them into his office. Hundreds of supporters and journalists waited on the marble-floored patio outside.

Standing near Bartlett's desk, Ibarra read the manifesto, "A Call for Legality," in a loud voice. "The voting that has just concluded represented a civic awakening," she said. "The citizens' desire to establish a democratic regime and abolish the authoritarianism that characterizes the current system was made clear." But electoral crimes had raised questions about the legitimacy of the voting, she said. "If the legality of the electoral process is not unequivocally reestablished, the below-signed presidential candidates will not accept the results, nor will we recognize the authorities derived from these fraudulent acts."

"Let's not prejudge the events!" Bartlett jumped in when Ibarra had finished. "These are baseless accusations."

Sharp words were exchanged. Heberto Castillo asked Bartlett to explain the problem with the computers. The Secretary quickly inventing a whopper of a lie, said that only 160 phone lines had been installed to receive the election data and a flood of returns had overwhelmed the lines, causing the computers to fail. He said he was working to install another 300 telephone lines to feed a parallel system, but the candidates had interrupted him.

"I don't get it," Castillo said. "So far, you've released no results at all. So what were all the calls that supposedly clogged the lines?"

Bartlett cleared his throat. The phone lines had been clogged in part by opposition parties phoning their out-of-state representatives, he answered. The candidates groaned.

"Frankly, that's just not credible," Castillo said.

The protesters stalked out. Rosario Ibarra read the manifesto again, this time to hundreds of journalists.

Bartlett called Newman, De Lasse, and Calles again to his office and berated De Lasse for shutting down the terminals at the voter registry.

"You nitwit! Don't you see how you've aroused suspicions?" Bartlett said.

Rosario Ibarra, flanked by Manuel Clouthier and Cuauhtémoc Cárdenas, reads the opposition manifesto, July 6, 1988

To buy time, he ordered Newman to convene the commission and explain that because of rain and communications problems it would take time before the data would begin to flow again. Newman, who had always considered De Lasse's plans for preliminary returns harebrained, refused to take on the messy job of lying to the opposition parties now.

"Manuel, I'm not doing it," Newman said.

Stunned, Bartlett stared briefly at Newman, pondering this insubordination. "Well, you're a shithead," he said. He ordered Calles to explain the delays to the commission members, who were furious minutes later when they gathered in Calles's office.

"We want some results! Quit hiding information!" Alcocer said. All the opposition representatives began to badger Calles at once.

"We're tired of waiting!" said Leonardo Valdés, another representative of Cárdenas's alliance. "What's going on with the computer?"

The opposition parties had already been told one lie, that the main computer processing the election results was on the eighth floor of the voter registry. Now Calles lied again, claiming that the computer at the registry, which had never existed, was overwhelmed with data. He said his staff was working to get a support computer running.

"What support computer?" the commission members shouted. "We want to see it!"

Finally Calles had no alternative. Trapped in his own bluff, he agreed to take the opposition representatives on a tour through the Secretariat. They walked down some stairs, across the flagstone esplanade, and down more stairs into the vast basement.

There, they beheld a sprawling computer center that looked crisply efficient. The Unisys mainframe was whirring peacefully in a glass-walled, air-conditioned chamber. Hundreds of data-entry personnel wearing white smocks and carrying sheets of election data were circulating among rows of tables lined with telephones. There was no chaos. The system looked anything but overwhelmed.

"Who's the boss?" inquired Fernández de Cevallos.

A short, heavyset technician named José Luis Urbina stepped forward. Calles tried to intervene, but Fernández de Cevallos waved him aside. "This is a very large computer," the *panista* told the technician, assuming the tone of a trial attorney beginning a cross-examination.

"Yes, sir," the technician answered, expertly describing its huge memory and powerful processing capabilities.

"It's large enough to store all the electoral information?" Fernández de Cevallos said.

"Yes, sir," Urbina answered.

"You haven't had problems this evening?" Fernández de Cevallos asked, his eyebrows rising.

"No, sir," Urbina said.

"How long have you been preparing this system for the election?" Fernández de Cevallos asked.

"Since about four months ago," Urbina answered, unknowingly contradicting Calles's assertion just minutes earlier that the system was a support center called into emergency service only that night.

"How many precincts have reported so far?" asked Leonardo Valdés.

"Eleven hundred," the technician answered.

"Oh! Print them out!" Valdés said. "We want those eleven hundred precincts immediately."

Calles intervened. The high-speed printer was out of order, he protested.

"But Mr. Urbina just said everything was working fine," Valdés countered. Calles was trapped again and agreed. When the opposition leaders left the basement, their suspicions had turned to certainty that Bartlett was fiddling with the count.

When Calles and Newman got back upstairs to Bartlett's office, the Secretary had already heard about the disastrous tour, but he kept his composure. He ordered De Lasse to print out results from the eleven hundred precincts. When delivered to the commission at about 10:30 p.m., they showed Cárdenas ahead.

Bartlett then locked himself in his office for the next two hours, refusing to receive anyone. Well after midnight he reappeared and, convening a final late-night Election Day session around the U-shaped table, offered new printed results, this time reflecting four thousand precincts, including many from Chiapas. He portrayed the four thousand precincts as the total number that had reported to that point. But he knew that they in fact were the four thousand precincts most favorable to the PRI, which De Lasse had hurriedly selected from many thousands of precincts reporting by that time. They showed Salinas with 45 percent of the votes, Cárdenas with 38 percent, and Clouthier with 17 percent.

Manuel Camacho, Carlos Salinas's friend since their university days, arrived at PRI headquarters that evening to find Salinas in an upstairs office, deeply depressed. His campaign coordinators were collecting vote results from the party's state committees. Salinas was phoning governors. Everybody had bad news. None of the governors had delivered the vote quotas they promised during the campaign. Mexico City was a rout: Cárdenas was leading Salinas by two to one.

Yet Jorge de la Vega, the PRI president, and other leaders were urging Salinas to make a victory speech. Camacho counseled caution, saying he should wait until he had numbers to back up any statement. President de la Madrid himself phoned Salinas and advised him to claim a triumph. "Carlos, this is going to give people cause for suspicion, because the PRI candidate traditionally appears around 11 p.m. or midnight to proclaim his victory," de la Madrid insisted. "If you don't, there will be problems."

"But I don't feel I have sufficient grounds," Salinas replied.

A couple of hours passed. Finally de la Vega, worried about the 1:30 a.m. deadline for Mexico City newspaper headlines, once again urged Salinas to deliver a victory speech. Salinas again refused.

Finally de la Madrid, the Harvard-trained technocrat, the forward-looking President, reverted to his authoritarian core to keep the PRI system in power. He had already authorized Secretary Bartlett to withhold the early election figures that were negative for the PRI. Now he encouraged de la Vega to ignore Salinas and declare a PRI victory. "Go ahead," the President told the PRI party leader. "Do it."

Well past midnight, in the dawn of July 7, de la Vega walked to the microphone at PRI headquarters. "Today's elections have culminated in a great triumph for the nation and for democracy," de la Vega said in a nationwide broadcast. "At this hour, even from the most remote areas of our country we are receiving from representatives and delegates of our party information that confirms our smashing and irrefutable triumph."

The next morning, however, all that was irrefutable was that the election was tainted. During the campaign the PRI had promised Salinas

20 million votes. Now the PRI candidate realized that he had received fewer than 10 million. Even the PRI brass didn't know whether all the chicanery had assembled enough votes, legitimate or bogus, to give Salinas a victory or whether the PRI would win a majority in the Congress, which the electoral laws empowered to certify the presidential voting.

Salinas faced a choice. He could wait and hope that the vote count would go his way, or he could follow de la Vega's lead and claim victory outright. The afternoon after the election he chose the latter option, but with a subdued speech in which he acknowledged that the opposition had shown far more strength than ever before. "The era dominated in practice by a single party is ending," Salinas said.

As it happened, the PRI retained control of the Congress, and thus of the electoral machinery; over the next ten weeks the authorities would wield it to impose a questionable victory and to sweep aside evidence of official skulduggery.

On election night the ballots were hand counted in each of the fifty-four thousand polling places, and the totals for each candidate were marked on a precinct tally sheet. In those where the opposition parties had managed to post poll watchers, the PRI faced some restraint in tampering with the count. In thousands of polling places, however, PRI officials had worked alone, free to report virtually any results.

Immediately after the vote counting, the ballots were trucked from the fifty-four thousand precincts to the offices of the Federal Electoral Commission in each of the three hundred districts. The ballots and precinct tally sheets were stored for three days in the custody of officials who technically worked for Secretary Bartlett but in most states were controlled by the PRI governors. Academics who have studied the 1988 vote have concluded that this three-day period was a riot of vote manipulation, with PRI officials all over the country systematically boosting Salinas's vote totals.

On July 10, the Sunday after the Wednesday of the voting, the officials in the Federal Electoral Commission's three hundred district committees met to add up their precinct votes to arrive at a district total and telephoned their numbers in to Bucareli.

The government first announced the official results on Wednesday, July 13, one week after the balloting, based on the district-by-district totals. Deputy Secretary Calles took his place at the U-shaped table, surrounded by TV cameras. He said that Salinas had received 9.6 million votes, or 50.4 percent; Cárdenas, 5.9 million, or 31.1 percent; and Clouthier, 3.3 million, or 17.1 percent.

Meanwhile, opposition parties collected stories of election fraud. Cárdenas's backers pulled together an account of the balloting in ten towns in Guerrero, for instance: teams of children had been recruited to mark blank ballots for Salinas; ballot boxes had been stolen, often at gunpoint; PRI mayors had entered polling places to suspend the ballot counting, only to resume it later inside their own town halls; ballots marked for Cárdenas had been burned.

Over the next weeks the opposition parties disputed the official results fiercely in three successive arenas. During July and August the Federal Electoral Commission reviewed the presidential and congressional elections, although it was only empowered to designate the winners in the country's three hundred congressional races. In late August the congressional candidates designated as winners by the commission formed an electoral college to review the legislative elections anew, this time from the floor of the Congress, and to formally certify their own victories. And in September the newly elected Chamber of Deputies debated whether to certify Salinas's triumph. At each stage of the process the opposition presented evidence of generalized fraud but was outvoted by the PRI.

The opposition parties got their first chance at a systematic review of the election documents at the Federal Electoral Commission in the third week of July. In a vast hall on the second floor of one wing of the Government Secretariat, officials set up tables and laid out in three hundred piles the electoral materials from each district. These included the approximately 180 tally sheets for the precincts within that district; a *sábana*, which was a paper spreadsheet the size of a large desktop, showing the results from each of the presidential, Senate, and congressional races in each precinct along with their combined vote totals; and the minutes of the July 10 vote-tabulation sessions at the district committees.

Cárdenas's representatives at the electoral commission, Leonardo Valdés and Jorge Alcocer, were among the most vigorous in their scrutiny of these documents during the commission's proceedings in late July and early August. Valdés and Alcocer worked from 8 a.m. to 4 p.m. each day reviewing the tallies, then rushed out for dinner, returning by 6 p.m. and remaining until midnight.

Even working every minute at this exhausting pace, Valdés and Alcocer found a review of all the country's precinct tally sheets an impossible challenge. With one tally for each of the presidential, Senate, and congressional races in the fifty-four thousand polling sites, there were 162,000 tallies. All the hours available during the twenty-four days that the commission was in session left the opposition parties, on average, less than five seconds to look at any one tally sheet. Still, their review allowed Valdés and Alcocer to learn a great deal about how the votes had been tabulated on July 10 at the country's three hundred district committees.

The tabulations followed the same procedure in the district committees all across Mexico. An official would page through the pile of precinct tallies one by one, calling out in a loud voice—in Spanish, *cantando*—the votes for each candidate as a secretary wrote the totals onto the district spreadsheet. The scribes who recorded the minutes of these meetings often clearly described the tactics used to inflate Salinas's vote totals.

The minutes of the tabulation session in one district in Puebla were particularly vivid, Alcocer discovered, and he studied them, fascinated. Soon after the July 10 session in Puebla began, the PAN representative interrupted to complain, the minutes indicated. Each time Salinas's votes from a precinct were read out loud, the PAN representative complained, the district committee secretary was adding a zero to Salinas's total on the spreadsheet, changing 73 votes for Salinas to 730 votes, for instance.

"That can't be," the president of the district committee replied.

"But that's what he's doing," the PAN representative insisted.

"Let's vote to see if the complaint from the PAN representative is accepted," the committee president said. The PRI had a majority on this as on all other district committees, so the PAN complaint was rejected. The tabulation continued. Soon a representative of one of the parties in Cárdenas's coalition interrupted to complain that the secretary was still adding zeros to Salinas's totals.

"We've already voted on that complaint, and since everything is democratic here, please stop interrupting!" the commission president replied. "Please respect our democracy!"

At that, all the opposition party representatives walked out, and the PRI officials continued the tabulation without opposition interference.

Alcocer carefully noted the scribe's account of the July 10 proceedings in the Puebla district and protested the abuses before the Federal Electoral Commission later that evening in late July around the U-shaped table. Bartlett ruled Alcocer out of order.

Valdés and Alcocer found that Salinas's vote total ended in a zero in thousands of precincts, many times more than was statistically probable had the digits appeared following the laws of random probability.

In thousands of precincts the tally sheets showed that Salinas had won with 100 percent of the votes. In a town where 990 voters had cast ballots, for instance, not a single soul would have voted for Cárdenas or Clouthier. Many precincts where Salinas won every last vote bordered precincts in which he received barely 30 percent, a pattern that was inexplicable in terms of political demographics.

Valdés and Alcocer identified another anomaly. In each of the three hundred districts, Mexicans had voted for the Congress as well as for President, and the number of votes cast in the congressional election should have been roughly equal to those cast for President. But the tallies showed far more votes for President than for deputies almost everywhere. In some states the differences were extreme, with Salinas receiving hundreds of thousands more votes than the PRI congressional candidates. There was only one logical explanation: as PRI fraudsters had altered thousands of tally sheets after the balloting, adding votes for Salinas, they had not wasted time touching up the congressional tallies as well.

Alcocer, Valdés, and other opposition representatives sought to have the elections annulled. They delivered impassioned speeches about the anomalies, held up charts, and occasionally beat the table in frustration. The PRI representatives would listen impassively, then proceed to certify the election.

In the first hours after the July 6 vote Cárdenas and Clouthier stood shoulder to shoulder in demanding that the vote be annulled. But Cárdenas opened an irreparable breach three days later, when he unilaterally declared himself the election winner. He had become convinced of his own victory, he said, by studying partial election returns gathered by his alliance as well as "reliable information from inside the government." "Any attempt to consummate this fraud" by installing Salinas in the presidency, Cárdenas said, "would be the technical equivalent of a coup d'état."

His declaration delighted his supporters but provoked strains with the PAN, because it abandoned the common demand that had united the right and the left opposition: to annul the election. Now he wanted instead to rectify the July 6 results.

The antagonisms between the supporters of Cárdenas and Clouthier traced back to 1939, when Manuel Gómez Morín founded the PAN. The Mexican Left despised the new party partly because it included far-right extremists; even Gómez Morín appeared at times to be anti-Semitic. President Lázaro Cárdenas had ordered Mexico's delegation at the League of Nations to condemn Nazi persecution of the Jews. Gómez Morín said Mexico ought not to help "factions that are foreign to us." For his part, Gómez Morín viewed President Cárdenas as a power-hungry socialist and believed the land reform stifled productive farming and that the official labor federations manipulated the working class.

Despite this historical ideological breach and Cárdenas's unilateral victory declaration, Clouthier continued to work with the leftist alliance for months, coordinating street demonstrations and staging a hunger strike to protest the fraud.

Manuel Camacho, meeting with Clouthier at Luis H. Álvarez's apartment days after the balloting, saw Clouthier's democratic commitment. Camacho, representing Salinas, was seeking to erode the PAN's determination to nullify the balloting.

"There's no reason for us to talk further," Clouthier interrupted. "I'm sick of this system and want a democratic change. The election is unacceptable. We want it annulled."

Other PAN leaders, however, never forgave Cárdenas for proclaiming himself President-elect, and their passivity after the balloting helped Salinas consolidate power.

Cárdenas's breach with the PAN came as the leftist alliance was debating the best tactics for resisting the fraud. Should the Frente Democrático Nacional contest the elections only within the Federal Electoral Commission, the courts, and the Congress, all controlled by the PRI? Or should Cárdenas orchestrate acts of civil disobedience like those that had paralyzed Chihuahua two years earlier?

Raúl Álvarez Garín, the 1968 student leader who in 1988 was publishing an influential leftist journal, urged Cárdenas to organize militant civil resistance. So did Porfirio Muñoz Ledo. On July 16, three days after the announcement of official results, Cárdenas summoned 200,000 defiant Mexicans—bearded university students, peasants clutching straw hats, factory workers, middle-class twenty-somethings in jogging suits— to the Zócalo. Many in the crowd expressed hopes that Cárdenas would lead them into open confrontation with the PRI system. But Cárdenas left unclear how far he was willing to push.

He launched a nationwide tour. In Guerrero his followers displayed thousands of burned ballots, marked for Cárdenas, some that were found dumped in ravines and others floating in a river. He was testing the people's mood, and perhaps his own. In Michoacán his backers spontaneously occupied town halls in several municipalities. Everywhere Cárdenas went, crowds shouted support for vigorous action to defend the vote.

Watching the groundswell, PRI officials began to issue thinly veiled threats of violence. At a PRI forum attended by Salinas, one General, Bardomiano de la Vega, echoed rhetoric that Díaz Ordaz had applied to student demonstrators before Tlatelolco, accusing Cárdenas of "verbal terrorism."

"We see street demonstrations organized to generate acts of repression," the General said. "Mr. President-elect, we will not let minority parties put at risk what has cost our nation so much blood."

Cárdenas, impassive, pursued his tour. In early August he called on citizens to turn off the lights in their homes each evening to protest the fraud. His closest supporters darkened their homes, but his call was not heeded nationwide, disheartening him about possibilities for civil resistance.

In Hidalgo, a state just north of Mexico City, thousands of Pemex workers and PRI dissidents surged around him, shouting his praise. On

Cuauhtémoc Cárdenas addresses protesters in the Zócalo in the summer of 1988

the fringes protesters set a torch to a paper effigy of Salinas. "We have scores to settle with the government," Cárdenas told the crowd, but then urged caution. "This is not the moment to seize city halls or to block highways," he said.

Several protesters in the crowd were waving a banner, trying to get Cárdenas's attention. "We'll do anything you order, Mr. President," the banner said.

In mid-August the Chamber of Deputies went into session, with the certification of the elections atop its agenda. The PRI's 260 deputies faced off against 240 from the opposition.

One PAN deputy was Vicente Fox. Then forty-five years old, he showed up at the Congress wearing a beard and jeans. Since his resignation from Coca-Cola in 1979, Fox had been living on his Guanajuato ranch, helping run the family businesses, and to his friends he seemed bored. In November 1987 he had received a call from Clouthier. "Get into politics and help change things," Clouthier had urged.

Fox registered with the Guanajuato PAN and ran for the Congress. At first he could barely manage to make a pleasing stump speech, but Guanajuato voters were fed up with the PRI, and he won election. On August 15, he took his seat in the Chamber of Deputies, then acting in its role as an electoral college.

Fox and other lawmakers learned that all the ballot boxes from the fifty-four thousand voting places were stored in the basement of the Congress. There was an easy way to resolve the election crisis, they reasoned: open the boxes and recount the ballots in disputed precincts. The PRI insisted that a recount would be illegal. But the weekend after their swearing in, Fox and thirty other congressmen descended to the basement anyway. They were met by soldiers.

Fox wrote later that the soldiers shouted, "Take one more step and you die, motherfuckers!" A journalist who witnessed the events was less melodramatic. She said a lieutenant colonel stepped forward to say that the head of the PRI congressional delegation was the only person with a key to the storage area warehousing the ballots.

If the lawmakers' foray into the congressional basement was disappointing, however, they found plenty of action upstairs. Fox called the debate over the 1988 elections "the thirty most enjoyable days of my life."

As an electoral college, the lawmakers had to certify the 300 separate congressional elections, in 255 of which there were accusations of fraud. The deliberations became an endless cycle of angry opposition speeches and PRI steamroller tactics. Exasperation led the opposition legislators to challenge the proceedings any way they could. They heckled and whistled. They tried to take the podium by assault, and fistfights resulted. They walked out en masse. They folded ballots into paper airplanes and sailed them across the chamber.

On September 1, President de la Madrid delivered his final State of the Union address. When he described the presidential balloting as "the beginning of a new and improved stage in our political development," he was hooted down by the Congress.

"Fraud! Fraud!" the opposition legislators yelled. Muñoz Ledo, who had been elected senator from Mexico City, led a walkout of oppositionists.

"Stinking traitor!" PRI lawmakers shouted. As Muñoz Ledo walked up the aisle, several tried to pummel him.

Days later the debate over Salinas's certification got under way, with opposition deputies storming the podium and tearing up the document formally declaring Salinas's triumph. Thereafter, PRI deputies formed a defensive line at the front of the chamber. The verbal and physical violence reached such a crescendo that one opposition deputy slumped to the floor with a heart attack. On the last day of the debate more than a hundred orators stood to decry the elections.

One was Fox. Standing at the microphone, Fox tore slits in two ballots, fashioning them into gigantic ears, which he slipped over his own. His imitation of the outsize ears of the President-elect sent opposition lawmakers into gales of laughter. In his speech Fox pretended to be Salinas talking to his family. "My children, I'm feeling sad because I've had to ask many friends to ignore their moral principles and help me obtain this triumph. I had to do it because I don't think Mexico is ready for democracy," Fox said, mimicking Salinas. Several times the PRI legislator presiding over the session attempted to silence Fox. But he plunged ahead with his caustic parody. Salinas, watching the proceedings on closed-circuit television, missed the humor.

A twenty-hour debate preceded the PRI's final vote to certify Salinas's

Vicente Fox denouncing
Carlos Salinas in the
Chamber of Deputies, 1988

election. Every PAN deputy voted against, and the 136 members of Cárdenas's alliance stalked out before the vote.

Four days later Cárdenas's supporters overwhelmed the Zócalo in a demonstration that Manuel Camacho, from his vantage point in the Salinas camp, saw as "the most powerful and most radical concentration of people in our history."

What would Cárdenas tell the thousands of angry citizens facing the gates of the National Palace? He had exhausted all legal recourse. Some in his party, perhaps mindful of the velvet revolution that had deposed Ferdinand Marcos in the Philippines two years earlier, were still urging him to incite the crowd to fury—to rush the palace, to defy police, to take over the city.

Cárdenas stepped to the microphone. For some minutes he reviewed in his methodical engineer's way the dismal course of ten weeks of fraud. He appealed to Salinas's conscience, urging him to resign as President-elect and rectify the fraud. But he warned his followers not to give authorities a pretext for repression. "They want us to issue a call to drag them from power by any means possible, in a disorganized and unprepared manner, so that they can respond with a bloodbath and a devastating wave of repression," Cárdenas said. Then he offered his alternative.

"We need to generate appropriate conditions for this struggle," he said. Instead of summoning a national insurrection, Cárdenas urged his followers to create a new leftist political party to mount a more organized electoral challenge to the PRI. "We need to form base committees in every part of our country," Cárdenas said. "Committees that express our great revolutionary unity. Disciplined. Effective."

In 1988 Cárdenas helped Mexicans overcome their fears of the PRI monolith. He showed that a nationwide democratic opposition could challenge the system.

By turning from violence, Cárdenas led the Mexican Left away from the lure of revolution and set it on the path to change by peaceful means. For many of his followers the events of 1988, more than a crushing setback, were a compelling sign that the Left could win power at the polls if the elections were clean and fair.

In 1989 Cárdenas and his backers founded the Partido de la Revolución Democrática. It grew to become the third force in Mexican politics, ensuring that a moderate socialist agenda was a permanent part of Mexico's political discourse. Cárdenas never regretted his decisions. "I was not part of a subversive movement," he recalled years later. "I was determined to stay within the law."

7

The Carlos Salinas Show

arlos Salinas was sworn in on December 1, 1988, with the legitimacy of his mandate in grave doubt. To overcome this weakness, he seized the great power of the presidency and used it to transform himself into a giant leader in the eyes of the Mexican people.

Although Salinas shared most of the free-market economic views of his predecessor, Miguel de la Madrid, his political persona was radically different. Whereas de la Madrid was essentially an administrator, Salinas made himself into a full-bore caudillo. He restored the presidency to the original monarchical grandeur conceived by the founders of the PRI system.

The hallmark of Salinas's presidency was the image of forceful and all-encompassing command. It even showed in his walk. Whether leaping onto the podium at a rally in Guadalajara or striding up the steps to the White House, he moved, despite his small stature, in long, brisk strides, so that his aides and security contingent had a problem keeping up with him. Not satisfied to leave his work on his desk, he did much business by responding to questions on file cards that his personal secretary would pass to him in hurried handoffs at any moment when he was not occupied, whether he was sitting on a dais before a speech or walking fifty yards from a limousine to a door. His relentless energy earned him the nickname Atomic Ant.

With his keen intelligence and capacious memory, Salinas demanded to be kept apprised of events at all levels of society and to have the last word on an encyclopedic range of issues. He was constantly on the phone to his cabinet secretaries, to a degree that they sometimes found maddening, getting updates on their projects and prodding them to produce more quickly. He even liked to decide the menu for the presidential meals at Los Pinos.

If Salinas was a centralizing workaholic, he was also an entertainer. He relished the pageantry of his office and used it expertly. For his annual *informe* he rode down the Paseo de la Reforma under a confetti shower, standing in an open limousine. He revived the tradition of the *besamanos* (the hand kissing) after the address, when the political elite would wait in an interminable line for a fleeting handshake with him, the latter-day equivalent of touching the royal robe.

Salinas also made intense use of the *gira*, or presidential tour. Throughout his term he spent two days of each week on the road. On a typical trip, a swing through Baja California during his first year in office, Salinas, carefully casual in a brown suede windbreaker and loafers, inaugurated two navy ships, a conference on ecology, and a boxing ring in a public park—during the morning. In the afternoon he handed out credits to dirt farmers in a string of villages many miles down the coast. At every stop he hugged grandmothers, kissed babies, and spread around his government's largesse.

Mexican culture was also part of Salinas's strategy to enhance his aura. At one point he sponsored a breathtaking mega-show of Mayan stele and Aztec snake goddesses at the Metropolitan Museum of Art in New York. "Splendors of Thirty Centuries," it was called, a bold bid to position Mexico's heritage right there alongside the Egyptian mummies and Greek marbles.

Salinas was a virtuoso of media relations. He read newspapers voraciously and understood the reporter's delight in anything that seemed like exclusive information from the chief. He was a master at talking without revealing. At the same time, correspondents in Mexico City got used to getting phone calls at dawn in which he browbeat them about some analysis in their copy or urged them to consider angles he deemed overlooked.

Salinas gained his aptitude for the exercise and display of power from his family. He was born into PRI aristocracy and raised from a young age to wield authority. His father, Raúl Salinas Lozano, had made a conspicuously successful career in the PRI system. Hailing from a northern fam-

President Carlos Salinas was a master of political showmanship, starting from the day of his inauguration, December 1, 1988

ily of modest means, Salinas Lozano had risen up through the ranks to become Secretary of Industry and Commerce from 1958 to 1964, under President Adolfo López Mateos. At the end of that *sexenio* his name was bandied about briefly as a possible PRI candidate for President.

Salinas Lozano's political lessons to his son Carlos carried two different and sometimes clashing messages. On one hand, the talk around the Salinas dinner table was of politics through the prism of PRI ideology and practice, at a time when the system was in its classic period. The family spoke of the winners and losers in the Mexican Revolution; of the rise and fall of famed caciques; of current power contests inside the party; and of the President, his gestures, chance remarks, and other hints about who was in his favor and who was not.

Young Carlos learned by direct experience that a feature of political success in the PRI system was financial prosperity. When his father was a mid-level bureaucrat, Carlos attended public school in Mexico City, rode the bus, and helped his schoolteacher mother to pinch pennies. By the time Salinas Lozano was Commerce Secretary, Carlos and his older brother, Raúl, had begun riding horseback at a fancy equestrian club in Mexico City. Both brothers became accomplished horsemen. They look effortlessly elegant in a 1960s photo taken with their father at a showring, both boys in velvet-covered hard hats, white ties, and jodhpurs. Carlos won a silver medal for Mexico in the equestrian competition at the Pan American Games in 1971.

Salinas Lozano's affluence once he attained the top ranks of government was regarded by his family, and by Mexican society, as routine. From the 1930s on, Mexico was largely closed to international trade and investment, and the state was the central force in the economy. With business heavily dependent on government contracts, the lines between the public and the private sector were often blurred. An executive receiving a substantial government contract would include in his cost calculations, as a matter of course, a commission for the official who approved the deal. Through *prestanombres*, third-party front men who took fees to sign their names to contracts, government officials often became silent partners in deals they authorized.

Alejo Peralta, a Mexican entrepreneur who built a copper-cable company into a billion-dollar manufacturing conglomerate, gratefully acknowledged that Salinas Lozano, as Commerce Secretary, had granted the permits that allowed him to import materials and machinery to set up his first plant. Before long Peralta became the primary supplier of cable to Mexico's state-owned electric and telephone companies—both monopolies. Although no documents have surfaced to confirm transactions, it is a common supposition in Mexico that Peralta's gratitude contributed to Salinas Lozano's upward mobility.

During Salinas Lozano's tenure as Secretary, Mexico enjoyed sustained growth, and his term was considered a solid success. The idea that his enrichment might be questioned did not enter the thinking of the Salinas family—or of the political class in general in that period.

It turned out that the cabinet post would be the zenith of Salinas Lozano's political career. In the succession of 1964, after it became clear that he would not be tapped as candidate, Salinas Lozano bet on the wrong horse, backing a rival of Gustavo Díaz Ordaz. Once Díaz Ordaz became President, he put the elder Salinas in the deep freeze. After that, Salinas Lozano was forced to invest his presidential ambitions in his two oldest sons, first Raúl and later Carlos. In the small, personalized world of the PRI, his father's example taught Carlos some basic procedures of self-protection in machine politics: pick your allies shrewdly; be loyal, but only to a point; keep your options open; depend on no one, but make others depend on you.

On the other hand, while wisdom about the PRI world was one part of the knowledge that Salinas Lozano passed down to his son, when he was a young man Salinas Lozano had also moved in another, very different world. He had studied for a master's degree in economics at Harvard (Carlos claimed that his father was "the first Mexican to graduate" from that university), and he encouraged Carlos to go there as well. Carlos lived in Cambridge for several years in the mid-1970s while completing two master's degrees, and he finished his Harvard doctorate in government and political economy in 1978. At Harvard, Carlos was exposed to a European and American tradition of rigorous academic research and critical analysis and also was immersed in progressive thinking about global economics and the lagging development of the Third World.

The two worlds of Carlos Salinas's upbringing converged in his presidency. On one hand, he carried out the most ambitious and forward-looking program of economic change in Mexico since the land reform and petroleum nationalization of Lázaro Cárdenas in the 1930s. However, he did so through the personalized top-down control and backroom deal making of the old-time authoritarian PRI.

Salinas adopted with a passion one of Mexico's great twentieth-century obsessions: the search for modernity. It was an especially enthralling fascination to a country as bound by its past as Mexico. Modernity's promise was that it would free the country from its historical cycles of tumult, allowing it to take its place among the orderly, prosperous, and technologically advanced nations.

For Salinas modernity went far beyond infrastructure like roads, airports, communications grids, and computer networks. Rather than close itself off to defend its much-battered sovereignty, Salinas argued, Mexico needed to do an about-face, to gain a secure place in the globalized world by seeking economic integration with its superpower neighbor, the United States. Mexico, he maintained, had to dismantle the obsolete paternalist state that had arisen from the revolution and give markets and independent groups in society the freedom to operate. "The majority of the reforms of our revolution have exhausted their effects and no longer guarantee the new development that our country demands," Salinas said in his first *informe*. Recent crises had shown that "a bigger state is not necessarily a more effective state, a property-owning state is not necessarily a more just one. The reality is that in Mexico, more government meant less response to the social needs of our people."

Salinas's modern Mexico would sell off to the private sector state business enterprises—government-owned banks, tourist hotels, funeral parlors—to raise money for core functions and social services. Slimmer, more efficient government agencies and greater private-sector growth and productivity would work better than government subsidies in advancing the condition of the needy, he believed.

Salinas was purposeful and disciplined in laying the economic foundations of the modernity he sought. His great achievement was the North American Free Trade Agreement, his signal contribution to Mexico's progress. Conceiving NAFTA, negotiating it with Washington and then Ottawa, and securing its ratification in all three countries were monumental tasks that occupied five of the six years of his term. The accord brought down the knotted net of regulations that protected Mexican business from foreign competition, opening up vast new markets to the country's entrepreneurs but also forcing them to change their ways, to learn to improve performance and control costs. NAFTA was admired and imitated in many developing countries, and it elevated Salinas (while he was in office at least) to the status of a world-class statesman.

But as he pursued *Salinastroika*, as the economic reforms came to be called, he was less clear about modernizing Mexican politics. He acknowledged that the economic opening should eventually bring more democratic government. But he contended that it was neither practical nor prudent to liberalize in both spheres at the same time. "Mexicans do not seek adventures, abrupt changes, or unnecessary risks," Salinas said in his second *informe*. "Electoral democracy cannot be attained by engaging in practices that jeopardize the country's stability or the continuity of its institutions."

Again, a year later, when he was facing a rising chorus of criticism of his administration as despotic, Salinas said, this time in an interview with

The New York Times, that he was in no hurry for a political opening. "I think each reform has its own rhythms, its own times," he said.

As his term advanced, Salinas seemed to conclude that as the main architect of the reforms, he was also the only one with the vision and clout to carry them out; that if he did not exercise uncompromising leadership, the reforms would founder. As the trade barriers came tumbling down, there could be no doubt that Salinas was serious about economic reform. But, as had often happened in Mexican history, his political reforms turned out to be mainly for show.

The two political sides of Carlos Salinas were evident from the day he took office. He named a cabinet that was so clearly split between modernizing technocrats and PRI dinosaurs that columnists immediately labeled it the "Janus cabinet."

To be his Finance Secretary, Salinas, who was only forty when he became President, named his peer Pedro Aspe Armella: thirty-eight, economist, doctorate from MIT. The Trade Secretary was Jaime Serra Puche: thirty-seven, economist, doctorate from Yale. The Budget Secretary was Ernesto Zedillo Ponce de León: thirty-six, economist, doctorate from Yale. Manuel Camacho, who was forty-two and had done master's degree studies at Princeton, was rewarded, for deft mediation he had carried on behind the scenes with Cárdenas and Clouthier during the election crisis, with the job of Mexico City mayor (which was still an appointed cabinet position). Salinas's chief of staff, who would become his most influential confidant, was José Córdoba Montoya: thirty-eight, trained in political economics at Stanford. To head the PRI, Salinas chose Luis Donaldo Colosio Murrieta: thirty-eight, economist, master's degree from the University of Pennsylvania.

At the same time Salinas bestowed a cabinet post on Carlos Hank González, El Profesor, the former mayor of Mexico City whose name was the first to spring to mind whenever the word "dinosaur" was mentioned. Hank became Tourism Secretary, but was really a political adviser to Salinas. As the Government Secretary, his second-in-command, Salinas chose one of the PRI system's darkest princes, Fernando Gutiérrez Barrios.

Don Fernando, who was sixty-one, was a professional intelligence cop. He had served for eighteen years in the Federal Security Directorate, the secret political police known by its Spanish initials as the DFS, and had risen to the top job. He had commanded the DFS agents deployed in Tlatelolco on October 2, 1968, who led the operation to capture the student strike leaders. That year the DFS, under Gutiérrez Barrios, also oversaw the work of an agent provocateur named Ayax Segura, who infiltrated students' meetings and goaded them to do something violent, in order to give his boss a justification for rounding them up.

In the 1970s, when Don Fernando was promoted to Deputy Government Secretary, the country's highest intelligence post, he was the authority assigned to eliminate the Liga Comunista 23 de Septiembre and other underground guerrilla organizations. The DFS, and other secret paramilitary squads under his authority, did their job. The guerrilla groups were dismantled, but the list of torture victims and of young people murdered and missing grew to hundreds.

Indeed, from the scraps of information Rosario Ibarra de Piedra had put together, she believed that Gutiérrez Barrios knew more about the disappearance of her son Jesús than anyone else in Mexico. So she had no illusions about Salinas, and from the first hours of his term Rosario, as everyone called her, pressed on with a crusade that had already established her as one of the most tenacious adversaries the PRI system ever confronted.

On the day of Salinas's inauguration, December 1, 1988, she and eleven other women staged a sit-in at the Angel de la Independencia in Mexico City. They had learned that Salinas was going to lay a wreath there with some of the heads of state who had come to pay homage to the longevity of the PRI and get to know its new President. Among them were Cuban President Fidel Castro and Daniel Ortega, the Sandinista President of Nicaragua, the reigning statesmen of the Latin American Left. That a convinced capitalist like Salinas was able to attract such guests was due to the PRI system, which, while dealing harshly with leftists at home, had supported Cuba and Nicaragua in their confrontations with the United States. Rosario found herself demonstrating against Latin leaders who should have been her ideological brethren.

Suddenly police rushed the monument and surrounded the protesters, closing in. The other women were terrified. "Don't you go getting weak knees now!" Rosario harangued as she walked up to the police and demanded they step back. "We are just like the Twelve Apostles. The Apostles didn't get weak knees!"

The police backed off; the women sat. Salinas never came. On the first day of his term Rosario fouled up his plans, at least a little.

It was a small consolation after she had just been defeated by Salinas in the election, her second presidential bid. In the years since her son Jesús Piedra Ibarra had disappeared, Rosario had devoted her life to finding him and hundreds of other missing Mexicans. She had adopted the form of a presidential campaign not because she coveted power or had a profound commitment to pluralism but because she discovered that it gave her credibility that she had lacked when she was only a distraught mother looking for a wayward son. Many Latin Americans had hesitated to accept her claims at a time when Mexico seemed to be a haven of freedom as one country after another in the region fell under rightist military dictatorship.

"When I became a candidate, I saw how people's thinking changed," Rosario said. "They said to themselves: 'Look at this woman. She is running for President, and she says that people have disappeared in Mexico. So it must be true.'"

The search for her son gave Rosario the slightly crazy fearlessness of someone living on the edge, in permanent conflict with the authorities. She and about eighty women who had missing relatives had amazed the public by undertaking a hunger strike in August 1978 in the atrium of the Mexico City cathedral, right under the windows of the National Palace. Police looking for Jesús (very probably under orders from Gutiérrez Barrios) had once seized and tortured Rosario's husband, a physician, breaking several of his ribs. Later, when Rosario ran for President for the first time in 1982, her husband received more than forty death threats.

She kept going after she discovered, in that first campaign, that she had an identity of her own. "First I had been the daughter of Mr. Ibarra, the civil engineer," she mused. "Then I was the wife of Dr. Piedra, the physician. Then I was the mother of Jesús Piedra Ibarra, the guerrilla fighter. But when I became a presidential candidate, I finally started to be Rosario Ibarra. I was up on the podium, and the people cried out, 'Rosario! Rosario!' That was when I began to be me.

"I have to say that I never minded being dependent on those men," she said, completing her thought. "They were men I loved: my father, my husband, my son. They were men I loved very much."

Even as her reputation grew, Rosario retained the moral authority of a housewife forced into politics by persecution. Her campaigns were low-budget, and she never adopted any of the modern trappings. She would have nothing of salon hairdos but always wore her shoulder-length wavy hair pulled back with a barrette. Her main base of operations was her living room, where she kept fresh roses in crystal vases. Her curtains were lace, her picture frames belle epoque. There were snapshots of Jesús, with his black eyebrows making him look thoughtful beyond his years. There were photos of her other children, of Rosario with Teddy Kennedy, with Fidel Castro.

For all her motherly spirit, Rosario associated mainly with narrow left-wing groups. Both of her presidential runs were backed by the Partido Revolucionario de los Trabajadores, the Revolutionary Workers Party, a Trotskyist organization. Although she never espoused violence or participated directly in an armed group, she took the position, because of her son, that armed resistance was not her choice, but she would not censure others for choosing it.

Moreover, Rosario was never a brilliant strategist. In 1988 she had failed to follow the lead of Heberto Castillo and resign her candidacy in favor of Cuauhtémoc Cárdenas. Consistent with her tactics from the heart, however, she immediately joined Cárdenas to fight the PRI's fraud once it was clear that he was the most popular opposition candidate.

Late on Salinas's inauguration day she and her apostles joined a march Cárdenas led down the Paseo de la Reforma. While Cárdenas was addressing the demonstrators, Rosario learned that plainclothes police had seized three people from the rally. She marched straight to the Government Secretariat on Avenida Bucareli and demanded to see Gutiérrez Barrios. He had not even laid out his pencils in his new office. Rosario, who had pursued him doggedly as he ascended through the regime, was the first person he saw as Government Secretary. He greeted her with a gentlemanly handshake. He was, as always, impeccably groomed, his pompadour arching up perfectly.

"Don Fernando," she said, also careful to preserve the courtesies, "the *sexenio* is getting off to a very bad start."

"I am sorry to hear it," he replied. Salinas's enforcer had no choice but to release the three people his police had snatched from the rally.

To consolidate his leadership, Salinas made several bold moves early in his term. The most stunning was the arrest, in January 1989, of Joaquín Hernández Galicia, the oil-workers union boss, known as La Quina.

La Quina was a welder who had risen up through the ranks of the 200,000-member union that represented the workers of Petróleos Mexicanos, the state petroleum monopoly known as Pemex. In 1988, after twenty-four years in the union leadership, he held only a ceremonial position in the hierarchy (head of the social-works committee), but everyone knew that he was the main man. He was called the "moral leader" of the union, a wild misnomer, since morality definitely was not an element of his management style.

With its center of operations in Ciudad Madero, a tar-coated town in the Gulf Coast state of Tamaulipas, the Mexican Petroleum Workers Union was a principality of corruption. Its most flamboyant phase began during the short-lived oil boom under President López Portillo, when the director of Pemex agreed to grant half of the company's construction contracts to the union without bidding. La Quina had also won an accord under which 2 percent of the value of all Pemex contracts was paid to "social projects" controlled by the union. The union also sold jobs, charging as much as ten thousand dollars for a white-collar position in the oil monopoly.

La Quina (his odd feminine nickname was a hybrid between his first name, Joaquín, and the Spanish word for "quinine," which he took for a childhood illness) was a small, fast-talking, wiry man with a mischievous gleam in his eye. His personal tastes were simple, and unlike many of his union sidekicks, he did not appear to lavish the union's riches on himself. He often dressed in a blue Pemex jumpsuit, and he lived in a nondescript house behind a white cinder-block wall in a proletarian neighborhood of Ciudad Madero. He liked to drive his own pickup truck, although he was always followed by a squad of rifle-cradling bodyguards. He had two families, one with his wife and another with a long-term mistress. He referred to them all as "my loved ones" and took care of his offspring on both sides. By the standards of Mexican labor, that made him a caring husband and father.

La Quina used the torrent of cash from Pemex to buy farms and build factories, stores, and housing, creating a socialist protectorate. Oil workers shopped at union supermarkets, ate union-grown produce, wore union-made shoes, convalesced in union hospitals, and mourned in union funeral homes—often at subsidized prices.

"We were not slaves to anyone," La Quina said of the union's heyday. "Not to the government, not to the Communists. We were the owners of our own factories and the lords of our own wages. Our money didn't come from Vanderbilt or Rockefeller or George Bush. It was money from the sweat of thousands of Mexican oil workers."

Supplicants lined up every day outside La Quina's home to ask him to give them work, resolve their property disputes, and mend their marriages. He defended them staunchly. His workers retired with pensions equivalent to their full salaries, and jobs were passed down from father to son to grandson.

"My workers were drunken and corrupt, but they were fearless," La Quina said, with typical candor. "They were never servile."

Unfortunately, La Quina's union was crippling Pemex. Once the boom went bust, the company's resources for new drilling and technology were severely strained as the union continued to leech away its cash. Negligent maintenance by the union was suspected by government investigators of being partly responsible for a fireball explosion in November 1984 at a Pemex liquid-gas storage terminal at San Juan Ixhuatepec near Mexico City, in which 452 people were killed.

La Quina, meanwhile, brooked no opposition. He and his inner circle came under suspicion after one unionist who challenged him died in a strange car accident. Another dissident was said by the union to have committed suicide, even though he had been shot three times.

For Salinas, La Quina represented another potential problem. Salinas and his economic advisers believed they would eventually have to open some areas of Pemex to foreign investment in order to obtain the huge amounts of capital needed to keep the company up to date. La Quina made it clear that there would be foreigners in Pemex over his dead body.

"I'm a scoundrel, but I'm a nationalist scoundrel," he fulminated. "I believe the property of the nation should be for the people, not for the President. My papa taught me that the oil should always be in the hands of the Mex-i-cans," he said, breaking up the word for emphasis.

On the morning of January 10, a little more than a month after Salinas became President, federal police and army troops in combat uniform mounted a lightning strike on La Quina's home in Ciudad Madero, blasting through his front door with a bazooka and hauling away the labor leader in his skivvies. The police reported that one of their detectives had been killed in a spray of bullets from La Quina's bodyguards. They also said they had found a stash of weapons in the house big enough to arm a brigade: two hundred Uzi submachine guns and thirty thousand rounds of ammunition.

The union immediately declared a nationwide wildcat strike. But it subsided within two days as approval for Salinas's action surged. Mexicans were surprised and encouraged by the assault on the oil union, that bastion of the PRI machine, and they admired Salinas for showing La Quina who was the real boss. A group of intellectuals, including Octavio Paz and Enrique Krauze, signed an open letter saying that Mexico "would advance, no doubt, on the road to democracy" as a result of the arrest. Overseas the arrest was taken as a sign that Salinas was serious about attacking corruption in order to attract foreign investment. With one stroke, Salinas did much to establish the authority he had not been able to get ratified through the polls, and to demonstrate that he had more than a rhetorical commitment to the modernization he had announced in his inaugural address.

But much about La Quina's arrest was anything but modern.

In the first place, Salinas was motivated in no small part by political and personal pique. He and La Quina hated each other. Back when he had been Budget Secretary, Salinas had imposed sealed bidding for well-drilling contracts that had previously gone to the union automatically,

Joaquín Hernández Galicia (front right), known as La Quina, was arrested on January 10, 1989, at his home in Ciudad Madero by army and police troops, who claimed they found a cache of hundreds of weapons

depriving La Quina of millions. The labor leader had retaliated during the presidential succession struggle. Hundreds of Mexican journalists were mailed an anonymous screed, "A Murderer in the Presidency." The pamphlet recalled a 1951 episode, documented in Mexico City newspapers, in which a Salinas family maid, all of twelve years old, had been shot and killed while playing with five-year-old Raúl Salinas, three-year-old Carlos, and an eight-year-old friend. The boys had found a .22-caliber rifle that their father had left in his closet—loaded, as it turned out—and decided to have a game of execution. The maid knelt down, and one of the boys shot her; the reports did not say which one. The authorities ruled it an accident.

Word got out in PRI channels that La Quina had paid for the mailing. Then, during Salinas's campaign, La Quina spoke admiringly of Cuauhtémoc Cárdenas and refrained from ordering the oil workers to vote for the PRI candidate.

If some of Salinas's motives for toppling La Quina were less than en-

lightened, the methods he countenanced to get it done were downright backward. After La Quina was arrested in Ciudad Madero, he was whisked by
jet to Mexico City and confined in an inner room at the Attorney General's headquarters. Guillermo González Calderoni, a top commander of
the Federal Judicial Police, was called in for the interrogation. He was instructed directly by the deputy attorney general who was his chief that the
job was very important, because he was going to help *el Señor Presidente*
project the idea overseas that he was tough on corrupt unions.

González Calderoni knew that the arsenal displayed to reporters was
made up of rifles belonging to the Mexican army that had been planted
in La Quina's home by the federal police during the hubbub of the arrest. It was his job, however, to get La Quina to sign a confession saying
that the guns belonged to him.

A cop with long experience, González Calderoni weighed the different techniques his police customarily used to make a prisoner talk. He
could pump mineral water laced with chili peppers up La Quina's nose,
or submerge his head in a bucket of excrement, or give him electric
shocks. But he surmised that La Quina was probably a shrewd and practical man, so crude coercion would probably not be necessary.

For many hours La Quina either showered his captors with insults or
lapsed into resolute silence. But González Calderoni was not in a hurry.
From time to time he strode into the room, shouted ferociously, and
marched out again, leaving La Quina with two milder inquisitors. Finally, when La Quina was weary and hungry, González Calderoni sat
down with him for a talk.

"Look, man, it's over for you," he said. "I know it, and you know it.
The orders to arrest you and bring you here came right from the top,
from the President. I wouldn't be doing this work if the President hadn't
ordered it."

González Calderoni spoke in terms of power, and that was La
Quina's language.

"Those aren't my weapons," La Quina retorted. "I know it, and you
know it."

"Look, Joaquín, I'm not going to touch a hair on your head, not one
hair," the cop said. "You are going to say that those weapons belong to
you, and you will say it because those are the instructions."

The hours dragged on into a second day. González Calderoni picked at La Quina with the news that his union's strike was petering out. When La Quina approached exhaustion, the policeman played a bluff. "When you are ready to sign a confession about *your* weapons, I will let your family go," he said, faking.

La Quina shivered. "You detained my loved ones? Where do you have them?" he asked.

"You tell me where you got those weapons, and I'll tell you where we have your family," said González Calderoni, bearing down.

"The weapons aren't mine," La Quina protested. "How am I supposed to tell you where I got them?"

González Calderoni waxed generous. "I'll help you with the story," he said. "But you will have to say why you needed those guns. Why don't you say that you had them to defend the headquarters of the union?"

The labor leader could see that he had lost a round in his fight with Carlos Salinas. The two men started to pencil out the details of his confession. "Do you want me to confess to the Kennedy assassination while I'm at it?" La Quina asked, determined to keep the dignity of his humor.

Afterward González Calderoni insisted that he had not tortured La Quina, and La Quina never claimed that he had been tortured. But several other union leaders arrested with him were tortured cruelly. In addition, after González Calderoni got the weapons confession, the Attorney General made sure that La Quina would remain in jail for the rest of Salinas's term by adding a charge of first-degree murder for the death of the federal agent who was allegedly killed by a gunshot from La Quina's compound.

"No one ever saw that body inside my house!" La Quina fumed when he spoke about it in the Mexico City jail cell where he was soon confined. "That was one dead man who just got up and walked away."

Eventually both La Quina and González Calderoni, separately, heard the story of the dead federal agent. He was a police detective named Gerardo Antonio Zamora, who had been assigned to help concoct the gun case against La Quina. How he was killed was never fully clarified (González Calderoni heard that a careless army soldier shot him accidentally), but the government's own autopsy showed that he had died of a bullet wound at least twenty-four hours before La Quina's arrest and not in Ciudad Madero but in Tampico, fifteen miles to the north. The federal police had solved the awkward problem of disposing of the body of one of their own men by shipping it down to Ciudad Madero to frame La Quina.

La Quina was convicted and sentenced to thirty-five years in prison. Soon after, González Calderoni fell out with the Salinas government. Accused by Salinas's Attorney General of taking bribes from drug traffickers and torturing suspects, he fled into exile in Texas. Mexico's attempt to extradite him failed after witnesses told an American judge that some of the evidence against him was fabricated.

"I don't remember exactly how many charges they threw at him," González Calderoni said when he thought about La Quina. "What I can tell you is this: That guy probably committed a lot of crimes. But he didn't commit the ones that Salinas put him in jail for."

He went on somewhat wistfully. "At the time, you think to yourself that what the President wants must be what the country needs. I see now that I was wrong. I recognize that I made mistakes. Lots of mistakes. But I assure you that when I did the jobs that I was assigned, I thought that I was serving my country."

In the first year of Salinas's term NAFTA was not part of his plans. He insisted repeatedly that he did not want a bilateral deal with the United States. After de la Madrid had spent his entire administration disciplining inflation to stabilize the peso, Salinas's priority was to restart growth. By early 1989 he was close to freeing the economy from one millstone. He was deep in negotiations to reduce Mexico's foreign debt, which amounted to 45 percent of the gross domestic product when he took office, on the brink of an accord that would decrease Mexico's debt burden by a huge $20 billion.

In February, Salinas, already feeling like he was on a roll, made a spin through Europe, meeting with British Prime Minister Margaret Thatcher and German Chancellor Helmut Kohl. To his dismay, both were lukewarm about Mexico. He went on to the World Economic Forum in Davos, Switzerland, the annual gathering of political leaders and big thinkers, and there he got even more yawns. He discovered that even if he was walking the fiscal straight and narrow, his country was not a particularly attractive investment. The world was regrouping into commercial mega-blocs, and Mexico wasn't part of the reshuffling.

Salinas was stung, diplomatically but also personally, by the indifference of the power countries. One morning in Davos he rousted his Trade Secretary, Jaime Serra Puche, out of sleep in the dawn hours. Breathlessly he ordered Serra, still in his pajamas, to approach American officials with a proposal to begin negotiations on a bilateral trade accord. If Mexico could provide investors with both cheap labor *and* privileged access to the U.S. market, Salinas said, its dance card would look very different.

Soon the campaign for NAFTA became a driving principle of domestic politics. In order to clean up Mexico to make it a suitable trading partner for the United States, Salinas accelerated his efforts to control the drug trade and capture the most notorious drug lords. The privatization of state industries went into high gear, and neoliberal laws were hustled through the Congress by the PRI's majority.

After 1988 it was clear to all sides that the old election system had collapsed. As his NAFTA project got going, Salinas also moved to reorganize Mexico's elections. The PAN regarded Salinas as a de facto ruler. But the conservative party took the view that he was, for better or worse, still the President, and decided to build an informal pact with Salinas.

In 1989 and 1990 the PRI and the PAN joined forces to pass laws and constitutional amendments that initiated a thorough renovation of Mexico's elections institutions. The main achievement of that round of reforms was a new agency, the Federal Electoral Institute. Whereas under the old laws elections had been entirely managed by the Government Secretary and his henchmen, the new institute was separate from the Secretariat and endowed with its own staff of professional, nonpartisan elections experts. The Government Secretary continued to be the ultimate elections authority but was no longer the only one. The Secretary became the chairman of an executive council that included federal lawmakers from different parties, party representatives, and—in the most important advance—six nonpartisan citizens.

For the first time rules were written requiring the media to balance its campaign coverage. José Newman's old voter registry (the one with the special codes to mark the PRI's phantom voters) was scrapped and a fresh one was ordered up.

However, amid many concessions the PRI made in the negotiations, it also achieved one crucial gain to protect its hold on power. The PRI insisted on a statute that automatically added to the margin of the leading party in a congressional election, boosting it up to 51 percent of the seats in the national legislature. Since the PRI expected to be Mexico's biggest party indefinitely, the measure, called the "governability clause," assured it of a congressional majority for just as long.

As these reforms were nearing completion, the governor's election in Baja California, on July 2, 1989, produced an unprecedented outcome. When the PAN candidate, Ernesto Ruffo Appel, won by an irrefutable margin, Salinas quickly accepted the victory. Baja California Norte became the first state to be governed by the opposition since the Mexican Revolution. Salinas won approval both abroad and at home for displaying a new tolerance for pluralism.

Yet many in the PAN who were followers of Manuel Clouthier, doubts about Salinas arose again after Maquío was killed in a strange car crash on October 1, 1989, on a highway in Sinaloa. His supporters were not satisfied that there was a thorough investigation, and the suspicion of political murder was never dispelled.

Nonetheless, Salinas continued to consort with the PAN, even while he engaged simultaneously in a brutal confrontation with Cuauhtémoc Cárdenas and the organization he founded, the Party of the Democratic Revolution. The discrimination against Cárdenas's followers was so stark that it became known, with sour irony, as Salinas's "selective democracy." The unsolved murders of Cárdenas's campaign aides, Francisco Xavier Ovando and Román Gil, set the tone for the blood feud that the Salinas government waged. The President never openly encouraged the attacks, but neither did he categorically condemn them.

Salinas harbored a visceral enmity for Cárdenas, in part because of the vituperation that Cárdenas had heaped on him in the presidential election, in part out of lingering insecurity about his own mandate. The

PRD in turn rejected Salinas's government as illegitimate. Cárdenas maintained that Salinas had come to power through a palace coup that was no less lawless for having been accomplished with ballots instead of bazookas, and refused to collaborate with him in any way. Salinas's loathing of Cárdenas was one reason why he hesitated to embrace democracy more fully. He seemed to fear that if he opened the system too much, his nemesis would resurge.

The intensity of the clash also stemmed from the social origins of the PRD's supporters. Because of the memory of Lázaro Cárdenas's land reform, his son's party attracted a militant following of discontented peasant farmers, especially in agricultural states like Michoacán (the Cárdenas family's home), Guerrero, Oaxaca, Puebla, and Morelos. Before the PRD, the PRI had dominated the confederation of *campesinos*, the peasant farmers. But small farming had been devastated by the neglect of PRI governments and by their terrible macroeconomic management. Cárdenas's party spread quickly in the countryside, becoming a resistance front for *campesinos* doing battle with PRI warlords, their enforcers in the police, and trigger-happy army troops. In some regions the presence of the PRD disrupted partnerships between PRI authorities and local marijuana and cocaine dealers. Since the peasants had never given up the custom of carrying rifles, which they acquired during the Mexican Revolution, the arrival of the PRD in villages long controlled by the PRI often led to armed hostilities.

The most intense assault on the young opposition party came in 1990, after elections in several states where PRD candidates contended for the first time against the PRI for town mayoral posts. In Guerrero, where the balloting was in December 1989, the state's elections system was so corrupt that in many towns it simply was not possible to determine the vote results. The PRI decided not to give up any towns at all, and the PRD, taking Cárdenas's example from 1988, refused to roll over. In early January its activists occupied twenty of Guerrero's seventy-five town halls, inaugurating alternative mayors who went to work administering village affairs.

The governor of Guerrero was José Francisco Ruiz Massieu, a rising star in the PRI who was close to Salinas both politically and personally. The two men had been college buddies at the UNAM, and Ruiz

Massieu married Salinas's sister Adriana. Although the couple had divorced, Salinas and Ruiz Massieu remained friendly. An urbane and well-spoken politician in the style of the PRI elite, Ruiz Massieu wrote essays on Mexican democracy and frequented the circle of Mexico City intellectuals sympathetic to Salinas's modernization. But when Salinas made it clear he wanted to go hard on the PRD, Ruiz Massieu rose to the task with discipline.

In February 1990 the PRD stepped up its protests against the elections fraud by taking them to the airports of the tourist resorts of Acapulco and Ixtapa. On February 27, Guerrero state police beat one protester to death and shot another to halt the airport demonstrations. Salinas's Government Secretary, Gutiérrez Barrios, invited the PRD leaders from Guerrero to peace talks in Mexico City, but they soon learned that the invitation was a decoy. At dawn on March 6, as the PRD leaders were leaving their villages for the meeting with Gutiérrez Barrios, Governor Ruiz Massieu dispatched eight hundred state police to evict PRD protesters from eight town halls. In Ometepec, a village in the southern sierra, the police moved in shooting. The PRD shot back, and at the end of the day there were four dead (three of them policemen), eight PRD followers missing, thirty wounded, and a dozen arrested.

"The state has returned to normal," Governor Ruiz Massieu announced in the evening. "Peace has been restored."

In Michoacán, where the PRD won 53 of the state's 113 mayoral posts in elections in the same period, there were dozens of clashes between PRD and PRI followers, and the deaths rose to the dozens. But as the discord fell out in blurry incidents in backcountry villages, the violence was little noticed outside the regions where it was taking place.

Still, some of Salinas's political advisers, particularly Manuel Camacho, warned him that he would soon be called to account for the vendetta if he did not distance himself from it. And indeed, in June 1990 Americas Watch, a human rights group based in New York, published a report recounting the rural killing succinctly titled *Human Rights in Mexico: A Policy of Impunity*.

As it happened, in the same period Rosario Ibarra finally, after tireless browbeating, got Salinas to meet for the first time with her and half a dozen other mothers of disappeared children. For the mothers it was a stunning encounter. Whereas earlier Presidents had shunned them and denied that the government had ever held their missing children, Salinas was cordial, even solicitous, saying he was deeply troubled by the disappearances. Then, at the close of the meeting, he promised them they would have news of their children "within twenty days."

The mothers were overwhelmed. "When the most powerful man in the country tells you that yes, finally, you are going to know something, it really ignites a mother's hope," Rosario said. Salinas asked to have a photo taken with the group. In the image even Rosario is grinning.

On June 6, 1990, almost exactly twenty days after he met with the mothers at Los Pinos, Salinas created the National Human Rights Commission, the first ever in Mexico. Even though it was a government agency, it was endowed with a modicum of independence to investigate abuses. At the inauguration, Salinas told the agency to proceed with confidence to expose the misdeeds of government officials and security forces, no matter what their rank.

The commission began its work with a task ordered by Salinas, to investigate a killing that had nothing to do with the PRD. It was the murder, on May 21, 1990, of a human rights crusader, Norma Corona Sapién, who had been battling drug dealers and their police accomplices in the state of Sinaloa. After a suprisingly aggressive investigation, the commission issued a report demonstrating that a top federal police commander, Mario Alberto González Treviño, had ordered the killing. He was promptly arrested.

The local elections in the State of México, a populous state that curves around Mexico City, were held on November 11, 1990. It was another race where Cárdenas's PRD competed against the PRI for the first time, and once again PRI fraud reduced the outcome to chaos. On December 12, Heberto Castillo, who by then had folded his own political party into the PRD and was part of its national leadership, went with his wife, Teresa, to speak at a fraud protest in the country town of Tejupilco.

Castillo felt his chest tighten when he climbed onto the rattletrap podium and saw dozens of state riot police on guard inside the town hall. He feared that someone from the PRD would summon the crowd to seize the building. But none of the speakers called for rash action. Instead, one after another they demanded more respect for elections. When it was his turn, Castillo refined the point. "The purpose of the Party of the Democratic Revolution is to open legal pathways to democracy," he said, dwelling on the word "legal." "We have to use the law and the Constitution to defend our rights."

No sooner were his words out of his mouth than a scuffle erupted between the police and a cluster of village women at the back of the crowd. A woman shouted that a policeman had grabbed her breast. The police fired tear gas into the crowd and sealed off the exits from the plaza. Trapped in the riot, Castillo's wife saw police beating women and children with rifles. She also saw PRD militants nearly stone one policeman to death and begin to lynch two others, stopping only when PRD leaders intervened.

By the end, two policemen and one villager had been killed and dozens of townspeople had been shot or beaten. The PRI president, Luis Donaldo Colosio, said the bloodshed had exposed "the real face of PRD intolerance." PRI officials blamed Castillo and accused him in a press bulletin of murder.

Instead of fleeing, as the authorities apparently hoped he would, Castillo went directly to the state governor's office and turned himself in. Taken aback, state officials declined to carry out their own arrest warrant.

"It is very dangerous to attack a tiger in its cage," Castillo wrote of the incident in a column in *Proceso*. "If you attack a crowd, like the one in Tejupilco, it will respond. I hope, Carlos Salinas, that you will reflect on this. That was not the way to social peace. What we need is respect for democracy."

After Tejupilco the PRD killings continued. (PRD records would later document that 250 PRD activists were slain during Salinas's *sexenio*.) The party took Salinas at his word and brought the cases of its dead assiduously before the National Human Rights Commission. But in cases involving the PRD, the commission proved ineffective. Out of eighty-two rulings the commission issued under Salinas in PRD cases, not one was fully executed by state authorities. Only 8 percent of the party's murder cases were ever clarified.

Nor did Salinas's commission make any progress in clarifying the case of Jesús Piedra Ibarra or any but a few of the missing people on Rosario's roster. Yet Rosario learned that Salinas had reprinted the photo of her standing beside him at Los Pinos with a big smile on her face and had it sent to Mexican embassies to distribute to foreign human rights groups.

It made her so mad that she would shout, "Judas! Judas!" every time Salinas's name was mentioned at a rally.

In August 1991, when Salinas was halfway through his term and nearing the apex of his power and prestige, Mexico held nationwide elections for federal senators and deputies and for seven state governors.

Mexicans were mesmerized by the dynamic, self-assured control Salinas had asserted over their rowdy country. The NAFTA negotiations were fully under way, giving Mexicans the heady experience of sitting at the table as peers with the United States and Canada. The economy was finally emerging from a decade of doldrums.

So when the people went to the polls in August, they gave a startling, resounding vote of confidence to Salinas and the ruling party. The PRI won 61 percent of the congressional vote, gaining invincible majorities in both houses and giving Salinas the power to make laws without having to seek any support from the opposition.

But one election that both Salinas and the public were watching very closely that day was the governor's race in the state of San Luis Potosí. There, things went wrong for the President.

The PRI candidate in San Luis was Fausto Zapata Loredo, "a man of the system," as he described himself. Zapata had fully expected to give Salinas, his President, an important victory in San Luis, but it did not work out that way. Zapata won the difficult election, but Salinas was hardly grateful. Without knowing quite how, Zapata became a shadow on the portrait that Salinas was painting of a progressive Mexico. In the course of the events Zapata learned a great deal about the ambiguities in Salinas's approach to democratic change.

Zapata was an example of the sort of talented Mexican drawn to the PRI. Since his youth his views had been mainstream: he was suspicious of the United States but not a national chauvinist, and he embraced the ideals of the Mexican Revolution, albeit loosely. Zapata was articulate and good-looking, if short of stature; he was a natural diplomat. From adolescence he had worked as a journalist in his hometown, the capital of San Luis Potosí (the state and its capital have the same name). Since the PRI was the only party in Mexico with a nationwide structure and direct channels to power, it offered Zapata, and ambitious young people like him, a route out of the provinces and into national play.

Zapata had been a PRI federal deputy when he was still in his twenties. He did well in the Congress and caught the eye of Luis Echeverría, who chose Zapata, when he was just thirty, to be his presidential spokesman. Zapata's job was to inform the press occasionally and control it continually, by rewarding publications that favored the President and undermining those that were critical. Zapata handled his responsibilities artfully, and toward the end of the *sexenio* Echeverría rewarded him by making him a senator. Later he was ambassador to Italy and China.

The trouble for Zapata in the San Luis governor's race was his unusually strong opponent. Salvador Nava Martínez was an elderly ophthalmologist who was admired throughout the state as a long-standing leader of democratic causes.

Nava had started out in the PRI, forming an association in the 1950s to represent the nascent middle class of urban professionals in San Luis. In 1958 he had won election to be mayor of the state capital. There Nava clashed with a formidable PRI cacique, a rancher named Gonzalo N. Santos, who liked to be called the Sorrel Stallion. His followers were organized into gunslinger posses that enforced his control in San Luis as Santos served a term as state governor and then became an "adviser" to two other governors whom he selected to succeed him. With his power base in the countryside, the Sorrel Stallion regarded Nava as a city-boy upstart. When the election for San Luis governor came around in 1961, Santos blocked the PRI from nominating the doctor.

Nava surprised both Santos and the state PRI by running anyway as an independent. The PRI made sure he was defeated, and the army laid siege to the San Luis capital to prevent protests. But Nava's campaign,

Even though he was suffering from cancer, Dr. Salvador Nava waged a strong campaign against the PRI candidate for the post of governor of San Luis Potosí in 1991

which centered on his call for greater political freedom, quickly coalesced into a statewide movement.

On September 15, 1961, while the outgoing PRI governor was presiding at Independence Day celebrations in the main square of San Luis city, the lights went out and shooting erupted. Several reporters in the crowd saw the barrage begin with sniper fire from the roof of the city hall, aimed into the governor's palace directly across the plaza. But then army soldiers posted in the plaza responded by firing into the crowd (in a pattern that eerily prefigured the events at Tlatelolco seven years later). The official toll was six dead and twelve wounded. But at least forty people with gunshot injuries, including both *priístas* and Nava supporters, were seen lying in the hallways at the city hospital. With no independent press or human rights groups to investigate at the time, the facts of the massacre were consigned to mystery.

A cub reporter for a local newspaper, Fausto Zapata, then twenty, was in the main hall of the governor's palace when the gunfire broke out, sending bullets ricocheting off the walls around him. Zapata knew Nava—whose brother was the Zapata family's physician—and he doubted that Nava would have started the shooting. But the Mexican army accused Nava of sedition. He was jailed briefly, then released. Two years later, however, army agents picked him up again and gave him a beating that left him unconscious.

After that Nava withdrew from politics and busied himself with his eye practice for two decades. In 1983 he got the itch again, risked a second run for San Luis mayor, and won. He governed decently, enhancing his profile and renewing his political ambitions. But in 1990, when he was seventy-five, Nava learned he had prostate cancer. He underwent a severe course of chemotherapy in Mexico City.

Because of Nava's illness, as the San Luis gubernatorial vote approached, both Zapata and Salinas were relatively confident that the doctor would not run. Zapata believed the time was right for him, but he thought it would be a mistake to run against Nava, a proven democrat with an untarnished name, the courtly eye doctor who strolled the streets of San Luis in a tweed cap, greeted by patients and supporters wherever he went. Salinas even made the unusual move of going to the hospital to visit Nava, an outspoken opponent of the PRI, in an attempt to assess the doctor's health and intentions. But neither Salinas nor Zapata got a clear answer about whether Nava wanted to attempt another campaign.

One day in January 1991 Salinas invited Zapata to ride in the presidential helicopter. "If Nava runs for governor, can you beat him?" Salinas asked. Zapata was surprised by the blunt question. Political calculations seemed to be buzzing like voltage in Salinas's head.

Zapata ventured that the doctor's base of support had probably eroded during the long years when he was out of politics, so Zapata could probably beat him. That seemed to be all Salinas wanted to hear. The President gave the word, and the PRI spun into action to launch the campaign of Fausto Zapata for governor of San Luis Potosí.

One week later Nava announced his own candidacy. He was backed by a rare coalition that included both the PRD and the PAN. It embodied Salinas's worst political fears, a reincarnation of the one that had emerged in 1988 to challenge his right to take presidential power.

The PRI machine in San Luis went to work for Zapata at full throttle.

Government offices and vehicles were mobilized, and the press, led by local television, turned ferociously against the doctor. Zapata portrayed himself as a modern, globe-trotting politician and, abandoning any deference, belittled Nava as an outmoded grandpa while also warning darkly that the left wing of Nava's coalition was prone to violence. Nava, knowing that the race would probably be his last, traded blow for blow, blaming Zapata for all the corruption in the state.

However, a new factor in the San Luis contest substantially altered the terms of the competition. For the first time independent Mexican elections observers scrutinized both the campaign and the vote. Before the election a group of researchers from the UNAM did a study of the voter rolls, concluding that the lists had been shaved in urban areas, Nava's stronghold, and inflated in the pro-PRI countryside. On Election Day more than three hundred Mexicans, with special training as observers, watched the balloting. They were organized by Sergio Aguayo.

Through the 1970s and 1980s Aguayo had juggled academics and activism. He was teaching at the prestigious Colegio de México while also working on an ambitious list of social projects to help Indians in the southern state of Chiapas, assembly-plant workers in the north, and immigrants heading illegally for the United States.

The phases of Aguayo's life were marked by death threats. The first one came after 1968, back when he was a young radical in Guadalajara. Pursued by a squad of thugs whom the PRI organized to combat the student rebellion, Aguayo was forced to leave Guadalajara to hide in the anonymity of Mexico City. The monkish discipline he adopted in his academic studies stayed with him for years, until he became a university professor.

The second threat came in 1981 from political police in Chiapas who wanted to put an end to Aguayo's social work with the restive Indians. The note left in Aguayo's car wasted no words: either he left the state immediately or he would be dead. It made him realize that he and other government foes needed more solid organizations to backstop their risky work.

Three years later Aguayo founded the Mexican Academy for Human

Rights. Unlike Salinas's human rights commission, Aguayo's academy had no connection to the government. It both investigated violations and educated Mexicans about their rights. Among the academy's board members were intellectual luminaries like Carlos Fuentes and Elena Poniatowska. In 1990 Aguayo was elected the academy's president. The day afterward he received a visit in Mexico City from an old friend, Robert Pastor, who was running former President Jimmy Carter's elections observation program at the Carter Center in Atlanta. Pastor invited Aguayo to travel to Haiti as part of Carter's contingent to observe a presidential election there.

Aguayo had his doubts. "I'm going with Yankee imperialists to a foreign country to judge somebody else's election?" he wondered. But he went. For four days he hiked around the hills of northern Haiti, amid the crudest poverty in the hemisphere, watching Haitians choose a leader to help them recover from the Duvalier dynasty. Aguayo's teammate was a man from the Philippines who had been part of the movement for free elections that toppled the dictator Ferdinand Marcos. By the time Aguayo came home, he had become convinced of the need for a national clean-elections movement in Mexico.

Mobilizing the observers in San Luis Potosí was Aguayo's first move toward that goal. He joined forces with a local human rights group, and most of the observers were from San Luis. The volunteers were taught that observing an election was an exercise of their civil rights. Aguayo was amazed by the response. From peasant farmers to society dames, the volunteers were delighted to participate in politics without getting tangled up in the political parties.

On Election Day, 330 volunteers managed to cover about a third of the twenty-two hundred polling stations in the state. They saw PRI ward heelers seduce voters with cash and free lunches and drive Nava's representatives away. They watched as thousands of Nava supporters with valid voter cards were barred from voting because their names had been shaved from the list. Their report was published in full in *La Jornada*.

"We have doubts about the legality of the entire election process," the observers said. "The irregularities we describe lead us to question the legitimacy and morality of the election we observed."

Aguayo had been tempted throughout the campaign to side with Dr.

Nava. He was sympathetic to Nava's uncomplicated call for democracy and to the grassroots movement Nava had galvanized. But Aguayo believed that his own clean-elections campaign would only grow if it remained nonpartisan. It was an unorthodox view, because Mexicans had little experience with civil rights activism separate from political parties and ideological debates. Indeed, Aguayo's stance infuriated many of Nava's followers, who wanted Aguayo to adopt their position and issue a direct call to have the election annulled.

As Zapata basked in ovations on election night, he felt satisfied: he had turned out the votes and kept his pledge to Salinas. He had not commanded any Election Day fraud operations; he simply let the PRI machine go about its business. According to the official returns, Zapata crushed Nava by nearly two to one: 329,292 votes for him, 170,646 for the doctor. In his victory speech at PRI campaign headquarters he called the results "a vote of confidence for President Carlos Salinas de Gortari."

But Zapata failed to anticipate the impact of the reports of Aguayo's observers. Only a small percentage of the poll-station reports were challenged by Nava's poll watchers at the close of balloting. So Zapata felt confident because of his wide margin, that Nava would not be able to contest the vote. But Nava was persuaded by the observers' conclusions that the irregularities put the whole election in doubt. On election night he pulled his representatives out of the state electoral commission, denouncing the whole system as corrupt and partial.

Salinas, to whom Zapata dedicated his vote of confidence, did not congratulate the governor-elect on election night. Instead, he called to instruct Zapata curtly to avoid violent disorders at all costs. "We are in very important trade negotiations with the United States," Salinas said, forthright about his overriding concern.

Salinas grew even cooler after Zapata made a tactical error at a press conference the day after the vote. A reporter from La Jornada issued a challenge: Would Zapata be willing to reopen the ballot boxes for a complete recount?

Zapata hesitated, contemplating the logistical headache, but finally said yes. The reporters rushed away with their story. Only afterward did

Zapata think back to 1988. After the presidential election the opposition had demanded a recount of the original vote tallies and of the ballots themselves. Salinas had managed to bury that demand in the first three years of his *sexenio*, and he was just then negotiating a final deal to have the ballots destroyed.

Salinas put through a call after reading Zapata's statement in the papers the next day. "I understand that you are willing to open the ballot boxes for a recount?" Salinas asked icily. Zapata, confirming what he had said, heard only silence on the other end.

Nava confounded Zapata by refusing to present any formal complaints to state election authorities and embarking instead on a campaign of nonviolent resistance to block Zapata from taking office. Eight days after the election Nava packed the stately Plaza of the Founders in San Luis city with a somber rally, haunted by the music he chose as the theme of his protests, the lament of Hebrew slaves from an opera by Verdi.

"I have to ask for your pardon," Nava told his followers. "I trusted the highest authorities, who promised that they would respect the triumph of the majority. We trusted, but our trust was betrayed."

Nava's voters waved their registration cards slowly over their heads, as if to let Salinas see them. YOU FAILED US, SALINAS! read the posters they held aloft.

One day Nava's followers closed down all five highways leading to San Luis city. A group of women started a sit-in of prayers and fasting on the statehouse steps, blocking Zapata's way to the governor's office. Women marched through the streets banging pots and comparing Zapata to the Chilean dictator Augusto Pinochet. Nava's movement, despite its fervor, retained a certain country civility. A placard at one rally read: FAUSTO, PLEASE STEP DOWN. THE MARTÍNEZ FAMILY.

As Nava's protests intensified, Zapata started to suspect that Salinas was also working against him. The President ordered him to cancel a huge rally he planned for his inauguration. He started to get telephone calls, sometimes two or three times a day, from Government Secretary Gutiérrez Barrios. On orders from the President, Gutiérrez Barrios said, he wanted to brief Zapata about secret intelligence he had gathered, showing that Nava's movement was about to turn to violent insurrection.

Later, when Zapata sought to sort out the events, he realized that the intelligence reports were false, apparently designed to throw him off balance.

One day Zapata traveled to Mexico City at the invitation of Raúl Salinas, Carlos's older brother. Raúl had no formal role in government at that time, but he was one of his brother's busiest and most trusted emissaries. Zapata and Raúl went for a slow stroll around a lake in Chapultepec Park. "Fausto, you should be looking for a solution to this crisis, to help out the President," Raúl said.

Then, coming to his point, he added: "If I were you, I would not want to become an enemy of Carlos Salinas."

The President began negotiating with Nava without informing Zapata. While Gutiérrez Barrios was telling Zapata that Nava's movement was on the brink of insurrection, the President hosted Nava at Los Pinos, offering to oust Zapata and install him as governor. Salinas, however, wanted to retain the right to name the senior officers in Nava's cabinet. Nava refused.

During Zapata's modest inaugural on September 26, Nava held a counter-inauguration, where he took an oath as the "legitimate and moral governor" of San Luis Potosí. Beside him on the podium were Cuauhtémoc Cárdenas for the PRD and Diego Fernández de Cevallos, a veteran leader of the PAN. Nava pledged "to stop the usurper, night after night, from even dreaming that he will ever govern this state!"

The President consented to attend Zapata's inauguration, but used the few hours he spent in San Luis to distance himself from his party's new governor. Still, Zapata pressed on, sustained by the belief that despite the irregularities, the majority of San Luis voters had chosen him. Four days after his inauguration he mobilized a group of *priístas* and tried to enter his new offices, barging through the Nava protesters on the statehouse steps. An ugly scuffle broke out and several of the fasting women were trampled.

On September 28, Dr. Nava, in a windbreaker and running shoes, set out from San Luis city at the head of a procession of thousands of protesters to walk 265 miles to Mexico City. He called it his March for Dignity. His complexion was sallow and he was obviously in pain from the cancer. Along the way he was briefly joined by Cuauhtémoc Cárdenas and his son Lázaro; by Luis H. Álvarez, the president of the PAN; and by Vicente Fox, the PAN candidate for governor in Guanajuato who was embroiled in a battle of his own against fraud, Nava expected to reach Mexico City by October 15.

On October 9, Gutiérrez Barrios summoned Zapata to his Avenida Bucareli offices. He was very uneasy. "The President asks you to present the state congress with your resignation as governor," he said. "As you know, I am here to carry out his orders."

Gutiérrez Barrios explained that he had an awkward problem. On Salinas's instructions he had done an analysis of a three-volume dossier of election irregularities that Nava's movement had presented to the President. The only formal complaint that Nava ever lodged, it was said to include evidence of fraud in 341 ballot boxes. But, the Government Secretary said, Nava's people, apparently out of haste, had included documents from seventy-eight boxes where Nava—not Zapata—had won. On that basis alone, the opposition's evidence was insufficient to overturn the election, Gutiérrez Barrios told Zapata. Now he would have to suppress his own study, he said uncomfortably, to conform to Salinas's decision.

Zapata went to see Salinas at Los Pinos. He said he would agree to resign, citing his loyalty to the system. But he insisted on one point of pride. "You know that I won those elections," Zapata said, and Salinas did not disagree. In the resignation statement he gave later that day, Zapata said he would "never put at risk the peaceful relations among the people of San Luis Potosí."

Nava halted his march and went back to San Luis. Salinas named another *priísta*, Gonzalo Martínez Corbalá, to be interim governor. The state PRI promptly rebelled. In the last of the ironies for Zapata, he had to step in to quell a mutiny on his behalf by his own supporters, by making it clear to them that he would not retract the resignation that he had never wanted to present.

Even then Zapata, still a *priísta*, did not break with Salinas. He accepted the post of Mexican consul in Los Angeles and continued to serve as a diplomat until the end of the *sexenio*. But he disengaged from party politics and moved for a time to the private sector as a media executive.

Reflecting later on the debacle in San Luis, Zapata called it "an au-

thoritarian act behind a democratic mirage . . . Salinas looked for strata-
gems that would make people think that in Mexico, by magic, reforms
were under way to make the country into a democratic regime supported
by the President," Zapata said. "I don't think he ever intended to carry
out a real political reform."

Salvador Nava died of cancer in San Luis on May 18, 1992.

There was a postscript to the crisis. When it came time in 1993 to replace Martínez Corbalá as governor, Salinas came up with an unusual
candidate: Martínez Corbalá. Since the Mexican Revolution the only
constitutional principle that had been consistently upheld was the one
barring government officials from reelection. But Salinas was so popular
at that point he began to toy with the idea of a second term. He apparently reasoned that if the people of San Luis would allow Martínez Corbalá, the appointed governor, to run to become the elected governor, it
might open the way toward reelection of the President.

Martínez Corbalá, a PRI veteran, warned Salinas that it would never
work, and he was right. At the PRI state convention the rank and file
balked, and Martínez Corbalá had to withdraw his candidacy. If Salinas
had reelection hopes after that, he kept them to himself.

San Luis Potosí was not the only election in August 1991 in which Salinas fiddled with the results. The governor's election in the state of Guanajuato, just south of San Luis in the cactus-desert plateau of central
Mexico, also took place on August 18. The three main candidates were
Ramón Aguirre, who had been the feckless PRI mayor of Mexico City
during the 1985 earthquake; Porfirio Muñoz Ledo, who broke from the
PRI with Cuauhtémoc Cárdenas in 1988, running for the PRD; and Vicente Fox for the PAN.

As an indication of the status of the rule of law in Guanajuato at the
time, none of the three leading candidates had met the registration qual-
ifications. Muñoz Ledo had not been a resident of Guanajuato for five
years before the election, as the law required. Adopting an offensive defense, Muñoz Ledo pointed out that Fox had missed the legal deadlines
for renouncing his Spanish citizenship (Fox's mother, Mercedes Quesada, was born in Spain). Muñoz Ledo also revealed that Aguirre had
forged his voter registration in the state and did not even have a valid cre-

dential as a member of the PRI. In the end all three scraped through on the creative jurisprudence of Muñoz Ledo, who argued that if the elections authorities disqualified one, they would have to disqualify them all.

Fox's campaign had started out erratically. The Guanajuato state PAN was afflicted with the syndrome of the predestined loser that so often handicapped the party at the national level; it was not organized to compete. Fox would drive his Suburban with a couple of aides to a country village where his appearance had been scheduled for weeks and find no platform, no sound system, and, worst of all, no people. But Fox kept his good humor. He would take off down the street in broad strides, knocking on doors along the way, his small campaign crew scrambling behind him.

"Señora, take off your apron," Fox would say heartily to astonished housewives who came out to see a stranger in a beard and dungarees, looking very much like a cowhand. "Come out and meet your new governor!"

Fox bounded through open-air markets, the nerve center of any Guanajuato village, handing out business cards with his name and instructions on registering to vote. What struck people most about Fox was his determination to win. Before Mexicans would take the risk of voting for the opposition, they scrutinized the candidates carefully to make sure they wouldn't buckle when the PRI bore down.

Soon Fox's campaign took off, clearly inspiring more enthusiasm than Aguirre's machine. But on Election Day, Fox suffered another case where "*se cayó el sistema,*" the system crashed—only this time, depressingly, it was his system. At his family's boot factory in León, the business capital of Guanajuato, Fox set up a bank of computers to conduct his own vote tally. But the system suffered a technical failure almost as soon as data started to flow in from the polling stations. From then on, the succession of events was all too familiar: PAN poll watchers called in frantically from the countryside to report the usual roster of PRI fraud tactics; Aguirre declared victory shortly after the polls closed; the opposition felt cheated and helpless.

It was almost too much even for Fox's stubborn optimism. But he received a boost from an unlikely quarter, from a pair of leftist outsiders who had come to Guanajuato as informal elections observers.

Jorge G. Castañeda was the scion of a dynasty of the system; his fa-

ther, Jorge Castañeda, had been López Portillo's Foreign Relations Secretary. But the younger Castañeda was anything but a PRI loyalist. He
was a left-wing gadfly, an *enfant terrible* intellectual to whom nothing
was sacred. His friend was another young apostate from the system,
Adolfo Aguilar Zinser. In the 1970s, after finishing graduate studies at
Harvard, Aguilar Zinser had been a protégé of Luis Echeverría's, leading
a think tank the President set up to propagate his Third World philosophy. But during the next decade Aguilar Zinser moved away from the
establishment until he was drawn to Cárdenas in 1988. By 1991 he had
begun organizing anti-PRI, pro-democracy citizens groups.

Both Castañeda and Aguilar Zinser were pleasantly surprised by what
they saw of Fox in action, even though neither had much in common
ideologically with the PAN candidate. So they stepped in to mediate between Fox and Muñoz Ledo, and on the day after the vote the two candidates came together at a press conference to protest the fraud. To Fox's
delight, Muñoz Ledo grabbed his fist and held it up over his head, declaring Fox the winner and creating a news photograph that made front
pages all over Mexico.

Fox mobilized his supporters and nearly paralyzed the state for a
week with PAN protests. Meanwhile, the final tally showed that Aguirre's
vote rigging had been overenergetic: he had given himself twice as many
votes as Salinas had claimed in Guanajuato in 1988.

Alarmed, Salinas summoned the top leaders of the PAN, Luis H. Álvarez and Diego Fernández de Cevallos, to Los Pinos. "I have made the
most difficult decision of my presidency," he said. Salinas announced
that he was prepared to sacrifice Aguirre, more or less acknowledging
that the PRI had not really won. Then, making a very unusual offer, he
said he would let the PAN choose Aguirre's replacement for governor.
But there was a condition: "I want you to promise me," Salinas said, "that
Vicente Fox will never again be a PAN candidate."

Álvarez stared at the President. He knew Salinas despised Fox, because of the way Fox had ridiculed him in the Congress during the debate in 1988. For a moment Fox's future in politics was up in the air.

Then Álvarez rose from his chair to his full height and looked down
on Salinas. "How dare you ask that of me?" he roared, abandoning his
normal mildness. "You're asking me to go to a Mexican citizen and tell
him to renounce his political rights?"

Salinas was taken aback. "Well—no, no, Don Luis," he stammered. "I just wanted to tell you about the decision I have made to find a new governor in Guanajuato." Álvarez was not assuaged. "You know the reasons for your decisions. They are entirely up to you. But there is absolutely no way that I am ever going to tell Vicente Fox that he can't run for political office." With that, Álvarez marched out.

In the following days, however, Álvarez stopped short of breaking off the negotiations with Salinas entirely. The PAN leader was no longer the daring idealist who had fasted almost to death in the kiosk in Chihuahua in 1986. After decades of confrontation with the PRI, he was convinced—in spite of the doubts surrounding the death of Manuel Clouthier—that the system had become more flexible since 1988.

To argue this belief, Álvarez would often make comparisons with an episode in which a much earlier PAN leader had gone to President Luis Echeverría to protest a grossly fraudulent PRI victory. "Those are the results, and if you don't like them, you can go jump in the lake," Echeverría had said. Carlos Salinas, by contrast, had recognized the PAN's victory in Baja California on the very night of the election, Álvarez would note. "Gradualism" was what he called his new approach.

"We studied the circumstances of each political moment and the correlation of forces," he explained. "Based on that, we tried to achieve the greatest gain for our party."

In Guanajuato, Salinas was offering the PAN another governor—a substantial gain, to Álvarez's mind. That the citizens would not get the particular PAN governor they had voted for seemed secondary.

So Álvarez and Diego Fernández de Cevallos, then a top PAN leader, called Fox to a meeting at a coffee shop in Mexico City. Salinas would let the PAN keep the governor's job, they said, but he would not let Fox keep it. At first Fox could not believe that his party would ask him to make such a sacrifice. But eventually PAN leaders persuaded him of "the correlation of forces." Fox recognized that for the time being at least, there was no way he could take office if the President was determined to block him.

"I'm not fighting for personal victories," Fox told his party's leaders, looking for a heroic phrase to mark the moment as he accepted his fate. He even recommended someone to take his place as governor: Carlos Medina Plascencia, a *panista* technocrat who was the mayor of León.

So the deal was struck. But then several days went by, and Salinas did nothing. On the morning of August 29, the foreign press weighed in. *The Wall Street Journal* published a column by Enrique Krauze saying the fraud in Guanajuato showed that the PRI system had become completely debased. "Mexico cannot go on being ruled by an antediluvian monster," he wrote. On the same day the *Journal* also ran an editorial calling for the Guanajuato elections to be annulled.

The overseas editorials moved Salinas to act. The same night, just after 11 p.m., Ramón Aguirre summoned the press to PRI campaign headquarters in Guanajuato city. "I have taken the most difficult decision of my life," he said, echoing Salinas's language—appropriately, since it was Salinas who had taken the decision. Aguirre declined to take his oath of office, and Medina was inaugurated as interim governor on September 1.

Fox returned to his Guanajuato ranch, his future in politics uncertain. But his new friends Jorge Castañeda and Adolfo Aguilar Zinser went back to Mexico City thinking how Fox stood out from the PAN, especially with his disposition to parlay with the leftist opposition. "This is a ballsy guy," Castañeda thought to himself. "This guy might be presidential material."

Fox's campaign staff was not so sanguine. His closest supporters felt betrayed by the PAN and Medina. They wanted Fox to retaliate, but that wasn't his style.

"Enough. Turn it down, please," he kept saying.

Finally he called his closest followers to a strategy session in Mexico City, away from the sour environment in Guanajuato. To impress their dissatisfaction on him, they showed up at the appointed location but hid in a back room. When Fox arrived, only one of his supporters was at the meeting table, feigning despair. The others made Fox wait without them for a long while, to make him think they had abandoned him because he wasn't a big-shot governor. Then they burst in, laughing.

Fox got the message. To kick off the discussions, he picked up a red marker and went to the white board. He wrote the year, 1991, then drew an arrow, then wrote another year, 2000, and alongside 2000 he made a box. Inside it he wrote in big letters: PRESIDENT.

It was the first time they had heard the idea. "We thought he was just trying to calm us down," recalled Leticia Calzada, a friend and supporter from Guanajuato. "Not one of us took it seriously. No one."

Although Fox didn't like the outcome in Guanajuato, many opposition leaders and intellectuals at first welcomed the results of Salinas's intervention there and in San Luis Potosí. It seemed to show that the system would no longer summarily impose its questionable victories and to prove that the opposition, in the provinces as well as in Mexico City, could effectively mobilize everyday citizens from different class backgrounds to challenge the PRI's electoral malfeasance.

But it soon became clear that those two elections were part of a pattern of arbitrary decision making by Salinas. By the end of his term Salinas had removed seventeen PRI governors, affecting fourteen of the thirty-one Mexican states. During his presidency more than 60 percent of the Mexican populace was governed by officials chosen by Salinas, not by the voters. Even while Salinas encouraged legal reforms to make the elections more credible, in practice he sapped legitimacy from the electoral process. He would decide, based on his political calculus of the moment, whether or not to allow the outcome of an election to stick. As in San Luis Potosí, his decisions often made Mexico appear more democratic at home and to the outside world but did little to make the country more democratic in practice for its citizens.

Over time Salinas's undoing of so many governors undermined the autonomy of the states and centralized ever more decision making in the President's hands. In the PRI's vertical system the governors were key intermediaries between the people, the party, and the President. With so many governors coming and going under Salinas, they no longer provided reliable channels of communication for political demands from the bottom of the pyramid. By concentrating power, Salinas weakened the substructure of presidential authority.

He also alienated his own party, routinely ignoring the PRI's recommendations for candidates for key posts and paying no attention to *priístas* who protested when he swept away officials whom they had labored to elect. That there was no PRI uprising while Salinas was in office was a measure of how deeply the party was guided by the principle of loyalty to the President.

In fact, the PRI's loyalty held even as Salinas relentlessly enacted an extraordinarily ambitious series of reforms that dismantled many cornerstones on which the ruling party had rested. The reforms cut the bottom out from under the PRI, but they only added to the popular luster of the PRI President.

Throughout his term Salinas attacked the federal bureaucracy, a stalagmite of accumulated PRI patronage, with an aggressive program to trim it down. One of his first moves, whose impact was huge, had been the sale of the state-owned telephone monopoly, Teléfonos de México, or Telmex. Virtually every Mexican had to deal in some way or another with Telmex. But because of its indolent service, it could take as long as three months to get a new phone line in most major cities, and the cost was beyond the reach of working-class Mexicans. On the grounds that service would improve, Salinas's administration sold Telmex to a group of private investors led by the Mexican financier Carlos Slim Helú.

By 1991 Salinas had also made good progress on reforms to restore the legal rights of the Catholic Church, reversing an anticlerical tradition in Mexico that dated back to Benito Juárez. The year before, in May 1990, Pope John Paul II had visited Mexico, to an outpouring of Catholic fervor. His trip had helped Salinas launch constitutional amendments and new laws to allow churches once again to own property and teach religion in private schools and to authorize priests to vote and wear clerical dress in public. The reforms, which took effect over the second half of the *sexenio*, were immensely popular. They freed devout Mexicans from double lives they had always maintained, in which they pledged allegiance to the secular PRI but sent their children to Catholic schools (technically illegal) and were regulars at Sunday Mass.

In 1992, amendments to Article 37 of the Constitution put an end to land reform in Mexico and, consistent with Salinas's free-market philosophy, opened the way for private development of millions of acres of farmland that had belonged to the state. For the Mexican working class this change was every bit as profound as the free-trade agreement. The land reform had been one of the central promises of the 1917 Constitution, the great legacy of those who fought the Mexican Revolution, and a cornerstone of the country's nationalist ideology. Lázaro Cárdenas's land distribution was remembered by working Mexicans as the PRI system's most forceful and enduring action to take from the rich and give to the poor.

Unfortunately, by the time Salinas was President, there wasn't much land left to distribute, and the descendants of land-reform beneficiaries were withering away on collective plots, called *ejidos*, in which no one wanted to invest because the land was the property of the nation, not the farmer.

"The massive distribution of land is over," Salinas said, explaining his new policy. "Now agrarian reform means supporting agricultural production." Under Salinas's reforms the peasant farmers themselves became owners of the collective property, and he was photographed countless times handing titles to *campesinos* in sandals and muslin shirts. Outsiders were allowed to invest in or rent the *ejidos*, and private commercial enterprises were allowed to buy farmland.

The controversial side of the reform was that it permitted farmers to sell their *ejido* stakes. The PRD vehemently opposed it, arguing that whenever the inevitable economic downturn came, peasants would be forced to sell en masse. Critics also raised doubts about the wisdom of carrying out the reform just when NAFTA would force Mexican agriculture to compete with the United States. There was great resistance inside the PRI. But as with many of his reforms, Salinas did not so much persuade his party as command it, relying on the PRI's obedience to win passage for his bills in the Congress.

Salinas's fiscal policies, which cut government spending and scaled back traditional subsidies in order to control inflation, were hard on those at the bottom of society. Salinas sought to alleviate the harshest effects of his economic liberalization through a hugely ambitious effort called the Programa Nacional de Solidaridad, generally known as Solidarity. Quickly becoming the face of Salinas's presidency for everyday Mexicans, Solidarity streamlined the government's social programs and centralized many of them under one organization, which Salinas kept close under his watchful eye. Its projects paved streets, built or repaired schools, brought electricity to faraway communities, and remodeled rural hospitals. In six years Salinas's government spent $18 billion on Solidarity.

In a break with past practice, the government did not merely give away services, but required villagers to organize themselves to provide labor and small amounts of their own resources for the projects. Salinas insisted that one of Solidarity's great innovations was that it encouraged grassroots participation. "And not just any type of participation," he said. "It had to be organized democratically, from the bottom up." Under his orders the program was heavily advertised on television and radio, touted as both government assistance and a channel for Mexicans to express their demands.

Solidarity was a big hit with the people, and it became completely identified with Salinas, a kind of quasi party parallel to the PRI. In May 1992 Salinas named Luis Donaldo Colosio, the PRI party president, to head the program. Colosio was so effective in that role, and built such a following for the President and for himself, that Salinas would choose him the following year to be the PRI candidate to succeed him.

But as Salinas gained political momentum from the brisk march of his reforms, he was also kicking out the foundations of the PRI system that brought him to power. The *ejido* reforms undermined the PRI's hold over the countryside by undercutting its farmworker unions. In the NAFTA negotiations Salinas undid privileges and protection that had been afforded to truckers, bus companies, construction companies, and manufacturers who supplied the government and the domestic market. Many of these sectors were organized into corporatist confederations named with endless acronyms that were attached directly to the PRI. Solidarity centralized under Salinas benefits that had formerly been distributed through the government at large and the PRI, sidelining PRI patronage handlers at all levels. The re-enfranchisement of the Catholic Church appalled PRI stalwarts like Manuel Bartlett and others in his generation, who regarded it as the vanguard of a rightist antirevolutionary conspiracy.

Carlos Salinas greets an eager crowd during a tour of Solidarity program projects, in Hidalgo state

Meanwhile, the reforms, ironically, helped to build the PAN's influence. The marriage of convenience between Salinas and the PAN was crucial to the adoption of the agricultural and church reforms. The PAN used the leverage it gained from playing ball with Salinas to advance an agenda of its own.

In 1992 Francisco Barrio ran once again for the Chihuahua governorship that had been stolen from him in 1986. In contrast to de la Madrid, Salinas dispatched one of his top elections officials, Carlos Almada, to Chihuahua weeks before the vote to work with Barrio's people to clean up the voter lists. On election night, July 12, Government Secretary Gutiérrez Barrios called Barrio in the early evening to congratulate him and assure him that he would see to it that the Chihuahua PRI did the same. At the end of 1992 PAN mayors governed 30 of the 160 largest townships in Mexico.

Salinas replaced Gutiérrez Barrios as Government Secretary in January 1993 because of his resistance to the church reforms. The PAN also succeeded that year in pushing through another round of electoral reforms. Under the new laws campaign-finance statements were required for the first time, and it became illegal for a political party to receive campaign money from the government (a statute that the PRI continued to honor primarily in the breach). They also barred foreign financing of political campaigns and gave formal status to elections observers, like the ones Sergio Aguayo had been organizing.

While the PAN was cutting deals with Salinas, Vicente Fox was using his downtime from political office to go on the road all over Guanajuato, building political alliances from the ground up, an activity the PAN had often treated as beneath its dignity.

"He's a politician who grows by eating dust," his friend Leticia Calzada would say of Fox to people who didn't know him. "He eats the dust of the trail; he wears down his boot heels. He talks to people."

Fox was preparing for another run for governor but also thinking about a larger goal. In 1993 Calzada got a phone call from him. "*Tengo un proyectito.* I have a little project for you," Fox said, using the diminutives typical of his country talk. "Let's organize a little struggle, *una luchita.*"

It turned out that Fox wanted to amend a "little article" in the Mexican Constitution. It was Clause 1 of Article 82, which stipulated that only Mexicans whose parents were born in Mexico could run for President. That clause would have to change, Fox said, because there was no changing the fact that his mother, Doña Mercedes Quesada, had been born in Spain.

Calzada took on the task. She summoned constitutional experts to gauge the prospects for Fox's amendment. Impossible, they said; the clause was a keystone of Mexican nationalism.

Casting about, Calzada went to Enrique Krauze and Héctor Aguilar Camín, the historians. After a bit of research they both reported that there was no august nationalist principle behind the troublesome clause. It had been the product of a petty maneuver by the Constitution writers of 1917 to eliminate some foes from contention.

Calzada went to Santiago Creel. Creel was a lawyer, even if his practice was corporate. He did not know Fox well and was not convinced of his presidential potential, but he liked the legal challenge Fox had posed. With some comparative research, Creel determined that none of the modern countries in the world that Mexico strived to emulate had such an exclusion clause. The way to overturn it, he proposed, was to assert the higher political rights of all Mexicans to compete for and hold public office, to argue that the clause was dividing Mexico into first- and second-class citizens.

In another inspiration Creel proposed that they take a petition to two dozen Mexican intellectuals to get them to sign it. The first person they went to, on July 6, 1993, was Octavio Paz. Paz pulled out his blue pencil and looked over Creel's draft preamble. "Aware that democracy can only flourish in a climate of equality among citizens, and that such conditions call for superior rights, characteristic of free peoples, and in the spirit of advancing our democracy . . ." Paz paused. Then, treating the words with the precision of a poem, he crossed out "advancing" and wrote "perfecting."

He signed. Others to sign were Carlos Fuentes, Sergio Aguayo, and Jorge Castañeda. The amendment campaign went on to gather hundreds of thousands of citizen signatures. Significantly, despite initial opposition from Salinas, it garnered support within the PRI. And even Salinas finally came around to the measure when he realized that the change would mean that Jaime Serra Puche, the talented NAFTA negotiator, could one day run for President. Serra's parents were both Spaniards.

The amendment to Article 82 passed the Congress on September 3, 1993. But in the final hours before the vote, Fox faced an end run from within his own party. Diego Fernández de Cevallos was determined to be the PAN candidate in 1994. Quietly he worked with the PRI to write a little clause into Fox's amendment, saying it would not come into effect until the presidential race of 2000.

So Fox was cut out of the 1994 contest. But he would stand in special elections for Guanajuato governor in May 1995 and win by a landslide.

The North American Free Trade Agreement was ratified by the U.S. House of Representatives on November 17, 1993. It had taken nearly five years of negotiations to reach a pact that both the White House and the Congress would accept. The treaty had first been signed by Salinas, President George H. W. Bush, and Canadian Prime Minister Brian Mulroney on December 17, 1992. But then Bill Clinton took over from Bush, and to satisfy the left and labor wings of the Democratic Party, he insisted on reopening negotiations to write additional accords providing protections for labor and the environment (those were signed on September 14, 1993).

It remained unclear right to the end whether Mexico would garner enough support in the U.S. Congress for ratification. Clinton lent his support, but many officials in his administration had political doubts about the treaty. A lobbying blitzkrieg that Salinas and Serra organized in Washington had a decisive impact, turning around many opponents of the accord at the last minute.

NAFTA was Mexico's first bloodless revolution. It brought enormous changes not only in the alignment of its economic interests but also in the country's self-perception. The central focus of Mexico's economy shifted. Businesses producing for export were in, while those that supplied a sheltered domestic market were out. With the agreement going into effect only on January 1, 1994, the benefits of NAFTA in terms of growth were not felt in Mexico during Salinas's term, although the economy did grow that year, by 4.4 percent. But in anticipation of NAFTA, Mexican businesses across the board were forced to scramble to retool and upgrade, to get ready for the new competition.

Salinas's trade pact forced Mexicans to rethink the defensive, self-isolating nationalism that was a key article of PRI revolutionary doctrine. Whereas the traditional PRI regarded the United States as an imperialist bully, NAFTA called on Mexicans to see their neighbor as a partner, even a friend. As it turned out, the leap was not that hard for most. For decades Mexicans by the millions had been crossing over to the United States, some legally but most not, to find jobs. Someone in practically every Mexican family had worked, studied, done business, or vacationed in the United States. Although Mexicans did not admit it too loudly, there was much about America that they liked. With NAFTA, Salinas brought the government in line with underlying views of many of his people.

NAFTA brought Salinas recognition as a world-class leader. "President Salinas is leading Mexico through an era of exciting, unprecedented reform," President George Bush said during one of Salinas's visits to the States. "Like the Aztec eagle, Mexico is rising again. The Mexican renaissance has begun."

President Clinton said Salinas had given Mexico "better leadership than ever in my lifetime." The foreign press, especially *The Wall Street Journal*, looked favorably on Salinas's reforms. (After Salinas stepped down as President, Dow Jones invited him to join its board of directors.) In Mexico intellectuals of the stature of Octavio Paz, Enrique Krauze, and Héctor Aguilar Camín subscribed to Salinas's modernizing crusade and threw their prestige behind his policies. Even María Félix, Mexico's adored movie queen, liked Salinas. She graced him with an autographed photo addressed to "Carlos Salinas, our hope."

As the final year of the *sexenio* approached, his performance reached its climax. Although the country was roiled by economic change, Mexicans were optimistic, as they had not been for decades, that it would take them to a new level of progress. Salinas seemed perfectly suited for the part and the times: an old-style caudillo with modern ideas.

However, he still had one more year to go.

8

1994

Salinas knew that his chief task in the final year of his term was to make a smooth handoff to another PRI President. It would be bad for the country and disastrous for the PRI system to suffer another upheaval like 1988, and if he did not ensure an orderly transition, his own legacy could be vulnerable. He could see what had become of José López Portillo, who could not go about in public, because Mexicans would bark at him, reminding him how he had failed in his pledge to defend the peso "like a dog."

But as Salinas's administration drew to a close, his political control, frayed by tensions in the system and the country, began to unravel. Violence erupted, first in Chiapas and later in the upper echelons of the PRI. The imperial height Salinas had attained became a place of isolation; the PRI mechanisms he might have used to rally support did not work because he had neglected them.

Signs of trouble had appeared the previous year. On May 24, 1993, narcotics gunmen ambushed one of Mexico's most important Roman Catholic prelates, Juan Jesús Cardinal Posadas Ocampo, as he was pulling into the parking lot of the Guadalajara airport. When Salinas flew to the city on the evening of the murder, he was greeted by heckling crowds outside the cathedral shouting, "Justice! Justice!" Authorities eventually ascribed the execution to cocaine-dealing assassins who fired on the Cardinal after mistaking him for a rival trafficker. But that explanation left many Mexicans wondering how professional killers could have confused a drug lord with an elderly gentleman in a flowing black habit.

Salinas's problems had deepened with the *destape*, or unveiling, of

Luis Donaldo Colosio as the PRI presidential candidate in November 1993. At that point his command was so firm that he might have encouraged the party to hold an internal election or a convention. But Salinas was not interested in giving up presidential prerogatives. He picked Colosio through the most conventional PRI rituals, hinting of his favor to three or four competitors with small gestures of approval and oblique dinner party compliments, then standing back to watch them vie like courtiers for his tap.

But after Salinas chose Colosio, and PRI leaders went through the time-honored motions of pretending the choice had been theirs, Manuel Camacho, the Mexico City mayor, committed heresy. Feeling seduced and abandoned by Salinas, Camacho refused to fall in behind the winner as PRI protocol required. On the morning of the *destape*, when he should have come out to hail Colosio, Camacho remained silent.

Colosio called him later that day. "Aren't you going to congratulate me?" the candidate asked jovially. Camacho, humorless, said he would make no statements about Colosio until he had words with Salinas. Then he gave a press conference in which he complained about the arbitrary selection process and demanded more democracy within the PRI.

Phone calls coursed across the scandalized PRI establishment. Finally Salinas got on the line with Camacho, demanding that he congratulate Colosio in public. "Your presence is very important. Those are the rules of the system."

There were hard negotiations, but finally Camacho agreed to end his insubordination and leave his job as Mexico City mayor to take the more prestigious post of Foreign Secretary.

In the first moments of January 1, 1994, the day NAFTA came into force, Salinas was met with a frontal challenge. While the President was celebrating the New Year and the pact with a band of mariachis in Mexico City, Indian rebels calling themselves the Ejército Zapatista de Liberación Nacional, the Zapatista National Liberation Army (or EZLN), seized several towns in Chiapas, denouncing the trade agreement and summoning the masses to overthrow the government. Salinas, deciding quickly against sending the army to crush the rebels, moved to halt the hostilities and opened negotiations. But the uprising jolted Mexicans and foreigners alike. The picture Salinas had projected of a progressive and tolerant Mexico was confronted with images of rifle-bearing Indians in black ski masks who said they had taken up arms to defend their survival and most elemental rights.

Manuel Camacho was the only high official in Salinas's administration who had maintained any ties to the Left, and he soon persuaded Salinas to send him to Chiapas as his negotiator. As Camacho opened talks with the guerrillas in a cathedral in the Chiapas highlands, the press published startling photos of him in jeans and shirtsleeves holding up one end of a Mexican flag while the Zapatista leader, Subcomandante Marcos, held up the other.

Soon Colosio's campaign was eclipsed by Camacho's pyrotechnics. It started to look like Camacho was carrying on an undeclared presidential bid parallel to the party's official candidate, breaking every rule in the PRI book. At one point Colosio threatened among his campaign staff to resign, although he never repeated the threat to Salinas.

By mid-March the uncertainties over the presidential succession had begun to rattle the Mexican financial markets. Finally, on March 22, Camacho yielded to the pressure and made a public declaration renouncing any intentions to run for President.

Just one day later, as Colosio was moving through a thick crowd of supporters in a shantytown in Tijuana, a man shoved his way to the candidate's side, put an old pistol to his head, and shot him dead. The gunman, Mario Aburto, was immediately subdued and captured.

The assassination rocked Mexico as few events have in modern times. Mexicans knew that the PRI system had been created in reaction to the 1928 murder of General Álvaro Obregón to put an end to internecine bloodletting in the revolutionary elite. Under PRI rule there had always been murderous violence at the bottom of the system, in the farming villages and city slums, but not at the top. The PRI's commitment to national "social peace" was one of the few that the system had consistently kept. The significance for Mexico of Colosio's killing was not in the facts of who did it and why but in the impression it caused. Indeed, federal authorities would not complete their investigation of the case until October 2000, six and a half years after the crime. (At that point the special prosecutor concluded that Aburto had acted as a deranged single gunman.) But within hours after the shooting, Mexicans formed a collective conviction that Colosio's killers were to be found within the PRI. To the public the assassination was a sign that the ruling party, consumed with ambitions and jealousies that Salinas had stirred, was destroying itself.

Even many within the PRI establishment harbored these fears. The timing of the killing left Colosio's family and followers full of suspicions that Camacho was somehow involved. When Camacho appeared at the funeral, the slain candidate's wife, Diana Laura, asked him to leave. Ernesto Zedillo, Colosio's campaign manager, refused to greet him.

Salinas cast about for a new candidate, summoning PRI leaders, opposition figures, and intellectuals to give their recommendations. Those who saw him in that period found a Salinas they had never known before: hesitant, searching. His demeanor convinced several visitors that he was not behind the killing, as the public believed. He seemed agonizingly aware that Colosio's death had annihilated his master plan for a triumphal end to his term.

In the middle of the crisis Salinas's five-year dalliance with the PAN also failed him. He hoped to name Pedro Aspe, his Finance Secretary, to replace Colosio as the candidate. But in order to do so, he had to amend

The assassination in Tijuana of Luis Donaldo Colosio, the PRI presidential candidate, on March 23, 1994, rocked Mexico

a clause in the Constitution stipulating that presidential candidates had to be out of government office for six months before Election Day. He needed PAN votes for the two-thirds majority required for a constitutional change, but the PAN turned him down. The party finally balked at altering the Constitution to benefit one person, especially when that person would be the PRI candidate to run against the PAN.

The only person who had the basic credentials—because he had served key positions in Salinas's cabinet and was also indisputably eligible under the Constitution—was Ernesto Zedillo (he had been the Secretary of Planning and Budget and later Education). Although Zedillo was never part of Salinas's circle of confidants, he did have the backing of someone who was, José Córdoba Montoya, Salinas's former chief of staff. So Zedillo got the tap.

He stood against Cuauhtémoc Cárdenas from the PRD, who was running for President for the second time, and Diego Fernández de Cevallos from the PAN. A determining factor in the race was the odd behavior of Fernández de Cevallos. With his cropped beard and high rhetoric, he cut a dashing figure on the stump. His nickname, El Jefe Diego, or Boss Diego, reflected his viceroyal demeanor. Fernández de Cevallos was a PAN aristocrat, a brilliant exponent of the party's most conservative political and social orthodoxy. A skilled orator of the old school, he handily defeated Zedillo and Cárdenas in Mexico's first-ever televised presidential debate, held in May, which was watched by 40 million Mexicans, the largest audience for any Mexican television show up to that time. His standing in the opinion polls took a leap.

Then, bizarrely, Fernández de Cevallos disappeared from view. For a month he hardly campaigned. When he was finally out on the trail again, it was too late. His non-campaign was so eccentric that it earned him the suspicion of many Mexican voters, who concluded that the only possible explanation was that Salinas had paid him off.

Zedillo, meanwhile, played unabashedly on fears of anarchy awakened by the Zapatista rebellion, stressing that no opposition party could maintain control as well as the PRI. In the August 21 election Zedillo won with 50.1 percent of the vote. Fernández de Cevallos drew 26.6 percent, and Cárdenas, hurt by being associated with the Zapatistas and by an ineffective campaign, fell to 17 percent. The most remarkable statistic of the day was the turnout: 78 percent of the registered voters, or 35.2 million Mexicans, went to the polls. They left no doubt that they wanted to manage their differences through orderly elections, not shooting wars.

Even though the Zapatistas espoused armed revolt over political debate, their uprising had an immediate positive effect on the progress of Mexican democracy. The revolt overwhelmed the Mexican press and mesmerized national attention. Since it was general knowledge that racist abuse was the common lot of Mexico's Indians, the public was strongly sympathetic to the Zapatistas' cause, although not to their violent methods.

The rebels had despaired of electoral politics as a means to change Mexico. In their First Declaration of the Lacandon Jungle, the rambling broadside in which they explained their uprising, they said they had adopted the desperate strategy of armed rebellion because they were "convinced that there is no other way to obtain justice and preserve the true dignity of our people." Subcomandante Marcos mocked Mexican elections as a trick that the PRI played regularly on the Mexican people. Thus the Zapatistas' guns had the effect of putting all of Mexico's political leaders up against the wall, especially those on the Left, forcing them to clarify whether or not they were fully committed to electoral democracy.

Their answer came on January 27, 1994. The leaders and presidential candidates of the three main parties and five small ones signed an accord in which they agreed that "the advance of democracy, closing the way to all forms of violence, should take place within the scope of the political parties and the republican institutions." They said it was time to create "trust and certainty in all the institutions that take part in the electoral process," to make it easier "for those who have opted for confrontation to join in the task of transforming our political life." Colosio signed for the PRI, Fernández de Cevallos for the PAN, Cárdenas for the PRD—the first time the PRD had endorsed an electoral reform.

The reforms, forged around a big table in government offices on Calle Barcelona in Mexico City, tumbled out one after another. Porfirio

Muñoz Ledo, despite his self-aggrandizing tirades, proved able at conceiving and drafting the necessary legislation. One negotiator for the PRI was José Francisco Ruiz Massieu, the former governor of Guerrero and sworn enemy of the PRD. But after battling the leftist party throughout his term over tainted voting in his state, Ruiz Massieu had come to believe that even the PRI might benefit from less controversial elections. He and Muñoz Ledo managed to deal.

In the new reforms the independence of the Federal Electoral Institute, established in law in 1990, was codified in the Constitution. The importance of the institute's citizen councillors was enhanced. All the political parties, including the PRI, lost their right to vote on the governing council; instead, each registered party was represented by one nonvoting member. Suddenly the PRI had no vote and just as much voice in elections decisions as the Labor Party, a left-wing micro group whose following did not surpass 2 percent of the voters. The six citizen councillors were to be elected by the Chamber of Deputies; there was no way for the President to get his hands directly on the selection.

Campaign-finance limits were set. The activities of Mexican elections observers were expanded, and the parties, in a supreme effort to overcome their nationalist suspicions, also decided to allow foreign observers, although they partially concealed them behind the euphemistic label "foreign visitors."

One of the first six citizen councillors to be elected by the Chamber of Deputies was José Woldenberg. He had started out in politics on the militant Left, as a socialist labor organizer who helped create a union for the blue-collar workers of the UNAM. In 1986 he changed course. When Manuel Bartlett was Government Secretary, he held some hearings as a prelude to minor changes in the elections laws that President de la Madrid would call his electoral reform. Bartlett, yielding something on form so as to yield nothing on substance, decided to allow a question-and-answer period during the hearings; before that, debate had been barred from such discussions.

Woldenberg was dispatched to Bartlett's hearings to represent his small socialist party. Worried that he might appear "provincial," as he put it, he dived into the books, reading up on electoral systems in Mexico and around the world. Even the limited repartee at the hearings intrigued him. He began writing about elections in columns in *La Jornada* and soon became a scholarly expert on Mexican voting, a field in which he had very little company at the beginning.

Another new councillor was Santiago Creel, whose political origins were poles apart from Woldenberg's. Creel was descended from generations of aristocracy, although his bloodlines were ideologically mixed: his great-great-grandfather was Luis Terrazas, a legendary liberal General from the time of Benito Juárez; and his great-grandfather had served as Foreign Minister to Porfirio Díaz. Creel studied law at the University of Michigan in the late 1970s and returned to Mexico to a corporate-law practice that quickly bored him. He had gone on a whim to Chihuahua in 1986 and from there became fascinated with the clean-elections movement.

Creel was a longtime friend of Adolfo Aguilar Zinser's (and, by extension, Jorge Castañeda's). Their fathers had been friends, and as boys they both liked to ride horseback. Aguilar Zinser recalled that their game was to dash toward a tree, then leap off onto a branch and let their horses gallop on without them. Seizing the branch didn't frighten Creel, but he was so small that dropping to the ground often did. Although Creel was instinctively more conservative than Aguilar Zinser, by the end of the 1980s both men had been drawn to the cause of getting rid of the PRI.

Even with the citizen councillors and many new laws in place, the 1994 election was far from perfect. Prodded by Sergio Aguayo and a national observer group he had formed in early 1994, the Federal Electoral Institute began to monitor campaign spending and media coverage. The inequities were glaring. In its first report, on July 5, the institute found that the PRI had received 41 percent of the television and radio campaign coverage, while the PRD received 18 percent and the PAN even less.

For Aguayo in particular, 1994 was not an easy year. His new group, Alianza Cívica, or Civic Alliance, had grown into "a gigantic animal," as he described it, a nationwide coalition of 470 grassroots elections-observer groups capable of tracking elections in every corner of the country. From the modest start in San Luis Potosí in 1991, Aguayo had built an observer organization that was ready to take on a presidential election.

But in January, during the days after the Zapatista uprising, Aguayo received his third death threat. This one was left in a hole in a light post, and an anonymous phone caller alerted police to pick it up. The writer made it clear that he did not like Aguayo or his work and was getting ready to "execute" him. The note included several intimate details about Aguayo's life, suggesting it had come from someone with access to government intelligence transcripts of his personal phone calls who knew a lot about his regular movements.

As soon as he learned of the threat from the police, Aguayo, afraid to go home and draw danger toward his family, went straight to the offices of *La Jornada*. There he received a call from the Government Secretary, Jorge Carpizo, asking him to accept government protection.

"I'm not a hero, but I'm not suicidal either," Aguayo reasoned with his appalled friends. If anything happened to him, he argued, the Civic Alliance's plans to monitor the presidential election might be crippled. In an irony not lost on him, Aguayo agreed to be tailed for the rest of the year by two bodyguards from the Government Secretariat, the agency that he suspected had generated the troubling threat. He sent his two children out of the country until the election was over.

On Election Day the Civic Alliance had observers in 1,810 polling stations around the country, selected to provide a scientific sample. Although the observers witnessed thousands of irregularities, they acknowledged that there were improvements over the past. "There is no doubt that the inequities of the campaign and the irregularities of the vote affected the result; but it is impossible to go beyond that general affirmation," the alliance concluded in its report. "We can't say what the different parties' percentages might have been if they had competed under equal conditions without anomalies. We are sure the results would have been different, but perhaps the outcome would not have changed."

That outcome, Zedillo's victory and the renewal of the PRI system, left Aguayo with painful mixed feelings. He had to keep reminding himself of his goals. "We pushed and pushed as hard as we could, and in the end the PRI won," Aguayo reflected. "But I had it fairly clear that our job was not to defeat the PRI in the elections. That job belonged to others. Our job was to achieve clean elections in Mexico so that the larger transition would be more solid."

Still, he could not help feeling a little used by Salinas. "He needed to have a peaceful and legitimate election that would gain international recognition," Aguayo said. "After we put out a report, he saw to it that the media coverage was more balanced for a month. Then, during the last three weeks, the bias returned, and it was too late for us to do anything about it. Afterward he cited us to prove that the election had been the cleanest one Mexico ever had."

But Aguayo was philosophical. "He used us, but in a way we used him, too," he acknowledged. "We pushed him, and we ended up with fundamental reforms."

Just when Salinas was savoring the election results and regaining confidence that his presidency would end in triumph, another murder brought savage rifts inside the PRI into public view. On September 28, 1994, as José Francisco Ruiz Massieu was leaving a breakfast meeting, a gunman strode up to him on a street just off the Paseo de la Reforma, in the very heart of Mexico City. The shooter, Daniel Aguilar Treviño, killed his target but was nabbed at the site by a lowly bank guard.

At the time of his murder Ruiz Massieu was the secretary-general of the PRI, the party's second-highest official, and his career was on a rising curve. After Ruiz Massieu had proven his loyalty by carrying out the vendetta against the PRD in Guerrero, Carlos Salinas had moved him to the PRI as a presidential agent in the increasingly fractious party. During Colosio's campaign Ruiz Massieu had grown close to Ernesto Zedillo, and the rumor was that Zedillo might make him Government Secretary.

Amid the horror over the new assassination, and with two assassinations in the PRI in one year, it seemed clear that the system was no longer channeling the violent impulses in its ranks. Based on the gunman's confession, the police investigation quickly closed in on Manuel Muñoz Rocha, an obscure PRI deputy from the northern state of Tamaulipas who seemed to have no ideological commitments other than fealty to the PRI machine. Within days after he became a suspect as the organizer of the murder, Muñoz Rocha disappeared, just after making several phone calls to the home of Raúl Salinas, the President's brother.

President Salinas made a strange move. He appointed Mario Ruiz

Massieu, a second-tier official in the Attorney General's office who was the victim's younger brother, as special prosecutor to head the investigation, waving aside legal restrictions that barred prosecutors from investigating crimes involving their relatives. Mario Ruiz Massieu soon ruled out any participation in his brother's murder by Raúl Salinas.

But Mario did not last long in charge of the probe. One week before the end of Salinas's term, on November 23, he gave one of the most peculiar histrionic performances in a *sexenio* full of theatrics. At a packed press conference in Mexico City, he announced that he was resigning, saying that his probe of his brother's murder had been stymied by dark forces within the PRI.

"The demons are loose, and they have prevailed," he said apocalyptically. He blamed the alleged cover-up on, among others, María de los Angeles Moreno, a matronly PRI official with a reputation as one of the party's few unquestionably decent members. With Mario Ruiz Massieu's inscrutable resignation, the PRI system seemed to have gone mad.

Attracted by Salinas's bold economic policies, Mexican and foreign investors had flocked to the Mexican stock market during his administration, making it exceptionally lucrative and adding billions of dollars to the country's foreign reserves. But the turbulence of 1994 gradually eroded their confidence.

The Zapatista uprising had shocked Wall Street at first. But when it became clear that the guerrillas were operating only in Chiapas, far from the centers of power, and that Salinas was looking to negotiate a settlement with them, relative calm returned to the markets. On February 15, Mexico still had $29 billion in reserves.

After the Colosio assassination those reserves plunged: on March 28, Mexico lost $1.15 billion in a single trading session. The following day the PRI announced Ernesto Zedillo's nomination as its presidential candidate, and both he and Salinas thought that would quell the panicky speculation; Zedillo held an economics doctorate from Yale, and as Budget Secretary he had been a straight-arrow fiscal conservative. However, the international markets did not know Zedillo. He seemed drab, lacking Salinas's flair and sure grip. The welcome Zedillo received from foreign investors was that Mexico lost another $1.2 billion in reserves between March 29 and 30. It was a surly greeting that Zedillo never forgot.

In April, adding light to the chiaroscuro of the year, the Organization for Economic Cooperation and Development admitted Mexico as a full member, giving Salinas the ultimate ratification of Mexico's modernity. The OECD is a sort of country club of world nations; only aspirants that are up to its income and social standards can get in. Back in the 1970s and 1980s Mexico had been proud of its place in the Third World and vigorously championed the causes of what were then called the under-developed nations. But Salinas had convinced Mexicans there was no reason why their country couldn't play in the big leagues. After the OECD ratified his thesis, Salinas began to consider running to be the head of the new World Trade Organization after his term ended.

Other events, however, clashed with the concept of a First World Mexico. On March 14, 1994, the chairman of Mexico's largest bank, Al-fredo Harp Helú, had been kidnapped, apparently by a cell of Marxist guerrillas. He was held for three months and paid tens of millions of dol-lars in ransom to gain his release. Months later Carlos Cabal Peniche, a businessman from Tabasco state whom Salinas had praised as a model of Mexican enterprise, went into hiding, fleeing from multimillion-dollar fraud charges.

In the background were weaknesses in the economy. Amid the appar-ent prosperity of the Salinas years, Mexican consumers had begun spending on credit as they never had before, with a special taste for im-ported goods, which had to be purchased abroad in dollars. Savings within the country dropped to a dangerous low. The banking system was overextended, and the deficit in the current account—which balances imports of goods and incoming investment flows against exports and out-going flows—was increasing. Economists began to warn that the peso was overvalued. By early 1994 the U.S. Federal Reserve had started rais-ing interest rates, luring money out of Mexico back to the United States.

Yet Salinas was confident of his administration's economic manage-ment. His Finance Secretary, Pedro Aspe, had prodigious professional skills as well as a cosmopolitan bonhomie that made him an easy inter-locutor for the fund managers and equities analysts on Wall Street. Aspe's showmanship was key, because the people in New York were working with few hard facts about Mexico's economic health. Even while Mexico was throwing open its trade, it kept its finances enveloped in secrecy. Basic figures such as the reserves and the current-account balance were published as rarely as twice a year. But big Wall Street investors had confidence in Aspe and no trouble getting him on the phone whenever they had questions. So even though some economic indicators began to deteriorate with the political turmoil, Salinas and Aspe were sure they could work things out gradually, without the kind of jarring devaluation that had bedeviled every presidential handover since the 1970s.

However, as the end of the *sexenio* approached, Salinas and Aspe shared their knowledge of the economy's deficiencies less and less with other members of the government, abandoning the rigorous collective decision making that Salinas had required up to that point from his cabinet secretaries. Before 1994 the economic cabinet had been meeting once a week, bringing together the Secretaries of Finance, Budget, Labor, and Trade as well as the chief of the central bank, all convened by José Córdoba, Salinas's chief of staff. Each official came armed with dossiers of facts and arguments to defend his position in hard-fought debates that often produced brilliant results.

But in 1994, when the economy needed careful handling, Salinas turned his attention to the political crisis, losing his focus on the economic policies that had been the priority and anchor of his administration. Córdoba, the convener, left Los Pinos in April, exhausted from a personal scandal and all the heat he had absorbed on behalf of Salinas. In all of 1994 Salinas's economic team met only seven times. At the same time, Salinas did not invite his economic team to his meetings with his political advisers. As the year advanced, crisis piled upon scandal, but the economic team got little explanation from the President, who kept his decisions increasingly to himself and his closest confidants.

On November 1, when Salinas delivered his final *informe*, he gave no hint of economic danger. Three weeks later, on the morning of Sunday, November 20, Jaime Serra Puche, Salinas's Trade Secretary, was not sure what awaited him when he received a call from an officer of the presidential general staff, Salinas's security contingent. Serra was instructed to report at mid-morning to the President's home in the Coyoacán neighborhood for a meeting. (It was so late in his term that Salinas had already moved out of Los Pinos.) At that point Serra was also a leading contender to become Zedillo's Finance Secretary, although nothing had yet been formalized.

As the tireless, quick-witted negotiator who had brought the marathon NAFTA negotiations to a successful close, Serra was on excellent terms with Salinas. But between Serra and Zedillo there was a bond that went beyond professional esteem. Although their backgrounds were different, the two men had become friends when they were economics graduate students together at Yale. Serra, whose parents were worldly Spanish exiles, came from a thinking elite in Mexico City; Zedillo grew up in a working-class family in the border town of Mexicali. Winning a graduate-school scholarship to Yale was an enormous break for Zedillo. He had arrived in New Haven in the fall of 1974 and struggled through his first year while he mastered English. So when Serra showed up the next year with similarly shaky command of the local tongue, Zedillo reached out to him, inviting Serra to Sunday night dinners in his tiny graduate-student apartment. The friendship had endured.

"What do you think of all this?" the President-elect asked when Serra stopped by to pick him up on the way to Salinas's home.

"What do I think of what?" Serra said.

"What do you think of what happened on Friday?" Zedillo insisted.

"Well, what did happen on Friday?" Serra asked. He was swamped with work to close out his affairs at the Trade Secretariat and had not been briefed on the government's confidential information about financial developments.

Zedillo looked at him in disbelief. He explained impatiently that there had been a market debacle in which $1.65 billion in foreign reserves had left the country in one day, coming after four days of continuous dollar bleed. Salinas had called the meeting, Zedillo said, to decide how to stop the drain.

The team assembled in the serene, newly paneled library of Salinas's home: Salinas, Zedillo, Serra, and Aspe; Miguel Mancera, the head of the central bank; Arsenio Farrell, the Labor Secretary; and Luis Téllez, an economist who would soon become Zedillo's chief of staff. Mancera gave a measured account of the severe damage the peso had sustained, and the talk turned immediately to the exchange-rate policy.

Salinas said up front that if it were necessary to make "an exchange-rate adjustment," he would do it.

Throughout his presidency the peso had traded within fixed upper and lower limits, known as a band, which restrained its fluctuations. When the currency hit the top of the band, the government spent some reserves to buy pesos and bring it down. Over the course of the *sexenio* Aspe had allowed the peso to slide by more than half of its original value. But he had always done it by widening the band in small increments that caused no alarm.

Now the discussion was about whether to widen the band by a bigger increment. Even though Serra had come to the meeting with no preparation, he got involved, thinking he had the necessary information to make educated judgments. From his position in the Trade Secretariat, he knew that the ballooning current-account deficit was a problem. Zedillo shared Serra's view, so they both argued for a substantial expansion of the band, by as much as 15 percent.

But Aspe expressed reservations. The markets were accustomed to his gradual increments, he argued. To make a change so late in the *sexenio* would rattle them, undermining the confidence he had built so painstakingly and raising doubts at a critical moment about the outgoing team, and the one coming in.

In Salinas's cabinet Aspe and Zedillo had fought countless bureaucratic skirmishes because Aspe, as Finance Secretary, was in charge of revenues and Zedillo, as Budget Secretary, was in charge of spending. Now the friction surfaced again as Aspe took a swipe at Zedillo, suggesting that the peso was falling because of "a perception" that the President-elect was not ready to shoulder the political costs of defending the band—in other words, that he was weak.

At the end of a morning of heated talk, Salinas broke off the meeting, saying that his men seemed to be approaching agreement on moving the band and instructing them to decide on how much. Then Salinas and Zedillo went off into another room to talk privately, inviting Serra to join them a few minutes later. The President informed Serra that Zedillo wanted to name him immediately as the President-elect's economic policy coordinator, to signal to the markets that the new economic team was in place. Serra's tenure as Trade Secretary was over, and on December 1, inauguration day, he would take over the far more powerful job of Finance Secretary.

"Okay, whatever you ask me to do," Serra said. The three men agreed that Zedillo would go to his own offices to put out a press release announcing Serra's appointment immediately.

Serra stepped out of the room to make some phone calls, and Aspe went in. Not ten minutes later Aspe left, sober and silent. Salinas called Serra back again. "There's been a change of plan," he said. "Pedro says he will resign. He wants you to take over as Secretary right away. He wants you to do the devaluation. It will be yours."

At first stunned, Serra quickly became exasperated. "Look, we just spent the whole morning talking about this. We all agree that we want to minimize the trauma," he said. "Well, if Pedro resigns, that will be traumatic. Very traumatic."

"He doesn't want to stay," Salinas insisted. "He wants you to take it over."

They did not agree. So Salinas called Zedillo at the President-elect's offices to tell him of Aspe's position. Salinas and Zedillo did not agree either. Zedillo argued that Aspe's resignation would send disturbing signals of dissension between Salinas's team and his.

In the afternoon Salinas summoned everyone back to his library. Amid high tension, he and Zedillo went out to the garden by themselves; their talk was agitated, but they still reached no agreement. With all the side discussions, not everyone present in Salinas's library was fully informed of the terms of the debate. Aspe had argued in private to Salinas that a devaluation could only be carried out properly if it was accompanied by a package of coordinated anti-inflationary measures. He said there wasn't enough time left in Salinas's term to devise such a package. Aspe's view was sound economics, but Serra never heard him make that case.

Once all were assembled, Mancera, the central bank chief, said calmly that if Mexico's foreign reserves were allowed to drop below $10 billion without an exchange-rate adjustment, he would feel obligated to resign. Aspe finally asked for the opinion of Labor Secretary Farrell, a crusty PRI veteran. Farrell observed that any devaluation would erode workers' salaries and could spell political disaster for the government in the final days of Salinas's term.

Farrell's comments seemed to seal it for Salinas: he wanted to avoid devaluation. The outgoing and incoming Presidents eyed each other, unable to agree on moving the peso. Zedillo and Serra felt they had little leverage to demand a widening of the band, since they were not yet in positions of authority. The decision was still up to President Salinas.

In the end the group opted for a third, default option. That evening, with Salinas's assent, Zedillo and Serra appeared with Aspe and Mancera before a roomful of labor and business representatives. Known as El Pacto, the Pact, the group had been convened regularly since the time of de la Madrid to endorse the government's economic policy changes. Zedillo, talking tough, pledged to enforce fiscal discipline and keep the economy on an even keel; he didn't say a word about devaluing the peso.

On Monday morning Aspe followed up with an intensive round of his famous telephone diplomacy. By that afternoon the markets' upset had begun to subside, and the markets remained tranquil through November 30, the last day of the *sexenio*.

Indeed, Salinas completed his term on a high note. Late in the afternoon of his final day in office, he, along with a number of officials and diplomats who had served in his government, was riding back to Los Pinos in the presidential bus after having spent the day in the streets of Mexico City—inaugurating social works and doling out property titles and kisses to the end. As dusk fell, Salinas received a phone call on the presidential hot line from Pedro Aspe, who was calling with his report on the final day of business in the markets.

As he heard Aspe's brief message, Salinas's face opened into a smile of relief and satisfaction.

"I am the first Mexican President in thirty years who didn't devalue," he said.

Jaime Serra went to work on December 1 in the Finance Secretary's suite atop an office tower on the Avenida de los Insurgentes. From the first day he encountered difficulties gathering all the information he needed and assembling a top-flight staff. Many of the Secretariat's most proficient officials, following the traditional group dynamics of the PRI system, had left to follow outgoing mentors to other agencies. Even though he was taking over from a PRI administration, his own camp, Serra found surprisingly little continuity.

As part of his preparation for the post, Serra had received from Pedro Aspe, days before the presidential handover, a thick volume of briefing papers known as the "100-Day Book." It was a compendium of all the information, both public and confidential, that the outgoing Finance Secretary considered his successor would need to guide the economy during the first three months of the new administration. Only nine days into his tenure, Serra was scheduled to present the federal budget for the following year at a hearing before the Congress.

The "100-Day Book" described an economy that was ailing but manageable, Serra concluded, although one confidential item gave him a chill when he first saw it: Aspe and his team had projected an immense deficit in the current account for 1995, a total of $30 billion.

But after he took office and saw all the Secretariat's most closely held figures, Serra realized there was a troubling omission in Aspe's briefing book. Nowhere did it mention the *tesobonos*. These were short-term treasury bills, which Mexico had begun to issue under Aspe, denominated in pesos but pegged to the dollar. For investors these bills were very nearly as good as dollars; the burden was on Mexico to provide enough pesos to pay for them at whatever rate the dollar was trading. In his strategic planning Serra had not been factoring in the overall *tesobono* debt—a confidential figure—because the briefing book didn't refer to it. The *tesobonos* had never been discussed in Salinas's economic cabinet, and Salinas had not said anything about them to Zedillo.

But the Secretariat's figures showed an ominous picture. On December 1, the reserves stood at $12.5 billion. But over the past year Salinas's government had issued twice that much—$25 billion—in *tesobonos*. In sum, Serra realized that there was a staggering short-term foreign debt about which he had known virtually nothing before taking office. In 1993 the *tesobonos* had been 3 percent of the total foreign debt. By 1994 they had reached 40 percent.

Moreover, Aspe's team had not included the debts of the state development bank in the overall federal budget deficit. In practice, Serra understood, the deficit was also much larger than reported.

On December 6, three days before his congressional budget presentation, Serra finally received all the data he needed from the outgoing team. In a marathon session with his aides, Serra devised a *tesobono* strategy. If he could just hold the line through December, he concluded, in early 1995 he would negotiate with Washington, where he had many friends, a fast-trigger credit arrangement that would reassure investors. Given the exceptional credibility of Zedillo's election, Serra felt confident that he had the political wherewithal to finesse December. Then, he calculated, with NAFTA in full swing the economy would almost certainly start to grow in early 1995.

Serra's budget presentation to the Congress on December 9 went well enough. The PRI-dominated lawmakers did not balk at his report of the lopsided trade figures and asked only one question about the *tesobonos*. The following week he gave an interview to *The Wall Street Journal*. He said the economy was well in hand and he did not expect to make any changes in exchange-rate policy. (What am I supposed to say? he thought as he listened to the reporter's question. *Yes, we're going to devalue next week?*)

Then suddenly everything started to come undone. After a year of cease-fire the confrontation with the Zapatistas sharpened once again, reviving the markets' jitters. On December 15, the central bank stepped in to prop up the peso, but it didn't help. The following day Mexico lost $855 million in reserves. On December 19, the Mexican press was filled with declarations from Subcomandante Marcos saying that the Zapatistas had occupied thirty-eight Chiapas villages. Reporters rushed to the area. It turned out that the guerrillas had briefly seized one town and blocked some highways, then vanished back into the rain forest. But the peso and the Mexican stock index both plunged.

Serra decided that a peso policy change could no longer be postponed. So he called a meeting on the night of December 19 between the financial authorities and the business and labor leaders in El Pacto. The purpose of that organization, established over a decade of practice, was to secure the support of PRI labor leaders for economic adjustments, ensuring their help in holding down workers' wages and discontent through one punishing anti-inflation program after another. Serra recalled that all changes in exchange-rate policy, dating back years, had been discussed with El Pacto. That was certainly what Salinas had done.

Serra informed Zedillo, who was on the road outside Mexico City, about the planned session. With Zedillo's assent, and after consulting the rest of the economic cabinet, Serra and Miguel Mancera, who had remained as head of the central bank, went into the evening meeting prepared to argue that it was time to stop holding up the peso and let it float. But they met resolute resistance from bankers, industrialists, and agribusiness leaders, who argued that abandoning the limited peso band would be a psychological shock to investors that could sink the currency far lower than its real value. With the businessmen adamant, Mancera finally signaled Serra to step out of the meeting for a moment. Mancera consulted by phone with Zedillo. Then he and Serra decided to give up on floating the peso for the time being and settle for a 15 percent increase in the range of the fluctuation band.

The meeting ended after midnight. Serra rose at dawn on December 20, and on Zedillo's orders he started giving interviews, before the Mexican markets opened at 9 a.m., to Mexican television and radio stations announcing the 15 percent band increase. Serra insisted, undiplomatically, on a narrow economist's definition of the change, saying repeatedly that widening the band did not constitute a devaluation. He blamed the financial instability on the Zapatistas.

After several hours of interviews Serra returned to his office at midday to find mayhem. Top people from Wall Street had been calling and were livid that they could not get hold of Serra in person, especially when they realized that he was out talking to the Mexican public instead. Pedro Aspe would never have left them out in the cold, the American money managers fumed. Several Wall Street callers demanded to know why Serra had not warned them of a devaluation. It rankled him that they had expected he would inform New York before Mexico.

All in all, though, December 20 did not end badly. The leakage of reserves came to only $90 million, a minor scratch compared with the hemorrhage of earlier days.

But the next day it all fell apart. Panic seized the markets. By the afternoon Mexico had lost $4 billion of its reserves and had only $6 billion left. The gap between the reserves and the *tesobonos* went to $16 billion. In just a few hours the country ran out of money to pay its debts. Serra saw that even foreigners were unloading their *tesobonos*, the safest investment Mexico had offered the world. The government, his government, had lost all credibility.

In the evening Serra met again with the Mexican business and labor leaders in El Pacto. They quickly relented and agreed that the peso should float freely and also agreed to a sixty-day freeze on wages and prices. Just after 11 p.m. Mexican television announced the government's decision to let the peso float. The next morning it dropped by 20 percent.

Serra flew that same day, December 22, to New York to face the money managers, representing hundreds of thousands of middle-class Americans who had sustained sudden, huge, and baffling losses. Even in the roughest hours of the NAFTA negotiations Serra had never encountered that kind of unveiled hostility. Staunchly defending his decision to consult the players in El Pacto about the peso change, he offered the American investors a primer lesson in the dynamics of Mexican decision making. The investors were incensed that Serra was patronizing them while billions of dollars of their firms' money were draining away. They felt betrayed; they longed, none too discreetly, for Pedro Aspe. Serra was shocked to see how psychological factors he regarded as secondary could generate a stampede in the globalized economy. It seemed absurd to him that such complex and weighty economic decision making had gone awry to some degree because he lacked Aspe's touch.

In the following days Zedillo and Serra turned to the U.S. government for help and began to get it almost immediately (even though Washington was also in a transition between Treasury Secretaries). Whereas Wall Street did not know or trust Serra, Washington did, because of his role in NAFTA. Officials there quickly activated a standing mechanism providing $5 billion in credit for Mexico in an emergency. (Later, in the spring of 1995, Mexico would be aided with a $52 billion bailout led by the Clinton administration.)

After his trip to New York, Serra realized that to restore investors' confidence, Zedillo would need a completely new economic program, one that would be very hard on the Mexican people—but that Serra now lacked the political means to carry out. On the day after Christmas he sent a note to the President attached to a proposal for the new adjustment program. Addressing the President as Ernesto, and using the familiar *tú*, Serra wrote that his credibility was shot. As Trade Secretary, Serra pointed out, he had defended the big balance-of-payments deficit, arguing that it was necessary to get NAFTA off the ground. Now he would have to blame the devaluation on a policy he had vigorously promoted.

For several days Zedillo wouldn't hear of Serra's resigning. In the first predawn hours of December 28, Serra, exhausted, arrived home from his Secretariat offices to find his wife in labor. He drove her to the hospital. There he received a call from Los Pinos, where Zedillo was waiting to see him.

The President had realized that Serra would have to go, and he could not conceal his desolation. "This is unfair," Zedillo said.

"Ernesto, this is not a problem of fairness. This is a problem of state," Serra replied. "You have to put it all on me. I'll take the hit."

Zedillo had never expected that he would have to govern without Serra, one of the few people in the government whom he trusted as a friend. Zedillo was discovering the solitude of the Mexican President just when he had to face the fury of his people over another economic catastrophe.

For a moment the two men were overwhelmed with sadness. Then it dawned on them that Serra's brief career as Finance Secretary would end with a moment of the absurd. That day, December 28, was the Mexican equivalent of April Fools' Day. Serra could not announce his resignation on this day, because half of Mexico might think it was a tasteless joke.

He resigned on December 29.

Mexicans had been through peso plunges before; it had become an end-of-*sexenio* routine. But this devaluation was humiliating: it left Mexicans feeling that they had allowed Carlos Salinas to play them for fools. He had persuaded them to set aside their native skepticism and to believe that Mexico had finally escaped the Third World for modernity. In the end that turned out to be another illusion.

"I really thought we were growing and that our economy had reached new stability," a carpenter named José Romero told a *New York Times* reporter in the first days of January 1995. As he hammered together a simple roof for a one-room shack, he was still wearing the cap that showed he had voted for the PRI in 1994, but only because he could no longer afford another. He had concluded that the government's promise of progress had been a simple lie. "They've just been trying to trick us," he said.

For poor people, especially in the big cities, the 1994 devaluation brought the return of hunger. Despite the government's freeze, the prices of basic goods shot up. People had to forgo meat, chicken, oranges, and squash and go back to beans and tortillas, the fare of the bare-bones villages from which so many had fled.

But the most painful devastation came to the middle class, the Mexicans who had believed in Salinas the most. During the Salinas years the credit card reached the Mexican masses for the first time. People confidently used their cards to buy big-screen televisions, video players, and home computers. After the devaluation the value of their savings collapsed, and many lost their jobs. When they didn't pay their bills, the banks treated them like criminals. Even more disastrous was the plight of those who bought into the dream by signing adjustable-rate mortgages to purchase homes. (With the country's history of chronic inflation, Mexican banks did not offer fixed-rate mortgage loans.) By February 1995, when interest rates soared to over 100 percent, those debtors faced the choice of becoming credit renegades or being turned into the street by the banks.

On January 3, 1995, Zedillo announced his first program to revive the economy. It was harsh, but not harsh enough; investors stayed away. In that environment the new government began to blame the old one more vocally for the catastrophe. While Zedillo and his new Finance Secretary, Guillermo Ortiz, acknowledged that the devaluation was mishandled, they also pointed up the weaknesses of the economy they inherited from Salinas. At first Salinas, watching from his Coyoacán home, maintained the silence that PRI tradition demanded of former Presidents.

But PRI tradition was blown away on February 28, when federal agents set a trap for Salinas's brother Raúl and arrested him at their sister Adriana's home on charges of masterminding the murder of José Francisco Ruiz Massieu. In all the PRI's years of corruption and foul play, no immediate relative of a former President had ever been arrested. A bold stroke by Zedillo against impunity in high places, it was also nothing less than a declaration of war with his predecessor.

That same afternoon Carlos Salinas called the news show on Televisa, saying he wanted to set the record straight on the peso crisis, because Zedillo's version "did not take into account the errors that were made in December." In other interviews that day Salinas blamed Serra for starting the whole calamity at the meeting with the business and labor groups in El Pacto on December 19. Salinas charged that Serra had tipped off the Mexican bankers there that the government could no longer sustain the peso and they had rushed out with that privileged information to send $13 billion out of Mexico "in a single day."

In the next days Salinas turned once again to political theater to try to salvage his reputation. He showed up on March 3 at a home in a working-class neighborhood in Monterrey that belonged to a beneficiary of his government's social programs. Sitting on a sagging bed in a cramped room, Salinas said he was joining a "battle for truth, for honor, and for dignity" by starting a hunger strike. But the protest didn't even last long enough for him to work up an appetite. Three hours after it started, he flew back to Mexico City in a private jet for talks with Zedillo.

In the meeting, on the evening of March 3 at the Mexico City home of a man who had served in Salinas's cabinet, Zedillo was keen to describe the details of Raúl Salinas's indictment, as if he hoped to persuade his predecessor that he had been right to proceed with it. Salinas countered that his hunger strike was not to protest Raúl's arrest. He was concerned about his own reputation. The press was filled with accusations, blaming Salinas for the financial fiasco and for engineering a cover-up in the Colosio murder investigation. Salinas demanded that Zedillo order his Attorney General to make a public statement clearing him in the Colosio case, and correct the imbalance in the public blame for the economic disaster. Zedillo gave his word that he would.

Zedillo did not try to force Salinas to leave Mexico, nor did he offer him any guarantees if he did. No deal on Salinas's future was reached or even proposed.

In the following days the Attorney General did make a statement exonerating Salinas in the Colosio case, but Zedillo continued to deflect public rage about the peso crash toward the former President. On March 10, Salinas left Mexico, forced by the events into self-imposed exile.

Sam writes:

Salinas flew to New York City, where he arrived unperceived by the media and dropped from public view for three days. On Sunday, March 12, Zedillo's aides told Tim Golden, the *New York Times* bureau chief in Mexico City, a version of the events, saying that Zedillo had forced Salinas into exile. Golden wrote a story outlining a power struggle unmatched in Mexico since President Lázaro Cárdenas had forced his predecessor out of Mexico in 1936. News organizations across the hemisphere went hunting for the former President.

On Tuesday morning, March 14, Salinas telephoned the *Times* in New York, the only American publication he contacted, saying he wanted to get together with Joe Lelyveld, the executive editor. Lelyveld, however, was busy. I was then an education reporter on the *Times's* metro desk. Because I spoke Spanish and had some reporting experience in Mexico, I was asked to accompany the new foreign editor, Bill Keller, to interview Salinas.

I had about an hour to refocus from New York City's schools to the turmoil in Mexico. Keller and I took a taxi from the *Times* offices across town to the official residence of Mexico's ambassador to the United Nations, an elegant five-story brownstone on East Seventy-second Street, where Salinas had been at lunch with the envoy.

We were ushered up a carpeted stairway to a sitting room on an upper floor. Salinas, smiling affably and dressed in a double-breasted suit, rose to greet us, then sat back again into an easy chair, drinking herbal tea.

The interview was a tug-of-war. We wanted to hear how President Zedillo had forced him into exile. He rejected that notion. "Can I return to Mexico?" Mr. Salinas asked rhetorically. "At any moment! Yes!" He paused. "But I don't have plans now to do so."

He only wanted to talk about the Mexican economy. He was seeking to set the record straight, he said, and plunged into a lengthy discourse on the financial debacle. But for once Salinas did not want his remarks to be quoted.

"Then why did you phone our newspaper?" we asked.

"I phoned to speak with Lelyveld," Salinas reminded us.

"But we're a newspaper," we insisted. "Our role is to publish news stories."

We went back and forth. We talked mostly in English, but he and I conversed for a time in Spanish.

"Your Spanish is very good," Salinas lied, eyeing me as he poured on the flattery, as he had with many foreign correspondents who covered his presidency.

He talked about the strengths of the economy he had turned over to his successor. Events had spiraled into crisis, he argued, because of the way Zedillo and his team had managed the economy in their first weeks in office, not because it was ailing at the end of his presidency.

Could we quote his saying that?

Not now, Salinas insisted. Such comments, if published, could undermine what little stability Zedillo had been able to restore, he said.

"The situation in Mexico is delicate," he said. "It is important not to disturb that." Eventually Keller and I persuaded him to allow us to quote him on those two sentences.

At the end I decided to get personal. What did it feel like for a Mexican President, who has enjoyed all the storied powers that go with the post, to leave office and return to being a mere citizen?

"This has been a difficult ninety days," Salinas said, sipping forlornly at his tea. "A former President of Mexico has to adjust to a different way of life. You have so many duties and responsibilities that end sharply. And that's it."

The story ran the next day on the front page of *The New York Times*. Salinas had made himself into a media phenomenon during his presidency, and his buzz was only amplified by the mysteries about his exile and whereabouts. So even when he said almost nothing, Salinas was still big news.

— — —

As Zedillo struggled to rebuild the economy during the spring, Jaime Serra and Pedro Aspe remained silent. In July, Aspe wrote an article that appeared in the Mexican newspaper *Reforma* and in *The Wall Street Journal*, defending his opposition back in November to a devaluation. Serra took a more muted approach, airing some of his views in a letter to the magazine *The Economist*. Months later the central bank put out a technical report on the devaluation containing an item of information that undercut Salinas's central contention: that Mexican bankers who attended the December 19 meeting of El Pacto, where Serra had discussed devaluation, had rushed out to protect their positions ahead of the game. The final central bank figures confirmed that on December 20, the trading session after the notorious meeting, there had been no run on the reserves, as Salinas had charged. The peso sell-off was on December 21.

The recriminations were not surprising, given the bitter times, but they were misplaced. The peso crisis was not primarily the result of the mistakes of one official or another—of Pedro Aspe or Jaime Serra—although mistakes were made on both sides. The crisis resulted from a systemic breakdown in the transfer of power from one PRI President to another.

The critical moment had occurred on November 20 in Salinas's library when he and Zedillo failed to agree on devaluation. In a time of mounting crisis there was no longer any stable institutional framework for transferring control of the economy from one President to the next. Like so much of Salinas's *sexenio*, it boiled down to a confrontation between a handful of politicians and spur-of-the-moment choices by the President. Even though both he and Zedillo were within the PRI system, Salinas held the only effective power in the final weeks of his term. As he hesitated to devalue, asserting the political interests of his presidency over those of his successor's, consensus and even communication about the economy broke down between the two men and their administrations.

The peso crisis marked the failure of the *dedazo*, which had been the central pivot of the PRI system, as the mechanism for transferring power. It was a delayed consequence of the doubtful mandate with which Salinas started his term. During his *sexenio* Salinas had tried to overcome the doubts about his legitimacy by reinforcing his own power, centralizing more and more decisions in his own hands rather than fortifying the democratic process in Mexican society. But the trade opening that Salinas carried out made economic decision making infinitely more complex, while it also stimulated political diversity at the grass roots. By 1994 it had become too much for Salinas to handle. The lack of a pluralistic foundation, democratic method, and institutional armature for the presidential turnover made the whole system unstable. At the moment of the handoff, when Salinas needed to convey control of a wavering economy to his successor, the system cracked.

As for Salinas, after he left, Mexicans turned against him with an almost pathological vengeance. In a few brief months the imagery of progress that had sustained his presidency dissolved, and his reformist achievements were banished from popular memory. He had to withdraw his candidacy to head the World Trade Organization and was denied any credit for the trade explosion under NAFTA that soon took place. The PRI tried to expel him, and its leaders rushed to show that none of them had ever been close to him. Not more than a handful of Mexicans dared to admit publicly that they had ever admired him, and his presidency was treated in Mexico as a historical void, six years left blank. His principal public monument was a rubber mask with a bald head and floppy ears that sold briskly to motorists on the Paseo de la Reforma. After his presidency Mexico made Salinas play one more dramatic role, that of the unredeemable villain.

He did have one small victory. His phrase "the errors of December" became the folk term for the devaluation, giving some life to the notion that it was not entirely his fault.

9

Ernesto Zedillo, the Outsider

Until just a few days before Ernesto Zedillo was tapped by President Salinas to replace the slain Luis Donaldo Colosio as the PRI presidential candidate, no one really thought he could be the next President of Mexico—least of all Zedillo himself.

One of the rare light moments at Los Pinos in Zedillo's early days in office came after his private secretary, Liébano Sáenz, made a casual mention of something Colosio had done in his effort to win the tap as the PRI candidate. Sáenz, who had been part of Colosio's inner circle, recalled that he had ordered his staff to prepare secret profiles of all his competitors. Colosio wanted to study them to figure out how to outshine them in Salinas's eyes. His staff had gone to work to uncover the idiosyncrasies of Pedro Aspe, Manuel Camacho, and several others whom Sáenz named for Zedillo. When he came to the end of the list, Sáenz stopped short, embarrassed.

Zedillo asked the logical question. "No profile of me?"

"No profile of you," Sáenz said. "We didn't think there was any chance that you would be President."

Zedillo chuckled. "Neither did I," he said.

Because he wasn't a player in the PRI system, few people considered Zedillo a contender. Even though he had served for more than a decade in government and held two cabinet posts, he remained something of an unknown to the PRI elite. They weren't sure what he stood for or wanted. They regarded him as an outsider.

In many ways he was. Zedillo had never joined the Revolutionary Family, as the extended PRI dynasty was known. Although he was born (in 1951) in Mexico City, when he was a boy his working-class family moved to Mexicali, a Baja California border town that grew in the desert around sand-blown industrial parks. He went to public schools and, according to the folklore, shined shoes in the street to help his mother make ends meet.

It was no accident that Baja California had been the first state to be taken over by the opposition. It was on the outer orbit of the PRI galaxy, largely ignored by the central powers in Mexico City. In Mexicali there was a lot of raw Mexico for a boy to see: a constant flow of migrants hunting for assembly jobs or nighttime crossings to the United States; thriving markets for marijuana, stolen cars, and other sleazy border commodities. At the same time, U.S. territory is within plain sight of Mexicali's downtown. The more prosperous and orderly way of life beyond the border was right there for the young Zedillo to examine.

At age fourteen he was sent back to the capital for secondary school, and he stayed there to attend university at the Politécnico, that great conduit for lower-middle-class social mobility. At that time the Mexican welfare state's meritocracy, one of the enduring positive legacies of the revolution, was at the peak of its efficiency, and Zedillo was a meritorious student. After getting a respectable and practically free undergraduate education at the Politécnico, Zedillo won government scholarships that paid for him to take an economics doctorate at Yale. He finished his doctoral studies in 1978, when he was twenty-seven.

Although Zedillo had joined the PRI when he was twenty, he was never especially active in party affairs. He never sought to run for public office, instead beginning his career in government in 1978 at the Banco de México, the central bank. Even though the bank was very much a tool of the President in that period, it was regarded as one of Mexico's most serious and professional institutions, generally isolated from PRI politicking. Central bankers were aware of the kleptocracy in the government but did not on the whole participate in it. Zedillo had mentors, not cronies, and he advanced by excelling as a brainy and diligent technocrat. Probably his most innovative accomplishment at the bank was a program he devised to protect struggling Mexican corporations against currency fluctuations. It played a crucial but inconspicuous role in reviving the economy in that period.

Zedillo moved into a more political arena in 1987, when he took a job at the Planning Secretariat, which managed federal spending. Just a year later, Salinas chose him to be the Secretary there. Zedillo proved an efficient but not outstanding member of Salinas's cabinet; he never displayed the panache of Pedro Aspe or the populist imagination of Manuel Camacho. In 1992 Salinas shifted Zedillo to be Secretary of Education, a post where he smoothly implemented a reform to streamline and decentralize the monstrous public-education bureaucracy.

Perhaps the most severe test of Zedillo's political mettle before 1994 was a scandal over some textbooks the Education Secretariat published, at President Salinas's behest, when he was in charge there. The texts gave a modestly nuanced portrait of Porfirio Díaz, going beyond the conventional rendering of the odious dictator to note his efforts to modernize Mexico's economy and consolidate its national government. They also included a gingerly mention of the Mexican armed forces' role in the Tlatelolco massacre. The Generals were furious, and the PRI establishment was filled with revolutionary outrage. Salinas, disturbed by the controversy, withdrew his support for the texts, and Zedillo accommodated the system's orthodoxy by revising them—censoring them, the authors said.

Going into the 1994 presidential year, Zedillo even looked callow: he wore big square glasses and an eager grin. Colosio chose him to manage his campaign, apparently in recognition of Zedillo's loyalty and economic smarts rather than his political acumen.

Even after the Colosio shooting, President Salinas made it no secret that he was not thinking of Zedillo to replace him but working to get a constitutional waiver for Pedro Aspe. Support for Zedillo among PRI bosses was negligible as the old guard pressed Salinas to tap Fernando Ortiz Arana, a dinosaur who was then the head of the party.

Zedillo's *destape*, or unveiling as the candidate, on March 29, 1994, at PRI headquarters in Mexico City served only to highlight the party's lack of enthusiasm for its new standard-bearer. Party leaders, miffed that their man had been passed over, balked at raising the customary street crowd for Zedillo, convening only a small gathering in an inner salon. The applause for the new candidate was subdued, and his anxious smile seemed to reveal that he was keenly aware of his party's indifference.

Then, during his campaign, Zedillo engaged in little of the bonding with the national PRI party apparatus that had always been the main point of the campaign exercise under the PRI. For example, Zedillo was supposed to pick his firmest allies in the party as candidates for the prime seats in the Congress to ensure maximum cooperation from the legislature. But he just wasn't interested in selecting the candidates. Instead, he wondered out loud time and again to his staff why the PRI had no procedures for its members to choose their candidates.

Nevertheless, the accidental candidate and his party closed ranks as the election approached. Like a PRI stalwart, Zedillo pressed every advantage the system afforded in terms of media exposure and campaign finance. (Figures released later showed that the PRI accounted for 71 percent of the money spent by all the campaigns, whereas Cuauhtémoc Cárdenas, for example, spent 6 percent of the total.) With Zedillo's 50.1 percent tally and high turnout, his was the most credible PRI presidential victory in decades.

As a result, Zedillo reached his inauguration, on December 1, 1994, with solid electoral backing and extraordinarily few political debts. He was a young president—just a few weeks shy of his forty-third birthday. Since he belonged to no PRI clique and had made no effort to create one, he brought no corps of cronies with him to office, only a few trusted professional colleagues like Jaime Serra.

He also came to power with many ideas that owed little to the PRI canon. Steeped in neoliberal economics, he believed in the virtues of free markets, global commerce, and international capital. He opposed protected trade, big government, social patronage, and foreign indebtedness, policies that were still firmly enshrined in PRI doctrine, even after more than a decade of neoliberal Presidents. Moreover, Zedillo maintained that sound economic policy required transparent accounting and straight talk from government rather than the PRI's opaque, clubby rhetoric. He did not like simulation, either economic or political; he didn't like magical fiscal management or fake elections. In addition, as a matter of personality and experience, Zedillo had little patience and no talent for the baroque machinations of PRI-style rule. In Zedillo, Mexico now had a President who was seriously uncomfortable with the gap between declaration and action in the workings of the state.

Carlos Salinas, of course, was also a neoliberal economist, but there was a crucial difference between them. Whereas Salinas believed that democratic reform should come after an economic opening, lest it destabilize market conditions, Zedillo was convinced that democracy was a prerequisite of flourishing markets.

"Economic reform is not enough," Zedillo would tell a gathering of American businessmen in a speech in New York City early in his term where he expounded his concept in detail. "That is the lesson that the whole world has learned in this era of global change: prosperity depends on the free market, and the free market, in the end, requires a democratic society."

After the bloody events of 1994 the new President also appears to have reached one more unorthodox conclusion: that the old system was falling apart and could no longer provide the stability and social welfare that had been its central promise.

Zedillo first laid out his agenda in his address to the Congress at his inauguration. "We must acknowledge that our democratic progress so far has been insufficient," he said. "The time has come for democracy to extend to all areas of life in our society." What Mexicans needed and wanted, he said, was "a new democracy that offers a better relation between the citizens and the government, between the states and the federation; that offers a new code of ethics between political contenders, and a definitive electoral reform." There should be a "better balance" between the President and the Congress and courts, he said. He proposed to "liquidate centralism" and share the President's powers with state and town governments.

"I am ready to assume my responsibility for building a fairer elections system," he went on. His "definitive reform"—he used the same words twice for emphasis—would "dissipate all the doubts, suspicions, and recriminations that tarnish our elections."

He even acknowledged that his own election had been flawed, an admission that no prior PRI President had ever been willing to make. He said he wanted new campaign-finance laws with spending limits; regulations to ensure fair media coverage; and a fully independent agency to oversee elections, supplanting the hybrid developed by Salinas, which was headed by the Government Secretary.

Zedillo's earliest statements of his goals served mainly to open a gap of skepticism between him and the Mexican public that would persist throughout his term. The *priístas* had been calling their regime a democracy for decades, so nothing the new President said sounded novel to them. The opposition was used to being told that the ruling party was just about to perfect its democracy. In short, everyone heard Zedillo talking about democracy, but few Mexicans thought that he really meant it.

From his first days in Los Pinos, Zedillo was a loner who engaged in a minimum of palace politics. He instructed Luis Téllez, another economist who was his first chief of staff, and Sáenz, his closest aide, to cut out all meetings that were not essential to his immediate policy objectives.

"He didn't invite the political elite to Los Pinos to shoot the breeze with them and coddle them," Téllez recalled later. "So some people felt uncomfortable because they were used to having the President listen to them and, while he was listening, to do them some favor or other. And that was what President Zedillo didn't do, period."

Whereas it had been customary for *el Señor Presidente* to be courted and petitioned by supplicants of all stripes, Zedillo regarded such entreaty as undignified. In the sitting room of his office at Los Pinos he hung a lithograph by a Oaxacan artist, Francisco Toledo, of a large cricket. In Mexico the Spanish word for cricket, *grillo*, also denotes someone who is always engaged in cheap political maneuvering and gossip—"a third-rate politician," as Zedillo once defined the term. If he felt that a visitor had come to press some personal interest on him, he would sit the guest in an armchair under the painting, then point to the *grillo* on the wall behind. "Don't try to lobby me!" Zedillo would say, shaking his finger.

Manuel Camacho was among several visitors who did get to see Zedillo at Los Pinos during the first grueling months of his *sexenio* and found him in shirtsleeves, transfixed by a computer terminal displaying spreadsheets of economic data. Like a college professor in the throes of research, Zedillo got out his graphs and set about to convince his guests of his thesis about the way out of the financial crisis. (He argued that Mexico not only had to reduce its foreign debt but also had to build up a deep reserve of savings within the country to buffer against future crises.)

Zedillo moved methodically to reduce the ostentation of his office. He did not host or attend the leisurely three-hour tequila luncheons where business typically got done in Mexico City. He would either have a taco in the office or walk over to his residence for a bite with his wife and five children. Officials in his government had to tuck away their Rolexes, because the President was wearing a Casio with a black plastic band. At times didactically puritan, Zedillo threatened to expel smokers from cabinet meetings.

Following the peso crash just three weeks after his inauguration, Zedillo was even more intent on removing any splendor from his presidency. At his first State of the Union *informe*, on September 1, 1995, he trimmed his speech to one hour, instead of the usual four. He canceled the traditional bank holiday that day, as well as the confetti parade, and skipped the *besamanos*, the hand kissing. Two weeks later, at his first celebration of the *grito*, the Independence Day festivities, Zedillo slashed the guest list for the cocktail party at the National Palace and allowed no hors d'oeuvres. The hungry guests huddled in a half-empty hall.

At the appointed hour of 11 p.m., Zedillo stepped out onto the balcony of the National Palace, above the teeming Zócalo, and intoned the traditional phrase: "*¡Mexicanos! ¡Viva México!*" His voice was so small and tentative that he left the crowd dissatisfied.

Zedillo's plans for democratic reform were quickly overshadowed by the trauma of the peso collapse. Amid the hardship Zedillo began to articulate a new concept of national stability. Throughout its rule the PRI had kept "the social peace" by stifling pluralism, on the premise that if the system relaxed its grip, *el México bronco* would leap out. After the peso crisis Zedillo started to argue that in order to restore and maintain stability, Mexico urgently needed better democratic representation to channel diversity instead of suppressing it.

On January 17, 1995, in the worst days of the peso disaster, he called together the leaders of all the political parties. He persuaded them to sign a document, called the Pact of Los Pinos, in which they agreed—although with much skepticism—to get to work on the "definitive reform." With the economy in ruins, more political freedom was all Zedillo had to offer opposition leaders to win a minimum of their cooperation for the harsh fiscal recovery program he was proposing. Still, he said he hoped to achieve the changes with the consensus of everyone in the pact. "Democracy cannot be imposed by a government or a party or an ideological faction. Democracy must be built with the participation of everyone," Zedillo told the party leaders.

To dispel the opposition's doubts about his commitment, Zedillo agreed in the pact to resolve yet another election dispute, this time in the governor's race in the Gulf Coast state of Tabasco. As a result of this pledge, however, Zedillo's pact, which was supposed to live in history, did not survive to summer. Zedillo found himself pitted against a wily lord of the system, who showed him that brave declarations from Los Pinos would not be nearly enough to open Mexico.

Unlike Zedillo, Roberto Madrazo was born into the Revolutionary Family. His father, Carlos Alberto Madrazo, had been a populist governor of Tabasco in the late 1950s. Later, as president of the PRI, the senior Madrazo had tried to abolish the *dedazo* and allow party members to elect their candidates for local office. He ran headlong into the party machine and President Díaz Ordaz, who quashed his reforms. In 1969 he died in a plane crash, which raised enduring suspicions that he had been killed by reactionaries within the ruling party.

His son Roberto acquired a taste for power growing up in the Quinta Grijalva, the palm-shaded governor's mansion in Tabasco's languid delta capital, Villahermosa. Roberto was active in the PRI when a teenager, and after earning a law degree from the UNAM in 1974, he was named to head the party's National Revolutionary Youth Movement, a post he used to forge ties with party members all across Mexico. In 1981 he was appointed to serve as president of a borough of Mexico City by Carlos Hank González, El Profesor, the fabled Mexico City mayor who was then very busy using his office to amass a fortune; Hank became Madrazo's political godfather.

In 1988 the PRI made Madrazo a senator as well as president of the

Tabasco state party, and he rapidly built his following among the state's truck farmers, oilmen, and ranchers. He became a cacique in the old style, munificent with the faithful and unforgiving with foes.

Madrazo did not look the part of a good ole boy. He was fair-skinned, bird-boned, and always fastidiously groomed; his enemies loved to spread rumors that he was homosexual. Although he could be soft-spoken in one-on-one conversation, on the stump he demonstrated gifts as a demagogue. A cheerleader for President Salinas and his economic modernization when both were on the rise, Madrazo shifted quickly when Salinas fell into disgrace. He began to assail the federal government and champion the little people of Tabasco, offering to stand up to the callous bureaucrats and lapsed nationalists in *el centro,* Mexico City. Madrazo showed early on that he was not afraid to spend the taxpayers' money in his crusade for his particular brand of states' rights.

His most formidable rival in Tabasco politics, Andrés Manuel López Obrador, was his equal as a populist and even more gifted as a grassroots organizer. López Obrador's career also started in the Tabasco PRI but not from a position of privilege: in the 1970s he served as the state director of the federal agency in charge of Indian affairs. In 1982 he was tapped to manage the PRI gubernatorial campaign, and he became the state party president the next year, five years before Madrazo held the post. During that period López Obrador also represented the state in hard negotiations with Pemex, demanding the cleanup of polluted oil sites.

In 1984 he left Tabasco for a job with a federal consumer-rights agency in Mexico City. There his frustrations with the PRI grew, and as the 1988 elections approached, Cuauhtémoc Cárdenas's criticism resonated with him. He returned to Tabasco to run for governor representing Cárdenas's breakaway coalition.

Defeated amid the nationwide fraud of 1988, López Obrador galvanized a voters' rights movement of civil resistance, leading marches, sit-ins, and roadblocks across Tabasco. He was telegenic, and his plain-spoken eloquence, in the sibilant tongue of the Gulf Coast, appealed to the poorest people of his state. He did not allow the protests to flag; in 1991 he walked for six weeks with a hardy group of protesters from Tabasco all the way to Mexico City.

López Obrador and Madrazo faced off in the governor's contest, scheduled for Sunday, November 20, 1994—days before the end of Carlos Salinas's term, due to an awkward fluke in the electoral calendar. López Obrador ran a shoestring campaign, while Madrazo laid out huge sums of money, buying up media time and paying journalists, effectively shutting his rival out of Tabasco television and radio. López Obrador's workers caught the Madrazo campaign handing out cold cash to voters in some districts.

Madrazo's stretching of even the very loose campaign-finance limits in Tabasco were conspicuous. Zedillo, then still President-elect, dispatched an operative from his transition team in the days before the vote to try to persuade Madrazo to curb his excesses and to convince López Obrador to be patient and accept the election results, whatever they might be. Zedillo's envoy did not succeed on either front.

The official results showed Madrazo winning by 56 percent to 37 percent, a margin of ninety-seven thousand votes. López Obrador rejected the tally. In protest, his supporters occupied dozens of Pemex facilities and wellhead sites, partially paralyzing the oil monopoly's huge operations in Tabasco. López Obrador meanwhile set off on another march to Mexico City, demanding that the election be annulled.

Thus Zedillo took office in the midst of a crisis that threatened his central political initiative, the effort to bring the political parties into negotiations on election reform. The situation demanded a savvy, hands-on response—precisely the sort of political management that Zedillo didn't do. Immersed in the peso crisis, the President delegated Tabasco to his Government Secretary, Esteban Moctezuma, a forty-one-year-old Cambridge-trained economist who was bright but even more guileless than the President.

In an unusual move Moctezuma ordered an investigation of the Tabasco vote from outside the government, giving the job to Santiago Creel and another independent lawyer. Initially Moctezuma got both López Obrador and Madrazo to agree to the probe. Creel and his team, mobilizing polling experts to take scientific samples of the tallies, detected considerable mischief. Their final report to Moctezuma detailed a host of irregularities but stopped short of calling for the vote to be annulled.

Madrazo was furious anyway. He denied ever having signed on to the investigation and distributed a bowdlerized version of the report, elimi-nating references to PRI misdeeds, all across Tabasco. Moctezuma, on the other hand, found the lawyers' report persuasive. Concluding that Zedillo's plan for political reform could not advance if fraud in Tabasco was allowed to stand, he set out to persuade Madrazo to step aside.

But Zedillo's next move was to surprise Moctezuma, as well as the en-tire PRI power structure, by announcing that he would not attend Madrazo's inauguration. To general disbelief, Zedillo insisted that he was not seeking to distance himself from Madrazo. Rather, he said, he re-garded the customary presence of the President at all governors' inaugu-rations as an unacceptable federal intrusion in state politics. Zedillo said he would not attend such ceremonies ever again.

Madrazo was not impressed with Zedillo's principles and was out-raged at the snub. It seemed unlikely that he would survive a week in of-fice without the blessing of the President.

Madrazo's inauguration did come off, if only because thousands of state police patrolled the streets of Villahermosa. Although not a single important federal official attended the ceremony, many PRI state gover-nors traveled to Villahermosa to show their solidarity, incensed at the af-front to a colleague by a President they regarded as fumbling. During the ceremonies PRD demonstrators occupied the Plaza de Armas, Villaher-mosa's main square, and soon advanced to block the entrance to the gov-ernor's palace. Madrazo could not start work in his office.

The blockade dragged on into weeks. Madrazo started shuttling be-tween Villahermosa and Mexico City, where he slipped quietly back into negotiations with the Government Secretary. Eventually Moctezuma proposed that Madrazo give up the Tabasco statehouse and become Sec-retary of Education; that post, the Government Secretary suggested, could position Madrazo for a presidential bid in 2000.

In mid-January, Madrazo told Moctezuma he agreed to the offer, promising to ask the Tabasco state congress for a leave from the gover-nor's post. But Madrazo said nothing to his restive *priísta* supporters back in Tabasco, including the businessmen who had bankrolled his cam-paign, who were anxious for him to get down to work as their governor.

On January 17, when Zedillo and the opposition party leaders signed the pact at Los Pinos to initiate the new electoral reform, Moctezuma thought he had everything nailed down. Zedillo promised the opposition leaders that he would end the Tabasco strife, and they all assumed that meant that Madrazo would soon be removed as governor.

But Madrazo had other ideas. That same day he left a meeting at Los Pinos and went to a columned mansion of green stone in the hills alongside Chapultepec Park to see his mentor, Carlos Hank González. Although retired and withdrawn from everyday party affairs, Hank still held tremendous influence in the PRI. El Profesor told his protégé that the new President seemed not only weak but also indifferent to the interests of the revolution. He advised Madrazo to hang on to his governor's post and create a grassroots force within the PRI to confront Zedillo and his technocrats, a force that could carry Madrazo—and Hank's wing of the PRI—back to the presidency in 2000.

By January 18, when Madrazo flew back to Villahermosa, a PRI insurrection had already begun. The party's state legislators had locked themselves in their chamber, determined to block any request from Madrazo for a leave (and threatening, for good measure, to secede from the nation). Calls were pouring in, from the ruling party's president and from governors across the nation, telling Madrazo to stand firm. Tabasco's business leaders made it clear that they were not prepared to lose their investment in Madrazo because of some whim from *el centro* to placate the opposition.

With state troops surrounding the city center, López Obrador's toughest PRD street fighters fanned out across the main square, bracing for battle.

Madrazo made his way to the Quinta Grijalva. Just before midnight he received a phone call from Zedillo. As a group of PRI militants stood by listening, his voice became calm. "No, no, Mr. President, this is just a natural catharsis for the people," Madrazo said smoothly. "There is some frustration here that I am not going to be their governor. They think we made a concession to the PRD. But you, Mr. President, and I both know that it isn't true, don't we?"

He paused to let Zedillo comment, then responded evenly. "I think we will have it all back under control by the morning. We just need to let them calm down, let out their natural frustration," Madrazo said. "Once things have calmed down, I will go ahead and request my leave," he assured the President. "I will see you soon in Mexico City."

Madrazo spent the rest of the night on the phone trying to placate his supporters. But Villahermosa awoke the next morning to a business strike that shuttered practically every store in town. *Priístas* blocked the main roads to the city and seized the state television station, where they broadcast footage of PRI crowds shouting at Zedillo to fuck his mother—the Mexican national epithet—until the Government Secretariat pulled the plug.

At mid-morning Madrazo instructed an emissary to convey a message to Secretary Moctezuma and Zedillo. "Today," Madrazo said, "I will sit in the chair where my father sat."

At just the same time hundreds of PRI toughs armed with rocks, clubs, and torches surrounded López Obrador's followers in the main square, led by the highest-ranking PRI state congressman, who brandished a baseball bat. Over several hours the *priístas* beat and kicked the PRD protesters until, bloodied, they fled the square. Then came the state police, spraying tear gas and arresting PRD supporters who refused to flee.

The head of the Tabasco state elections council, a *priísta*, cast off the impartiality he had feigned with little enthusiasm during the campaign, calling on citizens to show their support for Madrazo by burning their voter cards. Speaking live on the radio, Madrazo expressed his gratitude "for the bravery with which the people of Tabasco have acted." He took his place behind the desk in the governor's palace a little after 9 p.m.

Madrazo's defiance was a galling embarrassment for Zedillo. Coming in the midst of the peso crisis, it deepened Mexicans' impression that the President was losing control. *El Señor Presidente* had allowed a regional bad boy to provoke a rebellion in his party—and get away with it. When López Obrador saw that Madrazo would not step down, he accused Zedillo of bad faith, and his party, the PRD, pulled out of the electoral reform negotiations. Before long the PAN left as well. Secretary Moctezuma, having lost the confidence of every political party, including his own, resigned in June.

The Tabasco episode made it clear that Mexico's election reform could no longer be postponed, but it also laid bare the resistance to change. In much of Mexico the building blocks of PRI government were still fiefdoms commanded by regional strongmen whose power was held in check only by the President. Self-appointed heirs to the Mexican Revolution, they owed their wealth to the moneymaking mechanisms of the PRI, and after decades of entrenched rule their sense of entitlement was deep. It was one thing to ask them to make more room for their opponents but quite another to demand that they compete seriously for power. After Tabasco, it was evident that Zedillo would never get them to do so by standing on principle and remaining aloof.

By mid-1995 Zedillo would be forced to make peace with Tabasco's de facto governor. The President announced that he and Madrazo would "govern together" until the end of their terms in 2000. Then he traveled to Villahermosa and gave Madrazo a bear hug on the tarmac in front of the presidential jet, with eager photographers clicking away.

If Zedillo's footing was unsure at first on electoral reform, he seemed to be outright flailing on economic policy. In the weeks after the December 19 peso crash, as he and Jaime Serra were buffeted by the events, Zedillo appeared bewildered and overwhelmed. His January 2 package of emergency recovery measures (announced five days after Serra resigned) was dismissed by the markets as vague. As the peso continued to fall, Zedillo sought billions of dollars in rescue funds from the United States and the International Monetary Fund. In Washington the Congress heaped scorn on Mexico and balked at the bailout.

The spectacle made Mexicans begin to think the unthinkable: they wondered if Zedillo was really fit for his office. The traditional reverence was abandoned. "The President can't handle it!" decreed the cover of *Proceso* magazine. Porfirio Muñoz Ledo derided Zedillo's inexperience, dubbing him "Ernesto the Unborn," and Cuauhtémoc Cárdenas demanded that he resign.

Gradually, however, Zedillo regained his balance by implementing his hard-numbers, straight-talk approach to economics—often against the political counsel of his advisers. "The development of Mexico requires that we recognize, with complete realism, that we are not a rich country. We are a nation with grave needs and wants," he said, unveiling his new method in a gloomy televised address in early January.

By the end of February, Mexico had hit bottom. President Bill Clinton, after his bailout proposal was spurned by the Congress, reached into an executive reserve fund to provide $20 billion in emergency loans. But Mexico, in a new humiliation, was obliged to put up some of its petroleum holdings to guarantee the debt. On March 9, Zedillo and Guillermo Ortiz, the new Finance Secretary, finally announced an emergency program that seemed viable, slashing government spending while raising the cost of gasoline and electricity and increasing the national sales tax.

However, the only way Zedillo could get the PRI to swallow the austerity measures was by exercising the presidential fiat that he claimed he wanted to forswear. Unhappy PRI legislators, bowing to the President's will in a vote on March 10, passed the bill to raise the sales tax, known as the IVA, from 10 to 15 percent. On the floor of the Chamber of Deputies, the opposition delegates denounced their PRI colleagues as "ass lickers" and waved eggs at them, a reference to their testicles meant to encourage them to stand up to Zedillo. Adolfo Aguilar Zinser, then a deputy for the PRD, articulated the majority view. "This program is not viable, for a very simple reason: it does not have the support of anyone in the society," he said from the podium. "Ernesto Zedillo, alone against the rest of the country, will not be able to make this program succeed."

Two nights after the IVA vote Zedillo gave another grim television broadcast. He had taken measures that were "hard, painful," he acknowledged, because there had been new "deterioration and disorder" in the financial markets that could bring "a financial and productive collapse that would paralyze job-giving companies and services." There were "no easy or pleasant routes" out of the crisis, he said, and he expected "discipline and constancy" from the Mexican people to carry out his program. However, Zedillo promised, if everyone stuck to his plan, Mexicans would see recovery within a matter of months.

After the confrontation in Tabasco, Andrés Manuel López Obrador, unlike Zedillo, did not relent. He continued for months to stoke protests, bringing them from provincial Tabasco to the heart of the nation in Mexico City.

One day in June 1995, when he was addressing an antifraud rally in the Mexico City Zócalo, two strangers in a pickup truck pulled into the square and unloaded a bulky cargo: forty-five boxes full of documents. After a cursory inspection López Obrador rented a room in a nearby hotel and hired workmen to carry the boxes there, stacking them neatly in rows up to the ceiling.

The boxes—evidently purloined by a disgruntled Tabasco *priísta* from the party's Villahermosa offices—contained political treasure for López Obrador. They were original documents (not copies) from the PRI's financial files from Madrazo's campaign. For the first time the opposition had solid evidence of the ruling party's illicit campaign spending. López Obrador took the documents to the Attorney General, Antonio Lozano Gracia, and called on him to bring a federal case against Madrazo for campaign-spending violations.

After auditing the documents, Lozano concluded that Madrazo had spent $38.8 million to win the governor's seat in Tabasco. That was thirty-three times the state limit and, with fewer than 500,000 registered voters in the state, about $135 for every vote won.

For any determined prosecutor the documents would seem to have contained ample evidence for both state and federal charges against Madrazo. But even Lozano, although he hailed from the opposition, was not determined enough. Madrazo was able to use his vast network of political connections, and his understanding of the inner workings of the Mexican legal system, to defeat every attempt to pursue a prosecution against him.

While Madrazo remained firmly in charge in Tabasco, López Obrador sustained a running battle against him that enhanced his national profile as an opposition leader of vigor and tenacity. Mexican media coverage was growing more pluralistic, and López Obrador's crusade against the PRI made great television.

As the months of 1995 went by, Santiago Creel could see that Zedillo's democratic reform negotiations were going nowhere. So he gathered together some of his buddies and began to brainstorm. If the government couldn't do it, they thought, perhaps they should design the "definitive reform" themselves. This simple notion was radical in Mexico, where the Government Secretary had always initiated and controlled any effort at reform.

Creel had been one of the citizen councillors at the Federal Electoral Institute who helped organize—and criticize—the 1994 presidential balloting, an experience that gave him a rare look inside the PRI elections machine. After reprising that role in Tabasco, he began to think of election reform as his calling. "They thought they were bringing us in to be decorative," Creel said of the new breed of independent elections officials. "They took me into the living room of the system, then the dining room. But I was rude. I didn't stop there. I went back into the kitchen, rifled through the pantry. I got down into the basement."

Creel and his group decided to invite representatives from the political parties and elections activists to a series of drafting sessions. Not wishing to be too conspicuous, they labeled the meetings a "seminar." But they needed a venue, one that was unequivocally Mexican and would also lend a sense of moment to the proceedings. It was Creel who thought of Chapultepec Castle.

Surrounded by broad verandas, *el castillo* stands on a plateau rising from Chapultepec Park, with a commanding view (when smog allows) of the entire Valley of Mexico. Mexican schoolchildren know it as the promontory from which young military cadets leaped to their deaths in 1847 to avoid capture by invading U.S. troops. But the castle is also a gilded monument to Mexican aristocracy and despotic power: the emperor Maximilian once lived there, as did Porfirio Díaz.

It was precisely the range of Mexican political currents that converged at the castle that attracted Creel to it. But he knew that if he asked permission to use it for his electoral intrigue, the government would say no. So he marched one day into the director's office, announcing that she should prepare a salon with a long table because many of Mexico's most influential leaders would be arriving for meetings. The flustered director refused, as predicted, but Creel's group issued their invitations anyway. Chapultepec Castle was taken over once again, only this time very politely.

Creel soon learned that the chamber where the seminar was held had once been the living quarters of President Plutarco Elías Calles, the founding architect of the PRI system. Creel was delighted to think that he was using the bedroom of the Maximal Chief to plot the demise of his system.

Even as the Government Secretary's negotiations on Avenida Bucareli faltered, the meetings at Chapultepec Castle moved briskly forward. Among the leaders were Porfirio Muñoz Ledo, then president of the PRD, and Carlos Castillo Peraza, his PAN counterpart; other participants included intellectuals, elections experts, and citizens with ideas. The meetings were closed and by invitation only, giving them the ambience of an insurgent cabal. Before long PRI leaders called to see if they could join, like children cadging invitations to an interesting birthday party. In June 1995 the PRI officially joined the talks.

Muñoz Ledo's crucial contribution was to bring the disputatious PRD to support the reform. Many in the leftist party doubted that negotiations without militant protest would ever lead the system to change. After Cárdenas's humbling in the 1994 vote, the PRD had become fascinated with López Obrador and his confrontational tactics. But Muñoz Ledo convinced a party congress in August 1995 to embrace institutional reform. "Dialogue is not just one method of struggle. It is the form itself of democratic change," he insisted in a thundering address. "Our challenge is to rebuild the state as a democracy, not to destroy it irresponsibly." His proposals were finally adopted in the congress's conclusions.

The Chapultepec seminar concluded in January 1996, producing a sixty-point document that made detailed proposals in every area of electoral reform and some others not directly related to elections. In the final days, however, the PRI representatives suddenly bolted. Seeing that the castle talks had far outrun the official process at Bucareli, the PRI members wanted to make sure that credit for any reform went to them, not to Santiago Creel and his effete crowd—and certainly not to Porfirio Muñoz Ledo.

Creel was vexed by the PRI's attitude. "This is no time to be declaring false paternity for the reforms," he said in his deep, stern voice at the seminar's closing session. Still, at core his remarks were not unlike the ones that Zedillo had made when he launched the negotiations at Los Pinos. "In times such as these," Creel said, "political change must belong to all Mexicans equally."

After the success of the Chapultepec seminar, everyone seemed to be talking about election reform. The negotiations at Bucareli revived, and new ones started in the Congress. But the momentum stalled yet again when the PAN pulled out of the Bucareli talks once more. The PAN was annoyed at the PRI for stealing a mayoral election in an unexceptional corn-farming town named Huejotzingo, in the state of Puebla, whose governor was Manuel Bartlett.

He had never been shy about his belief that the PRI system was the most appropriate one for Mexico and had served the country well. Bartlett observed with alarm that opposition parties were winning town and state elections across the country, chipping away at the PRI's hegemony. Whenever a race was close, he would stand and fight. The Huejotzingo race was very close, but the PAN was certain it had won. After the PRI candidate took office anyway, the PAN appealed to the state elections commission, where Bartlett applied his influence. The commission found for the PRI after crudely annulling just the right number of PAN votes.

Weeks went by, and the PAN refused to return to the Bucareli talks, citing the situation in Huejotzingo. Zedillo, exasperated, recognized that the impasse demanded his involvement. He invited Bartlett to Los Pinos, sitting him down on the other side of a bare round table in the presidential office under the exacting gaze of the portrait of Benito Juárez. "Listen, Manuel, the trouble in that little town is holding up a political reform that is the most important item on my whole agenda," Zedillo said, pointing his finger at Bartlett for emphasis. "Manuel, I want to know: Did we win in Huejotzingo?"

Bartlett was taken aback by the bluntness of the question. He began to describe the fine points of the case. Zedillo interrupted. "No, Manuel. What I need to know is: Did we win or not?"

Bartlett hesitated. He wasn't sure where he stood with Zedillo. Few Mexicans had accumulated more prestige and power within the system than Bartlett, but he didn't know what that meant to this President. "Of course we won," Bartlett replied at last. "But you know there are always different visions, different interpretations of what it means to win . . ."

"Manuel, did we win or not?"

"Well, there were a few things that might be in dispute . . ."

"So we *didn't* win?"

Bartlett fell quiet. Zedillo's anger flashed. "I don't care how you do it, but you go back there right now and you recognize the PAN's victory and you bring the *priístas* in that town into line."

Bartlett, at a loss, restrained his temper out of respect for presidential authority. But once he was outside Zedillo's office, he vented his irritation to some of the President's advisers. "If we start giving in on things like this," Bartlett said, referring to the Puebla town, "one day we're going to lose the whole show!"

The President's aides found Zedillo at his desk, shaking his head about his party's leaders. "They keep underestimating me," he said.

In mid-May 1996 the PRI mayor in Huejotzingo resigned, a PAN mayor took over, and the PAN returned to the reform negotiations.

By this time the reform had become a great stew enriched with ingredients from many, many Mexicans. President Zedillo, the Congress, the PRI, the opposition parties on left and right, the Federal Electoral Institute, and a panoply of nongovernmental experts and informed citizens had all added something to the mix.

On the evening of July 25, 1996, the party leaders trooped once again to Los Pinos, this time in a buoyant mood. They signed an agreement to adopt seventeen constitutional amendments and a number of other laws that created a whole new framework for elections in Mexico. Almost all of the opposition's original goals—which had seemed mere pipe dreams at the outset—were addressed. The reform banished the government once and for all from organizing and overseeing elections. The Federal Electoral Institute, now fully autonomous and run by a council chosen by the Congress, was entirely in charge. The political parties were permitted to receive both public and private financing for campaigns, with the public funds distributed proportionally among them and the private funds subject to limits. A special elections court was created, and the institute was authorized to monitor media coverage of campaigns to ensure fair treatment for all candidates.

Mexicans were guaranteed the right to join the political party of their choice. No longer would they have to enroll in the PRI in order to join a labor union or get a government job. And, in a breakthrough that spelled evident trouble for the PRI, the reform gave the residents of Mexico

City, that hotbed of opposition, the right to elect their mayor for the first time.

Zedillo tried to remain solemn when he addressed the gathering, but he was clearly overjoyed. Here was the "definitive reform" of his inaugural promise; in his speech he added the words "decisive" and "irreversible" as well. As he had pledged, the reforms were supported by the consensus of the entire political spectrum. Even Santiago Creel rejoiced. The Congress convened a special session to approve the legislation, with passage expected to be pro forma, taking no more than a week or two.

But several months came and went without a vote as the congressional debate became deadlocked over the issue of campaign finance. The PRI insisted on allotting nearly $290 million in public funds to the political parties for the upcoming 1997 congressional campaigns, a sixfold increase over the government funds allocated for the presidential campaign of 1994. Suspicious of the PRI's motives, both the PAN and the PRD said the amount was exorbitant. The opposition parties assumed that the PRI brass was driving the finance dispute, trying to maximize its own funding, but they were wrong.

It was Zedillo himself. During his presidential campaign Zedillo had come to some staunch views on the issue. Believing that campaigns in Mexico were terribly vulnerable to bad money, he not only favored public financing; he wanted to ban private contributions entirely. He often cited the cautionary case of Ernesto Samper, the President of Colombia whose tenure had been clouded by revelations that drug lords were among his campaign backers. But Zedillo also had reasons closer to home to be worried about damage from dirty contributions. A fugitive Mexican businessman named Gerardo de Prevoisin, the disgraced former head of the Mexican airline Aeroméxico, had claimed in a Texas court that he was forced by the PRI to make huge donations from the company treasury to Zedillo's campaign. Zedillo denied any knowledge of the contributions. There were also unconfirmed but persistent reports that drug traffickers had tried to inject money into the Colosio campaign while Zedillo was its manager.

In the midst of the legislative impasse there was one bright moment. On October 29, the Congress, by a unanimous vote, chose the first truly independent governing council for the Federal Electoral Institute, with no representative from either the government or a political party. One new councillor was Juan Molinar, ten years after his study had exposed PRI fraud in Chihuahua. Another was Jesús Cantú, a newspaper editor who had crusaded against vote theft. The council president was José Woldenberg, whose roots were in the socialist opposition.

In early November came the first stirrings of the campaigns for the federal congressional elections on July 6, 1997, and the time for bickering over finance reform ran out. On November 14, the PRI congressional steamroller suddenly went into action. In a matter of hours PRI lawmakers, ignoring irate objections from the opposition, whisked the reform legislation, including the disputed campaign-finance measures, out of committees and through a vote. The bill passed by 282 votes in favor, including every PRI deputy except one, while the entire opposition, 142 deputies, voted against. The consensus that was supposed to legitimize the reform was shattered.

To be sure, most of the major agreements of July had survived. But the PRI had imposed Zedillo's high public-campaign-finance budget, and it also raised the limits on private donations and removed the teeth from the sanctions for violating them. In a measure especially dear to PRI leaders, the law made it much more difficult for other parties to form coalitions to run against the ruling party in the 2000 presidential vote.

The package even included a personalized dart for Santiago Creel. Tired of his badgering, PRI leaders dropped a clause into a constitutional amendment that banned people who had been elections councillors once from ever serving in that function again. That put Creel out of his job, "laid off by constitutional mandate," as he later mused with ironic pride.

The opposition decried the PRI bill. Enrique Krauze called on Zedillo to veto it, and López Obrador (who had succeeded Muñoz Ledo as president of the PRD) said that his doubts had been confirmed. "Now we know for certain that change in Mexico is not going to come through legal reforms," he said in disgust. "It will only come from the mobilization and the votes of the people." Both opposition parties refused the first payouts of money. The PAN made a media show of returning the check.

At Los Pinos, Zedillo listened to the clamor for a few days. Then, during an appearance at a business convention, he announced that he alone—not the PRI—had overruled the opposition and broken the consensus and, furthermore, he wasn't sorry for doing it. He insisted that public funding offered the "best guarantees that the financing of a political party or a campaign does not lead to undesirable subjection to private interests, including unmentionable ones."

Since the business gathering was closed to the press, reporters had to rely on a transcript of the President's remarks provided by his staff. When Zedillo's aides saw his unapologetic retort, they decided he must have gotten carried away, and, without asking him, they struck his comments from the official text.

Zedillo was greatly irritated when his sharp words did not turn up anywhere in the press the following day, and his aides were forced to confess to him that they had censored them. To get his campaign-finance point across, Zedillo made it all over again, even more forcefully, at his next public appearance.

Parallel to his efforts at political reform and economic recovery, Zedillo worked throughout his term on another theme: expanding the rule of law in Mexico. His strategy was straightforward: he sought to fortify and depoliticize the courts and the justice system, and then set an example, as President, by hewing to the letter of the law and letting the institutions do their work without interference from him.

"Whatever past Presidents did was above the law," remarked José Angel Gurría, the Foreign Secretary in the first years of Zedillo's administration. "Now this President always asks, 'What does the law say?'

"And we say, 'But, sir, there are political realities,'" Gurría continued. "But he believes that if we just follow the law, we'll be okay."

One of Zedillo's very first actions as President had been to clean out the Supreme Court, summarily retiring all twenty-five magistrates, all of them appointees of earlier Presidents. He reduced the Court to eleven justices, to be nominated by the President but ratified by two-thirds of the Senate. Zedillo said he hoped to generate a ripple effect from the highest court down that would encourage the judiciary to take more distance from politics. He also took the unprecedented step of naming the *panista* lawyer and congressman Antonio Lozano Gracia to be his Attorney General, the first opposition politician ever to serve in a PRI cabinet.

However, "political realities" posed problems from the outset for Zedillo's lofty approach. After decades of PRI rule, all too often the legal institutions that Zedillo left alone to function were, for practical purposes, nonfunctional. The only thing that could get them working was a push from the President, and that was what Zedillo thought he should not provide. His strategy faced many tests as holdups and kidnappings soared in the wake of the peso collapse and turf vendettas erupted among drug gangs. But one test that was especially painful for Mexico was a crime that took place at a dip in a backwoods dirt road in the state of Guerrero.

It was called Aguas Blancas, or White Waters, for the stream that coursed up over the weeded embankment during the rainy-season floods to cross the gravelly roadway. Only in farm country as poor as the hot slopes of the Guerrero sierra, where every inch of rock-strewn earth is examined by peasants for possible planting, would such a solitary site even have a name. The nearest town was Coyuca de Benítez, a hungry village where residents had been in some state of uprising against the PRI regime for generations. In the 1990s their resistance had taken the form of a group called the South Sierra Campesino Organization (known by its Spanish initials as the OCSS), which did battle with the state government over land titles, farmworker wages, teacher salaries, police violence, uncontrolled logging, and arbitrary arrests of citizens who had protested any of the above.

The governor of Guerrero, Rubén Figueroa Alcocer, was another scion of the system: four of his forebears had served as Guerrero governors. They ran the state like a plantation, and when a band of peasants and schoolteachers took up arms in rebellion in the 1970s, Rubén Figueroa Figueroa, the fourth and most powerful of them, called in the army and wiped them out. Traveling around the state in a serape poncho and fedora, Rubén Figueroa Sr. liked to have his picture taken loading his rifle and six-shooters in preparation to go forth and meet his constituents.

"There is a Mexican saying that when you kill a rabid dog, you kill the rabies. Well, when you kill a guerrilla, you kill the guerrilla war," he said to summarize his anti-insurgency doctrine. He had once been kidnapped by rebels whom he met for a peace negotiation, a betrayal that hardened his son Rubén's attitude toward all opponents of PRI power.

The youngest Rubén Figueroa guided his administration by the principle "much police, little politics," according to Juan Angulo, one of the few newspaper editors in the state who dared to criticize the Figueroas regularly. Among the political assets that Figueroa Alcocer liked to advertise was a claim that he was the *compadre* of President Ernesto Zedillo. Normally that would mean that Zedillo had been the baptismal godfather of one of Figueroa's children or vice versa; but in the Guerrero governor's case, it seems to have been that Zedillo once attended a Figueroa family wedding. At any rate, Zedillo never contradicted Figueroa, and PRI officials believed that the President quietly admired what he thought was Figueroa's common touch, so unlike his own.

On the morning of June 28, 1995, two dozen farmers from the OCSS, along with perhaps a dozen other passengers, squeezed into the back of a blue wood-slat cattle truck for the journey to a protest rally in a nearby town. As they rolled through Aguas Blancas, they found their path blocked by several dozen state policemen in black uniforms, armed with combat rifles, who emerged from the surrounding brush. The police ordered the farmers out of the truck, and they began to climb down apprehensively. Suddenly shots rang out, and the police began to shout. Then came a barrage of rifle fire so dense that it seemed to meld together into one explosion.

When it was over, blood seeped from the truck's tarpaulin, and slack bodies lay jumbled in the roadway. The dead numbered seventeen. Another twenty people were wounded, some gravely, but they survived, and a handful of passengers suffered no injuries.

These eyewitnesses gave reporters detailed cross-corroborating accounts of the shootings. No one in the truck had fired a gun or was even carrying one, they agreed. The police had opened up, shooting to kill, as though carrying out a precise order. The survivors recognized several top state police and justice officials among those commanding the operation. They also observed that Mario Arturo Acosta Chaparro, an army General well known to the farmers for his role in crushing the guerrilla rebellion a generation earlier, arrived by helicopter to inspect the scene moments after the shooting. Several of the wounded also remembered a man who leaned over them, not to help stanch their bleeding, but to film their wounds with a video camera.

By evening Governor Figueroa had sent local and national television networks a brief, blurry videotape supporting his own account of the events. It shows a man in a white shirt, seen from the back, aiming a pistol at uniformed police: a farmer from the radical group, the voice-over says. Figueroa's video includes no footage of the actual shooting, but it has pictures of dead farmers sprawled on the road with pistols in their fists. Figueroa said he had sent the police to Aguas Blancas to engage the peasants in dialogue and "dissuade them from their mission" of attending the antigovernment rally. The shooting had started, he said, with an "aggression" against the police.

In Guerrero the governor's version had begun to unravel by dawn the next day. *El Sol*, a daily newspaper in Acapulco, the resort on the Guerrero coast, carried two big photos on its front page. One was a color shot by its own photographer, the first to reach the scene, of a slain farmer splayed facedown in the mud. The other was a black-and-white photo of the same man taken hours later by a different photographer. The farmer lies in the same position, but his fist is now clutching a pistol. *El Sol* had never been known for hard-hitting reporting, but even its complacent reporters were offended at the security forces' crude deception.

The PRI machine went to work to spread Figueroa's version, courting the press while hounding the witnesses, whose accounts were soon buried. Figueroa handed the state investigation to a prosecutor who was his associate in a side business and had a second job as a police commander. This first prosecutor wrapped up his probe in three days, arresting fourteen state police officers of the lowest rank and upholding the thesis that the police had acted to repel an attack.

President Zedillo declared the killings a matter for the state authorities, and, consistent with his principles, he pledged not to interfere.

That was when Samuel del Villar got involved. An attorney and law professor with a doctorate from Harvard Law School, he had served since 1988 as chief counsel to Cuauhtémoc Cárdenas and the PRD. Del Villar believed, like Zedillo, that Mexico needed to strengthen the rule of law, but he had come to this conviction decades before the President. When he returned to Mexico from Cambridge in 1971, del Villar, then twenty-six, began to think that the way to change Mexico was to strengthen the Supreme Court. His mentor was Jesús Reyes Heroles, the distinguished PRI politician who was soon to become Government Secretary.

One day del Villar asked Reyes Heroles, "Why don't you try to become the chief justice of the Supreme Court?" He imagined that a brilliant man like Reyes Heroles could play the role that John Marshall had played in nineteenth-century America, establishing the independence and clout of the judiciary. But Reyes Heroles just laughed.

"Are you crazy?" he asked. "To be on the Supreme Court is to be nowhere, in limbo." That was when del Villar realized the scant value of the law in Mexican culture.

Although del Villar joined the PRI, as ambitious young Mexicans commonly did, in the 1970s he wrote a series of essays on the authoritarian system's corrosive effects on the legal fabric of the society. On the basis of del Villar's writings, Miguel de la Madrid named him to become Mexico's first anticorruption czar. But de la Madrid's commitment to the cause soon flagged, and del Villar left the administration. In 1988 he joined forces with Cuauhtémoc Cárdenas, drawn to his natural air of probity.

By 1995 del Villar had become a rumpled dissident intellectual of fifty, a chain-smoker whose words spilled out when he got onto a subject that intrigued him. As a teacher, he was philosophical and often very funny, but in legal practice he was notoriously stubborn. Once he had made up his mind about a case, he pursued his conclusions singlemindedly and would not be swayed. Aguas Blancas was one of the cases where del Villar had made up his mind.

Designated by the PRD to represent the victims' widows, he traveled to Guerrero to interview the witnesses in their dirt-floor shacks. With smoldering outrage, del Villar concluded that he was dealing with two premeditated crimes, mass murder and cover-up, both probably involving Governor Figueroa himself. "What they did to those men was a firing squad," del Villar decided, "an execution pure and simple."

On July 7, he presented a brief to the Attorney General's office in

Mexico City, trying to persuade federal investigators to step in. His petition was dismissed in four days without explanation. A month later, however, the National Human Rights Commission (Salinas's creation) issued
a report that bolstered del Villar's view. Making maximum use of its limited subpoena powers, the commission had conducted an unsophisti-
cated but thorough investigation of the crime scene. It proved that the
police had planted pistols on the victims, destroying Figueroa's thesis of
the victims as aggressors. The commission recommended that the original Guerrero prosecutor be prosecuted for cover-up. But it stopped short
of making any charge against Governor Figueroa.

Months passed, and several special prosecutors in Guerrero, all
named by Figueroa, came and went. Del Villar filed every sort of motion, brief, and complaint he could think of in state and federal courts,
mustering all his legal imagination to try to force the authorities to expand the investigation and move it away from Figueroa's influence. He
traveled the state, lodging in musty village hostels, gathering documents,
and grilling witnesses. He discovered, for example, that Figueroa had
held a closed meeting with Guerrero businessmen at the statehouse two
days before the massacre, where he said that he had intelligence indicating that leaders of the farm group were organizing a new guerrilla underground that would finance itself from kidnappings. Figueroa had
assured the businessmen that he was taking measures to deal with the
threat.

In January 1996 one Guerrero special prosecutor jailed eighteen
more state officials, including several Figueroa aides, on homicide-
related charges. But he took pains to absolve the governor, saying that
crime happened because the police had lost their heads. President
Zedillo monitored the developments closely and let the institutions do
their work without his interference.

Over the decades Televisa, Mexico's major television network, had never
given much coverage to topics like killings of peasants, preferring ano-
dyne newscasts and sentimental soap operas. But Ricardo Rocha helped
change that.

A quick-tongued television talk-show host, Rocha had made a career of pushing the boundaries a little at a time. He had worked for Televisa since it was born in 1972. It was a private company controlled by the Azcárraga family, but the terms of its license made it a virtual monopoly, and its ties to the PRI power structure were so intimate that it might as well have been state-owned. For years Rocha hosted both a zany Friday night entertainment show and a more cerebral Sunday afternoon talk show. Between the two, he managed to put a fully naked woman on mainstream Mexican television for the first (and probably the last) time. He invited two professional sexologists to teach Mexicans new positions for making love, and on one show a homosexual came out of the closet on the air, another first.

In the 1980s Rocha began to invite critics of the system to bring their views to his Sunday program, although he was always careful not to over-step invisible bounds laid down by Emilio Azcárraga Milmo, the Televisa patriarch who was known as El Tigre, the tiger. When Imanol Ordorika was leading a strike at the UNAM in 1986, he had marched on Televisa, expecting to be turned away. Instead, Rocha put him on the air. In those clamped-down times it felt to the students like breaching an iron curtain.

Eventually Rocha created a serious weekend newsmagazine called *Detrás de la Noticia* (Behind the News). He had aired several segments about Aguas Blancas, giving voice to the eyewitnesses. One day in February 1996, eight months after the killings, a woman who declined to identify herself came to the door of his studios and handed the security guard a videotape with a plea for Rocha to watch it. Something about her intensity made Rocha's staff think he should pay attention.

Rocha was alone the first time he saw the tape, and it left him immobilized. He ordered his chief editor to examine it for signs of doctoring. There were none, so he and his producers planned an episode around the tape for his Sunday night show.

First, however, Rocha knew he had to get Televisa's permission. He went to the network's studios on Avenida Chapultepec to see Alejandro Burillo, an Azcárraga relative who was the head of Televisa's news division. After Rocha showed the tape, Burillo, a tough-minded former soccer entrepreneur, sat for a long time in silence, drained.

"This is a kick in the balls," he said finally.

The twenty-minute tape, with the date and time stamped in the lower-right corner (beginning on June 28, 1995, at 10:28 a.m.), started with the footage that Governor Figueroa had shown. First a red truck rumbles down to the place where the stream flows across the road. Police step out of the bushes to stop the truck, but after looking over the passengers, they let it go. Close behind comes the blue truck, with passengers hanging out the top and sides.

Then begins footage that was not in Figueroa's version. At the sight of the blue truck the police rush onto the roadway and yell at the passengers to climb down. The passengers hurry, and the police order them to lie in the mud, kicking several of them as they crouch. After only a few seconds several single rifle rounds are fired. The police start running, and one voice commands, "Ready rifles! Ready rifles!"

Then, after two shots in quick succession, another policeman shouts at the peasants: "Is that what you want? Eh? Is that what you want?"

Shooting begins, so wild and loud that the cameraman careens and the camera sways, filming sky and then dirt.

After a full minute, the gunfire subsides. The cameraman refocuses, slowly filming the dead and the wounded. Piled together, they are wet with one another's blood. One man's moans rise and fall with the agony of each breath. "Don't shoot anymore," another man says wearily. "I'm going to die. Don't shoot anymore."

Once the tape ended, Burillo turned to Rocha. "You bastard, did you bring this to me to ask if you could put it on the air?"

Rocha nodded.

"Of course you can put it on the air, you goddamned bastard," Burillo said.

"That's good," Rocha said, "because if you had said no, I would have to quit."

Aguas Blancas, the Whole Truth aired on Sunday, February 25, 1996. Rocha reviewed what was known to date about the killings and replayed Governor Figueroa's statements and videotape. Then he played the entire tape of the massacre, about ten minutes, without commentary.

President Zedillo was watching the show during a Sunday evening with his family at his home at Los Pinos. When it was over, he was furious. He wasn't angry that Rocha had broadcast the videotape, he told his aides. But the President of the Republic, he said, should not have to learn what really happened at Aguas Blancas from Sunday night television. His Government Secretary, his intelligence services, and his friend the governor of Guerrero had obviously all failed him, the President seethed.

Rocha's show left no doubt among ordinary Mexicans that Figueroa had orchestrated a cover-up. The very existence of the videotape suggested that Figueroa had ordered police to film the shootings so his state security apparatus would have footage to work with later to create a misleading version.

Nevertheless, two days later the latest special prosecutor in Guerrero issued a final report that exonerated Figueroa once again. Acting on this recommendation, the PRI-controlled state congress retired the prosecutor and closed the case. Del Villar tried frantically to obtain a stay, but state authorities dismissed his motions without reading them.

At that point President Zedillo began to detect that the institutions were not working as well as he hoped they would without his interference. On March 4, he sent an unusual petition to the Supreme Court, asking the nation's top magistrates to investigate possible federal civil rights violations in the Aguas Blancas case. (Under Mexico's legal system, judges investigate as well as adjudicate.)

On hearing the news, Figueroa went to Mexico City, where Zedillo's staff turned him away from Los Pinos. But no one told him explicitly that his tenure was in trouble. He returned to Guerrero emboldened, since he enjoyed immunity from prosecution as long as he was governor. A week later he brought truckloads of PRI supporters to the state capital for a big rally, telling them that he didn't need any backing from Mexico City to govern Guerrero. "I will always work side by side with my elders, who made the revolution, against the jokers of this country," he said, referring to the massacre victims and their supporters. "In Guerrero we have men, brave men, not cowards." The crowd jeered at Zedillo and Ricardo Rocha. "Tell the truth, Televisa!" they hooted.

Within hours a phone call came from the capital. The taunts had pushed Zedillo too far. On March 12, Figueroa asked the Guerrero congress to grant him a permanent leave from his post.

The anonymous video of the Aguas Blancas massacre that Ricardo Rocha broad-cast on February 25, 1996, showed that police had carried out the killings

Five weeks later, on April 23, the Supreme Court issued an extraordi-nary report about the massacre. The justices found that the first shot fired was not aimed at the police, as Figueroa and his various special prosecutors had alleged, but was "an order or signal for the police to fire their automatic weapons in a barrage on defenseless civilians." This signal "provoked the police, with their powerful firearms, to begin to fire compulsively and indiscriminately on the passengers." The police acted "coldly and arrogantly, completely in command of the situation." Figueroa, the justices affirmed, had ordered top state officials to the scene "not to investigate and identify those responsible, but rather appar-ently to hide them and create information confusion."

The report concluded that there had been "grave violations of the in-dividual rights of citizens of Guerrero" and placed Governor Figueroa at the top of a list of officials to be held responsible. The Court sent its find-ings to Attorney General Lozano with instructions for him to complete the investigation and prosecute the federal violations.

Revealing as it was, the report left del Villar with mixed feelings. On one hand, he saw that the Supreme Court was coming alive, attacking the impunity of the politically privileged with candor and eloquence. At the same time, del Villar knew that the President, by ordering the report, had short-circuited the legal process. After such a finding, how could the Supreme Court now also serve as the instance of last appeal in the case?

Indeed, Attorney General Lozano, even though he was from the opposition, was not ready to prosecute someone as powerful as Rubén Figueroa unless the President gave the nod. Lozano was only looking for some small sign from Zedillo, but he didn't get it. Zedillo was letting the institutions work without interfering. So Lozano ignored the new avenues the Supreme Court had opened to him, reported yet again that he found no federal crimes at Aguas Blancas, and sent the case, yet again, back to the state authorities, who closed it down yet again. As del Villar had feared, the Supreme Court declined any further consideration of the matter.

Rubén Figueroa was never prosecuted. A number of top officials from his government went to jail but most were freed when public attention subsided.

"The problem was that someone had to make the point that a society can't live decently if people get killed like dogs," del Villar reflected some years later. "Someone had to say to Figueroa: you know, you really shouldn't go around killing people like that."

As Zedillo moved through the second year of his term, he felt the need to mend relations with his party, so he asked PRI leaders to organize a national party assembly.

The chill between Zedillo and the PRI had set in much earlier, even before he was elected. In the last days of his 1994 campaign he had called state-level party leaders together in an auditorium at PRI headquarters in Mexico City that was named for Plutarco Elías Calles, the man who gave the PRI its identity as a single government party at the service of a mighty President. The party leaders thought the young candidate had come courting, but instead he asked for a separation.

"I firmly believe that democracy demands a healthy distance between my party and the government," Zedillo told the audience. He added a punch line: "We *priístas* don't want a government that appropriates our party, or a party that appropriates the government."

The dinosaurs in the front row applauded with due respect. But in the aisles behind them heads swung to and fro as party officials asked each other: "*We don't?*"

Once Zedillo took office, he made other moves that his party regarded as slights, or worse. Probably the most important was his decision to cut off the secret flow of funds between Los Pinos and the party. Although it wasn't a secret that the PRI lived off the public till, the party had by and large been careful to conceal the transfer of resources. Local party headquarters were housed in municipal buildings without paying rent; full-time party staffers were paid by local government treasuries; the PRI took its cut of fees and union dues. But the party's most strategic resources came from a secret discretionary fund controlled by the President. It provided the walking-around money during election campaigns, the timely donations to community causes, the payments to journalists and hardworking party hacks. Soon after Zedillo took office, he realized that Carlos Salinas had secretly paid millions of dollars to Colosio's — and by extension his own — presidential campaign. As Zedillo argued in public for generous government financing of campaigns, he told PRI leaders privately to get ready to break their dependence on cash from Los Pinos.

Sergio Aguayo and his group, Alianza Cívica, had helped to spur Zedillo. They started a program they called Adopt a Functionary and made the President their first adoptee. Citing long-overlooked transparency clauses in the Constitution, they demanded information about the President's budget and spending as well as his personal patrimony. They found buried in the government's accounts a rubric titled Branch 00023, which in 1996 gave the presidency more than $4 billion just for salaries, including a reserve of $86 million the President could spend without reporting to a soul. Alianza Cívica sued Los Pinos in federal court, claiming its right to know about the government's use of taxpayers' money. Zedillo initiated steps to change the presidential accounts (and would reduce his discretionary spending to zero by the end of his term).

Zedillo's moves to distance himself from the PRI came as the party bore the brunt of the popular rage at the peso collapse and after Zedillo forced PRI lawmakers to adopt his emergency economic-adjustment measures, which most of them abhorred. Thus the PRI went into its seventeenth national assembly, in September 1996, roiling with resentments.

The PRI's periodic assemblies had been much like the great congresses of the Communist parties, convened to ratify ideological course corrections previously decided in closed meetings by national potentates. But going into the seventeenth assembly, the party found the directive from Los Pinos—the expected *línea* from the President—exceptionally vague. As a result, wildcat proposals sprang up from the floor of the assembly. Chiefly, the PRI rank and file wanted to revise the party statutes to set new requirements for the party's candidates for President. The militants were demanding what they called "padlocks," which required that anyone seeking the PRI nomination must have held elected public office at least once, been a PRI militant for at least ten years, and held some leadership post in the party. The message was plain: technocrats not allowed. Indeed, Zedillo himself would not have qualified to be the presidential candidate had the proposed conditions been in place in 1994.

The assembly delegates gathered in the Calles auditorium on the final evening, September 21, to adopt the assembly's conclusions. The Tabasco delegation, with Roberto Madrazo working in the background, was the first to abandon the canned party line that the leadership loyal to Zedillo had prepared. Others quickly followed suit.

"We have to suffer the whims of powerful technocrats who send their buddies to be governors and senators when they don't even know what our party stands for!" cried a delegate from Puebla, Antonio Hernández. A woman from the state of Querétaro called Zedillo's cabinet "that bunch of junior-league parvenus." Delegates excoriated Zedillo's economic policies and portrayed him as a direct heir to the dreaded Carlos Salinas. Finally an orthodox PRI senator from Veracruz state, Eduardo Andrade, declared that he had heard enough. He pushed his way to the front of the line of speakers waiting for the podium. "You are sending our enemies a wrongheaded message that we are breaking with our President," Andrade bellowed at the upstarts. "You are forgetting that the President of the Republic is the basic strength of our party!"

Jeers erupted from the floor. The old-guard *priísta* who was chairing

the meeting, Fernando Ortiz Arana, appeared at first to welcome Andrade's performance but soon thought he was becoming provocative. Ortiz motioned Andrade to sit down.

Andrade exploded. "You're telling me to sit down? You were the one
who told me to come up here and deliver this party line!"

The chairman, exposed, shut off Andrade's microphone, leaving the
senator gesticulating without words. When the rank-and-file rebels saw
that party leaders had silenced one of their own allies, they rioted, storming the stage. Green leaves and crockery littered the floorboards as priístas trampled a row of potted plants at the front of the proscenium.
Andrade joined in on the side of the rioters, throwing punches.

After hours of skirmishes and shouting, the rebels finally agreed to a
vote. The plank barring technocrats from being the PRI presidential candidate was approved. The rebels also pushed through a statement attacking Zedillo's plan to sell off part of Pemex, sinking in one stroke the
President's most important privatization initiative.

Zedillo was scheduled to close the assembly with an address to his
party colleagues the following morning at a giant indoor gathering at the
National Auditorium in Chapultepec Park. But after the events of Saturday night the presidential general staff (the elite unit in charge of
Zedillo's security) feared he might face physical violence from his fellow
priístas. The staff's top General decreed that the President would walk to
the main stage through a hidden side entrance, avoiding the march
down the long center aisle past all the party members.

After appeals from his political advisers, Zedillo rejected the security
measures. He delayed his entrance by a few minutes, then marched
straight down the main aisle, shaking hands and clapping people on the
back as he went. The gamble worked. Seeing that he was not intimi-
dated, the PRI rebels calmed down.

"This time the party line was that there was no party line!" Zedillo
said in his speech, giving his most optimistic interpretation.

The PRI's seventeenth national assembly turned out to be a pivotal
moment in Mexico's passage toward democracy. PRI militants tied their
party's hands by narrowing the field of potential candidates for the 2000
presidential race. For example, a capable official like José Angel Gurría,
Zedillo's last Finance Secretary, was eliminated from contention be-

cause he had never held elected office. More important, after the assembly the PRI never again managed to unify behind Zedillo. Because he insisted on denying the PRI privileges it had taken for granted, Zedillo grew more popular with the public but ever less so with his party. Authoritarian at heart, the PRI showed that it didn't really understand the uses of democracy. It seized on the greater leeway that Zedillo had offered to move backward, toward a political universe free from competition, a universe that no longer existed.

Julia:

"I don't believe in authoritarianism," Ernesto Zedillo said. "I believe in law and politics."

Sam and I interviewed Zedillo at Los Pinos two days after the PRI assembly. The turmoil in the party was not the only trouble in the air. An obscure ultraleftist guerrilla group, the Popular Revolutionary Army, had erupted with coordinated bombings in several states and eclipsed his second *informe*, where he had planned to broadcast the success of the political reform.

His aides said he had agreed to the interview reluctantly. He distrusted the press, and most of our Mexican colleagues never got a chance to talk with him. But the international economist evidently saw a point in speaking to the *Times*. We sat at the round table to one side of his office, under Benito Juárez. A Baroque fugue played quietly.

We made the blunt observation that many Mexicans regarded him as a weak leader.

"I think perhaps I have a different way of exercising power than many opinion makers here expect from the Mexican President," Zedillo replied. "I don't believe in authoritarianism, and perhaps that makes some people think that I am less powerful." He pointed out that he had worked deliberately to diminish his own influence.

"I took a personal decision to impose self-control on the authority of the President in order to give more space to the Congress, to have a more independent judiciary, to promote effective decentralization and federalism in the life of the country," he said. He pointed to political reform and economic recovery, both well under way by that time. We asked why he thought these achievements had not had more impact out in the streets, where people were still struggling and angry. He said it was because he had refused to take measures to satisfy interest groups or provide short-term economic relief. "I can't pretend to be a populist politician," he said, "even if that would give me some temporary popularity points. Why? Because it just doesn't work for me."

We asked him how he felt about the scorching he had taken at the PRI assembly. He wanted us to believe that on his terms, it had been a success. "My responsibility as President is to do my part to make sure the PRI has a life of its own," he said, sounding like the parent of an errant adolescent. "So I thought this assembly was the way assemblies ought to be, with a lot of debate and confrontation. I didn't interfere in any aspect that had to do with the internal life of the party."

Our exploration of the thinking of this antipolitical politician progressed smoothly when we spoke of principles but grew tense when we went to some specifics. We brought up the case of a colleague of ours named Razhy González, a journalist from Oaxaca state who had been abducted by an unidentified gunman less than a block from the governor's palace in Oaxaca City and interrogated in a secret facility nearby that looked like a professional intelligence unit. Razhy had been publishing stories about the new guerrilla group, which had a cell in Oaxaca, in a shoestring alternative magazine he published. When we saw him, Razhy had raw wounds on his forehead where his captors had ripped off his skin with the duct tape they used to blindfold him. He was convinced his kidnappers were from army intelligence.

Zedillo dismissed the incident out of hand. "I have no information that this is related to any government authority whatsoever," he said. We asked if he thought that someone else besides government security forces might be running a late-model interrogation chamber in Oaxaca. He was not interested in that line of inquiry.

So we asked him about Aguas Blancas.

He stiffly cited Attorney General Lozano's findings that there were no federal crimes. "On that matter there was no communication at all between me and the Attorney General. I have to respect his decision because I am not a judge or a prosecutor. The Attorney General, like all public officials, faces public criticism from time to time, but he has to perform his job according to law, not according to public opinion."

We started to point out that the general public and many human rights and lawyers groups had questioned whether justice was done in the case. He cut us off.

"I'm sorry," he said, lecturing, "but my responsibility as President is to work to better our institutions by all means available to me so they will inspire more public confidence. I am not going to reestablish that confidence by trampling the law. That confidence will be reestablished if we improve the professionalism of the institutions and establish new standards of ethics and behavior."

Both Sam and I had seen the videotape of the massacre. We remembered how the police had goaded the kneeling farmers before shooting them, then strolled past the bodies in the crimson mud to assess their work. We recalled Governor Figueroa's claim that the real victims of the attack had been the police.

"There are measures you can take in these situations that make you popular for a day or two," Zedillo continued, referring to demands that he intervene to ensure Figueroa's prosecution. "But that sort of popularity backfires, because sooner or later people see that you have broken with the rule of law and committed a great inconsistency. I believe that what we need in order to establish a new culture of respect for law is great consistency with the law."

Somehow, his argument seemed to be that it was all right for a major figure in the government party to get away with covering up a mass murder as long as the President didn't interfere with the judicial proceedings.

What we learned from the interview was that Zedillo was a reformer of institutions but not of people. He was a schematic thinker with a progressive view of how to alter the flowchart of the Mexican state to make it more responsive to its constituents and at the same time more stable. Like an architect restoring a national monument, he laid out his blueprints and built on them with determination. This politics of concepts often served Zedillo well, allowing him to pursue a consistent course toward reform and tune out the incessant nay-saying of Mexican politics. During his first three years, in addition to eliminating presidential control over elections, he helped complete reforms that granted autonomy to the Banco de México, the central bank, and gave the Congress powers to ratify the Attorney General and Supreme Court justices.

His steadiness certainly worked for economic recovery. In 1995 the economy had shrunk by 6.5 percent (the worst contraction in a single year since the Great Depression); the following year it grew by 5.2 percent, restoring nearly 1 million jobs. In both 1995 and 1996 Zedillo resisted pressure on the public purse and turned in balanced budgets. He paid back the foreign bailout loans early. Investor confidence was restored, the peso was stabilized, and trade through NAFTA began to flow. At the end of 1996 foreign reserves, which had dwindled to $6 billion two years earlier, stood at $17.5 billion and growing.

For everyday Mexicans, however, hard economic problems remained: high inflation persisted, and the banks were weak and corrupt. Many new jobs were in flighty and oppressive low-wage assembly industries that contributed little to the development of their environs. The recovery was lopsided, favoring wealthier classes and regions and bypassing the poorest ones.

But Zedillo, in his self-imposed remove, had little understanding of how dysfunctional the PRI system had become for many citizens, both economically and politically, or what it was like to be on the wrong side of it. Even though he was an outsider from the traditional PRI, the system as a whole had been good to Zedillo. He had no sense of the fear that shadowed a farmer at war with the PRI in Guerrero, or a journalist dodging secret police in Oaxaca. With Mexico's most disaffected, Zedillo could be just as authoritarian as his predecessors. As a result, he could help construct the framework for democracy, but the job of making it work for the system's outcasts would fall to Mexicans in the society at large, far from Los Pinos.

Moreover, it would become clear that Zedillo's commitment to the rule of law did have limits, and, despite his denials, they were eminently political. Several times during his term the opposition tried to get the Congress to investigate him. Adolfo Aguilar Zinser sought to start a probe into some allegedly fishy payments Zedillo authorized while he was Secretary of Planning. Andrés Manuel López Obrador led an effort to investigate Zedillo's 1994 campaign finances. Each time, PRI lawmakers stepped in to shut the investigations down.

———   ———   ———

In preparation for the midterm elections of July 1997, José Woldenberg and the new citizen councillors at the Federal Electoral Institute worked to consolidate one of the most advanced voting systems in the world. In the years since the 1988 fraud, Mexico had spent more than $1 billion on election reform. Citizens nationwide had been canvassed door-to-door several times to create a reliable voter list. The institute issued tens of millions of credentials with an embedded digital photo, part of a high-tech system that eventually purged 135,000 duplicate names by comparing voter photos.

The councillors moved into the institute's huge modernist campus at the southern edge of Mexico City, taking charge of a vast agency with offices in all thirty-one states and three hundred election districts. Sweeping aside the PRI's apparatchiks, they systematically appointed independent local citizens—dentists, photographers, butchers, physicians—to oversee the offices. They recruited young Mexican computer whizzes to design an Internet network that could monitor every stage in an election, from the training of poll workers to the tracking of unused ballots. It allowed Mexican citizens to monitor the returns in federal elections in real time, as votes were counted.

Many Mexicans did not realize how fundamental these changes were until the newly independent institute staged its first vote on July 6, 1997.

That was the night Cuauhtémoc Cárdenas smiled.

Since his defeat in the 1994 election, Cárdenas's famously long face seemed only to have gotten longer. He had worked stolidly to regroup the PRD. Finally he decided to run to become the first elected Mexico City mayor in the sixty-eight years since the PRI system had been in power.

He won a huge victory, taking 47 percent of the vote, while the PRI scored 25 percent and the PAN barely 16 percent. The PRD also won a decisive majority in the city council, whose powers were newly enhanced. The voters felt they were doing an act of justice to Cárdenas, finally making it up to him for 1988 while also rewarding him for his steadfast opposition to Carlos Salinas. So when Cárdenas came out into the camera lights at his party headquarters just after ten o'clock that night, he gave a broad, beautiful smile.

He was also savoring a turning point in Mexico's democratic struggle. In the federal voting the PRI lost control of its majority in the Congress for the first time since the system was founded, winning only 239 seats in the 500-seat Chamber of Deputies. The PRD surged to become the second-largest political force in Mexico, with 125 deputies; the PAN came in close behind with 122. (Splinter parties accounted for the rest.) As the independent council's first election, it was a resounding success: in more than five hundred races nationwide there were no more than a handful of challenges to the results.

The results also brought vindication for Zedillo, although the opposition parties would never acknowledge it. A crucial factor had been the huge campaign budgets they received from the government, funds they had attacked Zedillo for demanding. Once the parties realized how their appeal was amplified by the television and radio time they could buy with the windfall, they had quietly dropped their objections.

Zedillo, always the outsider, would face such doubt and ambivalence throughout his term. After Carlos Salinas left office, he was reviled in Mexico as an autocrat; but when Zedillo curbed his own powers, he was condemned as a weakling. Once the peso crisis abated, however, the

Cuauhtémoc Cárdenas gave a historic smile when he declared victory in the election for mayor of Mexico City on July 6, 1997

public's trust in Zedillo grew. Credited as hardworking and unpretentious, he saw his popularity polls climb steadily. The political class, by contrast, never stopped doubting the sincerity of his reformist intentions, and was never willing to acknowledge the cause and effect between his inaugural proposals for democratic change and the opposition gains in the elections of July 6.

Zedillo came out on television at eleven o'clock that night to recognize Cárdenas's victory. He used his familiar terms no longer in the future tense but in the past: "The nation has taken a definitive, irreversible, and historic step toward a normal democratic life," he said.

With such a wide vote margin the declaration was unnecessary, but Mexicans were pleased that Zedillo made it. He offered Cárdenas the federal government's help, saying, "I wish him the greatest success in his delicate task." In 1988, only nine years earlier, it had been impossible for the PRI regime to make such a gesture. But Zedillo made it look easy.

10

Raúl

The first time María Bernal saw Raúl Salinas de Gortari, he was sprawled in the doorway of a men's boutique where she worked on a chic shopping street in Seville, Spain. It was morning, and the stranger was soiled with vomit and still groggy after a night of melancholic drinking.

Pleading for Bernal's help, Raúl pushed his way into her shop. He washed up in the bathroom, then solved the problem of his dirty suit by purchasing a new one, together with a pair of shoes, spending well over a thousand dollars. When Bernal showed surprise, he told her not to worry: "I'm a multimillionaire," he explained. He paid with a gold Visa card under his real name. But Bernal found out later that Raúl also shopped that day at a store across the street, where he used another credit card under a different name. It was June 1992, and although Bernal did not realize it that day, Raúl's younger brother Carlos was at the apex of his presidency back in Mexico.

From the inauspicious encounter in Spain sprang a transnational romance that was to become legend in Mexico. Raúl brought María, a shapely young lady with a long mane of dark curls, to his country, installing her in the home of his father, Raúl Salinas Lozano, then shipping her from place to place so he could see her as he traveled around on business. For one of their first trips together Raúl rented a yacht in Acapulco Bay, and he and María went for a day cruise along with two other Salinas brothers, Enrique and Sergio, and some young consorts they had arranged. At one point María climbed up to straddle Raúl's lap as he sat in the prow of the yacht. A deckhand snapped a photo, with María looking coquettishly over her shoulder at the camera and Raúl flashing a broad, self-satisfied grin.

Those were glory days for Raúl Salinas. In April 1992 he had resigned from the government after an undistinguished sixteen-year career as a bureaucrat, during which he toiled always in the shadow of his younger brother Carlos and rumors of graft followed him wherever he went. Carlos had finally forced Raúl out because talk of his sibling's corruption was proliferating beyond the ability of Los Pinos to control it. Raúl had become known in Mexico City as El Señor Diez Por Ciento, Mr. Ten Percent, a reference to the off-the-books commissions he was said to charge on the many lucrative government contracts and other deals he secured for his friends.

Raúl evidently didn't mind the early retirement. On his final civil servant's financial declaration, he claimed that he had never made more than the equivalent of $190,000 a year, which he said was his salary plus perks and bonuses. In fact he already had tens of millions of dollars stashed away in bank accounts under false names in Mexico. Soon one of his buddies, Carlos Hank Rhon, the financier son of the PRI dinosaur Carlos Hank González, introduced him to a senior private-banking executive at Citibank in New York. The banker, Amy Elliot, set up a financial labyrinth to move and shelter Raúl's growing fortune, including accounts in the Cayman Islands, London, and Switzerland.

María Bernal, through her dalliance with Raúl, gained a uniquely intimate view of his way of life. She had a fine eye for detail, and several years later, when she was an embittered former mistress, she would share her knowledge with the Mexican people in a highly entertaining tell-all book. She would tell of her visits to all the major properties in his real-estate catalog, starting with his two spacious homes, within a few blocks of each other, off the Paseo de la Reforma in Lomas de Chapultepec, the most expensive patch of terrain in Mexico City. She had romped with Raúl at his beach house in Acapulco and at the big home he rented in La Jolla, California, when he tried to appease his brother the President by appearing to pursue academic studies at a research center there for a year. She went skiing from his chalet in Aspen and helped him fix up a new apartment in New York, on Fifth Avenue overlooking Central Park.

She also helped him adorn and run his two ranches. One, called El Encanto (for enchantment), was in the hills above Mexico City, ten minutes from his home. Always an avid horseman, Raúl kept a small stable there and could stop in for a ride or a tryst with Bernal (or some other mistress) anytime during his working day. The other, called Las Mendocinas, was a hacienda in the shadow of the spectacular Popocatépetl volcano, three hours from Mexico City, with a staff of dozens, a stable of thoroughbred rodeo horses, and an original El Greco (or so Raúl said) on the wall. In the closet hung his cherished collection of some sixty suits (many in suede) in the style of the Mexican cowboy, or *charro*, complete with sombrero, bolero jacket, and narrow pants trimmed with silver buttons down the outside.

Because Bernal was pliant and not a little ambitious, her affair with Raúl endured beyond what many women would have tolerated. She was not even dissuaded when, a year after they met, Raúl married another woman, a beauty named Paulina Castañón. He told Bernal that he had been forced to take on a trophy wife for practical reasons, because she was rich and Mexican. His brother the President, he explained, was preparing to make him governor of the northern business state of Nuevo

María Bernal and Raúl Salinas took a spin in an antique car from his collection, in the days before he shunned her to marry a wealthy Mexican, Paulina Castañón

León, and a Mexican governor couldn't very well have a Spanish tart for a wife.

Julia:

Other than his money, it was never very clear what Bernal saw in Raúl Salinas. But at the *New York Times* Mexico bureau, we were able to form a precise idea of what Raúl saw in her as a result of some photos she sent to our office, offering them for sale at a time when she needed cash. The shots, which posed María nude in a variety of goddess stances, were taken by Raúl himself, or so she claimed. Alas, since the *Times* does not have a centerfold, we were not able to publish them.

—   —   —

Over time Raúl's new marriage forced Bernal to rethink their liaison. For several months toward the end of 1994 she acceded to a tactical demotion, from fiancée to housekeeper. Raúl persuaded her that he needed her help with some urgent packing, because he was closing down some homes, moving his money out of the country, and putting all his properties under the names of third-party *prestanombres*, getting ready for the end of the presidential term, when the Salinas family's untouchable status would abruptly expire.

"It was very close to the end of the *sexenio*, and it wasn't convenient for Raúl to appear as the property owner, because Mexico would never forgive him for it," Bernal wrote in her book, in a comment that would prove exceptionally prescient.

Indeed, Mexico did not forgive him.

It can be argued that Raúl Salinas de Gortari did more than any other living Mexican to contribute to his country's transition to democracy. His, however, was not a hero's role; his impact stemmed from the compelling force of his negative example. He did more to discredit the PRI system in the eyes of the Mexican people than anyone else in seven decades, and in so doing, he significantly hastened the demise of authoritarian rule.

After Carlos Salinas left office, events caused countless details of his brother's profligate lifestyle to flood into the public domain. The revelations began early in Ernesto Zedillo's *sexenio*, after Raúl's stunning arrest on February 28, 1995, on charges that he had ordered the murder of his former brother-in-law and political rival, José Francisco Ruiz Massieu. The pace of the disclosures became dizzying after Paulina Castañón, Raúl's wife, was arrested in Zurich, Switzerland, on November 15, 1995, as she was removing a false passport bearing Raúl's picture from a safe-deposit box. The Swiss let Paulina go, but they froze about $130 million they found in Raúl's secret accounts and opened an investigation to discover the origins of the money, saying they suspected it came from narcotics money laundering.

After that, as Raúl sat silenced in a maximum-security prison, layer upon layer of scandal engulfed him. Investigations into his alleged financial foul play made front-page news throughout the Zedillo *sexenio*. Mexican congressional inquiries exposed lucrative deals he had done while he was in government office, especially when he held management positions at two government food-distribution agencies. Investigations in Mexico and Switzerland revealed business endeavors in which Raúl and his friends secretly moved tens of millions of dollars, often on little more than a handshake, into funds or investments that benefited from inside government information and influence peddling. Swiss officials ultimately ruled that at least some of the millions Raúl deposited in his accounts in that country had come from the drug trade, and they seized about $90 million of the money.

Most damaging for the PRI system, a federal investigation in Mexico alleged that $38 million were transferred during Carlos Salinas's tenure from the President's accounts to private bank accounts under Raúl's aliases.

And to top it all off, there was María Bernal's sensational book.

Although Mexicans were shocked by the Ruiz Massieu murder, they were most outraged to learn how Raúl had grown fabulously rich because of dubious privileges he enjoyed as the brother of the President. Raúl himself acknowledged the advantages of his position in a ten-page letter he wrote on October 23, 1997, to *The New York Times* in Mexico in response to questions conveyed to him through an American lawyer. His handwritten answers, which his lawyer smuggled out of the tomb-like Almoloya penitentiary, constituted the first interview he had given to a foreign publication since his imprisonment.

"I always have had private businesses," he wrote, "and when you are the brother of the President of Mexico, many huge opportunities come to you, as happened to me."

He made this point to support his categorical denial that he had anything to do with drug traffickers. Raúl's argument, which seemed completely sensible to him and his family, was that with so many ways to get rich through political nepotism, he didn't need to take drug payoffs. "There is no need, at the position that I had, to get involved with drug traffickers," he wrote.

Raúl's fall was especially long because, in engaging in forms of corruption that were routine for the PRI system, he had failed to observe the requisite proportions. He went to excesses that offended even his allies in the ruling party and was insufficiently generous in spreading the proceeds.

Moreover, details of the wealth and impunity that Raúl had enjoyed through his proximity to power rained down on the Mexican people in the years when they were struggling to recover from the 1994 peso crash, rebuilding from yet another economic catastrophe wrought by a PRI government. This time their tolerance was exhausted. With Raúl it became clear to the people that the PRI system was still working to spread wealth among the political elite but was no longer providing welfare for the working class.

One deal that typified Raúl's entrepreneurial style was his secret investment in a state-owned national television network that was sold into the private sector in 1993 by Carlos Salinas. The TV Azteca network was purchased in an auction by a young Mexican magnate, Ricardo Salinas Pliego, the head of a domestic appliance empire. The sale was part of the vaunted privatization campaign in which President Salinas, working to raise cash and pare down the government, also sold off Telmex and many other state-owned assets. Once in private hands, TV Azteca was expected to become the first serious competition to the near monopoly of Televisa. Documents that came to light through the various investigations of Raúl's finances revealed the transactions in a loan he made to Salinas Pliego at the time of the network purchase.

On May 24, 1993, the Salinas government published the terms for the sealed bidding for TV Azteca. During that same week, well before the government made public the identities of any bidders, Raúl set up a new bank account under a front name in the Cayman Islands. Later, after the sale was completed, payments from Salinas Pliego to Raúl would begin to show up there.

When the government disclosed a few weeks later that Salinas Pliego was among the bidders for the network, Mexican business took little note. The young executive in the bohemian goatee had made his fortune selling stoves, was only forty at the time, and had no important management experience in the Mexican media, so he was not regarded as a serious contender for an asset so crucial to Mexican politics and civic culture.

On June 30, more than two weeks before the auction results were announced, Raúl sent a total of $25 million to accounts controlled by Salinas Pliego in three Swiss banks (after first bouncing the money among his own Citibank accounts in Europe, apparently to obscure the money trail).

On July 17, the Salinas government awarded the sale of TV Azteca to Salinas Pliego, astonishing the Mexican business world. He had won with a huge bid of $642 million, reportedly about $100 million higher than the next-best offer.

Raúl's transfers to Salinas Pliego remained secret for three years but came to light after financial documents that he presented in his defense to Mexican and Swiss authorities leaked in Mexico. As their transactions began to become public, Raúl and Salinas Pliego at first both lied, the latter with vigor. In an interview with Andrés Oppenheimer of The Miami Herald, Salinas Pliego denied he had ever done business with Raúl. He said it was all a case of mistaken identity in which Swiss investigators had been confused by seeing the name "R. Salinas" on the records of some of his own transactions.

However, when confronted with court documents detailing Raúl's transfers to his accounts, Salinas Pliego was forced to admit, at a press conference in Mexico City, that he had in fact received a loan from Raúl. He acknowledged that the full amount was a little more than $29 million, for six years at 12 percent interest.

Both Salinas Pliego and Raúl then insisted that they had agreed on the loan *after* the auction of TV Azteca. Like most of Raúl's deals, there was nothing resembling a contract on paper, which might have shown a date. "No documents were needed because the word of Ricardo Salinas was good enough for me," Raúl told Mexican investigators.

But Raúl's bank statements showed that the money had changed hands while the confidential bidding for the network was still under way. There was never a full investigation to determine whether Raúl or Salinas Pliego had inside information about the TV Azteca auction.

Like many of Raúl's business associates, Salinas Pliego seemed surprised and offended by all the fuss about the TV Azteca deal. He said that he and Raúl had become friends because of their common love of horseback riding. He offered what seemed to him an elementary explanation of the dynamics between political power and business in Mexico. "Raúl was not just some middling bureaucrat," Salinas Pliego said. "He was the brother of the President. At that time, and for a long time before Salinas, if the brother of the President came and said, 'I want you to invest my money,' very few businessmen would have said no." Besides, Salinas Pliego argued, the sum in question was minor. "Twenty-nine million may be a lot of money to some people," he remarked, "but in this operation it was an irrelevant amount."

For his part, Raúl, even from behind bars, kept insisting that the deal was good business. In his October 1997 letter to the *Times*, he wrote that he knew "I would get the money back with a profit (a good one)." Under questioning by Mexican prosecutors, Raúl explained what he called the "rich man's logic" behind the transaction, and others in which contracts and tax statements were deemed unnecessary for Mexican financiers like himself: "Money works for rich men, while people who are not rich think they have to work for money. Rich men believe only two things: that they deserve all the money they can get, and that money should work for them."

This same logic also apparently applied to a deal Raúl did with Carlos Peralta Quintero, another wealthy scion. Peralta was to cellular telephones in Mexico what Salinas Pliego was to television. In 1993 Peralta, then in his early forties, had been awarded an extraordinarily valuable license by Salinas's government to start up the most important private Mexican cellular company to compete with Telmex, the state telephone giant that was in the process of privatization.

It was bad news for Peralta when the Swiss, in late 1995, froze Raúl's accounts. After Swiss authorities showed they were serious about investigating Raúl for narcotics violations, Peralta stepped forward to admit that $50 million of the money in Raúl's frozen accounts was actually his. Peralta and Raúl claimed the money was for an investment fund—whose purposes, they acknowledged, had not yet been agreed on. Peralta presented the Swiss with a five-hundred-page dossier, which demonstrated that the funds came from legal transactions and mapped every turn they had taken on their way to Raúl's Swiss accounts. Peralta's dossier made a convincing case that none of his money had originated in narcotics.

His problem was that for all his stacks of papers, Peralta had no record of the investment fund. There were no writs of incorporation or business plan, and the transactions were handled in secret. Peralta said he had turned over the millions to Raúl on a handshake. They had been friends since childhood, Peralta said, so that "was clear enough."

Unconvinced, Swiss officials noted that under their laws, if any part of the money in a blind account could be traced to narcotics, the whole account could be seized. When the Swiss finally confiscated most of the money in Raúl's accounts, they took Peralta's millions as well. The Mexican justice system did nothing to confirm or dispel the unavoidable suspicion that Peralta's money was a reward to Raúl for some assistance he gave Peralta in obtaining the cellular-phone license from Carlos Salinas's government.

Raúl and his business partners always defended themselves by saying they had played by the rules of the game that prevailed in Mexico before and during the Salinas *sexenio*. Secret money changing hands between businessmen and politicians? What was wrong with that? After all, Raúl was the President's brother.

The allegations that Carlos Salinas's *hermano incómodo* (uncomfortable brother) had done big business with cocaine lords were the ones that most electrified the Mexican press. Stoked primarily by Swiss prosecutors, international and Mexican drug investigations of Raúl went on for years, turning up evidence that was often damning but not always conclusive or legally actionable.

For example, several different secret informants told U.S. drug-enforcement agents of a 1990 meeting Raúl hosted at a family ranch with representatives of the drug don Amado Carrillo Fuentes, where, the sources said, money had changed hands.

Another episode, described by participants, was a 1995 dinner banquet in Tamaulipas state put on by an oil businessman close to the PRI, where guests passed around a photograph of Raúl posing side by side with Juan García Abrego, the cartel leader who was Carrillo Fuentes's main rival. There was a third man in the photograph, a PRI politician, and the setting appeared to be a cattle fair. The party took place not long after Raúl was jailed on the Ruiz Massieu murder charges, and the host joked with his guests that the arrest had made the photo more valuable. But the photo has never been published.

The most extensive narcotics evidence against Raúl was compiled in a dogged three-year investigation by Swiss police under the direction of Carla del Ponte, the Swiss Attorney General. In the brief justifying the seizure, in a civil proceeding in October 1998, of about $90 million of Raúl's money from his Swiss accounts, the police said that "when Carlos Salinas de Gortari became President of Mexico in 1988, Raúl Salinas de Gortari assumed control over practically all drug shipments through Mexico." The Swiss portrayed Raúl as the toll collector at the gateway through which all cocaine passed as it flowed through Mexico to U.S. markets.

The Swiss evidence seemed, in fact, to support only a sketchier picture. Perhaps the Swiss prosecutor's most substantial witness was Guillermo Pallomari, who had been an accountant for one of Colombia's top cocaine dons. Pallomari fled Colombia in August 1995, underwent a three-month debriefing by American drug agents, and became a protected witness in the United States. Several years later he testified to the Swiss that he had been instructed by his former boss to pull together $80 million to spend on bribes in Mexico. He claimed he arranged for $40 million of it to go to Raúl, in return for help expediting drug shipments through Mexico.

One problem with Pallomari's testimony to the Swiss was that it wasn't clear why he had failed to mention these details when he was first debriefed by American agents. But his charges against Raúl acquired some credibility when he showed Swiss detectives how to identify bribes paid in Mexico in ledgers that had been captured from Colombian cartel leaders by Colombian police in 1995.

Another witness who testified to the Swiss against Raúl was a drug convict named José Manuel Ramos. Before his arrest in 1990, Ramos had been a middle-ranking operative for the Medellín cartel deployed in Texas. Ramos described in detail an episode in 1989 where he claimed that Raúl intervened with local authorities to help him recover a shipment of cocaine from a Colombian airplane that had made a forced landing in northern Mexico. Ramos's claims, like Pallomari's, were strengthened by his references to cartel accounting documents seized at the time of his arrest. According to the Swiss, those papers showed that Ramos paid Raúl $28.7 million during two years after 1987.

American drug investigators, however, were skeptical, noting that Ramos only came forward to accuse Raúl after he had been sentenced to two life terms in American jails and that some of his statements in other drug cases had proven unreliable.

Raúl denied that he had ever had anything to do with the drug trade, insisting that the charges against him were "narco-fiction" concocted by jailed drug dealers seeking to trade on false information to lighten their sentences.

"Very bad people have told many lies to harm me and help themselves just because I am Carlos's brother," Raúl wrote in his letter to the *Times*. While it is not surprising that Raúl would issue such denials, his argument proved right about several of the witnesses in American jails, whose statements against him did not stand up under scrutiny. Also, lacking in the whole discussion were details of how and from whom Raúl secured the official cooperation for which he was reportedly paid.

Because of the weakness of the evidence, Raúl was never indicted in the United States or in Mexico on drug charges. Of all the corruption charges he faced, those involving drugs were the least well documented. But they enhanced Raúl's image in the eyes of the Mexican people as the personification of everything about the PRI system that they now wanted to reject.

It is difficult to overstate Mexico's horror after the slaying of José Francisco Ruiz Massieu. It came just six months after the Colosio assassination (on September 28, 1994) and was just as baffling. For many months justice officials offered no explanation of who had done it or why, leaving Mexicans to ask who would be next.

President Salinas waited no longer than the wake to decide that the special prosecutor in the case should be Mario Ruiz Massieu, the justice official who was the victim's brother. Despite the conflict of interest, Salinas reached agreement with Mario during the funeral services and also secured the consent of President-elect Zedillo on the spot.

Mario started out with some material to work on: the triggerman had been captured at the scene of the crime. Daniel Aguilar Treviño, a twenty-eight-year-old ranch hand, had given a confession after eighteen hours of interrogation, in which the police applied electric shocks and all but drowned him in a bucket of excrement. Aguilar Treviño said he had been hired for the hit by the chief of staff of Manuel Muñoz Rocha, the PRI congressman. But on the day after the assassination, before police had begun to hunt for him, Muñoz Rocha disappeared without a trace.

Mario Ruiz Massieu began to report immediately to President Salinas about his investigation. But in early October he also went calling on Zedillo. "Some of the witnesses are saying that Raúl was behind the killing," Mario told the President-elect.

Zedillo did not like Raúl Salinas. They'd had several run-ins over financial matters early in Carlos Salinas's administration, when Raúl was a top official in a government food-distribution agency and Zedillo was the Secretary in charge of the federal budget. Nevertheless, Zedillo doubted Mario's account, smelling a plot to frame President Salinas in his lame-duck period. Zedillo limited himself to advising Ruiz Massieu to deepen his investigation.

Mario returned several times to Zedillo to insist that the evidence was pointing to Raúl, although he cautioned that he did not have conclusive proof. He sought Zedillo's guidance about how to handle such explosive stuff. The President-elect's advisers began to suspect that Ruiz Massieu was using the case to convince Zedillo that he should be the new Attorney General. But Zedillo was not persuaded, and, impatient, he instructed Mario to deal directly with President Salinas.

Ruiz Massieu stopped consulting about the case with Zedillo, but in the final weeks of the Salinas *sexenio* he became a frequent visitor to Los

Pinos. The President took an encouraging, even solicitous attitude toward the special prosecutor. Then, in mid-November, Zedillo received a phone call from Salinas. "All of the Presidents of Mexico, when they leave office, ask their successors for two or three cabinet posts," Salinas said. "I'm not presumptuous. I'm only going to ask you for one," he said, referring to Zedillo by the informal *tú*.

"Which one is that?" Zedillo asked, wary.

"The Attorney General," Salinas replied firmly.

Zedillo demurred. Then, switching to formal terms of address, he said: "Mr. President, I've already taken my decision about that, and I know you will like it."

Zedillo and his staff never knew for sure whom Salinas wanted to place as Attorney General, but they had little doubt that the outgoing President hoped to retain control over the Ruiz Massieu investigation, perhaps by leaving Mario in charge. As the days passed and Zedillo had not unveiled his Attorney General, the matter contributed to the deterioration of relations between President Salinas and his successor.

When Zedillo finally chose Antonio Lozano of the PAN, promising him a free hand to pursue the assassination investigations, Salinas did not like it at all. On learning the news, Salinas held intense consultations with Mario Ruiz Massieu.

On November 23, a week before Zedillo's inauguration, came the strange press conference where Mario Ruiz Massieu resigned and accused top PRI leaders—but not Carlos Salinas—of blocking his probe of his brother's killing. He made no mention of Raúl Salinas. Zedillo immediately challenged the credibility of Mario's accusations by naming one of the accused PRI leaders to his cabinet and another to head the party.

With his presidency soon overwhelmed by the peso crisis, Zedillo did not focus on the Ruiz Massieu investigation again until February, when Attorney General Lozano came to him with a proposal. Key witnesses in the Ruiz Massieu murder had changed their testimony, Lozano said, and were now saying that Mario Ruiz Massieu had tortured them to make them omit Raúl Salinas from their accounts of the assassination. Lozano said he had enough evidence to put Raúl on trial as the intellectual author of the murder.

The battle of blame between Zedillo and Salinas over the peso disaster was escalating sharply. Zedillo knew that arresting Salinas's brother would shatter the PRI's tradition of protecting its former Presidents and could further destabilize the situation. Yet indicting Raúl might also help Zedillo consolidate his presidential position just when he needed to regain control of the economy. Zedillo told his advisers he wanted to proceed according to law. In practice, however, he short-circuited the judicial process by discreetly turning to the Supreme Court, asking the chief justice to read Lozano's indictment and advise him whether it was solid. The chief justice said it was—and thus became the first instance of judicial review in Raúl's murder trial rather than the last.

Raúl's arrest for murder, on February 28, 1995, brought both trauma and political gain for Zedillo. It was hailed as a daring act of defiance against the code of impunity for PRI Presidents, but it also set in motion the most devastating rift between two Presidents in the history of the PRI system.

In the middle of the tumult, on March 3, Mario Ruiz Massieu was arrested at Newark Airport in New Jersey, en route to Madrid with forty thousand dollars in cash in his bags. Three days later Mexico brought felony charges against him for a cover-up in the investigation of the shooting of his own brother and opened proceedings to extradite him.

Attorney General Lozano—the PAN's power-sharing pioneer—was given an unprecedented opportunity to fortify Mexican justice by solving the Ruiz Massieu murder. Instead, he conducted a trial investigation so inept and reckless that it stood out even in the tawdry annals of Mexican justice. Raúl Salinas's rights were flagrantly, vigorously violated until he became, in practice, a political prisoner.

The episode that most colorfully displayed the incompetence of Lozano and his team transpired on October 9, 1996, at El Encanto, Raúl's ranch in the pine-forest hills in the Cuajimalpa suburb on the western rim of Mexico City. The contingent of detectives and forensic experts who marched down the winding cobblestone driveway to Raúl's property that day was led by Pablo Chapa Bezanilla, the special prosecutor named by Lozano for the Ruiz Massieu case, a twitchy detective with white hair. With him came María Bernal, looking fetching in a black uniform and bulletproof vest with the logo of the federal police, provided by Chapa; and a stocky woman named Francisca Zetina, a clairvoyant who was called La Paca and favored dresses of violet satin. Raúl had been her client, and she testified to police that she had conducted regular spiritual-cleansing sessions for him in the year before his arrest.

After looking over the yard for some time, La Paca pointed to one spot that she felt "drawn to." The workmen started to dig, and several feet down they found a skeleton. "From the vibrations I feel, I know that those remains are Muñoz Rocha and that he rose up from his tomb to point to his assassin," La Paca said, swooning from the cocktail of psychic forces that she detected at the site.

Crouched on the edge of the brown mud pit, Chapa grew more excited as each bone emerged. If the remains of Manuel Muñoz Rocha, the missing PRI congressman and murder conspirator, turned up in the ferns at Raúl's ranch, the charges against Raúl in the Ruiz Massieu murder would become airtight, and Chapa might be able to indict Raúl for the murder of Muñoz Rocha as well.

In his elation Chapa paid little attention to some curious features about the skeleton. All ten of its fingers were missing, as well as the lower jaw. One detail was particularly worrisome to Chapa's team: a clean horizontal saw-cut through the skull above the eyes, which made it look like a music box with a lid that opened and closed. Not only was the fellow dead, some of Chapa's agents observed quietly; he apparently had already had an autopsy.

Nevertheless, Lozano summoned a press conference that same evening. Both he and Chapa were beaming. The Attorney General stopped short of declaring that the bones belonged to Muñoz Rocha, saying they would undergo more forensic examination. But he noted repeatedly that an anonymous source who had alerted police to the location of the bones "had said we would find Muñoz Rocha." He praised the diligent work of his police and all but declared victory against Raúl.

The Mexican people seized with delight on the mystery of Cuajimalpa Man, as the fossil was dubbed, for the suburb where the ranch was located. Over the next few days, however, it became clear that the discovery of the body had not been the result of sharp police work. Instead, Chapa had been led to the corpse by a dramatic note delivered to him by La Paca.

The unknown writer said he had finally been moved to tell his story by unbearable bad conscience. He recounted that he happened to have gone to Raúl Salinas's home in late September 1994 to ask for a job. By a stroke of misfortune, he reported, he was let in the front door just moments after Raúl had broken the skull of one of his guests in the foyer with a baseball bat. "Imagine my surprise!" exclaimed the writer, with a literary flourish. "The person with the bat (who I now know was Raúl Salinas de Gortari) stood there looking at me stupidly."

Having arrived at such an inconvenient moment, the job seeker was made to wait, while a doctor "with a foreign accent" cut off the corpse's fingers and pulled out its teeth, for reasons not precisely specified, then folded the body into a gunnysack. He decided that under the circumstances he might not want to work for Raúl Salinas after all, and was allowed to leave. Weeks later one of Raúl's bodyguards, after several rounds of beer, told him where the body was buried.

Since Cuajimalpa Man had turned up inside the Mexico City limits, the forensics work went to the city's police lab, where the medical examiner's unit was relatively professional. After withstanding attempts by Lozano and Chapa to suppress their findings, lab officials announced in late November that the Cuajimalpa remains were not those of Muñoz Rocha.

By this time the tales of the seer and the skeleton had begun to compete with the soap operas as nighttime television entertainment—to the mortification of Los Pinos. On December 2, Zedillo fired Lozano and Chapa. The PAN made only pro forma protests. Two months later the district attorney in Mexico City announced that the Cuajimalpa bones belonged to a late relative of La Paca. The missing fingers and mandible turned up in the grave where the man was originally laid to rest after dying of an accidental head wound. The anonymous note was composed by La Paca herself, who, it emerged, had done a tidy business with Special Prosecutor Chapa: he had paid her almost $150,000 as an informant against Raúl.

La Paca, six of her relatives, and María Bernal all were sent to jail for planting the corpse. The Mexico City police put Chapa's house under surveillance, so he fled, becoming the second special prosecutor in the murder case, after Mario Ruiz Massieu, to become a wanted man.

Julia:

The longer the Ruiz Massieu case dragged on, the flimsier seemed the charges against Raúl. At the *Times* bureau we might have regarded it all as high farce, except that Raúl remained in harsh confinement in Almoloya, in conditions reserved for Mexico's most dangerous convicts. He lived in a tiny isolation cell, had no communication with the outside, and was allowed visits with his family only once or twice a month. Yet he had never been convicted of any crime.

After Lozano, the case was taken up by the new Attorney General, Jorge Madrazo Cuéllar, a respected human rights lawyer. Madrazo's team found some new evidence, but the central weakness persisted. The case hinged on the testimony of one man: Fernando Rodríguez González, Muñoz Rocha's chief of staff. The gunman, in his confession extracted under torture, had said that Rodríguez, on orders from the congressman, had designed the assassination plan and instructed the shooter how to recognize José Francisco Ruiz Massieu on a busy street.

Jailed soon after the assassination, Fernando Rodríguez gave at least four sworn depositions in the fall of 1995 to detectives working for Mario Ruiz Massieu and didn't mention Raúl Salinas in any of them. Then, in February 1995, after Mario left the case, Rodríguez changed his account. He was the witness who told Lozano that Mario had brutalized him to make him drop Raúl from his statements. In his new version he said that Raúl had asked Muñoz Rocha to prove his political loyalty by doing Raúl the favor of getting rid of José Francisco. Soon after Rodríguez changed his testimony, Pablo Chapa, the special prosecutor, had paid his family $500,000.

This seemed a thin plank on which to build a murder conviction. Moreover, none of the prosecutors had ever been able to produce a motive.

Those were busy times in Mexico, and soon our reporting focused elsewhere. Then, in the final weeks of 1998, the prosecution rested its case, and a countdown started for the judge to render his verdict. We began casting about for an original way to cover the end of the trial. That was when Sam and I remembered the tape.

It was an audiocassette that had come into our hands through Craig Pyes, a freelance investigative reporter who was often our partner. Craig had received it many months earlier from a source who worked closely with the Mexican federal police. The source had said the tape had never been turned over to the Attorney General. Craig had badgered us to do a story on it. A meticulous reporter, Craig had gathered interviews and court documents to assemble an hour-by-hour chronology of the assassination and its aftermath, to situate the tape and clarify its significance. Now, with the case drawing to a close, I dug the tape out of a drawer at the office and sat down to listen to it. And then listen again. And again.

The astonishing recording seemed to be the voice of Jorge Rodríguez González, Fernando's brother. Jorge had helped Fernando recruit the gunman and stood watch on a street corner as the shooter closed in on José Francisco Ruiz Massieu. Like Fernando, he was serving a multidecade sentence for his participation in the crime.

Passing references in the dialogue established that the tape was recorded on the night of September 29, about thirty-six hours after the assassination, in the northern city of Matamoros. With every cop in Mexico on a manhunt for the killers, Jorge Rodríguez had flown back to Matamoros, his hometown, and strolled into the federal police station there, where he had a few friends. As he talked, one of them apparently turned on a tape recorder. It was a primitive recording, with buzzers going off and two-way radios crackling in the background. There were some tense words but no obvious sounds of coercion on the hour-long tape.

The only other witness who had been questioned in those thirty-six hours was Aguilar Treviño, the gunman, in Mexico City and under torture. So the tape of Jorge Rodríguez, if it proved authentic, would be the only statement in the entire tangled four-year case to have been given *before* the authorities began to manipulate the witnesses (and vice versa, in the case of La Paca) to suit their political and personal ends.

Jorge described the assassination matter-of-factly, boasting a bit now and then. In all, he mentioned Raúl Salinas eleven times, saying that he understood that Raúl had given the orders to "eliminate" José Francisco

Ruiz Massieu. He said that Raúl and Carlos's elderly father, Raúl Salinas Lozano, also knew of the plot. He said he had learned who was behind the assassination from his brother Fernando.

"What did Fernando tell you about the operation?" a man asks.

"He just said that they have orders from above that there was going to be an operation," Jorge replied.

"What operation?"

"They were going to eliminate a person whom they did not want to have around," Jorge said.

"Who gave the orders from above?" the same man asks.

"As I understand it, what I heard there, was that Raúl Salinas de Gortari and his father were the ones who handled that," Jorge said. He said his brother told him that Raúl had promised to find them both government jobs if they helped with the murder plot.

To be sure, all of Jorge's statements about Raúl were hearsay. But the tape was compelling because Jorge freely admitted his own role in the shooting. At that early moment he also mentioned many details of the events that were borne out in the investigation—but only much later. He seemed to be trying to warn the police in Matamoros that they should back off, because this was a murder that was ordered from the very top: by the President's brother.

It dawned on us that we had inadvertently been sitting on a key piece of evidence in the case. To put together the whole picture, I obtained a copy of Jorge Rodríguez's testimony from the court record. It showed that he had undergone an abrupt change of heart in the twenty-four hours after the Matamoros tape was recorded. Instead of letting him walk away, as he expected, the federal police, on orders from Mario Ruiz Massieu, took him to Mexico City. There he was subjected to twelve hours of beatings, in which two of his ribs were broken. At the end of that session—not even twenty-four hours after the Matamoros tape was made—Jorge gave his first sworn deposition for the record. His references to Raúl Salinas dropped from eleven to none.

Still, the possibility existed that the tape itself was a fake. So I negotiated a visit to prison to see Jorge Rodríguez.

Because of a confusion with the prison authorities, the first inmate who came into the tiny visitors' room was not Jorge, but Fernando. I played a bit of the tape for him, and he immediately confirmed that it was his brother's voice.

Then Fernando was taken away, and Jorge was brought in. He was much more of a workman than Fernando, who had held city jobs for years in PRI politics. Jorge immediately acknowledged his own voice. He quickly identified the place and time: Matamoros, federal police headquarters, the day after the killing. Then, as the tape rolled and the questioning got under way, his mind seemed to race forward, recalling what he had said that night. His hands began to tremble.

Although Jorge had originally confessed to the crime, his lawyers had more recently contested his conviction on the grounds of self-incrimination under torture. Hearing himself describe his own complicity so bluntly on the tape, he began to cry. He offered a muddled explanation, then gave up, and instead described his hellish life in prison. He begged me not to do anything with the tape that would make things worse for him. When we parted, his hand was shaking so severely that he could barely extend it to say goodbye.

Clearly the tape was authentic. Before publishing a story, I made a copy of the tape available to the third, and last, special prosecutor in the case. He was amazed by its implications. But he dejectedly pointed out that he had already rested his case, so the tape could no longer be introduced into evidence in the trial.

— — —

The tape story appeared in the *Times* on January 14, 1999. Raúl Salinas's defense lawyers dismissed it as a fabrication. They implied, and most of the Mexican press believed, that the special prosecutor had leaked the tape to us in an eleventh-hour ploy to bolster his case.

On January 21, the federal judge found Raúl Salinas guilty of masterminding the Ruiz Massieu assassination and sentenced him to fifty years in prison. The judge acknowledged that the prosecution had provided no "direct proof" of Raúl's participation and no clear motive. But he said that the "interlocking" circumstantial and hearsay evidence was persuasive. The sentence was later reduced to twenty-seven years.

More than any other judicial ruling in modern times, Raúl's conviction meant that the politically mighty in Mexico were no longer above the law. At the same time, Raúl's trial had been an outrageous miscarriage of justice, which went forward only because it confirmed his black image in the public's mind. Although the criminal conviction of a presidential sibling was unprecedented, it could not be said that the verdict achieved any break with Mexico's history of subjugating law to politics.

What the Ruiz Massieu case did show with clarity was how the decomposition of the PRI system had reached into the lives of the elite that sustained it, how political jealousy and loathing were corroding the families at the center of the ruling establishment. José Francisco Ruiz Massieu had once been Raúl and Carlos Salinas's brother-in-law, the husband of their sister Adriana. Although the exact motive for his killing may never be known, it seems clear that he became a target because of his rapid political ascent. The Rodríguez González brothers, anxious to promote the career of their PRI boss, turned into killers. Mario Ruiz Massieu, perhaps to advance his own fortunes, apparently ordered the torture of witnesses to suppress evidence in the murder of his brother. While Mario was under house arrest in New Jersey, American authorities discovered that he had shipped about $9 million in cash, stuffed in duffel bags, to the United States while he was a senior justice official in Mexico. In March 1997 a civil court jury ordered the confiscation of most of the money, finding that it came from drug bribes.

On September 15, 1999, Mario Ruiz Massieu, facing a criminal indictment in Houston on narcotics charges, took an overdose of antidepressants to commit suicide.

11

The General and the Drug Lord

With a shaved head and a bulldog's jutting jaw, General Jesús Gutiérrez Rebollo had a fearsome look. When President Zedillo named him to head the Instituto Nacional para el Combate a las Drogas, Mexico's antidrug agency, in December 1996, officials in both Washington and Mexico City liked him that way. He seemed to embody the drug war as they wanted it fought: ruthlessly, but with military efficiency.

"He's a butt-kicking General," Barry McCaffrey, President Clinton's drug czar and a retired General himself, said admiringly of his new counterpart. As the General in command of thousands of troops based at garrisons all across central Mexico, Gutiérrez Rebollo had presided over the arrest of several major traffickers.

Just nine weeks after his appointment, however, Gutiérrez Rebollo was himself arrested by military police and charged with racketeering—specifically, with using his official powers to assist and protect a narcotics cartel, the very sort of illegal enterprise he was supposed to wipe out.

In the official story, a young lieutenant who served as Gutiérrez Rebollo's driver had stepped forward to report the General's involvement with a drug mafia. Though stunned by the allegations, the Defense Minister, General Enrique Cervantes, investigated them fearlessly, and once he confirmed their veracity, he promptly arrested Gutiérrez Rebollo and reported the terrible news to President Zedillo. The moral of the story was clear: the Mexican military's own internal mechanisms were working to root out and punish corruption, even among its top officers.

The official story was a crude fabrication. No young lieutenant ever alerted the army to Gutiérrez Rebollo's corruption, and no one in the

General Jesús Gutiérrez
Rebollo served nine weeks
as Mexico's drug czar before
his arrest on narcotics
charges

Defense Secretariat informed President Zedillo. In fact, the President
and his staff stumbled upon Gutiérrez Rebollo's ties to the cartel by
chance, and Zedillo was forced to summon all of his presidential authority to order the army to arrest him. Thereafter, although the President
heaped public praise on the military for its courageous stand against corruption, only his continued pressure on the top Generals kept them from
brushing the scandal under the rug.

Gutiérrez Rebollo's crimes constituted a grave threat to Mexico's national security. He forged an alliance with a drug ring controlled by
Amado Carrillo Fuentes, a billionaire cocaine, heroine, and methamphetamine trafficker; he put soldiers and weaponry, bases and airfields, at
the mafia's disposal; he sent army troops, in their black uniforms and
head masks, to abduct and murder rivals; he had members of other drug
gangs detained and tortured on his military bases.

In his growing recklessness, the General sought to undermine Mexico's opening to democracy. After decades of service to the PRI, the rest
of the armed forces had begun to accept a nonpartisan role—except for
Gutiérrez Rebollo, who stirred a police mutiny in Jalisco to destabilize
the state's first opposition government.

In the 1980s and 1990s citizens had watched the acid of narcotics corruption corrode virtually every Mexican institution, from the ruling party and the presidency to the courts and the financial system, even the Church, because drug lords financed some parish construction projects. Only the military—it appeared—had largely been left unblemished. Zedillo had named Gutiérrez Rebollo to head the national drug agency precisely because he knew that narcotics bribes had broadly compromised the civilian police. The General's arrest, however, proved that the army was as vulnerable to corruption as the rest of the discredited law-enforcement system.

That made it a particularly searing episode in Mexico's opening. The country was seeking to build a regime of laws and an impartial means of enforcing them. But criminal gangs, flush with profits reaped in the huge North American market for narcotics, were undermining its entire legal edifice.

Throughout Mexico's history, power and wealth had commanded more respect than laws. In the years after independence the reins of government changed dozens of times, and the police and the courts were primitive institutions. In exchange for their loyalty to the President, the ruffians and brigands who served in the police and rural constabularies were given wide latitude to carry on criminal activities for their personal gain and empowerment.

The judiciary was traditionally the weakest branch of government, and a legal principle that has become central to the operation of the Mexican system symbolized the bench's limited powers: laws ruled unconstitutional by the Supreme Court remained in force for all citizens except those who filed the legal challenge. The principle was pioneered in 1847 by Mariano Otero, an eminent constitutional lawyer. To this day the Otero principle has forced all Mexicans except for a handful of wealthy litigants to obey laws already ruled unconstitutional and obligated the country's highest tribunal to spin its wheels endlessly, reviewing the constitutionality of the same laws again and again.

After the 1910 revolution a constitutional congress in 1917 sought to strengthen the judiciary's independence by giving the Supreme Court justices life tenure. But the successive Presidents who governed in the revolution's aftermath paid little respect to the Constitution, using their domination of the Congress to amend it at least four hundred times in seventy years. Many passages became incomprehensible to all but a handful of constitutional lawyers.

In 1928 General Plutarco Elías Calles, the President who founded the party that would evolve into the PRI, fired all eleven justices and appointed a larger court more to his liking; six years later President Lázaro Cárdenas did likewise.

Thereafter, authoritarian rule tended to breed corruption. Because PRI officials were finally accountable to no one but the President, it behooved special interests to ply them with bribes, and with the President drawn from the same party over the decades, incoming administrations had little incentive to clean house or punish abuses by their predecessors.

Moreover, the PRI system provided few incentives to obey the law. Most disputes were resolved not in the courts but in political negotiations, and the contender with the most ties to power was likely to win. Everyone from poor squatters to factory owners routinely ignored zoning, environmental, labor, traffic, and other laws. From time to time citizens who despaired of official justice wrought their own mob vengeance, lynching accused robbers and rapists in broad daylight.

The legal scholar Samuel del Villar was among the first Mexicans to comprehend the threat that the narcotics trade posed to lawful government. Del Villar earned his doctorate in jurisprudence at Harvard Law School in 1971. During the Echeverría and López Portillo presidencies, he had worked as a political science professor and journalist, crusading for government reform. In the corrupt final years of López Portillo's administration he wrote a series of columns in the Mexican press pointing out the systemic flaws that gave rise to graft.

The columns attracted one very influential reader. When Miguel de la Madrid ran for President in 1982, he invited del Villar to join his campaign as an anticorruption adviser. Del Villar gave him a list of reform proposals, which he used to make "Moral Renovation" a central theme of his campaign. Once elected, de la Madrid appointed del Villar presidential adviser for special affairs, with a mandate to fight corruption. Del Villar had an office twenty blocks from the presidential compound, a ten-person staff, and some impressive-looking badges, but his powers were severely limited: he could not issue subpoenas and saw de la Madrid only occasionally.

Still, del Villar threw himself into the work. He opened several broad investigations, focusing especially on the graft surrounding the oil-workers union and on the increasingly obvious ties the narcotics lords had forged with the government.

He studied the history of the drug trade. Mexicans had cultivated marijuana for centuries. During World War II, U.S. authorities had encouraged Mexico to plant poppies in the western state of Sinaloa to supply the Allied armies with morphine; after the war, shrewd Sinaloa traffickers began processing the crop into black-tar heroin. But drugs remained a cottage industry until the 1970s, when cocaine barons in Colombia began to contract with Mexican traffickers to smuggle their product into the United States. Almost overnight, del Villar realized, Mexico's drug industry had begun to generate hundreds of millions of dollars annually.

Del Villar put together a family tree of Mexico's major trafficking families. He discovered that a frightening evolution had taken place in a single generation. Narcotics kingpins like Ernesto Fonseca Carrillo and Miguel Angel Félix Gallardo, the sons of rough-hewn Sinaloa mountain families, had formed a sophisticated trafficking federation that negotiated head-to-head with Colombian producers; transported, stored, and smuggled cocaine in Mexico; and operated wholesale networks in the United States.

Inevitably, the traffickers had found allies in PRI governments. Del Villar's attention was drawn to the Dirección Federal de Seguridad, the Federal Security Directorate, a secret plainclothes corps founded (with CIA help) during the postwar presidency of Miguel Alemán, who maintained it under direct presidential control; after he left office, it became part of the Government Secretariat. Piecing together an informal history of the DFS, del Villar concluded that traffickers had used this agency to consolidate a partnership with federal authorities.

The DFS had stumbled into the drug business almost by accident. In 1976, after a leftist rebel group kidnapped his sister, President-elect José López Portillo had given the DFS authority to wipe out the insurgents by any means necessary. Working with the military police in a secret unit called the Brigada Blanca, the White Brigade, DFS agents kidnapped, tortured, and executed hundreds of Mexican rebels. During raids on narcotics warehouses thought to be guerrilla safe houses, they came into contact with drug traffickers, and soon they were protecting them from arrest in exchange for a healthy cut of their profits.

Under de la Madrid, the DFS director was José Antonio Zorrilla, and del Villar realized that he had elevated the relationship with traffickers to a new level, reorganizing the directorate into half a dozen regional offices whose commanders had become, in effect, the branch directors of the Mexican drug trade.

The way del Villar understood it, Zorrilla had turned the traffickers' search for official protection into one-stop shopping. By negotiating each shipment of cocaine and other drugs with the DFS and paying officials a percentage of its value, the traffickers ensured that no government security force would interfere at any level, local, state, or federal. For their part, the DFS commanders got rich; so, presumably, did more senior PRI officials, although del Villar could never determine how high up in the government the corruption had spread.

Del Villar outlined his alarming findings in a series of reports to de la Madrid, who urged him to continue investigating but took no action. In 1984, for example, when del Villar learned in advance that Fonseca Carrillo, Félix Gallardo, and other big traffickers were going to meet in Guadalajara, he urged the President to give him powers as a special prosecutor and to send a company of paratroopers to Guadalajara to raid the traffickers' summit. De la Madrid told him to share the idea with Jorge Carrillo Olea, a retired General who was the Deputy Secretary for Security Affairs. In a meeting, del Villar explained his proposal to Carrillo Olea, but the General took no action.

Del Villar's relations with the President and his top aides deteriorated. The aides began to give del Villar the cold shoulder. Someone leaked his confidential memos to the government-controlled newspapers, putting his life at risk. Del Villar finally resigned in 1985, after about two and a half years in office.

"My job is to fight corruption," he told de la Madrid. "Instead, it's getting worse."

Not long after del Villar resigned, a brash young trafficker in Guadalajara named Rafael Caro Quintero, who was an apprentice of Fonseca Carrillo and Félix Gallardo, committed an excess that brought trafficking into the public eye. He arranged for his henchmen to kidnap, torture, and execute an American agent of the U.S. Drug Enforcement Administration, Enrique Camarena, and made sure they were protected by badge-carrying DFS agents. Caro Quintero and Fonseca Carrillo were arrested and jailed. But the scandal forced Government Secretary Manuel Bartlett to disband the DFS altogether in the summer and fall of 1985.

What would happen to Zorrilla? Instead of being remanded to federal authorities for prosecution, he was recast as a PRI candidate for the Congress. After new evidence emerged of Zorrilla's criminal involvement, Bartlett forced him to resign his PRI candidacy, but Zorrilla was not charged. He was allowed to go into exile in Spain; not until 1989, after de la Madrid had stepped down and Bartlett had left the Government Secretariat, was Zorrilla tried, convicted, and sentenced to thirty-five years in prison for the 1984 murder of Manuel Buendía, a journalist who had been investigating official ties to the drug trade.

Meanwhile, the DFS's fifteen hundred commanders and agents— many of whom had ties to organized crime—were merely dismissed and allowed to drift away. Hundreds found jobs on state and federal police forces, where they continued to manage myriad criminal ventures. Some left government to become powerful traffickers in their own right.

In the 1980s drug money corroded other agencies as well, including the Procuraduría General de la República, Mexico's equivalent of the Justice Department; the Federal Judicial Police, a police corps controlled by the Attorney General akin to the American FBI; and even the Defense Secretariat.

The army was the best trained and most professional of Mexico's security forces, and therefore initially more of a challenge for criminals to penetrate than the slipshod agencies of civilian law enforcement. But the evidence suggests that during the de la Madrid administration the traffickers proved spectacularly successful. The Defense Secretary himself, General Juan Arévalo Gardoqui, took a hand in providing them with army protection. In two separate trials in U.S. federal courts, witnesses and prosecution affidavits prepared by the U.S. Justice Department accused Arévalo of accepting huge bribes from traffickers.

The Mexican government filed angry diplomatic protests with Washington over the imputations against General Arévalo's good name. The de la Madrid administration never investigated their veracity, at least not publicly. When Carlos Salinas took office, General Arévalo was allowed to retire quietly.

One of General Arévalo's last official acts as Defense Secretary was to promote Jesús Gutiérrez Rebollo to division General, the army's highest rank. Up to that point, however, there was no sign of the drug corruption that had infected the Defense Secretariat during Gutiérrez Rebollo's career.

After graduating as a second lieutenant in 1957 from the Heroic Military Academy, Mexico's equivalent of West Point, Gutiérrez Rebollo had excelled, by army standards, everywhere he served. He was posted in garrisons all across Mexico, held a string of staff positions at army headquarters, and taught as a professor for a time at Mexico's Senior War College. But his career really took off after he served as General Arévalo's top staff officer and then Arévalo was appointed Defense Secretary. During Arévalo's tenure Gutiérrez Rebollo rose from a one-star to a three-star division General in a period so short that his rivals suggested his ascent had violated army codes.

After 1988, when Gutiérrez Rebollo took command of the Ninth Military Zone headquartered in the sweltering western city of Culiacán, Sinaloa, his responsibilities included anti-narcotics tasks. He seems to have performed them capably and honorably.

Soon after taking office, Carlos Salinas struck out against traffickers, hoping to impress the United States, a potential trade partner. Gutiérrez Rebollo did his part. In April 1989 he participated in a regional dragnet that brought the arrest, in Guadalajara, of Miguel Angel Félix Gallardo, then considered Mexico's most powerful trafficker. Gutiérrez Rebollo detained the commander of the State Judicial Police, the chief of police of Culiacán, and nine hundred Culiacán officers, accusing them of collaborating with Félix Gallardo.

Three months later Gutiérrez Rebollo led hundreds of troops in a raid on a Sinaloa mountain village, striding past a cortege of drunken bodyguards to arrest Amado Carrillo Fuentes, Ernesto Fonseca Carrillo's nephew and a rising lieutenant in the Juárez cartel, the mafia that controlled the lucrative smuggling route from Ciudad Juárez into El Paso, Texas.

"General, I'll be glad to accompany you," Carrillo Fuentes told Gutiérrez Rebollo. "But let me explain . . . ," he added, in a classic opening to a bribe negotiation.

"I have orders to bring you in," the General replied. "You don't have to explain anything to me."

But if Gutiérrez Rebollo seemed incorruptible, the record shows that in pursuit of an active sex life, he was already living beyond the means of a meager government salary. He had established separate residences for his wife, Teresa, and also for not one but two young mistresses. He had begun an affair with Esther Priego Ruiz when he was forty-three and she was in her twenties, and during the 1980s she followed him as he transferred from base to base with his wife and daughter. In Culiacán he continued the relationship with Priego while starting a second affair, with another woman, who was ten years younger than Esther.

In late 1989, when he was fifty-five years old, Gutiérrez Rebollo was given command of one of the army's most prestigious posts, the Fifth Military Region, based in Guadalajara, Jalisco, Mexico's second-largest city, with a metropolitan population of 5 million. His new headquarters occupied a four-story eighteenth-century colonial building, originally built as a Catholic convent. As the regional commander, he had authority over forty thousand troops on a dozen bases.

Politicians and prominent regional personalities climbed the stairs to meet the new regional commander: current and former PRI governors of Jalisco, mayors and police chiefs of Guadalajara and of neighboring Tlaquepaque, and, inevitably, drug lords.

By 1989 Guadalajara had become the capital of Mexico's drug trade, and major traffickers felt secure enough to live there openly with their families. They did business with the military through a self-appointed intermediary: Irma Lizette Ibarra, a dark-eyed beauty who had won the Miss Jalisco contest in 1970. The drug don Félix Gallardo had given her a string of famously gorgeous gems. Many Generals, including General Vinicio Santoyo, the regional commander who preceded Gutiérrez Rebollo, had romanced her as well.

It was Ibarra's practice to organize an elegant dinner for new military commanders who arrived in Guadalajara, and to invite Fonseca Carrillo and her other trafficker friends. Not long after Gutiérrez Rebollo's arrival, Ibarra, resplendent in the jewels Félix Gallardo had given her, climbed the stairs to his office and invited him to dinner.

Once in Guadalajara, Gutiérrez Rebollo resettled his female entourage. He purchased a smart home near the Camino Real Hotel for his wife, a home in the northern suburb of Zapopan for Esther, and another in Tlaquepaque on the city's southern outskirts for his younger lover. He deployed platoons of young GIs to care for his women—as drivers, cooks, nursemaids, and gardeners. Soon he had three families, since his wife and his two mistresses bore him children.

Meanwhile, Amado Carrillo Fuentes was doing time in Mexico City's Reclusorio Sur, or Southern Penitentiary. Carrillo Fuentes was about six feet tall, with fair skin, green eyes, neat bushy hair, and a slowly swelling gut. Cocaine commerce had made him wealthy, and he was a favored client of Tomás Colsa McGregor, a jet-setting Guadalajara jeweler who sold emeralds and diamonds to most of the top Mexican traffickers. Although Carrillo Fuentes was being held in what was called a high-security cell block, the jeweler visited him at will, for he had enlisted onto his payroll both the prison director, Adrián Carrera, and the chief of security, who would greet the jeweler at the airport and escort him personally to the trafficker's cell.

Within a year charges against Carrillo Fuentes were dropped, and in June 1990 he was released from prison. Not long thereafter, Carrera became the director of the Federal Judicial Police, and Carrillo Fuentes kept him on the payroll, in one instance paying Carrera $1 million to appoint one of his cronies as the federal police commander for Sonora, the state bordering Arizona.

Carrillo Fuentes moved quickly to take control of the Juárez cartel. He compartmentalized the various groups within it—unloaders, warehousers, smugglers—so that if anyone was arrested, the others would remain at large. Once cellular phones became available in Mexico, he acquired sophisticated computerized scanners that allowed him to pirate cellular frequencies and thus avoid surveillance.

He brought the same know-how to murder. To eliminate rivals or undisciplined subordinates, he hired contract killers, often drawn from the ranks of the federal or state police, and stressed the need to dispose of evidence. Hundreds of his victims, especially in Juárez, were detained by police or soldiers and simply disappeared; their bodies were found only long afterward, dismembered and enclosed in barrels of acid.

Carrillo Fuentes was particularly skillful at syndicating large drug shipments among various investors, achieving economies of scale that other traffickers could only envy. He would buy old Boeing 727s and other passenger jets, remove the seats to make room for six tons or more of cocaine, and fly them from Colombia to airstrips in northern Mexico and back—or simply abandon them in the desert once the drugs had been off-loaded. A single flight could carry more than $100 million worth of powder. In awe, his Mexican admirers nicknamed him El Señor de los Cielos, the Lord of the Skies.

Carrillo Fuentes paid extraordinary bribes to such a broad array of senior officials that American officials eventually considered him the most insidious trafficker in Mexico. In 1994 analysts at a U.S. government drug intelligence center in El Paso, Texas, produced a lengthy confidential "Intelligence Assessment of the Amado Carrillo Fuentes Organization." They concluded that Mexican traffickers had organized a loose smuggling federation, headed by several *patrones*, or mafia bosses. "Amado Carrillo Fuentes is currently the premier *patrón*," the 1994 report said.

"Amado Carrillo Fuentes, through his familial ties and great wealth, has purchased influence at various key levels in the Mexican government," the report said. It called Manlio Fabio Beltrones, the governor of Sonora, an "associate" of Carrillo Fuentes's and accused him of using his state police to protect the traffickers' shipments throughout the state. It said that Jorge Carrillo Olea, who as Deputy Government Secretary had failed to act on Samuel del Villar's 1984 warnings of a drug kingpins' summit, had by the early 1990s become Carrillo Fuentes's "most influential associate in the Mexican government" and that as President Salinas's top antidrug coordinator from 1990 to 1993, he had used his influence to "insure safe passage of Carrillo Fuentes' aircraft" through Mexican airspace. In 1994 Carrillo Olea, who was not related to the trafficker, had taken office as the PRI governor of Morelos, the state south of Mexico City.

In the years after that intelligence report was issued, many other Mexican authorities were accused of ties to Carrillo Fuentes—federal judges, prosecutors, police commanders, and state officials. The most prominent was Mario Villanueva, the governor of Quintana Roo, the state where drug planes would refuel on their way north from Colombia. Villanueva was arrested and indicted in both Mexico and New York on charges that he rented out his state and its hundreds of remote airstrips to Carrillo Fuentes.

Even as he purchased loyalty from government officials, however, Carrillo Fuentes came to fear attacks by a rival drug mafia. He was most fearful of the Tijuana-based organization headed by Ramón Arellano Félix, the leader among four brash brothers who were the nephews of Miguel Angel Félix Gallardo. Ramón Arellano had commanded the helter-skelter May 1993 shoot-out at the Guadalajara airport in which the city's Roman Catholic Cardinal was riddled with bullets, a massacre that alerted Mexicans to the drug lords' growing power and reckless violence. Later the same year an Arellano assassination squad attacked the Mexico City restaurant where Carrillo Fuentes was dining with his family, and he barely escaped with his life.

In Guadalajara, General Gutiérrez Rebollo's most favored subordinates were the members of his intelligence group, a plainclothes unit of thirty soldiers who spent virtually all of their time on drug-related operations. The General gave them such unlimited powers that the rest of his staff dubbed them Los Intocables, the Untouchables. Their leader was a cocky captain named Horacio Montenegro.

In the summer of 1994 Montenegro led his troops in a raid on a methamphetamine laboratory in a Guadalajara suburb, confiscating a yacht, two Nissan farm trucks, and a Dodge Ram. Army protocol called for Montenegro to turn the seized property over to federal authorities. Instead, he treated it like war booty, giving the yacht and trucks to family and friends. Some months later Montenegro's father was stopped in one of the trucks at a routine highway checkpoint. Federal police uncovered a hidden compartment containing rifles and grenades. Gutiérrez Rebollo used his influence to free Montenegro's father without charge. The police never clarified why the man was driving a confiscated vehicle with a clandestine arsenal inside.

These were unmistakable early signs that General Gutiérrez Rebollo had begun to flirt with organized crime. Soon there were many more.

Gutiérrez Rebollo developed a friendship with a wealthy rancher, José González Rosas, who owned extensive lands adjacent to several Guadalajara bases, where he grazed cattle and baled hay. Gutiérrez Rebollo, a cavalry officer, had two prized horses, and soon González Rosas was supplying him with alfalfa. Gutiérrez Rebollo became a frequent visitor to his new friend's ranch.

Then, on orders of the Defense Secretariat, Gutiérrez Rebollo began investigating an air-force lieutenant suspected of drug ties. After some interrogation the lieutenant gave up a whopper of a confession: he said he had been a friend since boyhood of González Rosas's son Eduardo González Quirarte. In 1993 his old buddy had offered him a lucrative side job, which the lieutenant accepted, working for Carrillo Fuentes as an air-traffic controller, coordinating drug flights from Colombia. Normal procedure, the lieutenant said, was for the planes to refuel in Mérida, Yucatán, then proceed to Guadalajara and land at the Fifth Air Base, where their cocaine cargo was off-loaded into trucks and driven to González Rosas's ranch.

To the members of Gutiérrez Rebollo's staff who knew of his ties with the González family, these were stunning revelations. They expected the General, at the very least, to turn the lieutenant who had confessed to corruption over to military prosecutors for court martial; instead, Gutiérrez Rebollo released him, telling aides he was converting the lieutenant into an informant. They expected him to order an investigation of the González ranch; instead, he invited González Quirarte to his headquarters. González Quirarte became a regular visitor; he would pull up at military headquarters accompanied by a convoy of gunmen in armored Suburbans. The General would greet him cordially and usher him directly into his office.

Once, in 1995, on a rare occasion when González Quirarte was traveling with light security, an Arellano hit squad took advantage. Pulling alongside his vehicle in traffic, the gunmen opened fire, lightly wounding González Quirarte and one of his daughters. When González Quirarte recovered from his wounds, Gutiérrez Rebollo extended military credentials to him and half a dozen of his associates and assigned Fifth Region soldiers to serve as their escorts.

In return, González Quirarte gave the General several armored Jeep Cherokees and other vehicles as personal gifts. He donated sophisticated scanners that enabled the General and his men to monitor cellular-phone calls throughout Guadalajara and cellular phones with digital encryption devices that allowed the General and his people to phone the mafia without fear of detection. He paid large bribes to several of Gutiérrez Rebollo's aides. As for Gutiérrez Rebollo himself, there is no evidence that he received bribes on the scale of those paid to other top officials.

Instead, González Quirarte provided intelligence information on the Tijuana cartel, which the General used to plan his army operations. In early 1996 Gutiérrez Rebollo sent several plainclothes officers to Tijuana, where they worked alongside González Quirarte for three months, tapping phones and seeking to catch the Arellanos. Carrillo Fuentes paid for the soldiers' plane tickets, hotel rooms, and other expenses. They undertook similar operations in Chihuahua and throughout the Fifth Region. Gutiérrez Rebollo's intelligence partnership with the Carrillo Fuentes mafia enabled the General to maintain his reputation as a cunning and effective antidrug commander. Like generations of federal police commanders, he ingratiated himself with one mafia to attack another.

In the 1994 elections a PAN candidate, Alberto Cárdenas Jiménez, won the governor's post in Jalisco, making the state Mexico's third to be governed by the opposition and threatening to end this charade. In Baja

California and Chihuahua, where the opposition had previously won statehouses, the army had cooperated fully with the transition from PRI rule. The military's respectful attitude in those states had been a crucial but little-noticed advance in the country's democratic evolution.

When Cárdenas Jiménez (no relation to Cuauhtémoc Cárdenas) became governor in March 1995, he sought to establish friendly ties with Gutiérrez Rebollo. But the General responded by trying to undermine the PAN government at every turn, making clear the risks that organized crime posed to the democratic transition.

It was customary among PRI governors to allow Jalisco's military commander to choose the state police chief. Cárdenas asked Gutiérrez Rebollo for suggestions. The General urged the appointment of Captain Horacio Montenegro, and Cárdenas acceded. But no sooner had Montenegro taken charge than he clashed with Cárdenas's attorney general, Jorge López Vergara, a law professor and human rights activist. Montenegro ordered new anticrime checkpoints set up on highways across the state. López Vergara blocked the order, calling it an invasion of citizens' rights. He noticed that detainees turned over for prosecution were usually covered with bruises and traumatized, and warned Montenegro to respect the rights of the accused.

"The only human rights you worry about are the rights of criminals," Montenegro shot back.

A few days later Montenegro's state police stopped López Vergara's car and shoved his bodyguards around. Governor Cárdenas complained to Gutiérrez Rebollo, who defended Montenegro. Cárdenas held his peace until early 1996, when Montenegro's police crudely botched an attempt to rescue a kidnap hostage. Cárdenas fired Montenegro, who responded by organizing a police protest. Hundreds of uniformed officers swarmed into an anticrime conference at the Guadalajara Chamber of Commerce, carrying automatic rifles. Some jumped up on chairs and shouted, "Montenegro! Montenegro!" Others seized the microphone to harangue delegates with demands for Montenegro's reinstatement.

Still others shoved past guards at the governor's palace. Cárdenas heard angry officers gather outside his office door, shouting insults and cocking their rifles in a metallic clamor. "They're coming to finish us off," Cárdenas thought to himself.

Terrorized, he phoned President Zedillo. Ten minutes passed, then the police officers left the palace.

But over the next months Montenegro (backed by Gutiérrez Rebollo) stepped up his attacks on the Cárdenas government, accusing López Vergara and other PAN officials of ties to the Tijuana cartel. López Vergara sued Montenegro for libel, but Montenegro continued his attacks.

In July 1996 the war between the rival drug mafias bloodied the army. Gunmen working for Ramón Arellano went to Guadalajara intending to execute Carrillo Fuentes. Instead, they ambushed Chevrolet Suburbans driven by Gutiérrez Rebollo's plainclothes agents and killed a lieutenant and a sergeant—and one of González Quirarte's men as well. An investigation showed that the two trucks had been given to Gutiérrez Rebollo by González Quirarte.

The incident strengthened Attorney General López Vergara's misgivings. He tried to understand his adversary's motives. Was Gutiérrez Rebollo seeking to elbow him aside in order to consolidate his control over the Jalisco police? Why did Gutiérrez Rebollo target only the Tijuana cartel with his antidrug operations? He called federal Attorney General Antonio Lozano, a PAN member like himself, and suggested that Captain Montenegro and General Gutiérrez Rebollo could be involved with traffickers. Hearing this, Lozano agonized over whether to tell President Zedillo, then decided yes. Lozano has said that he mentioned the matter during a June 1996 meeting at Los Pinos and that the President grew irritated: "So it's come to this," he snapped. "Now they want to accuse the one man who's fighting the criminals with all his energies of being tied to the traffickers."

Zedillo has denied that Lozano ever raised suspicions about Gutiérrez Rebollo with him, but has also refused to answer questions about the matter.

If the ambush in July 1996 had worried Attorney General López Vergara, it infuriated General Gutiérrez Rebollo, who lost two of his men to the Arellanos' gunfire. Seeking revenge, he ordered a sweeping dragnet against the Arellano Félix gang.

The manhunt did not net any of the triggermen who killed the General's soldiers. But Gutiérrez Rebollo's agents did find one Arellano operative, a small-time crook named Alejandro Hodoyán Palacios. Alex (as he was known) had been dispatched by Ramón Arellano Félix to Guadalajara in September 1996 with the mission of renting a house that could serve as a base for the Tijuana mafia. Gutiérrez Rebollo's men seized him on September 11. While many suspected traffickers detained by the General disappeared without a trace, Hodoyán survived because Gutiérrez Rebollo came to view him as a useful informant against the Arellanos. Held in a makeshift prison for the next eighty days, Hodoyán experienced the General's brutality and lived to tell his story.

Alex Hodoyán was one of Tijuana's narco juniors, a generation of middle-class border youth who wandered into the drug trade looking for kicks. Alex was actually an American citizen, born in a hospital across the border in San Diego. He and his three siblings had come of age in Tijuana discos, where teenagers experimented with cocaine in the freewheeling way of wealthy American youth.

The Hodoyán kids met Ramón Arellano at a society wedding in Tijuana. In high desert summer the young trafficker was wearing a mink jacket and leather pants, as well as a gold chain with a cross encrusted with emeralds. His brash style impressed Alex, a law school dropout, and his younger brother Alfredo, and they soon joined the Arellanos' circle of riches and violence. Alex started by doing small favors and eventually helped the traffickers smuggle rifles and grenades into the United States. Alfredo, who was twenty-four years old in 1996, joined an Arellano assassination squad.

When Alex Hodoyán arrived in Guadalajara, he had not even heard of the ambush his gang had carried out days earlier, so he had little at first to tell the soldiers who seized him. They immediately began to beat him savagely and burn him with cigarette lighters. Then he was driven to a vacant army base on the city's southern outskirts that was Gutiérrez Rebollo's private interrogation center. Shackling him to a bed, soldiers forced soda water spiked with searing chili peppers up his nose. They scorched the soles of his feet and touched his eyelids and toes with live electrodes. Standing by to observe the proceedings was Eduardo González Quirarte. From time to time he suggested questions for Hodoyán to the torturers.

During his captivity Hodoyán heard the screams of other captives, all seized by Gutiérrez Rebollo's men and secretly held in the same illegal manner, without arrest warrants and in disregard of Mexican laws requiring criminal suspects picked up by the military to be turned over to civilian authorities within forty-eight hours.

For the first thirteen days Gutiérrez Rebollo directed Hodoyán's torment but did not allow his prisoner to see him. Then, on September 24, the General came forward. He was the consummate good cop, sweeping into Hodoyán's room, feigning shock at his condition, ordering his manacles loosened and his food upgraded. He let Hodoyán see him scolding subordinates for treating the prisoner harshly.

The ploy had a powerful effect on Hodoyán in his broken condition. Gutiérrez Rebollo, the gentle General, came to see his prisoner every day. Soon Hodoyán became devoted to his jailer. When allowed, he followed the General around the barracks like a dog.

But domesticating Alex Hodoyán was not enough for Gutiérrez Rebollo. In the early days of Hodoyán's detention, gunmen working for the Tijuana cartel had murdered a top Mexican antidrug prosecutor in Mexico City. Gutiérrez Rebollo had coaxed and tortured information about the assassination from Hodoyán and other prisoners. Putting together the fragments of testimony, he concluded that one of the assassins was Alex's brother Alfredo. Gutiérrez Rebollo was able to feed his superiors information about Alfredo's hideout, and soon U.S. agents arrested the younger Hodoyán brother in San Diego.

Mexican prosecutors sought to extradite Alfredo Hodoyán to Mexico to stand trial for murder, and they needed solid evidence to present to an American court. Gutiérrez Rebollo set out to persuade Alex Hodoyán to testify against his own brother. In late October he was sufficiently confident of his new informant's cooperation to move Hodoyán from the vacant military base to the Fifth Region headquarters in downtown Guadalajara, and he allowed Alex to call his family to say he was alive. His parents were elated. But as Hodoyán began to call them regularly, they realized that despite his guarded language, he was informing on the Arellano gang and under pressure to turn on his brother.

Alex's parents urged him to remain loyal to the family. But he was bitter that the Arellanos had sent him into an ambush. His allegiance had shifted to Gutiérrez Rebollo, a captor who aroused both terror and devotion. Cooperating with the General, Alex argued, was the only way he could survive to see his two young daughters again. "I love my brother, Mama," Hodoyán told his anguished mother in one conversation. "But my daughters come first."

In another, his father asked Alex what he wanted to tell his brother Alfredo. "Tell him I made a deal with the General, and the General is keeping his word," Hodoyán said. "He even bought new clothes for me. He spared my life, and I want to keep my word to him, too."

In another conversation Alex's father suggested to his son that he was suffering from Stockholm syndrome, in which kidnap victims become attached to their kidnappers. "Look, Papa, I don't want trouble," Alex responded. "I don't want them to kill me. I don't want that."

General Gutiérrez Rebollo eventually won the fight for Alex Hodoyán's soul. In November 1996 he summoned Mexican civilian prosecutors to Guadalajara. Hodoyán sat for eight hours before government video cameras, giving up the Tijuana cartel's secrets in legal testimony. He described the murders of police commanders, prosecutors, drug rivals, and innocent bystanders. His testimony was viewed on both sides of the border as another law-enforcement triumph by the Fifth Region's butt-kicking commander.

In early December 1996 President Zedillo appointed General Gutiérrez Rebollo to head the federal drug agency. How could he have made such a blunder?

Zedillo took office alarmed by the drug lords' rising power and audacity. Three weeks after his inauguration the director of the Federal Judicial Police, who had pledged a crackdown on traffickers within the force, was poisoned by his own bodyguards. Then the army detained the trafficker Héctor Palma Salazar virtually by accident—his Learjet had run out of fuel and crashed—and arrested thirty-two police officers working as Palma's bodyguards. All distinction between the police and the criminals seemed to be vanishing. Zedillo hoped that the army's discipline and cohesion could withstand the traffickers' corrosive onslaught.

Gutiérrez Rebollo took control with a characteristic show of force.

Hours after his swearing in, a SWAT team, wearing ski masks and carrying automatic rifles, took up positions on the roof of the drug agency's glass-and-steel headquarters and swept through hallways and offices, evicting the civilian bureaucrats.

But Gutiérrez Rebollo was loath to relinquish his lucrative command over the military in Guadalajara, and he felt out of his element in Mexico City. Reporters began to clamor for interviews. At a breakfast with foreign journalists he hunched over his plate of *huevos rancheros* while aides to Zedillo did most of the talking, then left scowling, refusing to take questions.

Seeking to maintain some personal stability, Gutiérrez Rebollo brought Montenegro and much of his Fifth Military Region staff from Guadalajara. He moved his wife into a suburban Mexico City home they had purchased a decade earlier, but left his younger mistress, now caring for two children, behind in Guadalajara. To rearrange his relationship with Esther Priego, he asked González Quirarte for help. "See if he has an apartment or a house he could loan me," the General instructed his driver, Second Lieutenant Juan Galván.

The trafficker was happy to oblige. He invited Galván to an apartment building in Bosques de las Lomas, a nouveau-riche Mexico City neighborhood. When Galván arrived, a man with green eyes and an aquiline nose sat in a stuffed chair.

"Meet Amado Carrillo Fuentes, the Lord of the Skies," González Quirarte told Galván. "Feel proud. Many would like to meet him, but you're among the few who've succeeded."

Carrillo Fuentes gave Galván the keys to three properties, including a second-floor apartment on the Sierra Chalchihui, overlooking a wooded ravine in the Lomas de Chapultepec neighborhood.

On December 10, 1996, Gutiérrez Rebollo and Priego moved into the apartment, furnished with garish overstuffed furniture and plastic plants. Esther bought an electric auto raceway for her son, now five, and set it up on the living room rug.

That day, as it happened, Barry McCaffrey traveled to Mexico City to meet with the Mexican Attorney General and with Gutiérrez Rebollo. After a morning speech McCaffrey spoke to reporters, giving his assessment of Mexico's new antidrug coordinator. "From the ambassador and his team, we know a lot about General Gutiérrez Rebollo," McCaffrey said. "He's a serious soldier, a very focused guy. He's spent most of his life in field command, the last seven years out in Guadalajara. He's a guy of absolute unquestioned integrity."

The General's arrest came just nine weeks later. In the official version of the events, an anonymous caller telephoned General Cervantes's office on February 6, reporting that Gutiérrez Rebollo was living in a trafficker's apartment. Prosecutors later claimed the anonymous caller was Second Lieutenant Galván, the driver. But the official story was a lie, hastily invented by the army in the days after Gutiérrez Rebollo's arrest.

In the end Gutiérrez Rebollo was undone by his hubris and sense of impunity. Among his new neighbors, it was well known that Carrillo Fuentes owned two apartments in the building on the Sierra Chalchihui. One day in early February one of them, a well-connected Mexican businessman, was working out in the building's gym when he noticed a sexy new resident, Esther Priego, walking a treadmill. He started a conversation, and Priego mentioned that she was living with General Gutiérrez Rebollo.

The businessman immediately understood the significance of her comment and reported to one of Zedillo's aides that the new drug czar was living in an apartment owned by Carrillo Fuentes.

Zedillo called Defense Secretary Cervantes to Los Pinos. "I want you to summon General Gutiérrez Rebollo and ask him if it is true that he lives at this address," Zedillo said. "If he confirms that he does, as commander in chief of the armed forces, I order you to arrest him immediately."

General Cervantes returned to the Defense Secretariat, gathered his top aides, and just before midnight on February 6 confronted Gutiérrez Rebollo, who claimed that he did not know that Carrillo Fuentes was his landlord.

According to the official story, Gutiérrez Rebollo went into a hypoglycemic swoon in the Defense Minister's office when he realized that his mafia ties had been discovered. He was taken to the Central Military Hospital for treatment and kept under guard.

The General's detention was kept secret for twelve days as the military police questioned his driver, bodyguard, typist, and a dozen others on his staff. On February 14, military police arrested Captain Montenegro.

All the while, some top Generals and even some of Zedillo's staff proposed that Gutiérrez Rebollo's arrest be kept secret until after March 1, when, in an annual exercise known as certification, U.S. President Clinton would report to the Congress on Mexico's cooperation in the drug war. Zedillo refused: "If we don't act, we're going to see Mexico's sovereignty exposed to ridicule in some hearing in the U.S. Congress," he said.

The army was still holding Gutiérrez Rebollo secretly on February 17, when reporters at the Guadalajara newspaper *Siglo 21* learned that military police were searching the General's homes in that city. With the paper planning to go to press, the Defense Secretariat was forced to act. Before dawn on February 18, military police drove Gutiérrez Rebollo and Captain Montenegro in shackles to the Almoloya penitentiary west of Mexico City.

That evening, reporters were bused to a ballroom at army headquarters, glittering with rococo chandeliers. The commanders of all thirty-six of the country's military zones had flown to Mexico City, joining hundreds of other Generals. Faces were grim. General Cervantes outlined Gutiérrez Rebollo's crimes and his decision to put him on trial. The harangue was designed to impress journalists and to warn other Generals against straying down Gutiérrez Rebollo's errant path.

In Jalisco the arrests of Gutiérrez Rebollo and Montenegro came as welcome vindication for Attorney General López Vergara and Governor Cárdenas. In Mexico City, Zedillo ordered that the national drug agency be renamed, hoping that would help citizens forget how Gutiérrez Rebollo had disgraced it. In Washington antidrug officials reviewed the secrets that Gutiérrez Rebollo might have leaked to the mafia, and in the spring of 1997 unmistakable signs of an intelligence fiasco appeared on the streets of Tijuana and San Diego: half a dozen DEA informants turned up dead.

During the six months after Gutiérrez Rebollo's arrest, three protagonists in his drama lost their lives or disappeared. Alex Hodoyán was flown in mid-January 1997 to San Diego, where American drug agents were offering to enroll him in a witness-protection program if he would testify against his brother Alfredo. Alex was in San Diego when he learned of Gutiérrez Rebollo's arrest.

During his captivity Alex had constructed a fragile vision of Gutiérrez Rebollo as a kindly General who had treated him fairly, a view that helped him to rationalize his role as an informant against his own brother. The news of the General's downfall shattered Hodoyán's illusions along with his personality. The morning after the announcement Hodoyán rose before dawn, bolted from his San Diego hotel, and crossed the border into Mexico, heedless of the danger from the Arellano Félix brothers, who knew that he was cooperating with authorities. He showed up at his parents' Tijuana home crying and beseeching them for forgiveness. Thirteen days later, when he was driving through Tijuana with his mother, armed men blocked their vehicle and kidnapped him. He was not seen again.

Meanwhile, it was becoming clear that the Lord of the Skies was yesterday's trafficker. Carrillo Fuentes had purchased government protection for a time, enriching himself and senior officials, but like other major drug lords who had risen and fallen before him, he had gained too much notoriety. One month before Gutiérrez Rebollo's detention, he barely escaped capture when army troops stormed into a Sinaloa ranch during a wedding reception for his sister. Ten days later, on January 14, González Quirarte met with several Generals to negotiate: if Carrillo Fuentes was allowed to keep some of his fortune and protect his family, he would minimize the violence associated with the drug trade and invest all his drug profits in Mexico. In the army's account of the meeting, the Generals rejected the offer. In other accounts, the Generals accepted a $6 million bribe, then reneged on the agreement. Carrillo Fuentes sent his family to Chile and took up residence in the Cayman Islands but returned to Mexico City in hopes that a change of appearance would allow him to live at home quietly. On July 3, he checked into a private clinic guarded by his gunmen. He died after eight hours of cosmetic surgery.

Three weeks later, on July 27, *Proceso* published a classified military report that identified Irma Lizette Ibarra, the former beauty queen, as an intermediary between the traffickers and the army. The next day the magazine's correspondent in Guadalajara, Felipe Cobián, telephoned Ibarra to request an interview. She declined but told Cobián: "If I were to talk, it would muddy the names of many Generals who are involved in narcotics trafficking." She said she was considering calling a press conference to outline her views.

The next afternoon a motorcyclist shot Ibarra eight times as she drove in Guadalajara traffic. Minutes after the murder, military intelligence officers searched Ibarra's home. The same summer two other men known as intermediaries between the traffickers and the military were assassinated. These murders were never clarified.

In private, even President Zedillo expressed fears about the Generals' potential for violence. The businessman who had first warned the President's men that Mexico's wealthiest trafficker had taken the drug czar as his tenant later boasted at a social dinner of his own involvement in the case. Word reached Zedillo, who dispatched an aide to quiet the man. "Tell that idiot to shut up or they'll kill him," Zedillo said.

Over the years political scientists devoted considerable study to the relations among traffickers, PRI leaders, law-enforcement officials, and the state. Some portrayed a hierarchical chain of control and corruption in which the Mexican government, from the President and his key aides down through the Government Secretariat and other security-related agencies, sold protection to traffickers. Other experts argued that patterns of corruption were more fragmented and complex, with temporary alliances of senior officials and criminal leaders coalescing for specific deals.

Gutiérrez Rebollo's arrest and subsequent conviction on racketeering charges set off a new debate about the power and evolution of organized crime in Mexico. The Zedillo and Clinton administrations argued that it was a major step in establishing rule of law, and the prosecution of several other Mexican Generals suggested that the army's impunity was at an end. On March 17, 1997, General Alfredo Navarro Lara was arrested in Tijuana and charged with offering a $1-million-a-month bribe on behalf of the Arellano Félix brothers. Later in Zedillo's presidency three other Generals were charged with narcotics crimes; U.S. officials, citing informants, said one had accepted a $16 million bribe from traffickers. Under Zedillo's prodding, the military seemed to have developed internal oversight mechanisms allowing it to prosecute corrupt Generals in at least some cases.

Some reform leaders argued hopefully that the advance of democracy in Mexico would make all public officials more accountable to constituents and the army in particular more responsive to congressional and other oversight, thereby suppressing corruption. But few Mexicans entertained illusions that reform would come quickly or easily. The growth of trafficking would continue to be one of the greatest challenges to democratic consolidation. As long as there was a huge demand north of the border for illegal drugs, the laws of the market guaranteed that traffickers would contrive the means to supply them, making the narcotics war a costly, often cruel, and generally futile exercise.

Some academics and media critics argued that journalists were writing too many stories about drugs and ignoring Mexico's efforts at democratic reform, giving an imbalanced image of the country to foreign readers. But how were journalists to ignore the drama? The country was struggling to develop a regime of laws after centuries of authoritarian rule, and the narcotics industry was turning police into kidnappers, politicians into cocaine brokers, and the courts into a marketplace where everything from documents to verdicts was up for sale.

The challenge was not to find corruption but to sort through the endless stream of accusations phoned and faxed to newspaper offices, besmirching the names of police and prosecutors, judges and Generals. In most Western democracies it is up to the courts to bring order to this swirl of imputations, punishing the guilty and exonerating the innocent. But in Mexico the PRI government often responded to criminal accusations not with investigation but with behind-the-scenes negotiation.

Sam:

We experienced this process personally during a seven-month legal skirmish provoked by a lengthy 1997 article that I co-authored with Craig Pyes. We began to work on the story after obtaining access to the extraordinary U.S. intelligence report, authored in 1994 by DEA analysts at the El Paso Intelligence Center, that called Carrillo Fuentes Mexico's "premier" trafficker and accused two PRI governors, Manlio Fabio Beltrones of Sonora and Jorge Carrillo Olea of Morelos, of protecting him. Drug rumors had swirled around both governors for years but had never triggered an official inquiry in Mexico.

The intelligence report, which had been distributed widely to U.S. government offices, went much further than any other official document we had seen in its specific drug accusations against senior Mexican politicians. Obviously, we did not rush its explosive findings into print. We carried out reporting in Sonora, Morelos, Mexico City, and the United States in a four-month investigation, during which we interviewed some of the government analysts who authored the report. They acknowledged that many of their insights about the Carrillo Fuentes mafia and its political patrons had come from the testimony of drug informants, by definition unreliable characters. But we concluded that they had based their claims on scrutiny of the intelligence information available, and we saw no sign of a personal vendetta against the governors.

We interviewed both governors in their offices, reading to them the accusations from the document, gauging their reactions, seeking to evaluate whether the accusations in the report were sufficiently credible to merit publication. Beltrones, a telegenic and popular politician who had forged his career as an understudy to Fernando Gutiérrez Barrios in the Government Secretariat, acknowledged that Carrillo Fuentes had established extensive operations in Sonora, but insisted that as governor he had worked to limit the trafficker's influence. We wondered, however, why he adamantly refused to provide us with a public statement of his personal wealth.

Until he took over the Morelos statehouse, Carrillo Olea had led a charmed life in the PRI system because of one serendipitous incident. When a young army officer during the 1970s, he had been at Luis Echeverría's side when students at the UNAM campus had thrown rocks at the President, and Carrillo Olea had whisked him to safety. The rescue rocketed Carrillo Olea to prominence within the PRI, and after retiring from the military as a General in the 1980s, he served as a Deputy

Secretary in Manuel Bartlett's Government Secretariat. He was the founding director of Mexico's federal intelligence agency under President Salinas, who later named him to coordinate Mexico's antidrug program.

Shortly before our interview with Carrillo Olea in Cuernavaca, the Morelos capital, Mexican newspapers had documented that Carrillo Fuentes had established a base of operations there as well. The drug lord's Learjets had been landing unchallenged at the Cuernavaca airport, and he had purchased a hacienda and three other mansions in the state. In our interview the governor not only denied all ties to Carrillo Fuentes but also pleaded complete ignorance of all the trafficker's blatant activities in his state, which strained credibility, given his career as a top intelligence official. He insisted indignantly that the Mexican newspapers had exaggerated when they reported that the trafficker had purchased a vast estate just two blocks from his own governor's residence in Cuernavaca. The estate in question was at least twenty blocks away, not two, the governor said. But after the interview we discovered that in fact Carrillo Fuentes's walled home was just around the corner from the governor's palace. It was inconceivable that the governor could have been unaware of the identity of his notorious neighbor.

Still, we remained unresolved about what kind of story to write. Then, in early 1997, we discovered in interviews that the two governors had not only been accused in the El Paso intelligence document but that the U.S. embassy had included both their names on a list of seventeen Mexican officials Washington suspected of corruption. The ambassador, James R. Jones, had delivered the list to Ernesto Zedillo shortly before the President-elect took office in 1994. That finding convinced us that the suspicions about the governors were held by many within the U.S. government, although it was clear that some in the Clinton administration felt that in the interests of fostering trade it was better not to press Mexican authorities about drug matters. Under the circumstances, we and the *Times*'s editors felt it would be irresponsible *not* to publish a broad story just to avoid stepping on toes.

Our thirty-seven-hundred-word story appeared the weekend after Gutiérrez Rebollo's arrest was announced and the week before March 1, when the Clinton administration was to certify whether Mexico was cooperating in the drug war, so it was not surprising that it aroused a tremendous clamor. The certification process is viewed all over Latin America as an exercise in Yankee arrogance, and many Mexican readers had difficulty believing that the story was not part of a plot to bully Mexico.

Our story intensified a debate within the U.S. government about whether to revoke Beltrones's American visa, a debate that turned on official opinions of the government's drug intelligence. Robert S. Gelbard, the head of the State Department's Bureau of International Narcotics Affairs, considered the intelligence sufficiently voluminous and credible to warrant revocation of the visa, and he was supported by the State Department's Bureau of Consular Affairs. Other officials, including Ambassador Jones, voiced skepticism about the intelligence gathered from drug informants in Mexico, saying that much of it was just hearsay and that in Beltrones's case it was inconclusive. Jones blocked the effort to lift Beltrones's visa.

Beltrones initially vowed to file a libel suit in New York, but his lawyers advised that his chances of persuading a U.S. court to punish journalists for quoting a government document were limited. Instead, both governors filed separate criminal complaints in Mexico, under the terms of a federal defamation law written in 1917 to give revolutionary leaders a tool with which to muzzle press critics.

The defamation case forced Julia and me for a time to devote much energy to our defense. Mexican newspapers quoted Carrillo Olea's lawyers saying that we had simply fabricated the accusations against the governors, even after we provided prosecutors with photocopies of the intelligence report. One magazine, Siempre!, headlined an article SAM DILLON CONSPIRES AGAINST MEXICO! The Morelos governor's lawyers even told reporters that I had gone underground and was a fugitive from justice.

If the justice system had been healthier, the official proceedings that followed might have inquired aggressively into the governors' associations, even as they forced us to defend the accuracy of our report. But there was never anything resembling a serious investigation, either of the governors or of us. It became apparent that we were involved not so much in a libel case as in a political negotiation. Although Jorge

Madrazo Cuéllar, the Attorney General who had replaced Antonio Lozano, had formal jurisdiction, our case was handled by the Government Secretariat, which called me in for a meeting. Julia came with me.

There, Alejandro Carrillo Castro, a PRI apparatchik who at the time was Deputy Government Secretary, greeted us jovially. He had just gotten off the phone with the governors of Sonora and Morelos, and now, he said, he knew what they needed. It was time to cut a deal.

It was not uncommon for Mexican journalists to be charged with criminal defamation by state governors, he said, seeking to calm us. The procedure was almost routine, he said. A journalist writes a story a governor does not like. The governor files a criminal complaint against the journalist. The journalist, he said, usually fights the complaint for a while but eventually tires. Then the journalist writes a second story, retracting the article that offended the governor.

All we had to do, Carrillo Castro said, was write a new story that would show we had erred in our first article, by saying that there was no U.S. intelligence document identifying the governors as associates of a drug mafia after all and by quoting some U.S. official praising their antidrug efforts.

We tried to be polite, but we told Carrillo Castro plainly that there was absolutely no chance that The New York Times would pursue that course. He was surprised, then furious. The Times's foreign editor, Bill Keller, reinforced our position in a letter to the Mexican government. "We do not, and will not, back away from a story we believe to have been accurate in order to appease someone who found the story troublesome," Keller wrote.

The PRI authorities eventually resolved the case in a way that reflected the system's profound limitations. In the fall of 1997 the Attorney General issued a brief announcement, saying that he would not prosecute us for defamation while claiming that he had conducted an investigation of the two governors and had found no truth to our article. This assertion was pure rhetoric, since as far as could be perceived publicly no authority had mounted anything resembling a vigorous investigation.

Although this Solomonic decision was designed for the benefit of the beleaguered governors, it finally did them, as well as the Mexican public, a disservice. If they were guilty of dealings with organized crime, for the good of the citizenry they deserved to be investigated and held accountable. But if, as they claimed, they had unjustly been tarred by American officials, the governors deserved a credible investigation and a clear exoneration. But the justice system was incapable of offering either, because its credibility was in tatters. How could it be otherwise when dozens of its senior officials had been found to be working with traffickers?

— — —

12

Testing Change, 1997

In the vote of July 1997 Mexicans elected 261 deputies from the opposition (including the PAN, the PRD, and two smaller parties) and only 239 from the PRI. If the opposition managed to hang together, it would hold a decisive majority in the lower house of the Congress for the first time in modern Mexican history.

The results reflected a pattern of the last decade of the century: pluralism was flourishing across Mexico like bougainvillea, from the ground up. José Woldenberg, the head of the elections agency, had a geography lesson he liked to give to explain why he was convinced that Mexico's progress toward democracy was irreversible. In 1988, he would observe, only 3 percent of Mexicans lived in municipalities governed by some party other than the PRI. By 1997 the figure had risen to 44 percent.

In 1988, Woldenberg would note, the PRI's monopoly in the statehouses was complete: not one of the thirty-one states or the Federal District had an opposition governor. In the eight years after Ernesto Ruffo of the PAN broke the barrier by winning Baja California in 1989, that party won governor's posts in Chihuahua, Guanajuato, Jalisco, Querétaro, and Nuevo León. Once the PAN took charge in Jalisco and Nuevo León and the PRD won Mexico City, the opposition was in command of the country's three most economically important states. Gradually, when convincing opposition candidates came along, Mexicans were voting the PRI out of power, starting in their own hometowns.

The opposition deputies elected to this first Congress without a PRI majority understood that they had been chosen by the voters to provide a new counterweight to the President, to be the checks and the balances—

literally, since it was the responsibility of the Chamber of Deputies to approve the federal budget. The PRI deputies, on the other hand, didn't seem to get it. The PRI leadership understood, in principle, that the loss of the congressional majority meant the end of business as usual. But they had no idea what it meant in practice not to be in control. As a result, they almost made Mexico's first pluralistic Congress crash during its maiden flight.

The Legislative Palace of San Lázaro, as it is grandly known, had been an appropriate venue for a legislature that was far more show than substance. A modern maroon rectangle on the edge of downtown Mexico City, the building was most noteworthy for its vast size. But after fire consumed nearly half of the building in 1989, the government did not think it worth the expense to rebuild. In 1997 one whole wing was still a wind-blown shell.

In August of that year the undamaged part of San Lázaro—the home of the Chamber of Deputies—was filled with newly intense activity. The leaders of the different party delegations came together for negotiations to divvy up committee seats in advance of the new session beginning on August 30 and to prepare for Zedillo's third *informe* on September 1. There was Porfirio Muñoz Ledo striding down the hallways, parleying and pontificating, entirely in his element. There was Pablo Gómez, a new PRD deputy. He had been a student militant and political prisoner in 1968 and later a youth leader in the Communist Party. With his mustache still bushy, Gómez represented the coming-of-age of the generation of 1968.

There also was Santiago Creel, who had avenged himself, after the PRI forced an end to his career at the Federal Electoral Institute, by running for deputy as an independent close to the PAN. Since the election Creel had hosted a series of meetings at his home on Calle Esopo—Aesop Street—in Mexico City (the name alone lent an air of sagacity to the gatherings) to forge a legislative alliance between the opposition parties. The talks had gone well, despite the party leaders' distrust of one other; they all knew that if they allowed the PRI to divide them, their majority would mean nothing.

José Woldenberg   Francisco Labastida   Manuel Bartlett
                              Ochoa

Roberto Madrazo Pintado   Andrés Manuel   Santiago Creel
                                  López Obrador

Manuel Camacho Solís   Jaime Serra Puche   Julio Scherer

Assembled in San Lázaro, the opposition lawmakers examined the Chamber's rule book to find the procedures for dividing up the committee posts. They found, quite simply, that there were no procedures: the rules had been written on the assumption that the PRI would control the Chamber of Deputies and all its committees to eternity. In fact, without a PRI majority, they discovered, it was technically impossible to bring the new Chamber into session. So the opposition parties—which included the PAN, the PRD, the small Partido del Trabajo, or Workers Party, and the even smaller Partido Verde Ecologista de México, the Green Party— went to work writing new rules for the newly diverse Congress.

As the session's opening approached, the PRI deputies began slowly to comprehend what was happening to them. First they were evicted from dozens of offices they had occupied along the hallways of San Lázaro to make room for the new opposition lawmakers. Then they were forced by the majority to relinquish the chairman's post on the budget committee, the floodgate through which all federal funds—the wellspring of patronage—had to flow. Then they were advised that a PAN deputy would be the chairman of the committee in charge of perks and favors within the Congress.

On Friday, August 29, on the eve of the session's inauguration, the PRI finally bolted from the negotiations. The last straw came in a dispute over the speaker who would give the traditional speech immediately following the President's *informe*. The opposition now had the right to choose the majority leader, the Chamber of Deputies' equivalent to the U.S. Speaker of the House, and one of that leader's established prerogatives was to respond to the *informe*. For the first time in sixty-eight years of the PRI system, an opposition speaker would share the limelight with the President, enjoying the last word in the principal rite of Mexico's political calendar.

The change from past practice was huge. The hardy few among the opposition deputies who had held seats in earlier legislatures remembered how the presidential guard would show up five days before the *informe* to order them out of their offices, on the grounds that the mere presence of anyone not with the PRI posed a risk to the chief executive's security.

For the *priístas*, having an opposition figure give the *informe* response seemed to violate the sanctity of the event, like sending an atheist to St. Peter's to rebut a prayer from the Pope. They were deeply uneasy with the idea of exposing their President's accomplishments to an instant opposition assessment on live television. But they were really shocked when they heard whom the opposition had chosen as the new majority leader: Porfirio Muñoz Ledo.

As soon as word reached the PRI offices, Arturo Nuñez, the normally phlegmatic leader of the ruling-party delegation, began pounding his fist on the negotiating table. "You didn't consult with us about Porfirio!" he said, apparently forgetting that the opposition, superior in numbers, was no longer obliged to clear its choice of leaders with the PRI. The PRI deputies demanded that they be allowed to vet the text of Muñoz Ledo's speech.

At one point Nuñez turned to Pablo Gómez, the former Communist. "You could do it, Pablo," Nuñez said hopefully, in a suggestion that indicated that the PRI would accept anyone but Muñoz Ledo.

The *priístas* despised Muñoz Ledo as a brilliant, volatile turncoat. When he was a young man, legend went, he had been the national champion of debating, boxing, and ballroom mambo all at the same time. Before he joined forces with Cuauhtémoc Cárdenas in 1988, he had been in the PRI for three decades, serving once as party president. He had held cabinet positions twice, had been Mexico's ambassador to the United Nations, and had twice come close to occupying Los Pinos, since he was on the *dedazo* list of two PRI Presidents.

But after his defection Muñoz quickly became one of the PRI's most biting critics, and the feeling was mutual. The PRI removed his oil portrait from the gallery of party presidents at the Mexico City headquarters. After he won an opposition Senate seat in 1988, PRI leaders greeted his request for a committee assignment with "hilarious laughter," he recalled, finally granting him a seat on the library committee. In more recent years Muñoz Ledo's political acumen had often been overshadowed by his stormy ego. By 1997 he had amassed many bones to pick with his former party mates, and the PRI deputies feared that he would launch a vengeful rhetorical assault on their President amid the spotlight and ceremony of the *informe*. So they went to work to block him.

By agreement of all the parties, the opening of the Congress was scheduled for 10 a.m. on Saturday, August 30. On Friday evening, however, a curious notice began to circulate in the halls of San Lázaro, announcing that the inauguration had been postponed until Sunday evening. The document appeared to be signed by Píndaro Urióstegui, a PRI deputy from the outgoing Congress who was in charge of the handover to the incoming one. But reporters who sought him out for an explanation discovered that Urióstegui had been hospitalized early Friday, apparently for cardiac arrest, and was lying semiconscious in an intensive care unit, in no condition to sign any documents.

Nevertheless, the PRI insisted that there would be a thirty-six-hour delay. Its deputies promptly took to the phones in a lobbying blitz, offering favors and privileges to potential swing voters, attempting to split the opposition majority and deprive Muñoz Ledo of his right to rebut Zedillo's speech. Among the busiest callers was Emilio Chuayffet, Zedillo's Government Secretary.

As dawn broke on Saturday morning, however, the PRI got a stunning surprise. The opposition deputies, sticking together, decided to ignore the PRI maneuver and proceed with the opening of the Congress—without the PRI. At 10 a.m. sharp they filed into the great plenary hall of the Chamber of Deputies—where they had always been the few, the powerless—and took their seats. They started the roll call to establish the quorum: they needed half plus one, or 251 deputies present.

The PRI deputies scrambled. Many were at home, confident they would have the whole day for their phone drive. They hastily pulled on suits, grabbed ties, and gathered in a war council at PRI party headquarters, across downtown Mexico City from San Lázaro. The party ordered up a fleet of buses to whisk them to the Legislative Palace in the event they were needed for an emergency show of voting force. Some eager *priístas* went to sit in the buses so they would be ready to roll at any moment. Hours went by, and the buses didn't move.

The PRI sent a stealth delegation of about a half-dozen deputies to San Lázaro to find out what was going on. Led by Fidel Herrera Beltrán, a brash *priísta* lawmaker, they crept down a back hallway, to avoid detection by the press, until they found an empty room with a closed-circuit television monitor showing the events in the hall.

The entire right half of the floor, where the PRI delegation was assigned to sit, was empty. With row upon row of vacant chairs with high, round backs, the PRI section looked like a cemetery. On the other side sat the opposition deputies, smartly dressed, poised to press the buttons on their desks that would register their presence electronically.

Herrera stared in disbelief at the big vote monitor screen at the front of the hall. Two hundred forty-one . . . 242 . . . 243 . . .

"Sons of their whore mothers! They're going to make the quorum!" Herrera shouted down the telephone line to Arturo Nuñez, the PRI delegation chief who was back at party headquarters. The internal television showed Muñoz Ledo on the floor of the Chamber, grinning.

"Look at him! It's Muñoz the Mad!" Herrera seethed. At headquarters the PRI leaders decided it was illegal for the opposition to ignore their decree canceling the session. It *had* to be illegal, didn't it? How could it be legal to open the Congress without the PRI?

Nuñez advised Herrera to head for the hall. "Go in there. Tell them they can't do this. Talk to Porfirio. Tell him that what he's doing is illegal," Nuñez said.

Two hundred forty-four . . . 245 . . . 246 . . .

"We'll fuck them," Herrera said, seizing on a plan. They would hold their own session on Sunday and get their own quorum, then declare the opposition inauguration illegal.

Herrera and his platoon of PRI deputies marched into the plenary hall and down the aisle toward the podium. They ran right into Muñoz Ledo.

"¡*Caramba!* Where the hell have you guys been?" he asked with a belly laugh at once jovial and sly.

"This ceremony is spurious!" Herrera charged.

"It's a coup, an assault on the legislature!" yelled another *priísta* behind him. A third one said: "We cannot allow an *artificial* majority to put a straitjacket on us when we are the *real* majority!"

Two hundred forty-seven . . . 248 . . . 249 . . .

"Porfirio, we have to talk," Herrera said.

"Why don't we just wait a little minute until the roll call is over?" Muñoz Ledo said, speaking slowly.

"No, now! Right now!" Herrera said.

Two hundred fifty . . . 251

A protocol committee led by a young PRD deputy climbed to the dais that rises high above the Chamber floor, with an enormous red, white, and green Mexican flag draped behind. On the podium they placed the silver inkwell and bell that symbolize the wisdom and decorum—such as they were—of the Mexican legislature. With a merry ring of the bell, they declared the Congress in session.

Herrera and his stalwarts turned angrily and left. In the first order of business the opposition deputies elected Muñoz Ledo majority leader, by a vote of 260 to 0. They chose Santiago Creel to be second in rank. Then they sprang to their feet, wrapped each other in embraces, and sang an atonal but impassioned chorus of the national anthem. More than one deputy wept with elation.

Later that day Muñoz Ledo swore in the other opposition deputies. The Senate, which remained under the control of a PRI majority, immediately retaliated by saying it would support the PRI deputies from the lower house and refuse to recognize the new Chamber of Deputies.

Thus came Mexico to the end of its first day of legislative pluralism: in a full-scale constitutional crisis. Because of the obstinacy of an eclipsed elite, the country, which had lacked a working legislature for so long, was on its way to having two.

President Zedillo's role in the events seemed inconsistent. On one hand, Government Secretary Chuayffet was busy on Friday and Saturday encouraging his fellow *priístas* in their resistance. But as the impasse hardened on Saturday night, Zedillo made a statement that seemed at odds with Chuayffet.

It was vintage Zedillo, a declaration about all the things he was *not* going to do. The dispute was within the legislative branch, he said, so he was not going to interfere. What was important was to respect the law.

The trouble was that there was no clear law to apply to the unprecedented congressional conflict. What was worse, the apparent disconnect with Chuayffet created the alarming impression that both Zedillo's top political operator and his party had run out of his presidential control.

By Sunday morning, with the standoff unresolved, the *priístas* started to talk about postponing the *informe*. At that point Zedillo went into action. Although he refused Muñoz Ledo's request that he meet with the opposition, his instructions to Chuayffet and Nuñez, the PRI congressional leader, were fierce. "Get your act together within the legislative branch. Get the Congress installed and get the crisis over," Zedillo said. "We don't want a crisis. We want the speech."

The PRI deputies were stunned. Without the backing of the President, whom the PRI regarded as the source of all its power, the rebellion collapsed. By Sunday evening the PRI had agreed to take the oath of office at a ceremony on Monday morning, so the *informe* could go forward as planned at five o'clock that evening. The PRI extracted only one concession from the opposition: although protocol demanded that they be sworn in by the majority leader, Muñoz Ledo agreed to let another opposition deputy take their oaths so as to spare his former party humiliation.

In his *informe* Zedillo gave a concise but colorless account of his administration's accomplishments for the year, in words that did nothing to illuminate the historic significance of the proceedings. As soon as Zedillo was done, Muñoz Ledo took the podium. The PRI deputies gripped their chairs in frustration.

But Muñoz Ledo delivered an address so eloquent and measured, so masterfully attuned to the moment, that even Fidel Herrera admitted he was tempted to cheer.

"From this day forward, and we hope for all time, no power in Mexico will be subordinated to another, and all will serve to guarantee the rights of our citizens, the fortitude of our institutions, and the integrity and sovereignty of the nation," Muñoz Ledo declared in his thundering baritone. "To know how to govern is to know how to listen and correct mistakes," he said, equally addressing the President and the assembled legislators. "Most certainly, the democratic exercise of power is *mandar obedeciendo*, to command by obeying."

Taking a phrase from the earliest parliaments to arise under the monarchy of Spain, he put Zedillo cordially on notice that the days of the kingly presidency in Mexico were over. "Each one of us is equal to you," he told the President, speaking of himself and his fellow lawmakers, "*y todos juntos somos más que vos*, and all together we are more than you."

The crisis of the opening of the first pluralistic Congress showed how fragile Mexico's democratic transition seemed, and how sturdy it could be. The danger that Mexico faced on August 30 was great. After 1994 any sustained constitutional standoff might have shaken the confidence of foreign investors and started a capital stampede. Mexico might have looked foolish to the world, not ready for the big leagues of democracy and development. Mexicans might have lost their delicate faith in the process of change. But none of this happened.

In 1988 Cuauhtémoc Cárdenas had refrained from forcing change through violence, thereby opening new possibilities for peaceful reform. Nine years later, when the knives were drawn again, all sides opted for restraint. The crisis was resolved by authoritarian method, when Zedillo ordered his party to obey. Yet the outcome showed that his orders were, in effect, for the PRI to obey the will of the people.

After that, San Lázaro never again lacked for life. With the pluralistic Congress installed, it immediately became the noisy battleground of clashes between the legislature and the President, and between rival parties. Most of the time the debates were civil, but sometimes they most definitely were not.

There was the time when deputies from an opposition party poured glue into the electronic voting buttons at the seat of one of their members after he sided with the PRI on a hard-fought issue. One group of PRI delegates earned the moniker "the Bronx" because of their incessant razzing of the opposition. Also memorable was the speech by a PRD deputy named Félix Salgado, who opposed the adoption of daylight saving time on the grounds that he was a *mañanero*, a morning person. Whereas others preferred sex at night, he said, he liked a tumble with his wife in the morning and was afraid the new schedule would throw off his manly body clock.

The Chamber hall resembled a parade ground for a day when a dozen members of a farm debtors group dramatized their fight with the banks by charging in on quarter horses. Striking sugar workers from Veracruz drew attention when they stormed to the front of the hall, turned around, and dropped their pants, mooning the lawmakers as well as the television-viewing public. Behind these antics was a serious point: they proved that the Chamber of Deputies was no longer the President's doormat.

Protests by sugar workers from Tabasco and other grassroots groups made for lively sessions of the new pluralistic Congress

Nowhere did the Congress exercise its clout more conspicuously than on the issue of the government's controversial bank bailout.

The banks' problem had originated under President Salinas. After the banks were disastrously nationalized in 1982 by José López Portillo, Salinas, in the soaring optimism of the middle of his term, sold them back to the private sector. To preserve nationalist appearances, he insisted that the banks be sold only to Mexicans, limiting the pool of buyers to the handful of entrepreneurs who could muster the necessary capital, and he stipulated that his primary goal was to achieve the highest proceeds possible for the government.

Salinas named Guillermo Ortiz, the Stanford-educated economist who was then an Undersecretary of Finance, to head the sell-off committee. Ortiz hired several Wall Street firms to help organize the complex auctions. Financial privacy laws in effect in Mexico at the time made it difficult for Ortiz and his foreign advisers to evaluate potential buyers. Nevertheless, the government sold eighteen banks and collected more than $12 billion, an amount 3.4 times the book value of the properties. Salinas was satisfied, and the international financial community hailed the privatization as an example of probity and good finance.

But trouble was not long in coming. Two banks, Banco Unión and Banca Cremi, had been sold to a shrimp merchant from Tabasco named Carlos Cabal Peniche. Cabal had flashy tastes and talked an impressive game, and he carefully cultivated relations with Roberto Madrazo and the PRI in Tabasco. Soon Salinas singled him out for praise as a model of the NAFTA-age Mexican business leader.

But after Cabal missed several large payments to creditors, Ortiz started watching him more closely. In mid-1994 Mexican government investigators discovered that Cabal was engaged in a vast shell game, taking money from one of his new banks to fund the other and using both to make loans to himself. The authorities filed charges for fraud in the amount of $700 million. Cabal went into hiding; both his banks failed and were repossessed by the government.

Then the peso crisis hit, sending the interest rates in early 1995 to more than 100 percent. Since fixed-rate loans are rare in Mexico, citizens and businesses were quickly forced into default, and soon many banks were on the verge of collapse. Because Mexicans pay most of their household bills through the banks, the entire economy was at risk.

Zedillo and Ortiz, who took over as Finance Secretary after Jaime Serra resigned, cobbled together a bailout. In their haste, they did not seek the pro forma approval of the PRI-controlled Congress. Under the program the government took over insolvent banks, protecting 100 percent of account holders' deposits, while shareholders lost their entire investments. In the case of banks that were in trouble but not yet bankrupt, the government took over portfolios of unrecoverable loans and injected new capital, giving the banks a fresh start, on the condition that their owners contribute new capital as well.

The day-to-day management of the bailout was handed off to an obscure and understaffed agency under the aegis of the National Banking Commission, the bank regulator. With few stringent standards and little oversight, the agency took over thousands of failed loans that the banks should never have made in the first place.

In light of the dangers that Mexico faced, the early results were positive. There was no run on the banks, and no Mexican depositor lost a peso from an account.

Then more problems started to turn up with the nouveau bankers. Angel Isidoro Rodríguez Saez had purchased a bank called Banpaís. Mexicans called him El Divino, after a stylish Mexico City restaurant by that name owned by his family. After federal regulatory authorities seized his bank in 1995, they uncovered evidence that showed, prosecutors alleged, that El Divino had made illegal loans to himself and others worth $400 million. Facing a fraud indictment, he fled. A year later police in Spain tracked him down as he was sunning himself on the deck of a yacht in the Mediterranean.

Extradited to Mexico, El Divino posted bond and went free, since Mexican law at the time did not treat charges of bank fraud as a serious crime. Soon he was back in business, this time running luxury resort hotels. He became a personification of the inequities that Mexicans despised in their financial and justice systems.

By the time the new Congress opened in 1997, twelve of the eighteen banks originally privatized had failed and fallen back to the government. While a few of the bankrupt banks were allowed to disappear, most were kept on life support by the bailout agency, which readied them to be sold. Even banks that were still sound were allowed to unload on the government the worst of the bad loans on their books. But the program made few provisions for banks that recovered through the bailout to use subsequent profits to lighten the government's debt burden. Some owners of rescued banks became hugely rich.

In January 1998 Zedillo sent Ortiz to head the central bank and named a new Finance Secretary, José Angel Gurría. Possessed of a confident bravado, Gurría was an intelligent and worldly economic strategist, equally articulate in English and Spanish. As Mexico's lead negotiator in foreign debt talks in the 1980s, he had done much to restore the country's credibility overseas. But like Zedillo, he had never confronted an adversarial Mexican Congress.

A few weeks after Gurría assumed his post, he and Zedillo slipped an unusual item into the federal budget proposal for 1999. They wanted to take all the debts the government had assumed piecemeal through the bank bailout, which was not registered on its basic accounts, and incorporate them in one lump in Mexico's overall public debt. Gurría described the move as an accounting shift that would make it cheaper to finance the bailout debt through global markets.

But when the proposal landed in San Lázaro, it received a new kind of scrutiny. How much exactly, some deputies asked, was the debt that the government was proposing to put on the shoulders of the Mexican taxpayers? Well . . . it was $62 billion.

The opposition deputies leaped out of their seats when they heard that figure, equivalent to 16 percent of Mexico's gross domestic product for a year. They quickly united to say that there was no way they would allow the Mexican public to assume that liability—not without a big fight.

The PAN and the PRD both declared that the taxpayers should not have to pay for any improper or illegal debts that had found their way into the bailout fund. To evaluate how much of the bailout debt might be fraudulent, the opposition parties demanded more information about the debt portfolio of the bailout agency (which was called Fobaproa for Fondo Bancario de Protección al Ahorro, or Bank Savings Protection Fund). Zedillo, Gurría, and the PRI deputies closed ranks to stonewall, insisting that Mexico's bank secrecy laws barred them from providing information to the Congress about any specific debts and debtors whose loans had been passed by the banks to the bailout fund.

The confrontation exposed many of the new Congress's inherited weaknesses. Each deputy had barely enough budget to pay for a secretary to answer the phone, much less conduct a massive investigation. Committees had no power to subpoena witnesses or documents. Moreover, since consecutive reelection was unconstitutional, the great majority of the five hundred deputies were parliamentary rookies.

Help came from an unexpected quarter when Carlos Cabal was arrested in Australia. In hopes of avoiding extradition to Mexico, he began to tell a few secrets. He said that he had worked with PRI officials to funnel $25 million from his banks to the party before the 1994 elections, before his banks collapsed and were taken over by the bailout agency. He produced documents that he said showed that about $4 million went directly to Zedillo's campaign. Opposition lawmakers accused Zedillo of asking taxpayers to pay for illegal loans that were taken out for illicit donations to his own campaign. But Zedillo still adamantly refused to divulge any information about the loans in the bailout portfolio.

Andrés Manuel López Obrador, then the president of the PRD, sensed the public outrage over the scandal and launched a nationwide campaign against the bailout. "It only occurred to President Zedillo to save those at the top, to buy the debts of the rich and the powerful and the friends of the government," he said in rousing rally speeches. "Mexicans, does it seem right to you that the profits go, once again, to the few, while the losses go, once again, to the majority?"

López Obrador and the PRD campaigned against the bailout across the country throughout 1998, while the Chamber of Deputies negotiated over legislation to settle the issue. López Obrador caused a sensation by releasing a list, obtained by artful hackers of thousands of names of Mexican people and businesses whose loans were said to be in the bailout portfolio. The PRD stopped short of calling for a default on the debts, a move that might have shaken confidence and imperiled the banking system. The debate dragged on for months, drowning out nearly everything else on the congressional docket.

Gradually the PAN gained the initiative in the negotiations, with Santiago Creel once again at the center. He found to his discomfort that the PRD's hard line was pushing him, and others among the conservative attorneys and businessmen at the core of the PAN, into a tactical alliance with the PRI in order to produce a workable bill to salvage the Mexican banking system. Seeking to exact a price for their uneasy cooperation, Creel and his PAN colleagues fixed their sights on Guillermo Ortiz, demanding that Zedillo fire him from the central bank as punishment for creating the bailout. But Creel and the *panistas*, in all their efforts, never established that Ortiz had done anything illegal. Ortiz's political position was strong because, as Finance Secretary, he had guided Mexico back to growth. Moreover, it was all but impossible for anyone—even Zedillo—to remove Ortiz as head of Banco de México because of new laws to protect the independence of the central bank— laws written by the PAN.

On December 12, 1998, the PRI and the PAN finally won passage of a new bank-rescue bill. The PRD deputies voted against it. In a compromise, the new law put the bailout debts into a special category on the government's books but not in the general public debt. It created a new bailout agency with stricter oversight and standards, but also more flexibility to finance debts and sell assets, and funded a program to help small debtors. The banks were required to pay a bigger piece of the debt. The law barred Ortiz from sitting on the board of the new agency, but he kept his job at the central bank. The markets surged with relief, and the economy remained stable.

As part of the bailout agreement, the opposition insisted on an outside independent audit of the bailout fund. The deputies selected a Canadian auditor, Michael Mackey, who delivered his report in July 1999. In the cool terms of accounting, Mackey's audit described a system riddled with fraud and incest. He found irregular loans worth $7.7 billion that the banks had passed to the bailout fund, including $638 million in loans that he deemed obviously illegal. Conflict of interest was rampant; loans worth $4.4 billion were made from one bank to another or to customers with whom the lender had direct business ties.

Mackey wrote in his report that the Zedillo government had fought him every inch of the way. He was never able, for instance, to examine the trust fund that Carlos Cabal had set up in one of his banks to channel his secret donations to the Zedillo campaign.

All in all, the bailout debate showed the possibilities and limitations of the new opposition-controlled Chamber. It pried open some of the PRI system's secret sanctums, exposing the decay in new detail, a sight that the voters would not quickly forget. But the opposition deputies did not succeed in saving the Mexican people from footing the bill for corruption and blunders that left the country with a bailout debt that eventually spiraled to $100 billion. At best, the bailout agency revitalized some Mexican banks only to have them purchased at fire-sale prices by foreign corporations. Citigroup, arguably the greatest beneficiary of the program, bought two Mexican banks after the government had cleared away their bad loans. The opposition parties, largely because of their divisions and inexperience, never managed to force a single government official to resign over the mess.

Indeed, as a result of the bailout debate, the opposition alliance was permanently broken. From then on all the parties in the legislature would move continuously around the dance floor, going from partner to partner based on the specific issue at hand. The PRI regained some power in that process.

But in general the practices of political monopoly were banished forever. Indeed, a fundamental shift of power occurred in Mexico after 1997. The pluralistic Congress showed the executive branch that someone would always be watching. A proposal from Los Pinos was no longer a fait accompli but rather the beginning of a negotiation. The opposition-dominated Chamber, although often raucous, was reasonably productive. Many Mexicans had foreseen disaster in a legislature not controlled by the PRI, but they were proven wrong.

Cuauhtémoc Cárdenas and the PRD team that took over the Mexico City mayor's office in December 1997 opened another front in democratic territory. If the opposition deputies were often plowing untilled soil, the Cárdenas administration was cultivating a swamp.

Before 1997 the governance of Mexico City had been an extreme form of the PRI pyramid. The city was neither a municipality nor a state in its own right, but a Federal District, a protectorate of Los Pinos. The President had appointed the mayor since 1824, a full century before the inception of the PRI system, but the PRI intensified the authoritarian logic governing the capital. Mexico City was the seat of the federal government; the federal government belonged to the President; therefore the capital city was also the President's, to attend to as he saw fit.

The nomenclature reflected the city's position. Mexicans do not call their capital Mexico City, as English-speaking foreigners do. They call it the D.F., for Distrito Federal, or simply México, showing how the capital overshadows the country much as the city of New York overshadows its state. Before 1997 the Mexico City mayor was called *el regente*, the regent, making it clear that he had no independent authority.

The population of the Federal District that Cárdenas would govern stood at 8.5 million, large but not exceptional by world standards. However, the Mexico City metropolitan area was approaching 20 million people—a figure that put it not far behind Calcutta and Tokyo. The majority of the population was spread out through a series of gigantic municipalities, gritty expanses of humanity in the State of México, which bordered the Federal District on three sides. As Cárdenas took office, Mexico City was very nearly ungovernable, because its most intractable problems—overcrowding, traffic, pollution—originated outside the limits of his mayoral jurisdiction.

On the day before his inauguration Cárdenas released a gloomy fact sheet. Some 182,000 of the 8.5 million residents had no underground sewage at all, and almost as many were without drinking water. Law enforcement was failing: of 229,605 serious crimes reported to the police since January of that year, 90 percent had gone unsolved. Armed bank robberies occurred at a rate of one every three days. With the job base dwindling as industries moved north to Mexican states with lower costs and closer access to the U.S. market, about 22 percent of the population was jobless or underemployed (a term referring to residents who were working in the informal economy—selling pirated CDs, plastic masks of Carlos Salinas, and the like on street corners). At least 330 days a year the smog reached levels that would be treated as a public-health emergency in any American city (including Los Angeles). Moreover, the ground was literally falling out from under the capital. When it wasn't racked by earthquakes, the city, built on the dried bed of old Lake Texcoco, was sinking, in some areas by as much as a few inches every year, as voracious water use sucked dry its underground aquifer.

It wasn't just that Cárdenas was the first mayor chosen by the residents. He had promised them that he would break with the patterns of PRI rule and govern in a radically new way, attacking corruption instead of living by it and incorporating them as citizens, not clients of patronage.

If Cárdenas was the commander of this assault on the ramparts, his captains were the *delegados*, or delegates, of the city's sixteen boroughs, its *delegaciones*. Several of the people Cárdenas chose for these jobs had followed similar paths: from 1968, through the first civic awakenings in 1985, through the UNAM student movement of 1986, to Cárdenas's campaign in 1988, and the feud with Carlos Salinas in the early 1990s. One of the new delegates, Salvador Martínez della Rocca, known as El Pino, had been one of the most prominent student leaders in 1968. He was asked in an interview at the beginning of his term what it meant that a man who had once been a revolutionary had become a suit-and-tie politician. He looked shocked. "I'm still a revolutionary!" he exclaimed.

An urban affairs expert named Jorge Legorreta was the delegate of the Cuauhtémoc borough, named not for the new mayor but for his Aztec warrior namesake. Cuauhtémoc was one of the largest boroughs, and the first among equals because it included the old city center. In theory, Legorreta was splendidly qualified for the job, since he had dedicated his professional life to the study and celebration of Mexico City. From a tiny office in the basement of the onetime home of a Mexican poet, Ramón López Velarde, Legorreta published literature about the city's history and social mores, conducted studies of its smog problem, led walking tours of its historic center, and compiled a guide to its venerable bars. With his hair swept back from a high forehead and a broad salt-and-pepper mustache, Legorreta looked the part of a bard himself. But from the first day in his new job he understood that his long romance with Mexico City would serve little to help him govern it.

The outgoing PRI mayor was Óscar Espinosa Villarreal, who was closely associated with Zedillo because he had been the treasurer for Zedillo's by now controversial 1994 campaign. Legorreta, like the fifteen other new borough delegates across the city, discovered as they moved into their new offices that Espinosa and the PRI had purged computers and emptied file cabinets. Contracts for public works, bidding that was in process, permits and licenses already authorized—all gone. Later the PRD delegates would hear from borough workers how they had been ordered to load files into dump trucks for removal in the days before the handover. Legorreta did not even have a roster of the names and positions of his eighty-five hundred employees, or a flowchart to explain the organization of borough hall.

It did not take long, however, for him to discover the basic rules of the regime he inherited from the PRI. First he learned, to his dismay, that the borough delegate was not supposed to resolve the problems of the borough residents. The delegate was merely a messenger for the mayor. So, for example, in the morning, when Legorreta would walk out the door of his home onto Avenida de los Insurgentes, a main boulevard that runs through his borough, he would see potholes and broken trash cans. He quickly found out that he did not have the power to fix them, or anything else on Insurgentes, or on any other major thoroughfare. If the problem was on a side street, Legorreta could arrange an asphalt patch or a repairman with a few phone calls. But under the PRI, big boulevards had been regarded as important sources of off-the-books commissions. According to established custom, only the mayor could designate the workers who would handle the care of Insurgentes and other avenues of its stature, and reap the income in tips and bribes that they offered.

In general, Legorreta learned, the city government had been run as a business, not a public service. A job with the city was primarily a platform on which employees could construct moneymaking enterprises. Wages were kept brutally low: a clerk or secretary made the equivalent of $450 a month, a policeman about $700. As a result, most workers, even honest ones, were forced to supplement their salaries with informal tips, outright bribes, and other schemes. These arrangements, in turn, were the foundation of the power of the PRI's unions and other corporatist organizations. They managed the distribution of jobs, reserving those that offered the best profit opportunities for PRI allies.

Take garbage, for example. The borough's garbage collectors would not pick up trash that people left in bags outside their doors unless the garbagemen were paid a tip. So, every day that some trash was cast on the street without the corresponding remuneration, it would sit in the heat, festering.

"How do you solve this problem?" Legorreta said, recalling his conversation with himself. "Obviously, this is the result of corruption among the garbage collectors. So you realize that this is your moment of truth, your challenge. You strap on your armor and your sword, and you sally forth on your crusade."

The foe in this case was the garbage haulers' local of the city employees union, the Unified Union of the Federal District Government, one of the largest in Mexico, with over 100,000 members, still very much controlled by the PRI.

"You bring your staff team, and you sit down across the table from them," Legorreta recounted. " 'Gentlemen,' you say, 'this business about the tips has got to stop. The city is paying your salaries so that you will collect garbage no matter where you find it.'

"They sit there and listen and nod for a while. 'Yes, of course, señor,' they say. 'We share your concerns, señor.'

"Then," Legorreta said, "they tell you how things work."

The union officials explained that every garbage truck in the borough was manned around the clock by twelve workers, on the average, in two shifts. But of those twelve workers, the only city employee was the driver. The other eleven were "honoraries."

"Honoraries?" Legorreta asked.

The honoraries were all employees of the driver, who was, in effect, the CEO of a small enterprise. In many cases the garbage truck was a family business, staffed by the driver's brothers, uncles, and nephews. In addition to the tips, the truck crew made money from recycling, with several men busy sorting the garbage from the moment it was dumped into the truck. In middle-class neighborhoods like Legorreta's borough, all kinds of stuff ended up in the trash that wasn't trash at all to Mexicans in the poorest slums. As the union officials spoke, Legorreta realized that recycling was one source of their power. The union decided not only which city worker would get to drive a truck but also which drivers would be sent to the neighborhoods where the recycling pickings were richest.

"These honoraries live off tips, señor, because the city government doesn't pay them a salary," the union leaders went on. "We completely agree with you, señor. Why don't you take them all onto your payroll and give them decent jobs? We've been asking the city to do that for thirty years."

Legorreta responded that he didn't have a budget to hire even one more garbage worker, much less thousands.

"Very well, señor. But in the meantime the honoraries have to pick up the garbage and collect their tips," the union leaders said. Their closing line packed a punch: "Or would you prefer that they didn't?"

Later the *delegados* would discover yet another source of income from the garbage trucks. One delegate found out that the trucks in his borough were using eighty liters of gasoline for every kilometer they traveled, or about thirty gallons for every mile—176 feet per gallon. Resale of gasoline siphoned from garbage trucks was a lucrative business for the union.

Legorretta was stymied. "When you govern," he reflected sadly, "you realize that you don't have enough money to change the old machinery. Private systems have grown up over all the years when the PRI was milking the treasury and reducing public investment in the city. If you break up those private systems, the whole city would go into crisis. It isn't enough for a guy like me to come in with an academic speech, ready to join the struggle against corruption. You have to keep going with the old systems so that the city can keep going."

Legorreta also discovered that he had to make a constant effort to avoid being ensnared by corruption. Although he declared war on it many times, he found out, months into his tenure, that borough employees were continuing to collect payments in his name, just as they had done under PRI delegates, in a practice called the *entre*. Unlicensed taxi drivers and street vendors, squatters, prostitutes, and countless others who lived at the edge of the law were paying bribes to borough officials, just as they had always done, in order to carry on their illicit enterprises. The bureaucrats were setting aside small portions of these bribes for the delegate, just as they had always done. The cash was piling up.

The first time some of his employees mentioned that he needed to collect his share of the money, Legorreta, not quite understanding what they were telling him, paid no attention. Then a former city official of his acquaintance came to see him. Apparently at the behest of Legorreta's staff, the man urged him to take the money. The cash flow coming up through the bureaucracy was his treasury, his friend argued, the only real money he would ever have to make improvements in the borough. He urged Legorreta to regard the money not as graft but as informal taxation. Since the borough staff knew that Legorreta was an honest man, he said, they would be confident that he wasn't keeping the money for himself. If he didn't take it, the former official argued, Legorreta would disrupt the whole system in unpredictable and perhaps dangerous ways.

Legorreta conferred with Cárdenas. They agreed they would not touch the money. Legorreta resolved that even if he couldn't stop the upward cash flow, he could still build a dam at the door to his office. But after that he was never sure where the gusher went, or when some conflict might erupt with someone who thought he had paid off the delegate and was enraged at getting no return.

As it happened, Legorreta never met with violence in his efforts to change the Cuauhtémoc borough. Some of his colleagues were less lucky.

For the first years of the Cárdenas administration Ricardo Pascoe Pierce was the *delegado* in the Benito Juárez borough, a teeming and diverse district in southern Mexico City. Pascoe had been a founder of the PRD in 1989 and was a key strategist in Cárdenas's 1997 mayoral campaign. He held a doctorate from the London School of Economics and had written extensively about the Mexican working class and the transition to democracy.

After two years as delegate Pascoe was promoted to become the city's *oficial mayor*, the senior administrative official. In that post he embarked on a drive to eliminate a particularly malignant form of corruption that he had first detected when he was a delegate.

Under the PRI, Pascoe discovered, the city government had been buying a complete change of clothing for every employee twice a year. In addition to new uniforms, complete with boots and gloves, for workers who labored outdoors, there were business suits for men and cocktail dresses for women—more than 1 million items per year at a cost of $25 million.

The clothing purchases were mandated by the city's contract with the union, which, under the PRI, had found several imaginative ways to profit from them. The union, after securing the right to decide where the clothing should be purchased, had set up a network of factories to supply the clothes—at inflated prices. Union bosses and city officials (or their wives, cousins, or in-laws) were often partners in the clothing businesses.

The city government paid for the clothing but turned it over to union-local chiefs to distribute to the workers. They charged each worker ten pesos, or about one dollar, for "transportation costs" for each set of clothes. Workers who were loyal to the union received the finest clothing, while those who were out of favor might not get any at all. The bosses, Pascoe discovered, had told the workers that the union, and not the city, had paid for the clothing, and then charged extra dues for it. Finally, the union withheld some of the clothing from the workers and sold it in open-air markets around Mexico City.

When Pascoe moved up to city hall, he vowed to put an end to the union's manipulation of the clothing deal. He knew he couldn't eliminate the clothing handouts without sparking an uprising among the rank and file. Instead, he summarily cut the union out of the distribution process. In no time the union's thirty-nine local chiefs and its secretary-general, Alfonso Rojo, were in his city hall office.

"Get this straight," Pascoe said, hardening his voice. "There is no way, *no way* that I am going to let you distribute those clothes ever again."

"There are going to be strikes and stoppages all over the city!" the secretary-general yelled. "This government is going to stop functioning!"

"Go ahead. Organize your strikes," Pascoe replied. "Prove to me that the workers are with you. I don't think they are. I think the people know that you have been stealing from them."

The bosses exploded with rage. After they left, Pascoe felt he had done the right thing, but he was shaken. "They hated me like they never hated anyone else in life," he said.

Soon the threats began. Strangers called his office, then his home. People shadowed him in the street. Even in the most dangerous hours of Cárdenas's campaign against Salinas, when the PRD was threatening the PRI's hold on power as never before, Pascoe had never felt so unsafe. For the first time in his life he got a bodyguard.

One day he was traveling in his official car on a principal street in downtown Mexico City when a car pulled up in front of his vehicle and stopped. Then another car tried to pull in behind, in the pincer action that is the classic prelude to a Mexican kidnapping. By a stroke of fortune, the thick traffic prevented the rear car from closing in completely. While Pascoe's bodyguard flashed his pistol at the assailants, his driver maneuvered into a side lane and darted away. Pascoe was left with the belief that his adversaries had tried to abduct him, a top city official, in broad daylight on one of the busiest streets in town. "They clearly think they are invulnerable," he thought.

Cárdenas and his officials tried to stem the corruption by encouraging new citizen participation and oversight. One borough delegate, Jorge Fernández Souza, organized a civilian review board of the police. Top police commanders started to attend monthly hearings where citizens aired complaints and reported trouble spots; the following month the commanders were required to report how they responded. Citizens were able to overcome their fear of the police, and the police were often relieved not to be seen as goons. The PRD government organized elections to select new neighborhood committees throughout the city, supplanting small-time cacique ward heelers named by the PRI. The neighborhood committees set up a system by which police officers had to check in with them once a day and get a signature to show they had been patrolling their assigned beats. The PRD team managed to make some neighborhoods run in a more just and orderly way, and in general, although corruption persisted, citizens were aware that it was no longer encouraged.

The public's number-one demand for Mayor Cárdenas was a reduction in crime. Cárdenas appointed Samuel del Villar, the PRD's longtime counsel who had defended the Aguas Blancas victims, as his district attorney. For del Villar it looked to be a gratifying culmination of his years of analyzing corruption and fighting losing battles against it as a lawyer.

But the D.A.'s job was almost impossibly difficult. The city's law-enforcement system was so riddled with graft that he found it difficult even to assemble an honest staff. After a headhunt, del Villar named a man as his top police commander who, the Mexican press reported, was under investigation for links to drug traffickers. Del Villar fired him and was forced to fill the post by promoting a young police officer, just over thirty, whom he had known from his legal work, because he found no one else he trusted.

Even so, he scored some early successes. Del Villar worked in tandem with Alejandro Gertz Manero, a university president whom Cárdenas chose to be the Mexico City police chief in August 1998. They installed tracking devices in patrol cars, so the police couldn't sneak away from their beats to carry out private extortion. They named a respected human rights activist to head the police academy. Del Villar restructured the justice bureaucracy to eliminate lapses between arrests and bookings that allowed criminals to dance away. With the help of the PRD-controlled city council, he rewrote laws that had set impractically high standards of evidence for prosecutors to bring indictments.

Early in his term del Villar won a $37.5 million settlement from IBM for procurement fraud in a computer contract with the city. Bank robberies, which had soared to twenty-three per month by the end of 1998, had dropped to one per month by June 1999.

Soon, however, del Villar found himself in a frontal conflict with an array of Mexico's most entrenched interests. It happened, strangely, because of the murder of a television comedian. On June 7, 1999, Francisco "Paco" Stanley, a sort of Mexican Jay Leno, was shot to death by two gunmen as he was leaving a popular taco restaurant in southern Mexico City in the clear light of late morning. Both of the major television networks, Televisa and TV Azteca, reacted with immediate outrage, citing the shooting as a shocking example of Cárdenas's failure to curb the crime wave in the city. Ricardo Salinas Pliego, the chairman of TV Azteca, which carried Stanley's show, made an unusual live appearance on the network that same afternoon to demand that Cárdenas resign.

The broadsides against Cárdenas made the Stanley case especially important for del Villar, and he devoted tremendous energy to the investigation. Within hours his detectives established with hard evidence that Mexico's beloved funny man was a cocaine addict and a dealer to other celebrities. The police soon arrested Stanley's straight man and several other colleagues who allegedly were partners in his drug business and charged them with putting out a contract for his murder in order to take over the enterprise.

But then the investigation degenerated into an unseemly battle between del Villar and Salinas Pliego. On the suspicion that Stanley's murder was part of a larger entanglement of TV Azteca with narcotics interests, del Villar expanded the probe to include the company's finances. Salinas Pliego countered with a campaign on his news shows against del Villar. Night after night TV Azteca's news announcers portrayed del Villar as an incompetent and vengeful tyrant. At one point the network broadcast video of a Mexico City mugging that was later discovered to have been staged, in an apparent effort to stoke the public's anticrime frustrations.

Del Villar made a critical error in his prosecution, basing his murder case heavily on one witness. In the later stages of the trial the man changed his story. There were signs that the witness had been pressured, but del Villar couldn't prove it, and his case collapsed. Nor was he able to assemble sufficient proof of his broader narcotics conspiracy hypothesis. In the end, a judge, sweeping aside evidence against some of Stanley's associates, acquitted everyone the district attorney had indicted.

Del Villar had struggled for years to reform the system from the outside. Better than almost anyone, he knew how drug money had saturated public life and how past Presidents, the PRI, and the media had colluded to protect criminal conduct. Once he was on the inside, however, he did not find an effective strategy for his crusade. He took on many powerful interests with no better weapons than his wits and the failing law-enforcement system he inherited, and his aspirations were frustrated.

Nevertheless, the justice system was changing, albeit slowly, and Mexicans were able to see some results in 1998, when the nation commemorated the thirtieth anniversary of the Tlatelolco massacre.

For three decades, long after President Díaz Ordaz's death in 1979, PRI authorities had clung to the official version of the events, blaming the violence on the demonstrators, who in fact were its victims. Each year on October 2 the victims' relatives had gathered almost furtively at the Plaza de las Tres Culturas, bearing candles to mourn their loved ones in silence.

But October 2, 1998, was different. Cárdenas was the mayor in Mexico City. The students who had risen in protest in 1968 were middle-aged, and many had ascended to posts of importance, not only in Cárdenas's administration and in the Congress, but also in academia, journalism, and the arts.

Cárdenas held a memorial ceremony on the roof of city hall, overlooking the Zócalo. He signed a proclamation calling the 1968 student movement "a decisive factor in Mexico's democratic opening" and ordered the city to observe a day of mourning, with the huge Mexican flag in the center of the Zócalo lowered to half-mast.

Elena Poniatowska was now sixty-five, and her book *La noche de Tlatelolco* was in its fifty-seventh printing. At Cárdenas's invitation, she stood at his side at the ceremony.

Tens of thousands of Mexicans marched from the Zócalo to the Plaza de las Tres Culturas. Speaking from the third-floor balcony of the Chihuahua building, a dozen former leaders of the National Strike Council, starting with Raúl Álvarez Garín, recalled the exhilarating sense of liberation they felt in the summer of 1968. The city council unveiled a gold-lettered inscription honoring the "Martyrs of the 1968 Student Movement," alongside other icons like Emiliano Zapata and Miguel Hidalgo.

The official version of Tlatelolco was under siege. Working independently but to collective effect, academics, journalists, attorneys, city leaders, and congressional deputies systematically dismantled the government's wall of propaganda. Enrique Krauze, the historian, who had participated at the margins of the 1968 protests as a university engineering student, gained exclusive access to Díaz Ordaz's memoirs. In a broader work of Mexican history published in 1997, he revealed Díaz Ordaz as a paranoid leader who viewed the demonstrators as participants in a worldwide conspiracy to undercut his authority. "The president's account is riddled with fantasies and lies," Krauze wrote.

Sergio Aguayo, who had been forced by a death squad in 1968 to flee his home in Guadalajara, produced perhaps the most ambitious of the revisionist books, drawing on archives in Mexico, the United States, and Europe, including reporting on the massacre by U.S. intelligence agencies and files disclosing the Mexican government's strategy for covering it up. Interviewing scores of police and military officers, Aguayo established that the conventional troops deployed to the plaza had orders only to disperse the demonstrators. They had opened fire only after coming under attack from snipers, whose shooting had started a pitched battle involving troops from a dozen military and police agencies.

Aguayo marshaled evidence that the Tlatelolco snipers had exercised unchallenged authority as they prepared their attack. Sir Peter Hope, who had been the British ambassador to Mexico in 1968, told Aguayo that armed men had commandeered the apartments of three British families overlooking the plaza, turning them into sniper nests. Aguayo also found a report, buried in declassified Government Secretariat records, indicating that army soldiers had captured many of the snipers. Yet the records showed that none of them had been charged with crimes. Instead, they were quietly released.

Solving the question of the snipers' identity fell to Julio Scherer García, the founder of the newsmagazine *Proceso*. In 1998 he was seventy-two, with a tousled shock of white hair, an eminence in Mexican journalism with a host of sources in the elite. Among them was General

Marcelino García Barragán, Díaz Ordaz's Defense Secretary, with whom Scherer had cultivated a long friendship.

In anguish over the stain of the massacre on the army's reputation, García Barragán, a decade later, had penned an account of the events, calling it "The Truth for History." He left it, along with other secret army documents, with his son before he died in 1979. For twenty years Scherer intermittently beseeched the General's son to allow him to read the papers. When the son died in November 1998, the papers passed to García Barragán's grandson. In a matter of weeks he turned them over to Scherer, who published them in 1999.

According to the documents, on the night of October 2, 1968, Defense Secretary García Barragán was monitoring the army operation at Tlatelolco by telephone. In the evening the commander of the main force of troops at the plaza called to request authorization to search buildings from which, he reported, snipers had been firing on his troops. García Barragán gave it. About fifteen minutes later he received an urgent call from General Luis Gutiérrez Oropeza, the commander of the special army unit charged with protecting the President. General Gutiérrez reported directly to Díaz Ordaz, not to the Defense Secretary.

"My General, I placed officers armed with automatic rifles to shoot on the students," General Gutiérrez told the Secretary bluntly. He said that eight of his ten snipers, who were in civilian clothes, had fled after other troops began to return their fire, but regular army troops had detained two of them.

"I'm afraid for their lives," General Gutiérrez told Secretary García Barragán. "Don't you want to order that their lives be respected?"

"Why didn't you inform me about the officers you're referring to?" the Defense Secretary asked.

"Because those were my orders," General Gutiérrez replied, leaving no doubt that he had carried out instructions from the President.

General García Barragán's documents showed that Díaz Ordaz himself had laid a trap. Loathing the youthful protesters, the President wanted a pretext to strike out at them. Without informing Secretary García Barragán, he ordered plainclothes marksmen from his presidential guard to take up positions above the plaza. The snipers had fired not only on the protesters below but also on their own army comrades, making them believe that students were shooting at them and provoking the chaotic firefight in which so many Mexicans had died.

Because of the new conditions in the country, the Mexican people finally knew the core of the truth about Tlatelolco. Justice for the perpetrators, however, would have to wait.

After only twenty-one months in charge of Mexico City, Cuauhtémoc Cárdenas resigned to launch his third presidential campaign. He had proven a competent but lackluster mayor. His granitic personal integrity did not make him a captivating or dynamic administrator, and his early departure kept him from making really substantial improvements in everyday life in the capital city. What he did do was stop the city's decline and set a new tone for its government.

His administration repaved thousands of miles of streets; reconditioned the city's leaky water system; cleaned up the air a bit; devised a more efficient health care system, relying on greater community participation; built thousands of public housing units; and distributed nearly 1 million free textbooks. But Cárdenas, always disdainful of the media, declined to publicize his successes, insisting that his was a "silent task." When he stepped down, a poll showed that 53 percent of city residents in the survey disapproved of his performance, while only 41 percent praised it.

His mediocre results hurt Cárdenas's prospects for becoming President. Yet Mayor Cárdenas had done a service to all opponents of the old system: he disproved once and for all the PRI's warnings that chaos would erupt if the opposition took over. Ironically, by not making more waves in the capital, Cárdenas did much to legitimize the possibility of change for Mexicans elsewhere. He failed only to convince the Mexican people at that time that he should be the one to make it.

Cárdenas fostered at least one political heir who did resonate. Rosario Robles had been his deputy in the city government. He named her to take over when he stepped down, making Rosario, at forty-four, not only the first woman mayor of the capital but one of the most powerful Mexican women of all time. The daughter of a middle-class Catholic family, Rosario (another woman who was generally known by her first name) had been radicalized at the UNAM and started her career in politics working with the university workers union, a group with a Maoist streak. After meeting Cárdenas in 1988, she helped him found the PRD and was a key player in developing its grassroots outreach. Rosario was fiercely loyal to Cárdenas, and even after she became mayor, she always consulted with him, addressing him as *ingeniero*, the word in Spanish for "engineer," a term of respect.

Awkwardly for both of them, Rosario, practically unknown to the public when she took office, quickly emerged as a far more appealing mayor than her mentor, with a gift for political theater.

One day President Zedillo decided to make an inspection tour of some federal projects in Mexico City, informing the mayor, as was customary, just a few hours ahead of time. Instead of dropping everything to accompany the chief, as PRI mayors had always done, Rosario told Los Pinos that she was sorry, but her schedule was already booked.

The people loved it, especially the women.

"They felt avenged," Rosario said in an interview during a breakneck ride in a Jeep Cherokee on a day of visits to neighborhoods around the city. "Men are always leaving us in the lurch. This time, for once, it was the other way around."

She managed to be both informal and commanding. In girlish bangs and spike-heeled sandals, she reminded Mexicans of their sisters and girlfriends. Since she hated helicopters, she used the jeep to move around the city, and when traffic was snarled, she would jump out and hop on behind one of her motorcycle police escorts to weave through the cars.

In one afternoon of suspense Rosario took on the anarchist students who had shut down the UNAM for months with an intractable strike. They insisted on calling a protest march on the Periférico, the main beltway ringing Mexico City, threatening to cause a huge and provocative traffic jam. Rosario authorized them to hold the march, but not on the beltway. When the day came, she sent unarmed police on horseback— rather than riot squads—to block the entrance ramps to the highway. She dispatched her top deputies, including well-known veterans of earlier student movements, to negotiate with the student leaders in the street.

The drama unfolded at one entrance point with a phalanx of edgy horses, a swarm of reporters, the students eye to eye with their leftist elders, and Rosario issuing instructions by cellular phone. Mexican television carried the standoff live for several hours. Some students lunged forward but were stopped by the horses. Finally the student leaders agreed to divert their march to a side street. No one was hurt, and the whole city sighed with relief.

"I wouldn't say it was risky. I would say it was bold," Rosario said of her approach. "It was a test of whether or not I was going to be able to govern. It was our only way to show that we were really committed to dialogue."

Rosario made progress in the delicate task of clearing downtown streets of sidewalk vendors and fought furiously with President Zedillo over the city budget, which still came through Los Pinos. Taking on the Catholic Church, she introduced legislation in the city council to allow abortions in the capital in cases of rape or threats to the mother's health, broadening the exemptions to a national ban on abortion. When she left office in late 2000, polls showed that 66 percent of city residents approved of her performance. She was one of only a handful of Mexican politicians whose ratings actually improved after they served in office.

13

The Earcutter

The gunmen seized Raúl Nava Ricaño one sunny afternoon in 1997. He was twenty-seven years old, the son of a man who had grown prosperous by trucking up bananas from the Chiapas plantations and wholesaling them in Mexico City. Family snapshots show Raúl with wavy hair and soft eyes smiling easily at his mother during vacations in Rome, Montreal, and Santiago during and after the years when he earned his university engineering degree.

He had worked off and on with his father since the age of ten at the family business, Navafrut, in the Central de Abasto, a thirty-minute drive southeast of the Zócalo when traffic is merciful, a vast complex of docks and cement-and-steel warehouses that is Mexico City's main market for vegetables, flowers, fruits, meat, and seafood. Thousands of truckers, stevedores, and vendors converge on the market each dawn in a chaotic din of shouts and honks and whistles to deliver and pick up much of the food eaten by perhaps 20 million Mexicans. Raúl had earned a reputation as a bright fellow, and his family had some connections in the government. In 1996 Ernesto Zedillo's aides picked Raúl to accompany the President on a 1996 trip to China as part of a delegation of young Mexican entrepreneurs.

On May 6, 1997, Raúl left the Navafrut offices just past 3:00 p.m. It appears that he walked out of the main banana terminal and down a flight of cement stairs to one of the immense parking lots around the Central de Abasto, where he was grabbed and dragged into a van, although authorities never located eyewitnesses. Minutes later, as he was driven to the improvised dungeon in a suburban slum where his abductors would chain him to a wall, their chief dialed the cellular phone of Raúl's father and let the young man talk. "They've got me tied up, Dad," Raúl said. Grabbing the phone back, the kidnapper demanded a $3 million ransom.

Raúl's parents had a few friends in government who put them in touch with both the Mexico City police and the federal intelligence agency. The abductors phoned frequently to the Nava Ricaño home in the nouveau-riche Bosques de las Lomas neighborhood, and the authorities began to tape the calls. Domingo Tassinari, a senior police detective, instantly recognized the nonchalant savagery in the kidnapper's voice.

"It's Daniel Arizmendi," Tassinari said, sounding a bit cocky as he described several of Arizmendi's abductions in detail to Raúl's parents.

"If you know who he is, then why haven't you arrested him?" asked Raúl's mother, Josefina Ricaño de Nava.

Seven days into the kidnapping, Arizmendi ordered the family to retrieve a package, hidden at the base of a streetlight along a Mexico City boulevard.

It turned out to be a small bottle with a screw-on lid containing a human ear.

The next day Arizmendi called back. "Give us the money now, or we kill him," he said. Private British security consultants who were advising Josefina and her husband told them to disregard the threat, that it was just a pressure tactic. But they were wrong. Arizmendi had called the Nava Ricaños for the last time. They waited for weeks, then months, in excruciating distress. Josefina ate, slept, and bathed with her cell phone within reach. Police claimed to be working the case, but their inattention became obvious.

Finally, in October 1997, five months after the abduction, Josefina's brother Fausto Ricaño, Raúl's uncle, decided in desperation to start visiting morgues. At his very first stop—Mexico City's main forensic center, in a central neighborhood five minutes' drive from the Zócalo—after passing a frightening statue of a snake-headed Aztec god of death adorned with skulls and going up a flight of stairs that smelled of disinfectant, the uncle met with an official in a white smock who handed him an album filled with grisly photos of anonymous cadavers retrieved from the city streets. Leafing through it, the uncle identified a body as Raúl's. It had been found, naked, minus an ear, with one gunshot wound in the head, lying in the gutter of a boulevard on the city's industrial east side on May 15, 1997, nine days after the kidnapping. Raúl's remains had lain unrecognized in the morgue for five months, as police "investigated."

As word about the discovery of Raúl's mutilated body spread among his old high-school and university classmates, it fed a wave of anger over similar outrages occurring all across Mexico. In 1995 alone, experts compiled information on fifteen hundred abductions in Mexico, a third again as many as in Brazil, a country nearly twice as large. In Latin America only Colombia, world center of the coca trade and a focus of endemic guerrilla insurgency, reported more. The next year the Sanyo Corporation paid a $3 million ransom to obtain the release of one of its Japanese executives abducted in Tijuana. While the case attracted much news coverage, most of the abducted were poor and working-class Mexicans: pig farmers, bus drivers, schoolteachers had their children or elderly parents snatched in crudely amateur abductions that often ended with the hostage slain. In Cuautla, Morelos, kidnappers demanded a sixty-six-hundred-dollar ransom for the son of a man who sold chili peppers in an open-air market. In Mexico City gunmen abducted, and eventually murdered, a Jesuit priest.

In time, Mexico's long-suffering people grew outraged. For nearly two decades, pollsters had consistently found the average citizen's main concern to be Mexico's troubled economy; by 1998 "public insecurity" had become the country's number-one worry.

How had one of the safest countries in the hemisphere become a place where bulletproofing automobiles was a growth industry?

In part it was the economy. Rafael Ruiz Harrell, a professor at the UNAM, charted annual figures for all reported crimes between 1930 and the late 1990s and found that rises in the crime rate coincided with peso devaluations and other cyclical crises. For the fifty years after 1930, for example, as Mexican workers enjoyed an almost uninterrupted rise in the standard of living, the crime rates remained stable. But between

1981—when oil prices plunged, sending the economy into a tailspin—and 1983, the crime rates grew about 20 percent. After the peso devaluation of 1995, the surge in reported crimes was sharper still, about 50 percent in two years.

The soaring delinquency rates also stemmed from defects in the criminal-justice system, which, according to Ernesto López Portillo, a legal expert with access to confidential government statistics and investigations, "simply doesn't respond to most crimes." Many victims preferred not to report crimes, and few of the crimes that *were* reported were investigated. A study in 1997, the year of Raúl Nava's kidnapping, suggested that of every one hundred criminal complaints, only about three resulted in the arrest and trial of a suspect. A World Bank study of crime in Latin America concluded that would-be criminals base their decisions to extort or steal on a kind of personal cost-benefit analysis. They estimate a crime's payoff, the costs associated with committing it, and the probability and severity of punishment. Those who applied this calculus in Mexico during the 1990s could see that robbery and abduction were extremely lucrative and punishment rare.

Prosecutors, judges, and police all contributed to the system's ineffectiveness. The unprofessional work of prosecutors, known as *ministerios públicos*, was one of the country's most serious but least understood problems. Crucial gatekeepers to the justice system, the *ministerios públicos* were often young men or women just out of law school, with monthly salaries of only a few hundred dollars. Since they enjoyed considerable discretion over which arrest warrants would be served and which cases sent to a judge, they were easy targets for bribes. They were not infrequently accused of writing mistakes into criminal complaints, for a price, thus forcing judges to dismiss charges.

Judges were better trained and paid, but a national survey in 1999 found that about 75 percent of Mexican adults expressed little or no trust in the courts they controlled. Behind much of the public irritation were abuses associated with the constitutional writ known as the *amparo*, the procedure by which Mexicans appeal sentences, file habeas corpus petitions, seek injunctions, and contest the constitutionality of laws. Anyone targeted with a criminal investigation could, if sufficiently wealthy to muster the legal fees, file an *amparo* suit requesting a federal judge to shield him or her from arrest. One U.S. Justice Department official based in Mexico during the 1990s called the *amparo* a "get-out-of-jail-free card." Most Mexicans would never seek *amparo* protection even once in their lives, yet not a few of Mexico's five hundred federal judges routinely extended *amparo* protection to narcotics traffickers, kidnappers, and other criminals.

Police were an even worse problem. Most city forces did not strive to prevent or punish crime; they administered it. In exchange for a cut of the profits, police would allow criminals to go about their business as long as they did not overreach. The parasitic relation between police and the criminal class was so institutionalized that successive PRI governments never bothered to pay police a living wage. Instead, on federal, state, and municipal forces all across Mexico, police were given mere token payments, in the knowledge that they would garner their living by shaking down criminals, as well as the everyday citizens they were supposed to protect. A 1998 study by two Mexican sociologists found that young officers were taught techniques of extortion from the moment they entered the police academy, where instructors were shaking down cadets for payments before promoting them onto the force.

Successive PRI administrations tolerated the corruption as long as it remained within reasonable bounds. But during the 1980s and 1990s police involvement in organized crime raged out of control just as the system was losing the authoritarian powers that had allowed Presidents in earlier decades to keep a lid on police graft.

Police were committing thousands of crimes. In one three-week period in 1998, Mexican newspapers published articles detailing thirty-nine separate cases of spectacular police criminality. One article said that Mexico City police were using a government computer to identify, and later threaten, citizens who reported crimes. Another told of the arrest of eleven policemen who were trafficking in migrant workers in Veracruz state. Another said that a police official from a state neighboring Mexico City was heading a car-theft ring. Another reported that a federal agent had organized a prison break in Tamaulipas state, bordering Texas.

Mexicans suffered not only a frightening crime wave but also a new kind of criminal, cunning in the ways of the old system but terrifyingly independent of it. Daniel Arizmendi López was a notorious example. In his mid-twenties, working as a State Judicial Police officer in Morelos, he watched carefully as his colleagues tormented prisoners. Dismissed during a purge of officers, he began to steal cars for a living in Ciudad Nezahualcóyotl, the Mexico City squatter slum where he had grown up.

He was arrested for auto theft in 1990 and served a brief stint in the penitentiary. Once back on the streets, he organized a gang: one man stealing cars, another bribing government officials to obtain replacement plates, Arizmendi himself reselling the cars through his own street-corner auto dealership. The group stole about 150 cars a year.

During 1994 and 1995 Arizmendi was charged with auto theft seven times. If the justice system had been working at all, he would have been identified as a hard-core recidivist. But he had forged ties to corrupt federal *ministerios públicos* who introduced him to José Angel Vivanco, a federal police commander turned lawyer, who became his defense attorney. Vivanco persuaded judges to dismiss all seven cases.

One day in 1995 Arizmendi complained to his wife that he no longer considered stealing cars worth his while. A few days later he told her that he "had a person" and expected to make some money out of it. The person was a local merchant, practically their next-door neighbor: the ransom came to sixty thousand dollars.

Arizmendi moved up to prosperous businessmen, especially from Mexico City's wealthy Spanish expatriate community. He submitted each of his hostages to vicious interrogation, wringing out names of vulnerable friends or business associates for inclusion on his list of targets.

As he gained experience, he compartmentalized his subordinates into distinct cells. One group was in charge of gathering intelligence on the finances and habits of targets. Another performed the abductions. Another group tended to hostages, keeping them in makeshift cages. Arizmendi was in charge of negotiation. Heedless of wiretaps, Arizmendi in his early kidnappings negotiated brazenly by telephone for fifteen minutes or more, often allowing relatives to hear the cries of his hostages.

"I'm a man who keeps his word," he told one family. "And I'm going to hurt him."

He would demand ransom, then send relatives to pick up a severed ear, tucked into a jar or plastic bag left on a highway median or under a park bench. He brought an industrial rhythm to his criminality, often kidnapping a new person the same day he picked up the ransom from the last.

The most vital part of his operation was the wall of official protection he cemented together with bribes to police, to *ministerios públicos*, and (many suspect) to higher officials as well. He operated with credentials from the federal Attorney General's Office and from the Chamber of Deputies. From 1995 to 1998 he seemed untouchable.

Some of those kidnapped died; those who lived were left traumatized. The seventy-nine-year-old owner of a chain of grocery stores died of heart failure weeks after he was freed by a $3 million ransom payment. A restaurateur sank into a profound depression, refusing to leave his bedroom.

Understandably frightened, thousands of wealthy Mexicans sought to buy the protection the government no longer provided. The number of private security companies nearly doubled after the Arizmendi case made front-page news, and by late 1999 about ten thousand security firms, most of them ad hoc and unregulated, had cropped up. The streets of Lomas de Chapultepec, Polanco, and San Angel were filled with armored Mercedes-Benzes, escorted by cars driven by sullen gunmen in ties and black suits.

In contrast, Josefina Ricaño, who was forty-nine years old when Raúl was abducted, resolved not to suffer her pain in isolation. After Raúl's funeral and a week of Masses and mourning, she reached out to other Mexicans to share her story and to listen to other crime victims, becoming the catalyst for an important citizens' movement that demanded of authorities that they respond more effectively to the tide of criminality.

Ricaño started by seeking to meet with President Zedillo. A friend knew the President's chef, so Ricaño wrote Zedillo a letter, asking for an audience, and handed it on to the cook for delivery. There was no reply. Another friend knew the wife of Liébano Sáenz, Zedillo's chief of staff, and Ricaño spent several hours with her, pouring out Raúl's story. The next morning Sáenz phoned Ricaño, but when she asked to meet with the President, even only for a moment, Sáenz said the President was too busy.

Next Ricaño and a dozen of her friends called a meeting, using their home phones to invite victimized families to the Chapultepec Golf Club. Some 120 people showed up, including the rector of the Iberoamerican University, several newspaper editors and radio hosts, and kidnapping survivors from the Spanish, Jewish, and Lebanese communities. Ricaño opened the meeting by reading a brief statement. How was it possible that in Mexico the reward for years of study and work was now abduction and violent death? "I can't get my son back, but I don't want even one more family to suffer what we've been through," she concluded. "How can we work together to stop the atrocities?"

One man stood to say he had been released just one month earlier from a kidnapping in which he lost an ear, but was overwhelmed with tears. Another man said that after his release from a kidnapping months earlier, he learned that police had recovered a journal of handwritten notes in which his captors had recorded daily comments on the course of his captivity and their ransom negotiations. The police, however, said it had been lost. Thereafter he began to receive calls from police commanders offering to sell him parts of the journal, page by page.

The meeting turned into a brainstorming session. There were calls for a tax boycott and for a business-sector strike. Finally the group agreed to organize a silent anticrime protest march along Paseo de la Reforma to the Zócalo. Its slogan would be: "¡Ya basta! We've had enough!"

The group allowed less than three weeks to pull the demonstration together, but crime victims practically organized themselves. Ricaño and her friends handed out leaflets in subway stops and markets. Others spread the word in their churches and synagogues. One circle of wealthy women rented a helicopter to scatter thousands of handbills across the Federal District. Dozens of citizens organizations signed on, including many newly formed neighborhood anticrime groups.

The November 29, 1997, demonstration attracted upwards of forty thousand participants, drawn from across the class lines that segregate Mexico. There were wealthy people whose relatives had been kidnapped and homes robbed; middle-class and working-class people who had been assaulted at subway stations; politicians from the three main parties — some of whom were crime victims themselves. Margarita González Gamio, upon returning from a posting as ambassador to Hungary, lost all her possessions when thieves (apparently working with police) hijacked the moving van. The writer Carlos Monsiváis had been robbed at gunpoint while getting out of a taxi just three days before.

"This is a historic moment in Mexico's civic history," the novelist Carlos Fuentes told reporters. "It's easy to forget people's rights, especially in a system that until recently had been authoritarian, in which leaders, who weren't elected, saw no need to respond to anybody. Today citizens are active, mobilized, and aware. And they're here today, seeking to defend themselves and their loved ones."

Rossana Fuentes-Berain, the editor in charge of investigations at the newspaper *Reforma*, learned of Raúl Nava's kidnapping during a dinner at a friend's house. Hearing crime stories over meals had become a dismal routine in Mexico City. Many hosts, in fact, were establishing a rule, and only partly in jest: each guest was entitled to tell of only one mugging, car theft, or other attack.

Even in this atmosphere, however, Raúl Nava's abduction seemed extravagant in its cruelty. The next day Fuentes-Berain assigned a *Reforma* reporter to call his law-enforcement sources, and he quickly confirmed the details.

Lacking reliable government records, Fuentes-Berain assigned investigative reporters to comb a database of all newspapers published in Mexico to analyze the press coverage of kidnappings during the first three years of the Zedillo presidency—and by extension to investigate the crime war itself. They found reports of the seizure of 269 people; most were mere announcements, two or three paragraphs long. Police had received reports of at least twice that many in 1996 alone. Fuentes-Berain concluded that kidnapping, though common, was receiving almost no serious coverage.

Meanwhile, reports of out-of-control crime flowed into the paper. Readers phoned to describe abductions of relatives, although few callers would speak on the record. Businessmen reported the seizure of colleagues.

In a staff meeting in October 1997, in the days after the discovery of Raúl Nava's body, *Reforma's* editors decided to undertake sustained cov-

erage of the kidnap crisis. Within days the paper got a scoop. A young reporter, César Romero Jacobo, obtained copies of the Mexico City police's investigative file on Daniel Arizmendi, which linked him to twelve
kidnappings in which he had collected nearly $5 million in ransoms. *Re-
forma* used the file as the basis for a front-page story—the first to make
Arizmendi's name and brutal tactics public and to suggest that law-
enforcement officials were protecting him from arrest.

Within weeks Romero filled out the picture with more specifics. He
reported that senior prosecutors had begun to suspect that the chief of
Mexico City's anti-kidnapping unit was shielding Arizmendi. This was
Domingo Tassinari, the senior detective who had recognized Ariz-
mendi's voice on tape at the Nava Ricaños' house. Romero reported that
in June 1997, four of Arizmendi's men, arrested after a botched ab-
duction, led detectives to Ciudad Nezahualcóyotl and pointed out
Arizmendi, sitting in a parked Volkswagen van. The detectives phoned
Tassinari. He ordered them to wait while he came to the scene himself.
By the time he arrived, hours later, Arizmendi had left.

Reforma reported that, when pressed, Tassinari had requested *amparo*
protection, and a federal judge had granted it.

As the paper exposed the corruption that allowed the abductors to
thrive, Fuentes-Berain felt it was crucial to give voice to the victims.
Through the friend of a friend, she put Romero in contact with a university student whom Arizmendi's men had abducted and held, naked
and chained, for nine days, and *Reforma* published a three-part series:
"Kidnapping, Like Dying a Thousand Deaths." It included the student's
first-person account of one of Arizmendi's mutilations:

As you're talking with the chief kidnapper, someone ties your
arms behind your back. They use lots of tape to immobilize your
legs.

"I'm afraid," you say.

"Calm down," he replies.

They are covering your head and face. You don't pay much attention, but later you remember the exact movements. First the
eyes, taking care not to cover the ears, going round and round
with the tape, and then your mouth.

One hand is placed on your back. You feel a blow to the nape of your neck. You fall down. You are flat on your back. You feel a man sit down on your legs. Another guy sits on your stomach and holds your head rigid.

With professional movements, the boss inserts a metal blade under the central part of your right ear. With one hand, he pulls the ear away from your head, and with precision cuts the skin and the cartilage in a single movement, vertical and perfect.

"I heard how they began to cut the left ear. I heard the sound that the blade made as it cut me," you recall. "First he cut this one. Then he switched sides and cut the other one."

At that moment the man shouted something. His voice changed. "It's as though it gave him tremendous pleasure. He grabbed me by the armpits, picked me up, and threw me against a wall.

"Untie the hands," he ordered. "He put a rag over my head. He grabbed my hands and put them on my wounds."

"Press!" he shouted.

You feel the blood on your neck and shoulders. There's a lot of it.

Cocking a 9-mm pistol, he put it to the back of my neck.

"If you scream, I'll kill you."

Crime shot to the top of the political agenda. Two of Mexico's most powerful businessmen, Emilio Azcárraga Jean, the heir to the Televisa broadcasting empire, and Roberto Hernández, the president of Banamex, the country's largest bank, visited Los Pinos to urge Zedillo to crack down on kidnappers. Others phoned Liébano Sáenz, begging for help in freeing their relatives. Sáenz's office became a clearinghouse for the distraught.

Eventually Zedillo was moved. He gave orders for the government's intelligence agency, called the CISEN (for Centro de Investigación y Seguridad Nacional, Center for Research and National Security), to focus more of its wiretap and other capabilities on tracking kidnappers. He put out word that he wanted Arizmendi arrested "by whatever means necessary." The Attorney General's Organized Crime Unit, usually devoted to narcotics investigations, went to work on the case. The Attorney General offered an extraordinary reward, 5 million pesos, the equivalent of $500,000, for information about Arizmendi, more than for any drug trafficker.

The first major blow against Arizmendi came in December 1997. Six weeks after city detectives located a safe house used by Arizmendi's right-hand man, Daniel Vanegas, they arrested Vanegas in downtown Mexico City carrying $220,000 and several automatic rifles. Shortly thereafter city detectives arrested his wife and mother, who placed Arizmendi at a hotel in Cuernavaca. There, detectives burst into Arizmendi's hotel room. He had fled minutes earlier, apparently, leaving behind a freshly drawn bath. Evidently one of his protectors had paged him a warning.

The discovery that Arizmendi was living in Cuernavaca was hardly a surprise. Morelos had been overrun with abductors ever since 1994, when Jorge Carrillo Olea, the retired army General, took office as governor. In 1995 the head of the state police anti-kidnapping unit was tried and imprisoned for collaborating with abductors. By 1996 thousands of citizens had taken to regularly marching through the streets of Cuernavaca in protests organized by Carmen Génis, a travel agent who had been stirred to action by a friend's abduction. During two visits by President Zedillo, Génis and several kidnapping victims positioned themselves along sidewalks to shout anticrime slogans at Zedillo and Carrillo Olea as they walked past. But it was not until a sister of Bill Richardson, the U.S. ambassador to the United Nations who had grown up in Mexico, was kidnapped in Morelos that Zedillo finally focused on the crisis.

"This is the sister of the U.S. representative to the United Nations!" one presidential aide said in a meeting at Los Pinos. "This could become a world scandal." A senior Mexican official phoned Richardson to assure him that the Mexican government would do everything possible to ensure his sister's safety. She was released unharmed—after payment of a ransom.

Zedillo's patience snapped after Carrillo Olea's *second* anti-kidnapping chief, Armando Martínez Salgado, was also found to be a criminal. On January 28, 1998, Martínez Salgado was arrested in Guerrero state, just beyond the Morelos line, in a pickup truck laden with the body of a seventeen-year-old boy; the officer had been preparing to dump the cadaver into a ditch. A federal investigation concluded that Martínez Salgado had tortured the boy to death; that he had masterminded several Morelos kidnappings; and that the Morelos attorney general knew of his crimes.

In state elections the previous summer, candidates from the two major opposition parties, the PAN and the PRD, had for the first time won a majority—eighteen of the thirty seats—in the Morelos legislature. During the spring of 1998 the opposition legislators combined forces to demand Carrillo Olea's ouster; the Morelos state police chief and the attorney general were arrested and charged with cover-up in the homicide of the tortured teenager; and Zedillo sharply criticized Carrillo Olea's government in a public speech.

On May 12, 1998, Carrillo Olea stepped down, taking a leave of absence that had not ended a year later, when the Morelos congress voted his formal impeachment. It was the first time that a citizens movement in Mexico had deposed a PRI governor.

Investigators never found conclusive evidence that either the Morelos governor or any of his aides had protected Arizmendi. The circumstantial evidence, however, was telling. Only nine days after Carrillo Olea was driven from office, Arizmendi's wall of official protection seemed to crack. Federal police arrested his son Aurelio in Cuernavaca, and he led them across the city to a sumptuous home, located just a few blocks from Carrillo Olea's mansion, telling them Arizmendi would be there.

He had slipped away again. But the officers detained his wife, daughter, and daughter-in-law and confiscated the equivalent of some $5 million in cash, stashed in various cabinets and under the kitchen sink. Arizmendi had never even bothered to unwrap much of the ransom money.

Two weeks later an odd call came to the *Reforma* newsroom—a gruff man, speaking from a public telephone, asking to talk to the boss. The executive editor was in a meeting, so a switchboard operator sent the call to the office of senior editor Roberto Zamarripa.

"I'm Daniel Arizmendi," the man said. Astonished, Zamarripa activated the speakerphone, turned on a tape recorder, and began firing questions. At first he sought to fill in biographical details that the paper had never previously been able to confirm. Where and when was Arizmendi born? Who were his parents and siblings?

"If you ask details about my children, I probably won't know, frankly, because I'm really distracted," Arizmendi said. He seemed by turns demented and chillingly lucid. Zamarripa asked if he would turn himself in if police agreed to free his family.

"Definitely not," the kidnapper said. "I'm not afraid of death, but I fear poverty and jail more than you can know."

Rambling, he reminisced about his brief police career, recalling the torture inflicted on detainees by his former colleagues. "It's really ugly," he said. "When they've got you, you want to die. But by then you're blindfolded and tied up, and how can you kill yourself?"

He confessed that he had carried out about twenty kidnappings, and he calmly incriminated his wife and children in the laundering of ransom money. No, he was not a drug addict, he said. Yes, he was an alcoholic. He expressed indignation about reports that he starved and beat his hostages. He had never done that, he insisted.

But did he cut off ears? Zamarripa asked.

"Oh yeah, that I do," he said. He viewed the mutilations as a kind of personal class warfare: "Even though their relatives have all that money, they don't want to give it to me," he said. He reflected for a moment. "I guess I'm going to go to hell, right?" he said, and rang off.

Arizmendi's call to the *Reforma* newsroom was an audacious move. Four years earlier he had seduced Dulce Paz Vanegas, the teenage sister of one of his lieutenants. She had become his partner in abductions, riding for a time with him, the Bonnie to his Clyde. Then she gave birth to a baby girl, and he installed her in a suburban safe house along with a teenage errand boy who kept her supplied with Coca-Cola, pizza, and cigarettes.

At this time Arizmendi was wearing shoulder-length hair and a tangled beard that gave him a certain resemblance to Charles Manson. He traveled to Querétaro, a quiet colonial state capital north of Mexico City. There he rented a new safe house and began stalking new victims. He eventually settled on Raúl Nieto del Río, the thirty-four-year-old son of a wealthy Querétaro cooking-gas distributor. Arizmendi contracted out the abduction to a squad of Mexico City gunmen, but when they attacked Nieto, ramming his Porsche sports car from behind with their vehicle and surrounding him, he put up a fight. The gunmen shot him in the chest, dragged him into a van, and drove him, bleeding profusely, to Arizmendi's Querétaro safe house.

When his men arrived carrying a cadaver instead of a hostage, Arizmendi ordered two of them to crack open the cement of his bedroom floor and bury Nieto under it; a third accomplice phoned the family and demanded a $15 million ransom. Querétaro police, however, had already discovered Nieto's Porsche, bathed in blood, and the family demanded proof that their son was still alive.

After reflecting for a day, Arizmendi had Nieto's body dug up—rigor mortis had by now set in—and bathed in hot water to restore some flexibility. He applied rouge to its ashen face and propped it up in a bed, perching a newspaper from that day, August 6, 1988, in its hands. He hung a sack of intravenous solution over the bed to simulate medical treatment of a living hostage. He took a Polaroid snapshot of the corpse. One of his gunmen again phoned the family, telling them to retrieve the photo, inserted in a box of cornflakes hidden at a Querétaro fruit stand.

A vast manhunt with hundreds of federal and state police, ordered by President Zedillo, was closing in on Arizmendi.

A secret unit at the CISEN was leading the investigation. Officially it was headed by a senior detective from México state, Alberto Pliego Fuentes. A pudgy, balding officer, forty-nine years old, Pliego had never attended a police academy. He had begun his law-enforcement career as a bodyguard for a corrupt Mexico City police chief. Pliego was accused of accepting a twenty-five-thousand-dollar bribe from Arizmendi in 1986 to refrain from searching the kidnapper's properties. He denied the accusation.

But Pliego was taking orders from Wilfrido Robledo Madrid, a retired navy rear admiral who headed a counterintelligence unit within the

CISEN, and from Robledo's deputy, Genaro García Luna. The main work in the Arizmendi investigation was taking place at the CISEN's intelligence compound in eastern Mexico City. There, intelligence officials analyzed the voices of kidnappers all across Mexico, taped during ransom calls to their victims' relatives. Not long after the killing of Raúl Nieto, an agent identified Arizmendi's voice in a ransom call to the family, and CISEN began to set a trap.

Through wiretaps and other investigation, CISEN had pieced together a profile of Arizmendi's gang, including the license plates of the van used in the Querétaro assault. The plates led Pliego and other agents to a home in a Mexico City suburb. On a hot Sunday afternoon in mid-August 1998, Pliego arrested four men, along with their wives and at least half a dozen children, during an afternoon barbecue.

Pliego made the gunmen an offer. If they would cooperate by acting as bait in trapping Arizmendi, he would cede some of the ransom money they were hoarding to their families while they were in prison. If they refused, he would hold their women and children indefinitely—as hostages, in effect. He had no legal authority for these actions, but senior CISEN officials approved them.

Arizmendi's men accepted Pliego's terms. One of them was carrying a cellular phone, and the day after the arrest a call came from Arizmendi. As CISEN agents eavesdropped, Arizmendi arranged to meet his henchmen that same evening outside a bank along the frontage road of a freeway in the eastern Mexico City district of Iztacalco.

Two hours later the agency's trap was set: the van parked outside the bank, Arizmendi's accomplices in its front seats, four intelligence agents crouched behind them, weapons drawn. As Arizmendi edged toward the van, his hair and clothes as disheveled as a hobo's, the agents sprang out and wrestled him to the ground.

Whimpering, Arizmendi begged them to kill him on the spot. Then he acknowledged that Raúl Nieto was twelve days dead. After an all-night interrogation he was taken by plane to Querétaro to his former safe house, where forensic agents dug up Nieto's cadaver.

In a press conference in Mexico City, Attorney General Madrazo gave a fictionalized account of Arizmendi's arrest, apparently to shield the prosecution's case from legal challenges and to keep CISEN under cover.

President Zedillo and his aides sought immediately to capitalize on Ariz-mendi's arrest. They scheduled a ceremony for the following week in which Zedillo and Government Secretary Francisco Labastida would an-nounce a National Crusade against Crime and Delinquency. To give the event the appearance of citizen participation, they called on Josefina Ri-caño.

In the months following the November 1997 anticrime march to the Zócalo, Ricaño and others who had convoked it had founded a national citizens organization, Mexico United against Crime. The organization urged citizens to set aside their justifiable distrust of the authorities by re-porting crimes, resisting police bribes, and forming neighborhood crime-watch groups.

Ricaño herself developed friendly relations with Wilfrido Robledo, the CISEN official investigating kidnappings, who had been attentive to her case. Zedillo's aides had repeatedly rebuffed her requests to meet

Daniel Arizmendi on display to the press, August 1998

even briefly with the President—until the national crusade got under way. After Robledo assured her that she would be permitted to express her views candidly, she agreed to participate.

Days later, however, two of Zedillo's aides showed up at her home to offer "orientation" about what to say in her speech. Ricaño thanked them but insisted that as the mother of a young man murdered during a kidnapping, she would have to speak from her heart. They went away reluctantly; the day before the ceremony, an aide phoned and insisted that she fax her speech to Los Pinos. She resisted, then did so.

An official called her back within minutes, scolding her for a phrase that seemed insufficiently respectful to the President. Ricaño put her foot down. If the officials wanted her participation, she said, they had to respect her freedom to choose her own words. If not, they could seek other speakers.

The ceremony took place at Mexico City's National Museum of Anthropology on an immense stage. In attendance were all the state governors, most of Zedillo's cabinet, and the Supreme Court—in short, most of the country's political elite. It began like all such events, with an announcer exclaiming breathlessly: "Ladies and gentlemen, he's in our presence, the citizen President of the United Mexican States!" Zedillo strode in and took his seat at the center of the vast tableau.

When it was Ricaño's turn at the lectern she related the events leading to Raúl's death, calling him "a magnificent son and an exemplary Mexican." She reminded the politicians that "criminality has become a business often fomented by the same authorities to whom the state has entrusted our security." Then, turning to Zedillo, she addressed him directly: "Mister President, since we have entrusted our security to you through our vote, I ask of you as a Mexican mother—and I respectfully demand of you in the name of the entire citizenry—that you use your power and will to end the wave of violence."

It was the "demand" that had seemed so impertinent to the President's handlers.

Mexicans were overwhelmingly relieved to see Arizmendi behind bars. His arrest, however, demonstrated not that the police were mastering modern law-enforcement techniques but that the system continued to rely on the authoritarian and extralegal methods that, in the view of some experts, had provoked the crime crisis in the first place.

Still, there were positive developments. Anticrime advocates like Josefina Ricaño in Mexico City and Carmen Génis in Morelos were a new breed of citizen—gutsy Mexicans who demanded more effective law enforcement so insistently that they finally forced the government to respond. Independent of both the system and the opposition parties, they empowered themselves to represent their own grievances. The concept of citizens' political rights, codified in the 1917 Constitution, was finally at the end of the century taking hold among common Mexicans. And as pluralism advanced across Mexico at the local level, citizen initiatives were finding support within the government.

Under the PRI system, politicians like Governor Carrillo Olea had seen little need for attentiveness to citizen complaints. President Zedillo's determination to bring Arizmendi down reflected, in part, his awareness that his party would, at the end of his term, have to beg for citizens' votes.

Even with a more assertive citizenry and more responsive government, however, organized crime would remain a daunting challenge. The economic disparities that brought about the crime crisis of the 1990s only grew during the decade. And like other emerging democracies, Mexico was searching for ways to replace the old controls on criminal behavior that had been suitable for an authoritarian regime with new ones based on the rule of law. Yet the sturdy law-enforcement and criminal-justice institutions that embody democratic rule were yet to be built.

14

Opening Minds

Anyone who sought evidence that a transformation had gotten under way in Mexico by the late 1990s had only to pick up a morning newspaper in the capital city. The most influential dailies—*Reforma, La Jornada, El Universal, El Financiero*—had all but abandoned the deferential self-censorship they practiced for decades and were seizing on topics that had long been untouchable. The competition for fresh, unvarnished news had turned into an unfettered press war.

Generations of reporters had been trained to accept that three subjects were not open to scrutiny: the sitting President, the armed forces, and the Virgin of Guadalupe. But in 1998 a newspaper in Guadalajara broke a story revealing that a brother of President Zedillo had done business with drug money launderers—unwittingly, he claimed; most papers reported unfavorably on the military's show trial of a dissident General, José Francisco Gallardo; and several papers even took up a debate about whether Juan Diego, the humble Indian to whom the Virgin was believed to have first appeared in 1531, had actually existed.

The end of an era of information control, often exercised by journalists on themselves, was marked on January 20, 1998, when Jacobo Zabludovsky anchored his last broadcast of *24 Horas* (24 hours), the nightly prime-time news show on Televisa and still the public's main source of news by far. As the program's anchor for twenty-seven years, Zabludovsky had developed a near-perfect sense for information he should leave out because it might upset the PRI government. Although he had demonstrated considerable skills as a journalist, he would also be remembered for declining to report on Cuauhtémoc Cárdenas throughout the 1988 election, then attacking him openly in the 1994 presidential campaign, in coverage so skewed that even Ernesto Zedillo, its primary beneficiary, later admitted that it was unfair.

In an interview with *The New York Times* on the morning before his last *24 Horas* broadcast, Zabludovksy explained, with unusual candor, that the government's media police "didn't issue orders. They gave advice, suggestions, requests . . . We had to observe those requests to a considerable degree," he said, characteristically taciturn.

Although the press still printed reams of innuendo and inaccuracy, new quality was emerging. Mexican journalists were acquiring the skills of investigative reporting, like the *Reforma* series that alerted the public to Daniel Arizmendi's crimes. *La Jornada* provided deep coverage of the Zapatista rebel movement in Chiapas, including full texts of Subcomandante Marcos's antigovernment tracts.

A parallel emancipation was taking place among Mexico's intellectuals. Their most freewheeling debates about the future of the political system had long been conducted within a lettered elite, in erudite journals like Octavio Paz's *Vuelta* and Héctor Aguilar Camín's *Nexos*. Now many of them crossed over into the mainstream press. Carlos Monsiváis—sympathizer of the Cuban Revolution and gay-rights activist—wrote a cultural column in *El Norte*, a paper in conservative Monterrey. Aguilar Camín, Enrique Krauze, and Sergio Aguayo all inveighed regularly against the system in *Reforma*, and they were by no means the most radical editorialists.

By the last years of the decade the feisty press and noisy political argument had come to seem commonplace. But, like so much else in Mexico's opening, they were the result of an accumulation of ideas and changes over decades.

The PRI system was not totalitarian; it was never as rigid or intolerant as the Communist regimes in the Soviet Union or China. But it did have its dogma, and as its hegemony advanced, its ideas became part of the fabric of life.

As the Institutional Revolutionary Party, the PRI saw itself as the 1910 revolution's sole heir, whose purpose was to carry out in an orderly way the ideals emanating from that upheaval. Over the years "the Mexican Revolution" came to refer not only to the tumult between 1910 and 1917 but also to the political canon of the system it spawned.

Above all the system was nationalist: suspicious of the United States and zealously protective of Mexican sovereignty. It favored a centralized state overseeing a protected capitalist economy. It was socialistic; it never sought to eliminate private property but followed egalitarian principles and sometimes carried out mass redistribution of landholding. In the land reform in the 1930s the government created the *ejido*, a hybrid form of social property, by expropriating private land and granting peasants long-term rights to farm it. Finally, the PRI was committed to *presidencialismo*, in which all essential power was invested in the chief executive, as the natural form of government for Mexico.

Although the system claimed to be democratic, the principles of democracy were never integral to its practices. The PRI did not promote representative government, free elections, competition among political parties, separation of powers, checks and balances, judiciary independence, government accountability, rule of law, civil liberties, citizen activism, or an independent press.

Yet for a single-party state the PRI system was unusually flexible. While its leaders were well versed in the doctrine of the Mexican Revolution, they rarely let it stand in the way of a good political deal. The PRI could expand and bend to encompass contending ideological factions within its ranks. The only principle on which the PRI did not compromise was the one holding that it was entitled to remain in power indefinitely.

As a result of its adaptability, the authoritarian system was able to maintain strong ties with the country's intellectuals, a unique situation among Latin American nations. The government's National Institute of Fine Arts supported artists and writers. Its universities, especially the UNAM, were generously funded. On occasion the state incorporated progressive ideas from Mexican thinkers into its policies. It recruited writers and thinkers to serve as ambassadors abroad and public officials at home, making the intelligentsia part of the power structure.

These customs made intellectuals a prominent caste in Mexican society, like a House of Lords based on brainpower. However, the regime coddled the thinking class largely to further its own ends: to burnish its image and keep them from straying into dissent. As a result, Mexican intellectuals faced a permanent dilemma in their relations with the PRI government, their "philanthropic ogre," in the phrase of Octavio Paz. They were always searching for the balance between influencing the state and being used by it.

Homero Aridjis, the poet, novelist, and environmentalist, described his life as an intellectual with the system as a "perverse game." He lived happily under the PRI tent for many years. When a young man, he served as Mexico's ambassador to the Netherlands and Switzerland. After returning home in 1980, at age forty, he went to work as Secretary of Culture for Cuauhtémoc Cárdenas, then an ascendant figure in the PRI and governor of Michoacán state.

From the state government Aridjis began to see the PRI system's view of Mexican culture. Once, he recalled, he was asked to entertain the wives of several visiting senior officials from Mexico City. He took them to one of his favorite country churches, a sixteenth-century Augustinian monastery. In a musty chapel hung a collection of ex-votos, small hand-painted plaques that the faithful had offered over many decades to the local saint, to thank him for answering prayers for help with a philandering husband, a sick child, or a lost cow.

The ladies admired the plaques. Then they took them down and put them in their handbags to take back to the capital, leaving the church wall bare. Taken aback, Aridjis tried to persuade them to buy similar plaques that the church had selected for sale in a nearby antiques store. But the PRI wives ignored him—the country's artistic patrimony was theirs, was it not?

In 1981 Aridjis organized a grand poetry festival, bringing writers from Europe and Latin America. President José López Portillo, who fancied himself a writer, gave the inaugural speech, promising to grow a beard after his term ended and dedicate himself to writing poetry. With the government at the height of its petroleum largesse, the festival's major participants were given solid-gold coins as mementos.

Although Aridjis counseled against it, Cárdenas scheduled a reprise for the following year, in the first days of September 1982. But on September 1, López Portillo nationalized the banks, and the economy careened. Cárdenas, evidently on orders from the President, ordered Aridjis to cancel the festival—even though many of the invited poets had already arrived in Mexico. When Aridjis resisted, Cárdenas dismissed him.

Aridjis scrambled around Mexico City, pleading with painters to donate canvases to raise funds and begging for hotel rooms and auditoriums. The festival went forward on schedule. However, for years afterward, Aridjis felt he continued to pay a price for defying the President. Although his work had already won international recognition, he was passed over for national literary prizes and fellowships, which were bestowed by the government. The Foreign Relations Secretariat scratched his name off invitations to conferences from foreign governments.

After 1985, when he founded the environmental Group of 100, the petty harassment grew more persistent. His telephone was either tapped or out of order. Then, from time to time, some official would try to draw Aridjis back into the fold. In the late 1980s, when Raúl Salinas, then a government food agency official, was trying to woo environmentalists, his chief aide offered to give Aridjis a car. Hoping to avoid a confrontation with the Salinas brothers, Aridjis responded, truthfully, that he had never learned to drive.

Raúl's aide promptly offered him a driver as well. He declined again.

The system recognized two kinds of intellectuals, Aridjis said. "Either you were co-opted or you were a traitor."

There was always lively debate within Mexico's universities and intellectual circles. But even there, the discussion remained largely within the bounds of the Mexican Revolution. In 1965 the distinguished sociologist Pablo González Casanova wrote a book called *Democracy in Mexico*, a pioneering work drawing on Marxist analysis in which he analyzed social indicators and election results to show the huge class inequities and lack of representation that working Mexicans suffered under PRI rule. However, the remedy González Casanova advocated was internal reform in the PRI. At no point did he propose replacing the authoritarian system with a democratic one. In 1965 the idea of Mexican democracy had not yet germinated. Its cultivation came over the next two decades, the specialized work of a small cluster of Mexican intellectuals.

The first among equals was Octavio Paz. *The Labyrinth of Solitude*, a political psychoanalysis of the nation published in 1950, had given Mexicans rare insight into their collective psyche of reserve, showing how it stemmed from the catastrophe of conquest. With his resignation after the Tlatelolco massacre, Paz had opened a breach in the system's monopoly of letters. When he returned to Mexico in 1971, he was a hero to the intelligentsia.

They were clamoring for Paz to join Heberto Castillo and Carlos Fuentes to form a socialist party that would take on the PRI from the left. (Fuentes, a good friend of Paz's, had written two novels, *Where the Air Is Clear* and *The Death of Artemio Cruz*, which had established him as a leading raconteur of the amorality of Mexican politics.) But Paz surprised his admirers. During his years in the foreign service, he had read about the concentration camps of Stalinism and the abuses of the revolution in China. Now he announced his disaffection with Communism and started to chastise the Mexican Left as vehemently as the government.

And instead of founding a party, Paz stepped back from politics to found *Plural*, a monthly literary review. Some of his inspiration came from Julio Scherer, who was still the editor in chief of *Excélsior*, then Mexico's most influential daily. *Plural* was edited at *Excélsior*'s offices and distributed by its delivery boys. For once, a journal of letters was available on street-corner newsstands.

With Paz moving to the right, a group of leftist writers coalesced around the popular weekly magazine *Siempre!* (meaning "always"). In 1972 Carlos Monsiváis took over as the editor of its literary supplement. When a young student, Monsiváis had joined Mexico's Communist Party, but in 1960, when he was twenty-two, he had been harshly expelled in a dispute over an obscure issue of orthodoxy. Even so, he had remained loyal to Fidel Castro's revolution, although he had grown increasingly dismayed by its persecution of homosexuals. A rumpled figure with a sardonic sense of humor, Monsiváis had recently published *Días de guardar* (Days to Remember), a rambling chronicle of the events of

1968 that, like Elena Poniatowska's account, was embraced as a work of defiant reportage.

Among the young writers who gravitated to *Siempre!* under Monsiváis were Enrique Krauze and Héctor Aguilar Camín, who in the early 1970s were both graduate students in history at the Colegio de México. Though friends, the two had very different personalities. Krauze was the son of a Jewish entrepreneur who manufactured boxes in Mexico City. Even while he was in graduate school, he was already something of a businessman, since he had helped out at his family's plant from the time he was a boy and had studied industrial engineering as an undergraduate.

Aguilar Camín, in contrast, grew up in Chetumal, in the jungle state of Quintana Roo, in what he called "a shipwrecked middle-class" life. His father drove the family lumberyard toward ruin, and then a hurricane came along to finish it off. When Aguilar Camín was fifteen, his father left home for good.

Krauze had never been drawn to the Left. His historical research was about Manuel Gómez Morín, the founder of the PAN. Aguilar Camín, on the other hand, wrote his doctoral thesis about the Mexican Revolution, focusing on the Generals who led the fighting in Sonora state. Both young men, however, had been inspired by the antiauthoritarian spirit of the 1968 student movement, although neither had played an important role in it.

The battle between the *Siempre!* group under Monsiváis and Paz's *Plural* was soon joined. Although Paz's group was eclectic, it united behind the poet and his increasingly fervent rejection of Marxism and Communism. Paz warned that the mayhem of class conflict and the tyranny of the one-party, one-class state were the gravest dangers facing modern society. He favored those strains of Mexican liberalism, dating back to Benito Juárez, that defended individual rights. He remained a nationalist, however, wary of U.S. domination, and he did not fully embrace free-market economics. On the other side, the leftists at *Siempre!* advocated sharp confrontation with the United States, supported the insurgencies arising in many Latin countries in the wake of the Cuban Revolution, and defended the need for militant, even armed, action to bring equality and justice for the poor.

Those in the *Siempre!* group identified their mission as two-pronged:

to assail both the government and the "reactionaries" at *Plural*. At one war council they agreed to train their fire on Paz. *"Tenemos que darle en la madre a Paz,"* one member of the group proposed, using a colloquial phrase alluding to the poet's mother that promised him very rough rhetorical treatment.

The prospect made Krauze uncomfortable. "Perhaps we should just read him and criticize him," he ventured. Nevertheless, he and Aguilar Camín collaborated on an essay that assailed both Paz and Carlos Fuentes, although their critique was mainly literary: they accused the two writers of allowing their political personae to eclipse and diminish their artistic works. It was published in an issue of *Siempre!*, coordinated by Monsiváis, which announced that Paz and his associates had made themselves irrelevant to the events in Mexico and proposed to "expel them from the discussion."

Paz and Fuentes responded with a far more artful essay in *Plural* that memorably ridiculed the two graduate students, calling them "one brain in two bodies." Krauze was mortified but also felt drawn to some of the arguments Paz and Fuentes had made to defend their role. Over the next four years Krauze migrated toward Paz's liberal views. In 1975 he published an article in *Siempre!* announcing a break with Monsiváis and his socialists, and parted ways with the magazine.

The ideological rivalry was taking place against the backdrop of a new effort by the government to court the intelligentsia. When Luis Echeverría took over in 1970 from President Díaz Ordaz, he was determined to bring the intellectuals, alienated in 1968, back to his camp. He adopted outspoken anti-American policies that pleased the Left. Announcing an *apertura*, he raised professors' salaries and lavished funds on artists and research institutes, pledging to steer the state back to the true course of the Mexican Revolution.

Carlos Fuentes was the most prominent man of letters to believe him. In 1975, seven years after Paz resigned in India, Fuentes agreed to be Mexico's ambassador in France.

However, Echeverría soon demonstrated that he was no friend of free expression. Under Julio Scherer, *Excélsior* had become increasingly bold in its critique of the President, accusing him of corruption and complicity in new episodes of violence against antigovernment demonstrators. Finally Echeverría, in the final months of his presidency, sent his operatives to provoke, with bribes and threats, a split in the cooperative that controlled the newspaper. On July 8, 1976, Scherer was forced out. Almost two hundred of his staff, virtually all the serious journalists, went with him.

Echeverría's coup at *Excélsior* proved to be one of the most costly miscalculations the PRI regime ever made. The President's aim was to silence annoying dissent. But Scherer, drawing on his loyal staff, rapidly organized his own weekly newsmagazine, *Proceso* (its first issue appeared on November 6), and encouraged others who had followed him out of *Excélsior* to start a newspaper, *Unomásuno*. With his exodus from *Excélsior* Scherer became, quite simply, the father of the independent press in Mexico.

Among those who left the paper in solidarity with Scherer were Octavio Paz and his crew at *Plural*. Paz obtained funding from a publisher who was angry at Echeverría for closing down a lucrative skin magazine and was happy to switch from porn to poetry to annoy the President. Rufino Tamayo, the painter, donated a canvas to raise money.

The first issue of *Vuelta*, meaning "turn," was dated December 1976, but to spite Echeverría it came out on November 15, two weeks before the end of his term. Among its offerings was an essay by a poet and political economist, Gabriel Zaid, decrying Echeverría's inept handling of a recent peso devaluation. Titled "Alice in Fluctuationland," it described the departing President's economic policies as "science fiction."

Paz, believing that the insular PRI regime had isolated Mexico, wanted *Vuelta* to import advanced thinking and literary analysis from around the world while also serving as a platform for his critique of the Left in Latin America. In February he and Zaid invited Krauze to join. With his business skills, Krauze became both deputy editor and publisher. He devised a plan to give the magazine a new financial base to free it from depending on the government ads that sustained all press publications in Mexico.

Krauze decided to accept some advertising from the government, from less political institutions like Pemex, the state oil company. He also increased revenues from ads from Televisa and other private Mexican corporations and from subscriptions and newsstand sales. His strategy was to maintain a balance, with no source providing more than about a third of the magazine's income. For Krauze this three-legged stance, although precarious, was key to ensuring the magazine's independence.

At one point early on, the Secretary of Education, Fernando Solana, offered to buy seventy-five hundred subscriptions. The leap would have nearly doubled the circulation and put an end to *Vuelta's* financial distress. But Zaid insisted it was too risky, and the editors agreed to decline.

Vuelta came on strong, but not everyone was fascinated. "They made the mistake of not inviting the Left," said Aguilar Camín. He regrouped with Monsiváis and others from *Siempre!* and other leftist academics like González Casanova. After several brainstorming sessions at Chapultepec Castle, they launched *Nexos* in 1978. Rather than be a literary journal, *Nexos* proposed to bring academic research on Mexico's socioeconomic problems to bear on public policy, and to take on topics the mainstream press clearly saw as too hot to touch.

Over the next decade the adversaries fired away at each other, exchanging polemics for and against socialism in the Soviet Union, Cuba, and Nicaragua and the guerrilla uprising in El Salvador and assessing the promise and perils for Mexico from the capitalist United States. Both factions attacked the PRI. But in the early years of the rivalry, neither side offered a vision of Mexico without the ruling party. They talked about reforming the Mexican Revolution from within.

"Each one of us had a little *priísta* inside," recalled Aguilar Camín, who became one of the top editors at *Nexos*. "The PRI way of politics was our national culture. Its domination was so effective that proposing to defeat the PRI seemed utterly utopian and remote. The only sensible possibility seemed to be to reform the PRI, to make it less cynical, less overweening; to make the President more responsible and the system more transparent.

"Our criticism of the PRI was systematic and frontal," he said. "What we could not visualize was how its hegemony was going to end."

One writer, however, had begun to imagine the end. Gabriel Zaid was reclusive by nature. He never participated in the late-afternoon lunches

and elaborate book parties where political discourse was conducted in
Mexico City. He was not interested in the cocktails at Los Pinos and jun-
kets with *el Señor Presidente* that were routinely offered to intellectuals of
a certain renown.

"Zaid is a man who has never seen a President," Krauze observed of
his friend, describing him as "something of a Christian anarchist."

Zaid had originally set out to write poetry, not political essays. Born in
1934, he was from Monterrey and had completed studies in industrial engineering at an institute of technology there. Unlike many talented Mexicans of his generation, Zaid was never attracted to a job in government.
His goal was to protect his independence in order to have time to write.

When young, he had read and admired Paz, who was twenty years his
senior. Spotting Paz once in a restaurant in Monterrey, Zaid approached,
and to his amazement Paz made him go right home and bring back
some of his poems. "These are better than the ones I wrote at your age,"
Paz said, giving Zaid an electrifying thrill. Only years later did Zaid meet
other Mexican poets whom Paz had flattered and galvanized with precisely the same words.

Moving to the capital, Zaid went to work in publishing and wrote poetry and literary criticism. Living at the geographic center of power but
disengaged from it, he began to see the PRI regime as a big corporation,
a hive of competing units and factions, with the cultural establishment
being one of them.

Zaid was publishing his literary essays in *Siempre!*, and he began to
lace them more frequently with political commentary. One day he sent
Monsiváis an article that directly accused President Echeverría of break-
ing his word about his *apertura* — essentially calling him a liar. Cautious,
Monsiváis showed the piece to the editor in chief of *Siempre!*, José Pagés
Llergo, a man well attuned to the prevailing rules of play.

"Zaid will write about poetry. *I* will write about politics," Pagés decreed.

Monsiváis phone Zaid, probing for a compromise. "How about if we
change it to read: 'The *system* has broken its word . . .'?" Zaid refused,
thinking it was the famous Monsiváis irony.

But *Siempre!* never published the essay, and Zaid left the magazine
and started to write for Paz.

In his monthly column in *Plural* and then *Vuelta*, Zaid laid out a sharply honed liberal critique that owed nothing to the Mexican Revolution. He showed with facts and figures how Mexico's state-heavy economy was failing to produce jobs and goods for the poor, as it had promised. He called for wider political freedom, denouncing the regime's democratic claims as a sham. His essays were short, and his humor biting; he exercised none of the Mexican intellectual's habitual restraint.

In a 1972 letter published in *Plural*, Zaid assailed Carlos Fuentes for his support for Echeverría. Comparing the President to Porfirio Díaz, Zaid wrote: "Even if you don't intend it, your position is a surrender of independence. A totally gratuitous surrender." After López Portillo took over, Zaid broadened his economic critique. In 1979 he published a book called *El progreso improductivo* (Unproductive progress), demanding that the Mexican state step back to make more room for private enterprise.

Later that year Zaid published a small editorial—barely six hundred words—in *Vuelta*. He called it "How to Make a Political Reform by Doing Nothing."

"Let us suppose," Zaid wrote, "that the majority of the voters in Nayarit (or any other state) moved to vote for . . . any opposition party . . . At first the losing candidates in the PRI, the winning opposition candidates, and the voters would all be disconcerted, wondering if they were dreaming or if the end of the world had come . . . Let us suppose that amid that astonishment . . . another majority of voters also voted against the PRI. And . . . all the power of the President, the entire government apparatus . . . was concentrated on the Herculean task of—doing nothing.

"A reform of unknown dimensions would be under way," he concluded. He never used the word "democracy." But he was describing the overthrow of the PRI by ballots.

Like Zaid, Krauze had started out in *Plural* writing essays that were not about the politics of the day. They were historical, often based on his biographical research on Gómez Morín and on Daniel Cosío Villegas, the grand old man of Mexican historians and Krauze's mentor at the Colegio de México. Both men were scholars of the orthodoxy of the

Mexican Revolution, and both had dissented from it, turning toward the liberal ideas embedded in Mexican history.

Outraged by López Portillo's bank nationalization, Krauze was moved to write his first essay about current Mexican politics, for *Vuelta*. Although his tone was respectful, he argued that López Portillo, because his power was so little constrained, had veered disastrously out of control—and perhaps lost his mind. In his summation Krauze listed reforms he thought Mexico needed right away. "In a new cycle," he wrote, "the state must try to accomplish the hardest part: construct its own limits." He called for decentralization; an independent Chamber of Deputies; "a professional press that reports on events but does not invent them"; and intellectuals "who do not confuse homage and protest with analysis and criticism and who appreciate truth more than dogma or employment.

"It follows," he concluded, "that our only historic choice is to respect and exercise political freedom, law, and, above all things, democracy."

The issue of *Vuelta* with his essay sold almost twenty thousand copies.

The following year Luis H. Álvarez, the PAN leader, won the mayoral race in Chihuahua. Krauze felt no attraction to the PAN, not least because he was Jewish. But Don Luis's victory got him thinking further about the possibilities for electoral democracy in Mexico. As often happened with Mexico's thinkers, Krauze's ideas raced forward once he got away from the country. As a visiting professor at Oxford University in the fall of that year, he delved into English history, on the notion that the monarchy had much in common with the PRI.

The result was a wide-ranging essay called "For a Democracy without Adjectives," which appeared in *Vuelta* in January 1984. Mexico's mistake in handling the oil boom, Krauze said, was that "we wanted to be rich before we were democratic."

He demanded that López Portillo be put on trial for corruption. "The lack of limits on the presidential chair has reached its limits," he wrote, arguing that the PRI would not change "from within" without vigorous competition from other parties. "The point is to begin on all fronts and understand . . . that democracy is not a solution to all problems but rather a mechanism—the least bad, the least unjust—to resolve them."

He said it was time for Mexico to go from being a "formal democracy" to becoming a democracy plain and simple. No adjectives.

The essay caused a commotion. Manuel Camacho, a government official at the time, wrote a rebuttal defending the PRI as the only viable
route to democracy in Mexico. Pablo Gómez and other leftists rejected
Krauze's democracy as bourgeois, saying he had proposed no convincing
approach to enfranchising the downtrodden.

Paz, Krauze, and Zaid came back with an issue of *Vuelta*, in June
1985, with a cover that announced, PRI: TIME IS UP. Taken together, the
articles they contributed drew the outlines for the first time of a liberal
democracy with a distinctly Mexican shape. Even Paz, the most cautious
of the three, wrote: "Until a few years ago I believed, like so many, that
the solution was internal reform in the PRI. Today that is not enough."

To be sure, Paz's prescriptions were not radical. Instead of reform in
the party, Paz wanted the party to reform the Mexican state, returning it
to the democratic goals of Francisco I. Madero. Paz saw no other alternative. He dismissed the Left as doctrinaire and the PAN as lacking a
"new and viable national project."

While democracy was becoming the central goal for the liberals at
Vuelta, the socialists in the *Nexos* camp tended to think of it as one goal
among many, a matter of electoral reform, with social justice as their
paramount aim. Democracy "was one part of our agenda," said Aguilar
Camín, who became the editor in chief at *Nexos* in 1983.

Other leftist academics added to the debate. In 1985 Jorge Castañeda
wrote an essay in *Foreign Affairs* magazine warning that Mexico's stability could "no longer be taken for granted" because of the inadequacies of
the PRI system.

The result of the ferment was the extraordinary meeting of minds that
took place after the Chihuahua elections in 1986, when Krauze reached
out to the Left to sign the letter protesting the fraud. In the end the
signatories included Krauze, Paz, and Zaid as well as Aguilar Camín,
Monsiváis, and Poniatowska. That rare moment of unity marked the
culmination of the diverse thought process that had begun two decades
earlier. Abstract notions about challenging the system through party

competition, which had incubated so long in intellectual drawing rooms, broke out into real politics and played out in an actual election. Mexican democracy was no longer just an idea.

The harmony was short-lived. The presidential election of 1988 shattered alliances across the board. Many on the Left, naturally, supported Cuauhtémoc Cárdenas and his campaign to contest the victory that Carlos Salinas claimed. Monsiváis said it was the only time in his life when he yelled political slogans. "When they approved the measure making Salinas President in the Chamber of Deputies," he recalled, "I started shouting, 'No to Fraud!' "

But many leading intellectuals did not back Cárdenas's insurgency or his protest after the vote. Octavio Paz was suspicious of Cárdenas, believing him to be less a reformer than a demagogue. Paz thought that Cuauhtémoc still had too much of the socialist faith of his father, Lázaro. Paz was not convinced that Cárdenas had won the election and remained unimpressed by his claims of fraud. Above all, Paz, then seventy-four, was wary of uncontrolled change.

"To accept the positions of the opposition was to start a civil war," he explained to Tim Golden of The New York Times, reflecting on the events of 1988 in an interview four years later. He said that the turmoil of Cárdenas's campaign had raised the danger of a return to Mexico's chronic cycle, in which "we would expose ourselves to Mexico's old history, of going from a just order to disorder and from disorder to violence and from violence to dictatorship."

Unexpectedly, Héctor Aguilar Camín did not support Cárdenas either. Although by then a veteran critic of the PRI system, he was also a historian of the Mexican Revolution. He, too, believed that Cárdenas looked to the past and would bring a return to his father's outmoded statist and populist traditions. Like Paz, he was not convinced that the vote fraud had actually robbed Cárdenas of a victory.

Moreover, once Salinas secured the presidency, he proved adept at winning the support of key intellectuals and reestablishing the traditional complicity between the PRI regime and the thinking class. He divided and conquered, and under his administration prominent intellectuals, instead of refining their rejection of the system, fell to squabbling among themselves, losing the momentum of the push toward democracy.

Salinas undoubtedly posed a challenge to Mexican intellectuals. With his American doctorate he was almost one of them. "His first name is Harvard-educated," Jorge Castañeda often quipped. "Harvard-educated Carlos Salinas."

Salinas courted writers assiduously. José Córdoba, his chief of staff, read widely and maintained a corps of readers to keep Salinas up to date. When a writer or scholar would come to Los Pinos, Córdoba would slip Salinas a note card with a nugget from the author's recent work. The writers were inevitably delighted by the President's interest.

But the main point was that Salinas, more than any PRI President, came to office offering modernizing policies that were clearly at odds with the tired orthodoxy of the PRI. His program was particularly appealing to Paz, who had advocated, in the pages of *Vuelta*, paring down the state and bringing down the walls of protectionism. Paz had met Salinas when he had given a lecture series at Harvard while Salinas was a graduate student there. Now he saw Salinas as the President who was going to carry out his proposals for reform. The impact of Paz's support for Salinas's policies was immeasurably enhanced after the poet was awarded the Nobel Prize in literature in 1990.

"I applaud the opening with all the world and especially the opening with the United States," Paz said in the *Times* interview, four years into Salinas's term. "It's the first time in my lifetime when I feel there have been important changes in the country."

Paz helped Salinas set up a program to provide lifetime fellowships, in the form of a yearly stipend, to Mexico's most distinguished artists. The sinecure—which Paz himself also received—was PRI co-optation in its classic form. Nevertheless, because of Paz's prestige, Homero Aridjis, Carlos Fuentes, Carlos Monsiváis, and Elena Poniatowska, among others, accepted fellowships, convincing themselves that the money came from the government and not from President Salinas.

Paz did set some limits. He rejected offers from Salinas to be ambassador in France and Secretary of Culture, and he turned down the grand celebrations Salinas tried to organize for him in honor of the Nobel.

"At heart Paz remained always a man of the Mexican Revolution,"

Through his literary magazines *Plural* and later *Vuelta*, Octavio Paz dominated
intellectual and political debate

explained Krauze, who knew Paz's thinking better than anyone.
"He thought it was a corrupt regime, imperfect, but the lesser evil. He
thought Salinas was the incarnation of his dream: the revolution, which
had done so many good things for Mexico, finally reformed from within.

"Octavio was more liberal than democratic," Krauze added. "His
democracy always had some adjectives."

Paz's enthusiasm for Salinas created an awkward problem at *Vuelta*.
Both Zaid and Krauze supported Salinas's economic liberalization (although Zaid wanted better programs to spread growth to the poor), but
both strongly rejected as superficial his gestures at political reform. Zaid
continued to blast away in the pages of *Vuelta*, but Krauze felt uncomfortable disagreeing with Paz in his own magazine. Krauze began to send
his political columns to *La Jornada*, even though the *Vuelta* crowd had
often dismissed it as a leftist screed. During the Salinas administration,
Krauze later acknowledged, "*Vuelta* lost some of its critical edge."

A similar crisis arose at *Nexos*. Aguilar Camín was also drawn to Salinas's modernizing policies. In a book called *Después del milagro* (After

the miracle), published in November 1988, he detailed the decay left across the Mexican social landscape by an eroding corporatist state. He offered a blueprint for change that included decentralizing the federal bureaucracy, creating government incentives to decentralize investment, and dismantling the state's subsidy and control of unions and other social organizations. He declared that the recent elections turmoil had been a summons to "a profound change in our political system by the institutional means at hand, gradually but drastically." The book was another call for reform of the Mexican Revolution—radical, but from within.

"To my great surprise," Aguilar Camín said, once Carlos Salinas took office "the book began to turn up letter for letter in several major government initiatives." Salinas tried to lure Aguilar Camín into his cabinet and also offered him the job of governor of Quintana Roo. Aguilar Camín declined.

"That was never a problem for me," he said. "I have never been tempted to be a public functionary."

But some regular *Nexos* writers did join the government, and others, committed leftists, bolted from the magazine in disgust. Aguilar Camín steered what he thought was a middle course, making *Nexos* a contractor of the Salinas government. On government contracts Aguilar Camín carried out Mexico's first national poll of educational needs and values and organized a team of scholars to write new history textbooks for public grade schools. Salinas also gave him the task of creating a PBS-style television network. Soon Mexicans were calling Aguilar Camín Salinas's *intelectual de cabecera*, his "bedside intellectual."

Parallel to the divisive debate about Salinas, another feud was poisoning relations among Mexican intellectuals.

In June 1988 *The New Republic*, the American political magazine, published a review by Enrique Krauze of two books by Carlos Fuentes: an autobiographical anthology called *Myself with Others* and a novel, *The Old Gringo*. The review's title, which Krauze conceived, was "The Guerrilla Dandy." For eight full pages Krauze poured scorn on Fuentes and his work. Noting that Fuentes had grown up in foreign embassies following his diplomat father, Krauze said the novelist was "a foreigner in his own country" and his autobiography showed a "lack of identity and personal history."

"For Fuentes," Krauze wrote, "Mexico is a script committed to memory, not an enigma or a problem, not anything really living, not a personal experience . . . Lacking a personal point of view and an internal compass, Fuentes lost his way through the history of literature and found himself condemned to the histrionic reproduction of its texts, theories and personages."

Some readers saw elements of truth behind Krauze's derision, which appeared in *Vuelta* two weeks later. After his extraordinary early novels, and several plays and some seminal literary criticism in the 1970s, Fuentes, though prolific, seemed to be stuck in place. It was his perennial misfortune to be compared with Paz, whose modernist poetry evolved to become more intelligent and innovative, more probing of a distinctly Mexican universe while also more universal.

Even so, Krauze's criticism struck many Mexican readers as disproportionate. Fuentes seemed clearly to have earned his stature as a statesman of letters. Aside from writing novels, he had deeply studied the history of Mexican politics and art, and his mesmerizing lectures had made him an eloquent interpreter of his country to the rest of the world. He had never taken a fiercely principled stand, as Paz had in 1968. But he maintained his integrity, worked for progressive causes, and showed younger generations of Mexicans the way to make a distinguished independent life of writing.

Krauze's assault, an expression of the sense of intellectual superiority prevailing in the *Vuelta* camp, was doubly wounding because of Fuentes's long friendship with Paz. Fuentes was certain that Paz had put Krauze up to the review. He was not mollified when Leon Wieseltier, the literary editor of *The New Republic*, wrote a letter clarifying that he had assigned Krauze to write it. Paz said that Krauze had shown him a draft and that he had strongly urged him not to publish it. But to stop Krauze outright would have been censorship, Paz said.

The reaction from Fuentes, his supporters, and the Left in general was beyond outrage. Bile spilled out in letters, columns, and seminars that denounced Krauze as a mercenary and an arrogant fraud. Fuentes broke with Paz, and they were never reconciled. The quarrel between intellectual Left and Right gained a sharp, personalized edge.

In the second year of Salinas's term the animosities flared into war. After enduring years of insult from the leftist establishment in Mexico, Paz and his crowd felt vindicated by the fall of the Berlin Wall. In August 1990 *Vuelta* organized a showy symposium in Mexico City to discuss the implications for Latin America of the new world order. They called it "The Experience of Liberty" and invited dissenters from Communism from around the globe, including Leszek Kolakowski, Czeslaw Milosz, the American sociologist Daniel Bell, and the Peruvian novelist Mario Vargas Llosa. The sessions were held behind closed doors, but they were videotaped and broadcast in the evening by a cable channel of Televisa, which was also a major sponsor of the event. Each participant received a five-thousand-dollar stipend. Paz and Krauze made a point of insisting that the funding came entirely from private businesses.

The Latin American Left was represented sparsely, by Carlos Monsiváis and only a handful of others. Several names were conspicuously absent from the invitation list, notably those of Carlos Fuentes and Gabriel García Márquez, the Colombian novelist and a Nobel laureate, like Paz.

"We did not invite any pseudo intellectuals who have been accomplices to tyrants," Paz said, referring to García Márquez's well-known friendship with Fidel Castro.

Paz dominated the proceedings, but he met unexpected resistance from Vargas Llosa, whose liberal politics were generally close to his. "I remember thinking many times that Mexico is the perfect dictatorship," Vargas Llosa said in one session. "It wasn't the Soviet Union; it isn't Fidel Castro's Cuba; it's Mexico. Because this dictatorship is camouflaged in such a way that it often seems that it's not one."

Paz was appalled. He broke in to make "a small rectification . . . What *I* said was that in Mexico we have a hegemonic system of domination," Paz snapped. "We *cannot* speak of a dictatorship."

Several of the sessions were thrilling for their erudition. But the self-satisfied neoliberal tone irritated the Mexican press and the Left.

Monsiváis wrote a letter to *La Jornada* charging that Paz had cut off his presentation. He questioned the role of Televisa. "On the subject of democracy, do you recall how Televisa silenced the opposition in the elections of 1988?" Monsiváis asked.

A year later the Left took revenge with a conference of its own about the end of the Cold War, more modestly titled "The Winter Colloquium." The list of organizers included the stars of Mexico's leftist firmament: Aguilar Camín, Jorge Castañeda, Pablo González Casanova, and, of course, Carlos Fuentes. They decided to hold the meeting on the UNAM campus, with funds provided by the Salinas administration's culture agency. No one from the inner circle at *Vuelta* was invited, not even Octavio Paz.

When Paz heard about it, he threw a temper fit. He objected to the very concept of the meeting, in which capitalism was put on trial right alongside Communism. "To equate Communism and democratic capitalism as if they were monster twins doesn't make sense," he said. He complained to the UNAM president and then to Salinas himself. When an invitation was hurriedly dispatched to Paz, he turned it down because there was none for Krauze.

The *Vuelta* group decried the colloquium as a breach of democratic ethics, contending that none of them could be excluded because the event was held at a public university and paid for with public money. "They don't have any right not to be pluralistic when they are receiving government funds," Krauze fumed.

A surreal shouting match filled the front pages. The leftists, with *Nexos* out front, argued that *Vuelta* had sold its soul to Televisa, whose money, they argued, was no less tainting than money from the PRI regime. The *Vuelta* group accused Aguilar Camín of selling *Nexos* to the devil by "doing business with the government" through his contracts, which they contended were morally different from the government advertising in their magazine. (Never more than one-third, Krauze stressed.)

However, the unavoidable reality was that both Paz and Aguilar Camín had embraced President Salinas and staked their publications on his policies. The flap was a regression to the intellectuals' old ruminations about who among them was more sullied by state power. From that time forward neither faction would add much new to the debate about democracy.

Indeed, the highbrow journals were starting to matter less as the mainstream press published a wider range of views for an ever wider audience. Dissidents were now able to hold forth for a rising generation of middle-class readers who had lost their taste for the pabulum of censored journalism. The press, like the intelligentsia, had its own evolution, pushing back the limits on expression story by story. But the press's ties to the regime had been especially intimate, and the system's corrupting influence on journalists was great.

PRI governments kept a grip on newspapers by controlling the fundamentals: their funding and their supply of paper. In an economy where the government was central, there was little private advertising. Newspapers derived their income from selling ads to the regime, which also had a monopoly on the distribution of newsprint, dating back to 1935, through a state-owned company called PIPSA.

Newspapers paid miserable wages, as little as four hundred dollars a month even in the 1980s, so for most reporters the primary source of income was not their publication but their sources. The lingo of the profession avoided the unpleasant word "bribe": the *chayote* (a squash) was an occasional payment for coverage of a major news event; *embute* referred to a regular cash-filled envelope. Reporters were also rewarded with commissions based on their paper's advertising revenues from the government agency they covered; they were sometimes asked to sell ads to officials they interviewed.

Reporters vied for the best beats based not on news value but on cash yield. Thus Los Pinos, the PRI, and Pemex, which had the most cash for *embutes*, received the most attentive coverage. These practices not only discouraged real reporting on the government's affairs, they also meant that sources who did not pay did not make the news. The typical Mexican newspaper was a compendium of vague declarations by inconsequential politicians. There were also stories, sometimes called *sablazos*, in which reporters and columnists savaged a politician for a fee from one of his rivals.

Journalists had to wage risky, dedicated struggles to escape such ingrown corruption. As a result, the opening of the press came haltingly and often met with traumatic setbacks.

In Mexico City it started with the diaspora that followed the 1976 coup at *Excélsior*. While Scherer turned his energies to *Proceso*, his deputy from *Excélsior*, Manuel Becerra Acosta, started *Unomásuno* (it means "one plus one"), a tabloid daily. First published in November 1977, the paper, unabashedly leftist, got off to a gutsy start. But Becerra eventually reverted to old habits, initiating a bid for autocratic control of the paper that drove his best staff to leave in protest in 1983.

On May 30, 1984, Manuel Buendía, a cantankerous and widely read columnist, was assassinated while investigating narcotics corruption in government; his death signaled the persisting dangers of pushing the boundaries. But that September 19, the forward march began again, when a group of refugees from *Unomásuno* put out the first issue of *La Jornada*. The new tabloid thrived, also with a proud leftist line. Meanwhile, Becerra quietly took a $1 million payment from the Government Secretariat in exchange for control of what remained of *Unomásuno*, resigned from the paper, and fled into exile.

The events of 1988 energized the press. The Salinas presidency brought some new freedom, but old constraints also reappeared.

As the press in the capital struggled, newspapers in the provinces struggled even more. There were some exceptions, most notably *El Norte*, a prosperous newspaper in Monterrey run by Alejandro Junco de la Vega, a young publisher trained at a Texas journalism school. There was an independent weekly in Tijuana, *Zeta*, and a respectable daily in Hermosillo, Sonora, *El Imparcial*. But it came as a surprise, in 1991, when an irreverent newspaper with a modern look appeared in Guadalajara, that most conservative and Catholic of Mexico's big cities. *Siglo 21* (Century 21) set out to shatter, not just reshape, the authoritarian mold of journalism, and it almost succeeded.

The paper arose from the frustrated political pretensions of a son of the system. Alfonso Dau, the scion of a wealthy Lebanese textile family in Guadalajara, had failed to persuade his party, the PRI, to nominate him for governor and was seeking other avenues to prominence. Though largely self-taught, Dau had broad horizons and was known in his city as a collector of fine art and books. During his foray into politics he had become fascinated by the role that the Madrid newspaper *El País* had played in Spain's transition to democracy from the dictatorship of Francisco Franco in the 1970s.

Knowing nothing of journalism, Dau sought help from a young friend who knew even less than he. Jorge Zepeda Patterson had grown up in Guadalajara but moved around the country as he studied to become a professor of economics and sociology. When Dau heard that Zepeda was headed for Paris to work on a doctorate at the Sorbonne, he handed him one thousand dollars in cash and asked him to travel to Madrid to check out *El País*.

Zepeda, introducing himself with a pipe dream about starting a newspaper in the farming heartland of Mexico, hit it off with top editors at *El País*. Another two thousand dollars from Dau persuaded him to write a blueprint for the fantasy daily. For Zepeda it felt like starting a novel on a sudden inspiration. In ten days of happy seclusion in an apartment overlooking the Montmartre cemetery, Zepeda finished his plan.

Then Dau went to Paris to persuade Zepeda that he had to be the editor in chief. Doubtful of his abilities, Zepeda kept laying down new conditions to prove to Dau that it would never work. As publisher, he insisted, Dau would not be allowed to talk to any reporter unless the editor in chief was present. Zepeda would hire the newsroom business manager and staff. When Dau kept saying yes, Zepeda finally decided it would be "irresponsible" not to accept.

Zepeda spent six months at *El País* learning to be an editor and several more months in Paris working with an Italian graphic designer on the layout of the paper. When he finally returned to Mexico, he had a dummy of the first issue in hand. *Siglo 21* was the product of virgin birth: a Guadalajara daily conceived in Europe and run by an editor who had never written a news story.

"We were totally uncontaminated by the heritage of Mexican journalism," Zepeda said. To keep things that way, he decided not to hire any reporters who had previously worked in journalism in Mexico. Instead, he would entirely train his own staff.

"They just had to be sharp, restless, inquisitive. And they had to be able to write," Zepeda said. He hired students fresh out of university and turned to Tomás Eloy Martínez, an Argentine journalist and novelist, to train them in secret workshops, explaining that their journalism would be so subversive that the forces of the status quo might try to stop them if they found out.

Zepeda's main idea was to shift the newspaper's target audience from the political class to the common reader. "Our idea was to carry new voices, to see things from some other perspective than that of the powers that be, and to expose the vices of public life," Zepeda explained.

So *Siglo 21* had a style manual, the first in Mexican journalism, which laid down rules to eliminate complicity between reporters and sources. The pay for reporters, while not lavish, was a living wage and noticeably more than other papers offered. Every reporter had a computer and an Internet connection. As editor in chief, Zepeda decided that he would be the coach of the newsroom instead of its boss. "The tradition was that the editor had to be a son of a bitch, to ridicule the reporters and show them all the things they didn't know," he said. "I was going to be the purveyor of a vision."

The first issue of *Siglo 21* appeared on November 8, 1991, promising, in a formal pledge on page 2, to win the public's respect by striking "blows of journalistic honesty and pluralism."

"We have a clear idea of the society we hope to serve," read Zepeda's editorial. "It is a society dissatisfied with the state of things, in which there are every day more people who believe that a balanced democratic life requires a free press committed to its readers."

That first issue carried a photo of Zepeda, in shirtsleeves and jeans, poring over page layouts with his staff; a photo of Dau in a pin-striped suit; and a profile in which the new publisher proclaimed that he was not out to promote his or anyone else's political career, but wanted only "a cultural enterprise that will be important for the region." Dau, who had invested $3 million, said he assumed that "a quality newspaper is a good business."

The paper started proudly but slowly. The competition to beat was *El Informador*, a stodgy Guadalajara broadsheet steeped in the conventions of crony journalism. Many readers at first thought that *Siglo 21*, with its arty front-page photographs and high-profile coverage of rock concerts and avant-garde gallery exhibits, was too adolescent to give them solid news. Zepeda and his staff learned that high ethics didn't help them much to beat the competition to stories. They were constantly outdone by reporters from other publications who had long-standing cozy relations with key sources. The paper's circulation did not rise above four thousand copies a day.

That was changed by one reporter and one very big story. The reporter was a woman just out of college whose byline was Alejandra Xanic. Her real name was Xanic von Bertrab, but Tomás Eloy Martínez had taken one look at that name, combining faux pre-Hispanic with German, and decreed it too much of a cultural conundrum for Guadalajara readers. Imbued with the paper's spirit of radical change, Xanic, as she was known to her friends, agreed to a new byline on the spot.

Editor Jorge Zepeda Patterson (seated, left) preparing the first issue of *Siglo 21*, in Guadalajara

One evening in April 1992, Xanic was dispatched to an industrial barrio of Guadalajara where residents were complaining of strong odors emanating from the sewers. She arrived in time for a press conference, where the city fire chief reported that there had been a leak into the pipes, apparently of solvents from one of the nearby factories, which included a cooking-oil plant, a plastics plant, and a huge Pemex storage facility. The chief assured the public that the department had things under control.

When the press conference was over, Xanic hung around, mindful of Martínez's teachings that the news does not come only from the mouths of officials. She searched for a way down into the sewers. She soon discovered that all the firemen who had been underground were coming up and, seemingly frightened, refusing to go back down.

A group of Pemex technicians were surveying the scene with an instrument that the firemen called an "explosometer." No one besides the Pemex crew knew what it was or how it worked, and they weren't explaining. But Xanic heard them say that it had registered "100 percent."

She called in every hour or so to Zepeda, who was fretting in the newsroom. He delayed the paper's close to 1 a.m. By then Xanic had gotten quotes from several firemen warning of danger and enough information for a map of the zone to be drawn, showing the web of streets where the leak had spread into the sewers.

After he read the story Xanic filed, Zepeda decided to make it one headline—but not the most important headline—on the front page. Inside, however, the first page of the city section shouted a warning of "imminent danger of explosion." *El Informador* carried only a small story reporting that the timely intervention of the fire department had stemmed the risk of disaster.

The explosion came just after 10 a.m. the next morning, April 22. More than six miles of streets were blown up. Facades were torn off buildings, cars hurled onto the roofs of two-story houses, body parts strewn over rubble where soda-pop stores, machine shops, and garages had stood. There was no fire, but the detonation had rocked the *Siglo 21* newsroom, miles away. The dead numbered in the hundreds. The streets where the sewers had blown were almost exactly the ones shown on *Siglo 21*'s map.

Zepeda put out a special afternoon edition (¡EXPLOTO!) and began to print a separate daily section on the explosion, which ran thirty pages in the early days. By April 24 the paper had sold more than twenty thousand copies a day.

The stunned PRI authorities dithered, quibbling over the death toll. Pemex pointed the finger at other plants in the neighborhood. Police roped off nearby blocks where the odor remained strong even after the explosion, denying reporters access.

Xanic found a hole in a wall. ("That woman is like a goat," Zepeda said, with respect. "She goes everywhere.") She fell in with a group of Pemex technicians making their rounds, who judged from her light blond hair and khakis that she was a visiting American accident expert. She discovered that the explosive was gasoline and that it was coming from a leak in a pipeline leading to the Pemex plant. The roped-off neighborhood, she learned, was still sitting on a river of the stuff. It was so volatile, she was told, that they didn't want people to approach who had metal nails in their shoes, for fear of the tiniest spark.

Pemex officials publicly denied responsibility, then were baffled day after day when their candid internal discussions turned up in *Siglo 21*. As the newspaper channeled the public's outrage, the Jalisco state governor and the Guadalajara mayor, both from the PRI, were forced to resign. It made no difference to *Siglo 21*'s coverage that the disgraced mayor was Alfonso Dau's cousin.

"The city began to pay attention to us," Xanic said.

The following year, 1993, Alejandro Junco de la Vega, the publisher of *El Norte*, founded *Reforma*, bringing his style of independent journalism to the capital city. *Reforma* paid better than other papers and trained reporters to check facts and get both sides of the story. A handsome broadsheet with a vivid color front page and sophisticated graphics, it offered food and fashion sections that were avidly read at middle-class breakfast tables. Junco's philosophy was to break the regime's economic stranglehold on the media. He believed that commercial success was fundamental to a free press. "We're fighting for the public's right to information, and that means developing . . . a healthy, arm's-length relationship with government," Junco said. "But we can't be quixotic about this; we have the challenge of surviving. We have to sell newspapers and advertising."

This philosophy made *Reforma* threatening to the government and also to other publications, including those that shared its goals. *La Jornada* continued to depend primarily on government ads. *El Universal* had stayed afloat because the government looked away when it failed to pay its Social Security taxes. Soon *El Universal*, the biggest of the serious papers in Mexico City, undertook a thorough editorial upgrade and moved to clean up its finances in order to compete with *Reforma*.

A year after *Reforma* started, the PRI-controlled union of street hawkers and newsstands said it would no longer sell the paper. In a nerve-racking confrontation, Junco led his reporters into the streets to sell the newspaper. He hired an army of vendors, giving *Reforma* its own distribution system, and the paper's independent image was made.

Throughout the Salinas *sexenio* the press advanced rapidly. Radio journalism also improved, growing more candid and incisive, led by a brilliant, hardworking, and durable Mexico City talk-show host, José Gutiérrez Vivó. But Televisa, which still dominated the media with its nationwide broadcast network, changed little. El Tigre Azcárraga's rule remained absolute, and his willingness to expand the network's political scope was at best erratic.

Azcárraga had taken a liking to Enrique Krauze through his dealings with *Vuelta*, and he invited Krauze to join the Televisa board. Krauze accepted, and Azcárraga soon invested in a multimedia company through which Krauze published history books and made a series of unusually revealing hour-long documentaries about Mexico's Presidents, which aired on Televisa on Sunday nights.

Yet Azcárraga once threatened, in a titanic rage, to drive Krauze out of the business and out of the country—by violence if necessary—after spotting a news photograph in which Krauze, a Jew, appeared to be laughing at the Virgin of Guadalupe, the national patroness. In the end Krauze had to humble himself before President Salinas, pleading for his intercession to calm El Tigre down.

In August 1993 Salinas ordered the sale of the government-owned television network that became TV Azteca, breaking Televisa's de facto monopoly. Yet Salinas made sure that Televisa stayed on the side of the

PRI. Indeed, the network's patent pro-government bias in the 1994 presidential campaign helped to mobilize a newly broad and influential group of intellectuals, opposition politicians, and journalists to protest. In June 1994, two months before the election, Carlos Fuentes appealed in a newspaper column for citizen action "so there won't be a train crash" in the vote. Fuentes phoned Jorge Castañeda, they both called a few friends, and before long more than sixty people from an array of professions and factions were meeting in Castañeda's living room. New faces joined old ones: Manuel Camacho, Adolfo Aguilar Zinser, Lorenzo Meyer, a historian from the Colegio de México. They were called the San Angel Group, after the neighborhood of cobbled streets and colonial portals where Castañeda's home was located.

The group, which received intense press coverage, presented a list of lightning reforms to be carried out before Election Day. A key demand was for Televisa to broadcast a series of shows covering issues in the presidential race. The network went some way to meet the demand: while Zabludovsky attacked Cárdenas on his news show, Ricardo Rocha hosted programs along the lines the intellectuals sought.

The San Angel Group signaled the passing of a torch among Mexican thinkers. A new generation came forward that was no longer focused on the theory of democracy. They were working on concrete steps to make democracy happen.

The impact of Ernesto Zedillo's presidency on freedom of expression was full of contradictions. Zedillo said that he considered a free press an indispensable element of a democratic system. But in practice he distrusted and disdained the news media, especially the Mexican media. At a press conference early in his term, a Mexican reporter, emboldened by the talk of new freedoms, asked Zedillo to comment on rumors that he might resign. The President dismissed the question indignantly; the reporter was fired from his newspaper; the press secretary was replaced; and Zedillo did not give another press conference in the remaining five years of his *sexenio*.

In general, however, Zedillo was not so much repressive as reluctant. Whereas Salinas had courted the media so as to manage his image,

Zedillo pursued the same end by avoiding the media. He avoided the intelligentsia as well. Under Zedillo intellectuals no longer had to agonize over their relations with the throne; he kept his distance from them all.

In Guadalajara, *Siglo 21* reached a circulation of thirty-five thousand readers, showing that a serious and independent paper could thrive in that market. Its objectivity was newly tested when PAN politicians won elections as Jalisco governor and Guadalajara mayor in February 1995. The paper was as critical of them as it had been of the PRI.

But success brought its own problems. The first sign came in the summer of that year, when new *panista* city officials called a press conference to charge, on the basis of a stack of documents, that Alfonso Dau, the publisher, had received fifty thousand dollars in cash from the city government in the final days of PRI rule, described in the documents as "an advance" against future advertising. Faced with the documents, Dau acknowledged accepting the payment. Zepeda was mortified, especially when he discovered that the payment did not appear on the books of *Siglo 21.*

Zepeda's relations with the publisher grew strained. He found evidence that appeared to him to show that Dau was taking money from the newspaper to finance real-estate projects. When the paper undertook an investigation exposing fraud in the Mexican Social Security Institute, reporters discovered that Dau had not been paying the paper's taxes to the agency. A bank sued Dau, claiming he had failed to repay a $3 million loan.

Dau had kept his word to Zepeda that he would not interfere in newsroom editorial decisions. But the newspaper's success had made him ambitious in his other business dealings, which Zepeda thought he was conducting in a way that compromised the maverick aims of the paper.

In the fall of 1996 President Zedillo went to Jalisco. Breaking with protocol, he asked to see Zepeda but not Dau. In a one-on-one meeting in the presidential suite of a Guadalajara hotel, Zedillo told the editor he was surprised by the "schizophrenic" character of *Siglo 21.* It had done much to show it was committed to democratic journalism. Yet Zedillo said that when he had met with Dau on a swing through Guadalajara during his campaign in 1994, Dau had told him outright that for $1.5 million he would put *Siglo 21* at the service of his campaign. "I have been a public official for nearly two decades, and no one ever proposed corruption to me as crudely as that man did," Zedillo remarked.

The next day Zepeda confronted the publisher. On the defensive, Dau announced that he would take over as editor in chief and told Zepeda he could leave if he didn't like it.

Zepeda bided his time. Six months later, in April, he resigned from the paper. He quietly went to work raising money and buying a printing press. On August 1, 1997, 235 of the 250 members of the *Siglo 21* staff resigned and went to work for Zepeda at a new paper called *Público*.

Público, which started with a robust circulation of twenty-two thousand, was a cooperative, with ownership partially shared among the employees. Because of the staff's experience, it was a better paper than its predecessor.

But when the new paper was still in its first year, it faced the most severe, and most ironic, challenge of all. Alejandro Junco decided to open a *Reforma*-style paper in Guadalajara. Zepeda's papers had shown Junco that there was demand for his kind of journalism in the country's second-largest city. Zepeda knew how to compete against the old school. But how would he beat a paper with much deeper pockets offering the same journalism he wanted *Público* to do?

To protect his staff, Zepeda decided to sell control of *Público* to a national media chain whose flagship paper competed against Junco's *El Norte* in Monterrey. Zepeda soon quarreled with what he regarded as its impersonal corporate management style. In February 1999 he resigned from *Público* and left Guadalajara.

For a time Zepeda worked at *El Universal* in Mexico City, lost in the pack. But the experience of Guadalajara was not lost. Soon he created a new Sunday magazine for the paper, and it achieved both independent journalism and commercial stability.

Although Zedillo intervened infrequently in the press, he exerted his influence more directly at Televisa, which he recognized as a more integral part of the power structure.

In 1997 El Tigre Azcárraga became terminally ill with cancer. The question of who would take over the empire, by then a $9 billion conglomerate, loomed large. Azcárraga was indecisive: he appointed his twenty-nine-year-old son, Emilio Azcárraga Jean, to be president, but he named Guillermo Cañedo White, a young executive from outside the family, to be chairman of the board. It was a formula for conflict, which erupted even while El Tigre was still alive, and Zedillo stepped into the succession struggle.

On March 4, 1997, the main contenders for control of the conglomerate went to Los Pinos to confer with Zedillo: Emilo Azcárraga Jean; Guillermo Cañedo White and his brother José Antonio, also a senior executive in the conglomerate; and Miguel Alemán Velasco, a PRI politician who was the son of a former President and a major Televisa shareholder. The four men informed Zedillo that they had agreed to act as a collective liaison with the government in the future. But the President would have none of that. He turned to the young Azcárraga. "Emilio, your father asked me to help you and look out for you," Zedillo said. "Between the government and the Azcárraga family there has always been a pact, starting with your grandfather, moving to your father. Now you have the responsibility . . . But the situation is changing, and we need to adjust to the new reality."

The President said he wanted to deal with only one person at Televisa, and no one in the room doubted who he thought it should be. He encouraged Alemán to sell his Televisa shares, and he said he wasn't certain whose interests the Cañedo brothers represented.

They all agreed that henceforth the President would deal directly and exclusively with young Emilio.

After the death of El Tigre on April 16, 1997, his seemingly callow son surprised everyone by vigorously modernizing the company's management and waging a series of aggressive battles, true to his father's style, to win undisputed control over the empire. The advantages of having Zedillo on his side became clear. The Alemán family sold its Televisa holdings. The Cañedos fought to hold on (coming to fisticuffs in one board meeting) but found themselves isolated and threatened. Guillermo retreated into exile for a year.

Emilio Azcárraga Jean retired Zabludovsky from the prime-time show and brought a more balanced approach to Televisa's newscasts. Before

long the former monopoly was getting higher marks for fair news reporting than the upstart, TV Azteca. Still, Azcárraga Jean made it clear that
he and Televisa would remain loyal to Zedillo.

Ricardo Rocha paid the price. During the March 1997 meeting
Zedillo had complained to Azcárraga Jean that Rocha was too hard on
the government. When Rocha was considered to replace Zabludovsky,
Zedillo's Government Secretary intervened to veto him.

Yet Rocha continued to irritate the government with tough documentaries on his weekend show. In December 1997 he broadcast a report from the Indian highlands of Chiapas, using unedited footage to
show the explosive tensions between the Zapatistas and pro-government
gangs and warning that bloodshed could be expected. Three weeks later
pro-government killers massacred forty-seven villagers as they kneeled to
pray in a hamlet chapel. Televisa responded by cutting back Rocha's airtime, moving his show later at night, and auditing his accounts.

In April 1998 Rocha prepared a documentary about the aftermath of
the Aguas Blancas killings, two years after his first powerful report. In it
he would expose the Zedillo government's failure to secure justice in the
case. The former governor Rubén Figueroa remained a free man, and
Rocha discovered that many of the police officials who had been convicted of the shootings had been freed from jail.

Just half an hour before the show was to air, an envoy from Azcárraga
Jean arrived in Rocha's studio and seized the master videotape of the
show, taking it away. With no program to broadcast, Rocha read the news
for five minutes, then the network switched to sports.

Rocha went to Azcárraga Jean and Alejandro Burillo, who had defended the first Aguas Blancas video. "I'm leaving, but I'm not breaking,"
Rocha told them. He remained grateful to El Tigre for his career at Televisa, he said, and would not turn against the network now. Instead,
Rocha formed his own news agency, providing television, radio, and
print coverage for all buyers. The business was a terrible travail, but
Rocha never spoke against Televisa.

There were many power struggles among Mexican journalists in the late
1990s as big egos that had been united for decades behind the cause of

greater freedom began to clash with one another once freedom was in sight. Journalism had been largely a poor man's profession, but now there was money to be made, and the profession's new leaders scrapped for profits and control of institutions.

Still, the environment was ripe for a new kind of media-savvy opposition politician, one who understood that the press was no longer the servant of the state and could, with smart campaigning, be used against it. A politician, for example, like Vicente Fox.

15

Chiapas

By the last years of the Zedillo *sexenio* the rebellion in Chiapas by masked Indians calling themselves Zapatistas had stopped being big news in Mexico. The armed uprising that had stunned the country on New Year's Eve in 1994—rudely interrupting President Salinas's mariachi party to celebrate the start of the North American Free Trade Agreement—seemed to have deteriorated into an array of narrow feuds between Indian communities in Chiapas that supported the Zapatistas and others that leaned toward the government. The Zapatistas' fight for justice for Mexico's indigenous peoples continued to draw sympathy throughout the nation. But in the federal elections of 1997, Zapatistas in black ski masks had disrupted voting at polling stations, burned ballots, and even attacked some Chiapas voters. Although their leader, Subcomandante Marcos, was admired to the point of adulation among leftists both in Mexico and abroad, his movement's militant tactics in that election seemed out of step with the progress toward democracy in the rest of the country.

But the EZLN—for Ejército Zapatista de Liberación Nacional, Zapatista National Liberation Army—was not as distant from the general trend as it appeared. In their communities, far away in torrid jungle canyons and chilly highland hamlets, the Zapatistas' followers were engaged in a democratic experiment of their own. It did not center on advancing electoral representation, as did efforts elsewhere in Mexico. Rather, inspired by the agrarian radicalism of Emiliano Zapata, the Christian socialist teachings of the Catholic Church in Chiapas, and Marcos's own sui generis anti-globalist doctrine, the Zapatistas undertook a utopian program of Indian self-government, seeking to create an enclave of popular rule within the authoritarian state.

The Zapatistas' quest for indigenous *autonomía*, or autonomy, was little known and less understood outside Chiapas. The Mexican and foreign press (including, we admit, *The New York Times*) focused on the seductive figure of Marcos, the guerrilla commander with the pipe and fraying fatigues, the mestizo among Indians, the onetime university professor who gave up the comforts of middle-class urban academia to join a revolutionary jungle underground. The press also followed the fervent pro-Zapatista solidarity movement that sprang up in the United States and Europe, spurred in no small part by the Subcomandante's exceptional talents for Internet communication. At the same time, the Zapatistas did not always publicize their experiment in home rule. Hemmed in and harassed by Mexican army troops, the Zapatistas restricted access to their villages, allowing visits only by foreign and Mexican leftist supporters who passed careful screening.

To be sure, the Indian townships of Chiapas, Mexico's southernmost and most impoverished state, had long been worlds unto themselves. In some communities time was still reckoned according to a Mayan calendar developed twelve centuries ago; their year ended not on December 31 but five days earlier, on December 26. Early in his term President Zedillo adopted daylight saving time for Mexico during the summer months, but many Indian communities, whether Zapatista or not, refused to go along. They scorned the clock change as "Zedillo's time," the work of a leader of the *caxlanes*, the Mayan term for people who are not Indians. They preferred to stick to their old schedule, deeming it *hora de Dios*, "God's time."

The stucco churches that dominate the central squares of Indian towns are nominally Catholic, but little of the ritual practiced within comes from the Vatican. The Indians have appropriated Catholic saints to embody spirits from the Mayan cosmos. Worshippers make altars on the floor of pine needles spread before braziers burning copal incense and adorn them with pop bottles filled with homemade sugarcane liquor, for libations to God. Women bring white chickens to Mass to have them blessed before sacrificing them to carry out cures prescribed by Indian healers.

The Indians had been excluded from *caxlán* Mexico by centuries of exploitation and racist abuse. In 1994, at the time of the Zapatista uprising, there were still *fincas*, or big farms, in remote Chiapas where the owners exercised *la pernada*, the right to sleep with an Indian bride on her wedding night before her new husband.

The Zapatistas' townships, called *municipios autónomos*, built on the Indians' sense of being separate in both politics and faith but magnified it. Although the EZLN had a clandestine army of as many as one thousand guerrilla fighters (most of them peasant farmers by day), early in their uprising they made it clear that they were not anxious to engage in combat. Rather, their method of defiance was to set up their own alternative town administrations with their own policies and social programs while rejecting all contact with government agencies. The Tzeltal, Tzotzil, Tojolabal, and Chol Indians (among others) who lived in the autonomous townships called their political philosophy *resistencia*: civil resistance to government authority. In the late 1990s there were thirty-eight Zapatista townships in Chiapas, including less than 10 percent of the 700,000 Indians in the state, but with a political impact in the indigenous communities that far outweighed their size.

The Zapatistas sought not to found a new Indian nation but to make a place for Indian self-determination within the Mexican state. In their townships they kept their own birth and death records, discouraging followers from registering with official bureaucracies. They stopped paying taxes to any government and refused to allow social workers from government health and welfare agencies to set foot inside what they considered their boundaries. They opened their own health clinics staffed by volunteer Mexican and foreign doctors and local herbal healers and organized agricultural and crafts cooperatives that operated mainly through regional barter. In some townships they held trials and set up jails.

The procedures by which Zapatista villagers chose their authorities varied between townships depending on the local *usos y costumbres* (habits and customs), a constitutional term for community tradition. In some places they held elections, formally inaugurating town mayors with the wooden staff, the *bastón de mando*, that is the traditional symbol of authority in Chiapas. In others village councils were drawn from leaders who had ascended through a traditional Mayan cargo system.

Zapatista doctrine required that their village leaders *mandar obede-ciendo* (that phrase that Porfirio Muñoz Ledo had used in the Chamber of Deputies in 1997); they should govern by obeying the will of the local assembly. Establishing a track record of honest service was meant to be the key to advancing to a higher post. "Nothing for us, everything for everyone" was an oft-repeated slogan of an organization that was radically egalitarian and suspicious of individual material gain. Its canon was infused with the beliefs and experiences of Catholic Indians who had participated in an extensive network of catechuists, or Bible teachers, organized in remote Indian communities in the 1970s and 1980s by Samuel Ruiz, the Bishop of San Cristóbal de las Casas who was a proponent of liberation theology.

The autonomous townships gave Zapatista Indians a sense of empowerment that they prized, enough to endure severe hardship to preserve it. In particular, Indian women were incorporated as never before in community life and leadership. Unusually, the EZLN also united Chiapas Indians across tribal lines, mobilizing Tzeltal, Tzotzil, and others in demonstrations that filled the streets of San Cristóbal.

Julia:

With constant clashes between the Zapatistas and the government in Chiapas, I spent a lot of time reporting there. I became convinced that the Zapatistas' townships were making an original contribution to the rich history of leftist revolution in Latin America, so I tried to visit as many of them as I could. It wasn't easy. Government troops kept them under continuous siege, making the Zapatistas suspicious of all nonpartisan outsiders—particularly a reporter from *The New York Times*, that well-known mouthpiece of American imperialism. After years of negotiations I managed to convince them to let me spend two days in a township.

Called Roberto Barrios, it was a Tzeltal community alongside a waterfall amid wild palms and rubber trees in the foothills in northern Chiapas. The Zapatistas had rechristened the town after a popular leader in the state who had defended Indian causes. A small river that crossed the only dirt road into the village could be forded by truck in dry winter but often became completely impassable with summer rains.

At the village entrance Zapatista women stood guard twenty-four hours a day, using shawls for cover in the cool of jungle night. A wooden sign in red-and-black lettering welcomed visitors to TERRITORIO REBELDE (rebel territory) and announced that it was an Aguascalientes, a term the Zapatistas used to designate a regional capital and meeting place. (The Aguascalientes sites were named for a central Mexican city where a revolutionary convention in 1914 marked a political high point for Emiliano Zapata and his followers.) Although unarmed, the watchwomen were fierce; there was no way to get past them without prior permission from Zapatista authorities. EZLN governance was firm but not always efficient, and even with the proper papers a stranger could wait a day or more to be cleared for entry to the village center, just a few hundred feet down the road, while the authorities sought instructions by radio from the central command, apparently hiding somewhere in the canyons of the Lacandon rain forest.

A hand-painted banner hanging over a fence by the entrance announced the township's raison d'être in terms that were hardly catchy: FOR THE CONSTITUTIONAL LEGITIMIZATION OF THE RIGHTS OF INDIAN PEOPLES. A mural on the side of a slat house showed Comandante Tacho, one of the EZLN's top Indian commanders, against a field of flourishing maize, with an inscription: BUT THE REBELLION CONTINUES AS LONG AS CORN GROWS AND SPARKS FLY FROM THE EYES OF THE ZAPATISTA COMMANDER.

By a muddy patio where scruffy turkeys went pecking was the Voices of the Mountain library, its simple wooden shelves filled with donated pulp novels, old textbooks, and leftist tracts, many in English. Nearby stood the Sleep of Hope visitors' dormitory, where the beds consisted of single planks of wood raised from the dirt floor on tree stumps and hammocks hung from log columns.

What most clearly distinguished Roberto Barrios from the non-Zapatista communities around it was that it had both a government primary school and a Zapatista one. The EZLN's autonomous school was a crude, half-finished cinder-block building; its windows had no glass, and the corrugated-tin roof radiated oppressive heat from the sun into the classrooms. Each classroom had a blackboard (although no nails to hang it up), a few pieces of chalk, and little else. Some classrooms had chairs and tables for the children; students in younger grades sat on dirt floors.

The girls, who were the majority, came to school nicely turned out in pink-and-purple satin dresses with pinafores and plastic shoes. Many of the boys were barefoot, their T-shirts tattered. Each student had one notebook and a pencil, but there was no sign of other materials. A teacher named Israel (all the teachers withheld their last names) was giving a course on pre-Hispanic history to a classroom of older students, probably sixth-graders. He spoke in Tzeltal, but he had written "Olmec" and "Maya" on the board in Spanish, and then a list:

They made colossal heads in stone
They used a number system based on twenty with zero
They built the ceremonial center at Palenque

The latter was now a booming commercial hub city and tourist venue in the region, and Israel sought to impress on his skeptical students that their forefathers had founded it. It was hard for Israel to keep the class focused. One boy penned a tattoo on the back of the neck of the boy next to him; another gazed at a dead scorpion dangling in cobwebs in a corner.

In a classroom of younger kids, a teacher named Ana, also speaking in Tzeltal, taught the Spanish alphabet. When the children got spunky, she poked and swatted them with a stalk of sugarcane. A round-eyed girl, Erica, was deaf and mute. The teacher showed her how to point to letters on the blackboard, and Erica read the students' lips as they pronounced them; she was clearly one of the most alert students in the class.

The last ten minutes of Ana's class were devoted to *integración*, a course in which the teachers applied Zapatista teaching to the realities of the community. Ana tried to engage the children in a conversation about the shortage of farmland in the community. She said Indian parents should demand more land from the "bad government," but the kids were too restless to listen. Good-humoredly, Ana dropped the subject and went straight into a few rounds of the Zapatista anthem, a lively folk march about *la lucha*, which the children sang with gusto.

A wrinkled Zapatista pamphlet explained the teachers' purposes in more detail:

1. We don't want a school where students are fined for missing classes.
2. We don't want a school where students are beaten or abused.
3. We don't want a school where corrupt teachers make us pay to get a passing grade.

1. We do want a school where Indian language and culture are respected.
2. We do want a happy school, filled with songs and theater.
3. We do want a school where we learn things that are useful to Indians.

After school a group of teachers—the Zapatistas called them *promotores*, rather than the more hierarchical *profesores*—gathered to elaborate even further. They were teaching in Roberto Barrios, they said, on orders from the EZLN. They were trying to make a school that was very different from the ones their parents had attended, where Indian children were barred from class if they did not have a uniform (which their parents were sometimes too poor to buy) or if they arrived late after working in the fields in the early morning. A *promotora* named Rosa said it was an important change for the children to feel they could speak and learn in their own language.

"We don't paint any other world here," Benjamín chimed in. "Here we paint the reality of our world, how we live and what we do."

Behind their idealism, the teachers hinted at problems. They were not paid by the EZLN, but lived on food donations from school parents and aid from foreign solidarity groups—all of which had grown scarce. Construction on the school had halted because the community volunteers who were working on it ran out of time and materials. The school had started with 150 students, but enrollment had dropped to 130 and was still declining. Although many parents professed to prefer the Zapatista curriculum, they worried because children at the autonomous school could not get certificates from the Education Secretariat showing the grades they had completed.

By the end of my visit I had come to realize that Roberto Barrios was a divided village. The Zapatistas were the majority, but a significant number of families actively supported the PRI and the government school. Its freshly painted building stood on the far side of the central plaza, with glass in the windows, blackboards on the walls, textbooks on the shelves, and a generator to power the lights. The teachers were not local but commuted in for the week and returned to homes elsewhere on weekends. During recess on the day 1 was there, they organized the students into platoons in the yard and had them goose-stepping up and down, carrying the Mexican flag and shouting pledges of fealty to the nation.

—   —   —

When the Zapatistas first burst out of the lowland jungles, seizing half a dozen towns in the Chiapas highlands, they barely mentioned the Indian cause. In the First Declaration of the Lacandon Jungle, issued in the early hours of the uprising, the EZLN's high command declared war on the "dictatorship" of Carlos Salinas and summoned its fighters to "advance to the nation's capital defeating the Mexican army" on behalf of all oppressed Mexicans. Even at that stage, however, the Zapatistas advocated not overthrowing the order established by the 1917 Constitution but only restoring it to its revolutionary origins by creating a "free and democratic" government for all Mexicans.

Within days, as the Mexican army counterattacked and rebel casualties mounted, Subcomandante Marcos, the EZLN's military strategist, realized that his force was seriously outgunned. With Salinas also reeling from the blow to his image, both sides adopted parallel unilateral cease-fires after only twelve days of hostilities. Marcos began to rethink his plans.

The defense of the Indian cause was still muted in the EZLN's Second Declaration of the Lacandon Jungle, in June 1994, but other ideas were evolving. "This revolution will end not with a new class, class faction, or group in power," the document stated, "but with a free and democratic 'space' for political struggle . . . born over the foul-smelling cadaver of the state-party and presidential system." The *comandantes* reported that they had conducted a referendum among their ranks, "a democratic exercise without precedent in an armed organization," in which the militants had voted to reject a government peace offer put for-

ward by the negotiator, Manuel Camacho. At that time they also unveiled their philosophy of *resistencia*. "We will accept nothing that comes
from the rotten heart of the government," they said, "not a single coin or
a tablet of medicine, not . . . a grain of food or a crumb of the alms it offers in exchange for our dignity."

By December 1994, in a new declaration issued as Zedillo took over
in Mexico City, the Zapatistas had begun to describe themselves as "a
Chiapas Indian rebellion." They de-emphasized military tactics and
stressed the importance of building a new opposition force, which they
called "civil society," in Mexico. With that in mind, they announced the
first *municipios autónomos*, saying they intended to put into practice in
three dozen Chiapas townships under their control the ideas they espoused for more just and egalitarian rule for Indians.

Two months later, in February 1995, President Zedillo, struggling to
assert his control amid the peso crisis, issued arrest warrants for Marcos
and other top Zapatista commanders and sent army troops into the Lacandon canyons to find them. On February 9, Zedillo revealed on national television that government intelligence had finally identified
Marcos. He was Rafael Sebastián Guillén Vicente, a Mexican but not an
Indian, who had been a communications professor at the Autonomous
Metropolitan University in Mexico City before dropping from view in
Chiapas some years earlier. The fighting ended within days without the
capture of Marcos (or any of the highest EZLN leaders).

Not since Emiliano Zapata had the Mexican Left had a more appealing
figure than Subcomandante Marcos. The revelation of his former civilian identity did nothing to diminish his aura. He was a living icon: always appearing in a brown shirt, olive green pants, high jungle boots,
and a black head mask that covered all but his eyes and mouth, which
he invariably topped with a battered brown cap. He wore wireless head-
phones with a microphone to maintain communications with his forces.
Marcos was a revolutionary Renaissance man: a guerrilla strategist and
theorist who was also a master of political stagecraft, an essayist and
raconteur, even a children's book author. Many of his writings were
framed as dialogues with a beetle he called Don Durito, Mr. Hardhead.

The insect had a low opinion of Marcos's political acumen, which he expressed freely in exchanges where Marcos tested his analysis of current events.

Although Marcos was clearly in charge, he retained the rank of Subcomandante, below the highest Indian commanders, to preserve the appearance of ruling by obeying. Time proved, however, that the Indian leaders—Tacho, David, Zebedeo, Esther, Trini, among others—had significant influence. The EZLN, despite constant hounding by the government, maintained its unity.

Marcos conceived a hybrid leftist ideology for the EZLN. He saw it as the spearhead of the new "civil society," which would be separate from any political party and eventually much more powerful. He framed the Chiapas Indians' struggle for justice as part of a broad attack on neoliberal economic policies, with the EZLN as a vanguard of the international movement against free trade. The Zapatistas' manifestos, which he composed, expressed their goals in terms of a quest for Mexican democracy. Yet Marcos generally disdained elections, and the EZLN undercut and even attacked Indians who chose to stand in local races in Chiapas as candidates for the PRD.

Julia:

I was inclined to like the Subcomandante because of his sense of humor. I had covered the guerrilla wars in Central America in the 1980s. The *comandantes* of the Sandinista regime in Nicaragua and the guerrilla front in El Salvador had been a humorless bunch, and I had grown tired of their turgid Marxist tracts.

The first time I met Marcos in person was in October 1995, when peace talks between the Zapatistas and the government were starting up again after a yearlong lapse. The EZLN had agreed to meet with a group of mediators, including several federal congressmen, in a Tojolabal village on the floor of a canyon in the rain forest. Aptly named La Realidad (Reality), the community had been penned in for months by army troops, so the villagers had not been able to sell their coffee crop and were starting to feel hunger.

Anticipation mounted throughout the appointed day, but the EZLN *comandantes* did not appear. Then, at dusk, the sound of marching feet on the dirt road announced the arrival of a phalanx of Zapatista girls, in lavender-and-scarlet satin dresses, with red or black bandannas concealing their faces. After they filed past into the village, and with the setting sun burnishing the valley with amber, up over a knoll came Marcos, on horseback, with a silver-handled assault rifle slung across his saddle and bullet belts strapped on his chest, flanked by two other mounted *comandantes*. The stagecraft dazzled the Indians who had gathered to see the Zapatista leader and provided the news photographers with striking images.

Marcos finally gave a press conference after midnight, by candlelight, sitting at a wooden table under a spreading tree. I was struck by his soft speech and thin hands, surprisingly smooth for a guerrilla fighter. He portrayed the EZLN as a reluctant army. "We know what it costs to rise up in arms," he said. "An armed rebellion shouldn't have been necessary for us to be heard."

He made no effort to play up his military capabilities. "We have many things to be proud of," he said, "but our arms are not among them." He insisted time and again that the Zapatistas were ready to disarm and sign a peace settlement; the question was not if but when. "There is no doubt at all that the Zapatistas will convert into a political force," he said.

But it was hard to pin him down on specific steps the EZLN was ready to take to advance the peace talks. He clearly was not interested in state elections that were about to take place. "We are not going to get involved in voting for someone we don't know who has done nothing for us," he said, slightly imperiously.

— — —

The Zapatistas gained new momentum after they signed a partial peace agreement with the government on February 16, 1996, in the Chiapas town of San Andrés Larráinzar, in what was described at the time as one step toward a permanent armistice and the eventual disarmament of the Zapatista force. In the accords the two sides agreed to establish "a new relation" between the Mexican state and the Indian peoples by reforming the Constitution to give the Indians rights to "free determination" within a "framework" of "autonomy" that "ensures national unity." This new status would give Indians legal latitude to choose their own form of village government and endow their communities with a special status under Mexican law that would allow them to create new collective forms of landholding and political association. The pact greatly increased the Zapatistas' stature, establishing them as representatives of Indian peoples across Mexico.

However, President Zedillo soon decided that the government's negotiators had gone too far. He made no move to implement the accords, and by September 1996 the peace talks had collapsed. But Zapatista leaders surprised the government by deciding to carry out the autonomy promised in the San Andrés accords anyway. Under Marcos's guidance the EZLN worked hard to extend the movement out of the canyons into highland communities, building a civil insurgency that challenged government authority in Chiapas, starting from the lowliest Indian villages.

Julia:

As I did more reporting in Chiapas, my view of Marcos changed. One jarring incident occurred during a grand international bash in August 1996 that the Zapatistas dubbed the Intergalactic Conference. Meetings held simultaneously at five or six sites across Chiapas drew Zapatista loyalists from the United States, Europe, and Latin America, mainly to inveigh against global free trade. The final session, which brought all the participants together in La Realidad, was held in a big corral that was a foot deep in soupy mud after weeks of rainy-season downpour. The assembly, which Marcos was scheduled to address, was supposed to start at 2 p.m., but 5:30 rolled around and no *comandantes* appeared. The sun was out, warming the mud until it steamed. By late afternoon many participants, all of them ardent Zapatista supporters, had started to reel from the heat and wanted to leave the center of the corral for the shade along the edges. But Marcos and Tacho, one of the most senior Indian *comandantes*, sent Zapatista security guards armed with truncheons to block people from leaving their seats, saying it would be a security risk to the EZLN leaders to have people moving around. A group of German volunteers cried out for relief, and several of them fainted. But the two com-

manders, who finally appeared in the cool of dusk, insisted on making
their point: their security was paramount.

— — —

The drive to build their new political "space" from the village up
brought the Zapatistas, unexpectedly, into a new phase of conflict as they
clashed with entrenched local PRI officials—who almost always were Indians like them. (Most of the *caxlán* landowners of large *fincas* in the Indian areas had fled with the uprising in 1994.) Indeed, in the Mayan
villages the traditional political organization was even more autocratic
than the PRI state, dominated by Indian caciques who had come to
power by following rigid ceremonial rules for political ascent and by maneuvering to secure a position in the local PRI patronage machine. Pluralism was largely unknown in the communities, which tended to be
homogeneous in ethnicity and faith and intolerant of other views. Long
before the Zapatista rebellion there was a turbulent history in the Chiapas highlands of Indian communities that had expelled members who
had tried to convert from Catholicism to evangelical Christian faith.

One place where the conflict with the EZLN turned vicious was
around the Zapatista township at Polhó, a hamlet built on a steep hill-
side in the Tzotzil highlands. The *municipio autónomo* had been
founded in April 1996 by Zapatista sympathizers who had tried to take
control of the larger township Chenalhó. After they lost the power struggle to *priísta* villagers, the Zapatistas seceded and set up a rival administration in Polhó, ten miles up a curving road from the township seat.

The rancor deepened during 1997, until both sides took up guns and
started shooting. In the last half of that year homicides claimed eighteen
victims in Chenalhó township: fourteen *priístas* and four Zapatistas, a
death toll that indicated that the EZLN was the more belligerent faction.
Chiapas state justice authorities ignored the killings, dismissing them as
the kind of chronic feuding that was to be expected among Indians. Finally the father of one PRI murder victim decided to take decisive
revenge. On December 22, 1997, he dispatched several dozen *priísta*
Indian vigilantes to Acteal, a settlement on the rim of a ravine filled with
unarmed refugees. The residents were not EZLN militants but members of an association of Catholic Indians committed to nonviolence, al-

though they were known to be anti-PRI because they had been driven out of villages controlled by PRI factions. The PRI gunmen killed forty-five people, including two infants and sixteen other children, as the refugees were praying in the mud-floor shack that served as their chapel.

After the Acteal massacre President Zedillo, even as he supported national democratic reform, showed his authoritarian side in Chiapas. By that time the EZLN had demonstrated that it was not an orthodox Marxist rebel army. The Zapatistas were doing what no other guerrilla organization in Latin America had done: trying to transform themselves gradually, on their own initiative, from an armed force into an Indian rights movement. Zedillo, however, chose to ignore this reality. He concluded that the massacre was the result of omission by federal and state officials who had allowed the Zapatista townships to usurp their authority and decided the remedy was to restore the sovereignty of the Mexican state. The President fired his Government Secretary, Emilio Chuayffet, replacing him with a smoother politician, Francisco Labastida. Together Zedillo and Labastida devised a dual strategy: they would try to lure Indian communities back into the fold by investing $3.5 billion, an enormous sum, in Chiapas social programs while crushing the Zapatistas' autonomous townships one by one.

One of the townships that federal army and police troops shut down was at the village of Taniperla, six hours by jeep up a punishing rocky road. The first thing the troops did when they arrived, in mid-April 1998, was take hammers and whitewash to a cheerful thirty-six-foot-long mural that the Zapatista villagers had just finished painting that morning on the side of a building that was to house a newly elected autonomous village council. The government forces set fire to the building and arrested nine people, none of whom was a Zapatista authority. (They included an observer from a Chiapas human rights organization and the art professor from Mexico City who had advised the villagers on the mural.) The Zapatista sympathizers in Taniperla all fled into the surrounding hills while the PRI faction was reinstalled in the mayor's office, in what amounted to a military coup d'état in the village.

At the same time, federal officials fanned a campaign of xenophobia in Chiapas, focused mainly on foreign volunteers working with the Za-

patistas. Dozens of foreign medical and aid workers serving in the autonomous townships were summarily arrested and deported, accused of
violating terms in the Mexican Constitution barring political activism by
foreigners. *Priísta* Indians, encouraged by the government's rhetoric, harassed and threatened American social workers.

The Zapatistas, seeing that the Zedillo government was determined
to destroy their alternative forms of self-rule, went into a defensive withdrawal. Their autonomous authorities went into hiding, and they closed
the townships to most visitors. The differences between *priísta* and Zapatista villagers hardened into hatred. The government's strategy also
forced new privations on Zapatistas who remained dedicated to their
townships. Besieged by army troops, the towns were cut off from regional
commerce, and the flow of international aid from leftist supporters was
not large or reliable enough to compensate. Since the Zapatista towns
refused to pay taxes, the authorities cut off their electricity, which was
supplied by a state-owned company. The want was especially severe in
Zapatista townships that took in refugees who had been driven out of
PRI-controlled villages.

But the Zapatistas also inflicted hardship on themselves. They expelled Telmex workers who came to string telephone lines, saying the
EZLN would not contribute to a private company's profits. (This was
ironic, since rural landline telephone service was a losing business that
Telmex undertook only to comply with government regulation.) They set
up blockades to stop government construction crews from opening roads
through their territories, saying the dirt tracks could serve as access routes
for army troop trucks. They rejected all government health services, so
their children went without vaccinations and treatments and suffered
epidemics of measles and malaria.

As time went by with no peace settlement in sight, the Zapatista communities became ever more isolated. The EZLN began to seem more
like a political cult than a civil rights movement with national aspirations.

Julia:

I went to Polhó in October 1998, looking for the Zapatista mayor,
Domingo Pérez Paciencia. He was not easy to find. Government officials

had been hinting that they were getting ready to launch an assault on the Polhó township, so Mayor Pérez was on the run, moving from one hiding place to another within the hamlet. By that time Polhó, like all the Zapatista townships, had been living for five months under a general "silence" imposed by the EZLN high command, which barred all its followers from talking to journalists without specific instructions from the top commanders. Across the highlands, Zapatistas had observed the directive rigorously, revealing the high level of discipline within the movement.

The village straddled steep hillsides that were slick with mud from seasonal rains. In addition to the regular population, more than eight thousand pro-Zapatista refugees, who had been driven out of nearby PRI villages, were living in crude shacks around the hamlet. The place had a picked-over look; practically every tree had been razed for firewood.

The people of Polhó, like Zapatistas in general, appeared to be civilians. Many of them probably owned black ski masks and guerrilla uniforms, but they rarely wore them. I had little doubt that there was a weapons cache somewhere in Polhó, but unlike the PRI gunmen who had flaunted their rifles, Zapatista fighters rarely displayed theirs.

The Mexican army was using psychological tactics to keep the Zapatistas rattled. On the roadway above the village, the army set up a tent base, from which a General and his troops peered down day and night into the streets of the hamlet. Army choppers clattered in and out of an improvised helipad nearby. Soldiers patrolled every footpath into the town, searching and questioning passersby.

One morning during my visit a group of Zapatistas ventured into the hills outside Polhó village in a desperate search for firewood. PRI followers from a neighboring village spotted them and, contending that the wood was theirs, called the army. The Zapatistas also called for reinforcements. A melee erupted when Indian women from the opposing factions starting hurling stones at each other. The soldiers pushed back the Zapatistas with bayonets, injuring several, and fired into the air to make them disperse. Eventually the Zapatistas decided to drop the fight and withdraw—with no firewood.

Despite the pressure on all sides, the Zapatistas were moving ahead with their projects to change Indian mores. By the entrance to Polhó were several public trash cans, a rare sight in any Indian village. These were labeled—incredibly—for recycling. (Someone had labored to find the right words in the Mayan language for "organic trash.") On rooftops here and there hung solar panels, which the Zapatistas had encouraged their townships to use as an independent electricity supply.

Signs announced the stern prohibition, applied in all Zapatista areas, of "alcohol or drugs of any kind." At one point I watched two young Zapatista policemen with truncheons march a giddy drunk off to the village jail. Of all the Zapatistas' innovations, the ban on alcohol was probably the most direct challenge to Mayan custom, since traditional political and religious rites required generous alcoholic libations. The measure was especially popular with women, who reported a sharp drop in street fighting and wife beating.

At a tortilla cooperative the cash box and books as well as the clanking automated tortilla press were handled by masked Indian women. One of them explained, with authority, that the cooperative was formed to undercut outside tortilla vendors who charged high prices and to serve

There were continual clashes between Zapatista followers and the army troops that surrounded and harassed them, like the one in January 1998 in the hamlet X'oyep

as an example of the new participation of women in the Zapatista way of life.

After days of waiting, I finally saw the elusive Mayor Pérez—very briefly. He would not answer any questions. But he was eager to impress on me that Polhó had defied the army harassment and been militant in its *resistencia*, spurning all government aid.

Everywhere I looked, I saw bony children and aching need, the most visible results of his constituents' devotion to the cause. There was no food to be seen in any of the houses in Polhó—not a piece of bread or a bottle of cooking oil, only near-empty saltshakers. On a narrow forest pathway outside the village, I came across two state health workers stopping to rest. They recounted how they had hiked out to a distant hamlet to bring medicine for an outbreak of malaria there. One small boy they saw was trembling with fever chills. But the Zapatista authorities had refused the medicine and demanded they leave.

One man whose hunger made him anxious to talk was Juan Pérez Vázquez, the leader of a cluster of refugees living on an outlying Polhó hill. On a sun-hardened knoll the refugees gathered to hear me interview their leader, whose tattered clothes made him look like he had just come from a brawl.

Pérez Vázquez said that PRI gunmen remained in control of their home village, so there was no possibility of going back for the time being. He described life in Polhó as very harsh. There was no place to plant, he said, no drinking water or firewood, no jobs, no market to buy fruit and no money to buy it with, no school for the older children, no shoes for anyone. His four children were all sickly.

Yet his zeal did not seem dampened. "We are Zapatistas, and we don't have to answer to the government," he said confidently, and his listeners hummed assent. "The Zapatistas are Indians who are in resistance, strong, powerful. We want democracy and justice and freedom." He paused, then added soberly: "We don't know yet if we are going to get them."

He endorsed the EZLN's rejection of government assistance. "We don't accept government aid, because we haven't won our struggle yet. Before we were Zapatistas, when we asked for help the government looked down on us and didn't give us anything. Now that we are in resistance, they want to help us, but even if we are living under a tree or in a cave, we will not take anything from the government."

— — —

After Acteal, when the Zedillo government began to dismantle the autonomous townships, Marcos became obsessed with the belief that the army was planning a full-scale attack to eliminate him and the Zapatista high command. "Recently it has become clearer that the government's strategy is to strike all around the Zapatista army and its leaders to isolate us, so that when they attack us no support or witnesses will be left," he said. Marcos warned of the possibility so often that he almost seemed to desire it.

Beginning in June 1998, after a shooting episode between Zapatista villagers and the army, and after Bishop Ruiz resigned as mediator in the peace talks, giving up on any hope of progress, Marcos dropped from view completely for many months. In November, Comandante Tacho and several other Indian commanders went to San Cristóbal for a weekend of meetings with the mediators in the peace negotiations to see if talks could be resumed. Marcos didn't go, but it was evident he was in close communication. The Zapatistas started off the session by accusing the mediators of racism because the rooms they had arranged for the *comandantes* lacked comfortable mattresses. The mediators, some of whom were longtime Zapatista supporters, were offended. The Zapatistas seemed to have lost their legendary populist touch.

Julia:
    The last time I saw Marcos was in La Realidad, in August 1999. It was clear that there would be no peace with Zedillo, and the Zapatistas were biding their time for the end of his term. Marcos convened a small group of Mexican followers to ruminate about the future of the EZLN. The Zapatista security guards for the event were surly. They enforced a new disposition that no journalist could be anywhere near Marcos while he was giving a speech. So they locked me and two dozen other reporters, most of them Mexicans, in a holding pen for the afternoon while Marcos addressed the gathering. When they finally let us out, we found Marcos

strolling around with an admiring entourage of foreigners behind him. He refused to speak to the press but was happy to have his picture taken with some Scandinavian groupies.

— — —

President Zedillo tried to defeat the Zapatistas by attrition. He carried out a new, selective round of agrarian reform in Chiapas, giving Indians who were not Zapatistas credit to buy small parcels of land of their choosing. The Zapatistas watched as a deluge of federal aid allowed other Indian communities in the state to thrive, reaping the benefits from the uprising they had fought. The long jungle exile of the *comandantes* and the persecution of their followers radicalized the Zapatistas, isolating them from the nation. Marcos and the EZLN continued to attract admirers in other parts of the country and the world. But because of intransigent leaders on both sides, their experiment with Indian self-determination in remote Chiapas was mostly lost to the rest of Mexico.

16

Democracy at Work

Mexico's Labor Day festivities on May 1, 1997, were emblematic of the state of affairs in the official trade-union movement.

Fidel Velázquez, the onetime milkman who had controlled the largest PRI labor confederation for half a century, lay dying. He was ninety-seven. Since the early 1990s he had been virtually blind and confined to a wheelchair, his speech often slurred into mumbling. He looked so cadaverous that at one point antigovernment posters, plastered on hundreds of Mexico City walls, featured a photo of Velázquez, his clouded eyes concealed behind his trademark tinted glasses. "This Is the Face of the System You Want to Change!" the poster said.

Don Fidel had been unfailingly loyal to ten successive PRI Presidents: suppressing labor dissidents, holding wage demands in check, and in recent decades even turning a blind eye to mass firings of thousands of members of his Confederación de Trabajadores Mexicanos, the Mexican Workers Confederation, known as the CTM. Following the 1994 currency crisis, as the devaluation wiped out worker savings and Don Fidel grew more decrepit, his passivity only deepened. He scorned calls for a general strike and signed agreements with the government prohibiting any wage increases that exceeded a benchmark set well below inflation—as he had every year since 1987.

Despite his feeble health, however, Velázquez remained keenly aware of the potential for violent protests. In 1995 and again in 1996 he canceled the traditional May Day labor parades through Mexico City. Instead, he marked each of those worker holidays by appearing alongside President Zedillo before audiences of handpicked union loyalists, safely assembled indoors and protected by police barricades.

In 1997 the CTM once again announced that the May 1 ceremonies would be held indoors, at the National Auditorium on the Paseo de la Reforma. This time, however, it became clear in advance that Velázquez was too feeble to make an appearance. For the first time in fifty-six years someone other than Don Fidel would have to preside over the PRI's official Labor Day festivities. Obviously, the CTM and the Congreso del Trabajo, the PRI-controlled umbrella group known as the Labor Congress that included several smaller federations as well as the CTM, needed rejuvenation. So PRI leaders picked a younger man to make the May Day speech: Leonardo Rodríguez Alcaine, the head of the electricians union. He was seventy-eight.

Thousands of petroleum workers, government bureaucrats, and other union members were bused to the auditorium on May 1 and paid a day's wages to sit through the speeches. Still, they showed little patience with Rodríguez Alcaine, a jowly man with dyed hair. From the moment he rose to the lectern, whistles and catcalls filled the air. "Shut up and let us sleep!" workers jeered.

President Zedillo watched in irritation as the heckling mounted, his jaw muscles working. Rodríguez Alcaine pressed onward with his speech. His hands trembled, and his face flushed. An insulting new chant swept the auditorium. "You belong at the Anthropology Institute!" workers yelled, referring to an institute associated with the museum where anthropologists studied ancient artifacts, which stood just across the Paseo de la Reforma. Finally Rodríguez Alcaine acknowledged the discontent. Drawing a deep breath, he looked up to face his hecklers. "I'm just about finished!" he blurted.

The workers, unsure as to whether Rodríguez Alcaine was referring to his speech or to his career, whistled even more raucously.

If Mexican labor came to the end of the twentieth century under the charge of enfeebled union bureaucrats like Rodríguez Alcaine, it had begun it with heroic developments that seemed to portend great strides for Mexican workers. Labor ferment was spreading rapidly when the revolution broke out in 1910, and radical workers, many inspired by the Wobblies in the United States, gave important support to the revolutionary armies that eventually triumphed.

At the 1917 constitutional convention in Querétaro, delegates enshrined much of labor's political agenda into the four-thousand-word Article 23 of the Constitution, focused on work issues and social welfare. Article 23 gave constitutional protection to the right to form unions and to strike, to earn a minimum wage and overtime pay, to work limited hours under safe conditions, even to share in corporate profits. Those provisions made the Mexican system seem more generous to labor, on paper at least, than the labor system in the United States.

The Federal Labor Law passed fourteen years later, however, gave the revolutionary state broad powers to control workers, through a federal office (the future Labor Secretariat) and through a national network of presidentially appointed labor boards, the Juntas de Conciliación y Arbitraje. A union could obtain the right to represent workers at a plant, for instance, only by persuading the local labor board to give it a *registro*, or license—not by winning workers' votes in a certification election. From the start the labor boards routinely refused to recognize unions that were out of favor with the party and the President. A union wishing to strike had to give six to ten days' advance notice, and the law empowered authorities to rule a walkout illegal if they considered it inconvenient.

In this way the system reduced organized labor to a string of officially sanctioned federations, with wide latitude to repress independent rivals. A pioneer was Luis N. Morones, a mechanic who during the 1920s forged the Confederación Regional Obrera Mexicana, known as the CROM. Morones believed that union leaders should exploit their ties to government, and his own career was an example. During the presidency of Plutarco Elías Calles, from 1924 to 1928, Morones simultaneously headed the CROM and served as Minister of Industry, Commerce, and Labor, using his cabinet post to increase his federation's membership and influence.

After Calles left office, Morones and his federation fell from favor. When he assumed the presidency in 1934, Lázaro Cárdenas called for the formation of a new national federation that could expand his government's political base and help press his social agenda, which included wage and other policies beneficial to workers. A convention of labor leaders responded to his request by founding the CTM. In 1938 Cárdenas reorganized the ruling party, formally incorporating the CTM into its structure and making the officially sanctioned labor movement one of four pillars that would sustain it. In later years an alphabet soup of smaller, mostly regional *oficialista* federations, including a now-humbled CROM, were absorbed into the PRI.

These federations eventually included millions of workers from across the economy, even families living at the edge of garbage dumps who gleaned an income from picking through trash. Velázquez himself, when a young man, had organized a union of milkmen, and his collaborators were mostly from low-skilled trades like dish washing, bricklaying, and street sweeping. Virtually everyone who scraped out a living on the street needed a government license, and these were withheld unless workers signed a union card. In this way the PRI organized everyone from lottery-ticket vendors to newspaper sellers, from mariachi musicians to shoe shiners, into *charro* unions, as they were called. It became difficult for a worker *not* to belong to one of the federations aligned with the government.

As the line between labor federation and governing party had disappeared, the boundary separating the CTM from the state itself blurred as well. Fidel Velázquez became secretary-general of the confederation in 1941 and maintained control until his death in 1997. The PRI guaranteed him or one of his closest subordinates a seat in the Mexican Senate for forty-eight years, from 1940 through 1988, nominating him and ensuring his election. (The equivalent in the United States would have been for George Meany, or an aide, to have served continuously in the Senate during his twenty-four-year presidency of the AFL-CIO, from 1955 to 1979.) The PRI reserved a dozen or more seats in every Congress for lesser leaders of the CTM and other PRI-affiliated federations. They were also allotted seats on each of the hundreds of municipal, state, and federal labor boards, along with the representatives of employers and the Labor Secretariat. With the labor boards empowered to rule on which unions were valid and which strikes legitimate, the PRI-affiliated officials sitting on the boards could legally suppress all rivals.

By the late 1940s the PRI labor system had taken shape. It was a domesticated union movement whose leaders enjoyed top posts within the PRI; a large, permanent presence within the Senate and Chamber of Deputies; and comfortable sinecures on the nationwide network of labor boards. The CTM and other *oficialista* federations, in turn, provided the government with political support, mobilizing workers by the tens of thousands to applaud for successive Presidents and PRI candidates at rallies. On Election Day the CTM and other PRI federations could deliver millions of voters and also mobilize precinct-level muscle for the official party, calling out union members to serve as poll watchers or PRI block captains and, in opposition areas, as goons to steal and destroy ballot boxes.

At the same time, the *charro* unions provided the government with a crucial means of control over Mexican workers, a system for co-opting idealistic young leaders and suppressing groups considered too left-wing or too independent by threatening them with the loss of their jobs.

Despite its subservience, the PRI-affiliated labor movement made a clear contribution to national progress during its first decades. Velázquez and other leaders used their influence vigorously with the broad aim of raising workers' living standards. They helped persuade PRI leaders to adopt in Mexico the development strategy common to most of Latin America, known as import substitution. The idea was to protect native producers and their employees from foreign competition in order to achieve rapid industrialization. The results were impressive for a time: the economy grew, wages rose, the government built thousands of schools and clinics accessible to workers, and Mexican businesses created millions of new urban jobs. The proportion of the population that was poorly fed, clothed, or housed dropped dramatically between 1940 and 1970.

The PRI favored labor only when doing so was convenient, however. In key industries at sensitive moments, successive PRI Presidents did not hesitate to use police or army troops to crush strikes and imprison independent leaders. Through the decades the lack of accountability within the official unions encouraged corruption and racketeering. As the decades passed, Velázquez and other aging PRI labor chieftains gave up all but the rhetorical efforts to seek betterment for the rank and file, instead using their failing energies to maintain their own power and privileges. They fought as fiercely as any within the PRI establishment to beat back ordinary Mexicans' democratic aspirations.

Arturo Alcalde knew the underbelly of the labor system as well as anyone. By the mid-1990s he had worked for twenty-five years as a lawyer for
underpaid workers and tiny dissident unions. Workers who came to Alcalde seeking help in forming an independent union were often surprised to learn that their workplace was already represented by a legally
constituted union, run by PRI officials or mere racketeers, who had
signed sweetheart contracts with management but whose identities and
addresses were kept secret under the terms of Mexican law. As a result,
much of the daily work of labor organizing centered on helping workers
break free from such parasitic unions and obtain recognition for another
of their choosing, a process known as decertification.

But the laws included onerous rules that helped the *oficialista* unions
withstand challenge. In decertification elections, for instance, authorities were allowed to force workers to cast their votes not by secret ballot
but orally, in full view of management and the established union leaders.
Employers were required to dismiss any worker who lost his or her union

Fidel Velázquez dominated Mexico's main workers' confederation for fifty-six
years, until his death in 1997

membership. Using this provision, incumbent labor leaders facing demands for more effective workplace representation could simply strip their challengers of union membership and the dissidents would lose their jobs.

Over the years this tactic had been used repeatedly against would-be union reformers, not only in tiny sweatshops but even in Mexico's largest, most modern plants. In 1985, for instance, after a CTM executive committee at a General Motors engine plant in northern Coahuila state made wage demands that management considered excessive, higher-ranking CTM leaders, in collusion with GM management, stripped the local leaders of their union membership, giving the company legal justification to fire them en masse.

In the fall of 1997, just ten weeks after opposition political parties had won control of the Congress in the midterm elections, Alcalde witnessed how the advance of electoral democracy had done little to change workplace life. Workers at a plant outside Mexico City were hoping that a new union could help them obtain better safety conditions. The factory, which produced disc brakes for trucks, was owned by ITAPSA, a Mexican affiliate of the Echlin Corporation of Connecticut. The workers knew they were already represented by the CTM, but its leaders had done nothing to respond to their complaints that they were routinely exposed to asbestos without adequate protective equipment. They sought to affiliate with the FAT.

Filing legal documents, Alcalde persuaded the local labor board to schedule an election to allow workers at the plant to choose between the CTM and the FAT. As the vote approached, management fired more than twenty workers suspected of opposing the official union, and carried out a campaign of threats and intimidation against others. When Alcalde arrived at the plant on September 9, 1997, the morning of the election, he found that CTM leaders and management, with the collaboration of local police, had bused to the plant nearly two hundred goons, armed with clubs and a few firearms. As Alcalde and two FAT colleagues walked through the factory gate for the vote, they were filmed by company cameramen and surrounded by thugs shouting threats and insults. Amid the din, Alcalde sought out the government labor board officials administering the vote to protest the unfair conditions. The officials ignored his complaints.

To cast their ballots, workers testified that they were forced to walk the same gantlet of screaming thugs, stand in a small room in a circle of CTM officials, and state their union preference out loud to a labor board official. It was such an intimidating experience that several workers wept. When one man plucked up his courage to vote for the FAT, the thugs shouted, "Who was that? Take down his name!" Not surprisingly, most of the plant's workers voted for the CTM. Four months later CTM goons physically attacked five ITAPSA workers who were distributing leaflets describing the rigged election, beating them senseless.

Presidents Plutarco Elías Calles and Lázaro Cárdenas wrote the rules of the labor system to ensure *oficialista* control over workers. But for most of the twentieth century there was a trade-off: if dissidents could be repressed, at least the nation's development strategy viewed workers not only as producers but also as consumers of Mexican-made goods. With the near collapse of the economy during the 1980s, however, Mexico adopted a new strategy, based on attracting international investment to increase production of export goods designed for *foreign* consumers, an approach that gained strength with the implementation of NAFTA in 1994. With that shift came an essential change in official labor policy: thereafter the central idea was not to increase workers' purchasing power but to keep wages competitive with cheap labor elsewhere in the world.

The new economic system encouraged the industrialization of remote areas of Mexico, especially across the north, where the PRI-dominated labor movement made little attempt to unionize workplaces. Most politicians of all parties, even the PAN leaders who eventually governed in the border states of Baja California and Chihuahua, ignored the government's previous commitment to a broad improvement in living standards.

Much of the foreign investment flowed into industrial parks hugging the border with the United States, financing construction of thousands of new assembly plants known as maquiladoras. One border town transformed by maquiladora production was Ciudad Acuña in Coahuila state, across the Rio Grande from Del Rio, Texas. For most of the twentieth century, Acuña had been a sleepy river settlement of just a few thousand residents. The backbone of the local economy was the taverns and whorehouses that catered to American airmen from the Laughlin Air Force Base near Del Rio.

One family had run Acuña and its border backlands like a private ranch for decades. The patriarch, Jesús María Ramón Cantú, served three times as Acuña's PRI mayor, between stints in the Mexican Senate and Chamber of Deputies, and his sons remembered his heroic drinking bouts with Lyndon Baines Johnson, who occasionally visited Acuña. As Ramón Cantú accumulated regional power, his family acquired vast swaths of ranchland along the Rio Grande. In the early 1970s, when the Acuña population had grown to forty thousand, the federal government began offering tax-exempt status to companies building assembly plants along the border. Ramón Cantú's oldest son, Jesús María Ramón Valdés, began to bulldoze the family's sagebrush tracts into industrial parks and to woo foreign corporations to lease them.

Alcoa, the Pittsburgh-based aluminum-products conglomerate, was one company that accepted the invitation. In 1982, when Alcoa built its first factory in Acuña, it was producing automotive wiring systems at two plants in Mississippi, but its Asian competitors were beginning to produce wiring components more cheaply. The company discovered that its executives could live in Del Rio and manage plants in Acuña. That coupled the advantages of cheap foreign production with the convenience of Texas golf courses, schools, and unpolluted drinking water. Alcoa shut down its auto-parts operations in Mississippi and built eight factories in Acuña during the 1980s and 1990s. It eventually became Acuña's largest employer. Subsidiaries of many other U.S.-based corporations, including General Electric and Allied Signal, also built factories.

Inside the plants, as in other maquiladora centers the length of the border, working conditions varied. Some were well organized, clean, and efficient. Others were chaotic sweatshops. But in almost all of them, wages were set at a subsistence level that forced workers to live in squalor.

Construction of the new plants set off a mass migration as thousands of dirt farmers and out-of-work laborers streamed in from all over Mexico. Many built shelters on vacant land. Hundreds of squatters even seized a railroad siding, building shanties on the tracks. By 2000 the town's population had quadrupled to 150,000 and was growing faster than any other city in northern Mexico. It was a squalid grid of dirt streets and rotting garbage.

Sam:

I first visited Acuña after Javier Villarreal Lozano, a Coahuila historian based in the state capital, cited the city as an example of how U.S.-based corporations were exploiting their Mexican workers. "Acuña is a disgrace," Villarreal told me. "A hundred years ago U.S. employers would have been ashamed of these conditions. Henry Ford's workers living in cardboard boxes? He'd never have tolerated it."

On my first day in Acuña a local environmental engineer told me that because the city had not built sufficient sewage lines for the exploding population, half of Acuña's residents were defecating in backyard latrines.

I arranged an interview with Jesús María Ramón Valdés, the industrial-park developer, and he flew back to Acuña from farther south in Mexico in his private plane. He treated me with courtesy, offering to show me around Acuña. As we drove through one of the shantytowns, the stench of the latrines wafted into his pickup truck. He noticed my grimace. "We have an odor problem that is very serious," he said.

Ramón Valdés had followed in his father's footsteps. He had been elected as the PRI mayor of Acuña in the early 1980s. He was proud of his role in attracting some sixty maquiladoras to the city, adding to the fortune he and his family had built as the local beneficiaries of PRI power. He was equally proud that he had worked from the start to keep out all unions, even PRI unions. "The American companies said they didn't want any unions, so I've always managed the situation so that there are zero unions here," he said.

How had he managed that? I asked.

"We made a leader of the CTM a partner in our first industrial park," he said. "And then we gave them the concessions for Acuña's bus lines. And since then nobody—nobody—has had unions in Acuña."

On another day I drove into a shantytown a mile south of the Alcoa plants. I parked my car and set out walking through Acuña's sweltering summer heat. At the top of one dirt outcropping I found the rusting carcass of a school bus up on blocks, which seemed to be somebody's residence. I knocked on the bus's metal door, and Óscar Chávez Díaz, an Alcoa worker, invited me in to see the home he shared with his wife, Nelba.

He kept his clothes in a pile where the driver's seat had been, and he had installed a tiny stove and refrigerator beyond the bed, near the rear emergency door. He had strapped an air conditioner to a side window, but the bus still felt like an oven. Chávez said he bathed standing on his bus's front steps, ladling water from a bucket.

I asked how much he earned, and he laid out his pay stubs on a table. They showed that his Alcoa take-home pay was sixty dollars for a forty-eight-hour week. He said he spent about eleven dollars a week for bottled drinking water. About five dollars went to rent the bus, twenty dollars for electricity, and ten dollars for buses and taxis. (He had no car.) There was little left for food or clothing. Nelba, who worked in another Acuña plant stitching leather seats for Chevrolet Corvettes, earned about the same as Óscar. She was spending about forty dollars a week on groceries.

Mulling the harsh arithmetic of their lives, I returned to my hotel room at a Ramada Inn full of traveling American plant managers on the Del Rio side of the border. I called to give the figures to Dr. Ruth Rosenbaum, a social economist based in Hartford, Connecticut, who was collecting data on food and other prices in eleven Mexican border cities for a study of the purchasing power of Mexican workers. After some calculations she called back.

Óscar, she said, had to work nearly a week just to outfit his six-year-old son, Raúl, for school. He worked sixteen hours to earn enough to buy the cheapest sneakers available in Acuña; twelve hours for a book bag; nine hours for a pair of boy's pants; three hours for a little white shirt. It took four hours of Óscar's work to buy notebooks and pencils.

As it turned out, the PRI mayor of Acuña at the time of my visit was Eduardo Ramón Valdés, the brother of the industrial-park developer. When he came over to the Ramada Inn for an interview, I learned that the town was nearly as broke as its citizens. Acuña's budget for 2000 was $9 million, which meant the city could spend just $60 on each resident. In contrast, the budget of Del Rio, population forty-five thousand, was

$32 million, allowing for a per capita expenditure of $777, thirteen times as high.

The mayor acknowledged that his government could not remotely address Acuña's needs. At the Acuña fire department the fire trucks were broken down, so the Del Rio fire department routinely sent its fire trucks across the bridge into Acuña, sirens wailing, to extinguish fires. Acuña's sixty-year-old, forty-five-bed hospital, a facility run by the federal social security system, the basic health service for most factory workers, was crumbling and overwhelmed. The mayor said that one of his most difficult tasks was fielding anguished calls from the Acuña schools. "Every week I get some new plea from our teachers," he said. "They need windows, toilets, drinking water. They want desks. They want a flag. It's an endless list."

The municipal government's dilemma was that with Acuña's workers earning such miserable wages, there was no point in trying to tax them. If Acuña had been an American town, its sixty factories would have generated millions of dollars in annual property-tax revenues to support local schools, streets, and police. But the maquiladora tax system was allowing U.S. parent companies to pay next to nothing to their host communities. Alcoa, for instance, was operating eight manufacturing plants in Acuña, a sprawling industrial enterprise. Yet Alcoa was paying no income, property, asset, import, export, sales, or value-added taxes. The other foreign corporations in Acuña enjoyed the same tax advantages.

—   —   —

The PRI unions had nothing to say about squalid conditions of work and life at the border. Their silence was a new thing. During the postwar years of rapid industrialization, Fidel Velázquez and the other PRI labor leaders, even while politically subordinate to the President, had often worked to bring government-funded street paving, sewage lines, and school construction to working-class districts. But during the 1980s and 1990s, as maquiladora construction was booming across northern Mexico, the PRI unions fell silent about the miserable conditions in the border towns.

In a few places independent unions sought to organize the maquiladoras. In Tijuana, workers at the Korean-owned Han Young truck-chassis plant fought for recognition of their local, affiliated with the FAT.

They fought yet another conflict with enforcers from a PRI-affiliated union that had signed a secret contract with Han Young.

In Acuña the group working hardest to challenge the status quo was not a union but the Comité Fronterizo de Obreras, the Border Workers Committee, led by Julia Quiñonez, a young working mother with a mane of dark hair and tireless energy for organizing. When a teenager, Quiñonez had worked in several Coahuila maquiladoras, eventually quitting to study for a public-health degree at a local university. Quiñonez and her colleagues were suspicious of the corruption and cronyism of the official labor movement and made no effort to gain legal union recognition for the workers who joined the committee. Instead, Quiñonez visited workers in their homes in the slums of Acuña and other border settlements, inviting them to learn their legal rights and to demand fair treatment from their employers.

By the mid-1990s she had organized scores of Acuña workers into weekly home-study groups. Workers would sit in a circle, reading Mexican labor laws aloud to each other, almost in the fashion of a Bible study group, and discussing ways of bettering conditions in and around the factories. With the backing of two American church groups that were owners of small amounts of Alcoa stock, Quiñonez and Juan Tovar, a thirty-year-old Alcoa worker, traveled in 1996 to Pittsburgh to attend the corporation's annual meeting.

Addressing Alcoa shareholders from a convention floor microphone—exercising shareholders' rights—Tovar embarrassed Alcoa's top executives simply by describing conditions in the Acuña plants. He reported that Alcoa managers had stationed janitors at the doors of factory bathrooms to limit workers to just three pieces of toilet paper. He recounted an incident in which more than one hundred Alcoa workers had been overcome by fumes and taken to hospitals.

Presiding over the Pittsburgh convention was Alcoa's chief executive, a well-regarded American business leader named Paul O'Neill, whom, five years later, President George W. Bush would name his Treasury Secretary. "Our plants in Mexico are so clean they can eat off the floor," O'Neill insisted to the assembled stockholders.

"That's a lie," Tovar shot back. He produced news clippings that documented his assertions.

O'Neill later acknowledged that many of Tovar's complaints were valid. He ordered a cleanup at the plants and a wage increase, from twenty-five dollars per week for the average worker to thirty dollars.

The Border Workers Committee, an upstart group of grassroots democrats, had won at least temporary improvement in workers' conditions, but there were few such worker victories to celebrate anywhere in Mexico during the final years of the century.

Under Presidents de la Madrid, Salinas, and Zedillo, the PRI federations acquiesced in the systematic suppression of wages, forcing workers to shoulder a disproportionate share of the costs of economic modernization. In 1980 the average hourly compensation of a Mexican manufacturing worker was 22 percent of the earnings of a comparable American worker. Sixteen years later, in 1996, the average Mexican worker's compensation had dropped to just 8 percent of the U.S. rate. The average hourly wage of an American production worker was $17.74, while Mexican workers earned $1.50.

Each year for a decade after 1987, Fidel Velázquez and other leaders of the PRI labor movement joined with government and business leaders in signing what was known as the *pacto*, a formal annual agreement that made the deterioration of workers' wages official. The PRI-affiliated labor leaders helped the government to minimize worker protests but paid a tremendous price in credibility.

When Velázquez died on June 21, 1997, the only workers to attend his wake in the echoing headquarters of the CTM in Mexico City were a few dozen autoworkers—all paid by the confederation to be there. Some labor analysts predicted that independent unions more in tune with the country's democratic mood might soon overwhelm the CTM. Instead, Leonardo Rodríguez Alcaine took the reins of a *charro* federation that was a bit like himself: enfeebled but not in collapse. The CTM remained Mexico's largest labor grouping, with official collective-bargaining rights to several million workers in tens of thousands of union locals.

Some Mexicans dreaming of reform pinned their hopes on the Unión Nacional de Trabajadores, the National Workers Union, known as the UNT. Its leader was Francisco Hernández Juárez, a shrewd labor politician formed in the CTM who had once been a protégé of Don Fidel's. The career of Hernández Juárez, the leader of the telephone workers union, prospered after he negotiated a deal during the Salinas administration to cooperate with the 1990 sale of Teléfonos de México, or Telmex, into private hands. But later in the 1990s he chose a rebellious path, gathering around him an array of independent union leaders. In late 1997, months after Velázquez's death, Hernández Juárez led 160 federations and unions in forming the UNT as a reform alternative to the PRI-affiliated movement. A number of important unions that had previously been with the PRI switched to join the new federation, including Hernández Juárez's *telefonistas* and the unions representing workers at social security hospitals and at the UNAM.

At first it appeared that the Sindicato Nacional de Trabajadores de la Educación, the national teachers federation, which was the largest union in Latin America and had helped the PRI win many an election, would also join the UNT. Its leader, Elba Esther Gordillo, met many times during 1997 with the leaders organizing the new federation, but finally her SNTE did not join it.

Still, she led the teachers union down the road of pluralism. Gordillo did not look like a fighter, with her face set in a perpetual smile after multiple face-lifts and capped by meticulously coiffed strawberry bouffant hair. But she was one of Mexico's shrewdest politicians, a consummate pragmatist, and she sensed the shifting political winds. A modernizing union with a vast and increasingly cosmopolitan rank and file could no longer confine its membership to one political party, she realized, and although she remained a PRI leader herself, she sensed that the teachers federation was no longer drawing strength from its links with the official party. She cut its formal tie to the PRI and advised her members that they could decide their political loyalties on a personal basis.

During the late 1990s upstart labor organizations that were anything but reformist were also making claims on worker loyalties. Many employers who in previous decades had signed collective-bargaining agreements with CTM leaders, hoping to retain good relations with the PRI, began to cut deals with federations of a new kind that were willing to negotiate sweetheart contracts, guarantee labor peace, and keep their businesses out of politics entirely.

The leaders of these federations were often attorneys acting as labor entrepreneurs. They provided employers with what were known as protection contracts, agreements favorable to management that shielded businesses from unionization by anyone else. One organization that expanded rapidly during the Salinas and Zedillo presidencies, for example, was the Federación Sindical Coordinadora Nacional de Trabajadores, a federation with such a low profile that few Mexicans had even heard of it. Its founder and secretary-general was Ramón Gámez Martínez, a wealthy, globe-trotting attorney whose passions included collecting antique Chinese furniture and African folk art.

His organization represented the more than ten thousand workers at all of Mexico's McDonald's restaurants, the employees at most of the country's thousands of movie theaters, and workers at most of the foreign airlines landing in Mexico, including United, Northwest, Air Canada, Air France, KLM, British Airways, and Aeroflot. In all, Gámez was administering more than two thousand protection contracts, with legal rights to bargain for 350,000 workers in businesses scattered throughout all thirty-two Mexican states. He was overseeing one of the country's most extensive labor empires, yet few of the workers he represented knew who he was, since the contracts were kept secret by the government.

Gámez was only one of many apolitical and cunning opportunists who were building union fiefdoms as the PRI federations declined.

In the late 1990s Mexico's main *oficialista* federations were thoroughly discredited, ruled by ailing octogenarians, and under challenge from rivals of all stripes. The PRI was no longer drawing strength from a labor movement that had previously been one of its main pillars.

17

Campaign for Change

In the last years of the millennium myriad events, large and small, were signaling the end of an epoch. The great men of twentieth-century Mexico and its one-party system were dying. Emilio Azcárraga Milmo, the broadcasting baron who pioneered Latin America's largest media empire, the PRI loyalist who called himself a "soldier of the President," died in in 1997. Months later, Mexicans marked the passing of Fidel Velázquez, the labor titan who served ten Presidents—one of the few men to influence the workings of the system even more than Azcárraga. The following year brought the death of Octavio Paz, the poet who had alternately scorned and courted the PRI, his "philanthropic ogre."

Patterns of everyday life were changing. Businessmen were forgoing their traditional three-hour tequila lunch, and the Veracruz cigar and game of dominoes that often followed it. Now young executives were gobbling a sandwich at their desks and washing it down with a diet Coke. The bittersweet November 2 Day of the Dead celebrations—when Mexicans traditionally stream into cemeteries with baskets of food for graveside picnics with the spirits of their departed—were giving way to the trick-or-treat processions of Halloween.

Many young men preferred soccer to bullfighting, and animal rights groups protested regularly outside the bullrings. The broad-brimmed sombrero had given way among rural men to the Stetson and, on construction sites, to the baseball cap. In a few ballrooms older couples still reveled in the graceful steps of the *danzón*, a Cuban beat that dominated Mexican dance halls at mid-century, but in the 1990s most couples were moving their hips to the racier *cumbia* and the merengue.

Only a third of Mexicans had landline telephones, because Telmex had been slow to make domestic service accessible in rural areas at affordable prices. Yet during the 1990s private telecommunications companies spent several billion dollars to lay fiber-optic lines around Mexico and erect cellular-phone antennas. As a result, upscale restaurants became a cacophony of beeping and buzzing, and the Periférico was jammed with BMWs driven by wealthy Mexicans with cellular phones pressed to their ears.

Mexico outgrew its reputation as an industrial backwater. Mexico had its own multinationals, like Cemex, the cement producer headquartered in Monterrey, which expanded operations to twenty-three foreign countries and was admired for its world-class efficiency. Mexican corporations made high-powered bioengineered seeds for agriculture, and the country's foreign-owned automobile- and computer-assembly plants were among the world's most efficient and technologically advanced manufacturing facilities.

Change was in the air—even in the air. Since the 1960s the people of Mexico City had been choking in smog, and in 1992 the United Nations had declared the city's air to be the worst in the world. But no-lead gas, catalytic converters, and legally mandated environmental testing for cars were slowly improving the atmosphere. On good days, residents could even look east and see the Popocatépetl and Iztaccíhuatl volcanoes; hidden for decades behind a dirty yellow haze, their magnificent snow-capped peaks now gleamed on occasion on the horizon.

Mexico was changing because Mexicans were changing. When the authoritarian system was founded in 1929, the population was just 16 million. During the four decades of development that followed, the population tripled, to 48 million in 1970. Then widespread use of birth control led to a plunge in the fertility rate. In 1965 women had seven children on average; by the 1990s only three. With smaller families to care for, Mexicans spent more of their money on their children's education, and women worked or spent more time outside the home. Life expectancy rose from sixty-one to seventy years for men and from sixty-five to seventy-five for women. The infant-mortality rate dropped from thirty-one to twenty-two deaths per one thousand live births in just seven years during the 1990s, despite the economic crisis. During the same years university enrollment jumped by 42 percent.

Even with slowing growth rates the population continued to increase, and the number of Mexicans more than doubled between 1970 and the end of the century, from 48 million to 97 million. The population of the Mexico City metropolitan area, which included the Federal District and thirty-eight suburbs that stretched into the neighboring states Hidalgo and México, reached 17 million in 1995. The farm-to-city migration that had been a major feature of Mexican life for sixty years continued. Now, however, rural Mexicans were no longer settling in the Federal District, where there was no more room for them. Instead, they went to once-sleepy villages many miles from the Mexico City center. Demographers projected that during the first decades of the twenty-first century, the megalopolis would extend out to a hundred-mile radius around the city center, encompassing some 50 million people.

Uprooted by the economic crises of the 1980s and 1990s, Mexicans were also migrating along new routes. Dirt farmers streamed north from states like Veracruz and Durango to the industrial parks proliferating across the northern border. Oaxacans left Indian villages to travel each year to harvest chilies in Sinaloa and Sonora. Out-of-work laborers from Chiapas and Guerrero gravitated to new beachfront developments near Cancún and Los Cabos. A strip of prosperous central states like Querétaro and Aguascalientes attracted hundreds of industries and thousands of new workers from elsewhere in Mexico.

In Mexico City and many regional capitals—like Monterrey, Querétaro, and Aguascalientes—urban squalor blended with stylish professional enclaves. New university graduates managed architectural firms, Internet-access companies, automobile dealerships, video-rental clubs, and medical centers. Many young Mexicans had traveled abroad, to Chicago, Montreal, Madrid. They had not grown up regarding the United States as Mexico's eternal enemy. On the contrary, they listened to B. B. King and Tupac Shakur on the radio and were in love with Julia Roberts's smile.

So powerful was the sense of impending transformation that even many capitalists who had built fortunes in the shadow of the PRI system began to acknowledge in private that it would not be such a bad thing for the PRI to lose the presidency. No one followed this shift more closely than Lino Korrodi, Vicente Fox's fund-raiser.

A close friend of Fox's since the Coca-Cola days, Korrodi had worked on Fox's two gubernatorial campaigns in Guanajuato. During the first, in 1991, begging money for an opposition candidate had been a sobering experience. A few of the men heading the country's twelve Coca-Cola bottling companies—buddies to both Fox and Korrodi—had secretly helped out. But those were the glamour years of the Salinas presidency, and no other entrepreneurs even returned Korrodi's calls, not even the shoemakers and vegetable packers from Guanajuato who knew Fox and his family well. "There was total rejection," Korrodi recalled.

During Fox's 1995 campaign a few businessmen were more receptive; Salinas had by then fallen into disgrace, and a few daring capitalists were so outraged about the peso crisis that they agreed to meet with Fox.

But the real sea change came after Fox declared his presidential candidacy in July 1997. Korrodi found to his surprise that now many big businessmen not only returned his calls but openly voiced discontent with the PRI. They complained of debts that had piled up during the 1995–96 financial crisis. They wanted their contacts with Fox and Korrodi kept secret, and many said that in public at least they would continue to support the PRI. But for the first time Mexico's wealthiest men made important donations to an opposition presidential candidate. It was a tectonic shift in the relationship between the entrepreneurial class and the ruling party.

"The peso crisis was a watershed," Korrodi recalled later. "The government had lost all credibility, and the *empresarios* [the businessmen] began to see that the system wasn't going to be able to sustain itself anymore."

Mexico's wealthiest men now wanted to meet Fox. The backgrounds of some of Fox's new business backers made their support understandable: Manuel Espinosa Yglesias, for instance, had been the president of the Banco de Comercio until López Portillo's 1982 nationalization, and he was still angry with the PRI. Alfonso Romo Garza, an industrialist of middle-class origins, had accumulated a $2 billion fortune in biotechnology and other industries, but he remained a bit of an outsider to the Mexican aristocracy.

Other industrial barons who now donated to Fox were young men whose forebears had never dared to finance the opposition, but had themselves come of age during the 1980s and 1990s, when it was no longer inconceivable that an opposition party might someday govern.

But the willingness of some plutocrats to back Fox was a great surprise, because only a few years earlier they had unabashedly sought to ingratiate themselves with the PRI. The memory was still strong of a 1993 PRI fund-raising banquet. Roberto Hernández, the billionaire president of Banamex, organized a private dinner that included President Salinas and Carlos Slim, who became Mexico's richest man after the government sold him Telmex in Salinas's 1990 privatization; Emilio Azcárraga Milmo of Televisa; Lorenzo Zambrano of Cemex; and about twenty-five other tycoons. Salinas and his aides told the billionaires that the party needed a campaign fund of at least $500 million. There was some good-natured grousing, but the group eventually accepted the goal of raising an average of $25 million apiece. The banquet became a storied example of the billionaires' gratitude to the PRI for favors received, and of their dread of an opposition victory.

Now, during 1997 and 1998, as Fox's presidential campaign picked up speed, Korrodi found that many of the men who attended the 1993 PRI banquet were agreeing to write checks to the Fox campaign: One was Roberto Hernández. Others included Lorenzo Zambrano and Carlos Slim.

Virtually all the magnates making contributions to Fox made it clear to Korrodi that they wanted them and their meetings with the candidate kept secret. Moreover, their decision to support Fox by no means meant that they were not writing checks to the PRI as well. Korrodi was certain that most of them were hedging their bets, backing Fox *and* the old system. Still, their financial support for Fox shattered the PRI's long monopoly on effective campaigning.

Why were the plutocrats willing to back Fox, when no one from their class had given serious money to an opposition presidential candidate for half a century?

Korrodi sensed that many industrialists, like millions of citizens, felt it was time to build a new system. In a 1998 booklet, *La transición mexi-*

cana (The Mexican transition), the country's largest private-sector lobby-ing group said this explicitly. "Mexico is living a transition," it declared. "We're passing from an old system to a new system. The transition exists. It's a fact. It affects us directly. Therefore, we can participate in the de-sign of what is coming."

Still, businessmen had reservations. How to keep the change moder-ate? Fox, with his Coca-Cola background, seemed like the candidate who might be able to ease the PRI from Los Pinos without stirring up a social revolution. But once in office would he want to excavate the secrets of Mexico's recent history? Was Fox a vindictive man who might punish businessmen who had made millions in cozy dealings with the PRI state?

The business class needed reassurances, and Fox provided them with the posture he adopted during the 1998 debate over the banking bailout. Andrés Manuel López Obrador and the PRD had demanded a broad in-vestigation aimed at forcing wealthy beneficiaries of the bailout to as-sume their debts. After infiltrating the bailout agency's records, López Obrador had released a list of thousands of names of debtors whose loans had ended up in the bailout. Even some PAN leaders were calling for the PRI to accept punishment for officials who had mishandled the bailout and for businessmen who had benefited from illegal loans.

With the confrontation polarizing the country along class lines, Fox stepped into the debate. He said he was appalled that López Obrador had publicized the names of people who had been unable to pay their loans, among them struggling shoe manufacturers and ranchers from his own state. Fox said he knew their plight; unpayable loans had almost sunk his own family's vegetable-packing plant. In a television commer-cial broadcast repeatedly by the PAN in December 1998, Fox urged a "responsible solution" to the bailout, and in press interviews was careful to signal to the business class that it had nothing to fear from a Fox pres-idency. With Fox's urging PAN lawmakers voted with the PRI to approve the final bailout law.

"We're going to be strict in enforcing the law, and we won't permit a single new dishonest act," Fox told the *Times* in that period. "But every democratic transition requires that a country look to the future. We're not going to waste time and energy pursuing vengeance for the corrup-tion of the past in some endless witch-hunt."

After that, wealthy donors began clamoring to meet Fox, prompting Korrodi to determine that unless they could guarantee that their meeting with him would generate at least 3 million pesos in donations (about $300,000), he would tell them Fox was too busy.

As Ernesto Zedillo began to focus on the presidential succession, he was concerned that the PRI had lost touch with the times. The party had helped him to approve the 1996 electoral reform, which gave Mexico one of the world's most advanced balloting systems. Yet the party's own election practices had not kept pace. Few of its leaders were young people, even though half of the registered voters were thirty-five years of age or younger. The clearest path to change, Zedillo argued, was for the party's candidate to be nominated in a legitimately democratic process. "Let's do primaries," Zedillo told his aides one day midway through his term, and in the following months he said the same thing in speeches and interviews.

The suggestion seemed so brash that at first hardly anyone took him at his word. The President was proposing to give up his unwritten right to exercise the *dedazo*—his most important means of power. Yet he doggedly pursued his plan, organizing a nationwide primary election.

His goal was to help the party hold on to the presidency by making it more competitive, but the plan involved considerable risk. The PRI was roiled with internecine jealousies; if Zedillo was proposing an open competition among rival presidential aspirants, how would he prevent the party from tearing itself apart?

He delegated to his aides the ticklish challenge of designing the primary. In 1998 and early 1999 Liébano Sáenz, Ulises Beltrán, the University of Chicago–trained historian who was the presidential pollster, and others discussed arcane topics like the role of New Hampshire in U.S. primaries and the theoretical defects of the Iowa caucus.

Sáenz carried out an experiment in Chihuahua, his native state, where a new governor was to be elected. The PRI wanted badly to win there, partly because of the state's symbolism: the incumbent governor was Francisco Barrio, the businessman turned PAN politician who had been defeated through fraud in 1986 but had won election on his second try in 1992. Barrio had governed ably and was leaving office in good favor with voters. The Chihuahua PRI machine, in contrast, was led by Artemio Iglesias, an *alquimista* from the old guard who was nicknamed Hereford, "after the cow," as one correspondent wrote.

Iglesias appeared to have the nomination locked up. But Sáenz secretly intervened, twisting arms in the name of the President, and the Chihuahua PRI suddenly announced that it would select its candidate in a gubernatorial primary open not just to the party faithful but to all registered voters. The experiment was a smashing success. Nearly a quarter of a million curious Chihuahuans cast ballots; that was about 25 percent of the total voters in the 1997 federal congressional elections in Chihuahua, which the PRI considered a great turnout for a party primary. The voters shunned Iglesias for Patricio Martínez, a real-estate executive who had been a mayor of the state capital. Most important, the Chihuahua PRI remained united, despite rancor within the Iglesias camp, and in July 1998 Martínez upset the PAN in the general elections.

In other states similar exercises in party democracy provoked infighting. In Guerrero warring PRI factions disputed a party election with gunfire. But the Chihuahua success overshadowed the failures. Beltrán drafted a detailed blueprint for a nationwide primary in which all registered voters, not just PRI members, would be eligible to participate.

Eventually four politicians competed to be the PRI's presidential nominee. Humberto Roque, a former congressman, ran with the encouragement of the presidential staff, but his candidacy attracted almost no support. Manuel Bartlett, who had just left office as the governor of Puebla, was taken more seriously until the first polls showed that he, too, was arousing little public enthusiasm. Thereafter most Mexicans viewed his candidacy with a certain irony: the stone-fisted autocrat who as de la Madrid's Government Secretary had presided over the fraudulent 1988 presidential election was now complaining that the process was insufficiently democratic.

The race came down to Francisco Labastida, who stepped down as Zedillo's Government Secretary to contend in the primary, and Roberto Madrazo, whom Zedillo had unsuccessfully sought to prevent from taking office as Tabasco governor in 1995.

Madrazo's term as governor had been a stylish display of his tropical demagogy. He built some roads and bridges and badgered Pemex into spending more of its oil revenues on local development. But despite his promises to carry on his father's legacy by implementing democratic reforms, he ran his party and his state "like a cattle ranch," as Raúl Ojeda, then a PRI congressman, described it. Madrazo allowed the Tabasco PRI to elect its state leader, but when his candidate was defeated in the vote, he drove the victor out of the party. A young executive whom Madrazo appointed to head the state's investment board also resigned, complaining of the kickbacks he said were demanded by the governor and his aides.

Nonetheless, Madrazo positioned himself shrewdly for a presidential run. During his final months in office he spent some $25 million of Tabasco state funds on a series of television commercials, broadcast nationwide, that were supposed to boost the state's image but mainly boosted Madrazo's. They made him a celebrity, and by the time the primary campaign got under way, he had shot to the top of the polls.

But Labastida had PRI advantages that not even Zedillo could smother. In the *dedazo* ritual, party leaders would rush, in the hours after the announcement of the President's choice, to congratulate the new candidate and future ruler, a display of loyalty known as *la cargada*, the charge. Once Zedillo had abolished the *dedazo*, there was supposed to be no more *cargada*.

Zedillo never offered any clear hint that he favored Labastida. But Labastida was the only member of Zedillo's cabinet to run, and millions of PRI members inferred as a result that he was *el bueno*, the President's favorite, and rushed to demonstrate their allegiance to him. On the afternoon in May 1999 when Labastida announced his candidacy at the Fiesta Americana Reforma Hotel in Mexico City, hundreds of government employees mobbed him, seeking desperately to touch him, all on the presumption that he would soon be President.

Madrazo tried to turn this anachronistic *cargada* to his own advantage. He styled himself as an insurgent and taunted Labastida as the *candidato oficial*. He lambasted the President's tight-money economic policies, which were popular in business circles but not in the streets.

Madrazo's loyalty was tested in the last weeks of the campaign as the party machine targeted him with dirty electoral tricks. PRI chieftains in one town blocked the main road, forcing Madrazo's supporters to get off the buses and walk a mile into the town to hear his speech. One senior Labastida aide, Emilio Gamboa, engineered the firing of a radio talk-show host in Sinaloa state after he broadcast an interview with Madrazo. The PRI governor of Chiapas, Roberto Albores, ordered his party's legislators to work against Madrazo. "Don't be assholes!" Albores shouted. "We have to guarantee a victory for Labastida!"

On November 7, 1999, the day of the vote, party operatives, as usual, stuffed ballots and monkeyed with the tally. In a town in Puebla someone snapped a photograph of a PRI thug brandishing a pistol at onlookers as his cohorts absconded from a polling station carrying ballot boxes.

Labastida won the primary in a landslide. Madrazo seemed to flirt with defecting from the PRI, but Zedillo headed him off. Early in the campaign the President sent a message to Carlos Hank González, the former Mexico City mayor who was Madrazo's political godfather. "I'm not going to worry about Roberto, because I know you'll make sure he doesn't leave," Zedillo told Hank. "Close ranks! You get the gold medal if he stays."

The 1999 primary: PRI gunmen steal a ballot box

Madrazo swallowed his defeat and remained in the party. The President and his aides celebrated the success of their bold experiment. But Zedillo's personal diplomacy had been necessary to keep the party from spinning apart.

As 2000 began, the PRI looked practically invincible—again! Zedillo was popular. The economy had grown at a lusty 6.9 percent during 1999. The primary seemed to have convinced at least some voters that the PRI would finally adopt certain democratic practices. At the same time, it had transformed Labastida from one more gray face in Zedillo's cabinet into a household name, and in polls he led all opposition candidates by a huge margin. "The PRI is enjoying a honeymoon with the Mexican electorate," *Reforma*'s chief pollster wrote weeks after the primary.

And another development made circumstances even more favorable to the PRI: months of negotiations, organized by Manuel Camacho, to unite all the opposition parties behind a single presidential candidate had collapsed.

Camacho's career had followed a tempestuous path since his refusal in 1994 to fall in line behind Salinas's presidential nominee. After Luis Donaldo Colosio's assassination newspapers insinuated that Camacho might have had a hand in its planning, but there was never a shred of credible evidence. But Ernesto Zedillo did not forgive his disloyalty and drove him from the PRI. Camacho formed a tiny political party and dreamed about a new shot at the presidency.

As a rising young associate of Carlos Salinas's, Camacho had aimed to revitalize the party's relations with the working poor and the Left. He also sought to make the selection of the presidential candidate more democratic for PRI members—and to give himself a better chance at becoming President. After his break with the system, he embraced broader democratic goals.

He had mastered the art of politics inside the PRI, where he learned to navigate the power contests between contending groups clustered around one or another cacique. He was as sharp as a blade and in perpetual motion, dodging and maneuvering, cutting deals, outflanking rivals. During 1999 he brought those skills to the opposition arena. Using his vast Rolodex, he organized negotiations among representatives of Fox, Cárdenas, and nearly a dozen tiny parties, aimed at uniting the opposition.

Powerful logic drove the effort. If both opposition parties fielded presidential candidates, they would split the anti-PRI vote and lose. Polls showed that nearly 60 percent of Mexican voters wanted the opposition to unite behind a single candidate.

With the public in favor, and Camacho shuttling between opposition leaders, Fox and Cárdenas agreed during the summer of 1999 to send their representatives into full-time talks. Diego Fernández de Cevallos offered his walled mansion in Lomas de Chapultepec as a negotiating venue.

The parties drew up a joint program of government and even began to discuss how a victorious coalition might divide up the cabinet. But soon a paralyzing dispute emerged: How would this grand coalition choose its single candidate? Cárdenas's representatives argued for a primary election. Fox, who was far ahead of Cárdenas in the polls, insisted that the parties should commission a nationwide poll, whose front-runner would be designated the nominee. The talks stalemated, yet neither candidate wanted to be blamed for pulling out.

To break the impasse, the parties invited a "citizens council" of fourteen academics, lawyers, and other intellectuals to design a mechanism for choosing the candidate. Sergio Aguayo agreed to participate. He was teaching at the New School for Social Research in Manhattan and began to shuttle between Mexico and New York. He quickly realized that the process unfolding in Fernández de Cevallos's living room was a sham. Cárdenas's people were unwilling to make any concessions that might jeopardize his right to be a candidate. Fernández de Cevallos, purporting to represent Fox, was blocking all paths to unity and seemed to be subtly undercutting Fox. Neither Fox nor Cárdenas was remotely willing to put aside his personal ambitions. Yet each man was eager to blame the other for the stalled talks.

The negotiations dragged on for months. It became obvious that neither Cárdenas nor Fox would ever stand down. Finally Fox pulled out of the talks, seeming to take the hope of genuine reform in Mexico with him.

Sam:

"Ending seventy years of dictatorship will be a great heroic exploit for Mexico," Fox told me one day during the spring of 1998, when he was campaigning village by village through Yucatán state. "Something like when you Americans put a man on the moon."

He was chatty and relaxed as his Chevrolet Suburban carried us through the tropical landscape of table-flat cattle pastures and palm trees. His driver stopped at every settlement to let Fox shake hands with surprised locals, most of them Mayan farmers about half Fox's height, so it was a day of interruptions.

But he kept steering our conversation back to the mathematical assumptions of his fledgling campaign. The PRI, he estimated, would win 40 percent of the votes in 2000. Sixty percent of the electorate would vote against the official party. If Fox and Cárdenas both ran strongly, they would defeat each other. "I have to beat Cárdenas," Fox said. "If Cárdenas and I split the vote, the PRI wins."

Yet he was brimming with confidence. He took it for granted that he would eventually win the PAN nomination and that beating Cárdenas and the PRI to Los Pinos was only a matter of hard work, careful planning, endless fund-raising, and clever marketing. Fox liked to say, quite unabashedly, that he was a good product.

We pulled to a stop at one Yucatán crossroads, and as two dozen men in straw hats gathered, Fox climbed up onto the bed of a truck. Cursing and shaking his huge fists, he vowed to drag the PRI out of Los Pinos by the scruff of its neck.

Sometimes, however, his vernacular got him into hot water. "I'm selling an irresistible product," Fox told a news agency reporter at one campaign event. "I'm honest, I work like a motherfucker, and I'm not an asshole." When newspapers in heavily Catholic Guanajuato published his vulgarities verbatim, they provoked an uproar. At his next public appearance he remarked: "Ladies, please cover your ears and take the children outside. Your governor is about to give a speech."

—   —   —

Fox could work this magic with Mexicans who had some connection with the country's ranchero past. But he had struggled to find a rapport with the Mexico City intellectuals who decorated their walls with por-traits of Che Guevara and preferred Pablo Milanés to Los Tigres del Norte.

Realizing this, Fox sought to cultivate another image for himself, as a social democrat. He received help from Jorge Castañeda, who had been his friend since his 1991 campaign in Guanajuato. Castañeda, the once-militant leftist, held a doctorate in economic history from the University of Paris and referred to himself as a "Frenchified intellectual." He had ties to progressive politicians all over Latin America, and in the years of leftist malaise after the fall of the Berlin Wall he invited many of them to the series of policy discussion groups he hosted at his San Angel home. He invited Fox, and at first the former Coca-Cola CEO in cow-boy boots seemed out of place sipping white wine with socialists and ex-guerrillas. But Fox soon learned the language of social democracy and began to argue that government had an important role to play in fighting poverty, leveling social inequality, and providing credit to small producers.

Fox's real challenge, however, was not to win the votes of the coun-try's few thousand intellectuals but to conquer the millions of working people in and around Mexico City who had voted for Cárdenas in 1988 and 1997. They were maids, street sweepers, market vendors, and three-dollar-a-day factory laborers. They lived packed into crumbling apart-ment complexes in the city center, in slums lining the freeways, and near the garbage dumps in the squalid eastern suburbs.

Fox hoped to inherit these voters by persuading Cárdenas to withdraw from the race during the coalition negotiations. One night soon after the talks collapsed, he met to plot strategy with Castañeda, Camacho, Por-firio Muñoz Ledo, and others at the Mexico City home of Adolfo Aguilar Zinser. Castañeda had a brainstorm.

The key to victory, he argued, was to transform the election into a ref-erendum on change and to insist that Cárdenas could not make that change, because he had no chance to win. Most of the opinion polls showed Cárdenas attracting no more than 15 percent of votes. If Fox could convince people that a vote for Cárdenas was a vote wasted, they would be left choosing between Labastida and the PRI, on one hand, and Fox and change, on the other.

Muñoz Ledo and Camacho supported Castañeda's reasoning, and Fox went home convinced. Over the next weeks he adjusted his campaign to portray the election as a plebiscite on change.

Francisco Ortiz, a young TV marketing wizard whom Fox had hired away from Procter & Gamble, came up with a one-word slogan that brilliantly expressed the new campaign: ¡Ya!, or Enough already! The logo was a hand with two fingers raised, superimposed on the letter Y, transforming the V for victory into a Y for *ya* signal.

Sam:

By March 2000, when I traveled again with Fox on his campaign, the gesture had become a subversive signal of defiance to the PRI. One evening as his campaign bus rolled slowly through Morelia, the capital of Michoacán, Fox leaned out the window, waving ¡Ya! to sidewalk crowds. Many pedestrians raised two fingers back at him and yelled out a greeting. Others glanced sideways before flashing it back more surreptitiously. The next morning, as we climbed into his Suburban for more campaigning, Fox said he was tickled about his marketing coup.

He had routinely referred to Labastida, a PRI insider who had served in three cabinet posts and as the governor of Sinaloa, as the *candidato oficial.* Ortiz, however, thought that phrase sounded too positive, like a product endorsement—like Gatorade becoming the "official beverage" of the Olympics. On Ortiz's advice, Fox began ridiculing Labastida as "the candidate of more of the same."

He had begun to speak of himself as a commodity. "Fox is an outsider," he said, describing the logic of his television campaign during a drive along a winding Michoacán road. "He's the citizen worried about his country who gave up his business life to work for change."

"Very few Mexicans believed you could beat the PRI," he said, turning in the front seat of the Suburban to look at me. "They needed to see an aggressive guy, a rough guy with boots and his sleeves rolled up, who wouldn't shrink from a fight for social justice. They needed a Lech Walesa, a Nelson Mandela, a challenger, a guy who's a winner, a guy with guts."

For an instant he broke out of his marketing spiel. "Really, I'm not

Vicente Fox boards a campaign jet provided by a wealthy patron

that tough guy," he said. "I'm human and emotional. But I'm building
up that image."

— — —

Labastida, too, was struggling to portray himself as the candidate of
change. Coordinating his strategy was Esteban Moctezuma, the young
economist who had been Zedillo's first Government Secretary and was
now Labastida's campaign manager. Studying polls that showed young
voters to be distrustful of the PRI, Moctezuma concluded the party could
no longer count on its base of aging, uneducated, mostly rural voters. It
needed a makeover.

He suggested rechristening the party El Nuevo PRI, the New PRI.
Labastida liked the idea, which became the core theme of Moctezuma's
modern, television-driven campaign. Moctezuma hired President Clinton's political consultant James Carville and his pollster, Stanley Greenberg, as advisers. Their track record in the United States was impressive, but neither spoke Spanish or had any background in Mexico. As
Labastida's main slogan, Carville adapted an old phrase from the Ameri-

can Left, "Power to the People." It translated poorly into Spanish, "*Que el poder sirva a la gente*," but soon was plastered on billboards all over Mexico.

Labastida made a public gesture to demonstrate his repudiation of PRI corruption. He dealt a slap to Carlos Hank González, still one of the PRI's most influential power brokers, by publicly refusing an offer for help from one of his sons, Jorge Hank Rhon, a playboy who owned a Tijuana car racetrack. Jorge had been seen in the company of drug traffickers and was once arrested smuggling illegal ocelot pelts into Mexico. To many Mexicans he was a symbol of sleaze.

Moctezuma was delighted. But another group of Labastida advisers, led by Emilio Gamboa, were not. A former chief of staff to President de la Madrid, Gamboa was Labastida's channel to the party hard-liners, who considered the concept of El Nuevo PRI an insult.

Gamboa believed the campaign should play to the PRI's strengths. It was Mexico's only truly nationwide party, with leaders in every village, neighborhood, labor union, and peasant cooperative. It was the party in power, and in his view every Mexican who received a government benefit was indebted to the PRI. Gamboa and his cohorts thought Labastida should call out the machine to mobilize loyal voters, entice the undecided, and frighten opponents.

In the first nationally televised debate, on April 25, Labastida stumbled, mouthing Carville's slogans in an effort to portray himself as the candidate of change.

"Labastida talks about change, but he's been in the PRI for thirty-seven years," Fox retorted. The TV commentators and newspaper columnists judged that Fox had cleaned Labastida's clock.

Labastida then sidelined Moctezuma and closed ranks with the old guard. The day after the debate he embraced Carlos Hank González at a hastily arranged luncheon, apparently believing the public would see no contradiction with his repudiation of Hank González's son. He invited Manuel Bartlett to tour the country to rev up the party faithful. Labastida never again referred to the New PRI; now he campaigned as the proud heir to the revolution's venerable traditions. Who carried out the land reform? he asked a crowd of farmers in Durango. Who created the social security system? Who expropriated the petroleum fields?

Behind the scenes, party hard-liners were trying to buy and coerce votes all over Mexico. Government officials began to warn welfare mothers and corn farmers that they would be cut off from government support payments unless they pledged to vote for Labastida. In Tabasco, PRI officials appeared suddenly with disaster funds, delayed since flooding eight months earlier, and paid six hundred dollars to homeowners identified as governing-party supporters.

These timeworn tactics had worked well when local officials held sway over voters who, rooted in their *ejido* land-reform cooperative or shantytown, were political captives. But in the new Mexico the tactics backfired. During the campaign's final weeks, hundreds of voters complained publicly about PRI arm-twisting. Senior officials at a federal welfare agency summoned its 150 top bureaucrats to a meeting during working hours, ordering them to campaign for Labastida. But a researcher, María del Refugio Montoya, reported the coercion to Alianza Cívica.

Ramiro Berrón, a Pemex technician in Tabasco, circulated a letter to colleagues reporting that he and other employees had been ordered to work for the Labastida campaign, using Pemex telephones and other resources, on threat of dismissal. Berrón soon discovered that his phones were tapped and he was being followed, but he stood by his accusations.

After the reports of vote coercion, Labastida's television commercials portraying him as an anticorruption crusader rang hollow.

Fox's campaign had inconsistencies, too. He was focused on the marketing, not on presenting a realistic plan of government to solve the country's intractable problems. Some of his contradictions emerged at the annual convention of the Mexican Bankers Association, held on March 4 at a beachside hotel in Acapulco. In times past the arrival of the PRI candidate would have been a key event, when bankers would have rushed to greet him. But this year Labastida received only a smattering of applause as he and his aides swept into the hall.

For months Fox had been courting the business elite in discreet fund-raising encounters. The moment he strode into the auditorium in his cowboy boots, the bankers leaped to a standing ovation. In his speech Fox addressed himself to "my friends in the banks," barely mentioned the scandalous bank bailout, and even praised the bankers for keeping their institutions afloat during the 1995 crisis. They roared their approval.

"Fox told us what we wanted to hear," Roberto González Barrera, the president of the Banorte financial group and a longtime PRI supporter, told reporters.

Four days later Fox told a group of small-business men what *they* wanted to hear. He met in the capital with a roomful of struggling entrepreneurs who hated the bankers, whom they excoriated for accepting billions in government rescue funds yet refusing to extend new loans to thousands of ma-and-pa enterprises that were sliding into bankruptcy for lack of credit. Fox listened intently, and then echoed their angry statements. He lashed the bankers as a class of inefficient drones and promised to prosecute those suspected of fraud in the banking rescue.

In a visit to New York he spoke favorably of privatizing Pemex, but back in Mexico he promised never to do any such thing. He raised the banner of the Virgin of Guadalupe during one of his rallies, then apologized after protests by Protestants and agnostics and after authorities reminded him that the use of religious symbols in political campaigns was against the law. Yet all the zigzags finally did Fox little damage. Voters seemed to understand that the 2000 vote was not about whether Fox or Labastida had put forward more coherent campaign proposals. They accepted Fox's argument that it was a referendum on PRI rule.

Every poll published by Mexican newspapers in the weeks before the July 2 vote showed Fox to be trailing Labastida. (One pollster, Rafael Giménez, said he was fired by the newspaper *Milenio* because he produced a national sounding in April showing that Fox was taking the lead, and PRI officials worked to suppress at least two similar surveys.) Labastida's U.S. pollster, Stanley Greenberg, released a poll ten days before the vote showing Labastida to be leading Fox by four points. Privately, however, Greenberg warned Labastida that the 20 percent of voters who said they were undecided would break overwhelmingly against the PRI on Election Day, meaning that Fox was likely to win.

Ulises Beltrán, Zedillo's pollster, told the President six weeks before the elections that Labastida was in serious trouble.

As a result, campaign insiders knew that Fox could likely win, but most Mexicans could only assume from the polls that he would lose. Still, there was electricity in the air. A great citizens movement had grown up across Mexico over three decades, an inchoate mass of voters from all regions, parties, and social classes, united in their desire for honest elections, for an end to corruption and organized crime, for a modern nation that could provide a better life for its people. They wanted change. During thirty years of democratic struggle, Fox had been first a spectator and later a bit player. But as the climax approached, he positioned himself so that voters viewed him as the one leader with the drive and will to bring the saga to a triumphant conclusion.

During the last candidates' debate Fox paid homage to the heroes who had fought despotism and been excluded from official history. He honored the sacrifice of the student protesters at Tlatelolco in 1968. He praised Rosario Ibarra's tenacity in her search for the disappeared, and Heberto Castillo's generosity in resigning his candidacy to Cárdenas in 1988. He lauded Manuel Clouthier's antifraud protests. He paid tribute to Salvador Nava's march for dignity in San Luis Potosí. "The road has been long and difficult," Fox said. "We're arriving at the end thanks to millions of Mexicans who have overcome the challenges of PRI authoritarianism with strength, character, and a bit of stubbornness. We're just five weeks from the change."

On July 2, 2000, at 8 a.m., when José Woldenberg brought down his gavel to open the Election Day session of the executive council of the Federal Electoral Institute, he had many reasons to be confident that the voting would go well. As both a student and a practitioner of election reform, Woldenberg knew that the institute he headed was the product of two and a half decades of careful improvements, starting as far back as the changes by Government Secretary Reyes Heroles in 1977. The independent elections process was now a reality in law and practice throughout the nation, and under Woldenberg's leadership the institute had finished creating one of the most sophisticated voting systems in the world. With $1.2 billion to spend on the presidential vote, the institute had trained nearly half a million people, chosen randomly from all registered voters born in April, to serve as polling-place officials. They were backed up by opposition poll watchers covering nearly every one of the more than 113,000 balloting places.

Woldenberg had overseen one innovation he was especially proud of: the design of a skinny little portable voting booth to be used in every polling place. There was no way that more than one adult could fit into it, and it had a curtain to allow voters to mark ballots in complete privacy. Voters could accept PRI bribes, tremble at PRI warnings—and then vote any way they wanted, because this time their vote would be secret.

Most of the balloting was orderly by any nation's standards. But there were clashes in the polling places between the new way and the old. At a voting station in a primary school in Toluca, about thirty-five miles southwest of Mexico City, a squad of PRI officials tried to eject a PAN poll watcher, accusing him of standing too close to the ballot boxes. Chappell Lawson, an MIT political science professor who was at the school as a foreign observer, watched as the PAN poll watcher, with his wife and eight-year-old daughter nearby, stood his ground, rejecting the PRI demands. The yelling made his daughter cry, but her mother was firm. "You must not cry, and you cannot go home. They will always try to make you feel afraid, but you have to stand up and fight for your rights," she counseled the child, who promptly marched over to tell a PRI official that her family would not go home, "no matter how mean he was." Mexico, Lawson decided, was building a civic culture "one eight-year-old at a time."

In the late afternoon on July 2, former President Jimmy Carter, together with his wife, Rosalynn, and others in a small observer delegation he had brought to Mexico, paid a brief visit to the PRI. They found the atmosphere strange. By that time news of the first private exit polls showing Fox with a substantial lead had begun to swirl through the corridors of Los Pinos and some campaign headquarters.

Labastida came briefly to greet Carter, and he seemed out of sorts and almost groggy, as if some blow had left him enervated. Other PRI officials did most of the talking. They reported stolidly to Carter that the PRI polls at that time showed Labastida, not Fox, ahead by three points.

Carter and Robert Pastor, his adviser, both had the distinct impression that the *priístas* were dissembling. From the funereal mood in the room, they surmised that Labastida probably knew the truth about the returns. Why wasn't he telling them? Was he having trouble accepting the outcome?

Zedillo, Liébano Sáenz, and the others at Los Pinos also feared that afternoon what the PRI might do. Throughout the many rounds of reforms and during its own primary, the PRI had made an effort to become the democratic political party it was never created to be. But in the hour when it had to let go of the presidency, the pillar of its power, Zedillo and his men worried deeply that the PRI hard core would rebel.

At eight o'clock the polls announced by Televisa and TV Azteca unveiled Fox's victory to the Mexican people. Over the course of his presidency, Zedillo had stepped back from the ruling party. Now, at a crucial juncture, he and Sáenz found they had less leverage to negotiate with Labastida and their own party than with Fox and the PAN. At midevening, when word arrived over at PRI headquarters that Zedillo was thinking of taking it upon himself to call the election rather than deferring to Labastida, the party heavyweights clustered in the war room unleashed their pent-up resentment against the President. What was that son of a whore planning? He was going to hand the election to Fox in order to ensure his niche in history? And abandon his party to the street?

During the evening Woldenberg faced unexpected pressures to waylay the process the elections council had planned. Zedillo, concerned that Labastida was not conceding, called Woldenberg to ask if he would consider moving up the time of his announcement of the institute's first official results, scheduled for 11 p.m. But in a straightforward exercise of their independence, Woldenberg and the council simply told the President no.

At the same time, calls were flying back and forth from Woldenberg's staff to Robert Pastor, who was at Jimmy Carter's outpost in a downtown hotel. At one point Woldenberg was informed by one of his aides that

Carter had requested permission to give a press conference at the Federal Electoral Institute, sometime before 11 p.m., apparently to announce the results of the balloting.

Woldenberg was dumbfounded. He and the other council members had been working day and night for four years to organize the election, surviving shouting feuds among the members and attempts by every one of the political parties to undermine them. And now an American, a gringo, a politician Mexicans disliked when he was President, a leader of the country that had once sliced Mexico in two and kept the top half, this man was going to announce the election results to the Mexican people?

As far as Woldenberg was concerned, Carter was "completely out of line." Pastor tried to explain that Carter had only intended to lend his support to whatever results Woldenberg announced. But the council wanted to make it absolutely clear that there would be no foreign interference in a Mexican election.

As was fitting, given the thirty-year effort that had gone before, Woldenberg, as council president, informed Mexico of the official results, at 11 p.m. sharp. "We are a country in which a change of government can be accomplished peacefully," Woldenberg said, "by means of a regulated competition, without recourse to force by the loser, without risk of retrogression."

Then came Zedillo, speaking from Los Pinos. "We have shown that ours is now a mature democracy, with solid and trustworthy institutions and especially with citizens who have a great civic awareness and sense of responsibility," he said.

At PRI headquarters the followers amassed in the central plaza at first hung around, disoriented. They started to get angry. Then a lifetime of training in the authoritarian party took hold. They furled their banners and began to leave. The mariachi musicians, who had been testing their trumpets for hours, packed their instruments disconsolately, wondering if they would even get paid for their time.

Across the country PRI militants stood down; their resistance had never been activated. The PRI rank and file yielded, not out of democratic conviction, but because neither their candidate nor their President told them to do otherwise. The party's leaders had never contemplated the possibility of broad defeat, and when it happened, they were paralyzed. Decades of change in Mexico had left them without the means or the will to commandeer another election.

In the PRI auditorium, after Labastida conceded, the party's leaders were overwhelmed. Manuel Bartlett was trembling. Leonardo Rodríguez Alcaine, the eighty-one-year-old PRI union leader who had blustered before the election that he would "draw a line" in front of Fox, now stammered, and then fell silent. The PRI president, Dulce María Sauri, tried to show that she was no pushover. "We do not have the disposition to be an eternal opposition," she said defiantly. The PRI wasn't out of power yet, and already the exile seemed too long to them.

When all the votes were officially counted, Fox won 43 percent of the votes cast, compared with 36 percent for Labastida and 17 percent for Cárdenas. The old rural, poorly educated Mexico that voted for the PRI was fading away. The new Mexico—young, urban, more educated—was now in the majority and had chosen Fox. He won 50 percent of the ballots cast by Mexicans eighteen to twenty-four years old, 59 percent of the votes cast by students, and 60 percent of the votes cast by Mexicans with a university education. Labastida earned far more votes than Fox among people who said they had no schooling at all.

Fox's key triumph came in Mexico City and its sprawling suburbs. In the Federal District, Fox beat Labastida by nearly two to one, racking up a margin of 870,000 votes. Virtually all the working-class-stronghold suburbs to the east that had voted heavily for Cárdenas in 1997 voted overwhelmingly for Fox in 2000.

Fox accumulated large margins everywhere there were sidewalks, winning a majority in all of the sixteen most urbanized states, while Labastida won majorities in the seven most rural states. In northern Mexico, Fox won every border state and sixteen of the nineteen electoral districts that touch the United States.

Mexicans used their ballots with considerable sophistication, splitting their tickets. Even as they swept Fox into the presidency, they elected

Mexico's most pluralistic Congress, giving none of the three major parties enough votes to pass legislation without making alliances. In Mexico City voters chose Andrés Manuel López Obrador to be their mayor, after he had focused his campaign not on Fox's middle-class followers but on the urban poor.

Voters played a final joke on the PRI. The size of Fox's victory suggested that many of them had accepted campaign gifts from the ruling party and even attended its rallies, only to vote for Fox. Mexicans were no longer selling their votes. After July 2, the country no longer belonged to the PRI or any other party or strongman, not even to Fox. It belonged to the Mexicans. They had voted for change, for a President who would be different from the PRI. More of the same—the taunt Fox had repeatedly thrown at Labastida during the campaign—would not be good enough.

Fox, after drinking his champagne on the balcony at PAN headquarters in front of thousands of cheering supporters, acknowledged that his was not so much a personal victory as the triumph of a citizens movement dating back a generation. "Today is the culmination of many years of struggle," he said.

Later he went to the Angel de la Independencia, which had formed the backdrop to countless pro-democracy demonstrations: by students protesting police violence before the 1968 Olympics, by Rosario Ibarra and other antifraud marchers after Carlos Salinas's election, by Josefina Ricaño and other crime victims in 1998. The crowd gathered on the steps of the monument was celebrating Fox's victory, but already Mexicans wanted to remind him that they intended to hold him accountable. "*¡No nos falles!*" they shouted as Fox raised his arms to acknowledge their cheers. "Don't let us down!"

Epilogue

Would Vicente Fox's victory merely mean the replacement of one self-serving governing party with another? As a candidate, Fox had promised not only to throw the PRI out of Los Pinos but also to engineer more fundamental transformations, to extend the rule of law, and to build an economy that worked for all classes, not just the wealthy elite.

In any nation, dismantling an authoritarian system and erecting democratic institutions to take its place is an extraordinary undertaking. Long-standing political rules no longer apply, and new codes of conduct have yet to be written. Those who held privileges in the old regime seek to retain them, and citizens' expectations for change run high. Few politicians have the statesman's skills needed to lead their people through such murky terrain.

Fox, gifted as a candidate though he was, proved to have only limited instincts and abilities as a President. It soon became obvious that his victory would not bring prosperity, equality, and justice overnight. During his first years in office many Mexicans began to question the depth of the change he represented. But nobody seriously questioned the essential vigor of the democracy Mexicans had constructed, and the country's peaceful transition remained a source of national pride.

Many Mexicans expected the transition from Ernesto Zedillo to Fox to be a chaotic one, especially for the economy. Currency collapse had darkened every presidential handoff since 1976, when Luis Echeverría devalued the peso two months after José López Portillo's election to succeed him. But this paradigm fell, too; the economy proved resilient. Well before the elections, Zedillo had outlined an economic strategy for avoiding a new end-of-presidency crisis, and it worked. Instead of capital flight, the summer of 2000 saw international investors pour dollars into Mexico, and the *bolsa* boomed.

Indeed, in the weeks after the governing party's defeat, the showdown Mexicans watched was between the last two PRI leaders of the twentieth century, when Zedillo and Carlos Salinas faced off in a public battle. During his years of exile Salinas had rarely spoken out. But as it turned out, he had spent the Zedillo presidency writing a 1,393-page book in which he defended his own administration like a street fighter, decree by decree, and claimed that Zedillo had Raúl Salinas tried for murder only to seek political revenge against his brother. Hoping to ride the book to rehabilitation, Salinas arranged a media blitz to accompany its Mexican release in the fall of 2000. In a Saturday night interview on Televisa he argued that Zedillo had used all the powers of the state to blame others for his own mistakes.

But Salinas blundered when he spoke of Raúl. The Salinas brothers, one in exile, the other imprisoned, had maintained a precarious mutual loyalty. Carlos had never blamed Raúl for the damage done to his presidential reputation by Raúl's corrupt exploits, and Raúl had never described what President Salinas had known about them while in office. But in the Televisa interview Carlos ruptured that balance, adopting a self-righteous attitude about Raúl's dealings and insisting that Mexicans were owed an explanation.

Raúl, watching the interview in prison, went into a slow burn. Shortly thereafter he put through a call to his sister Adriana. Days later, the same Televisa news anchorman who had interviewed Carlos broadcast a tape recording of Raúl's telephone conversation with her.

Raúl's tone and language were controlled, but his voice smoldered with fury as he complained that his brother's Televisa statements had undermined his defense against graft charges. Adriana, mindful that authorities taped inmate's calls, sought to silence him.

RAÚL: I'm going to clarify everything, where the funds came from, who was the intermediary, what they were for, and where they went. Because I think that, in fact, the society deserves a complete explanation, and more lies won't help.
ADRIANA: Uh-huh.

RAÚL: And I'm going to say which funds came out of the public treasury so they can be returned . . .

Raúl was incensed that Carlos had criticized him on television for having a false passport.

ADRIANA: He said he was hurt by the question of your false papers . . .
RAÚL: That's right, I got them from the Government Secretariat on instructions from him!

The tape cut off as Raúl revealed that Carlos had been asking him for money.

RAÚL: The money is *his*, and now he comes to say that he knew nothing about it . . .

Most Mexicans assumed that President Zedillo or his staff had engineered the leak of the tape in a Machiavellian counterattack on Carlos Salinas. Zedillo's chief of staff, Liébano Sáenz, denied that in an interview for this book. In the end, how Televisa obtained the tape mattered little: the Salinas brothers had wounded each other. None of Carlos Salinas's enemies had ever presented conclusive evidence that he was directly complicit in Raúl's transgressions, and at least some Mexicans had given the benefit of the doubt to a former President they had once admired. Now even faithful allies like Héctor Aguilar Camín, who had defended Salinas throughout the Zedillo years, cut their ties with him. Raúl's words were damning in a way that no one else's could ever be.

Vicente Fox enjoyed tremendous national goodwill when he took office on December 1, 2000, and many Mexicans welcomed the new informality that he made his presidential style. He went so far as to begin his inaugural speech—after Zedillo passed him the presidential sash but before he greeted the lawmakers and other dignitaries—by waving clownishly to his four children, seated in the congressional chambers. His choice of ministers reinforced the drama of regime change: several key posts went to protagonists in the democratic struggle. Santiago Creel became Government Secretary, moving into the offices on Avenida Bucareli previously occupied by Gustavo Díaz Ordaz, Luis Echeverría, and Manuel Bartlett. Jorge Castañeda took over the Foreign Secretary's post his father had occupied, returning to his elite origins after his odyssey through the deserts of the political opposition. Adolfo Aguilar Zinser became Fox's National Security Adviser; Francisco Barrio, Comptroller-General; Luis H. Álvarez, Fox's representative to the Chiapas rebels.

Yet within weeks of Fox's inauguration it was clear that he would not be able to deliver on many of his extravagant campaign pledges. He enjoyed a healthy popular mandate but held less power than any modern President, mainly because the PRI still had a slight plurality of congressional votes. His own limitations became apparent. As a candidate, he had been astute, decisive, and occasionally courageous. As a President, he often seemed inept, dithering, and too eager to appease the defenders of the authoritarian past.

He had vowed to resolve the conflict in Chiapas in "fifteen minutes," and once he took the oath of office he proceeded as though he believed his own rhetoric. He made an overture to the Zapatista National Liberation Army, releasing its prisoners, allowing the group to march to Mexico City, and permitting its masked leaders to address the Congress. But Fox needed to summon the power of his electoral mandate to bring balking conservatives in the PAN to back his peace proposals. Instead, Fox was outmaneuvered by two of his most formidable adversaries—Diego Fernández de Cevallos, from his own party, and Manuel Bartlett—who joined forces to adopt a proposal that the Zapatistas rejected. The chance for real peace in Chiapas was lost.

Midway through Fox's first year, reporters scrutinizing the presidential budget discovered that many of his advisers were being paid exorbitant salaries and that his family quarters at Los Pinos had been outfitted with four-hundred-dollar towels and thirty-eight-hundred-dollar bed linens. Not even his most cynical critics viewed Fox as a crook, but only astonishing insensitivity could have permitted extravagance that so smelled like the PRI. The news especially enraged working families, who, as the worldwide economy slid into recession, began to face layoffs.

There were other signs that Fox could be as heedless as his PRI predecessors of the interests of common Mexicans. Citigroup announced the $12.5 billion buyout of Banamex, the largest Mexican bank, whose principal stockholder was Roberto Hernández. The Zedillo government had injected some 30 billion pesos (more than $3 billion) of government funds to stabilize Banamex as part of the Fobaproa bailout. In approving the Banamex purchase, which landed Hernández a windfall profit, the Fox government did not require either bank to repay the bailout funds. The instant, no-questions-asked approval of the sale looked like a rich reward to one of Fox's generous campaign donors.

Sam:

When I returned to Mexico in September 2002 to review the country's progress, a majority of Mexicans were still expressing patience with Fox. But a deepening cynicism—so familiar during the PRI era—was in the air. Some were saying that Fox's only truly major achievement had been to get himself elected.

Sergio Aguayo was among those expressing disappointment with the Fox government. I caught up with him at a Mexico City community center, where he was up to his neck in the tasks of organizing a new center-left political party, México Posible. That day he was discussing with a roomful of regional party colleagues, most of them human rights activists, how to avoid picking opportunists when recruiting candidates.

"Our transition is passing through phases," Aguayo told me during a break. "For more than a decade Mexico's struggle was about clean elections. That's over. Now the task is to tear down the networks of corrupt special interests from the old regime and build institutions that work by democratic rules. This is more difficult."

——— ——— ———

In 2002, a citizens group had fashioned a democratic tool of the type Aguayo seemed to have in mind. PRI governments had as often as not treated basic information about their operations, not to mention official documents, as state secrets, and Presidents routinely purged records that might incriminate them. But a collective of university professors, lawyers, journalists, and others who called themselves the Grupo de Oaxaca

(Oaxaca was an early meeting place) drafted a freedom of information law. It required the executive branch, the legislature, the courts, the central bank, and other federal institutions to publish basic information on their decisions and operations and established sanctions for officials who withheld information or destroyed documents. On April 30, 2002, the Congress approved the law without a single lawmaker voting nay.

Fox signed it, but the law was a citizens' triumph. Because Fox needed PRI votes in the Congress to approve the economic changes that were his highest priority, his policies seemed designed mostly to avoid conflict with the officials and institutions of the old regime.

During Fox's first year the very survival of the PRI had seemed in doubt, since its defeat had provoked multiple schisms and the party had never existed without an umbilical connection to a President drawn from its ranks. Now those questions had been laid to rest. The party had elected Roberto Madrazo as its national president, pulled itself out of despondency, and won several state elections.

Senator Manuel Bartlett exemplified the party's adaptation. He had traveled to France to survey its quite successful state-owned electric-power industry and had studied the Enron case and the disastrous deregulation of power utilities in the United States. Armed with this new expertise, Bartlett was leading opposition to the Fox government's efforts to attract private capital to Mexico's electric-power monopoly. His opinions were open to debate, but Bartlett and most of his party colleagues were playing by democratic rules.

Not only the PRI had survived. Much of the old system that had served the party, the political culture and the patronage machine that Mexicans called the *aparato*, was also proving resistant to change, and that was less encouraging. Fox seemed by turns unwilling or unable to force the changes that would move the transition forward.

He had brought with him into government only a few hundred campaign aides and PAN supporters. They had made little dent in the army of more than one million federal bureaucrats who had accumulated under PRI rule as officials padded payrolls with cousins and sweethearts. Conchalupe Garza, the PAN veteran, was working in a government high-rise in the Zona Rosa; she was a mid-level official in Santiago Creel's Government Secretariat. When she took over her post, she asked her subordinates to explain the duties of their secretaries and assistants. The secretaries, she was told, dialed phones for their bosses, and the assistants served coffee. By the time of my visit some of these redundant federal workers had been given buyouts, but Conchalupe and four PAN colleagues were still leading an office of fifty workers, virtually all of them PRI holdovers.

The inertia was more extreme in other government offices. At Hacienda the Secretary was Francisco Gil Díaz, an economist who had worked for most of his career at the Banco de México and Hacienda. With stability his priority, he was careful not to shake things up; virtually the entire Secretariat was staffed by bureaucrats from the old days.

Luis González de Alba was one Mexican citizen who felt the impact. He was still writing books, but he earned his real livelihood as the owner of several gay bars. On one occasion he had imported $115,000 worth of Greek wine for his emporiums, but when the shipment reached the gulf port of Tampico, customs inspectors (who worked for Hacienda) embargoed it pending payment of a 30,000-peso import tax, about $3,150. González de Alba paid the tax immediately. But the wine nonetheless sat in a government warehouse for four months until the officials could get the paperwork sorted out—and then charged him 65,000 pesos, about $6,850, for storage. González de Alba saw only one noticeable change since the defeat of the PRI.

"Just that the red tape has gotten worse," he said.

Fox the candidate had promised to make an "educational revolution" his highest priority. Under the PRI, lower schools were controlled not by local boards, as in the United States, but by the federal Public Education Secretariat, which mandated a national curriculum, as well as thirty-one state departments, which kept academic records and licensed teachers. The same system, transferred to New York, would require a principal in Queens to negotiate even small curriculum changes with federal officials in Washington and to travel to Albany to register students' grades. Zedillo had begun to decentralize the system, but under Fox the Secretariat appeared paralyzed. Instead of shrinking, the number of bureaucrats in the central offices in Mexico City was growing.

Fox's policy of appeasing the old regime was most obvious in his relations with the PRI's discredited union leaders. Leonardo Rodríguez Alcaine, the CTM leader, had threatened before the July 2000 vote to call a general strike if Fox were to win the presidency. But after the election he changed his mind, saying he hoped he could become the President's "buddy." Fox, apparently mindful of the useful service the *oficialista* unions performed during the PRI era by cajoling workers to accept austerity measures, praised Rodríguez Alcaine's "vision."

Arturo Alcalde found that his efforts to obtain legal recognition for independent unions had become no less harrowing since Fox's victory. He represented pilots at a regional airline, Aviacsa, who were seeking to decertify a phony union with which the airline management had signed a protection contract. Midway through a decertification election on April 1, 2002, thirty goons charged into Mexico City's main labor tribunal, knocking Alcalde to the floor and kicking him with their combat boots. The goons retreated when a crowd of pilots ran to Alcalde's rescue, and he suffered only bruises. But the attack showed that the mafias were still in control of the labor underworld.

Nor did life seem any easier for the maquiladora workers across northern Mexico after the PRI's defeat. In Ciudad Acuña tensions between Alcoa and the Border Workers Committee, led by Julia Quiñonez and Juan Tovar, boiled over after Fox's victory. The committee was pressing for wage increases, and in the fall of 2000 Tovar led a wildcat walkout. Alcoa called in the Acuña police, who suppressed the strike by lobbing tear gas at workers huddled in an Alcoa parking lot. Management first responded with a modest wage increase. But a year later, when the Mexican and U.S. news media were focused on the September 11 terror attacks, Alcoa quietly fired Tovar and nearly two hundred other Acuña workers whom management had identified as troublesome.

The Fox government dealt some blows to the drug cartels, jailing a former PRI governor of the Quintana Roo province who had been indicted on drug charges in New York and Mexico and detaining one of the Arellano Félix brothers; police killed another brother in a gun battle. These events suggested that the ties formed during the PRI era between federal officials and the cocaine mafias were unraveling. But it was too early to conclude that the democratic government could remain immune for long from the traffickers' blandishments; the profits of the North American drug trade were too vast.

The government had made little progress against other types of organized crime.

Sam:

I visited Josefina Ricaño at her home in Bosques de las Lomas. Our conversation was interrupted several times by calls from the distraught relatives of a kidnap hostage who had been seized in the Valle de Chalco, a dismal suburb just south of Daniel Arizmendi's home turf in Nezahualcóyotl.

"Samuel, make it clear that the kidnappings have gotten worse," Ricaño said. "The problem is growing."

— — —

Fox vacillated about how to deal with the historic crimes of the PRI era. During his first two years some advisers, including Adolfo Aguilar Zinser, sought to persuade him to appoint a Truth Commission, modeled on similar bodies in South Africa and Chile, that could sort through the PRI's long-secret files to clarify the facts and identify officials responsible for the Tlatelolco massacre, the 1970s extermination campaign against leftist rebels, and other episodes. Others, led by Santiago Creel, argued it was better to leave these skeletons undisturbed.

In June 2002 Fox ordered a compromise. He opened the files of the PRI's political police, the DFS, to public review and appointed a special prosecutor, Ignacio Carrillo Prieto, to investigate selected episodes of government-sponsored violence, including Tlatelolco. These were steps that no President before him would have taken, yet human rights leaders criticized them as another tactic designed to avoid confrontation with the PRI. Opening millions of files to public review was a far cry from empowering experts, backed by the authority of the democratic government, to sort through them with an eye to delineating responsibilities.

In July 2004, Carrillo Prieto brought an unprecedented indictment of a former President, charging Luis Echeverría with genocide for the killings on June 10, 1971, of some twenty-five student demonstrators by shock troops known as Los Halcones. But the action backfired: the judge dismissed the charges the following day without even studying the brief.

Yet it appeared that at least some authorities responsible for the worst abuses of the PRI era would be held accountable. In September 2002 the army itself announced that one of its own military tribunals had charged two generals, Francisco Quirós Hermosillo and Mario Acosta Chaparro, with overseeing the murder of nearly 150 leftists during the 1970s. Human rights groups had identified the two generals as leaders of the dirty war pursued under Presidents Echeverría and López Portillo years earlier. In the final weeks of the Zedillo presidency, military police had arrested them on drug charges, but few Mexicans had believed they would ever stand trial for political murder.

As his term progressed, Fox became ensnarled in a bramble of indecision and double standards, and Mexicans were frustrated. Still, few expressed nostalgia for the authoritarian Presidents of the past. The evolution in popular attitudes became apparent in a dispute over the government's attempt to build a new international airport twenty miles northeast of Mexico City. Its runways were mostly to cover a dry lake bed but also required the expropriation of some farmlands. Peasants protested. It was the kind of not-in-my-backyard conflict that has complicated development projects from Germany to Korea. Fox's aides, from the corporate world, drew up beautiful blueprints but ignored the escalating protests — until July 2002, when the peasants, machetes in hand, seized government offices and took a dozen hostages. PRI Presidents had over the years faced similar antidevelopment protests; the dissident leaders had invariably been bought off, jailed, or in some cases just "disappeared." Fox, in contrast, abruptly canceled the airport project, arguing that he could not in good conscience impose the airport by repressing the farmers.

Some businessmen criticized Fox for not crushing the protesters, saying his decision would only encourage other opportunist protests elsewhere. Common Mexicans, however, overwhelmingly approved his restraint, recognizing it as a democratic impulse. The nation with a historic admiration for caudillo leaders now had divided opinions about whether Presidents should rule with a strong hand.

Fox could not have ruled as an authoritarian caudillo even if tempted, because democratic checks were restricting his powers to a degree faced by no previous Mexican President. The opposition-controlled Congress had declared its independence from President Zedillo in 1997, but it had nevertheless approved almost every bill Zedillo proposed. By the time Fox took office, however, the Congress had become far more assertive, defeating a considerable percentage of the bills he proposed and rewriting everything. The Senate even prohibited Fox from traveling to the United States and Canada in April 2002.

The Supreme Court was also evolving into a more independent power. The Court had always been the weakest of the three federal branches; before the PRI's defeat it had never dared to rule against a President in a constitutional dispute. That changed just seven weeks after Fox's victory. The Court ordered Zedillo, a lame duck, to turn over to the Congress banking data he had insisted on keeping secret. Under Fox, the Court broadened its independence, ruling against the President three times in two years, overturning his decrees on everything from daylight saving time to a tax on corn syrup.

Power, after decades of concentration in the hands of a strongman President, was suddenly and dramatically dispersed. The state governors, for instance, exercised far more autonomy than they had previously exercised. Fox was obviously unable to issue orders to the seventeen PRI governors, and even the eight PAN governors maintained a cordial independence from him. PRD governors led six states plus the Federal District, where the mayor, Andrés Manuel López Obrador, soon became Fox's most powerful rival. One of the larger political risks Fox took early in his term was to promise much warmer relations with the United States, in order to achieve new measures to legalize the status of millions of Mexicans living and working there without papers. Fox was confident in this pledge because he had hit it off initially with President George W. Bush, a fellow rancher. But after the terrorist attacks of September 11, Bush's priorities shifted: he tightened border security and cracked down on illegal immigration, forgetting his friendship with Fox. In January 2004 President Bush finally presented a new immigration proposal, offering to create temporary three-year worker visas for undocumented Mexicans. But in the ensuing months he did not send it to Congress, so its only effect was to make it clear that his administration would proceed unilaterally, without negotiating an immigration pact with Fox.

Relations deteriorated further when Mexico gained a seat on the United Nations Security Council during the debate over the imminent U.S. war in Iraq. The Bush administration, using a crude diplomatic calculus, assumed that Mexico would ultimately have to give its backing for war. But Fox responded to overwhelming antiwar sentiment at home and remained aloof in the negotiations. By the end, both sides were bitter.

In midterm elections on July 6, 2003, Mexican voters let Fox know of their disappointment. Sharply reversing the extraordinary turnout of July 2000, only 41.8 percent of registered voters participated. The PAN lost 54 seats in the Chamber of Deputies, while the PRI enlarged its plurality. Aided by López Obrador's charisma, the PRD went from 54 seats to 95. Fox had even less support than before his reforms.

Although Fox had promised to create more than 1 million jobs a year, mainly in small businesses, Mexico lost jobs as the economy slowed with the recession in the United States and the flight of manufacturing jobs to China and elsewhere. In his fourth year employment was just beginning to grow again. In contrast to the past, under Fox's management the economy weathered the slowdown without a major crisis. But the tax reform he proposed to keep Mexico competitive in the globalized economy foundered in the adversarial Congress.

By 2004, Fox already governed like a lame duck. Many of the democracy movement veterans who joined his government had languished or departed, and some had even broken ties with him. Luis H. Álvarez had made no progress in coming to terms with the Zapatistas. Jorge Castañeda had resigned as Foreign Minister in 2003, frustrated by the lack of progress with Washington on immigration, and he left the Fox camp, deciding to launch an improbable independent campaign for president. Adolfo Aguilar Zinser, after being removed by Fox as National Security Adviser, was sent as ambassador to the United Nations. There he feuded with Castañeda and ultimately with Fox. After four years the President remained personally popular, but Mexicans had concluded that although his intentions were good, he could not govern effectively. At times he appeared unable to control his own wife, Martha Sahagún, whom he had married early in the *sexenio*. He allowed his presidency to be eclipsed for months by speculation about her presidential ambitions.

A new generation of democratic leaders had come forward, led by

López Obrador, an articulate populist who governed Mexico City by frequently challenging the President. When reports surfaced of Fox's extravagant remodeling expenditures at Los Pinos, López Obrador slyly revealed that he was living in a modest apartment. He arrived for work at his Zócalo offices at 6 A.M. each morning, to the horror of his bleary-eyed staff. As Fox's promises of millions of microcredits for small entrepreneurs went unfulfilled, López Obrador established a popular, municipally financed cash-stipend system, paying a 636-peso monthly check (about $60) to each citizen.

While López Obrador's innovative programs won him admiration beyond Mexico City, he, too, felt the impact of the new democratic scrutiny. In the spring of 2004 a member of his team, his onetime chief of staff, René Bejarano, was captured on video taking stacks of cash from a businessman who received construction contracts from the city. Instead of ordering a serious investigation, López Obrador blamed the scandal on a conspiracy he said was orchestrated by the PAN, and he summoned his supporters to the Zócalo to shout slogans in his defense.

As the nation looked toward a new presidential election in 2006, Mexico, so long defined by one party, had evolved into a three-party system, with each one struggling to adapt to the new reality. López Obrador's rise, instead of strengthening the PRD, had divided it, moving the patriarch, Cuauhtémoc Cárdenas, to resign from the party leadership. The PRI, with Roberto Madrazo as its leader, held on as the largest and best-organized party but remained in the grip of its old guard, tethered to the past. (Even Carlos Salinas returned from exile to live in Mexico and move behind the scenes in PRI politics, regaining some of his old reputation as the master string-puller, though none of his old power.) The PAN elders, clinging to narrow conservative views, never rallied fully behind Fox. Yet Santiago Creel performed well enough as Government Secretary to be a presidential contender. The 2006 race was shaping up to be polarized and unpredictable. But there were no signs that it would be destabilizing.

During his own presidentail campaign Fox had promised to end the increasing polarization between rich and poor. He had promised financial reforms that would allow working people to obtain small loans to buy houses and start businesses. He had promised to reinvigorate the social security and public-health systems. He had promised to end the depredation of forests that was turning watersheds into deserts, and to institute programs to make public servants more accountable. As Fox's government faced gridlock, most of these initiatives seemed forgotten.

Cynics said that Fox had allowed himself to be absorbed by the old system. Certainly he had aroused unrealistic hopes and offered only mediocre presidential leadership. It was also true that amid the malaise, a few voices, as elsewhere in Latin America, were complaining that democratic rule itself was too cumbersome to deal with the region's economic and social challenges. But a majority of Mexicans continued to express pride in the democracy they had achieved and were willing to give it more time.

Democratic government in the United States was born in the last decades of the eighteenth century with a brilliant constitution and tremendous grassroots vigor. Yet it took U.S. democracy eight decades to abolish slavery, and after a full century urban corruption as bad as any seen under the PRI was proliferating in the New York slums controlled by Tammany Hall. Did U.S. democracy produce efficient economic policies? The United States had experienced a century and a half of democratic government when the Great Depression put a third of its workers onto soup lines.

Democracy does not guarantee good government, but puts in place a set of rules and a culture for resolving differences that allow citizens to limit or correct bad government. Mexicans had been building their democracy in earnest for more than three decades, and it was a work in progress. They were now directing a drama in which Vicente Fox, López Obrador, and the lawmakers of the newly independent Congress were temporary players. If those politicians faltered, Mexicans now had the power to call forth other leaders to more boldly carry forward the nation's agenda.

Mexico's future, like its past, would undoubtedly include moments of turbulence. But it was a nation whose citizens had created an effective division of powers and a well-tested electoral system, and had achieved complete liberty of expression. Vigorous democratic institutions were prepared to endure the tests to come.

Mexico had seemed the perfect dictatorship. Now it was an imperfect democracy.

Notes

1. The Day of the Change

6–29 The account of Election Day, July 2, 2000, is based on the following author interviews: Federico Berrueto, Jan. 19 and Aug. 16, 2001; Cuauhtémoc Cárdenas, Dec. 12, 2000; Jorge G. Castañeda, June 6 and Nov. 19, 2000, and June 30, 2001; Vicente Fox, July 2, 2000; Emilio Gamboa, Feb. 8, 2001; Concepción Guadalupe Garza Rodríguez, Sept. 28, 2000; Francisco Labastida Ochoa, Oct. 12, 2000; Esteban Moctezuma, July 22 and Dec. 25, 2000, and Aug. 30, 2001; Nguyen Huu Dong, Nov. 17, 2000; Robert Pastor, April 24 and 26, 2001; Marco Provencio, Oct. 3, 2000; Liébano Sáenz, Feb. 21, March 2, May 9, Aug. 3, and Nov. 29, 2001; Javier Treviño, Sept. 21, 2000; José Woldenberg, Nov. 28, 2000; and Emilio Zebadúa, Nov. 27, 2000.

11 Labastida rattled off his plans for election night: Over the course of Election Day, the Federal Electoral Institute as well as pollsters working for President Zedillo, the candidates, and the two major television networks would produce polls estimating results with increasing accuracy. While the voting was still under way, they would give results based on exit polls, interviews with voters as they leave the polling station. These polls are not highly accurate, because voters will sometimes give false answers about their votes. As soon as the polls closed, the institute and other pollsters would produce quick counts, results based on statistical projections of actual vote tallies.

11–12 Details of Fox's activities: See Guillermo Rivera, "La historia no narrada del 2 de julio," *Reforma*, Sept. 17–20, 2000, four-part series.

15 José Luis Caballero: Reporting for *The New York Times* by Francisco Hoyos.

18 sharp exchange with former President Jimmy Carter: Carter and his longtime adviser Robert Pastor were both taken aback by Zedillo's reaction to their pre-election report. At a meeting on the Friday before the vote, Zedillo had been cordial. But he handed them a confidential letter that included an analysis of the document. It dismissed the complaints as fantasies concocted by the opposition to spoil the image of the election. "In our view the [report] fails to comply with the principles of objectivity and fairness," it said, in very tart language for a diplomatic exchange. "The report lacks adequate balance . . . The

emphasis on alleged irregularities leads the Carter Center to make statements that are out of proportion . . . We resent the unfair criticism."

19 phone calls from Los Pinos to PRI headquarters: During the afternoon Sáenz also received a call from Ricardo Salinas Pliego, the young chairman of Mexico's second-largest television network, TV Azteca. Salinas Pliego (no relation to former President Carlos Salinas) had bought the network from the government in 1993 in a sale designed to break the monopoly of Televisa, the country's broadcast giant. Mexicans hoped that TV Azteca's newscast would provide an alternative to Televisa, which had long been the willing tool of PRI Presidents. Instead, Salinas Pliego had been more obedient than his rivals. After looking at the results of TV Azteca's own exit polls, which showed Fox ahead by at least eight points, he called Los Pinos for guidance. He was tempted to put the news on the air immediately, breaking the embargo he had agreed to observe until after the polls closed throughout Mexico. But Sáenz, a master at handling the halfway-independent Mexican press, dissembled, saying he didn't have enough data to confirm TV Azteca's polls. Salinas Pliego did not violate the embargo.

2. From Disorder to Despotism

31–32 "rivers of blood": Enrique Krauze, *Mexico: Biography of Power: A History of Modern Mexico, 1810–1996*, trans. Hank Heifetz (New York: Harper-Collins, 1997), p. 98.

33 "Among us . . . there is no single time": Carlos Fuentes, "Kierkegaard en la Zona Rosa," in *Tiempo mexicano* (Mexico City: Cuadernos de Joaquín Mortiz, 1975), pp. 9–10. Translated from the Spanish by Julia Preston.

34 "In Mexico the Spaniards": Octavio Paz, *In Search of the Present: Nobel Lecture, 1990* (New York: Harcourt Brace Jovanovich, 1990), pp. 9–10.

34 Mexico City Zócalo: Manuel Toussaint, *Colonial Art in Mexico*, trans. and ed. Elizabeth Wilder Weismann (Austin: University of Texas Press, 1967).

37–38 *The Mouse Assembly: La asamblea de los ratones* (Mexico City: Lomas Altas School, 1997), mimeographed text.

40 by 1650 the Indian population had decreased to 13.6 percent: Michael D. Coe, *Mexico: From the Olmecs to the Aztecs* (New York: Thames & Hudson, 2000), p. 202.

40 "the country of inequality": Robert M. Buffington and William E. French, "The Culture of Modernity," in *The Oxford History of Mexico*, ed. Michael C. Meyer and William H. Beezley (New York: Oxford University Press, 2000), p. 397.

41 "governed by the will of the people": Henry Bamford Parkes, *A History of Mexico* (Boston: Houghton Mifflin, 1960), p. 160.

41 "increase the daily wages of the poor": José María Morelos cited in Krauze, *Mexico: Biography of Power*, p. 112.

41 Iturbide's reign: Michael C. Meyer, William L. Sherman, and Susan M. Deeds, *The Course of Mexican History*, 6th ed. (New York: Oxford University Press, 1999), pp. 288–96.

41 "a theatrical performance or a dream": Lucas Alamán cited in Krauze, *Mexico: Biography of Power*, p. 129.

42 Peasants were at times able to secure their lands and livelihood by backing a regional caudillo: Letter from Professor Friedrich Katz, Department of History, University of Chicago, Sept. 12, 2002.

44 Juárez's youth: Meyer, Sherman, and Deeds, *Course of Mexican History*, p. 360.

45 "scandal": Daniel Cosío Villegas, *El sistema político mexicano* (Mexico: Cuadernos de Joaquín Mortiz, 1976), p. 16. See also Daniel Cosío Villegas, *A Compact History of Mexico*, trans. Marjory Mattingly Urquidi (Mexico: Colegio de México, 1985), p. 135.

45 He eliminated much of the democracy: Letter from Professor Friedrich Katz, Department of History, University of Chicago, Sept. 12, 2002.

45 Creelman 1907 interview with Díaz: Krauze, *Mexico: Biography of Power*, p. 7.

45 "Effective suffrage, no reelection": Ibid., p. 202.

46 Madero on Díaz's absolute rule: Enrique Krauze, *Francisco I. Madero: Místico de la libertad* (Mexico: Fondo de Cultura Económica, 1987), p. 37.

46 Madero and Zapata: John Womack Jr., *Zapata and the Mexican Revolution* (New York: Knopf, 1969), pp. 97–128. Also see John Mason Hart, "The Mexican Revolution, 1910–1920," in *Oxford History of Mexico*, p. 440.

46–47 Madero's biography and presidency: See Meyer, Sherman, and Deeds, *Course of Mexican History*, pp. 475–503.

47–49 the revolution from 1910 to 1920 and the Constitution of 1917: See Héctor Aguilar Camín and Lorenzo Meyer, *A la sombra de la Revolución Mexicana* (Mexico: Cal y Arena, 1989). Also see John Mason Hart, "The Mexican Revolution, 1910–1920," in *Oxford History of Mexico*.

49 real decrease in the population: *Censo general de población 1910, 1921*.

49 "This circumstance": Calles cited in "El dinosaurio no da más," *Reforma*, July 3, 2000, pp. A12–A13.

50 Catholics killed in the *cristero* rebellion: Jean Meyer, *La Cristiada* (Mexico: Clío, 1997), p. 173.

50 the Generals . . . were not primarily concerned with ideals: See George Grayson, *Mexico: From Corporatism to Pluralism?* (Fort Worth, Tex.: Harcourt Brace College Publishers, 1998), p. 18.

50 Cárdenas's agrarian reform: Meyer, Sherman, and Deeds, *Course of Mexican History*, p. 577.

52 presidential succession: Jorge G. Castañeda substantially lifted the veil from the presidential succession in a book that includes interviews with the four living Mexican ex-Presidents: Luis Echeverría, José López Portillo, Miguel

de la Madrid, and Carlos Salinas. See Jorge G. Castañeda, *La herencia: Arqueología de la sucesión presidencial en México* (Mexico: Extra Alfaguara, 1999).

54 three-decade slide in the real value of workers' wages: Sergio Aguayo, ed., *El almanaque mexicano* (Mexico: Grijalbo, 2000).

54 "We came to power": Velázquez cited by Carlos Monsiváis, "Hacia la beatificación priísta," *El Universal*, July 11, 1999, p. 7. Monsiváis collected the lapidary phrases as well as the mixed metaphors, malapropisms, and revealing slips of tongue of the PRI's leaders. In the case of Don Fidel's phrase, there is dispute about exactly where and when he said it.

54 Miguel Alemán's presidency: See John W. Sherman, "The Mexican 'Miracle' and Its Collapse," in *Oxford History of Mexico*; and Aguilar Camín and Meyer, *A la sombra de la Revolución Mexicana*, esp. pp. 206–9.

55 The population had nearly tripled since the revolution: Mexico's population in 1921 was 14.3 million; in 1960 it was 34.9 million; in 1970 it was 48.2 million. Official statistics from the Instituto Nacional de Estadística, Geografía, e Informática.

55 postwar economic boom: Per capita gross domestic product grew by 117 percent in real terms between 1940 and 1965. Kevin J. Middlebrook, *The Paradox of Revolution* (Baltimore: Johns Hopkins University Press, 1995), p. 213.

57 "A politician who is poor is a poor politician": Quote from González, ibid., p. 7.

59–60 Vasconcelos's history: Luis Javier Garrido, *El partido de la revolución institucionalizada: Medio siglo de poder político en México* (Mexico: Siglo XXI, 1982), p. 274. Also see Alfonso Tarracena, *Cartas políticas de José Vasconcelos* (Mexico: Librera, 1959).

60 Almazán's history: Garrido, *Partido de la revolución institucionalizada*, p. 274.

60 Exactly how many were killed: Humberto Musacchio, *Milenios de México*, vol. 2 (Mexico: Raya en el Agua, 1999), pp. 1280–81.

60 He tended to see subversive threats: The account of Díaz Ordaz's thinking is based on his unpublished memoirs presented in Krauze, *Mexico: Biography of Power*, ch. 21.

61 A thriving Mexican hippie movement: José Agustín, *Tragicomedia mexicana 1: La vida en México de 1940 a 1970* (Mexico: Planeta, 1990), p. 245.

3. Tlatelolco, 1968

63 Arriving at the edge of the colonial center: The account of González de Alba's movements comes from interviews with him and from his book *Los días y los años* (Mexico: Era, 1971).

64 infuriated President Gustavo Díaz Ordaz: Díaz Ordaz's thinking throughout the 1968 crisis is based on the presentation of his memoirs in En-

rique Krauze, *Mexico: Biography of Power: A History of Modern Mexico, 1810–1996*, trans. Hank Heifetz (New York: HarperCollins, 1997), ch. 21.

64 Díaz Ordaz: See ibid.; and José Agustín, *Tragicomedia mexicana 1: La vida en México de 1940 a 1970* (Mexico: Planeta, 1990).

64 four hundred people had been hospitalized and one thousand arrested: *El Universal*, July 30, 1968, cited in Ramón Ramírez, *El movimiento estudiantil de México*, vol. 1, *Análisis/cronología* (Mexico: Era, 1969), p. 163.

64 more than fifty thousand students: The figure is from Krauze, *Mexico: Biography of Power*, p. 696. Ramírez, citing *El Universal* of August 2, 1968, says "nearly 100,000."

65 Raúl Álvarez Garín: The account of his movements and family is based on author interview with Raúl Álvarez Garín, Feb. 2, 2001.

65 "It was one of those emotions": González de Alba, *Días y años*, p. 57. Álvarez Garín also discussed that speech in an author interview, Feb. 2, 2001.

66 Eventually 200,000 Mexicans marched: The account of the August 13 march is from Ramírez, *Análisis/cronología*, p. 215.

66 not to overthrow the government: Raúl Álvarez Garín, *La estela de Tlatelolco: Una reconstrucción histórica del movimiento estudiantil del '68* (Mexico: Grijalbo, 1998), p. 164.

66 By day at the Politécnico: Author interview with Álvarez Garín, Feb. 2, 2001.

67 "It was a party": Luis González de Alba, "1968: La fiesta y la tragedia," *Nexos*, Sept. 1993.

67 400,000 Mexicans: Figure and account of the August 27 rally and its suppression by the army are from Ramírez, *Análisis/cronología*, p. 250.

67–68 In his annual State of the Union: The speech is reprinted in Ramón Ramírez, *El movimiento estudiantil de México*, vol. 2, *Documentos* (Mexico: Era, 1969). The selected quotations are drawn from pp. 203 and 205.

68 One of the university leaders: Castillo's biographical information comes from his curriculum vitae, published by the Heberto Castillo Foundation, and from the essay about him in Humberto Musacchio, *Milenios de México*, vol. 1 (Mexico: Raya en el Agua, 1999), p. 519. Castillo's participation in the university protests is drawn from Heberto Castillo Martínez, *Si te agarran te van a matar* (Mexico: Proceso, 1983).

68 Castillo's involvement . . . infuriated Díaz Ordaz: Krauze, *Mexico: Biography of Power*, p. 713.

68–69 meeting at General Cárdenas's Mexico City home: Author interview with Luis González de Alba, Feb. 16, 2001.

69 He also pooh-poohed Castillo's worries: Castillo, *Si te agarran te van a matar*, p. 82.

69 Castillo barely escaped capture: Ibid., pp. 84–88.

69 students defended the campus fiercely: Álvarez Garín, *Estela de Tlatelolco*, p. 78.

70 When González de Alba arrived: The account of González de Alba's partici-

pation and arrest at Tlatelolco is derived from *Días y años* and author interviews with González de Alba.

70 some one hundred foreign reporters: Sergio Aguayo, *Los archivos de la violencia* (Mexico: Grijalbo and Reforma, 1998), p. 221.

70 Perhaps eight thousand demonstrators: Ibid., p. 12.

71 ten thousand soldiers and police: Álvarez Garín, *Estela de Tlatelolco*, p. 87.

71 their shots were immediately returned: Some details of the events on the balcony are drawn from the first-person account by the Italian journalist Oriana Fallaci, who was injured by gunfire there. Reprinted in Ramírez, *Análisis/cronología*, p. 394.

72 Álvarez Garín had joined the rally: Author interview with Álvarez Garín, Feb. 26, 2001.

72 "When the gunfire was most intense": González de Alba, *Días y años*, p. 185.

72 Amid this firestorm: Ibid., p. 185.

72 the Chihuahua building caught fire: Elena Poniatowska, *La noche de Tlatelolco* (Mexico: Era, 1997), p. 185.

72 The gunfire continued intermittently: Álvarez Garín, *La Estela de Tlatelolco*, p. 87.

72 A young woman seeking to drive: Poniatowska, *Noche de Tlatelolco*, p. 181.

72 a photographer for the newspaper: Ramírez, *Análisis/cronología*, p. 400.

72 first of the 2,360 persons detained: Aguayo, *Archivos de la violencia*, p. 12.

73 soldiers were setting up camp: González de Alba, *Días y años*, p. 206.

73–74 Mexican radio and TV stations reported: Álvarez Garín, *Estela de Tlatelolco*, p. 89.

74 The official body count: Aguayo, *Archivos de la violencia*, p. 13.

74 Díaz Ordaz called Zabludovsky: Author interview with Jacobo Zabludovsky, Jan. 19, 1998.

74 Heberto Castillo was not at the plaza: Castillo, *Si te agarran te van a matar*, p. 89.

74 His wife stayed up with him: Aguayo, *Archivos de la violencia*, p. 271, citing Amalia Solórzano de Cárdenas, *Era otra cosa la vida* (Mexico: Nueva Imagen, 1994).

74–75 Elena Poniatowska: The account of her movements on October 2 and 3, 1968, and over the weeks thereafter is from author interview with Poniatowska, Feb. 13, 2001.

75 One of the women, Margarita Nolasco: Poniatowska, *Noche de Tlatelolco*, p. 174.

75 She had counted sixty-eight dead: Ibid., p. 172.

77 "What savagery!": Ibid., p. 231.

77 a senior committee official: He was Frederick Ruegsegger, the private secretary to Avery Brundage, the committee's president. See Aguayo, *Archivos de la violencia*, pp. 263–65.

77 "pageantry, brotherhood and peace": "100,000 See the Olympics Open in Mexico Stadium," *New York Times*, Oct. 13, 1968, p. 1.

77–78 British television documentary: Quotation taken from the International Olympic Committee Web site, where Internet users can stream a brief video-cast of the opening ceremony.

78 biggest story for Americans: John Durant, *Highlights of the Olympics: From Ancient Times to the Present* (New York: Hastings House, 1973), p. 185.

78 Scores had been arrested: Author interviews with González de Alba and Álvarez Garín, Feb. 2001.

79 smuggled González de Alba's manuscript out of Lecumberri: Author interview with Poniatowska, Feb. 13, 2001. Despite his friendship with Poniatowska, González de Alba sued her in 1997, arguing that in quoting material from *Los días y los años* for inclusion in her *Noche de Tlatelolco*, she had misidentified some student leaders.

79 Poniatowska's book: *La noche de Tlatelolco* is one of Mexico's all-time best-sellers. By 1998 it had sold out fifty-seven editions.

80 "We were experiencing": Octavio Paz, *Vislumbres de la India*, in *Ideas y costumbres II: Usos y símbolos*, vol. 10 of *Obras completas* (Mexico: Fondo de Cultura Económica, 1996). Cited in Guillermo Sheridan, "¿Aquí, allá, dónde? Octavio Paz en el servicio diplomático," in *Ensayos en Paz* (forthcoming). This account of Paz in 1968 and 1969 owes many details to Sheridan's carefully researched chronicle of Paz's tenure in New Delhi and 1968 resignation, and to Sheridan's additional insights during an author interview on February 13, 2001. From 1997 through 2001 Sheridan was the director of Mexico City's Octavio Paz Foundation.

81 a lengthy report: Paz's reply to Carrillo Flores is published in its entirety in "Un sueño de libertad: Cartas a la cancillería," *Vuelta* 256 (March 1998).

81 "I will not describe": Paz's resignation letter, ibid.

82 "Interruptions from the West (3)": Eliot Weinberger, ed. and trans., *The Collected Poems of Octavio Paz, 1957–1987* (New York: New Directions, 1991).

82 vilify him: Díaz Ordaz would articulate his loathing of Paz most bluntly in 1970, when the President was asked in a television broadcast what he thought of Paz's resignation. "I die laughing," Díaz Ordaz said. See Sheridan, "¿Aquí, allá, dónde?"

83 Carlos Fuentes and Gabriel García Márquez: Author interview with Guillermo Sheridan, who cited Paz's correspondence.

83 "The massacre of the students": *Le Monde*, Nov. 14, 1968.

83 Zavala arranged for a speech: Aguayo, *Archivos de la violencia*, p. 276.

83 When an embassy economist: ibid., p. 273.

84 "a privileged bureaucracy": *Le Figaro Littéraire*, Jan. 27, 1969.

84 Zavala cabled to Mexico City: Diplomatic message from Zavala to the Foreign Secretariat, Feb. 14, 1969. Copy on file in archives at the Octavio Paz Foundation, Mexico City.

84 *Posdata*: The title means "postscript," but the book was published in English in 1972 by Grove Press as *The Other Mexico: Critique of the Pyramid*.

84 "But the experiences of Russia": Paz, *Posdata*, p. 247.

84 "These days": González de Alba, *Días y años*, p. 145. And see final reference on last page, p. 207.

84 a poll carried out: Aguayo, *Archivos de la violencia*, p. 28, citing Princeton University poll.

84–85 "Democracy in Mexico": Consejo Nacional de Huelga, *Manifiesto a La Nación*, printed in Ramírez, *Documentos*, p. 503.

85 priests even refused to celebrate: Poniatowska, *Noche de Tlatelolco*, p. 270.

85 victims were the same two soldiers: Author interview with Álvarez Garín, Feb. 2, 2001; and Álvarez Garín, *Estela de Tlatelolco*, p. 208.

85 One was Ernesto Zedillo: Author interview with Liébano Sáenz, Feb. 21, 2001.

85–86 Fox also caught a brief glimpse: Vicente Fox, *A Los Pinos: Recuento autobiográfico y político* (Mexico: Océano, 1999), p. 40.

86 living with two roommates: They were Lino Korrodi and José Luis González, who recalled that Fox never, ever talked about politics in that period. Author interview with José Luis González, March 27, 2001.

86 "I was totally out of that world": Fox, *A Los Pinos*, p. 40.

86 Aguayo's experiences: Author interview with Sergio Aguayo, July 6, 2000.

87 paramilitary soldiers: Castillo, *Si te agarran te van a matar*, pp. 125–46. The Mexico City mayor, Alfonso Martínez Domínguez, claimed to have watched Echeverría orchestrate the June 10, 1971, massacre over the phone, ordering aides to burn the bodies. Martínez Domínguez told the story to Castillo. Also see "Luis Echeverría recibió informes de la matanza cada 10 minutos," *Proceso*, June 17, 2001.

87 convinced hundreds of youths: Author interview with Álvarez Garín, Feb. 2, 2001. The enumeration of twenty-nine dead comes from Tim Weiner, "Mexico Secrets: Envelope Holds Ghosts of 70's," *New York Times*, July 1, 2002, p. A1.

88 hundreds of Mexican rebels were killed: Author interview with Álvarez Garín, Feb. 2, 2001. One study of Mexico's 1970s counterinsurgencies estimated that fifteen hundred guerrillas were killed: Gustavo Hirales, "La guerra secreta, 1970–1978," *Nexos*, June 1982. In December 2001 the official Comisión Nacional de los Derechos Humanos reported after studying the government's previously secret intelligence files that 275 people disappeared after being detained by security forces. But human rights groups, based on their own interviews with relatives of victims, insisted that the number was as high as 500. See Ginger Thompson, "Flashback to Deadly Clash of '68 Shakes Mexico," *New York Times*, Dec. 13, 2001, p. 3; and Ginger Thompson, "Who 'Disappeared' in Mexico: A General's Sinister Story," *New York Times*, July 16, 2002, p. 3. The detail on the 143 rebel bodies hurled from helicopters is drawn from an interview with an army prosecutor; see Gustavo Castillo García, "Acosta Chaparro y Quirós, acusados de 143 asesinatos," *La Jornada*, Sept. 28, 2002, p. 1.

88 Ibarra never gave up her search: Author interviews with Rosario Ibarra, Sept. 21, 2000, and Oct. 20, 2000; also see Elena Poniatowska, *Fuerte es el silencio* (Mexico: Era, 1980).

88 details of Echeverría's coup at *Excélsior*: Krauze, *Mexico: Biography of Power*, pp. 750–51.

89 came out of the closet: Author interview with González de Alba, Feb. 19, 2001.

89 Arturo Alcalde Justiniani: This account is drawn from author interviews with Alcalde, March 14 and July 17, 2001.

91 involved in sectarian bickering: From the 1930s through the 1960s Mexico's electoral laws were written to give the PRI every advantage. The PRI became so strong that by the late 1950s, the opposition parties, especially the PAN, the largest opposition party, had considered withdrawal from the political arena. In 1958 opposition parties won only 8 seats in the Chamber of Deputies (out of 161), and the PAN leadership decided that its six winning candidates should not take their seats. As the lack of a credible opposition became a weakness for a regime claiming to be democratic, the PRI in 1963 rewrote the electoral laws to encourage tiny parties to win congressional seats. The laws were rewritten again in 1973 in ways that encouraged tiny parties but limited the congressional representation of the PAN. See Juan Molinar Horcasitas and Jeffrey A. Weldon, "Reforming Electoral Systems in Mexico," in *Mixed-Member Electoral Systems: The Best of Both Worlds?* ed. Matthew Soberg Shugart and Martin P. Wattenberg (Oxford: Oxford University Press, 2001).

91 "Intolerance is the sure path": Ricardo Becerra, Pedro Salazar, and José Woldenberg, *La mecánica del cambio político en México: Elecciones, partidos, y reformas* (Mexico: Cal y Arena, 2000), p. 87.

91–92 the 1977 reforms: Ibid., p. 148. Also see Molinar Horcasitas and Weldon, "Mixed-Member Electoral Systems in Mexico, 1964–1997," p. 4.

92 "We want to make it understood": Becerra, Salazar, and Woldenberg, *Mecánica del cambio político en México*, p. 103.

92 effects of the 1977 electoral reform: See Soledad Loaeza, *El Partido Acción Nacional: La larga marcha, 1939–1994* (Mexico: Fondo de Cultura Económica, 1999), pp. 317–18. For details of the Communist Party's legalization, see Arnoldo Martínez Verdugo, ed., *Historia del Comunismo en México* (Mexico: Grijalbo, 1983), p. 372.

92–93 Aguayo was a sought-after: Author interview with Aguayo, July 6, 2000.

4. Earthquake, 1985

95 "the creation of a new country": Héctor Aguilar Camín and Lorenzo Meyer, *A la sombra de la Revolución Mexicana* (Mexico: Cal y Arena, 1989), p. 250.

95 "a group of Mexicans": José López Portillo, *Sexto informe de gobierno* (Mexico: Presidencia de la República, 1982).

96 This chapter is based on interviews with Cuauhtémoc Abarca, Arturo Alcalde, Homero Aridjis, Imanol Ordorika, and Elena Poniatowska. It also
draws on reporting by Julia Preston for *The Boston Globe* and Sam Dillon for
The Miami Herald in Mexico City in September 1985.

100 de la Madrid in Tlatelolco: Carlos Monsiváis, *Entrada libre: Crónicas de la
sociedad que se organiza* (Mexico: Era, 1987), pp. 52–64.

101 "We are ready to return": José Agustín, *Tragicomedia mexicana 3: La vida en
México de 1982 a 1994* (Mexico: Planeta, 1998), p. 83.

101 "The truth is that": Enrique de la Garza et al., *Esto pasó en México* (Mexico:
Extemporáneos, 1985), p. 97.

104 "bad Mexicans": Agustín, *Tragicomedia mexicana 3*, p. 84.

104 "The only thing I can say": de la Garza et al., *Esto pasó en México*, p. 109.

107 In all, eight babies were pulled alive: Manuel Becerra Acosta et al., *19 de septiembre: Unomásuno* (Mexico: Uno, 1985), p. 52.

111 "We who live": "A Declaration by 100 Intellectuals and Artists against Con-
tamination in Mexico City," *News*, March 1, 1985, p. 18.

113 Probably twenty thousand people perished: William A. Orme Jr., "Thousands Still Homeless 1 Year after Mexico Quake," *Washington Post*, Sept. 20,
1968, p. A1.

113 "It's absurd to suggest": Monsiváis, *Entrada libre*, p. 82.

5. Chihuahua, 1986

117 Mexico's largest opposition party: The PAN had consistently won more votes
in congressional and presidential races than any other opposition party. In
the 1982 presidential elections, for instance, the PRI's Miguel de la Madrid
won 71 percent of the valid votes cast; the PAN's Pablo Emilio Madero won
16 percent; and candidates from five other tiny parties together won a total of
9 percent. Historical election results provided in a 1999 interview by a
spokesman for the Federal Electoral Institute.

119 three-to-one margin: Enrique Krauze, *Mexico: Biography of Power: A History
of Modern Mexico, 1810–1996*, trans. Hank Heifetz (New York: Harper-
Collins, 1997), p. 767.

119 "What good was it to be a critic": Author interview with Luis H. Álvarez,
July 7, 2000.

120 The army dispatched: Author interview with Lorenzo Meyer, Colegio de
México historian, March 13, 2000.

120 airplanes at his service: Gabriel Romero Silva, *Memorias del PAN, tomo V*
(Mexico: Estudios y Publicaciones Económicos y Sociales, 1993), p. 208.

120 did not have enough money to pay for a single campaign advertisement: Luis
Rubén Cuevas, "Luis H. Álvarez: El hombre que aró en el mar," *Dos Puntos:
Revista Dominical del Periódico Reforma*, March 10, 2001, p. 21.

120 organization of overworked volunteers: Author interview with congressional

deputy María Elena Álvarez de Vicencio, the wife of a former PAN party president, March 12, 2001. She struggled to raise money for the PAN from the 1950s through the early 1980s.

120 he would barnstorm Mexico by car: These and subsequent details of the 1958 presidential campaign are from author interviews with Luis H. Álvarez, July 7, 2000, and May 15, 2001, and from Romero Silva, *Memorias del PAN, tomo V*, pp. 143–233.

122 sign on facade of PAN headquarters: Salvador Beltrán del Río, *Partido Acción Nacional: La lucha por la democracia, 1939–2000* (Mexico: México Desconocido, 2000), p. 71, has a photograph of the sign.

122 academics sympathetic to the PRI: "The figures were very difficult to believe, if you consider the climate of protest in the months before July 1958 and the discontent that had been shown among groups of workers, precisely when López Mateos was Secretary of Labor." Soledad Loaeza, *El Partido Acción Nacional: La larga marcha, 1939–1994* (Mexico: Fondo de Cultura Económica, 1999), p. 276.

122 in just eighty-eight cases: María Elena Álvarez Bernal, *Municipio y democracia* (Mexico: Estudios y Publicaciones Económicos y Sociales, 1995), pp. 154–60.

123 in 1963 the government slightly altered the electoral laws: Juan Molinar Horcasitas and Jeffrey A. Weldon, "Mixed-Member Electoral Systems in Mexico, 1964–1997," in *Mixed-Member Electoral Systems: The Best of Both Worlds?* ed. Matthew Soberg Shugart and Martin P. Wattenberg (Oxford: Oxford University Press, 2001).

123 refused to talk: María Elena Álvarez de Vicencio, *Alternativa democrática* (Mexico: Estudios y Publicaciones Económicos y Sociales, 1986), p. 97.

123 economic crisis: Details on the financial developments of 1982 are drawn from Alan Riding, *Distant Neighbors* (New York: Knopf, 1984), pp. 147–51.

124 retirement compound: Ibid., p. 128.

124 prices for all basic goods: Alberto Aziz Nassif, *Chihuahua: Historia de una alternativa* (Mexico: La Jornada, 1994), p. 40.

124 Adalberto Almeida Merino: Ibid., p. 41.

125 six of Chihuahua's seven largest cities: They were Ciudad Juárez, Chihuahua, Delicias, Parral, Camargo, and Nuevo Casas Grandes. Cuauhtémoc was won by the leftist party. See ibid., p. 69, for a useful table of the results town by town.

125 aroused only backbiting: Ibid., p. 58.

125 "That book became our bible": Details about Barrio's career and campaign are from author interview with Francisco Barrio, April 24, 2001.

126 peso crisis marked a watershed: For a thorough discussion of the political impact of this generation of young Mexican entrepreneurs, see Blanca Rubio Heredia, "Profits, Politics, and Size: The Political Transformation of Mexican Business," in *The Right and Democracy in Latin America*, ed. Douglas A.

Chalmers, Maria do Carmo Campello de Souza, and Atilio A. Borón (New York: Praeger, 1992). "Never before had the authoritarian regime been forced to deal with entrepreneurs for whom political participation was important in and of itself," Heredia wrote. "Never, in short, had an important group of Mexican businessmen been able and willing to act as citizens rather than as members of a particular interest group" (p. 290).

127 "patriotic fraud": Juan Molinar Horcasitas, a PAN member and political scientist, and Enrique Krauze, an independent historian, cited Bartlett as using this line of reasoning in conversation with them. Author interview with Molinar Horcasitas, Nov. 16, 2000. See Krauze, *Mexico: Biography of Power*, p. 768. In an author interview with Manuel Bartlett on August 23, 2001, he denied ever using the phrase "patriotic fraud." "I know that people have quoted my saying that, but that's totally false," Bartlett said.

127 Chemax, Yucatán: Álvarez Bernal, *Municipio y democracia*, p. 143.

127 Agua Prieta, Sonora: Ibid., p. 149.

128 José Newman Valenzuela: This account is drawn from an author interview with Newman on March 28, 2001.

130–31 Saúl González Herrera . . . rammed through the state legislature: Loaeza, *Partido Acción Nacional*, pp. 388–89.

131–32 "They're having trouble understanding": Aziz, *Chihuahua*, pp. 30–31. Aziz's book is perhaps the only comprehensive account of the democratic cycle in Chihuahua, from the PAN victories in 1983 through the 1986 fraud and the PRI's eventual recognition of Barrio's victory in 1992.

132 "What has put the PRI up against the wall": Francisco Ortiz Pinchetti, "Los chihuahuenses quieren democracia y repudian al PRI," *Proceso*, May 5, 1986, p. 16.

132 "He invited me to join the PRI": Francisco Ortiz Pinchetti, "Por petición de Bartlett el Vaticano ordenó que hubiera misa en Chihuahua," *Proceso*, Aug. 4, 1986, p. 13. Biographical information on Almeida, *Proceso*, Aug. 4, 1986, p. 8. Many details of the 1986 electoral season in Chihuahua were drawn from Ortiz Pinchetti's reportage in *Proceso*, which was extensive, and an author interview with him on March 13, 2001.

133 "Lord, forgive them": "La homilia del hermano Baeza," *Proceso*, July 7, 1986, p. 9.

135 an alliance of thousands of peasants: For a description of the Movimiento Democrático Electoral in Chihuahua, see Francisco Ortiz Pinchetti, "El Movimiento Democrático Electoral rebasa a los partidos en Chihuahua," *Proceso*, June 30, 1986, p. 18.

136 Over the following weeks: The varied protests in Chihuahua are detailed in Francisco Ortiz Pinchetti, "Chihuahua: De la ira al cerrazón, del fraude al menosprecio oficial, "*Proceso*, July 21, 1986, p. 12.

136–37 "I'm not a symbol of anything": Francisco Ortiz Pinchetti, "Luis H. Álvarez, tres semanas en huelga de hambre: 'Quiero vivir, pero como hombre libre,'" *Proceso*, July 21, 1986.

137–38 "Last Sunday someone was seized": Pérez Mendoza, "Por petición de Bartlett el Vaticano ordenó que hubiera misa en Chihuahua," p. 6.

138 apostolic delegate: Prigione was the apostolic delegate instead of the papal nuncio because Mexico had no formal diplomatic relations with the Vatican until 1992.

138 The PAN had filed 920 formal complaints: Aziz, *Chihuahua*, p. 109. The commission's formal name was the Colegio Electoral. For a fuller analysis of its rulings, see Juan Molinar Horcasitas, "Regreso a Chihuahua," *Nexos*, March 1987.

138–39 Six weeks after the elections Castillo flew to Ciudad Juárez: The account of Castillo's meetings in Juárez and Chihuahua with the PAN leaders is in Francisco Ortiz Pinchetti, "En Chihuahua parece gestarse una alianza pluri-partidista de oposición, por la democracia," *Proceso*, Aug. 11, 1986, p. 18.

140 The events in Chihuahua had become: Francisco Ortiz Pinchetti, "Inci-piente organización opositora, respuesta a la política de arrasamiento," *Proceso*, Aug. 18, 1986, p. 12.

140 "The PAN got a lot of votes": De la Madrid interview with Ed Cody, *Wash-ington Post*, Aug. 10, 1986, cited in *Proceso*, Aug. 18, 1986, p. 13.

141 "Thieves who steal ballots": "Ante de la Madrid y Bartlett el PAN reiteró que no negociará," *Proceso*, July 28, 1986, p. 6. In an author interview on Au-gust 23, 2001, Bartlett said he had challenged the PAN representatives in this meeting to document the Chihuahua fraud but that they had no evidence. "Their claims of fraud had no backing," Bartlett said.

141 "Chihuahua today is living the revolution of democracy": Enrique Krauze, "Chihuahua, ida y vuelta," *Tarea política* (Mexico: Tusquets, 2000), p. 145.

141 tug-of-war: Author interview with Héctor Aguilar Camín, Dec. 7, 2000.

142 "The official results": The statement was published in newspapers on July 23 and in *Proceso* on July 28, p. 4. Author's translation. In an author interview on August 23, 2001, Bartlett argued that Manuel Camacho, who in 1986 was an aide to Carlos Salinas, had manipulated the intellectuals into signing the joint statement on the Chihuahua fraud as a way of harming Bartlett's presi-dential possibilities. He said the intellectuals lacked objectivity because they all opposed the PRI.

143 A long, civilized dinner debate followed: It is described in Héctor Aguilar Camín, "Una pequeña historia," *Nexos*, March 1987, p. 19. Some details from author interview with Héctor Aguilar Camín, Dec. 7, 2000.

144 "Elections with one candidate?": Author interviews with Juan Molinar, Nov. 16 and 24, 2000.

144 eight to five: The PRI's eight votes on the Federal Electoral Commission came from the PRI Government Secretary, a PRI member who was the com-mission's notary public, a PRI representative from the Chamber of Deputies, a PRI representative from the Senate, a PRI member representing the party, and the votes of the Partido Popular Socialista, Partido Socialista de los Tra-bajadores, and the Partido Auténtico de la Revolución Mexicana. The op-

position's five votes came from the representatives of the PAN, Partido Demócrata Mexicano, Partido Socialista Unificado de México, Partido Mexicano de los Trabajadores and Partido Revolucionario de los Trabajadores. For a discussion of these parties and votes, see Jaime González Graf, "La crisis del sistema," in *Las elecciones de 1988 y la crisis del sistema político*, comp. Jaime González Graf (Mexico: Diana, 1989), p. 140.

144–45 Molinar was developing an association with the PAN: He formed close friendships during the 1980s with Luis H. Álvarez and Diego Fernández de Cevallos and eventually joined Vicente Fox's government.

145 "The official statistics": Juan Molinar Horcasitas, "Entre la reforma y la alquimia: La costumbre electoral mexicana," *Nexos*, Jan. 1985.

146 "I want you to read this article and destroy it": Author interview with José Newman on March 28, 2001. In an author interview on August 23, 2001, Bartlett said Molinar's arguments in *Nexos* were biased because of his sympathies for the PAN. He did not recall ordering Newman to "read this article and destroy it."

147 When the article . . . was published: Molinar, "Regreso a Chihuahua."

6. 1988

150 Born in 1934, the year Lázaro Cárdenas took office: Biographical details for Cuauhtémoc Cárdenas are drawn from Paco Ignacio Taibo II, *Cárdenas de cerca* (Mexico: Planeta, 1994); James R. Fortson, *Cuauhtémoc Cárdenas: Un perfil humano* (Mexico: Grijalbo, 1997); Cuauhtémoc Cárdenas, *Nuestra lucha apenas comienza* (Mexico: Nuestro Tiempo, 1988); and author interviews with Cárdenas on April 17, 1997; July 4, 1997; and Dec. 12, 2000.

150 sought PRI nomination to the Senate: Cuauhtémoc Cárdenas pursued a political career against his father's admonitions. "If there was something he was very insistent about, it was that I not get involved in political affairs," Cárdenas recalled. See Taibo, *Cárdenas de cerca*, p. 14.

150 Echeverría's selection of a rival angered him: See ibid., p. 51.

151 flying back and forth to Michoacán: Author interview with a member of Cárdenas's state government.

151 Cárdenas protested the atrocity: Luis Javier Garrido Abreu, *La ruptura: La corriente democrática del PRI* (Mexico: Grijalbo, 1993), p. 19.

151 at an academic forum: Juan Pablo González Sandoval, "La emergencia del neocardenismo," in *Las elecciones de 1988 y la crisis del sistema político*, comp. Jaime González Graf (Mexico: Diana, 1989), p. 161.

151 pauperized millions of Mexicans: During de la Madrid's presidency, salaries brought home an ever-shrinking bag of groceries amid extraordinary inflation: 106 percent in 1986, and 159 percent in 1987. See Humberto Musacchio, *Milenios de México*, vol 2 (Mexico: Raya en el Agua, 1999), pp. 1701–3.

151 "We are responding": The full text is published in González Graf, comp., *Elecciones de 1988*, p. 209.

151 "As far as I'm concerned": Enrique Krauze, *Mexico: Biography of Power: A History of Modern Mexico, 1810–1996*, trans. Hank Heifetz (New York: HarperCollins, 1997), p. 769.

152 Bartlett, Salinas, and four other top contenders: The others were Ramón Aguirre Velázquez, the mayor of Mexico City; Alfredo del Mazo, the Secretary of Energy, Mines, and State Industry; Sergio García Ramírez, the Attorney General; and Miguel González Avelar, Secretary of Education. The *pasarela* is detailed in Larry Rohter, "Candidate Breakfasts Give Mexico Taste of Politics," *New York Times*, Aug. 29, 1987.

152 classic exercise of the *dedazo*: For a play-by-play account, see Jorge Castañeda, *Perpetuating Power: How Mexican Presidents Were Chosen* (New York: New Press, 2000), p. 75.

153 "Look at this goddamned *priísta!*": Author interview with Ordorika, Sept. 26, 2000.

154 formed an alliance: A description of the alliance's formation is in González Sandoval, "Emergencia del neocardenismo," p. 165.

154 Manuel Clouthier del Rincón: Biographical details are from Enrique Nanti, *El Maquío Clouthier: La biografía* (Mexico: Planeta, 1998); also Larry Rohter, "To Lay Waste a Dynasty: A Northern Barbarian," *New York Times*, May 3, 1988; and author interview with Manuel Clouthier Carrillo, Clouthier's son, 1999.

154 Monterrey Technological Institute: The full name is the Instituto Tecnológico y de Estudios Superiores de Monterrey.

154 electoral legislation: An analysis is in Juan Molinar Horcasitas, "Un código para un proceso," in *Elecciones de 1988.*

154–55 painful setback to Secretary Bartlett: The description of the atmosphere at the Government Secretariat in the months preceding the elections is based on author interviews with José Newman, March 28, 2001, and with Manuel Bartlett, Aug. 23, 2001.

155 For what purpose was De Lasse collecting: In an author interview on August 23, 2001, Bartlett said he created the SNIPE to be able to respond quickly and with good intelligence to potential Election Day crises in any of the three hundred electoral districts.

156 procedures were cumbersome: Outlined in Manuel Bartlett, *Elecciones a debate, 1988: Precisiones en torno a la legalidad, organización, y funcionamiento del procedimiento oficial de resultados* (Mexico: Diana, 1995).

157 "Long live the son of the patriot general!": Larry Rohter, "In the Footsteps of Cárdenas, Cárdenas Campaigns," *New York Times*, April 27, 1988.

157 "No matter where we go": Ibid.

157 resigned his candidacy in favor of Cárdenas: For an account of Castillo's decision, see Alejandro Caballero, "La unidad, el mayor logro de su vida," *Reforma*, April 6, 1997, p. A7.

157–58 Basáñez carried out a nationwide survey: Aides to Salinas pressured Basáñez and *La Jornada* not to publish the June poll. It finally appeared the day before the election, accompanied by Basañez's own "projection," based on political conjecture, that added six percentage points to Salinas's margin. Basañez acknowledged later that the projection adding percentage points to Salinas was an error because it was Cárdenas's candidacy, not Salinas's, that was gaining momentum. Furthermore, pollsters in the years that followed learned that opinion polls routinely attributed to PRI candidates several percentage points more than they eventually earned in elections. For an overview of 1988 polling techniques and results, see Irma Campuzano Montoya, "Una novedad: Las encuestas preelectorales," in *Elecciones de 1988*, p. 89. Basañez's experiences are drawn from author interviews, May 2001; and Miguel Basañez, "Investigación de la opinión pública en México," *Este País*, April 2000.

158 Salinas's older brother Raúl: Author interview with Guillermo González Calderoni, McAllen, Tex., Nov. 26, 1996.

158 aides were shot dead: They were Francisco Xavier Ovando and Román Gil. Cárdenas discussed the killing at length in Taibo, *Cárdenas de cerca*, p. 112.

158 Televisa . . . aired Salinas's every move: For details of the biased television coverage, see "La television, oficial y privada," *Proceso*, March 28, 1988; and "Televisa denigró a la oposición," *Proceso*, July 11, 1988, p. 15.

158–59 "The impression caused": Jorge Castañeda, "La víspera: Cárdenas en Guerrero," *Proceso*, July 4, 1988, p. 22.

159 elections computer system was supposed to be a secret: The account of the pre-electoral developments at the Secretariat is based on author interviews with José Antonio Gómez Urquiza, Leonardo Valdés, and José Newman. In an interview with the authors on August 23, 1988, Bartlett confirmed many of the basic events of the pre-electoral period but denied that he had overseen an attempt to mislead the opposition parties or the public about the election results.

159 The election law did not obligate: Bartlett outlined his views on the relation between the SNIPE and the official counting process in Bartlett, *Elecciones a debate*, 1988.

161 "It's very close, this election": Author interview with José Newman, March 28, 2001.

161 "Well, how bad is it?": De la Madrid recounted his conversation with Bartlett in Jorge G. Castañeda, *La herencia: Arqueología de la sucesión presidencial en México* (Mexico: Extra Alfaguara, 1999), p. 221. In an author interview on August 23, 2001, Bartlett confirmed the outlines of this conversation with de la Madrid.

161 "Interesting essays in futurology": Elías Chavez, "Jornadas de titubeos del Secretario de Gobernación," *Proceso*, July 11, 1988, p. 22. The article is a minute-by-minute account of the Election Day events at the Federal Elections Commission. Another detailed account: "Crónica de un fraude presidencial anunciado," *La Nación*, July 15–Aug. 1, 1988, p. 38.

161 Bartlett would often sit stone-faced: Author interview with Leonardo Valdés, April 23, 2001.
162 the terminal blinked: The account of the breaching of De Lasse's secret computer files is drawn from an author interview with Gómez Urquiza, May 23, 2001. It remains unclear why the young technician working for De Lasse helped Gómez Urquiza to open the forbidden computer files.
163–64 "the computer has gone silent": A transcript of Fernández de Cevallos's statements is in Bartlett, *Elecciones a debate, 1988*, p. 38.
165 The President approved the request: De la Madrid recounted his conversation with Bartlett in Castañeda, *Herencia*, p. 221. Without seeming to understand the gravity of his words, de la Madrid in his statements to Castañeda acknowledged primary responsibility for his government's handling of the 1988 election results. Bartlett has said that his own actions before, during, and after the 1988 voting complied strictly with Mexico's electoral laws. In a February 1998 interview with reporters and editors of *The New York Times*, he expressed disdain for Mexican detractors who have continued to hound him with criticism for his actions in 1988. He made his views known in his book *Elecciones a debate, 1988*.
165 written a joint opposition manifesto: This account of the opposition candidates' protest on election night was drawn from author interviews with Cárdenas, Ibarra, and Luis H. Álvarez and from Chávez, "Jornadas de titubeos del Secretario de Gobernación," p. 22.
166 only 160 phone lines had been installed: The account of Bartlett's explaining the computer problem is drawn from Chávez, "Jornadas de titubeos del Secretario de Gobernación," p. 22. In an interview with the authors on August 23, 2001, Bartlett repeated the argument that the flow of election results was interrupted because phone lines became saturated. In a separate interview with the authors José Newman, Bartlett's aide, called that argument a cover story, and it was never credible to opposition leaders.
167 He ordered Calles to explain the delays: Calles's tour of the computer center is drawn from interviews with Leonardo Valdés and José Newman. Written accounts include Yuri Serbolov and Fernando Gutiérrez, "Detectó el PAN 'fraude cibernético,'" *El Financiero*, July 11, 1988; and Leonardo Valdés and Mina Piekarewicz, "La organización de las elecciones," in Pablo González Casanova et al., *Segundo informe sobre la democracia: México, el 6 de Julio de 1988* (Mexico: Centro de Investigaciones Interdisciplinarias en Humanidades de la UNAM-Siglo XXI, 1990).
168 eleven hundred precincts: Two men who were political antagonists in 1988 reported the events the same way in separate interviews. José Newman, Bartlett's aide, and Jorge Alcocer, Cárdenas's representative on the Federal Elections Commission, said that Bartlett and De Lasse had selected precinct results that were favorable to Salinas from among several thousand precincts while excluding precinct results unfavorable to him. For Alcocer's detailed

account of the evening of July 6, see Jorge Alcocer, "6 de julio: Ayuda de memoria," *Enfoque*, Sunday supplement to *Reforma*, July 10, 1994, p. 18. Academics who have studied the elections have drawn similar conclusions. See Valdés and Piekarewicz, "Organización de las elecciones" and Castañeda, *Herencia*, p. 450. Carlos Salinas offers a slippery accounting of these figures in his self-serving review of the 1988 elections, *México: Un paso difícil a la modernidad* (Barcelona: Plaza y Janés, 2000), p. 951.

169 PRI headquarters: This account is drawn from "La fiesta del miércoles en el PRI quedó en preparativos," *Proceso*, July 11, 1988, p. 7.

169 "Carlos, this is going to give people cause for suspicion": The de la Madrid quotation is drawn from the ex-President's interview in Castañeda, *Herencia*, p. 223.

169 "Go ahead": Ibid., p. 223. Although history has largely left Bartlett with the blame for the 1988 fraud, Bartlett, unlike de la Madrid, refused to credit Salinas with victory on election night because he understood there were insufficient statistics to back such a claim. Author interview with Bartlett, Aug. 23, 2001.

169 "Today's elections have culminated": The text of de la Vega's victory statement is printed in *Elecciones de 1988*, p. 325.

170 received fewer than 10 million: The final official results, which according to many studies included hundreds of thousands and perhaps millions of votes, added to Salinas's totals after the balloting had concluded, adjudicated only 9.6 million votes to Salinas.

170 "The era dominated in practice": The text of Salinas's speech is printed in *Elecciones de 1988*, p. 327.

170 Academics who have studied: In a June 19, 2001 author interview Jorge Alcocer said, "The manipulation and the fraud of 1988 were carried out basically in the district committees." Silvia Gómez Tagle drew the same conclusion: "The greatest 'adjustment' of the electoral results must have been done in the district committees, because the PRI there had an absolute majority." See Silvia Gómez Tagle, "La calificación de las elecciones," in *Segundo informe sobre la democracia*, pp. 87–88.

171 official results: Larry Rohter, "Mexican Victor Urges Party to Adapt to New Challenge," *New York Times*, July 14, 1988, p. 3.

171 ten towns in Guerrero: Gómez Tagle, "Calificación de las elecciones," pp. 98–99.

171 three successive arenas: Soledad Loaeza explains these three distinct phases of the postelection crisis succinctly in *El Partido Acción Nacional: La larga marcha, 1939–1994* (Mexico: Fondo de Cultura Económica, 1999), pp. 451–52.

172 late July and early August: the Federal Electoral Commission was in session from July 21 through August 13. See ibid., p. 452.

172 Leonardo Valdés and Jorge Alcocer: The account of their experiences at the

Federal Elections Commission was drawn from author interviews with Valdés on April 23, 2001, and with Alcocer on June 19, 2001. Alcocer, who kept detailed notes of his 1988 work during the scrutiny of the voting materials, read from them extensively during the interview.

173 Bartlett ruled Alcocer out of order: In an author interview on August 23, 2001, Bartlett said Alcocer was out of order because the commission's legal mission was to certify the election for the Congress, not for the presidency.

173 But the tallies showed far more votes for President than for deputies: Author interviews with Valdés and Alcocer. This evidence is also detailed in Leonardo Valdés, "La ley y las cifras: La elección presidencial de 1988," in *Movimientos políticos y procesos electorales en México* (Mexico: Editorial Universidad de Guadalajara, 1989).

174 "reliable information": Cárdenas's statement is published in González Graf, comp., *Elecciones de 1988*, p. 329.

174 The antagonisms . . . traced back to 1939: See Krauze, *Mexico: Biography of Power*, pp. 476–78.

174 "There's no reason for us to talk further": Manuel Camacho, *Yo Manuel: Memorias ¿apócrifas? de un comisionado* (Mexico: Rayuela, 1995), pp. 17–18.

174 helped Salinas consolidate power: Vicente Fox later reproached the PAN leaders for their pragmatic stance with Salinas, calling them "a current of cowards." See Vicente Fox, *A Los Pinos: Recuento autobiográfico y político* (Mexico: Océano, 1999), p. 72.

175 "verbal terrorism": Elías Chávez, "Sin concertación posible, la oposición no cede y el gobierno enseña el puño," *Proceso*, Aug. 15, 1988.

175 disheartening him: Cárdenas interview in Taibo, *Cárdenas de cerca*, p. 123.

176 "We have scores to settle with the government": "Cárdenas pide mantener la movilización, pero sin violencia," *Proceso*, Aug. 1, 1988, p. 7.

176 Vicente Fox: The account of Fox's entry into politics and his participation in the Congress drawn from author interviews with Fox and José Luis González. Written accounts in Fox, *A Los Pinos*; and Miguel Angel Granados Chapa, *Fox & Co.: Biografía no autorizada* (Mexico: Grijalbo, 2000).

177 "Take one more step and you die": Fox, *A Los Pinos*, p. 69. The journalist's account is in Granados Chapa, *Fox & Co.*, p. 84.

177 The deliberations became an endless cycle: This account of the congressional debates is drawn from Gómez Tagle, "Calificación de las elecciones." Also see Pablo Gómez, *Mexico 1988: Disputa por la presidencia y lucha parlamentaria* (Mexico: Cultura Popular, 1989); and Larry Rohter, "Mexicans See Tumult Come to Congress," *New York Times*, Aug. 25, 1988.

177 final State of the Union address: This account is drawn from Larry Rohter, "Leader Booed in Mexican Congress," *New York Times*, Sept. 2, 1988.

178 Fox pretended to be Salinas: Granados Chapa recovered the text of the speech and described Fox's performance in *Fox & Co.*, p. 91.

178–79 the PRI's final vote to certify Salinas's election: See Larry Rohter, "In Stormy Session, Mexicans Certify President-Elect," *New York Times*, Sept. 11, 1988.

179 Cárdenas stepped to the microphone: The text of his speech is printed in Cárdenas, *Nuestra lucha apenas comienza*, p. 151.

7. The Carlos Salinas Show

181–82 Salinas's work style: "Carlos Salinas de Gortari," *Lideres Mexicanos*, Sept. 1994, pp. 65–82, special ed.

182 Baja California: Larry Rohter, "The Non-stop Roadshow, Starring Carlos Salinas," *New York Times*, June 30, 1989.

185 "the first Mexican to graduate": Carlos Salinas, *México: Un paso difícil a la modernidad* (Barcelona: Plaza y Janés, 2000), p. 315.

186 "The majority of the reforms": Carlos Salinas, *Primer informe de gobierno*, Nov. 1, 1989.

186 Salinas's modern Mexico: See Salinas, *México*, pp. 287–321.

186 neither practical nor prudent: When Salinas was in office, the concept of two-stage reform was widely endorsed in international policy circles. Also, looming especially large in Salinas's thinking was Mikhail Gorbachev, who had tried to carry off the two reforms at once and instigated the collapse of the Soviet system he was trying to preserve.

186 "Mexicans do not seek adventures": Mark A. Uhlig, "Mexico's Salinas Rains on His Own Parade," *New York Times*, Nov. 25, 1990.

187 "I think each reform has its own rhythms": Tim Golden, "In Mexican Politics, the More It Reforms the More It's the Same," *New York Times*, Aug. 25, 1991.

188 Gutiérrez Barrios biography: He started in the DFS in 1952 and was its director from 1964 to 1970. At Tlatelolco his men were in charge of picking student leaders out of the crush in the hallways of the Chihuahua building and hauling them off to jail. Sergio Aguayo Quezada, *1968: Los archivos de la violencia* (Mexico, D.F.: Editorial Grijalbo, 1998), p. 223.

188 Gutiérrez Barrios and the elimination of guerrilla groups: see Sergio Aguayo Quezada, *La charola: Una historia de los servicios de inteligencia en México* (Mexico: D.F.: Editorial Grijalbo, 2001).

188–91 Rosario Ibarra biographical details: Author interviews with Rosario Ibarra de Piedra, Sept. 21 and Oct. 20, 2000.

191 Its most flamboyant phase: George Grayson, *Mexico: From Corporatism to Pluralism?* (Fort Worth, Tex.: Harcourt Brace College Publishers, 1998), p. 58.

192 La Quina takes care of oil workers: Joe Treaster, "Mexican Union Chief Is King to the Oil Workers at Home," *New York Times*, Jan. 15, 1989, p. 1.

192 "We were not slaves" and other quotations: Author interview with Joaquín Hernández Galicia, Oct. 7, 1997.

192 Supplicants lined up: Author interview with George Grayson, Nov. 17, 1997.

193 On the morning of January 10: Joe Treaster, "Arrest of Oil Union Chief in Mexico Sets Off Strike," *New York Times*, Jan. 12, 1989, p. 1.

193 "would advance, no doubt": Salinas, *México*, p. 503.

193 With one stroke: The effect was amplified when, in this same period, Salinas ordered the arrest, on stock-fraud charges, of Eduardo Legorreta, a financier who had been a major backer of Salinas's presidential campaign.

193–94 He and La Quina hated each other: Grayson, *Mexico*, p. 59.

194 a 1951 episode: Andrés Oppenheimer, *Bordering on Chaos* (Boston: Little, Brown, 1996), p. 201.

195 who was his chief: the deputy attorney general was Javier Coello Trejo. His duties included supervision of the Federal Judicial Police.

195 La Quina and González Calderoni: Author interviews with Guillermo González Calderoni, Nov. 26, 1996, and Joaquín Hernández Galicia, Reclusorio Oriente prison, Oct. 7, 1997.

195 rifles belonging to the Mexican army: Carlos Fernández-Vega and Emilio Lomas, "Indicios de siembra de armas en la captura de La Quina," *La Jornada*, Sept. 1, 1996, p. 1.

196 the government's own autopsy: "Informe médico legal de autopsia de Gerardo Zamora Arreoja," Jan. 10, 1989, fol. B343002.

197 reduce Mexico's foreign debt: Salinas, *México*, pp. 14–37.

198 begin negotiations on a bilateral trade accord: Ibid., p. 50.

198–99 election reforms of 1989–90: Ricardo Becerra, Pedro Salazar, and José Woldenberg, *La mecánica del cambio político en México: Elecciones, partidos, y reformas* (Mexico: Cal y Arena, 2000), ch. 3.

201 deaths rose to the dozens: According to PRD records, Michoacán was the most dangerous state for the PRD under Salinas; sixty-eight activists were killed during the *sexenio*, most of them straw-hat farmers. Leonel Godoy, a lawyer and PRD federal deputy who was defending many party activists before Michoacán courts, was abducted, beaten, and robbed by armed men who took documents proving the corruption of the state police.

201 called to account for the vendetta: Author interview with Manuel Camacho, April 26, 2001.

203 "the real face of the PRD intolerance": Candace Hughes, "Mexican Vote Fraud Ignites Political Battle," Associated Press, Dec. 14, 1990.

203 "It is very dangerous": Heberto Castillo, "Tejupilco," *Proceso*, Dec. 17, 1990.

203 250 PRD activists were slain: Secretaría de Derechos Humanos, Grupo Parlamentario, and PRD, *En defensa de los derechos humanos: Un sexenio de violencia política* (Mexico: PRD, 1994), p. 19.

203 surprisingly aggressive investigation: The investigation took fifteen months.

204 8 percent of the party's murder cases: Secretaría de Derechos Humanos, Grupo Parlamentario, and PRD, *En defensa de los derechos humanos*, p. 20.

204 The PRI won 61 percent: Becerra, Salazar, and Woldenberg, *Mecánica del cambio político en México*, p. 273.

206 September 15, 1961: Sergio Aguayo, *Los archivos de la violencia* (Mexico: Grijalbo and Reforma, 1998), pp. 205–13.

206 army agents picked up Nava: Miguel Angel Granados Chapa, *¡Nava sí, Zapata no! La hora de San Luis Potosí: Crónica de una lucha que triunfó* (Mexico: Grijalbo, 1992), p. 57.

209 he had become convinced of the need: Author interviews with Sergio Aguayo, July 6, 2000; March 20, 2001; June 5, 2001.

209 "We have doubts": Academia Mexicana de Derechos Humanos y Centro Potosino de Derechos Humanos, "Entre la ilegalidad y la inmoralidad," *La Jornada*, Sept. 26, 1991, pp. ii–vi.

210 official returns: Tomás Calvillo Unna, "A Case of Opposition Unity: The San Luis Potosí Democratic Coalition of 1991," in *Subnational Politics and Democratization in Mexico*, ed. Wayne A. Cornelius, Todd A. Eisenstadt, and Jane Hindley (La Jolla, Calif.: Center for U.S.-Mexican Studies, 1999), p. 97.

210 "a vote of confidence": Carlos Mendoza, dir., *San Luis: Lección de dignidad* (Mexico: Canal 6 de Julio, 1991).

211 "I have to ask for your pardon": Ibid.

212 the President hosted Nava: Author interview with Jesús Cantú, June 14, 2001.

212 "to stop the usurper": Mendoza, *San Luis.*

213 "never put at risk": Carta dirigida al H. Congreso del Estado de San Luis Potosí, Oct. 9, 1991.

213–14 Fausto Zapata's account of his role in the San Luis Potosí governor's elections of 1991: Author interviews with Fausto Zapata, Oct. 5 and 19, 2000; May 8 and Aug. 20, 2001.

214 Martínez Corbalá . . . warned Salinas: Adriana Amezcua and Juan E. Pardinas, *Todos los gobernadores del presidente* (Mexico: Grijalbo, 1997), p. 145.

214 none of the three leading candidates: "Elecciones en Guanajuato," *Carta de Política Mexicana*, Aug. 2, 1991.

215 Fox's campaign had started out erratically: Author interview with Leticia Calzada, June 7, 2000.

216 Fox and Muñoz Ledo: Author interviews with José Luis González, May 14, 2001, and Jorge G. Castañeda, June 1, 2000.

216–17 "I want you to promise me": Author interview with Luis H. Álvarez, May 15, 2001.

218 "This is a ballsy guy": Author interview with Jorge G. Castañeda, June 1, 2000.

219 He wrote the year: Author interview with Leticia Calzada, Aug. 9, 2001.

219 Salinas had removed seventeen PRI governors: Amezcua and Pardinas, *Todos los gobernadores del presidente*, p. 12.

220 He also alienated his own party: Salinas even flirted openly with the idea of creating an alternative party, based on Solidarity, a nationwide network of so-

cial development programs that he had masterminded. He never moved beyond ideas, but the PRI faithful knew he had considered disenfranchising
them.

221 "The massive distribution of land": Salinas's first annual State of the Union
address, in 1989, in Salinas, *Mexico*, p. 683.

222 Its projects paved streets: According to figures provided by Salinas, in the six
years of his term Solidarity built or refurbished 128,000 schools, brought
electricity to fourteen thousand communities, rehabilitated 234 rural hospitals, and paved streets in ten thousand shantytowns; see ibid., p. 550.

222 "not just any type of participation": Ibid., p. 553.

223 Gutiérrez Barrios called Barrio: Author interview with Francisco Barrio,
April 24, 2001.

223 PAN mayors governed 30 of the 160 largest townships: Jorge Alcocer, "La ter-
cera refundación del PRI," *Revista mexicana de sociología.*

224 Clause 1 of Article 82: Author interview with Leticia Calzada, Aug. 9. 2001.
Also see Anthony DePalma, "Mexico Passes Electoral Change, but Foils a
Presidential Bid," *New York Times*, Sept. 4, 1993, p. 3.

226–27 "President Salinas is leading Mexico": *El hombre que quiso ser rey*, México Siglo XX series (Mexico: Clío, 1998), videocassette.

227 "better leadership": *Houston Chronicle*, Oct. 5, 1992.

227 "Carlos Salinas, our hope": Salinas, *México*, p. 153.

8. 1994

230 Camacho . . . committed heresy: Manuel Camacho, *Yo Manuel: Memorias
¿apócrifas? de un comisionado* (Mexico: Rayuela, 1995), p. 80.

231 Colosio threatened among his campaign staff to resign: See Procuraduría
General de la República, Subprocuraduría Especial para el Caso Colosio, *Investigación Colosio*, Oct. 20, 2000, videocassette.

232 Salinas cast about: Julio Scherer García, *Salinas y su imperio* (Mexico:
Océano, 1997), p. 41.

233 largest audience for any Mexican television show: Ricardo Becerra, Pedro
Salazar, and José Woldenberg, *La mecánica del cambio político en México:
Elecciones, partidos, y reformas* (Mexico: Cal y Arena, 2000), p. 342.

233 For a month he hardly campaigned: See Vicente Fox, *A Los Pinos: Recuento
autobiográfico y político* (Mexico: Océano, 1999), p. 94. Five years later,
when Fox was in the middle of his own presidential campaign, he pointed to
Fernández de Cevallos as an example of the PAN's chronic lack of will to
win. "I've always thought that when you are on the verge of conquering the
top spot, you need perseverance and stamina," Fox wrote in a campaign autobiography. "Diego Fernández de Cevallos reached the critical point in
1994, and at the crucial moment either they didn't tie the stone to him firmly
or he thought it was too heavy to carry. He just retreated."

234 78 percent of the registered voters: Becerra, Salazar, and Woldenberg, *Mecánica del cambio político en México*, p. 357.
234 "the advance of democracy": Ibid., p. 321.
235 In the new reforms: Ibid., ch. 5.
235–36 José Woldenberg: Author interview with José Woldenberg, Nov. 28, 2000.
236 Santiago Creel: Author interview with Santiago Creel, July 6, 2000.
236 Creel was a longtime friend of Adolfo Aguilar Zinser: Katia D'Artigues, "Adolfo Aguilar Zinser, el escalador," *Milenio*, April 30, 2001, p. 18.
236 Even with the citizen councillors: The other citizen councillors were José Agustín Ortiz Pinchetti, Miguel Angel Granados Chapa, Ricardo Pozas Horcasitas, and Fernando Zertuche Muñoz.
236 In its first report: Becerra, Salazar, and Woldenberg, *Mecánica del cambio político en México*, pp. 344 and 350.
236 For Aguayo in particular, 1994 was not an easy year: Author interview with Sergio Aguayo, June 5, 2001.
237 "There is no doubt": Alianza Cívica, *La calidad de la jornada electoral del 21 de agosto de 1994: Informe de Alianza Cívica observación 94*, Sept. 13, 1994, photocopied report.
239 "The demons are loose": "Los demonios andan sueltos," *Proceso*, Nov. 28, 1994.
239 $29 billion in reserves: Banco de México, *Informe anual*, 1994.
240 weaknesses in the economy: Jonathan Heath, *Mexico and the Sexenio Curse: Presidential Successions and Economic Crises in Modern Mexico* (Washington, D.C.: Center for Strategic and International Studies, 1999), p. 38.
241 economic team met only seven times: Author interview with Jaime Serra Puche, May 24, 2001.
242–43 Serra was also a leading contender: Another candidate for Finance Secretary at that moment was Guillermo Ortiz Martínez.
243–45 The team assembled: Pedro Aspe, "México en 1994: Las razones de la política cambiaria," *Reforma*, July 14, 1995; Jorge G. Castañeda, *La herencia: Arqueología de la sucesión presidencial en México* (Mexico: Extra Alfaguara, 1999), pp. 313–15; Carlos Salinas, *México: Un paso difícil a la modernidad* (Barcelona: Plaza y Janés, 2000), p. 1111; author interview with Jaime Serra Puche, May 24, 2001; Sidney Weintraub, *Financial Decision-Making in Mexico: To Bet a Nation* (Pittsburgh: University of Pittsburgh Press, 2000), p. 98.
245 "the first Mexican President in thirty years who didn't devalue": Author interview with Jorge Montaño, July 17, 2001.
245 Jaime Serra went to work: "1995: Sacrificios, confusión, y furia; Terminó la gran mentira," *Carta de Política Mexicana*, Jan. 6, 1995; *New York Times*, daily coverage by Anthony DePalma and Tim Golden; Salinas, *México*, pp. 1113–30; author interview with Jaime Serra Puche, May 24, 2001; Weintraub, *Financial Decision-Making in Mexico*, pp. 100–111.

246 deficit in the current account for 1995: See Anthony DePalma, "Casualty of the Peso: Investor Confidence," *New York Times*, Dec. 27, 1994.

246 $12.5 billion: Banco de México, *Informe anual 1994* (Mexico: Banco de México, 1995).

246 *tesobonos*: Banco de México, *Informe anual 1995*, table 6, p. 269.

247 lost $855 million in reserves: Salinas, *México*, p. 1120.

248 leakage of reserves came to only $90 million: Banco de México, *Informe anual 1994*, app. 5, pp. 154–61.

248–49 gap between the reserves and the *tesobonos*: DePalma, "Casualty of the Peso."

249 to face the money managers: One account is in Anthony DePalma, "With Peso Freed, Mexican Currency Drops 20% More," *New York Times*, Dec. 23, 1994.

250–51 "I really thought we were growing": Anthony DePalma, "In Mexico, Hunger for Poor and Middle-Class Hardship," *New York Times*, Jan. 15, 1995.

252 "did not take into account": *Cárcel a Salinas* (Mexico: Canal 6 de Julio), videocassette 27; Anthony DePalma, "Salinas Blames Successor for Peso Crisis," *New York Times*, Mar. 2, 1995.

252 In the meeting, on the evening of March 3: Salinas, *México*, pp. 1200–1205, author interview with Luis Téllez, Aug. 16, 2001.

254–55 Aspe wrote an article: Pedro Aspe, "México en 1994: Las razones de la política cambiaria," *Reforma*, July 14, 1995.

255 no run on the reserves: Banco de México, *Informe anual 1994*, app. 5, pp. 154–61.

9. Ernesto Zedillo, the Outsider

259 scandal over some textbooks: Author interview with Héctor Aguilar Camín, July 23, 2001.

259 Zedillo's *destape*: Elías Chávez, "Un día antes del destape," *Proceso*, April 4, 1994.

260 the PRI accounted for 71 percent: Ricardo Becerra, Pedro Salazar, and José Woldenberg, *La mecánica del cambio político en México: Elecciones, partidos, y reformas* (Mexico: Cal y Arena, 2000), p. 371.

261 "Economic reform is not enough": Ernesto Zedillo, "Discurso, Economic Club of New York," Oct. 11, 1995.

261 "We must acknowledge": See www.presidencia.gob.mx for the official transcript of the speech.

262 Zedillo was a loner: Author interviews with Luis Téllez, Aug. 16, 2001, and with Liébano Sáenz, Feb. 21 and March 2, 2001.

262 Zedillo's *grillo*: Author interview with President Ernesto Zedillo, Feb. 11, 1998.

262–63 Zedillo working on economic plans: See, among others, Federico Reyes Heroles, "El enigma," *Reforma*, Nov. 28, 2000, p. 18.

264 "Democracy cannot be imposed": Presidencia de la República, *Acuerdo político nacional*, Los Pinos, Jan. 17, 1995.

264 Elections crisis in Tabasco: This account is based on author interviews with Manuel Andrade Díaz, Oct. 20, 1999; Santiago Creel, July 26, 1999; Andrés Manuel López Obrador, June 15 and 21 and July 5, 1999; Roberto Madrazo, July 27, Oct. 27, and Dec. 3, 1999; Esteban Moctezuma, July 22, 1999; Liébano Sáenz, March 2, 2001; and Juan Gabriel Valencia, Aug. 24, 2001.

264 Roberto was active in the PRI: Madrazo's career is drawn from author interviews and from Humberto Musacchio, *Milenios de México*, vol. 2 (Mexico: Raya en el Agua, 1999), p. 1699.

265 López Obrador: His career is drawn from his "Semblanza biográfica," a political résumé distributed by the PRD in 1997.

266 The official results: Tim Golden, "Another State in Mexico Challenges the Government," *New York Times*, Jan. 20, 1995, p. 3.

266 Santiago Creel and another independent lawyer: The other lawyer was José Agustín Ortiz Pinchetti, the brother of the *Proceso* journalist who had covered the events in Chihuahua in 1986.

267 become Secretary of Education: Zedillo had fired the first Secretary after only a few weeks because he had falsely claimed on a résumé to have a master's degree from Harvard. The newspaper *Reforma* discovered that the official, Fausto Alzati, had not even finished his undergraduate degree in Mexico.

269 The head of the Tabasco state elections council: Alvaro Delgado and Armando Guzmán, "Miércoles 18," *Proceso*, Jan. 23, 1995.

269 "for the bravery": Ibid.

270 "The development of Mexico": The address was on January 3, 1995. Carlos Acosta, "Salinas pasó a la historia negra," *Proceso*, Jan. 9, 1995. Also see Anthony DePalma, "Mexico's Leader Gives the Nation a Recovery Plan," *New York Times*, Jan. 4, 1995, p. A1.

271 "This program is not viable": Gerardo Albarrán de Alba, "Solos, abucheados," *Proceso*, March 20, 1995.

271 "hard, painful": Ernesto Zedillo, "Mensaje a la nación," Los Pinos, March 12, 1995.

272 forty-five boxes full of documents: Piecing things together over time, López Obrador came to believe that some PRD supporters from Tabasco, who wanted to remain unknown for fear of reprisals from the state PRI, had grabbed the files after the 1994 election from a PRI safe house in Villahermosa. Author interview with Andrés Manuel López Obrador, June 15, 1999.

272 "he gathered together some of his buddies": The other organizers of the Chapultepec seminar were José Agustín Ortiz Pinchetti, the elections councillor, and Jaime González Graf, a political scientist who was an alternate on the elections council.

273 "They thought they were bringing us in": Author interview with Santiago Creel, July 6, 2000.

274 meetings at Chapultepec Castle: Ibid.

274 "Dialogue is not just one method": Quoted in Becerra, Salazar, and Woldenberg, *Mecánica del cambio político en México*, p. 389.

274–75 "This is no time": Santiago Creel, "El seminario del Castillo de Chapultepec," *Reforma*, Jan. 17, 1996.

277 Gerardo de Prevoisin: Carlos Salinas chose de Prevoisin, an insurance executive in his circle of friends, to be chairman of Aeroméxico, the ailing state-owned airline. After six years in the job, de Prevoisin left the airline $2 billion in debt and much closer to extinction. Forced out by creditors in September 1994, he vanished, and after auditors examined his books, he was charged with embezzling $72 million from the airline. In a statement he sent from hiding to a Texas court that heard part of the case against him, de Prevoisin said that at least $8 million of Aeroméxico's money that had passed through his personal Citibank account were a contribution to Zedillo's campaign. "Those payments were exacted from Aeroméxico by the incumbent party during election time in Mexico," de Prevoisin said. "They were made on behalf of Aeroméxico as a requirement of business life in Mexico in a presidential year."

His claim, published months later by *The New York Times*, was dismissed at first by PRI finance officials. Then they admitted that de Prevoisin had made large contributions, but argued that they didn't know the funds were from the airline. "In Mexico, as in the United States, political parties cannot be expected to know what undisclosed legal problems an individual contributor may have," a PRI press release said. Zedillo said he had no knowledge of the details of the money that went into the Colosio campaign when he managed it, or into his own.

277–78 first truly independent governing council: The councillors elected were José Barragán, Jesús Cantú, Jaime Cárdenas, Alonso Lujambio, Mauricio Merino, Juan Molinar, Jacqueline Peschard, and Emilio Zebadúa.

278 "laid off by constitutional mandate": Author interview with Creel, July 6, 2000.

279 "best guarantees that the financing": Zuniga, Mariel, "Defiende Zedillo financiamiento," *Reforma*, Nov. 19, 1996, p. 1.

279 "Whatever past Presidents did": Author interview with José Angel Gurría, Sept. 1996.

280 Antonio Lozano Gracia: As President-elect, Zedillo had first offered the job to Diego Fernández de Cevallos, his PAN opponent in the presidential race. Fernández de Cevallos eagerly accepted, until his party reminded him that he had pledged during his campaign that he would not take a post in government if the PRI won the race. Two days after he agreed, Fernández de Cevallos declined, and the PAN instead recommended Antonio Lozano Gracia.

281 "There is a Mexican saying": *La matanza de Aguas Blancas* (Mexico: Canal 6 de Julio, 1996), videocassette 30.

281 "much police, little politics": Ibid.

287 "I will always work": Miguel Angel Juárez, "Con este respaldo no necesito más," *Reforma*, March 11, 1996.

289 "an order or signal": Quoted in Samuel del Villar, Secretaría de Asuntos Jurídicos y Reforma del Estado, Partido de la Revolución Democrática, Memorial (para la Comision Interamericana de Derechos Humanos), June 18, 1996.

289 "The problem was that someone": Author interview with Samuel del Villar, May 13, 2001.

290 Alianza Cívica sued Los Pinos: Sergio Aguayo, "Demandar al Presidente," *Reforma*, June 12, 1996, p. 7.

293–95 "I don't believe in authoritarianism": Author interview with Zedillo, Sept. 24, 1996.

295 eliminating presidential control: See Alonso Lujambio, "Adiós a la excepcionalidad," *Este País*, Feb. 2000, pp. 2–16.

296 1995–96 economic figures: Oficina del Vocero de la Secretaría de Hacienda y Crédito Público, "Algunas puntualizaciones," Sept. 24, 2000.

297 purged 135,000 duplicate names: Author interviews with electoral councillor Jesús Cantú on June 14 and July 11, 2001. Many other details of the electoral reform are also drawn from Cantú's insights. As a result of the reforms, Mexico's electoral system was considerably more modern than the one in the United States—especially, as events would later prove, in Florida.

299 his popularity polls climbed steadily: Alejandro Moreno, "Popularidad en ascenso," *Reforma*, *Enfoque*, Nov. 26, 2000.

10. Raúl

301 María Bernal and Raúl Salinas de Gortari: Bernal recounted their relationship in *Raúl Salinas y yo: Desventuras de una pasión* (Mexico: Océano, 2000). She provided additional details in an author interview, July 20, 2000.

304 "It was very close to the end": Bernal, *Raúl Salinas y yo*, p. 74.

304 It can be argued: This chapter draws extensively on reporting for *The New York Times* by Julia Preston and Sam Dillon between 1995 and 2000.

305 $38 million were transferred: Francisco Gómez, "Dicta juez a Rául ortra orden de aprehensión," *El Universal*, July 31, 2002; Abel Barajas, "Dan nueva orden de aprehensión vs. Raúl," *Reforma*, July 31, 2002.

305 in response to questions: This written interview was conducted by Julia Preston and Peter Truell, published in *The New York Times* on October 31, 1997, p. A1, and arranged by Stanley Arkin, a New York attorney.

306 TV Azteca: For more detail on Raúl Salinas's role in the sale of the television network, see Julia Preston, "Mexico's Elite Caught in Scandal's Harsh Glare," *New York Times*, July 13, 1996, p. A3.

307 Raúl sent a total of $25 million: Mexican court documents showed transfers on June 30, 1993, from a Raúl Salinas account in Citibank Zurich to accounts controlled by Ricardo Salinas Pliego in the Union Bank of Switzerland, the Swiss Bank Corporation, and Banque Edmond de Rothschild.

307 In an interview: Andrés Oppenheimer, "Which Salinas? Mexican TV Tycoon Target of Bank Probe," *Miami Herald*, June 21, 1996. Ricardo Salinas Pliego was not related to Carlos and Raúl Salinas de Gortari, but the fact that he had the same last name added confusion to the case for investigators, reporters, and newspaper readers alike.

307 Raúl's loan to Ricardo Salinas Pliego: Even though Salinas Pliego was forced to admit that he had tried to deceive the Mexican public, the newest steward of Mexican television brought criminal libel complaints against several Mexican journalists who had covered the story, in an unveiled—and not unsuccessful—bid to harass them into silence.

308 Carlos Peralta Quintero: For more detail on this deal, see Julia Preston, "Mexican Fights Swiss for Honor and Millions," *New York Times*, Dec. 30, 1997, p. A3.

310 Carla del Ponte, the Swiss Attorney General: In August 1999 she was named by the United Nations to be the chief prosecutor in the war-crimes trial against former Serb President Slobodan Milosevic.

310 "when Carlos Salinas de Gortari": Tim Golden, "Swiss Recount Key Drug Role of Salinas Kin," *New York Times*, Sept. 19, 1998, p. A1.

310 Guillermo Pallomari's allegations against Raúl Salinas: Tim Golden, "Tracing Money, Swiss Outdo U.S. on Mexico Drug Corruption Case," *New York Times*, Aug. 4, 1998, p. A1.

311 José Manuel Ramos's claims of support from Raúl Salinas in drug trade: Jean-Francois Boyer, *La guerra perdida contra las drogas: Narcodependencia del mundo actual* (Mexico: Grijalbo, 2001), p. 119. Also see Golden, "Swiss Recount Key Drug Role of Salinas Kin," p. A1.

311 whose statements against him did not stand up: One case was Marco Torres. See, for example, Tim Golden, "Questions Arise about Swiss Report on Raúl Salinas's Millions," *New York Times*, Oct. 12, 1998, p. A10.

311 never indicted in the United States: A Swiss judge informed Raúl Salinas of criminal narcotics charges against him on July 23, 2001.

312 Daniel Aguilar Treviño: To protect themselves, the police who conducted the torture, ever mindful that the political currents around such an important killing could shift in unpredictable ways, kept a private tape recording of Aguilar Treviño's confession, and his screams. A Mexican official familiar with the case said that Rubén Figueroa, then the governor of Guerrero, who was always well connected in security circles, obtained a copy of the tape and made it available to Ernesto Zedillo in the days before he took office as President, during the commotion over Mario Ruiz Massieu's resignation. Zedillo listened to the recording of the gunman's agony. It deepened his distrust of

Mario. Zedillo turned the tape over to Antonio Lozano, the new Attorney General. But the tape apparently did not become part of the trial record until two years later, when someone leaked it to the press in Mexico City.

312 Mario Ruiz Massieu's meetings with Zedillo: Mario confirmed these meetings, which took place in October and November 1994, in a book. See Antonio Jáquez, "Testimonios por escrito, desde el 94, Mario Ruiz Massieu incriminó a Zedillo," *Proceso*, Sept. 20, 1999.

313 Mario Ruiz Massieu resigned: Ignacio Pichardo, one of the PRI leaders accused by Ruiz Massieu, has described the close coordination between Mario and Carlos Salinas in a memoir. See Ignacio Pichardo, *Triunfos y traiciones: Crónica personal, 1994* (Mexico: Océano, 2001), pp. 269–307.

313 Zedillo immediately challenged the credibility: He named Ignacio Pichardo to be Energy Secretary and María de los Angeles Moreno to head the PRI.

314 asking the chief justice to read Lozano's indictment: Zedillo took a similar course years later in the Aguas Blancas case.

314 Raúl's arrest for murder: Esteban Moctezuma, the young Government Secretary, helped devise a trap for Raúl and a decoy for Carlos. The former President was promised that he would see the indictment before Raúl's arrest; in practice Luis Téllez, who was Zedillo's chief of staff but also knew Salinas well, showed up at Salinas's home with the indictment on the evening of February 28, 1995, hours after Raúl was locked away in a maximum-security cell at the Almoloya penitentiary. Salinas started yelling: What did Zedillo think he was doing "with these actions that are so alien to the good practice of law and Mexican politics?" He sent Téllez away without a word of farewell. The story is recounted in Carlos Salinas, *México: Un paso difícil a la modernidad* (Barcelona: Plaza y Janés, 2000), p. 1196; and by Luis Téllez, author interview, Aug. 16, 2001.

314 he conducted a trial investigation so inept: Under Mexico's essentially Napoleonic justice system, there is no jury trial. The trial is a process in which the prosecution and the defense accumulate evidence and counterevidence in a voluminous written record. The judge decides the case and sets the sentence.

320 the third, and last, special prosecutor in the case: The special prosecutor was José Luis Ramos Rivera.

320 The tape story appeared in the *Times*: Julia Preston with Craig Pyes, "Secret Tape of Plotter's Confession Deepens the Mystery of a Political Murder in Mexico," *New York Times*, Jan. 14, 1999, p. A8.

11. The General and the Drug Lord

324 the President and his staff: Author interviews with Zedillo aides.

325 ruffians and brigands: A useful account of the history of the Mexican police during the nineteenth and twentieth centuries appears in Ernesto López Portillo Vargas, "La policía en México: Función política y reforma," in John

Bailey and Jorge Chabat, *Public Security and Democratic Governance: Challenges to Mexico and the United States; Report to Task Force* (Washington, D.C., Feb. 2001).

325 The principle was pioneered in 1847: The legal principle is discussed in Rafael Estrada Samano, "Administration of Justice in Mexico: What Does the Future Hold?" *United States–Mexico Law Journal* (1995).

326 to amend it at least four hundred times: Author interview with Alfonso Zárate, publisher of *Carta Política*, a political newsletter. Zárate cited Santiago Creel, who studied the Constitution during the Zedillo presidency as a congressional deputy. Creel said the Constitution was such a patchwork of changes that it was impossible to enumerate its amendments exactly.

326 successive dismissals of Supreme Court: See Michael C. Taylor, "Why No Rule of Law in Mexico? Explaining the Weakness of Mexico's Judicial Branch," *New Mexico Law Review* (Winter 1997).

326 Samuel del Villar: The account of del Villar's career and investigation of the narcotics culture is drawn from interviews with him in May and June 2001.

328 José Antonio Zorrilla: Zorrilla eventually became such a disaster that politicians traded accusations about who was responsible for his rise to the head of the DFS. He was first appointed to head the DFS in 1982 by José López Portillo, on the recommendation of Fernando Gutiérrez Barrios. De la Madrid's Government Secretary, Manuel Bartlett, recommended that Zorrilla remain in the post with the new administration. See Antonio Jáquez, "Siempre fiel al sistema que cayó: Gutiérrez Barrios, un policía-político que salió limpio," *Proceso*, Nov. 6, 2000.

329 disband the DFS altogether in the summer and fall of 1985: Dismissing the agents took several months. The DFS was formally disbanded on November 29, 1985. See Sergio Aguayo, *La charola: Una historia de los servicios de inteligencia en México* (Mexico: Grijalbo, 2001), p. 246.

329 recast as a PRI candidate: Miguel de la Madrid discussed Bartlett's decision to send Zorrilla to the Congress in Jorge G. Castañeda, *La herencia: Arqueología de la sucesión presidencial en México* (Mexico: Extra Alfaguara, 1999), p. 208.

329 Zorrilla was not charged: In an author interview on August 23, 2001, Bartlett said Zorrilla was not charged until after de la Madrid left office, because only then did prosecutors assemble evidence of his involvement in the Buendía killing. Zorrilla's sentence is drawn from Humberto Musacchio, *Milenios de México*, vol. 3 (Mexico: Raya en el Agua, 1999), p. 3350.

329 the DFS's fifteen hundred commanders and agents: For a fascinating account of the technique used in dismissing them, see Aguayo, *Charola*, pp. 243–44. In an author interview on August 23, 2001, Manuel Bartlett said that three DFS commanders were tried in absentia on charges of illicit enrichment, even though the government had not arrested them: Rafael Aguilar, Daniel Acuña, and Rafael Chao López.

330 two separate trials in U.S. federal courts: During a 1988 drug trial in Tucson

of a wealthy trafficker named Jaime Figueroa Soto, U.S. attorneys filed an affidavit asserting that Figueroa and Caro Quintero had in 1984 paid a $10 million bribe to General Arévalo, purchasing protection for a vast marijuana-processing center in Chihuahua, guarded by soldiers. In another federal trial the following year in San Diego, jurors heard taped statements by Pablo Girón Ortiz, a Mexican federal police officer, telling an American trafficker that by bribing General Arévalo through intermediaries, he could arrange protection for cocaine planes landing at clandestine airstrips in Mexico. "I can connect you with the army," Girón Ortiz said. "Everything is being controlled by the army." See Michael Isikoff, "Informer Ties Top Mexican to Drug Deals; Allegations Revealed in DEA Affidavit," *Washington Post*, June 4, 1988; and William Branigin, "U.S. Trial Implicates Mexican Officials in Drug Trafficking," *Washington Post*, Feb. 6, 1989. A senior official in the de la Madrid administration also said in an interview with the authors that he presented evidence to President de la Madrid that General Arévalo had accepted a $10 million bribe from Veracruz-based traffickers.

330 One of General Arévalo's last official acts: General Arévalo promoted Gutiérrez Rebollo to division General on November 16, 1988, but Arévalo's successor actually signed the certificate of promotion on January 17, 1989. Gutiérrez Rebollo's service record is drawn from military documents included in Court Files in the Trial of General Jesus Gutiérrez Rebollo, unpublished Mexican Judicial Files, 1997–98. During the General's trial we obtained twelve hundred pages of the trial record.

331 to arrest Amado Carrillo Fuentes: The trafficker's arrest was announced publicly on August 24, 1989, when authorities said he had been detained in Guadalajara by police. But one of the trafficker's lawyers, José Alfredo Andrade Bojorges, wrote that in fact Gutiérrez Rebollo made the arrest two months earlier, on June 27, 1989, in Badiraguato. Authorities routinely falsify arrest dates in Mexico in order to allow weeks or months for the interrogation of detainees held incommunicado. See José Alfredo Andrade Bojorges, *Desde Navolato vengo: La historia secreta del narco* (Mexico: Océano, 1999), p. 81.

331 affair with Esther Priego Ruiz: The account of Gutiérrez Rebollo's various romances and his relations with the politicians of Guadalajara and with Lizette Ibarra is drawn from Court Files in the Trial of General Jesús Gutiérrez Rebollo, unpublished Mexican Judicial Files, 1997–98.

332 It was Ibarra's practice to organize an elegant dinner: Felipe Cobián, "No soy narca, pero si hablara embarraría a muchos militares," *Proceso*, Aug. 3, 1997, p. 18.

332 a favored client of Tomás Colsa McGregor: Colsa McGregor told authorities of his relationship with Amado Carrillo Fuentes during March and May 1997 and was murdered shortly thereafter. Extracts of his testimony are published verbatim in an appendix to Andrade Bojorges, *Desde Navolato vengo*. The prison visit is detailed on p. 185.

332 paying Carrera $1 million: The bribe is detailed in legal testimony by José Luis Antu Martínez, a former agent of the Federal Judicial Police, an extract of which is published verbatim in ibid., p. 177.

333 old Boeing 727s and other passenger jets: Tim Golden, "Tons of Cocaine Reaching Mexico in Old Jets," New York Times, Jan. 10, 1995.

333–34 the 1994 report: The report was distributed to the U.S. embassy and consulates in Mexico and other government offices: "Intelligence Assessment of the Amado Carrillo Fuentes Organization" (El Paso, Tex.: El Paso Intelligence Center, 1994).

334 many other Mexican authorities: The list of officials whom Carrillo Fuentes allegedly corrupted is too cumbersome to detail in its entirely, but it included all three of President Salinas's antidrug coordinators and at least one federal judge. The first of the drug coordinators was Javier Coello Trejo, who headed Mexico's antidrug efforts during Salinas's first two years in office. Testimony in three separate federal drug trials in the United States later indicated that Coello Trejo had accepted bundles of cash from Carrillo Fuentes's drug mafia both during and after the trafficker's imprisonment, and Carrillo Fuentes's defense attorney wrote later in a book that the trafficker had bribed Coello Trejo to obtain his freedom. See Andrade Bojorges, Desde Navolato vengo, p. 86. In a 1998 author interview, Coello Trejo denied that he had ever accepted drug bribes. After Coello Trejo's 1990 resignation, Jorge Carrillo Olea succeeded him, serving until 1993. Salinas's third drug coordinator was Mario Ruiz Massieu, the man who in Salinas's final year engineered a cover-up in the investigation of his own brother's murder. Months after Salinas left office, Ruiz Massieu was arrested in New Jersey carrying a suitcase full of undeclared cash, and authorities found he had deposited $9 million in Houston banks during his tenure as drug czar. In federal proceedings to confiscate the funds, witnesses described huge bribes to him by Carrillo Fuentes's organization. After he was indicted in Houston on narcotics charges in 1999, Ruiz Massieu committed suicide. See Tim Golden, "Mexico's Ex-Drug Chief, Indicted, Is Found Dead in U.S.," New York Times, Sept. 16, 1999, p. 3. The federal judge was Teresa Irma Fragoso, who was dismissed from the bench in October 1997 amid accusations that a thirty-thousand-dollar bribe from Carrillo Fuentes influenced her decision to turn down federal prosecutors' request to search one of the trafficker's Mexico City residences. See Andrade Bojorges, Desde Navolato vengo, pp. 169–72. Villanueva was eventually arrested and indicted; see Tim Weiner, "Ex-Mexico Governor Arrested and Linked to Cocaine Traffic," New York Times, May 26, 2001.

335 Montenegro led his troops: This account of events at the Fifth Military Region is drawn from Court Files in the Trial of General Jesús Gutiérrez Rebollo, unpublished Mexican Judicial Files, 1997–98.

336 bribes on the scale of those paid to other top officials: After Gutiérrez Rebollo's arrest, anonymous federal prosecutors told reporters that he had sent

$500 million into overseas accounts during his eight years as commander of the Fifth Military Region. But during his trial those claims evaporated, and prosecutors documented only about $3 million that had passed through his Mexican accounts in his decade of power, some of which he used to buy a string of homes in several states. He had about $400,000 in the bank at his arrest. See Philip True, "Ex-drug Czar's Daughter Rips Illicit-Cash Story," *San Antonio Express-News*, April 8, 1997. The prosecutors' account of the $500 million in foreign accounts originally appeared in *El Universal* on April 7, 1997. The government's much-downsized estimates were reported in Luis Guillermo Hernández, "Investigan ingresos ilícitos a general," *Reforma*, Sept. 27, 1997.

337 trying to undermine the PAN government: The account of the dispute between the army's Fifth Military Region and Jalisco's PAN government is drawn from interviews with Alberto Cárdenas Jiménez, Jorge López Vergara, and Antonio Lozano.

338 "So it's come to this": Lozano quoted Zedillo in a June 21, 2001, interview. Lozano first told this story publicly in the spring of 1997. López Vergara said in interviews that he had several times passed on his suspicions about Gutiérrez Rebollo and Montenegro to Lozano. Governor Cárdenas also raised complaints with General Cervantes. President Zedillo said of Lozano's charges in an interview on May 2, 1997: "That's absolutely false. In his heart he knows he's lying."

341–42 Héctor Palma Salazar: His arrest is detailed in Andrés Oppenheimer, *Bordering on Chaos* (Boston: Little, Brown, 1996), pp. 298–300.

342 the Sierra Chalchihui: As it happened, the drug lord's pied-à-terre was just six blocks from the Mexico City bureau of *The New York Times*.

342 an electric auto raceway: It appears in military police photos of the apartment included in the court files.

342–43 "From the ambassador and his team": Authors' transcript of General McCaffrey's remarks to reporters after a speech in Mexico City in early December 1996.

343 the official story was a lie: This account is drawn from interviews with several senior Mexican government officials.

343 The businessman immediately understood the significance: The sources for this account declined to reveal the identity of the businessman on the grounds that his life continues to be in danger because of his role in General Gutiérrez Rebollo's arrest.

343 "I want you to summon": Zedillo met alone with Defense Secretary Cervantes but described the encounter to his staff.

343–44 General Cervantes . . . confronted Gutiérrez Rebollo: Cervantes described the events in a letter to Zedillo, later published in *Proceso*. Carlos Marín, "Documentos de Inteligencia Militar involucran en el narcotráfico a altos jefes, oficiales, y tropa del ejército," *Proceso*, July 27, 1997, p. 11. In an author interview on May 12, 1997, Gutiérrez Rebollo's daughter, Teresa de Jesús Gutiérrez Ramírez, accused the army of putting him in the military hospital in order to assassinate him there.

344 half a dozen DEA informants: Author interview with former DEA administrator Thomas Constantine, Jan. 30, 2001.

345 González Quirarte met with several Generals: General Marcial Macedo de la Concha, at the time the army's top prosecutor, confirmed the meeting in an author interview on September 19, 1997. An army intelligence document referred to the meeting: "Un documento de la exposición de diversas hipótesis del ofrecimiento de un narcotraficante." See Marín, "Documentos de Inteligencia Militar involucran en el narcotráfico a altos jefes, oficiales, y tropa del ejército," p. 12. The $6 million bribe was reported by John Ward Anderson, "Drug Kingpin's Life Is an Open Book, Now That He's Dead; Damaging Details about Influential Mexicans Often Aired Only after They've Lost Power," *Washington Post*, Nov. 25, 1997, p. 1.

345–46 a classified military report: Marín, "Documentos de Inteligencia Militar involucran en el narcotráfico a altos jefes, oficiales, y tropa del ejército."

346 Felipe Cobián telephoned Ibarra: Cobián, "No soy narca," p. 18.

346 political scientists devoted considerable study: The debate is outlined in John Bailey and Roy Godson, eds., *Organized Crime and Democratic Governability* (Pittsburgh: University of Pittsburgh Press, 2000), pp. 3–6.

346–47 three other Generals: They were Generals Jorge Mariano Maldonado Vega, Mario Arturo Acosta Chaparro, and Francisco Quirós Hermosillo. See Abel Barajas and Víctor Fuentes, "Cae otro narco general," *Reforma*, April 6, 2001, p. 1. A DEA official based in Mexico from 1997 through 2000 described the $16 million bribe.

347 Some academics and media critics: See Delal Baer, "Misreading Mexico," *Foreign Policy* (Fall 1997). A more recent article that also criticized journalists for exaggerating the drug threat in Mexico was Michael Massing, "The Narco-State?" *New York Review of Books*, June 15, 2000, p. 24.

348 a lengthy 1997 article: "Drug Ties Taint 2 Mexican Governors," *New York Times*, Feb. 23, 1997, p. 1.

12. Testing Change, 1997

353 growth of the opposition vote: Ricardo Becerra, Pedro Salazar, and José Woldenberg, *La mecánica del cambio político en México: Elecciones, partidos, y reformas* (Mexico: Cal y Arena, 2000), p. 499. Also see Alonso Lujambio, "Adiós a la excepcionalidad," *Este País*, Feb. 2000, pp. 2–16.

356 the majority leader: The formal title was Presidente de la Mesa Directiva.

357 had twice come close to occupying Los Pinos: See Jorge G. Castañeda, *La herencia: Arqueología de la sucesión presidencial en México* (Mexico: Extra Alfaguara, 1999).

358 the inauguration had been postponed: This account is based primarily on author reporting of the events for *The New York Times*, supplemented by an author interview with Fidel Herrera Beltrán, July 31, 2001; and the following newspaper accounts: Jorge Camargo, "Avísenle a Nuñez," *Reforma*, Aug. 31, 1997, p. 7; Miguel Angel Granados Chapa, "Legislatura instalada," *Reforma*, Aug. 31, 1997, p. 19; Gerardo Albarrán de Alba, "La maniobra de Chuayffet," *El Norte*, Aug. 31, 1997, p. 12.

360–61 "Get your act together": Author interview with Luis Téllez, Aug. 31, 1997.

361 From this day forward: author translation of live tape recording of Porfirio Muñoz Ledo, Palacio Legislativo de San Lazaro, Sept. 1, 1997.

363 collected more than $12 billion: Gabriel Székely, coordinator, *FOBAPROA e IPAB: El acuerdo que no debió ser* (Mexico: Océano, 1999), p. 201.

365 more problems started to turn up: The banker Jorge Lankenau was arrested on November 19, 1997, on charges of fraud worth $170 million. Court documents in the case showed that he had been taking his customers' money out of his bank, called Confía (the name means "trust me"), and depositing it in accounts in the Cayman Islands that were not reported to Mexican fiscal authorities.

365 police in Spain tracked him down: Luis Mendez, "Seguían a 'El Divino' desde 1995," *Reforma*, July 31, 1996, p. 4.

366 new kind of scrutiny: See Sergio Sarmiento, "El rescate," *Reforma*, June 14, 2001. Sarmiento compared Mexico's banking rescue to similar operations in South Korea and Chile.

366 he began to tell a few secrets: Author correspondence with Carlos Cabal, and examination of documents he provided, in June 1999.

367 Andrés Manuel López Obrador's speech: filmed on videotape. *El Fobaproa y Usted*, PRD, July 19, 1998.

367 the PAN gained the initiative: Among other *panistas* in the talks were Fauzi Hamdan Amad, Rogelio Sada Zambrano, Francisco José Paoli Bolio, and Gerardo Buganza Salmerón. Ricardo García Sáinz, Alfonso Ramírez Cuéllar, and Dolores Padierna were among the key players for the PRD.

368 outside independent audit of the bailout fund: At the insistence of the PRI, Mackey did not reveal any names in his original July 1999 report. Based on an agreement among the three main parties in the Congress, Mackey put a list of loans he determined to be illegal and the names of the loan holders on a compact disc and provided different codes to the PRI, the PAN, and the PRD. The CD could only be opened if all three parties agreed. However, in July 2000 the PRD, using hackers, unilaterally broke the codes. The names were disappointing to those who expected to find high-ranking government officials among them. Still, they included the brother of the head of Pemex, a son of Carlos Hank González, and a $422,000 loan directly to the PRI.

371 from the first day in his new job: Legorreta's experiences in the Delegación

Cuauhtémoc come from an author interview with Jorge Legorreta, April 12, 2001. Also, author interview with Jorge Fernández Souza, April 5, 2001.

371 Oscar Espinosa Villarreal: Carlos Cabal Peniche, the rogue banker, claimed that he had worked with Espinosa to make illegal donations to Zedillo's 1994 campaign. In author interviews in June and July 1999, Espinosa said that he knew of Cabal's contributions but argued that they had not violated any laws.

372 Unified Union of the Federal District Government: The name in Spanish is Sindicato Unico de Trabajadores del Gobierno del Distrito Federal.

373 another source of income from the garbage trucks: The study of gasoline use was ordered by Jorge Fernández Souza, the *delegado* of the Miguel Hidalgo borough in the Cárdenas administration.

375 a drive to eliminate a particularly malignant form of corruption: Author interview with Ricardo Pascoe Pierce, Dec. 11, 2000.

377 promoting a young police officer: Samuel del Villar's chief of detectives was Mauricio Tornero.

377 a respected human rights activist: He was José Luis Pérez Canchola.

379 a proclamation: "Acuerdo por el que se establece el 2 de octubre como día de duelo en el Distrito Federal," *Gaceta Oficial del Distrito Federal*, Aug. 27, 1998, p. 3.

379 Tens of thousands of Mexicans: Andrea Becerril and Mireya Cuéllar, "Verdad y justicia, exigieron miles en Tlatelolco," *La Jornada*, Oct. 3, 1998, p. 1.

380 "The president's account": Enrique Krauze, *Mexico: Biography of Power: A History of Modern Mexico, 1810–1996*, trans. Hank Heifetz (New York: HarperCollins, 1997), p. 725.

380 Sergio Aguayo: The account of his research is drawn from several author interviews with Aguayo and from studying Sergio Aguayo, *Los archivos de la violencia* (Mexico: Grijalbo and Reforma, 1998).

381 the commander of the main force of troops: He was General Crisóforo Mazón.

381–82 "Because those were my orders": The account of Scherer's relationship with General García Barragán was drawn from Julio Scherer and Carlos Monsiváis, *Parte de guerra, Tlatelolco 1968* (Mexico: Nuevo Siglo/Aguilar, 1999). The quotations are from pp. 38 and 44. In another important piece of reportage by *Proceso*, Scherer's daughter, a reporter at the magazine, established for the first time that a government movie crew had filmed the massacre with movie cameras. Cameramen told her that hours before the 1968 demonstration, on the orders of Government Secretary Luis Echeverría, they had gone to the twenty-story Foreign Relations building that towers over one side of the plaza, setting up their cameras behind the plate-glass windows of several upper floors. They shot five hours of film, using powerful five-hundred-millimeter lenses that allowed them to close in on individual faces of the wounded and dying. Its mission completed, the crew delivered its film directly to Echeverría, Scherer Ibarra's article said. But he refused to submit to congressional questioning in 1998, and the film remained missing. María Scherer Ibarra, "El Secretario de Gobernación sabía lo que iba a suceder: Echeverría recibió 120,000 pies de película, con los detalles de la masacre filmados desde seis cámaras," *Proceso*, March 16, 1998, p. 1. Which floors of the Foreign Relations building the movie crew occupied is in dispute. Scherer's story says floor 19. Sergio Aguayo says the crew was on floors 17 and 20. See Aguayo, *Archivos de la violencia*, p. 224.

382 a poll showed: "Cárdenas: Encuesta trimestral," *Reforma*, Sept. 17, 1999, p. 1.

382–83 Rosario Robles: Based on reporting by Julia Preston for *The New York Times*.

13. The Earcutter

386 demanded a $3 million ransom: See María de la Luz González, "Reconoce Arizmendi secuestro de Raúl Nava," *Reforma*, Aug. 26, 1998, p. 8.

387 Raúl's remains had lain unrecognized: The account of the Ricaño family's ordeal during their son's kidnapping comes from author interviews with Josefina Ricaño on March 30 and Aug. 24, 2001.

387 As word about the discovery: Nava Ricaño's abduction went unreported in the press until after his body was recovered. His relatives and the authorities kept it secret, believing that publicity could endanger Raúl's life.

387 compiled information on fifteen hundred abductions: Author interview with Christopher T. Marquet, managing director of Kroll Associates, the New York security firm, Aug. 1996.

387 the country's number-one worry: Crime fears first overtook economic insecurity in mid-1998. See *Seguridad nacional y opinión pública: Selección de encuestas de opinión* (Mexico: Instituto Nacional de Administración Pública, 2000), p. 61.

387 a professor at the UNAM: Author interview with Rafael Ruiz Harrell, June 1998. For the chart of reported crimes from 1930 to 1997, see Rafael Ruiz Harrell, *Criminalidad y mal gobierno* (Mexico: Sansores y Aljure, 1998), p. 13.

388 "simply doesn't respond to most crimes": Author interview in June 1998 with Ernesto López Portillo, co-author of *Seguridad pública en México* (Mexico: Universidad Nacional Autónoma de México, 1994).

388 of every one hundred criminal complaints: Guillermo Zepeda Lecuona, "Inefficiency at the Service of Impunity: Criminal Justice Organizations in Mexico," in John Bailey and Jorge Chabat, *Public Security and Democratic Governance: Challenges to Mexico and the United States: Report to Task Force* (Washington, D.C., Feb. 2001).

388 A World Bank study: Robert L. Ayres, *Crime and Violence as Development Issues in Latin America and the Caribbean* (Washington, D.C.: World Bank, 1998).

388 *ministerios públicos*: For a penetrating study of their work, see Zepeda Lecuona, "Inefficiency at the Service of Impunity." During the 2000 presidential campaign, PRI candidate Francisco Labastida said in a speech that 60 percent of Mexico's *ministerios públicos* failed a nationwide exam administered during his tenure as Government Secretary.

388 a national survey in 1999: *Seguridad nacional y opinión pública*, p. 67. Judges, of course, were held in marginally higher repute than police and prosecutors.

389 A 1998 study by two Mexican sociologists: Nelson Arteaga Botello and Adrián López Rivera, "Viaje al interior de la policía: El caso de un municipio de México," *Nexos*, April 1998.

389 the system was losing the authoritarian powers: Former agents of the Federal Security Directorate, the intelligence agency dismantled in 1985, co-authored a book that traced the growth in Mexican lawlessness to the 1970s, when President López Portillo gave the DFS and other police license to exterminate accused subversives. When the guerrillas had been suppressed, the police turned their extralegal skills to organized crime. "They went into drugs, car theft, kidnaps, piracy, truck hijackings," said Lucio Mendoza, one of the authors. "It was like a cancer that expanded." Author interview with Lucio Mendoza, June 1998. See Instituto Mexicano de Estudios de la Criminalidad Organizada, *Todo lo que debería saber sobre el crimen organizado en México* (Mexico: Océano, 1998).

389–90 Daniel Arizmendi López was a notorious example: This section profiling Arizmendi would have been impossible to write without the extensive, virtually day-by-day coverage of the Arizmendi mafia in *Reforma* starting on November 24, 1997, and lasting until well after his arrest in mid-August 1998. In writing this chapter, we studied that coverage, then went back to the principal figures in the case for interviews.

390 "I'm a man who keeps his word": César Romero Jacobo and Guillermo Osorno. "Identifican a secuestradores," *Reforma*, Nov. 24, 1997.

391 about ten thousand security firms: Bailey and Chabat, *Public Security and Democratic Governance*, p. 20, citing *La Jornada*, June 13, 1997. *La Jornada* quotes Horacio Cantú Díaz, president of the Asociación Mexicana de Sistemas Integrales de Seguridad Privada.

392–93 The November 29, 1997, demonstration: Alejandra Bordon and Luis Guillermo Hernández, "Ensordece el silencio," *Reforma*, Nov. 30, 1997, p. 1. González Gamio's story is told in Alejandro Caballero, "Roban pertenencias a ex embajadora," *Reforma*, Aug. 28, 1997, p. 2.

393 Fuentes-Berain assigned a *Reforma* reporter: Author interview with Fuentes-Berain, Dec. 6, 2000.

393 Fuentes-Berain concluded: Even in the years after *Reforma*'s reporting changed the journalistic environment, most kidnappings went unreported. Rafael Macedo de la Concha, President Fox's Attorney General, estimated in

a radio interview in August 2001 that of every ten kidnappings, only two were reported.

394 front-page story: Romero Jacobo and Osorno, "Identifican a secuestradores."

394 He ordered them to wait: César Romero Jacobo, "Protegen policías a los Arizmendi," *Reforma*, Jan. 21, 1998.

394 requested *amparo* protection: David Vicenteno, "Tramita juicio de amparo Tassinari," *Reforma*, Nov. 28, 1997. In 2001 *Reforma* reported that officials were still investigating Tassinari's ties to kidnappers, but by mid-2003 no charges had been filed against him. Francisco Rodriguez, "Relacionan a judicial con 'El Mochaorejas,'" *Reforma*, May 9, 2001.

394–95 "As you're talking with the chief kidnapper": This passage is from César Romero Jacobo, "El cautiverio," *Reforma*, March 26, 1998. The series ran March 25–27, 1998. Author translation, with some phrases trimmed for space.

395 Two of Mexico's most powerful businessmen: See César Romero Jacobo, "Si me agarran, me matan," *Reforma*, Jan. 21, 1998.

395–96 "by whatever means necessary": Author interview with Samuel González Ruiz, the head of the Organized Crime Unit, on May 25, 1998.

397 Zedillo sharply criticized Carrillo Olea's government: The Morelos police chief was subsequently convicted of the cover-up. The attorney general was never convicted. For details on Zedillo's criticism, see Fernando Mayolo López, "Critica Zedillo a priístas," *Reforma*, March 4, 1998, p. 4; and Raymundo Riva Palacio, "No soy el malo de la película: Carrillo Olea," *El Financiero*, March 9, 1998, p. 1.

397–98 an odd call came to the *Reforma* newsroom: Roberto Zamarripa, "Soy Daniel Arizmendi," *Reforma*, June 3, 1998, p. 4.

398–99 He traveled to Querétaro: Most of this account of the Raúl Nieto kidnapping is drawn from an author interview on December 16, 2000, with Alberto Pliego Fuentes, the state of México police commander who participated in Arizmendi's arrest and interrogation.

399 Alberto Pliego Fuentes: suspicion was never dispelled: In July 1998, less than a month before Arizmendi's arrest, authorities arrested his defense attorney, José Angel Vivanco, and charged him with racketeering. During his trial Vivanco accused Pliego of accepting the bribe from Arizmendi. He testified that in June 1996, he delivered 150,000 pesos, about $25,000, to a subordinate of Pliego's at the Nezahualcóyotl judicial headquarters. Vivanco said that Pliego's subordinate skimmed off 10,000 pesos, that he himself had skimmed another 10,000, and that Pliego kept 130,000. See Daniel Lizárraga, "Aceptó soborno Pliego Fuentes, acusa Vivanco," *Reforma*, July 26, 1998. In their respective press conferences on the day after Arizmendi's arrest, Attorney General Jorge Madrazo and the head of the Attorney General's Organized Crime Unit, Samuel González Ruiz, differed as to whether Vivanco's accusations against Pliego remained credible, despite Pliego's role in Arizmendi's ar-

rest. Madrazo said the accusations had lost credibility. González Ruiz disagreed.

400 Pliego made the gunmen an offer: Pliego's use of these technically illegal tactics would almost certainly have been supported by large majorities of the Mexican public. Still, Pliego's rationale for basing Arizmendi's arrest on extralegal tactics involved an acknowledgment of the weakness of Mexican police techniques in general: "I had to do things that a police officer cannot legally do," Pliego said. "But if I didn't do them, I'd never arrest him." Author interview with Pliego, Dec. 16, 2000.

400 Attorney General Madrazo gave a fictionalized account: Madrazo asserted falsely that the kidnapper had been seized not in front of the bank along the gritty freeway in eastern Mexico City but in the far western suburb of Naucalpan, Pliego said in the December 2000 interview. Madrazo omitted any mention of the CISEN's role. See the Attorney General's official transcript of Madrazo's August 18, 1998, press conference.

14. Opening Minds

408 The "perverse game" of being an intellectual in Mexico: The first part of this chapter, dealing with intellectuals, is based on author interviews with Héctor Aguilar Camín, Dec. 7, 2000, and July 23, 2001; Homero Aridjis, July 7, 2000, and March 14, 2001; Jorge G. Castañeda, June 30, 2001; Enrique Krauze, April 11 and July 2, 2001; and Carlos Monsiváis, Aug. 2, 2001. Comments were provided by Gabriel Zaid.

413 economic policies as "science fiction": Gabriel Zaid, "Alicia en el país de la fluctuación," Vuelta 1, no. 1 (Dec. 1976).

414 they launched Nexos: The first director was Enrique Florescano, a prominent historian.

415 Cautious, Monsiváis showed the piece: Reflecting on the episode in an interview in 2001, Monsiváis said, "If it had been today, I would have resigned. But to say that now has no point."

416 In a 1972 letter: Gabriel Zaid, "Carta a Carlos Fuentes," Cómo leer en bicicleta (Mexico: Joaquín Mortiz, 1975), p. 106.

416 "Let us suppose": Gabriel Zaid, "Cómo hacer la reforma política sin hacer nada," La economía presidencial (Mexico: Vuelta, 1987), p. 48.

417 first essay about current Mexican politics: Enrique Krauze, "El timón y la tormenta," Vuelta 6, no. 71 (1982), pp. 14–22.

418 "Until a few years ago": Octavio Paz, "Hora cumplida (1929–1985)," Vuelta 9, no. 103 (1985), pp. 7–12.

418 stability could "no longer be taken for granted": Jorge G. Castañeda, "Mexico at the Brink," Foreign Affairs (Winter 1985–86).

419 "To accept the positions": Transcript of tape-recorded interview with Octavio Paz by Tim Golden of The New York Times, Feb. 1992.

419 veteran critic of the PRI system: Aguilar Camín's most revealing exposé was a work of fiction, an inspired novel called *Morir en el golfo* (To die in the gulf) about a dissolute Mexican journalist and his run-in with a labor leader, who was based on La Quina.

420 lifetime fellowships: Sistema Nacional de Creadores de Arte, Creadores Eméritos. List provided by the Fondo Nacional para la Cultura y las Artes, April 22, 1998.

422 new history textbooks: These were the ones that caused trouble for Education Secretary Ernesto Zedillo.

422–23 a review by Enrique Krauze: Enrique Krauze, "The Guerrilla Dandy: The Life and Easy Times of Carlos Fuentes," *New Republic,* June 27, 1988, pp. 28–38. The books were Carlos Fuentes, *Myself with Others: Selected Essays* (New York: Farrar, Straus & Giroux, 1988) and *The Old Gringo* (New York: Farrar, Straus & Giroux, 1985).

423 an eloquent interpreter of his country: Fuentes taught for years at Princeton and maintained a home there.

423 Paz's comments on the Krauze review: Transcript of an interview with Octavio Paz by Tim Golden of *The New York Times,* Feb. 1992.

424 they were never reconciled: Paz died in April 1998.

424 "We did not invite any pseudo intellectuals": Armando Ponce and Gerardo Ochoa Sandy, "*Vuelta* inicia su encuentro de la libertad," *Proceso,* Aug. 27, 1990.

424 exchange between Paz and Vargas Llosa on "the perfect dictatorship": Octavio Paz and Enrique Krauze, general editors, *La experiencia de la libertad,* vol. 1 (Mexico: Fundación Cultural Televisa, 1991), pp. 160–62.

425 "On the subject of democracy": Armando Ponce and Gerardo Ochoa Sandy, "En las afueras del encuentro," *Proceso,* Sept. 3, 1990.

425 "To equate Communism": Transcript of interview with Octavio Paz by Tim Golden of *The New York Times,* Feb. 1992.

427 Becerra quietly took a $1 million payment: Larry Rohter, "Mexican Papers Want to Keep Tie with State," *New York Times,* Dec. 4, 1989, p. D11.

427–28 *Siglo 21*: This account is based on author interviews with Jorge Zepeda Patterson, Jan. 23, Feb. 22, and March 6, 2001, and with Alejandra Xanic von Bertrab, Aug. 2, 2001.

431 The dead numbered in the hundreds: The official death toll was 211, with hundreds more permanently injured and traumatized.

433 Azcárraga once threatened: Author interview with Enrique Krauze, July 2, 2001.

434 the San Angel Group: The group was a descendant of a series of informal discussion groups in which pro-democracy politicians and intellectuals from diverse political camps—as disparate as the left wing of Cárdenas's movement and the right wing of the PAN—got together to search for common ground. An early incarnation was the Council for Democracy, formed in 1989. One

of its prime movers was an executive from an industrial glassmaking dynasty in Monterrey, Rogelio Sada Zambrano. He was a *panista* who worried that the rancor created in 1988 could tear Mexico apart if nothing was done to build bridges among opposition factions and accelerate reform. The potpourri of about thirty people who attended the council's meetings included Jorge Castañeda, Porfirio Muñoz Ledo, Diego Fernández de Cevallos, Juan Molinar Horcasitas, Leticia Calzada (the friend of Vicente Fox, who was also an old friend of Sada), and Arnoldo Martínez Verdugo, former leader of the Mexican Communist Party. One offspring of the council was the group that organized a March 1993 referendum in Mexico City in which residents affirmed that they wanted to elect their mayor and city council and become the thirty-second state. The San Angel Group formed a year later. Among its participants were Tatiana Clouthier (daughter of Manuel Clouthier, El Maquío), Ricardo García Sainz, Enrique González Pedrero, Elba Esther Gordillo, David Ibarra, Javier Livas Cantú, Federico Reyes Heroles, and Demetrio Sodi de la Tijera.

435 Dau's financial troubles: Irma Salas, "Enfrenta *Siglo 21* demanda de quiebra," *El Norte*, Aug. 7, 1997, p. 5; Felipe Cobián, "Alfonso Dau utilizó al periódico," *Proceso*, Aug. 11, 1997; Miguel Angel Granados Chapa, "Dau en escena," *Reforma*, Aug. 25, 1997, p. 21; Joaquín Fernández Nuñez, "Los buenos divorcios," *Expansión*, Nov. 5, 1997, p. 64.

437 Televisa meeting on March 4, 1997, at Los Pinos: Author interviews with José Antonio Cañedo White, Oct. 26, 2000, and Liébano Sáenz, Nov. 29, 2001.

438 Zedillo's Government Secretary intervened to veto him: At the March 4 meeting at Los Pinos, President Zedillo told the Televisa executives that his Government Secretary, Emilio Chuayffet, "had complained a lot" about Rocha. After the meeting the executives went directly to Chuayffet's office to discuss the matter further. "You have to control Rocha" was Chuayffet's message. This passage based on author interviews with José Antonio Cañedo White, Oct. 26, 2000, and with Ricardo Rocha, May 10, 2001.

15. Chiapas

443 they kept their own birth and death records: For a detailed look at the Zapatistas' autonomous network of government, see Lene Lothe Gómez Palma, "Indigenous Resistance and the Construction of Autonomy: Power, Land, and Territory in Two Regions of Chiapas, Mexico" (thesis, University of Oslo, 2001). Gómez Palma first went to Chiapas through a Norwegian solidarity organization, and so gained rare access from the EZLN to their autonomous government at work.

447 "We don't paint any other world here": Interview by Anne Sorensen, Roberto Barrios Autonomous School, June 20, 2001. Julia and Sorensen, a reporter

for the Danish newspaper *Politiken*, made a trip together to Roberto Barrios. The Zapatista authorities allowed both of them to visit the school but only allowed Anne to interview the teachers in depth.

448 "advance to the nation's capital": For this and other EZLN declarations, see http://www.laneta.apc.org/porlapaz/ind/chis0.htm.

16. Democracy at Work

461 "This Is the Face of the System . . .": Miguel Angel Granados Chapa, "El siglo de Fidel," *Reforma*, June 22, 1997.

461 Don Fidel had been unfailingly loyal: Details of Velázquez's last years are drawn from Anthony DePalma, "At 95, Still Labor's King, but Ruling Party's Vassal," *New York Times*, Feb. 5, 1996, p. 4; and Anthony DePalma, "Fidel Velázquez, Mexico Titan, Dies at 97," *New York Times*, June 22, 1997, p. 26. Other biographical details are from Kevin J. Middlebrook, *The Paradox of Revolution* (Baltimore: Johns Hopkins University Press, 1995), p. 268; on Velázquez's acquiescence in mass firings, see p. 276.

462 "I'm just about finished!": Rodríguez Alcaine's 1997 May Day appearance is reported in Miguel Pérez, "Abuchean a dirigentes sindicales," *Reforma*, May 2, 1997.

462–63 it had begun it with heroic developments: This sketch of the evolution of the union movement and its relations to the state owes much to Middlebrook's terrific study of the twentieth-century labor movement, *The Paradox of Revolution*, from which a number of details in this chapter have been drawn. On Luis N. Morones, see pp. 77–83. On the CTM formation, see pp. 87–95. On Velázquez's reserved seat in the Senate, see p. 105.

465 The results were impressive for a time: See the social-poverty index for Mexico, 1910–70, in James W. Wilkie, "The Six Ideological Phases of Mexico's 'Permanent Revolution' since 1910," in *Society and Economy in Mexico*, ed. James W. Wilkie (Los Angeles: UCLA Latin American Center Publications, 1990), p. 16.

467 General Motors engine plant: Middlebrook, *Paradox of Revolution*, p. 275. For a discussion of the origin of the separation-exclusion clauses, see p. 96.

467 ITAPSA: The plant is in Ciudad de los Reyes and was owned at the time by Echlin Inc. of Branford, Connecticut. Echlin was purchased in 1998 by the Dana Corporation of Toledo, Ohio. Arturo Alcalde recounted the September 1997 confrontation at the Echlin plant. The events are also documented in a government report: U.S. National Administrative Office, *Public Report of Review of NAO Submission No. 9703* (Washington, D.C.: Bureau of International Affairs, U.S. Department of Labor, July 31, 1998).

469 two plants in Mississippi: Alcoa executives Robert Hughes and Jack D. Jenkins recounted the history of Alcoa's move from Mississippi to Mexico during an author interview in February 2001.

469–70 the town's population had quadrupled: Mexico's 2000 census counted 110,388 residents in Acuña, but state and local officials called that a gross undercount, estimating Acuña's population in the range of 150,000 to 180,000. The 2000 census found that only two other cities, Iztapaluca, a suburb of Mexico City, and Los Cabos, the seaside resort in Baja California Sur, were growing more quickly than Acuña.

470 "The American companies said": Author interview with Jesús María Ramón Valdés, Ciudad Acuña and Del Rio, Tex., Sept. 23, 2000.

471 Dr. Ruth Rosenbaum: She is based at the Center for Reflection, Education, and Action, in Hartford, Connecticut, a social economics research and education center.

471–72 Acuña's budget for 2000: Author interview with Acuña's mayor, Eduardo Ramón Valdés, on Sept. 24, 2000, and with Rafael Castillo, Del Rio's acting city manager, a few days later.

472 the maquiladora tax system: In response to questions, Alcoa released a written statement saying that in 1999 its Acuña factories paid a $450,000 Coahuila state payroll tax, $7.8 million to Mexico's social security system, and $2.4 million in federal taxes earmarked for low-cost housing. None of these taxes was being paid to Acuña's municipal authorities, and the statement indicated that Alcoa paid no other taxes on its Acuña operations.

473 two American church groups: They were the American Friends Service Committee and the Congregation of Benedictine Sisters.

474 wage increase: See José Aguayo, "Saint Benedict and the Labor Unions," *Forbes*, Feb. 9, 1998, p. 64.

474 suppression of wages: The figures are drawn from Sidney Weintraub, "Workers' 15-Year Nightmare," *Los Angeles Times*, Jan. 11, 1998. Weintraub cited data compiled by the U.S. Bureau of Labor Statistics.

475 cut its formal tie to the PRI: See Claudia Ramos, "Deben sindicatos revisar estrategias," *Reforma*, April 17, 1996, p. 14.

476 Its founder and secretary-general: Author interview with Ramón Gámez Martínez, Aug. 14, 2001.

17. Campaign for Change

478 Only a third of Mexicans had landline telephones: 36 percent of Mexican homes had phones, according to press release 59/2001 of the Instituto Nacional de Estadística, Geografía, e Informática, May 21, 2001. In small towns, defined as having fewer than twenty-five hundred residents, only 6 percent of homes had phones. See "Principales resultados del XII censo general de población y vivienda, 2000," on the INEGI Web site at www. inegi.gob.mx.

478 Cemex: Author interview with Lorenzo Zambrano, July 25, 2001. Also see Charles Piggott, "Cemex's Stratospheric Rise," *Latin Finance*, March 1,

2001; and James F. Smith, "Making Cement a Household Word in Latin America," *Los Angeles Times*, Jan. 16, 2000, p. C1.

478 automobile- and computer-assembly plants: Harley Shaiken, *Mexico in the Global Economy: High Technology and Work Organization in Export Industries* (San Diego: Center for U.S.-Mexican Studies, 1990).

478 Change was in the air: Tim Weiner, "Terrific News in Mexico City: Air Is Sometimes Breathable," *New York Times*, Jan. 5, 2001, p. 1.

478 by the 1990s only three: *La situación demográfica de México* (Mexico: Conapo, 1998), p. 17. The figures on the rise in life expectancy correspond to the years 1975 to 1995; see ibid., pp. 11–12.

478–79 infant-mortality rate: *México hoy* (Mexico: Instituto Nacional de Estadística, Geografía, e Informática, 2000), p. 42. For university enrollment, see ibid., p. 64.

479 the Mexico City metropolitan area: See Consejo Nacional de Población, "Escenarios demográficos y urbanos de la Zona Metropolitana de la Ciudad de México," *La situación demográfica de México*.

480 Lino Korrodi: His account of his fund-raising efforts from author interviews during the 1999–2000 campaign and on July 9, 2001, and from interviews with other Fox campaign officials.

480 During Fox's 1995 campaign: Korrodi collected more than $1 million before Fox's May 1995 victory in Guanajuato, he said. Author interview with Korrodi, July 9, 2001.

480 Mexico's wealthiest men made important donations: A senior member of the Fox campaign identified Manuel Espinosa Yglesias, Alfonso Romo Garza, Roberto Hernández, Lorenzo Zambrano, and Carlos Slim as Fox contributors. Author interview, July 2001. The identities of these and other Fox contributors became public in 2002, when *Proceso* published a series of investigative reports on Fox's campaign fund-raising. See Antonio Jáquez, "Aportaciones sospechosas," *Proceso*, no. 1334, May 26, 2002, p. 9. *Proceso* pursued the theme in subsequent issues: June 2, June 9, and June 16, 2002.

480 Alfonso Romo Garza: Carlos Acosta Córdova and Antonio Jáquez, "Los magnates regiomontanos empiezan a obtener su recompensa," *Proceso*, Aug. 6, 2000; and Porrita Varela Mayorga, "Un pura sangre en aprietos," *Día Siete*, July 2001.

481 1993 PRI fund-raising banquet: A detailed account is in Andrés Oppenheimer, *Bordering on Chaos* (Boston: Little, Brown, 1996), pp. 83–110.

481 no one from their class: In 1940 some Monterrey businessmen appear to have given financial backing to the dissident presidential candidacy of General Juan Andrew Almazán, who was nonetheless overwhelmed by the PRI. See Luis Javier Garrido, *El partido de la revolución institucionalizada: Medio siglo de poder político en México* (Mexico: Siglo XXI, 1982), p. 274. Twelve years later, Miguel Henríquez Guzmán, another PRI politician who left the official party to run for President on his own, also attracted some private-

sector donations. He also was crushed by the PRI. The historian Lorenzo Meyer, of the Colegio de México, said in an author interview on January 18, 2002, that both Almazán and Henríquez Guzmán had received financial support from wealthy backers during their 1940 and 1952 presidential candidacies. For details on the support given to Miguel Henríquez Guzmán by his brother and other wealthy backers, see Elisa Servín, *Ruptura y oposición: El movimiento henriquista, 1945–1954* (Mexico: Cal y Arena, 2001). The obvious lesson for the business class was that it was a waste of money, as well as a tremendous political risk, to donate to presidential candidates opposing the ruling system. In the half century that followed, no opposition presidential candidate received significant financial support until Vicente Fox. Some academics have hypothesized that Manuel Clouthier, the PAN candidate in 1988, might have received significant private-sector support. But the top-ten Monterrey capitalists, who were Clouthier's friends and might have donated to him, instead supported Salinas and merely gave Clouthier a dinner, hosted by Dionisio Garza Sada, a prince of Monterrey's founding industrial dynasty.

"We're not going to do politics," Garza Sada told Clouthier. "This is about friendship." Author interview on August 11, 2001, with Fernando Canales, governor of Nuevo León, who attended the 1988 dinner.

481–82 a 1998 booklet: *La transición mexicana y nuestra propuesta para un desarrollo sostenible en el largo plaza* (Mexico: Consejo Coordinador Empresarial, 1998).

482 The business class needed reassurances: The private sector's insecurities and the importance of Fox's pro-business position on Fobaproa in calming them are from an author interview with one of the most incisive observers of Mexico's private sector, Rogelio Ramírez de la O, June 8, 2001.

483 half of the registered voters were thirty-five years of age or younger: Author interview with Eduardo Badillo, the director of the Federal Voter Registry, May 2000.

483 "Let's do primaries": This Zedillo statement, as well as other presidential quotations and accounts of the participation of Los Pinos officials in organizing the 1999 PRI primary, was cited by Zedillo's senior aides in author interviews. Zedillo was at first coy about describing his plans to journalists and the public but eventually became more specific. Asked during an interview with *The New York Times* in February 1998 about whether he would exercise the *dedazo*, Zedillo said, "I think I won't play the same very strong role other Presidents have played." But in a visit to New York City four months later, in June 1998, he told newspaper executives he favored a "wide open" primary to choose the PRI candidate. See the wire story by Claude E. Erbsen, "Mexico President Seeks Open Primary," Associated Press, June 9, 1998.

484 "after the cow": The quotation is from a hilarious article by José De Cordoba, "Mexico's Ruling Party Dabbles in Democracy to Stave Off Decline," *Wall Street Journal*, July 1, 1998.

485 kickbacks: Author interviews in October 1999 with Madrazo, Ojeda, and the young executive Gerardo Priego Tapia.

485 spent some $25 million: Author interview with Madrazo, Oct. 1999.

486 engineered the firing: In a September 1999 interview, Gamboa denied that he had had any influence over the dismissal of the radio talk-show host.

486 "Don't be assholes!": Daniel Pensamiento, "Se enfrentan Albores y Congreso en Chiapas," *Reforma*, Oct. 21, 1999, p. 15.

486 a PRI thug: The photo was published on the cover of *Proceso*, and the accompanying article was a colorful roundup of the pro-Labastida chicanery all across Mexico. Alvaro Delgado, Julia Aranda, "El mismo de Salinas y De Córdoba: El 'nuevo PRI' tan viejo como sus mañas," *Proceso*, Nov. 15, 1999.

487 "The PRI is enjoying a honeymoon": Alejandro Moreno, "Impulsan internas a Labastida," *Reforma*, Nov. 29, 1999, p. 4.

487 drove him from the PRI: Fernando Gutiérrez Barrios struck the first blow, according to an official of the Zedillo government. The former secret-police chief obtained a copy of a draft of Camacho's memoirs and arranged for its publication under the sarcastic title *Yo Manuel: Memorias ¿apócrifas? de un comisionado*. It put Camacho's overweening ambitions on embarrassing public display. Emilio Chuayffet, the Government Secretary, followed up by insulting Camacho publicly, leaving him little alternative but to leave the party.

488 they would split the anti-PRI vote and lose: In the 1997 federal congressional elections, PRI candidates had received 39 percent of the national vote, far more than either the PAN, which received 27 percent, or Cárdenas's PRD, which received 26 percent, but far less than the opposition parties' combined vote of 53 percent. Those 1997 percentages seemed a good rough estimate of how the parties' presidential candidates might fare in the 2000 election. See "Resultados electorales, estadísticas elecciones federales 1997," Web site of the Instituto Federal Electoral: www.ife.org.mx.

489 "I'm selling an irresistible product": Reuters, "Entrevista, Vicente Fox," *El Norte*, Feb. 27, 1998, p. 8.

491 plebiscite on change: This account of the meeting at Aguilar Zinser's home is drawn from author interviews with participants. Castañeda outlined his argument in a lengthy opinion piece, "2 de julio: Los escenarios," *Reforma*, Feb. 4, 2000, p. A18.

493 refusing an offer for help: Daniel Moreno, "Rechaza Labastida apoyo de Hank Rhon," *Reforma*, Nov. 20, 1999, p. 1.

493 Jorge Hank Rhon: See Larry Rohter, "Tijuana Journal: 'The Cat' Clawed Many; Is One His Murderer?" *New York Times*, July 1, 1988, p. 4. On the smuggling of ocelot pelts, see Gustavo Alanís Ortega, "Especies en peligro de extinción," *Reforma*, June 1, 1995, p. 4.

493 he campaigned as the proud heir: Daniel Moreno, "Modifica su discurso Francisco Labastida," *Reforma*, May 13, 2000.

495 "Fox told us what we wanted to hear": Daniel Moreno, "Fox nos dijo lo que queríamos oír," *Reforma*, March 5, 2000, p. A6. Moreno also did great reporting on Fox's turnaround with the small entrepreneurs; see Daniel Moreno, "Recula Fox: Ahora pide carcel para banqueros," *Reforma*, March 9, 2000, p. 2.

495 worked to suppress at least two similar surveys: The other two pollsters were Ricardo de la Peña and María de las Heras. See Sam Dillon, "Mexican Party Reported to Quash Polls Predicting Its Defeat," *New York Times*, July 17, 2000, p. A9.

496 "The road has been long": Transcript of the second presidential debate, May 26, 2000, distributed by the PAN.

496–97 The account of Election Day, July 2, 2000, is based on the following author interviews: Federico Berrueto, Jan. 19 and Aug. 16, 2001; Cuauhtémoc Cárdenas, Dec. 12, 2000; Jorge G. Castañeda, June 6 and Nov. 19, 2000, and June 30, 2001; Vicente Fox, July 2, 2000; Emilio Gamboa, Feb. 8, 2001; Concepción Guadalupe Garza Rodríguez, Sept. 28, 2000; Francisco Labastida Ochoa, Oct. 12, 2000; Esteban Moctezuma, July 22 and Dec. 25, 2000, and Aug. 30, 2001; Nguyen Huu Dong, Nov. 17, 2000; Robert Pastor, April 24 and 26, 2001; Marco Provencio, Oct. 3, 2000; Liébano Sáenz, Feb. 21, March 2, May 9, Aug. 3, and Nov. 29, 2001; Javier Treviño, Sept. 21, 2000; José Woldenberg, Nov. 28, 2000; and Emilio Zebadúa, Nov. 27, 2000.

497 Chappell Lawson . . . who was at the school as a foreign observer: See Chappell Lawson, "What's New about the 'New' Mexico?" *ReVista: Harvard Review of Latin America* 1, no. 1 (Fall 2001), p. 8.

498 Labastida, not Fox, ahead by three points: See Charles Krause, "PRI, historia privada de un fracaso," *Gatopardo*, Aug. 2000.

500 Fox won 43 percent: Fox won 16 million of the 37.6 million votes cast. Labastida won 13.6 million, and Cárdenas won 6.3 million. These and other election figures were drawn from the Web site of the Instituto Federal Electoral at www.ife.org.mx.

500 The new Mexico: At the dawn of the twentieth century it had been an overwhelmingly rural nation populated mainly by illiterate peasants. At the century's end 60 percent of Mexicans lived in cities, 90 percent of adults could read and write, and about six in ten had a high-school degree. Most of those who remained illiterate were senior citizens. Cities defined here as settlements of fifteen thousand or more inhabitants. See the "XII censo general de población y vivienda, 2000," on the INEGI Web site at www.inegi.gob.mx.

500 He won 50 percent: The demographic analysis of the July 2, 2000, vote is based on the exit poll conducted by *Reforma* newspaper. See Alejandro Moreno, María Antonia Mancillas, and Roberto Gutiérrez, "Gana Mexico urbano y educado: Perfil de los electores," *Reforma*, July 3, 2000, p. 8.

500 Labastida won majorities in the seven most rural states: Oaxaca, Chiapas, Hidalgo, Zacatecas, Tabasco, Tlaxcala, and Guerrero.

501 Mexico's most pluralistic Congress: The PAN won 208 seats in the 500-member Chamber of Deputies. The PRI won 209 seats, and the PRD won 53. Five small parties won the remaining seats.

501 Voters played a final joke: "On July 2, Mexicans dismantled the machine," Denise Dresser, a political science professor, wrote in *Proceso*. "They accepted the bicycles and rode them away, leaving the PRI behind. They said thanks for the washing machines, turned them on, and washed the dirty linen of seventy-one years . . . They carried away their bags of cement and mixed mortar to build the foundations of a new country." See Denise Dresser, "Despertar en un país recobrado," *Proceso*, July 3, 2000, p. 11.

Epilogue

503 an economic strategy: Zedillo arranged new lines of foreign credit in case of a run on the peso, kept election-year government spending from growing exorbitant, and stuck by his sturdy exchange mechanism that allowed the peso's value to rise and fall with market demand. For a detailed discussion of the plan, see Jonathan Heath, *Mexico and the Sexenio Curse: Presidential Successions and Economic Crises in Modern Mexico* (Washington, D.C.: Center for Strategic and International Studies, 1999), p. 63.

504 a 1,393-page book: Carlos Salinas, *México: Un paso difícil a la modernidad* (Barcelona: Plaza y Janés, 2000).

504 the same Televisa news anchorman: He was Joaquín López Dóriga.

504–5 "I'm going to clarify everything": A transcript of the tape-recorded conversation between Raúl and Adriana Salinas, drawn from the Televisa broadcast, was published in Mexico City newspapers on October 11, 2000.

505 Most Mexicans assumed: Liébano Sáenz, Zedillo's chief of staff, insisted that neither he nor Zedillo knew anything of the Raúl tape before hearing it on Televisa. Author interview with Liébano Sáenz, Aug. 3, 2001.

506 Comptroller-General: Barrio's office was the Secretaría de la Contraloría y Desarrollo Administrativo.

506 resolve the conflict in Chiapas in "fifteen minutes": Reuters, "Pactaria con Marcos en quince minutos," *El Norte*, Feb. 27, 1998, p. 8.

506 exorbitant salaries: One presidential office with four employees had an annual payroll of 12 million pesos, about $1.3 million. See David Aponte and Daniel Moreno, "Las cuentas de Los Pinos," *Cambio*, June 10, 2001, p. 21, cited in Alfonso Zárate, "Fox en su laberinto: El *toallagate*," *Lectura Política*, no. 109, June 27, 2001. For the four-hundred-dollar towels, see " 'Toallagate,' " *Milenio*, June 19, 2002.

507 looked like a rich reward: Fox's cozy relationship with Roberto Hernández was evident in the days after his election victory, when Hernández hosted Fox on a Caribbean island he owns. Fox appointed as his Treasury Secretary Francisco Gil Díaz, a PRI economist who had two decades of service in the

Banco de México and the Hacienda Secretariat—but who had most recently been the CEO of Avantel, the long-distance telephone company owned by Hernández. Gil Díaz's instantly applauded Citigroup's purchase of Banamex.

507 still expressing patience with Fox: See the nationwide poll coordinated by Ignacio Rodríguez Reyna, "Mas tiempo para Fox; no al regreso del PRI," "*El Universal*, Sept. 2, 2002, p. A8. Sixty-seven percent of the one thousand adults questioned in their homes said that Fox should be given more time to bring about change; 33 percent said they thought the country had been better off under PRI rule, while 60 percent disagreed with that notion.

508 freedom of information law: The Mexican law was called the Ley Federal de Transparencia y Acceso a la Información Pública.

509 number of bureaucrats: Denise Dresser, "El tigre y la tortuga," *Arcana*, Sept. 2002, p. 38. The article provides a meticulous overview of the state of Mexican education two years into Fox's government.

510 But after the election he changed his mind: "Periquin va de visita," *Reforma*, Aug. 2, 2000.

510 praised Rodríguez Alcaine's "vision": Margarita Vega, "Elogia Fox a dirigente electricista," *Reforma*, Nov. 6, 2000.

510 suffered only bruises: For a more detailed description of the continuation of the corrupt PRI labor structure under Fox, see Miguel Angel Granados Chapa, "Bajo mundo sindical," *Reforma*, April 15, 2002, p. 25.

510 Ciudad Acuña: One irritant that helped provoke the wildcat strike was the extraordinary compensation given to Paul O'Neill, the Alcoa CEO. Based on Alcoa's 1999 profits, O'Neill exercised $33 million in stock options beyond his $3 million salary. The workers were familiar with the payments to O'Neill, which Alcoa detailed in its 1999 annual report, and were angry that the company paid its Acuña workers only $40 in profit-sharing payments. In 2001 O'Neill left Alcoa to become President Bush's Treasury Secretary. In January 2002 Alcoa announced that it had appointed Ernesto Zedillo to its board of directors.

510 The Fox government dealt some blows to the drug cartels: The former PRI governor was Mario Villanueva of Quintana Roo. See Tim Weiner, "Ex-Mexico Governor Arrested and Linked to Cocaine Traffic," *New York Times*, May 26, 2001.

510 detaining one of the Arellano Félix brothers: He was Benjamín Arellano, see Tim Weiner, "Drug Kingpin, Long Sought, Is Captured by Mexicans," *New York Times*, March 10, 2002, p. 7.

510 police had killed another brother: He was Ramón Arellano. See Tim Weiner, "The Bloodstain's Secret: Is Cartel Enforcer Dead?" *New York Times*, Feb. 28, 2002, p. A4.

511 appointed a special prosecutor: He was Ignacio Carrillo Prieto. His official title was Fiscal Especial para la Atención de Hechos Probablemente Constitutivos de Delitos Federales Cometidos Directa o Indirectamente por

Servidores Públicos en contra de Personas Vinculadas con Movimientos Sociales y Políticos del Pasado. For an interview with Carrillo Prieto, see Rafael Rodríguez Castañeda, "No tengo límites ni obedezco consignas," *Proceso*, Jan. 27, 2002.

512 one of its own military tribunals: See Tim Weiner, "Three Mexican Army Officers Are Accused in 70's Killings," *New York Times*, Sept. 28, 2002, p. A4.

512 overwhelmingly approved his restraint: See "Encuesta/Avalan cancelación del aeropuerto en DF," *El Norte*, Aug. 7, 2002, p. 5.

513 Congress had become far more assertive: The fifty-seventh Congress, which was in session from 1997 to 2000, the second half of Zedillo's presidency, approved 99 percent of the bills Zedillo proposed—often without changing a word. The Fifty-eighth Congress, which served from 2000 to 2003, approved only 82 percent of the bills Fox proposed and rewrote every bill in some way before it became law. Author interview with Jeffrey A. Weldon, professor of political science at the Instituto Tecnológico Autónomo de México, Jan. 22, 2002.

513 The Senate even prohibited Fox: Ginger Thompson, "Mexico Bars Its President from Trips Next Week," *New York Times*, April 10, 2002, p. A7.

513 ruling against the President: The Court on September 4, 2001, invalidated a presidential decree establishing daylight saving time; see Comunicado de Prensa de la Corte Suprema No. 2001/124. In May 2002 it invalidated changes in energy regulations Fox had made to permit private investors in the state-owned electric-power industry; see Mayela Cordoba, "Excluye SCJN a independientes," *El Norte*, May 23, 2002, p. 3, negocios. And it sided with the Chamber of Deputies in agreeing to hear a constitutional challenge to a presidential decree that exempted corn-fructose importers from an import tax; see Comunicado de Prensa de la Corte Suprema No. 2002/051.

513 The state governors: Mexico has thirty-one states, headed by governors. The Federal District now functions much like a state but is headed by a *jefe de gobierno*, often called *el alcalde*, or mayor.

516 voices . . . were complaining: See "Democracy Clings on in a Cold Economic Climate."

Acknowledgments

Much of the material for this book was drawn from interviews with 92 people, almost all of them Mexicans, which we carried out between July 2000 and December 2002. We were fortunate to undertake an intensive phase of research and reporting in the year following the presidential election of July 2, 2000, when many Mexicans—including quite a few who did not support Vicente Fox—felt liberated by the fall of the PRI. Many people spoke for hours at a sitting and agreed to several interviews. Those who consented to be identified are named in the notes. In some cases, people we interviewed agreed to be named as sources, but *not* for specific facts and episodes; they are cited accordingly. Political currents can change swiftly and treacherously in Mexico, and the people who shared their stories with us were often taking a risk. We are indebted to them for their candor and their interest in creating an accurate record of the history to which they contributed.

We have also drawn on hundreds of interviews we carried out during our five years of reporting as correspondents for *The New York Times*.

A number of people read drafts of chapters or passages and provided incisive comments. In this regard we are grateful to Cuauhtémoc Abarca, Rogelio Carvajal, Denise Dresser, Rossana Fuentes-Beraín, Luis González de Alba, Enrique Krauze, Jorge Legorreta, Imanol Ordorika, Liébano Sáenz, Fausto Zapata, and Jorge Zepeda Patterson. Others took time to help us understand the rituals and mysteries of Mexican politics, including Sergio Aguayo, Jorge Alcocer, Leticia Calzada, Manuel Camacho, Jose Carreño, Jorge G. Castañeda, Jorge Chabat, Federico Estevez, Jeff Hermanson, Lorenzo Meyer, Rogelio Ramírez de la O, and Samuel del Villar.

We are especially grateful to Friedrich Katz, who patiently shared his encyclopedic knowledge of Mexican history to help us—journalists accustomed to dealing only with the first draft—in our effort to understand the significance of the democratic vote of July 2000.

We are indebted to Jonathan Galassi at Farrar, Straus and Giroux for his conviction that Mexico is a country fundamental to the national security and cultural future of the United States. Paul Elie, our editor at FSG, skillfully consolidated and streamlined the work of two authors into a coherent whole. We thank him for his broad vision and his attention to fine detail.

Henry Kaufman read the manuscript with an exacting lawyer's eye. Ingrid Sterner treated our words with extraordinary care, correcting inconsistencies of fact and style.

Esther Newberg, our agent, understood our desire to write about Mexico's democratic revolution and worked effectively, as always, to obtain the resources for us to do it.

We received a generous grant from the Research and Writing Initiative of the Program on Global Security and Sustainability of the John D. and Catherine T. MacArthur Foundation, which greatly expanded our research capabilities.

The project would not have been possible if Joe Lelyveld, then the Executive Editor of the *Times*, and Andy Rosenthal, when he was Foreign Editor, had not allowed us both to take leaves from our daily duties at the paper. We also thank Roger Cohen, Foreign Editor, and Jim Roberts, National Editor, for comprehending the exigencies of book writing and allowing us to take additional time off.

We owe much to our predecessors in the *Times*'s Mexico bureau, whose coverage of the country's earlier democratic stirrings was an inspiration: Marlise Simons, Richard Meislin, Larry Rohter, Tim Golden, and Anthony DePalma. Alan Riding's *Distant Neighbors* remains a classic against which other books about Mexico are measured.

Alejandro Quiroz Flores was our sharp, insightful, and efficient research assistant in Mexico. He composed chronologies and essays that allowed us to understand the democratic transition in whole areas of Mexican life, such as the media and the intellectual sphere. Gabriela Warkentin provided quick, meticulous transcriptions of several interviews.

Our colleague and dear friend Gladys Boladeras, the manager of the *Times*'s Mexico City bureau, carried out photographic research and helped in countless ways to keep the project afloat, not least by informing us with her wonderfully deep and ironic knowledge of Mexico's political mores. Javier Cárdenas more than once saved our work from computer meltdown.

The visual perceptions of photographers, including Wesley Bocxe, Keith Dannemiller, Phillippe Diederich, Sergio Dorantes, Gerardo Magallon, and Pedro Valtierra, enriched our understanding of Mexican society.

Others who gave generously of their counsel, knowledge, or humor at crucial moments were Mario Campuzano, Alma Guillermoprieto, Susan Gzesh, Francisco Hoyos, Berta Lujan, and Janet Schwartz.

We also extend our appreciation to Silvia Reyes and Nelva Maldonado for their help, patience, and care.

While we have benefited from much wisdom generously given by others, the judgments in our book are all our own.

Julia Preston and Samuel Dillon
August 2003

Index

Photo Credits

592

Chapter 10
p. 303: Courtesy of María Bernal

Chapter 11
p. 324: Rodolfo Valtierra/Cuartoscuro

Chapter 12
Photo gallery, p. 355: José Woldenberg: Archive/Proceso; Francisco Labastida Ochoa: Archive/Proceso; Manuel Bartlett: Archive/Proceso; Roberto Madrazo Pintado: Benjamín Flores/Proceso; Andrés Manuel López Obrador: Benjamín Flores/Proceso; Santiago Creel: Tomás Bravo; Manuel Camacho Solís: Paco Martínez; Jaime Serra Puche: Francisco Daniel/Proceso; Julio Scherer: Archive/Proceso
p. 363: Gustavo Graf/Imagenlatina

Chapter 13
p. 401: Gabriel Jiménez/Agencia Reforma

Chapter 14
p. 421: Archive/Proceso; *p. 430:* José Hernández Claire/Siglo 21

Chapter 15
p. 457: Pedro Valtierra/Cuartoscuro

Chapter 16
p. 466: Archive/Proceso

Chapter 17
p. 486: Archive/Proceso; *p. 492:* Ulises Castellanos/Proceso